DATE DUE

OCT 0 4 2010			

Jews and Baseball

VOLUME 2

Jews and Baseball

Volume 2

The Post-Greenberg Years, 1949–2008

Burton A. Boxerman
and Benita W. Boxerman

Foreword by Ron Kaplan

McFarland & Company, Inc., Publishers
Jefferson, North Carolina, and London

LIBRARY OF CONGRESS CATALOGUING-IN-PUBLICATION DATA

Boxerman, Burton Alan, 1933–
Jews and baseball : / Burton A. Boxerman and Benita W. Boxerman ;
foreword by Ron Kaplan.
v.   cm.
Includes bibliographical references and index.
Contents: v. 2. The Post-Greenberg Years, 1949–2008.

ISBN 978-0-7864-3357-5
illustrated case binding : 50# alkaline paper ∞

1. Jewish baseball players—United States—Biography.
2. Jews—Cultural assimilation—United States.
3. Baseball—Religious aspects—Judaism.
I. Boxerman, Benita W.   II. Title.
GV865.A1B645   2010   796.3570922—dc22   2006034478

British Library cataloguing data are available

Cover art: *Koufax* ©2009 Arthur K. Miller; www.artofthegame.com

Manufactured in the United States of America

*McFarland & Company, Inc., Publishers
Box 611, Jefferson, North Carolina 28640
www.mcfarlandpub.com*

To every Jew
who has helped make
baseball America's pastime

Acknowledgments

We are deeply grateful to many people who provided time, knowledge, and materials as we researched, wrote, and acquired photos for this book. Many are referenced in the notes and bibliography, but we wish to give special recognition to the following:

Martin Abramowitz, whose baseball cards, Jewish Major Leaguers, were our authority for determining who was Jewish. He was also patient and very responsive in answering our requests for more information.

John Horne and Pat Kelly, in the photo department of the Baseball Hall of Fame, who were helpful in obtaining pictures for this book, especially of players who made the briefest of appearances in the major leagues.

Our good friend, Gary Kodner, partner in Nehman-Kodner Graphic Designs, who not only supplied us with photos for the book, but reformatted others to make them usable.

Marvin Miller, former executive director of the MLBPA, who was very generous with his time and very candid in his assessment of the role of the Players Association in baseball.

The players who took time to discuss their careers with us by e-mail or by phone and a special thank you to those who were able to send photos for the book.

Rollie Hemond, all-around baseball executive, who also made time for us in his busy schedule and was kind enough to answer our questions.

The following individuals who went out of their way to search their archives and send the authors a number of photographs: Chris Downey, Gwinnet Braves; Andrea Breen, Iowa Cubs; Megan LaBella, Boston Red Sox; Paul Kennedy, Fresno Grizzlies; Doug Scopel, Nashville Sounds; Jim Byers, Oklahoma City Red Hawks; Robert Vigon, Florida Marlins; Ian Locke, Norfolk Tides; Dave Sachs, New Orleans Zephyrs; Matt Nordby, Pittsburgh Pirates; Tina Urban, Philadelphia Phillies; Mike Kennedy, Minnesota Twins; Jarrod Rollins, Cincinnati Reds; Russell Luna, Houston Astros; and Jon Chapper, Los Angeles Dodgers.

Members of SABR, who could always be counted on for their support and their continued interest in the project.

Finally, we thank our family for their patience and understanding when we had to devote time to the book that we would rather have spent with them, and our many friends who followed the progress of the book and eagerly waited for its conclusion.

All these people greatly aided us in the writing of this book, but the authors take full responsibility for any errors.

Burton A. Boxerman • Benita W. Boxerman • St. Louis, Missouri • Fall 2009

Table of Contents

Foreword

by Ron Kaplan

The Jewish major leaguers included in the first volume of Burton and Benita Boxerman's watershed *Jews and Baseball* faced problems that were basically the tenor of times in the late 19th–early 20th century: stereotypes at best ("Jews make poor athletes") and outright anti–Semitism at worst (when a Jewish batter came to the plate, an unruly fan would urge the pitcher, "Throw him a ham sandwich. He won't bite."). Those players who stuck it out might have changed their names to hide their identity not only from those who would beleaguer them with taunts, but also to hide their profession from their families. Nice Jewish boys were expected to get an education and improve upon their situations, working towards a better life than their shopkeeper or laborer parents, not fool around with a roughhouse sport.

But an article in the *Jewish Daily Forward*, a Yiddish-language newspaper, urged parents to learn this strange game, to embrace it, and understand it, and so truly become American.

Many of the ballplayers from this period were raised in Jewishly-observant households, with parents who came over from "the old country" where religious observances were considered of the utmost importance. But after Detroit Tiger superstar Hank Greenberg—the original "Hebrew Hammer"—showed a Jewish ballplayer could be both an outstanding player and "true to his religion" (in the words of poet Edgar Guest), those who followed had a somewhat easier time of it. Sure, you still had a Ron Blomberg, who grew up in the Deep South and had Klansmen as teammates, but as the generations became further removed from their predecessors, hiding one's religion became less of an issue.

Some players—most notably Hall of Famer Sandy Koufax and Shawn Green—still felt obligated to refrain from playing games on Yom Kippur, the holiest day of the Jewish year, regardless of how crucial those contests were. Koufax passed on the opening game assignment for the 1965 World Series, causing Don Drysdale to fill in. When manager Walt Alston came out to relieve Drysdale following rough treatment by the heavy-hitting Minnesota Twins, the tall righty said to his skipper, "I bet you wish I was Jewish too right about now."

The post–World War II years have had their share of high-profile players, including Al Rosen, Mike Epstein, Art Shamsky, Ken Holtzman (who won even more games than Koufax), Cy Young–winner Steve Stone, and the afore-mentioned Blomberg (who used his fame as the DH for another meaning in his autobiography: *Designated Hebrew*).

Since the beginning of the new century, baseball has seen an unprecedented influx of Jewish players. More than a minyan (the Jewish quorum of 10 necessary to conduct services) appeared in 2009, including a few bordering on stardom such as Kevin Youkilis, Ryan Braun, and Ian Kinsler; and several touted rookies waiting for their chance.

The Boxermans have expanded their labor of love to include new generations of Jewish Major Leaguers. The profiles in this second volume reflect that story of progress and success (not always the same thing).

Like many of their coreligionists, these young men have become more assimilated with time and a debate has grown over who should be considered Jewish. Tradition holds that the mother's religion dictates that of the child; others, including the bi-monthly *Jewish Sports Review*, employ a more liberal criteria. JSR's philosophy: "an athlete is Jewish if they have at least one Jewish parent, do not practice another faith and identify ethnically as a Jew." So by their definition, Ryan Braun, the son of an Israeli father and Christian woman, is a Jew.

Several athletes are the products of "mixed marriages"; some celebrate parts of their Jewish heritage, some none at all. Like parents who love all their children, Jewish fans embrace all these players regardless of levels of observance. Nevertheless, they *kvell* all the more when a Jason Marquis recounts his bar mitzvah for a story in an Israeli newspaper, or a Kevin Youkilis appears in a documentary about the Israel Baseball League.

And it's not just players. Where would the game be without the contributions of Allan Roth? For better or worse, he's the one responsible for the plethora of statistical analysis that have given broadcasters the material to fill those interminable rain delays and pitching changes, not to mention opening the door for a new industry: fantasy baseball. And where would the players be if not for the yeoman's work of Marvin Miller, whose exclusion from the Baseball Hall of Fame is a *shanda* (shame)? Certainly a lot lighter in the wallet.

It doesn't matter if these players were just up for a cup of coffee or they enjoyed long and fruitful careers. Like any proud parents, we love all our children.

Ron Kaplan is the sports and features editor for the New Jersey Jewish News. *He hosts two blogs: Kaplan's Korner on Jews and Sports (njjewishnews.com/kaplanskorner) and Ron Kaplan's Baseball Bookshelf (rksbaseballbookshelf.word press.com).*

Prologue

When Hank Greenberg, probably professional baseball's all-time greatest Jewish player, retired after the 1947 season, World War II had been over for two years. The economy was operating at its highest pace and the nation boasted nearly full employment. Many economic historians describe the period following World War II as an age of prosperity far different from the 1930s and 1940s, when demagogues such as Henry Ford, Father Charles Coughlin, and Gerald L.K. Smith, made Jews the scapegoats for America's economic woes.[1]

During the 1950s, the police action against Communist North Korea and the strengthening of the Cold War did not deter America's economic upturn but did replace anti–Semitism with an obsession with Communism.[2] In fact, while anti–Semitism was rampant for more than three decades before World War II, the years immediately after the war did not produce a single major anti–Semitic political movement in the United States. On the contrary, legislation in some states banned discrimination in employment, and there was even a bill introduced in Congress making anti–Semitism a crime. The country's veterans' organizations officially condemned bigotry as un–American, and anti–Semitism was openly discussed on the radio, as the clergy often preached both religious and racial tolerance.[3]

In this more accepting atmosphere, Jews in the United States participated in the nation's growing affluence and became increasingly acculturated to American ideals. By the mid to late 1950s, many American Jews had completed the transition to the middle- and even to the upper-middle classes.[4]

Jewish communities also were strong participants in the 1950s' suburbanization movement. Many Jews left the nation's older regions of the Northeast and headed for warmer areas such as Los Angeles and Miami.[5]

Nowhere was the changing attitude towards Jews more apparent after World War II than in the field of education. The G.I. Bill paved the way for a vast flood of military veterans to enter the nation's universities. Not only did Jewish students take advantage of this opportunity, a demand for instructors opened up teaching slots for Jews. So did the postwar scientific competition with the Soviet Union. Finally, as Jews achieved middle-class status, many more were financially able to afford higher education.[6]

During the immediate postwar years, along with the various social movements taking place, a number of changes occurred in the game of baseball. During the 1950s, franchises began moving and new cities became home to major league teams. Milwaukee became the first of these new cities to field a major league team in fifty years when the Boston Braves moved there after the 1953 season. That same year St. Louis became a one-team city when the AL Browns sold their franchise to Baltimore, where the new team was renamed the Baltimore Orioles. In 1954 the Mack family sold the Philadelphia Athletics to Arnold Johnson, who promptly moved the team to Kansas City, Missouri, making the Athletics the westernmost team in major league baseball. Four years later, in 1958, baseball truly became a nationwide game when San Francisco and Los Angeles fielded major league teams for the first time. Their departure left New York City with only one team.[7]

Not all baseball activity was taking place on the field. The 1950s also became the television decade, as television revenues became an integral part of baseball finances. In 1950 Gillette paid $800,000 for television rights to the World Series; the radio rights for that Series went for only $175,000.[8] By 1955, the Brooklyn Dodgers were televising all their home games as well as more than 20 road games, earning the team close to $800,000 from radio and television.[9] In 1958, the New York Yankees got $1 million to televise 140 of their 154 games.[10]

Probably the most important postwar off-the-field baseball event occurred in 1957, when the Supreme Court declared that baseball was exempt from anti-trust laws.[11] The decision upheld the Court's 1922 ruling and delivered a severe blow to opponents of the reserve clause, which bound players to a single team. Without other teams bidding for their services, players were left to accept a club's salary offer or find another line of work.

Another influential trend that affected both baseball and the way Jews related to the game began in the early 1950s and continued throughout the twentieth century. An abundance of fictional baseball books appeared, including a large number by Jewish authors who wrote about the game in general or worked Jewish themes into the plots.

One of the earliest of these Jewish authors was Bernard Malamud, who was credited with transforming baseball fiction from juvenile to adult literature in his 1952 novel, *The Natural*.[12] The best-known book on the Black Sox Scandal of 1919, *Eight Men Out*, was likewise penned by a Jewish author, Eliot Asinof.[13]

Philip Roth's *The Great American Novel* included a hapless baseball team exiled from their New Jersey home field and forced to play their 1943 season as a visiting team, wandering from city to city throughout the league. This book was popular with first- and second-generation Jewish-American youth, many of whom saw the myths and legends in the Biblical stories as parallels with baseball.[14] Jewish writer Mark Harris became well known for his 1956 novel, *Bang the Drum Slowly*, a pastoral version of the Lou Gehrig story.[15]

Other authors not only wrote about baseball, they also had Jewish protagonists. Eric Rolfe Greenberg's *The Celebrant* focused on immigrants who attempted to assimilate by becoming supporters of America's national pastime. Peter Levine's *The Rabbi of Swat* featured a Jewish star pitcher. Both novels contained all the ethnic stereotypes—Jewish mothers, Sabbath meals, and anti–Semitism in both the opponents and teammates.[16] Irwin Shaw, in his 1965 novel, *Voices of a Summer Day*, also focused on how the game of baseball could be an integral part of Jewish father-son relationships.[17]

Eric Solomon, an authority on Jewish baseball writing, discovered that American Jewish authors have written far more books on baseball or with baseball sub-themes than writers of any other ethnic background. He reasons that Jewish writers were attracted to baseball because it was a means of becoming American and yet holding onto their identity as Jews, that they found appealing its strong foundation in statistics and history, and that as Philip Roth once wrote, "I couldn't play baseball professionally so it was realistic to write about the game and to raise realism to more intense forms."[18]

But a number of Jewish boys could and did continue to play professional baseball, a number of them entering the major leagues in the late 1940s and the 1950s. The stage was set for this next group of Jewish players in major league baseball.

1. A New Golden Age Begins

During the 1950s twenty-one Jewish baseball players, both first- and second-generation Americans, were on major league rosters for a minimum of one year. With one exception, all of them had their major league careers either delayed or shortened because they served in the armed forces during World War II or the Korean Conflict.

Marvin Rotblatt

When Marv Rotblatt appeared against the Detroit Tigers on July 4, 1948, he became the first Jewish player to debut in the major leagues since the end of World War II. Rotblatt was born on October 18, 1927, in Chicago, the eldest of three sons of Sol and Carolyn Rotblatt. After pitching for Chicago's Von Steuben High School, he enrolled at the University of Illinois where the stocky, five-foot, seven-inch southpaw became an immediate pitching whiz. His father was not enthusiastic about his son playing baseball after he saw Marv's cheek bone smashed when the opposing batter knocked the ball back to the mound so fast that his son never saw it. "That does it," he told Marv, "I hope now you'll give up baseball."[1] "I got an assist on that play," related Rotblatt. "Despite my father's protests, I was back on the mound 10 days later. To this day, I still have numbness on the cheek."[2]

Despite his father's protests, Rotblatt continued pitching for the Illini, and during summer break, billed as "Little David,"

Before Marv Rotblatt pitched in the major leagues, he was a star for the University of Illinois, leading his team to the 1947-1948 Big Nine championship. He pitched for his hometown Chicago White Sox in 1948, 1950, and 1951 before serving in the military from 1952 to 1953. He never returned to the major leagues (courtesy Marvin Rotblatt).

the diminutive pitcher hurled for the House of David baseball team where he won 14 games in a row. In a game with the Harlem Globetrotters baseball team, he fanned 17 players.[3]

While pitching for the Illini, scouts from several major league teams, including the New York Giants, were following him. Rotblatt was aware that the Giants were always looking for promising Jewish ball players to boost attendance at the Polo Grounds. He was also practical enough to understand that despite his 25 wins and .862 winning percentage, he was not yet ready for the majors.[4]

Rotblatt graduated from Illinois in 1948 with a degree in journalism, and was immediately offered contracts by all but two major league teams. He signed with the Chicago White Sox who promised him the most money—$6,000. "When I complained to the White Sox General Manager about the low offer, he told me either to sign or he would release me. Obviously, I signed. Personally, if I had to do it over again, I probably would have signed with the Brooklyn Dodgers who I always felt were looking for Jewish players."[5]

Rotblatt's debut on July 4, 1948, against the Detroit Tigers was in the Sox's home field, Comiskey Park. Although the Tigers won the game, Rotblatt's debut was auspicious, as he pitched two scoreless innings, giving up only one hit.[6] He pitched in six more games that year; his record was 0–1, with an earned run average of 7.85.[7]

One of the seven games in which Marv Rotblatt appeared his first year was against the Boston Red Sox. Rotblatt was on the mound to face Red Sox future Hall of Famer Ted Williams. As Rotblatt related the story later, "I'm sent in to face Ted Williams with the bases loaded. Luke Appling is playing a shallow third that day and I shuffle over to him and ask, 'Say, Luke, how do you pitch to this gorilla?' Luke never looked up. 'Low and inside, son,' he drawls, so I crank up, lay it in there, and Williams almost kills the first baseman with a line drive. 'How come,' I ask Luke and he says, 'Well, sonny, it's like this. I got a wife and two kids. Goldsberry on first, he's a bachelor—so I figure it's better you pitch inside to him and have it go that way, 'cause it's gonna go places no matter how you pitch.'"[8]

Rotblatt spent the 1949 season in the minors and did not pitch for the White Sox that year.[9] During the 1950 season, Rotblatt was in the minors for most of the year, but was called up to end the season in Chicago, appearing in two games; he had no decisions and an ERA of 6.23.[10]

His one major anti–Semitic incident while in the minor leagues occurred when Rotblatt was pitching for Charleston in a game against Indianapolis, managed by Kerby Farrell, who was also coaching at first base. "He rode me the entire game," recalled Rotblatt. "All I heard from him were slurs about my religion. I retaliated and called him every name I could think of."[11]

"I heard anti–Semitic taunts even before I played professional ball," said Rotblatt. "When I was 11, one of my younger brothers and I attended a Chicago Cub game, and in order to get a pass for the next day, we would pick up seat cushions after the game. One of the Cubs' greats was catcher Gabby Hartnett. After the game we followed him a couple of blocks to get his autograph. When we caught up with him, he chased us away with such terms as 'sheenie' and 'kike.' Thirty-five years later I attended a Jewish country club in Highland Park, Illinois, and whom did I see but Hartnett. I reminded him of the incident and he was the most embarrassed guy in the place."[12]

Rotblatt's last year in the major leagues was 1951. He appeared in 26 games that year, but started only two of them. He ended the year with a record of four wins and two losses and a 3.40 ERA. During the 1951 season, Rotblatt took part in one of major league baseball's innovations. That year marked the first time a major league team used an automobile to transport a pitcher from the bullpen to the mound. Before 53,000 fans, Marv Rotblatt was driven to the mound while the Yankees stood at attention in their dugout.[13] On July 30 of that year he was sent down to Memphis.[14] During his three-year career in the majors, Rotblatt appeared in 35 games, with an ERA of 4.82; he won four games, lost three, for a winning percentage of .571.[15]

He was to have been inducted into the Army on August 31, 1951, but got a reprieve when his draft board's quota was changed.[16] He did serve in the Army from 1952 to 1953 where he played on a military exhibition team with stars such as Don Newcombe, Bob Turley and a fellow Jew, Hy Cohen. During his time in service, Rotblatt hurt his pitching arm.[17]

After Rotblatt returned from the army, he continued in the minors. In 1954 he set a new Southern Association strikeout record of 202. In 1957 he suffered another injury and retired from baseball. After his professional baseball career ended, Rotblatt went into the insurance business.[18]

Rotblatt's baseball days may have ended in 1957, but he was not forgotten. In 1964 a group of male students at Carleton College in Northfield, Minnesota, founded a slow pitch softball league. They decided to name the league after a former major leaguer so obscure that his identity would test trivia buffs. The player they chose was Marvin Rotblatt and the league was called the Rotblatt Memorial Softball League. When some of the players felt Rotblatt was an "invention," one of the founders remembered he had a Rotblatt baseball card in his vast collection. They then discovered that Rotblatt was alive and well and selling insurance in Chicago. The league invited Rotblatt to the college to prove his existence, and the former White Sox hurler accepted the invitation. A softball game was held in Rotblatt's honor, and he happily mixed with the students. According to one of the participants, "We all had tears in our eyes as he left." Three years later, Rotblatt returned to the campus to pitch in the All-Star Game.[19] "It was one of the greatest weekends of my life," said Rotblatt.[20]

Joe Ginsberg

Myron Ginsberg, known throughout his baseball career as "Joe," was another post-war Jewish baseball player who debuted in 1948. Ginsberg was born in New York City on October 11, 1926, but he was raised in Detroit; the Tigers were his favorite team. His father's favorite player was Hank Greenberg, but Ginsberg idolized Ted Williams.[21] Much to his father's chagrin, the Tigers signed Joe after he graduated high school. His father was not opposed to his son playing baseball; he simply could not imagine how Joe would make it financially in the minors, earning only $100 per month. Joe assured his father that he would have no trouble, but at the end of each month, he usually had to borrow ten dollars.[22]

Ginsberg spent a total of five years in the Tiger minor league farm system before he made it to the big leagues. When he turned eighteen, the army drafted him. He was stationed in the Philippines where he played baseball with major leaguers including Joe Garagiola and Early Wynn. After he left the army, the Tigers sent him back to their farm system.[23]

When Detroit catcher Hal Wagner was sold to the Philadelphia Phillies late in the 1948 season, Ginsberg was brought up from Buffalo, the Tiger's AAA team, to replace him.[24] Ginsberg's debut with the Tigers on September 15, 1948, was auspicious; he walked and scored the game-winning run. Ginsberg recalled that the Tiger team in 1948 had some of the most outstanding players in the majors—stars such as Dizzy Trout, George Kell, Hal Newhouser, and Art Houtteman. "It was the outfield," stated Ginsberg, "that was our strength. Wertz, Evers and Groth—they were the Million Dollar Outfield, even though they played at a time when guys were making $5,000 a year. It was really a thrill to be playing ball in your hometown. But in Detroit, unless you were a superstar, the fans didn't take to you."[25]

Ginsberg spent 1949 and most of 1950 in the minors. He was recalled to Detroit late in 1950 to bolster the Tigers' American league pennant hopes.[26] Ginsberg appeared in only 36 games that year, but he became Detroit's regular catcher in 1951 and 1952, his only 100-game seasons.[27] In 1951 Ginsberg was one of eleven Jewish major leaguers to appear in at least one game that season. The Jewish roster included Cal Abrams, Al Federoff, Sid Gordon, Lou Limmer, Duke Markell, Al Richter, his teammate Saul Rogovin, Al Rosen, Marv Rotblatt, and Sid Schacht.[28] Martin Abramowitz, President of Jewish Major Leaguers Inc., noted that these players formed their own community, knew each other socially, played winter ball together, and, on at least one occasion, took part in a Passover Seder together.[29]

Detroit Tiger manager Red Rolfe was pleased with Ginsberg's play and although he had two more experienced catchers on his roster, Bob Swift and Aaron Robinson, Rolfe was encouraged by Ginsberg's versatility. "Imagine that," said Rolfe, "a rugged catcher who can throw and hit and run too." Rolfe pointed out that Ginsberg's speed eased the double play threat when the Tigers were batting. "We already have too many slow guys. These double plays were going to murder us, I knew. It wasn't much of a decision to move Ginsberg in there."[30]

In 1951, Ginsberg's first full season with the Tigers, he appeared in 102 games. That season he notched a .262 batting average, and clouted his single-season career-high eight home runs.[31]

One of Ginsberg's most memorable games was in 1952 when Ginsburg caught Tiger hurler Virgil Trucks' no-hitter. The no-hitter was especially meaningful to both Trucks and Ginsberg, as the two players became best friends. Ginsberg always considered Trucks easy to work with on the mound. "Virgil Trucks was one of my favorite teammates and we still keep in contact to this day," stated Ginsberg.[32]

Joe Ginsberg was born in New York, but raised in Detroit, and played five of his thirteen years in the big leagues for the Tigers. He also caught for the Indians, Royals, Orioles, White Sox, and Red Sox, and was the catcher in the first game of the inaugural year of the New York Mets. Ginsberg holds the distinction of having played for the American League team with the most wins and the National League team with the most losses (courtesy National Baseball Hall of Fame Library; Cooperstown, N.Y.).

Ginsberg supported Trucks when he pitched his no-hitter, but he did the opposite to New York Yankees hurler Vic Raschi. Ginsberg hit only 20 home runs in his long major league career, but he hit the most dramatic one against Raschi in the ninth inning of a game on June 13, 1952.

Raschi had pitched 8.1 innings of scoreless, no-hit ball when Ginsberg came to bat. Raschi ran the count to 2–2, and when catcher Yogi Berra went to the mound to speak to his pitcher, umpire Larry Napp commented to Ginsberg, "He's pitching quite a game." "Quite a game," Ginsberg replied. "No hits, no runs." As the wind began to shift, blowing toward Yankee Stadium's short right-field porch, Ginsberg told Napp, "You know, if he comes with that high fastball and I can hit it up in the air, it'll blow it out of the park." As Ginsberg predicted, Raschi delivered a fastball and Ginsberg turned it into a home run, spoiling Raschi's no-hitter and shutout with one swing of the bat. After Ginsberg rounded the bases, Napp gave him an expressive look and said, "Joe, Babe Ruth has not a thing on you."[33] Joe Ginsberg had a reputation for being a clubhouse comedian, but after he spoiled Raschi's bid for a no-hitter, Raschi, a fierce competitor, made it known that he was not all amused.[34]

Even though Ginsberg had a mediocre year in 1952, hitting only .221 in 113 games, he was still a sought-after player. At the 1952 winter meeting, the Washington Senators offered to trade their backstop, Mickey Grasso, for Joe Ginsberg, but the deal was never made.[35]

Ginsberg's two managers at Detroit were Red Rolfe and Fred Hutchinson. He worked well with all his managers, but admitted that his favorite was Fred Hutchinson. "Although I always felt that an everyday player made a better manager than a pitcher (which Hutchinson was), I still feel Hutch was great."[36]

Ginsberg appeared in 18 games for the Tigers in 1953 before he was traded on June 16, 1953, to the Cleveland Indians in an eight-player deal. Cleveland sent shortstop Ray Boone and three pitchers—Steve Gromek, Al Aber and Dick Weik—to the Tigers. In return Cleveland got pitchers Art Houtteman and Bill Wight, infielder Owen Friend, and catcher Joe Ginsberg.[37] Ginsberg finished the 1953 season with the Indians, appearing in 64 games. The following year, he played in only three games before the Indians sold him to their farm club in the American Association.[38] Unfortunately, he did not rejoin the Indians in 1954, the year the Tribe won the American League pennant, with 111 wins, the American League record that stood for forty years until the Yankees broke it in 1998.[39]

Nor was he back to the majors in 1955. Ginsberg spent the entire 1955 season in the minors, playing for Manager Lefty O'Doul's Seattle Rainiers in the Pacific Coast League, where he batted .295 and was named Player of the Year. Ed Mickelson, a former major leaguer, who also played in the PCL, remembers Ginsberg when he caught for Seattle. "I was in the batter's box many times when Ginsberg was behind the plate," said Mickelson. "When any batter came to the plate and tried to concentrate, Ginsberg would start his usual chatter saying anything just to distract the hitter."[40]

On August 17, 1956, the Kansas City Athletics purchased Ginsberg's contract from Seattle and once again he was a major leaguer. Ginsberg appeared in 71 games and was hitting .247 for the Kansas City Athletics, when the Baltimore Orioles obtained him in August.[41]

Ginsberg remained with the Orioles from August 1956 until June 1960, signing next with the Chicago White Sox as a free agent. His manager at Baltimore was former Detroit Tiger catcher Paul Richards. "I thought," said Ginsberg, "Here's a Detroit boy and I'm going to catch for him a lot."[42] Ginsberg was wrong; he had to share the catching duties with Gus Triandos—the left-handed-hitting Ginsberg faced right-handed pitchers, while Triandos, a right-handed batter, caught when facing a southpaw. Even though he disliked being platooned, Ginsberg understood Richards' move. "Richards was a great manager," said Ginsberg. "It seemed he always knew what he was doing."[43]

Ginsberg enjoyed his stint with the Orioles except when knuckleball pitcher Hoyt Wilhelm was on the mound. Neither Triandos nor Ginsberg was able to catch Wilhelm, and the two catchers began to set records for passed balls when Wilhelm pitched. In one of Wilhelm's outings, Ginsberg had a record of three passed balls in a single game. In order to catch Wilhelm's knuckleball, Joe used an oversized glove—one he called an "elephant glove" to make sure he could hold on to the ball. "I broke the glove in and used it whenever Hoyt came to pitch," Ginsberg recalled. "It worked fine except for one problem—when there was a man on first and he went to steal and you caught the ball, you knew that it was in there somewhere but not exactly where. You would be digging around in there looking for it, and sometimes the guys would be circling the bases while you were doing it."[44]

On June 12, 1960, the Orioles waived Joe Ginsberg, at the age of 33, the first step toward releasing him.[45] A few days later, the Chicago White Sox signed him again. He played 28 games for the White Sox in 1960 and six in 1961. He then signed with the Boston Red Sox in May of that year. Boston was the sixth American League club to hire Ginsberg since he had broken into the majors in 1948, making him the most widely traveled American League player since Bobo Newsom. Newsom pitched for nine major league clubs, six of them in the American League.[46]

Ginsberg played 19 games for Boston in 1961. He was in the Red Sox dugout when the Yankees' Roger Maris hit his record-setting 61st home run.[47] At the end of the season the Red Sox asked waivers on Ginsberg, prior to granting him his unconditional release.[48]

On January 31, 1962, the newly franchised New York Mets signed two baseball veterans, Gil Hodges and Joe Ginsberg, for the team's inaugural season.[49] Ginsberg played only two games for the Mets, but made history when as opening day catcher, he was the first Mets player to ever take the field. He had the distinction of having his name in the "How to Score" section of Shea Stadium programs for more than twenty years. The 1962 Mets were the "losingest" team in National League history.[50]

"[Casey] Stengel was some manager," recalled Ginsberg. "He called all his players 'son' because he could not remember their names. He told me that I'd be better known as a member of the Mets than anywhere else in my entire playing career. The only problem the Mets had is that they couldn't decide if they wanted veterans or young players. They went with veterans who were in the last years of their careers, and although they didn't play well, they drew huge crowds."[51]

On April 27, 1962, the Mets released Joe Ginsberg.[52] He had played his final major league game. Ginsberg spent thirteen years in the majors, playing for seven different clubs during his major league career. He appeared in 695 games, had 414 hits, 182 runs batted in, 20 home runs, and a lifetime batting average of .241.[53] After he left baseball, Ginsberg represented the Jack Daniel's Distillery for sixteen years prior to his retirement.[54]

He still followed baseball but noted sadly how the game had changed over the years. "It's a vastly different game today," he said. "You hardly ever see the hit-and-run and most of the players have no idea how to lay down a bunt. It seems all the non-power strategic moves have been taken out of the game."[55]

Saul Rogovin

The year after Joe Ginsberg became a member of the Tigers, Detroit added another Jewish player to its roster, Saul Rogovin. Except for the year when Joe was in the minors, the two were teammates until 1953.

Saul Rogovin was born in Brooklyn on October 10, 1923, the only child of Jacob and

Bessie Rogovin. He attended Abraham Lincoln High School where he played infield on his school's baseball team and helped his team win the Public School Athletic League title.[56]

After high school graduation, Rogovin tried out for the Dodgers but was unable to make the team. He then played with a Class D team in the Penn State Association, but the team folded. The following year, 1941, he took a job with Brewster Aeronautical Plant as an assembly line worker. During his spare time he played on the company team where Dolly Stark, a Jewish umpire, spotted him. Stark was confident that he could make another "Hank Greenberg" out of Saul Rogovin. Rogovin told Stark, "I have a strong arm, but I never could hit like Greenberg. The only thing we have in common is that we're Jewish."[57] Nevertheless, Stark recommended Rogovin to Mel Ott, manager of the New York Giants, who gave him a tryout at the team's wartime spring training site. Rogovin impressed Ott with his power and the Giants signed him to a contract in their minor league system, where he spent the remainder of 1941. He finished he year with Chattanooga of the Southern Association playing third base.

Red Lucas, one of Chattanooga's coaches, suggested that the six-foot, two-inch, 205-pound Rogovin try pitching. On the final day of the 1945 season, Rogovin started a game and shut out the Birmingham Barons on a four-hitter. Rogovin decided that pitching was his forte.[58]

"By that time," said Rogovin, "I could see that I wasn't going to make it to the big leagues as an infielder. I really had a good arm and I figured this was my best chance of going to the Majors."[59]

Rogovin never had the opportunity to become part of the Chattanooga starting rotation; in 1946 he was traded to Pensacola in the Southern League where he saw little action. That year many ball players were returning from military service and Rogovin faced fierce competition for a spot on the pitching staff. Wally Dashiell, Pensacola's general manager, contacted every team in the International League on Rogovin's behalf. Finally, Paul Richards, manager of Buffalo, a team affiliated with the Detroit Tigers, signed Rogovin in 1947. Richards had seen Rogovin pitch and was so impressed with him that he ultimately became Rogovin's mentor.[60]

Paul Richards was a former major league catcher who later managed in the big leagues from 1951 to 1961 and in 1976.[61] To this day Paul Richards remains an enigma. Called a "cold and hard man," yet he had been known to "charm a ball player right out

Brooklyn-born Saul Rogovin pitched in the majors for eight years. Although his lifetime record was 48–48, he had two outstanding seasons before a sore arm forced him to retire in 1958. Rogovin fought back from a period of depression after he left baseball, and returned to college to obtain a bachelor's degree. At the age of 56, he began a satisfying and successful teaching career in the New York public school system. He died in 1995 of bone cancer (courtesy National Baseball Hall of Fame Library; Cooperstown, N.Y.).

of his spikes." He had no formal education beyond high school, but he was a voracious reader, and for a man who was never without his Bible on long road trips, he had been thrown out of many games for using language that would embarrass Leo Durocher. Before he was a manager, he had been a catcher with the reputation of being able to work well with difficult pitchers.

Richards was more than Rogovin's manager at Buffalo; he was his personal catcher in every game Rogovin pitched. He altered Rogovin's delivery from three-quarters to straight overhand, making him a more effective hurler. Bringing him along slowly, Richards allowed Rogovin to start only six games in 1947.[62]

In 1948 Rogovin won 13 games for Buffalo, and Detroit exercised its agreement with Buffalo to select two players; they chose pitcher Saul Rogovin and catcher Joe Ginsberg. Rogovin did not make his debut with the Tigers until April 28, 1949. He appeared in only five games for the Tigers that year, pitching 5.2 innings with an ERA of 14.29.[63] Unhappy with Rogovin's pitching, the Tigers returned him to Buffalo where he won 19 games with an ERA of 3.50.[64]

In 1950, at an exceptionally cold and wet exhibition game in Memphis during spring training, Rogovin developed a sore arm that would last his entire career. He opened the season with Detroit and pitched briefly for the Tigers that year, appearing in 11 games with 2 wins and 1 loss and a 4.50 ERA. By August it was evident he was not improving and Tigers manager Red Rolfe sent him down to the Toledo farm club to try to work out his problems.[65]

Rogovin's only genuine accomplishment in the majors in 1950 was at the plate. On Sunday, July 23, 1950, against the New York Yankees in Yankee Stadium, a large contingent of family and friends watched the local New Yorker take the mound. With Eddie Lopat pitching for the Yankees, Rogovin came up with the bases loaded. Years later Rogovin recalled that his only concern was hitting the ball over the infield, avoiding a double play. "Lopat hung a curve ball in my eyes," said Rogovin, "and all I did was meet the ball. I thought the ball was going just over short, but the thing jumped into the stands. It was one of those times when everything went right and the first thing I knew I had a home run with the bases loaded."[66]

In 1951, Rogovin, his arm rested, was back with the Tigers. However, despite a record of 1–1, the Tigers were still not pleased with his pitching and announced that the righthander was being sent to the White Sox in exchange for 26-year-old southpaw Bob Cain. In Chicago, Rogovin was re-united with his old manager, Paul Richards.[67]

For the remainder of 1951, Rogovin was in the White Sox starting rotation, taking the ball every fifth day. He left the Tigers with a 5.25 ERA, but brought it down to an excellent 2.48 with the White Sox. Even with the high earned run average from Detroit, Rogovin ended 1951 with a combined ERA of 2.78, good enough to lead the American League. His combined won–lost record that year was 12–8. Seven of his eight losses were by only one run and the eighth was by two.[68]

At the end of the 1951 season, he explained to the press the reason for his success that year. "It was like being back home again. I knew Paul had confidence in me. I remembered how well he used to work with all the pitchers at Buffalo. If a pitcher had a sore arm or something bothered him, Paul would always give him an extra day or two of rest. Many managers don't give their pitchers the benefit of the doubt, but Paul is in a class by himself."[69]

Some of Rogovin's remarks about managers not giving their pitchers the benefit of the doubt were aimed at Red Rolfe in Detroit. Rogovin often stated that keeping him in that cold, rainy game in Memphis for a prolonged period exacerbated his already ailing pitching arm.

Rogovin had an excellent year for the White Sox in 1952. His record was 14–9, and he finished the season with an ERA of 3.85. The following season, however, proved less than successful. Rogovin's record was 7–12 with an ERA of 5.22. He was placed on the disabled at the end of July with what was diagnosed as a strain in the right elbow. In September Rogovin returned to Chicago to pitch a four-hit shutout against the Cleveland Indians, his final game in a White Sox uniform.[70]

Rogovin's arm continued to hurt and he was aware that some believed that his sore arm was all in his head. Rogovin, however, continued to deny this allegation. "After all," he said, "I'm not a complete dumbbell, nor am I a hypochondriac."

In addition to a sore arm, Saul sometimes fell asleep on the bench. After one night game he was found asleep in the dugout at Comiskey Park long after his teammates had showered and dressed. According to fellow pitcher, Marv Rotblatt, Rogovin was given the nickname "somnolent Saul." It was later disclosed that Rogovin was suffering from a sleep disorder.[71]

In spite of his brilliant victory against the Indians in September, Paul Richards finally gave up on him and on December 10, 1953, the White Sox traded Rogovin out of the American League to Cincinnati. Sox General Manager Frank Lane received three players from Cincinnati in return for Rogovin—outfielder Willard Marshall and infielders Connie Ryan and Rocky Krsnich.[72]

Rogovin threw one ball in the majors in a Cincinnati uniform. His sore arm persisted into the spring of 1954 and he was shipped to the AAA Havana Sugar Kings. Rogovin compiled an 8–8 record with the Sugar Kings in 1954.[73]

Prior to the 1955 season, the Baltimore Orioles acquired Rogovin and Rogovin acquired a wife. On January 30, Rogovin wed Doreen Lipsit at Rodeph Sholom Temple in New York City.[74] With the Orioles, Rogovin was again brought together with his "spiritual leader" Paul Richards, the new Orioles manager. In an exhibition against the Pirates, Rogovin impressed Richards by giving up just one scratch hit in four scoreless innings.[75] He made the big team and in his first start, defeated the Washington Senators in a 10-inning complete game. Rogovin was elated and told the press, "This was the best game I ever pitched."[76] Rogovin's joy was premature, for that outing was to be his only victory. He appeared in 13 more games with the Orioles, winning none and losing 8. His ERA was 4.56.[77]

Paul Richards decided he wanted a younger team at Baltimore and released most of the veterans. On July 4, 1955, Rogovin was given his unconditional release. A few days later, Rogovin signed with the Philadelphia Phillies as a free agent. Rogovin became the seventh ex–White Sox on the Phillies roster, which included Peanuts Lowrey, Roy Smalley, Gus Niarhos, Bob Kuzava, and coaches Wally Moses and Whitlow Wyatt.[78]

Rogovin's stint with the Phillies in 1955 was much better than his time with Baltimore. He pitched two consecutive shutouts and finished the season with a 5–3 record and an ERA of 3.08. He told sports writer Milton Richman that he had acquired a sinker and a change-up to supplement his fading fastball. "Somebody cracked that I now throw with three speeds, slow, slower and stop," stated Rogovin. "But who cares, as long as I'm winning? They can have the fastball."[79] In 1956, as a spot starter and reliever, he retired 32 batters in succession, had a 7–6 record, but his ERA rose to 4.98. Rogovin appeared in a major league uniform for the final time in 1957. That year, he pitched in only four games—no wins, no losses, and an ERA of 9.00.[80]

Rogovin had an eight-year career in the major leagues. He pitched in 150 games, with 48 wins and 48 losses, compiling a lifetime ERA of 4.06.[81] On July 2, 1957, the Phillies sold Rogovin to the Miami Marlins in the International League.[82] Rogovin took his release in stride. "I don't blame the Phillies," he said. "They have a bunch of promising kids who throw hard, but I never got a real chance." He had some success in Miami, but went on the disabled list in August and was released the following spring. He never again played professional baseball.[83]

After his retirement Rogovin worked as a liquor salesman, but was going through a period of depression. Many professional baseball players can retire from the game and never look back. This was not the case with Rogovin. He told columnist Red Smith, "Being out of baseball hurt me inside, hurt me so bad I couldn't go to a game for years. I wanted to go visit my old team, keep up my baseball contacts, but I couldn't. I got to be a loner. I'd be irritated with customers. I quit selling liquor and didn't do anything for a while."[84]

At the age of 56, Rogovin decided to return to college more than 30 years after he started. He applied to Manhattan Community College where a dean told him that he would have to take a physical education course despite his age. He showed the dean one of his baseball cards with his picture on it. The dean waived the physical education requirement.[85]

Rogovin spent two years at Manhattan College, and he then transferred to City College of New York where he earned a degree in English Literature. In 1979 he began his new career at Hughes High School in New York and later moved to Eastern District High in one of the tougher sections of Brooklyn. He spent the last eight years of his teaching career there. Rogovin was happy teaching and he often commented, "After I left the game there was a void, something empty I couldn't fill ... until I became a teacher."[86]

On January 23, 1995, Saul Rogovin died at St. Vincent's Hospital in New York of bone cancer at the age of 71. His second wife Evelyn survived him. He was inducted posthumously into the Jewish Sports Hall of Fame on March 28, 1998.[87]

Cal Abrams

Although Cal Abrams had an eight-year career in both the National and American Leagues with five different teams, most people remember him as the "shame of Brooklyn" when he was thrown out at home plate in the ninth inning of the final game of the 1950 season. If he had scored, Abram's run would have set up a special playoff between the Dodgers and the Phillies for the pennant.[88]

Calvin Ross Abrams was born March 2, 1924, in Philadelphia, the son of a Russian immigrant father and an American-born mother. While still a child, the family moved to Brooklyn in the shadow of Ebbets Field. Abrams had always dreamed of pitching for the Brooklyn Dodgers and that was the position he played while in elementary school. Although he was not on the school's baseball team until the middle of his junior year at James Madison High School, Abrams discovered he was better as an outfielder than a pitcher. "I happened to hit one of the longest home runs in the history of James Madison High when Joe Labate, a scout for the Dodgers, was sitting in the stands. He asked me if I would like to play for Brooklyn and I said yes, of course," related Abrams.[89]

If Abrams' father had had his way, Cal would have been a Giant rather than a Dodger. According to Abrams, his father was a frustrated man who was not good enough to play professional ball, so he began teaching his son how to handle a bat and ball when he was only three. "He kept nagging me to make baseball a career," said Abrams. "He took me to every tryout in New York and it seems that I never was good enough to play for the Giants. I never told my dad, but I was pleased to be turned down. I wanted to be a Dodger."[90]

After Abrams graduated from high school, the Brooklyn Dodgers signed him to a contract for $75 a month.[91] Two weeks after he reported to the minors, the United States Army drafted him. He spent three years in the army during World War II, seeing action in both Europe and the Philippines; he was honorably discharged in 1946.[92]

Cal Abrams spent three years in the minors before being promoted to the big leagues. He started with Danville in the 3-I League where he hit .345, skipped Class A ball and went to Mobile in 1947 where he helped them win the championship of the Southern Association with a batting average of .336.[93]

After his excellent year in 1947, Abrams fully expected to be

Although Cal Abrams played for five different teams during his eight-year career in the major leagues, he is best remembered as one of the Brooklyn Dodgers during their glory days in the early 1950s (courtesy National Baseball Hall of Fame Library; Cooperstown, N.Y.).

with the Dodgers in 1948, but General Manager Branch Rickey had other ideas. He had Duke Snider in center field and Carl Furillo in right and a bevy of candidates in left field. Rickey sent Abrams back to Mobile.[94]

In Mobile Abrams experienced anti–Semitism in baseball for the first time. He was the first Jew to play ball in that town, and it was not uncommon for Abrams to hear comments about "that Jew." Fans would ask Abrams if he was a Baptist Jew or a Methodist Jew, or if he were a Jewish Catholic or a Jewish Protestant.[95]

If Abrams faced anti–Semitism in baseball, his Jewish fans more than compensated for it. Even Mobile's small Jewish community adopted him, and three times during his career, his fans held "Cal Abrams" nights in his honor. These events started in 1948 when he played for Brooklyn's Baltimore farm club. A second "night" was in 1951 when he played in Brooklyn for the last time, and the third was in 1954 when he was traded from the Pittsburgh Pirates to the Baltimore Orioles. The Baltimore Jews embraced Abrams and his wife Mae as their way of saying, "what a source of pride it was for them to have a Jewish ball player."[96]

Cal Abrams, the son of a Russian working-class immigrant, was pursuing the American dream by playing ball, and Brooklyn's Jewish fans reacted when he put on a Brooklyn Dodger uniform for the first time in 1949. Here was a product of James Madison High School displaying his baseball skills just a few blocks away at Ebbets Field. It is not surprising that the *New York Post* spoke for its Jewish constituency in Brooklyn when it proclaimed, "Mantle, Schmantle, We got Abie."[97] Cal Abrams was the Great Jewish Hope to many Brooklyn fans in the late 1940s and early 1950s, but he never reached his expectations.[98]

He debuted with the Brooklyn Dodgers on April 20, 1949. His first major league hit was against future Hall of Famer Robin Roberts at Shibe Park, Philadelphia. Abrams played eight games for the Dodgers in 1949 before he was sent down to Fort Worth where he hit .333 and helped the club win the Texas League pennant.[99]

Rickey tried everything he could to make Abrams a pull hitter. He wanted him, as a left-handed batter, to take advantage of the short right field fence at Ebbets Field in order to hit more home runs. Abrams tried to accommodate Rickey, but he was never able to change his batting style, and accepted the fact but also asserted, "I knew that I could be a heck of a leadoff hitter because I had good eyes and could follow the ball, and could really hit."[100]

Cal Abrams split the 1950 season between the St. Paul Saints of the American Association and the Brooklyn Dodgers. He was called to the Dodgers when Carl Furillo got beaned and the team needed a right fielder. When he was permanently promoted to the Dodgers in 1950, Abrams changed his uniform number from 32 to 18. H explained "18 means a lot. The number 18 stands for the Hebrew word 'chai' which means life." He wore that number for most of his career. When Sandy Koufax came to the Dodgers he was assigned the number 32, which today is retired from the Dodgers.[101]

Abrams fully expected to see more action with Dodgers in 1950 but Furillo was not hurt as badly as the team had originally feared, and Abrams spent most of his time sitting on the bench. "I wasn't enjoying the life," said Abrams. "It reminded me of being overseas during the war. Most of the time I was busy packing and unpacking. Like a traveling salesman, you're living out of a suitcase. And that was one of the reasons I cut short my career. I wanted a home, wanted my family with me, wanted roots."[102]

Abrams finished the 1950 season hitting .205 with nine hits, no home runs, and only four RBIs.[103] He played only 38 games for the Dodgers, but one of the 38 games was the final game of the 1950 season. That game has become one of the most controversial in baseball history.

On September 19, 1950, the Philadelphia Phillies led the Brooklyn Dodgers by nine games with 15 left to play. By the final day of the season, Philadelphia's lead had dwindled to one game. If the Dodgers could defeat Philadelphia, they would tie the Phillies for the pennant and the two teams would have needed a one-game playoff.[104]

The score was tied, 1–1, in the bottom of the ninth. Cal Abrams led off the inning by drawing a walk on a 3–2 pitch. Pee Wee Reese, after two futile attempts to bunt, lined a single to left-center, sending Abrams to second and into scoring position. The next Dodger batter was Duke Snider; most fans and the Phillies fully expected Snider to bunt the runners over. Instead, Snider lined the first pitch into center field where Richie Ashburn was playing unusually shallow in preparation for a bunt. Even though Ashburn charged the ball, third-base coach Milt Stock waved Abrams home. Ashburn fired the ball to catcher Stan Lopata, who tagged Abrams out and the game remained tied.[105]

On the play at home, Reese went to third and Snider, who had singled, took second.

Abrams was the first out of the inning, but there were still runners on second and third. The Phillies, having no desire to pitch to Jackie Robinson with the pennant at stake, and also hoping to set up a double play, walked Robinson intentionally to load the bases. The next batter, Carl Furillo, swung at the first pitch and popped out feebly to first baseman Eddie Waitkus. With two outs, Gil Hodges hit the fly ball the Dodgers had so desperately wanted one batter earlier. Del Ennis, the Phillies right fielder speared Hodges' drive in deep right center near the scoreboard, forcing extra innings.[106]

In the top of the tenth inning, Dick Sisler hit a three-run homer. The Dodgers failed to score in their half of the tenth, and the 1950 Phillies, known as the Whiz Kids, won the pennant.[107] It was the closest Abrams ever got to the postseason.

After the game, Abrams told the press that he felt he should have been able to score on Snider's hit. According to Abrams, as he raced toward third he got the "go" sign from Coach Stock. "But it was the strangest 'go' sign I've ever seen," added Abrams. "He was half-heartedly waving me in with his left hand, while biting the fingers of his right hand. What happened was that, as he gave me the signal, he looked into the outfield and couldn't find the center fielder. Ashburn wasn't there anymore, but he kept signaling me in."

"Somebody was standing in my way when I rounded third, but when the base line cleared, I could see Stan Lopata with the ball," Abrams said. "Ashburn had made a bad throw that didn't come close to the plate. But he got to the ball so quickly; the throw was there in plenty of time, even if it was 20 feet up the line. All I could do was to try to knock the ball out of Lopata's hand. I hit him as hard as I could. It liked to have killed me, but he held on to the ball."[108]

The Dodgers' loss to the Phillies had two lasting results. First, it ended the season as well as the Dodgers' hope of going to the World Series in 1950. Second, Abrams' attempt to score on Snider's fly ball became the subject of heated conversations and debates. Even today, questions remain about where to place the blame for the Dodgers' loss.

New York Times sportswriter Roscoe McGowen wrote, "It will be hard to convince a lot of Flatbush fanatics that coach Milt Stock didn't make a bad decision."[109] Dodger Manager Burt Shotton, however, defended Stock's decision. "Milt played it right," he said after the game. "In a 1–1 game and with no one out, you send in the big run. Even though he was out, we still had runners on second and third and our three big hitters coming up."

At first, Shotton took the defeat graciously, placing the blame on nobody. However, Stock was let go as a Dodger coach shortly after the 1950 season; he never coached in the big leagues again.[110] Shotton did not blame Abrams directly for the play at home; he obviously forgot that Abrams was not a good base runner. In the spring of '49, Shotton had said of Abrams, "He don't score. He gets on base, and he's fast enough, but somehow he don't run the bases right and you have trouble moving him ahead. It takes two hits to score him from second base."[111]

Arthur Daley, bluntly wrote in his feature, "Sports of the *Times*," "The Brooks should have hit the jackpot in the ninth but the slot machine produced three lemons. The biggest lemon was Cal Abrams being thrown out at the plate with the winning run, an exceedingly foolish and disastrous bit of strategy."[112]

Richie Ashburn, who made the throw to retire Abrams at home, said, "I was surprised they sent him in. I was playing close—not unusually close, because you can't play Snider shallow—and the ball was hit sharp." Ashburn's manager, Eddie Sawyer, added, "The throw was the big thing. It was perfect. Ashburn's arm was weak early in the year and people got in the habit of running on him. But it's improved recently."[113]

Most baseball men agreed that Stock made the right play. If Ashburn did not make a good throw, Abrams scored, and even if he were out, Brooklyn had a runner at third base with only one out. The play would have been forgotten if Furillo had hit a ball out of the infield.[114]

The words of one Dodger fan summed up the feelings for the majority of Brooklyn's faithful. "I could have killed Cal Abrams for making that wide turn around third base. I never forgave him. That day I could have killed him with my bare hands."[115]

Even Abrams' most fervent Jewish fans were against him. Larry King, noted television host, minced no words when he spoke of the infamous play at home. "We were very Jewish and we wanted Jewish players to do well," he said. "Cal was a favorite. Cal had a lot of speed, and he was a good outfielder. But we uniformly despised him for the turn he took at third base in the final game against the Phillies in 1950. I loved Cal Abrams—until he got thrown out at home."[116]

Cal Abrams, the man most affected by the play, admitted that he was in a state of shock for quite a few days after the game. He read all the accounts of the play and maintained that that he was a victim of circumstance. "But as it turned out," revealed Abrams, "all these years I go out and make speeches and meet with people, and they all remember the play so vividly, and I'm very thankful that they do. Had I reached home, I don't think they would have remembered it as well, because many people get home safely and score."[117]

In all the interviews and accounts of the much-discussed play at home, there was never any mention of Cal Abrams' religion in connection with his being thrown out at the plate.

Prior to the start of the 1951 season, Charley Dressen replaced Burt Shotton as team manager. For a while Abrams was leading the National League in hitting with a .471 average, but appeared in only 67 games that year and finished the season with a batting mark of .280. Nevertheless, that was one of the years he was honored with a "Cal Abrams Night."[118] Abrams' Dodgers were leading the National League by 13½ games in August, yet their rivals, the New York Giants, caught them at the end of the season. Bobby Thomson hit his historic home run off Ralph Branca to win the pennant in the third and deciding game of the three-game playoff series. Although Abrams was on the bench when Thomson hit the home run, for the second consecutive year Abrams played for a team that lost the National League championship in the final game of the season.[119]

Abrams was perplexed about his lack of playing time. "I always had the feeling that Charley Dressen only played me enough to give me rope to hang myself. I remember one game, I hadn't been playing, and it's the ninth inning, bases loaded, and two outs. Dressen puts me in to pinch hit. I popped up. Meanwhile, there was an opportunity in the sixth and seventh for a left-handed batter, and the fans were yelling, 'We want Abrams,' and he wouldn't put me in. Then there was the time Pee Wee Reese had two strikes on him and Dressen sent me in to pitch hit. I don't recall in the history of baseball where any major league hitter ever had the same situation. Two strikes and to go up and pinch hit? Never in a million years. I could understand it if it was a rookie, but (Hall of Fame) shortstop Pee Wee Reese was up there. And two strikes? I popped out," said Abrams.[120]

Abrams never questioned Dressen about his lack of playing time in 1951. His manager told him that he was his number-one leadoff man because he had the best eyes in baseball. "Our coach, Clyde Sukeforth, would say in the newspaper, 'Cal Abrams can throw as hard and as accurately as Carl Furillo.' And all these clippings and you wonder why you never got a full season under your belt. If I went 0 for 15, they'd say, 'Cal is in a slump,' and I'd be out of the lineup. Yet other fellows, like Jackie, went 0 for 27, Hodges had 0 for 20, and they'd still play every day. So I'd say to myself, 'There has to be a reason why.' But you were so afraid to say anything that would in any way jeopardize your career. We had nothing but baseball. You had all your eggs in one basket, so you didn't dare voice your feelings or walk up to a guy like Charley Dressen and say, 'How come I'm not playing?'"[121]

For the first time, Cal Abrams felt that there might be a certain feeling of discrimination against him, but it was still too early to be sure. "As time progressed," stated Abrams, "I found out it was so and that Dressen did not particularly like the Jewish people."[122]

Although Cal Abrams did not publicly state that Charley Dressen was an anti–Semite or a bigot, Cal's son, David, said that his father painfully felt an anti–Semitic attitude, especially during his early years with the Dodgers. David said that Cal always suspected that Dressen had benched him after a torrid hitting streak because he couldn't visualize a Jewish player forcing his way into the everyday lineup. Sportswriter Maury Allen, who wrote about Abrams for the *New York Post*, checked old Dodgers box scores, and he discovered many games against right-handed pitchers when the lefty Abrams curiously was not in the starting lineup.[123]

If Cal Abrams was hesitant to talk about his manager and any anti–Semitism he might have faced, his wife, May, was not. In an interview she unhesitatingly stated that with her husband's ability, he would have been given more opportunity to play had he not been Jewish. "It's so subtle," she said, "it's under the surface, simmering all the time.... They don't have to come out and call you a dirty Jew for you to know that it's there. You feel it. I felt it with the wives all the time.... Cal and I never had a social life with ball players. We just didn't have the same values.... When I look back now, I think about things and I think that things would have different had we not been Jewish."[124]

Abrams played ten games for the Dodgers in 1952 and never got his job back. On June 9, 1952, the Cincinnati Reds purchased his contract. The trade took place between games of a doubleheader.[125] That day, with the Dodgers in first place playing two games against the Reds, Dressen told Abrams that if he wished to remain with the Dodgers he was to get on Rogers Hornsby, the Reds' manager. "Call him every goddam name you can think of. I want you to get him so mad he can't think straight." Abrams spent the first game of the doubleheader bellowing and screaming taunts at Hornsby. The Dodgers won the first game, 6–1, and Hornsby was raging. In the clubhouse between games, Dressen said to Abrams, "Don't bother to dress here. You've been traded. You're playing for the Cincinnati Reds. Abrams, your new manager is Rogers Hornsby."[126]

Despite Abrams' taunting, Hornsby was elated with the Abrams trade. "Abrams is doing right well out there," noted Hornsby. "He's suddenly started hitting to right field occasionally, even though he had the reputation as a dead left-field hitter. He is getting in more games and is getting around more on the ball." Hornsby was also pleased with Abrams' alertness when men were on base and his accurate throwing arm.[127]

In 71 games for the Reds in 1952, Abrams hit .278, with 44 hits in 158 at-bats. He also drove in 13 runs.[128] Abrams was especially proud that in 1952, he played in more games without making an error than any other National League outfielder.[129] The only disappointing aspect of the season was that the Dodgers won the pennant in 1952, but Abrams was not around to play in the World Series.

When Abrams was traded to the Reds in 1952 he was unaware that the Pittsburgh Pirates actually wanted Abrams on their team. However, in 1952, the new general manager was former Dodger executive Branch Rickey, and the Dodgers would not trade with him so

Rickey made a deal with Gabe Paul, the Reds' general manager. The Reds would purchase Abrams from the Dodgers, keep him in 1952, and then trade him to the Pirates.[130]

On October 14, 1952, the Cincinnati Reds sent Cal Abrams, catcher Joe Rossi, and outfielder Gail Henley, to the Pittsburgh Pirates for Gus Bell, a long-ball-hitting, 23-year-old outfielder.[131] It was with the Pittsburgh Pirates that Abrams had his most productive season in the majors. In 1953 he batted .286 with 15 home runs and a .435 slugging average—all career highs. On September 23, he hit his only career grand slam, off Giant hurler Ruben Gomez.[132]

Abrams started the 1954 season with the Pirates but was injured in the second game of the season. He played only 17 games for Branch Rickey, hitting a meager .143 before the Pirates traded him to the Baltimore Orioles for cash and pitcher Dick Littlefield. In his last 59 appearances at the plate for the Pirates, Abrams had only one hit.[133] His stats picked up when he joined the Orioles in 1954; he appeared in 115 games and ended the season with a .293 batting average. In addition, he ranked seventh in the American League with an on-base percentage of .400 and tenth in the league with seven triples.[134]

Abrams did well with the Orioles in 1955 also, posting a .413 OBP, and ranking eighth in the league in walks with 89. After the season ended, Baltimore traded Abrams to the Chicago White Sox, getting utility infielder Bobby Adams in return.[135]

Abrams ended his major league career with the White Sox in 1956. He appeared in only four games before Chicago sent the 32-year-old outfielder to the AAA Miami Marlins to make room on their roster for the newly-acquired Larry Doby.[136] Abrams retired from professional baseball at the conclusion of the 1956 season. He had played in 567 major league games with the Dodgers, Reds, Pirates, Orioles and White Sox. Ten years after he retired, Abrams was inducted into the B'nai Brith Jewish-American Hall of Fame in Washington, D.C.[137]

Towards the end of his life, Abrams had financial problems: one of his sons needed money for a kidney and pancreas transplant. For the first time, Abrams began charging for his autograph. Cal Abrams died of a heart attack on February 25, 1997, one week before his seventy-third birthday. According to his wishes, he was buried in his white Dodger uniform bearing the number 18. "He grew up in Brooklyn," said his widow. "We both grew up loving the Dodgers." Mrs. Abrams noted also that the most Cal had ever made in the majors was $22,000 a year with the Orioles.[138]

Writing about Cal Abrams, journalist Stan Izenberg, said, "Sing no sad songs for Cal Abrams.... He was a Brooklyn boy who made it to the Dodgers as a backup 'boy of summer.' If you were Brooklyn-raised and came to manhood in the Flatbush of the 1940s, nobody has to tell you that for the rest of his life, Cal Abrams could summon up the rarest of gifts from the back roads of his mind—the remembering of a childhood dream that came true."[139]

Lou Limmer

On May 2, 1951, at Briggs Stadium in Detroit, Philadelphia Athletics infielder Lou Limmer stepped into the batter's box to pinch-hit against Tiger hurler Saul Rogovin. Catcher Joe Ginsberg gave his pitcher the signal—Limmer swung and hit a line drive that cleared the right field fence for a home run. There is nothing unique about a home run, or even a pinch-hit home run. But on that May afternoon, Limmer's home run was indeed unique.

For the first and perhaps the only time in baseball history, the pitcher, the catcher and the hitter were all Jewish.[140]

Those attending the game might not have been aware of the situation, but home plate umpire Joe Paparella certainly was. When Lou Limmer stepped up to the plate, Paparella came from behind the plate, dusted it off, and said, "Boy, now, I've got three Heebs. I wonder who's going to win the battle." After Limmer rounded the bases and touched home plate, Paparella said, "I guess you're the winner, Lou."[141]

Lou Limmer was born March 10, 1925, in the Bronx, one of twelve children from an Orthodox Jewish household. He was a star athlete at Manhattan Aviation High School, also attended by Whitey Ford a few years later. Limmer, like many of his contemporary Jewish players, was in the military during World War II; he joined the Army Air Corps after graduation and served until 1946.

When he was discharged from the service, Limmer began his professional baseball career with Lexington in the North Carolina State League. Two years later, he was promoted to Lincoln, Nebraska, of the Western League. Two of his teammates there would become prominent major leaguers—pitcher Bobby Shantz and future Hall of Famer Nellie Fox. While playing for Lincoln in 1948, Limmer suffered a serious injury resulting in blindness for a few days. He recovered sufficiently to have an outstanding season and the following year, 1949, he led the Western League in both hitting and home runs.[142]

In 1950, the Philadelphia Athletics purchased his contract and he was sent to the St. Paul Saints in the American Association.[143] That year, 30 of the American Association's 36 baseball writers named Limmer the league's outstanding freshman.[144] Major league players were also taking note of Limmer's accomplishments. One was slugging Red Sox outfielder Ted Williams, who boldly predicted that Limmer would be a "great hitter." Ted Williams' playing abilities were much better than his eye for talent, for Limmer's career batting average fell a good deal short of greatness.[145]

Limmer's accomplishments at St. Paul, however, were sufficient for Philadelphia Athletics manager Connie Mack to sign the 23-year-old Limmer to a major league contract in 1951. Lou was one of the few Jews to play for the Athletics.[146] Philadelphia had high hopes for Limmer that year. The Athletics considered him the most likely of their 18 rookie hopefuls to make the team as a regular player and even debated trading their regular first baseman, Ferris Fain, to make room for Limmer.

The team's only concern was Limmer's ability to hit to left field. As a left-handed hitter, the six-foot, two-inch Limmer was strictly a pull hitter, hitting only one of his 29 home runs to left and having a batting average of only .197 in his home park. On the road, strangely, Limmer hit .354, for a composite average of .277, marking the first time in his four seasons in professional ball that he hit below .300. Limmer admitted his tendency to hit the ball to right field. "I can't even throw to left," he said.[147]

Limmer made his major league debut on April 22, 1951. The following day, Limmer had his first moment of glory. Sent in to pinch hit for Philadelphia catcher Joe Tipton, Limmer faced one of the top pitchers in the American League, Yankee Vic Raschi. Limmer got his first major league hit and his first home run as the ball sailed into the right field pavilion. His second high spot that year was his home run against Saul Rogovin.[148]

Unfortunately, Limmer could not unseat Fain as Philadelphia's regular first baseman. Lou appeared in 94 games that year but in 214 at-bats, he compiled a lowly .159 batting average, not withstanding his five home runs. Limmer remained with the club throughout the 1951 season, but on March 24, 1952, manager Jimmy Dykes dropped eight players from the squad. One of them was Limmer, who was sent to Ottawa of the International League.[149]

Both Jimmy Dykes and Philadelphia General Manager Arthur Ehlers agreed that sending Limmer to Ottawa was in his best interest. "With Fain entrenched at first, Limmer is certainly not going to improve sitting on the bench. He ought to be playing every day," Dykes pointed out. Said Ehlers. "The experience should do him a world of good. At the same time I know that he'll be able to do a lot of good for us in the International League until he's ready to come back into the majors. I don't think that will be too long."[150]

Limmer spent two years at Ottawa. Ferris Fain was traded to the White Sox following the 1952 season, but Limmer did not return to the Athletics until 1954. He still had to compete with two other candidates for the first base job—Vic Power and Don Bollweg. Bollweg won the job but suffered a minor break in the middle finger of his right hand and was unable to start on opening day. Manager Eddie Joost announced that Limmer would be the starting first baseman when the season opened.[151]

Despite the promising start, 1954 was Limmer's second and last big-league season. Lou hit 14 home runs and ten doubles in only 316 at-bats for a solid slugging average of .415, but his batting mark was a mere .213.[152] In his two seasons in the majors, Limmer had 107 hits in 530 at-bats for a lifetime batting average of .202.[153] He did manage to establish one record in 1954. On September 25, Lou Limmer hit the last home run for the Athletics before their move to Kansas City. It was his nineteenth career home run, but the A's still lost the game to the New York Yankees, 10–2.[154]

On May 2, 1951, at Briggs Stadium in Detroit, Lou Limmer pinch hit for the Athletics, facing Tiger pitcher Saul Rogovin. Behind the plate was catcher Joe Ginsberg. It is the only known time in major league baseball that a Jewish batter faced a Jewish pitcher with another Jew catching. Limmer hit a line drive over the right field fence (courtesy National Baseball Hall of Fame Library; Cooperstown, N.Y.).

When the A's moved west, Lou Boudreau took over as manager and made sweeping changes to the roster. On April 1, 1955, the Kansas City Athletics optioned four players to their farm club in the International League. One of them was Lou Limmer.[155] In 1958, Limmer ended his professional baseball career after seeing tours of duty with three more minor league teams.[156]

Limmer often stated that wherever he played in the minors, Jews reached out to him—whether it was a dairy owner in Lincoln or car dealers in Omaha and Toronto. He also recalled facing the first overt anti–Semitism of his life in the Deep South, seeing signs like "Jews, niggers, and dogs: Stay out." "I used to hang out with Jackie Robinson in Florida in spring training towns where neither of us was welcome. Jackie and I had a lot of trouble going into restaurants down south because they didn't allow blacks and Jews."[157]

After his retirement from baseball, Limmer went into the manufacture of commercial refrigeration. He also was very active in his synagogue and served a number of terms as president. What he enjoyed the most was visiting schools, talking baseball to the students and telling them baseball anecdotes. "I love it. These kids are something. They are so receptive to anything you say, whether it's politics, school, wartime experience, or whatever, I love to tell my audience all about it." Limmer never had a shortage of diamond tales to share with the children.[158]

Lou Limmer passed away April 1, 2007, in Boca Raton, Florida, at the age of 82.

Al Federoff

Al Federoff was another Jewish major leaguer of the late 1940s–early 1950s. Federoff began his professional baseball career after serving in the military until the conclusion of World War II.

Federoff was born on July 11, 1925, in Bairdford, Pennsylvania. He played both baseball and football in high school and enlisted in the army after graduation. After he was released from the service, he attended Duquesne University for two years before the Detroit Tigers signed him. A right-handed-hitting second baseman, Federhoff began his professional baseball career in 1946 in the Pony League, and he led the league in fielding in both 1946 and 1947. In 1947 he also led the league in assists.[159]

Fielding was not Federoff's only asset in baseball. When he was promoted to Flint, Michigan, in the Central League in 1948, he led that league in stolen bases as well as in both fielding and assists for a second baseman.[160]

By 1950, Federhoff had made it to Toledo of the American Association where he continued his outstanding defensive play. He set an amazing pace by taking part in 134 double plays in 133 games and even was involved in two triple plays.[161]

At the end of the 1951 season, the Tigers finally called Federoff to the big leagues.[162] Because of illness, he managed to play in only two games for the Tigers that year, and in his four plate appearances, he made four outs.[163]

Federhoff began the 1952 season with the Tigers' AAA farm club at Buffalo, but during the summer, the regular Tiger second baseman, Jerry Priddy, suffered a broken leg. The Tigers recalled Federoff in an effort to shore up a weakened infield.[164] He became the Tigers' regular second baseman for the final 74 games of the 1952 season, posting a .242 batting average. One of his teammates that year was starting catcher Joe Ginsberg. The Tigers finished the season in last place, but the one high spot for Federoff was the no-hitter Virgil Trucks hurled on August 25 against the Yankees. In a 1–0 victory for the Bengals, Federoff made the final putout.[165]

When Priddy's broken leg mended, he reclaimed the starting second-base assignment. Federoff played in the minors from 1953 to 1959, ending his playing career in 1959. He then managed various minor league teams from 1960 through 1970.[166]

Herb Gorman

Herbert Allen Gorman had the unfortunate distinction of being the shortest-lived of all Jewish major league players.

He was born December 19, 1924, in San Francisco, the son of Harry and Jennie Cohen Gorman. Gorman, too, played baseball in military service during World War II.

He began his professional career at the age of 22 as both a first baseman and an outfielder for Three Rivers of the Canada-America League in 1946. He continued to shine offensively for the next two years, reaching the AAA Hollywood Stars of the Pacific Coast League by 1949 where he played that year and in 1950.[167]

Gorman spent the last half of the 1951 season on the disabled list with Hollywood because of a broken foot. During the first half of the season, however, Gorman managed to hit .275 and drive in 53 runs, and the St. Louis Cardinals drafted him in 1952.[168] Also in 1952, before the season started, Gorman married Rosalie Bloom of Los Angeles.[169]

Gorman made his only major league appearance on April 15, 1952, with the Cardinals. St Louis was playing the Chicago Cubs at Wrigley Field, and Gorman was called on to pinch hit for pitcher Willard Schmidt in the seventh inning. He grounded out as the Cubs defeated the Cardinals, 8–1.[170]

In 1953, Herb Gorman was back in AAA and on the roster of the San Diego Padres, playing for manager Lefty O'Doul. On April 6, San Diego had a doubleheader scheduled with Bobby Bragan's Hollywood Stars. This was Gorman's first game of the season, as O'Doul wanted to try out some of his new players. When Padres coach Jimmy Reese informed Gorman that he was in the starting lineup, he appeared in good spirits. "Gee, that's fine," Gorman told Reese. "I'm ready."

Gorman doubled in each of his two at-bats, but when he took the field in the sixth inning, he called time out. Buddy Peterson, the Padres' shortstop, ran to him, then turned and called for help.

Gorman had collapsed on the field. He was taken to the dressing room where he lapsed into unconsciousness, and although he was given oxygen, he did not revive. An ambulance took the young outfielder, still in uniform, to Mercy Hospital where he was pronounced dead on arrival. It was determined that a massive blood clot, which normally forms over an extended period of time, caused Gorman's death when it reached his heart.

Word of his death reached the field in the ninth inning of the first game. The second game of the doubleheader was immediately cancelled, and O'Doul ordered Gorman's number, 25, taken off the roster, never to be used again.[171] (The number 25 was reissued later when the San Diego Padres became an expansion team in the National League.)

Outfielder Herb Gorman made only one appearance in the major leagues when on April 19, 1952, the St. Louis Cardinals used him as pinch-hitter for pitcher Willard Schmidt. The following year, while playing the outfield for San Diego in the Pacific Coast League, Gorman collapsed in the field and died of a massive heart attack. At age twenty-eight, he had the shortest life of any Jewish major leaguer (courtesy St. Louis Cardinals).

Among those watching the game was Clarence Rowland, president of the league, who said, "Herb Gorman was an outstanding character and a credit to the game. He will be missed." Similar sentiments were expressed by San Diego president Bill Starr and manager Lefty O'Doul.[172] O'Doul really spoke for all who knew Gorman when he said, "He never caused trouble—he just wanted to play. A quiet fellow who just minded his own business. It's a terrible loss."[173]

Hy Cohen

Many professional baseball players had their careers interrupted by World War II, but Hy Cohen was one of the earliest to be affected by the Korean Conflict. Two different professional teams seeking a Jewish ball player also drafted him.

Hy Cohen was born January 29, 1931, in Brooklyn to two immigrant parents. His father, Joseph, had come to America from Warsaw, Poland, and his mother, Bessie, was from Brest-Litovsk, Russia. In 1948, the New York Yankees, in their perennial search for a Jewish player, drafted Cohen, who was then just seventeen years old, and shipped him to their Class D farm club in LaGrange, Georgia. The six-foot, five-inch, 220-pound right-handed pitcher spent two years in the minors only to be told that his contract was not going to be renewed for a third year. The Yankees later informed him that this had been an oversight and it had nothing to do with his baseball skills.

Regardless of the excuse given him by the Yankees, Cohen signed with the Chicago Cubs in 1951. He started the season with the Cubs' Class A farm club and was promoted twice during the season, ending with the AAA Iowa Cubs. His season record there was 16–10; he had a 2.86 ERA, and three playoff victories. With this great showing in 1951, it seems likely that the Cubs would have added him to their roster in 1952, but he was drafted by the U.S. Army to serve in the Korean Conflict.[174]

Ironically, Cohen was sent to an army base in San Antonio and was assigned to play baseball, along with major leaguers Bobby Brown, Don Newcombe, Gus Triandos, Bob Turley, Dick Kokos, and Owen Friend. Also assigned to the army base was a fellow Jewish player, Marv Rotblatt. Cohen remained in San Antonio for two years before he returned to the Chicago Cubs minor league system in 1954 where he began the season with the AAA Los Angeles Angels in the Pacific Coast League. He soon returned to Iowa where he had a great year, ending with an ERA of 1.88; this time he was called up to Chicago at the end of the year but did not make his first appearance until the following season.

Hy Cohen debuted with the Cubs on April 17, 1955; he pitched his final game on June 2, 1955, starting only one of the seven games in which he appeared and allowing 28 hits in 17 innings for an ERA of 7.94.[175] His tenure in the majors was so brief that he did not even stay around long enough to see his Topps trading card produced.[176]

After he left the Cubs, Cohen played for a number of other minor league teams including the Toronto Maple Leafs of the International League. Leafs president Jack Kent Cooke had been seeking a Jewish star for his Toronto club, hoping to attract the large Toronto Jewish population. Shortly after Cooke bought Cohen's contract, however, Cohen began to develop arm problems and retired from baseball.[177]

Cohen returned to school after his retirement, and in 1966 he received his Master's Degree. Like Jewish baseball player Saul Rogovin, Hy Cohen began a second career as a teacher. The Los Angeles public school system hired him to teach social studies and physical education at Birmingham High School. He also coached football, baseball, and tennis. His baseball team won two city championships. In 1995, Hy Cohen was honored at Dodger Stadium for his outstanding achievement in baseball education. He rejoined one of his old army buddies, Don Newcombe, and his old Dodger rival, manager Tommy Lasorda.[178]

Al Silvera

Pitcher "Subway Sam" Nahem had a brief baseball career in the late 1930s and early 1940s, but his nephew, Al Silvera, had an even shorter one. An outfielder, Silvera played in only 14 games in 1955 and 1956, and had only seven career at-bats.[179]

Aaron Albert "Al" Silvera was born on August 26, 1935, in San Diego, California. He was an outstanding athlete at Fairfax High School; in freshman baseball at the University of Southern California, he batted .405 with 14 home runs, including 5 grand slams.[180]

The six-foot, 180-pound Italian Jew spoke neither Italian nor Hebrew, but he was able to converse in Syrian, which, along with English, was spoken in his home. Al's father had been born in Italy, but he grew up in Syria before coming to the United States. His father met Al's Jewish mother in Brooklyn; she helped him learn to speak English.

Silvera enrolled at Southern California for a good reason. As Al related, "The very athletic-minded officials of the USC made me a very attractive proposition to enroll there. It was a real good deal."[181] While at Southern Cal, Silvera was named Co-Player of the Year with another future Jewish major leaguer, pitcher Barry Latman. It was the first time that the university named co-players of the year in baseball.[182]

After playing college ball for one year, Silvera received offers from many major league clubs to turn pro. He chose to sign with the Cincinnati Reds on June 12, 1955, accepting a bonus of $50,000, and becoming the Reds' first bonus player under the then-existing rule which stated that once a major league team signed a bonus player, that player had to remain with the parent club for two years before he could be sent down to the minors. Cincinnati manager Birdie Tebbetts indicated that he intended to "break him [Silvera] into the lineup gradually."[183]

Bonus baby Al Silvera played for Cincinnati in 1955 and 1956. He appeared in just 14 games and had only seven career at bats, six of them as a pinch-hitter. When no longer a player, Silvera became active in the Los Angeles Jewish community and after battling brain cancer for 15 years, he passed away in 2002. The following year he was inducted into the Southern California Jewish Hall of Fame (courtesy Cincinnati Reds).

Silvera was put into the lineup very gradually, indeed, for throughout the entire 1955 season, he appeared in only 13 games for the Reds. He had one hit in his seven at-bats for an average of .143. Six of his seven appearances were as a pinch hitter. He did manage to score three runs and drive in two.[184]

In 1956 Silvera returned to play his second year for Cincinnati. The team had changed its name from the Reds to the Redlegs that year due to the "Red Scare" inspired by the witch-hunts of Wisconsin Senator Joseph McCarthy. This name change was to last for only one year.[185]

During spring training in Tampa that year, manager Tebbets gave Silvera a catcher's mitt and began assigning him to catch in the exhibition games. Silvera realized that he did not have the power or speed to become a standout as an outfielder, but that as a catcher, he might be able to prolong his major league career. Tebbets, a former catcher himself, was pleased with Silvera's performance behind the plate and told the press, "He looks as though he has been a catcher all of his life, and here I was afraid the kid might get killed when I put him behind the plate."

Silvera had no illusions that he could learn the techniques of catching overnight. "There is one thing in my favor," he stated. "The job's all new to me. I've got no bad habits to break. And my instructors are the best."[186]

Unfortunately for Silvera, he had no future either as a catcher or as a major league ball player. In 1956 he appeared in one game for the Redlegs and did not get any at-bats. He finished his career with a lifetime batting average of .143.[187]

On May 15, 1956, the Redlegs asked waivers for the purpose of an unconditional release for the 20-year-old player.[188] Silvera was the only player the Reds ever signed under the bonus rule as it existed in the 1950s. Gabe Paul, general manger of the Reds, explained that he was not "fed up" with bonus players, but "We have to have one that can play major league baseball right today. If we were building for a couple years ahead we might have kept Silvera, hoping some day he'd make our lineup."[189]

After his brief stint in the majors, Al Silvera moved to Los Angeles and worked for a manufacturing company. He also coached Little League for 15 years. Silvera also became active in the Los Angeles Jewish community and was honored by the city of Beverly Hills in 1983 for being a role model, mentor, and inspiration to legions of Little Leaguers.[190]

Al Silvera passed away July 24, 2002, at the age of 66 after a long battle with brain cancer. He was posthumously inducted into the Southern California Jewish Sports Hall of Fame in January 2003.[191]

Al Richter

Al Richter, one of 12 Jewish major leaguers to play for the Boston Red Sox, was born in Norfolk, Virginia, on February 7, 1927.[192] He was the youngest of three children of Sol and Flora Richter. In 1945 the Boston Red Sox signed Richter as an amateur free agent shortstop and assigned him to Louisville of the American Association.[193]

The Army Air Corps drafted Richter; he served for 18 months before returning to Louisville for the start of the 1947 season. He also enrolled at the University of Miami during the off-season.

Richter played the following two seasons with Scranton in the Eastern League before returning to Louisville in 1950. He continued to play for Louisville most of 1951 until the Red Sox brought him to the major leagues on September 20, 1951. He debuted two days later as a pinch hitter and hit into a double play. A week later he got his only hit that season. Richter appeared in just five major league games for the Red Sox that year, made 11 plate appearances, and hit .091 for the season.[194] At the end of 1951, Richter, in a ceremony at

Fenway Park, was awarded the Look Magazine Award, as the minor league All-Star short-stop of the year.[195]

In 1952 Richter played all season with the San Diego Padres in the Pacific Coast League;

one of his teammates was Herb Gorman. The following year Al came up from the minors for a very brief stint with Boston. On April 21, 1953, he played shortstop in one game for the Red Sox, but did not have an at-bat. Five days later, the Red Sox sent Richter and pitcher Ike Delock back to Louisville. It was the third time Richter had been optioned out. He stated that he would give it one more season and then quit if he could not make the grade.[196] That same year, Richter received his degree in business administration from the University of Miami.[197]

He played professional baseball two more years—in 1954 and 1955 with Rochester in the International League, a St. Louis Cardinal affiliate. After that season, he played winter ball in the Dominican Republic and then retired from baseball.

Richter began careers in real estate and food merchandising and also hosted a fifteen-minute television show prior to the "Sunday Game of the Week," called "Spotlight on Sports." In 1983, Richter was inducted into the Norfolk, Virginia, Sports Hall of Fame.[198]

Shortstop Al Richter, who played in six games for the Boston Red Sox during the early 1950s, was the first Jew to play for the Bosox since Moe Berg from 1935 to 1939. A graduate of the University of Miami with a degree in business, Richter played two more years in the minors and then retired from baseball to begin a career in real estate and food merchandising (courtesy Boston Red Sox).

Moe Savransky

Moe Savransky was another Jewish player whose career was interrupted by the Korean Conflict. Born Morris Savransky, on January 13, 1929, in Cleveland, he later changed his name to Moe. In 1947, a year before he graduated, Savransky pitched in the Amateur World Series in Brooklyn and the Ohio State High School Championships.

After a Cincinnati Red scout saw Savransky playing on a Cleveland sandlot team, he signed him for the Reds organization. Moe was sent to Sunbury, Pennsylvania, a Cincinnati Class B team. His record there was 6–4 with a 3.67 ERA. The young southpaw started the season poorly, but won his last six games. During the off-season he attended Ohio State University and also remained in the Reds organization, pitching for various Reds farm teams. Moe was a standout hurler with the Columbia Reds in 1950. He led the South Atlantic League in ERA (2.55) and shutouts (5). His record was 15–7 and he tossed the league's only no-hitter that year.[199]

In 1951, Savransky was promoted to AAA, and pitched for the Buffalo Bisons, compiling an ERA of 2.92 despite walking 104 batters in 185 innings. His excellent ERA ranked sixth in the International League, but he could not pitch the following two years due to military service.

When Savransky was released from service in 1954, he went directly to the Cincinnati Reds, making his major league debut on April 23, 1954. His record that year, the only year he pitched in the major leagues, was 0–2 in 16 games. He did not start any games; all his major league appearances were out of the bullpen.[200]

On June 25, when Umpire Frank Secory chased Moe Savransky off the Reds' bench in Pittsburgh, many of those present, and especially the Pittsburgh writers, learned for the first time that he was on the team.[201] Savransky retired from the majors at the end of the 1954 season, and after one year in the minors, retired completely from baseball.[202]

Moe Savransky, a native of Cleveland, spent his one-year major league career with the other Ohio major league team—the Cincinnati Reds in 1954. He pitched in only 16 games, compiling a record of 0–2 in 24 innings. Savransky retired from professional ball at the end of that year (courtesy National Baseball Hall of Fame Library; Cooperstown, N.Y.).

2. "...and Last in the American League"

"First in shoes, first in booze, and last in the American League" was a fairly accurate description of St. Louis for most of the years from 1901 through 1953. The city was a leader in shoe manufacturing and distribution and the location for a large number of breweries including the powerhouse Anheuser-Busch, Inc., the brewer of Budweiser and Michelob.[1]

St. Louis was also home to two major league baseball teams, the National League Cardinals and the American League Browns. Although the Cardinals certainly did not reward their fans with a spectacular performance every season during that period, the consistently disappointing Browns were almost always at or near the bottom of the standings in the junior circuit. In fact, the only pennant the Browns won during their tenure in St. Louis was in 1944 when many able-bodied players were serving in World War II. (And even then, they lost the World Series to the Cardinals that year, 4 games to 2.)

During their history, the Browns included a few Jewish players on their roster. Harry Kane (who changed his name from Cohen when he entered professional baseball) pitched in four games for the Browns in 1902, and Jim Levey was the Browns' regular shortstop in 1930. Right-handed pitcher Barney Pelty proudly bore the nickname, "The Yiddish Curver" and played for the St. Louis Browns from 1903 to 1912. Although he finished his career with a 92–117 record, he was considered one of the finest American League pitchers of his day.[2] Ike Danning, brother of Harry Danning, caught briefly for the Browns in 1927, and a fifth Jew, Bud Swartz, pitched for the Browns in 1947. In the 1950s, only two Jewish players, Sid Schacht and Duke Markell, were St. Louis Browns, and both had very short playing careers in the majors.[3]

Sid Schacht

Sidney Schacht, often confused with baseball clown Al Schacht, but no relation, was a right-handed pitcher for the St. Louis Browns and the Boston Braves. He was born in Bogota, New Jersey, on February 3, 1918. Schacht began his professional career in 1947 with Stamford, Connecticut. While he played there, he commuted to his home in the Bronx to care for his sick mother. Schacht was known as a control pitcher, and this enabled him to finish the '47 season with a record of 18–7. His outstanding work at Stamford earned Schacht a promotion to pitch for the San Diego Padres in the Pacific Coast League, but because his mother was still ill, he remained at Stamford where he compiled a record of 7–8 in 1948. His low ERA of 2.09, however, led the league. After his mother's death that fall, the Boston Red Sox organization purchased his contract.[4]

His new contract was a generous one, but it would have branded him a "bonus player," and Schacht objected to playing under the bonus rules of the day. He began the 1949 season pitching briefly for Birmingham until he was demoted to Scranton where he greatly improved, as was evidenced by his record of 19–5 and an ERA of 2.44. His excellent control was a major factor in his success in the minor leagues. From 1947 to 1949, Sid Schacht walked only 168 batters in 596 innings while fanning 353. At the end of the 1949 season, the St. Louis Browns purchased his contract.[5]

Bob Broeg, sportswriter for the *St. Louis Post-Dispatch*, covered the St. Louis Browns at their spring training camp in 1950. He was impressed with the progress Sid Schacht was making. "On the strength of his savvy and sneaky stuff," wrote Broeg, "Schacht, who originally was more or less earmarked for San Antonio, apparently could make the immediate jump from Scranton of the Class A Eastern League to the American League."[6]

Schacht began the 1950 season with the Browns, and on April 20, 1950, the 32-year-old righty made his major league debut at Sportsman's Park in St. Louis. Entering the game in the seventh inning, Schacht gave up one run. Unfortunately for Schacht, the game was called after the seventh inning, and the Browns lost 7–6.[7]

Schacht completed the 1950 season with the Browns, making eight appearances, starting one game and pitching in 10.2 innings. His control deserted him as he struck out seven batters while walking 19 and allowed 19 earned runs for an ERA of 16.03.

The following year Schacht was released by the Browns on May 14, and on the same day general manager John Quinn of the Boston Braves purchased his contract.[8] One of his teammates at Boston was another Jewish player, Sid Gordon. Less than two months later, the Braves announced that veteran infielder Gene Mauch and pitcher Sid Schacht had been released outright to Milwaukee of the American Association. Schacht retired from baseball at the end of the 1951 season. For 1951, his combined statistics with the Browns and Braves was a won–loss record of 0–2, both with the Braves, and an ERA of 3.05, a vast improvement over 1950.[9] Schacht died on March 30, 1991, in Ft. Lauderdale, Florida, at the age of 73.[10]

Duke Markell

Harry Duquesne "Duke" Markell was the last Jewish player to wear the St. Louis Browns uniform. Born Harry Duquesne Makowsky in Paris, France, on July 17, 1923, his family moved to New York City in 1930 and changed its name long before Markell was old enough to even consider playing professional baseball.

Duke claimed that from the moment he entered the United States, he fell in love with baseball and always had a bat and ball handy. His home in the Bronx was only four blocks from Yankee Stadium and he often remarked that he looked forward to the day when he could pitch in the "House That Ruth Built." When the Detroit Tigers came to New York, Tiger slugger Hank Greenberg would hire neighborhood boys to "shag" flies for him during batting practice. Although he had always wanted to be a pitcher, he later wrote, "Hank Greenberg was my inspiration"[11]

Markell had to delay his baseball plans because of World War II. Three years after he graduated from James Monroe High School, he entered the Army and won a field commission while serving in the Philippines. He was honorably discharged in 1945.

That same year, he began his minor league career. His first stop was Hickory, North Carolina, in the North Carolina State League, where he posted a 5–2 record and an ERA of 2.63, appearing in 15 games. One of his five wins was a no-hitter.[12] From 1946 through 1951, Markell pitched in the minors, moving up in class and setting strikeout records several years.

In 1947, he struck out 11 consecutive batters in one game and also set the Eastern Shore League record of strikeouts with 274. In 1948, he set a new Canadian-American league record when he struck out 270 hitters. Markell began the 1951 season with Oklahoma City in the Texas League. Although he had a record of 13–19, he allowed only 218 hits in 273 innings, had a strikeout-to-walk ratio of 211–129, and posted an ERA of 2.77.[13]

Markell was promoted to the St. Louis Browns when he completed his season at Oklahoma City, making his major league

Duke Markell was born Harry Duquesne Makowsky in France in 1923. The family name was changed to Markell when seven-year-old Duke and his family immigrated to the U.S. in 1930. Markell's entire major-league playing career consisted of 21.1 innings pitched for the St. Louis Browns in 1951. While still in the minors in 1953, Markell began working as a New York City policeman during the off-season. Duke Markell died in Ft. Lauderdale, Florida, at the age of 61 (courtesy National Baseball Hall of Fame Library; Cooperstown, N.Y.).

debut on September 6, 1951, by pitching three innings in relief of Fred Hutchinson. The Chicago White Sox defeated the St. Louis Browns, 9–4.[14] Three weeks later, Markell registered his only major league triumph when the Browns defeated the Detroit Tigers, 7–4, in the final game of the season between the two clubs.[15] That year, Duke Markell pitched in only five major league games, including two starts. His record was 1–1 with a high ERA of 6.33.[16]

Markell had a great record in the minor leagues, but after the 1951 season, he never again pitched in the majors. He saw little action during spring training in 1952. Browns manager Rogers Hornsby explained that he did not dislike Markell, but that the Browns were loaded with pitching talent in 1952.[17] Whatever the reason, at the end of March, the Browns optioned Markell to Toronto in the International League.[18] During the 1952 season the Philadelphia Phillies obtained Markell and sent him to Syracuse, also in the International League. He won 11 games for Syracuse in 1952 and led the league in strikeouts. At the beginning of 1953 spring training, the Philadelphia Phillies invited Markell to their camp, but he did not win a place on their roster.[19]

In the spring of 1953, Markell

began wearing a new type of uniform—he had become a New York City "cop" during the baseball off-season. But he also continued to play excellent minor league ball for a number of years. He pitched for Syracuse again in 1953, and on August 6, 1953, hurled a no-hit game against the Toronto Maple Leafs.[20] In addition, Markell led the International League in strikeouts for the second consecutive year.[21]

In 1955, while a member of the Rochester Red Wings in the International League, Markell pitched another no-hitter, this time against the Columbus Jets. The Jets were able to put only two men on base: Hector Lopez, who walked in the fourth inning, and former Athletics player and fellow Jew, Lou Limmer, who was hit by a pitch in the fifth. The closest the Jets came to getting a hit was a ball that bounced off Markell's glove. Fortunately for Markell, another Jewish player, shortstop Al Richter, made a fine play and threw the batter out at first.[22]

Markell pitched for his last team in 1956 and 1957, the Charleston Senators in the American Association. In 1958 he permanently retired from baseball and became a full-time policeman. On June 14, 1984, Duke Markell died in Ft. Lauderdale, Florida, at the age of 61.[23]

Max Patkin

Al Schacht and Max Patkin had much in common. Both were Jewish, both began their careers in baseball as pitchers, and both were major attractions for fans who attended a baseball game. At different times, both were known by the sobriquet "Clown Prince of Baseball."

They were also different in a number of ways. Patkin was physically much taller and lankier than Schacht and included more slapstick in his acts. While Schacht usually performed before or between games and, on rare occasions, between innings, Patkin always performed during the game itself, much to the chagrin of many fans, managers, and players who felt he was a distraction that interrupted the flow of the game. Unlike Schacht, Patkin today is recognized as the inspiration for the numerous mascots who entertain at both major and minor league games.[24] While Schacht never publicly expressed his feelings about Patkin, Max Patkin often stated, "[Al Schacht] never treated me nice."[25] Even though Al Schacht was the first to be called "The Clown Prince," many believe Patkin was the most memorable.[26]

Max Patkin was a first-generation American; his parents, Samuel H. and Rebecca Patkin, were both born in Russia and settled in Philadelphia where Samuel had relatives. Max, one of three children, was born January 10, 1920. In 1928, his Hebrew School teacher took the class to Shibe Park, and Patkin immediately became a baseball fan while watching Jimmy Foxx play.[27]

Patkin was not the greatest student; he even failed physical education at West Philadelphia High School. However, the coach of the baseball team was intrigued by Patkin's unusual high kick when he threw the ball, and Max soon became a pitcher for the school's second-string team. When his school's varsity team called a wildcat strike, the tall and gangly Patkin got a chance to start a game. He not only struck out 15 batters, he also won the game.[28] "I was a tall and skinny kid with a big nose," recalled Patkin, "and I was very sensitive about my looks. But when I went on the mound and threw a fastball, nobody laughed. I was a hell of a pitcher."[29]

After tryouts with several major league clubs, Patkin signed with the Chicago White Sox in 1941 and went to their farm club in the Wisconsin State League, the Wisconsin Rapids. Pitching in 17 games in 1941, Patkin compiled a record of 10–7. The following year, team officials asked Patkin to have an operation to remove bone chips in his shoulder, and when he refused, he was fired. Green Bay, also in the Wisconsin State League, picked him up, but he and his pitching coach never could get along, and when the 1942 season ended, Green Bay became the second team to fire him. While he was with Green Bay, however, the team used him as a first base coach where he would direct comments to the opposing team's bench, trying to needle the players. This was the earliest sign of what would become his "clowning act."[30]

While he played in the minor leagues, Patkin encountered anti–Semitism and also witnessed discrimination against black ball players. "I've caught my share of bigotry," he stated. "Overheard a fan once talking about a black player, saying 'He's nothing but a Jew turned inside out.' Fought a teammate in the Wisconsin State League who called me a "dirty Jew." And there was a brutal bus ride from Kinston to Durham, when I got a bigot kicked off the bus."

"And I had it easy compared with the black ballplayers in the South. There were separate water fountains for blacks, separate men's rooms. The black, minor-league players had to really want to make good, considering the conditions they had to endure. They'd have to take a bus ride to the other side of the tracks while their white teammates stayed in the one good hotel in town."[31]

Max Patkin, who was the second man termed the "Clown Prince of Baseball," performed at literally thousands of barnstorming engagements throughout his career. Tall and gangly with a face that was described as the world's biggest hunk of bubblegum, his slapstick routines amused both fans and players. Few were aware, however, that Patkin was a shy, lonely and insecure individual, who would rather have been a major-league ballplayer than a clown (courtesy National Baseball Hall of Fame Library; Cooperstown, N.Y.).

After his release from Green Bay, Patkin joined the Navy and spent most of his World War II service at Pearl Harbor. In 1944 he was pitching for a military team when Joe DiMaggio homered against him. In mock anger, Patkin threw his glove to the mound, twisted his head sideways and began to follow DiMaggio around the bases, much to the delight of the fans. DiMaggio was furious, and the madder he got, the louder the crowd roared. It was at that moment that Patkin sensed that his career was born. "I really could break 'em up on the base paths," he said.[32]

Following the war, Patkin pitched for Wilkes-Barre in the Eastern League and compiled a 1–1 record before he was given his release. Soon after, Lou Boudreau, manager of the Cleveland Indians, who had seen Patkin's antics, hired him to perform his comedy routine during an exhibition game between the Indians and its farm team at Harrisburg. Boudreau introduced Patkin to Indians' owner, Bill Veeck, who watched Patkin perform, and he also liked what he saw. He commented that Patkin looked as if someone having trouble reading the instructions had assembled him.[33] Veeck hired Patkin as his first base coach for the Indians for 1946 and 1947 with the understanding that his clowning was much more important than his coaching.

Patkin was six feet, three inches tall, but 30 percent of that seemed to be neck. He was described as having two miles of arms and a face that looked like the world's biggest hunk of bubblegum. One columnist wrote that his neck was so long he could read over the shoulders of two people and, when he wound up on the mound, he had to be careful his two arms did not send the rest of him somersaulting like a guy caught on a propeller. "He was 140 pounds of nervous tic. He looked as if he had a permanent case of the hiccups. His ears should have had lights on them," wrote columnist Jim Murray.[34]

One of his routines started out in the batter's box. First, he would dodge a brushback pitch. Then he would take a fastball over the heart of the plate and push the catcher over. Finally, he would connect on a lob thrown by the pitcher, run to third base, be tagged out, and engage in an epic argument that usually saw him tossed him out of the park. Before he left, he would show the third-base coach how to give signs while dancing to "Rock Around the Clock" and take long drinks of water and spew a geyser. Patkin estimated that throughout his career, he also dropped his pants in front of ten million people.[35]

Patkin normally would coach only during the early innings of the games when his capers would be less provoking. However, his constant mocking of umpire's calls often got him thrown out of games. Two clubs, the St. Louis Browns and the New York Yankees, actually lodged formal complaints against Patkin remaining in the first base coaching box.[36] If Patkin was concerned about the action taken by these two teams, Bill Veeck was not. Patkin apologized to Veeck who asked his clown, "Did they spell your name right?" Max replied "Yes," and Veeck then asked, "What can you possibly be worried about?"[37]

One of the loudest complaints to the American League office came from Clark Griffith, president of the Washington Senators. Griffith was the same man who had previously employed Al Schacht, Germany Schaefer, and Nick Altrock to clown on the coaching lines. Griffith charged that Patkin wasn't "dignified." He also asserted that his players were laughing at Max when they should have had their minds on the game. But Patkin stayed.[38]

In 1947 Cleveland got off to an excellent start and began to contend for the American League pennant. The Indians released their clown, Max Patkin, because he was so good at his trade he was a distraction to both the Indians and the visiting teams. Lou Boudreau admitted that the fans came to Cleveland's games to see the sideshow in the first base coaching box rather than to see the Indians make a run for the pennant.[39]

Steve O'Neill, who was managing the Detroit Tigers when Patkin coached for the Indians, called Patkin "Cleveland's tenth man." "The guy is wonderful," noted O'Neill. "But how can you play ball when you hear the fans laugh and know that everyone in the park is watching Patkin?" Eddie Mayo, O'Neill's second baseman echoed the sentiments of his manager. "Try as I will, I have to sneak a look at that clown, and when I do, I have to laugh. I'm always afraid I'll be laughing when I ought to be covering second base."[40]

Patkin fully understood why he was no longer an Indian coach. "I was first sent to the bench and then handed a pink slip. If I had thrown only slow ones instead of fast ones, I might have still been there," he said regretfully.[41] He then began entertaining in minor league parks, something he would do off and on for the next 50 years.

When Veeck sold the Indians in 1949, Patkin was barnstorming around the country, appearing in minor league stadiums throughout the United States and Canada. He always wore a baggy uniform with a question mark (?) on the back where a number should have been and a ball cap always off center over one eye.[42]

In 1950, Patkin signed with the Philadelphia Phillies to serve as their "club jester" and to entertain and distribute gifts from the Phillies to children in orphanages.[43]

Bill Veeck was back in baseball in 1951 when he purchased the lowly St. Louis Browns; he rehired Patkin to take his position in the first base coaching box. The following year, Veeck brought in baseball legend Rogers Hornsby to manage the St. Louis Browns. One of the first public comments Hornsby made after he was hired as manager was to set limits on the team clown. "Patkin can clown before the game, or between games of a doubleheader, but I don't want his clowning during the game. When I'm losing a ball game in the fifth or sixth inning, I'm in no mood for laughing or seeing any clowning. Losing a ball game never was fun for me."[44] Hornsby served only a few months of his three-year contract, and after his departure, Patkin resumed his full-time coaching and clowning for the Browns, continuing to amuse the sparse crowds attending their games.[45]

Patkin's final long-term job in the major leagues was 1953; the last year the Browns remained in St. Louis prior to their move to Baltimore. Ed Mickelson played on the 1953 Brownie team and remembered Max Patkin. "I swear," said Mickelson, "that Patkin appeared everywhere in organized baseball except the Pacific Coast League. He always liked to imitate first basemen, imitating their every move. He was a great contortionist. I remember he always used to say to us players—'I'm tired, I've been breathing all day.' Actually he could be a very serious guy, but he seemed to me he was very intellectual. The fans loved him— they loved how he could make his body into a pretzel."[46]

Patkin spent most of the remainder of his career all over the minor leagues. When he first returned to the minors in 1954, he was alarmed at how the minor leagues had deteriorated. "I travel around the country all season," bemoaned Patkin, "and I visit more of the smaller cities than any official in the game and I'm worried about what I see. The local sports pages play up the major leagues over the minors. The majors are mentioned first on the radio. Everybody's talking about the major league players. It's not a good situation."[47]

Even as he continued his annual tours, Patkin continued to predict the demise of minor league baseball. He numbered among the culprits for the bleak situation air-conditioned homes, television, outdoor theaters, automobiles, and the lack of colorful players. Patkin also blamed the lack of new minor league parks. "They aren't being built. In most places it's a disgrace to walk into the rest rooms. And there are no good promotions in the minor leagues. It's wrong to open the doors and let 'em in for nothing. You're giving away the product and it's cheapening it."[48]

Patkin received a great deal of static about his negative remarks concerning the future of minor league baseball. Several minor league executives threatened to cancel his future performances, and many promoters indicated they were less than enchanted with his words. This caused Patkin to recant some of his harsh comments. "I would like the record to show," Patkin stated, "There are more players in the minors than there ever were, and that the game is hardy enough to survive."[49]

By 1971, Patkin was going strong. He had jumped from a $350-a-month minor-leaguer to a comic earning between $20,000 to $40,000 or more a year. His biggest regret was that he had not built up a circuit of performances in major league cities.[50]

In 1972, Patkin performed in 65 minor league cities before 250,000 customers. In locations where the average game attendance was normally a couple of hundred, Patkin drew several thousand. Sports writer Leonard Koppett noted that Max offered something conceptually pure: the natural baseball movements made humorous, much as the Harlem Globetrotters applied comic art to the to the natural movements of basketball.

Part of Patkin's wishes about the majors came true. On April 21, 1973, it was announced that Patkin would perform at Shea Stadium in the annual charity exhibition game between the Mets and the Yankees.[51]

In 1978, Patkin joined the coaching staff of the Chicago White Sox, the organization that gave him his first contract in organized ball. His stay with the team was brief. By 1980, Patkin was back on the road. "It's a lonely, stinking life," he told an interviewer. "You check into a motel and it's outside of town. What's there to do but look at the four walls? I'm older and can't run around with the ball players like I used to. So I sit in my room." Despite his mood, Patkin reminded the interviewer that he had not missed a single one of his 4,000 performances.

"I really believe I belong in the Hall of Fame," declared Patkin. "Me and Al Schacht. There's no one else like me. I'm the last of my breed, as Joe Garagiola told me. But there's no category in the Hall of Fame for a baseball clown."[52]

In 1988, Max Patkin was featured in the hit motion picture *Bull Durham*, starring Susan Sarandon and Kevin Costner, who played a veteran catcher on his way out of baseball. In the movie, the 67-year-old Patkin performed two of his classic slapstick routines before dying in a car crash and having his ashes placed in a resin bag and scattered around the mound.[53]

Patkin officially retired on August 19, 1995, at ceremonies at Reading, Pennsylvania. His uniform and portrait were taken to Baseball's Hall of Fame in Cooperstown, New York, to be included in their collection. Patkin was also inducted into both the Philadelphia Sports Hall of Fame and the Pennsylvania Sports Hall of Fame. He retired to King of Prussia, Pennsylvania, a Philadelphia suburb.[54]

Four years later, on October 30, 1999, Max Patkin passed away at the age of 79. Doctors said Patkin was handing out his baseball cards from his hospital bed the night before he died.[55] He had had a history of heart problems and suffered a ruptured aorta on October 23 while staying at his daughter's home in Exton. His son-in-law, Roger Tietsworth, said that the phone had been ringing off the hook as fans and friends called to express their condolences. "Some were shocked, while others were saying that baseball would never be the same without Max," Tietsworth said.

Tietsworth noted that his father-in-law often commented that he never wanted to be a clown; he always wanted to be a major league ball player. Despite all the humor, Patkin once acknowledged that his life was often lonely, filled with fears and insecurities. He hid these fears behind the funny face.[56]

Bob Fishel

To the millions of people who follow major league baseball, Bob Fishel was probably was one of the least-known individuals involved in the sport. But to those who knew him best, he was a man of rare integrity and reliability. Many also consider him Bill Veeck's closest friend and confidant.

Fishel was born on May 15, 1914, in Cleveland, Ohio. He graduated from Cleveland's East High, and by his own admission, he was not very athletic. One reason was his small build and his five-foot, seven-inch frame. Fishel was, however, quite a baseball fan, thanks to his father and grandfather, who took him to see the Indians when he was six or seven. "I saw my first All-Star game in Cleveland in 1935," recalled Fishel. "My grandfather, who was a brewer, had a season box."[57]

He attended Hiram College in Hiram, Ohio, which he described as a "fine, small institution," for two years. He had every intention of obtaining a degree, "but the depression came along and I ran out of funds. So with two years to go, I had to quit college and start earning a living." Fortunately for Fishel, even before he entered college, he had some writing experience. He had written for a society magazine, *Bystander*, in Cleveland, and as he stated, "I hobnobbed with the polo set."[58]

In 1934 Fishel landed a job with a Cleveland advertising agency, Lang, Fisher and Stashower. "I was with that agency for 17 years," said Fishel, "from 1934 until 1951. I became production manager, then an account executive, and finally, in 1951, vice-president."

In July 1946, when Bill Veeck bought the Cleveland Indians, Fishel was handling advertising for the Cleveland Browns football team. Veeck wanted to promote the Indians and their newly created "Fans' Club" and he asked whether there was an advertising man in Cleveland who knew something about baseball. Someone told him that a young man named Fishel, who worked for an ad agency, was quite a baseball fans and a "regular" at the ballpark. Veeck met Fishel and told him, "I'll give our account to your firm, but on one condition. I deal only with you. You have to guarantee that no vice-presidents, no account executives, nobody butts in." It was on those specific terms that Bob Fishel began to handle the advertising and promotions for the Indians until Veeck sold that team and bought the St. Louis Browns.[59]

Fishel considered working for Veeck the beginning of a wonderful friendship and a rare experience. "Not everybody may like Veeck," noted Fishel, "but one thing is certain. He never has been commonplace and stodgy. It was a life of surprise every minute."

The two men got along very well. Fishel's advertising firm handled Veeck's ads, and Fishel worked with Veeck personally. Up to that time, the Indians had not broadcast their ball games, and one of Fishel's duties was to set up an Indian network. It ended up being a simple project to get started. In 1946, Veeck simply invited any radio station that wanted to broadcast Indians game to do so gratis. Three stations accepted his invitation.[60]

Veeck had been known for his baseball stunts in the minors, and he and Fishel worked in harmony to promote them for his major league club, the Indians. "I liked his thinking, his daring and brand new methods, his daffy looking ideas and his fireworks," said Fishel.[61]

Of course, the two men were not always in complete agreement. Fishel always remembered one of Veeck's stunts that he argued against, but Veeck prevailed in the end. In 1949, Veeck was greatly disappointed that the Indians did not repeat their pennant-winning season of 1948, but finished in third place behind the New York Yankees. When the Indians were mathematically eliminated from the pennant race, Veeck staged a mock funeral and buried the 1948 championship flag in Municipal Stadium. While thousands cheered, Veeck, clad in his usual sports shirt along with a stovepipe hat, drove the coffin bearing the pennant to the flagpole in center field. The last rites were read from the *Sporting News* and the coffin was lowered into a grave, covered with flowers, and marked by an imitation tombstone inscribed "1948 Champs."[62]

At the end of the 1949 season, Bill Veeck sold the Indians to a syndicate headed by former baseball great Hank Greenberg and Ellis W. Ryan, an insurance executive. Fishel, however, remained with his agency in Cleveland and continued to handle the Indians' advertising. In 1951, Bill Veeck bought the St. Louis Browns, causing John Lardner, journalist and son of noted sportswriter Ring Lardner to write, "It came as a surprise to many fans to hear that the Browns were sold, because they had not realized they were owned."[63] Once the deal for the Browns was completed, Fishel left Cleveland and came to St. Louis to work for Veeck. "Veeck and I had no misgivings. We were determined to see St. Louis battle its way back to the first division and profits. I thought so much of the chance that I put my own money into the enterprise."[64] In fact, he bought $10,000 worth of stock in the team.[65]

One of Fishel's tasks was to help Veeck sign players for the Browns. Since Fishel was not a tall man, he specialized in signing players of somewhat less than average stature. One was former 20-game winner for the St. Louis Cardinals, Harry Brecheen, who inked a three-year contract at $14,000 a year as a pitcher-coach. He was small, weighing only 160 pounds. Brecheen pitched for the Browns in 1953, and when the team moved to Baltimore, he became an Oriole and went along as a coach.[66]

Veeck brought with him to St. Louis his talent for wacky stunts. In 1951 Veeck dreamed up a special promotion as a birthday celebration for his team's sponsor—Falstaff Brewery. He promised the beer people,

Bob Fishel was one of the most beloved public relations men in professional baseball. An aide to Bill Veeck during the years Veeck owned the Cleveland Indians and the St. Louis Browns, he did much of the work in arranging Veeck's best-known stunt of the midget at the plate. In 1954, Fishel joined the New York Yankees where he served as PR director for close to 20 years, resigning in 1973 when George Steinbrenner purchased the team (courtesy National Baseball Hall of Fame Library; Cooperstown, N.Y.).

"I'll do something so spectacular it'll get you national publicity." It was Bob Fishel's job to sign a very small man who would appear in a Brownie uniform at a birthday party at Sportsman's Park during a doubleheader against the Detroit Tigers.

"The agent kept trying to send us dwarfs," Fishel said, "grotesque gnomes you couldn't present in a baseball uniform. Veeck held out for a midget and we finally got Eddie Gaedel, a nice-looking little guy. The uniform was no problem. The seven-year-old son of Bill DeWitt, our vice-president, had one hanging in the clubhouse. We swiped it and had a number $\frac{1}{8}$ sewn on the back."

Veeck and Fishel hid Gaedel, who weighed only 65 pounds and stood three feet, seven inches, in a hotel a few blocks from the ballpark. Fishel drove his old Packard to a nearby street intersection, parked, and the waiting Gaedel climbed in and signed two standard player contracts for $15,400 a season, or $100 a game. Fishel mailed one copy of the contract to the American League office and entrusted the other to Brownie manager Zack Taylor in case the umpires questioned the legality of the signing.

Before the first game, a seven-foot birthday cake was wheeled out, appropriate greetings extended to the sponsor, and the tiny Brownie popped out of the cake. "I should have been fired right then," remembered Fishel. "I was so nervous I forgot to alert the photographers to stay around."

By the time the second game started, only the Associated Press camera man was still around. It was a good thing for everyone that he was there when Eddie Gaedel led off the second inning as a pinch-hitter. When Gaedel stepped to the plate, home umpire Ed Hurley said, "What the hell!!" Manager Taylor showed the man in blue the signed contract and the roster of players, and play resumed. Tiger pitcher Bob Cain got down on his knees to pitch to Gaedel, but he still could not find the strike zone. The midget walked on four straight pitches and was replaced by a pinch runner, who was stranded on first base. The Browns, to no one's surprise, lost the game, 6–2.[67]

An interesting sideline to the Gaedel incident is that even though the scorecards, which were sold that day listed the name and number—⅛ Gaedel—no one in the crowd bothered to ask Bill Veeck anything about it as he moved through the stands during the first game. Harry Mitauer of the *St. Louis Globe-Democrat* did ask Fishel about it up in the press box, but Fishel was able to avoid the question.[68]

More than three decades later, Fishel visited St. Louis and located the site where the old Sportsman's Park had stood. He was in St. Louis for the 1985 World Series between the Cardinals and the Kansas City Royals and was showing a visiting newspaperman where Eddie Gaedel had come to the plate. Fishel pointed to a spot alongside a curb on the west side of Grand Boulevard and said, "It was right about here."

As much as he had disapproved of the entire incident, Fishel said of the promotion, "The Tigers were in fifth place and the Brownies occupied the American League basement as usual. One thing about Bill, he wasn't going to do anything that would affect the pennant race." Even 34 years later, Fishel, as he had always done, was defending his old boss, Bill Veeck.[69]

After the 1953 season, both the Browns and Bob Fishel left for Baltimore. The Browns became the Baltimore Orioles, and Bob Fishel took a temporary job with the National Brewery Company as public relations director.[70]

But it was not long before Fishel was back in baseball. Late in 1954, Bob Fishel became the publicity director for the New York Yankees. Even though he had enjoyed his job in Baltimore, he told *The Sporting News* he could not get baseball out of his system. He was elated to be working for the Yankees, a team that, unlike the Browns, never had a problem coming up with the money when the expense was justified.[71]

Bob Fishel was public relations director for the New York Yankees from 1954 to 1973. The longer Fishel remained with the Yankees, the more his duties and influence increased.[72] A bachelor, Fishel worked seven days a week, at least 12 hours a day when the Yankees played day games, and 16 hours when the games were under the lights. He disseminated club news and statistics to the press, arranged the spring exhibition schedule and the yearly Old-Timers' Day, handled the team mail, supervised the Yankee Speakers' Bureau, prepared the team yearbook, and was in charge of the expanded television and radio business of the New York Yankees.[73]

In 1972, the Baseball Writers awarded him the Bill Slocum Award. Named for a well-known sportswriter in New York City during the 1920s, it honored those judged to have had a long and meritorious service in baseball.[74]

A group headed by George Steinbrenner purchased the Yankees in 1973 and the following year Fishel moved to the office of the American League as a public relations director and assistant to the president, Lee McPhail.[75]

Other honors came Fishel's way. In 1981, Commissioner Bowie Kuhn announced the establishment of the Robert O. Fishel award to be presented annually to the baseball personality who best exhibited public relations excellence. The first award was given to Fishel.[76]

Bob Fishel died on June 30, 1988, in New York at the age of 74 of apparent complications from an asthma attack. Commissioner Peter Ueberroth said, "Bob Fishel embodied the characteristics of the game he loved. He was a man of style, patience, wit, strength, and grace. We will miss him terribly."[77]

The Yankee Stadium pressroom was dedicated on April 1, 1989, in memory of Bob Fishel.[78]

3. The Next Jewish Superstar

During Hank Greenberg's last year as an active player, Al "Flip "Rosen made his major league debut. Throughout the first half of the 1950s, Rosen would follow in Greenberg's footsteps and become not only one of the most outstanding Jewish players in the majors, but also one of the best players in all baseball at that time. Like Greenberg, Rosen would fight anti–Semitism and would gain the respect of Jews and non–Jews alike for his observance of the Jewish traditions.[1]

Albert Leonard Rosen was born February 29, 1924, in Spartanburg, South Carolina. He was a sickly child who suffered from asthma. While still a youngster, his parents, Louis and Rose, were divorced. Because of his asthma, Al and his brother Jerry went to live with their mother in Southwest Miami, an area called at that time, "Little Havana."[2] Rose worked as a salesperson in a dress shop while Al's Polish-born grandmother, Gertrude Levine, looked after him and his brother.[3]

His mother encouraged Al to participate in sports to improve his health. "As a boy," said his mother, "I'd watch him playing with the other boys, gasping as if each breath would be his last. But he would never stop playing."[4] He learned to fight because many of the children in his neighborhood taunted him with anti–Semitic remarks. To learn to defend himself, Rosen began to spend time at a gym, watching professional boxers; soon he began to box. After that, he heard "Jew boy" less frequently, as the neighborhood bullies realized it was much less painful to accept the Jew than to challenge him. As Rosen recalls it, "Although I didn't look for trouble, when it came to me, I wanted to end it and damn quick."[5]

Al Rosen attended Miami High School his freshman and sophomore years. When he was 14, he went on a tour with a team of Miami softball all-stars, playing the infield and pitching occasionally. While he was pitching, he earned the nickname "Flip" because of the way he flipped the ball to the batter.[6] Others insist that the way that Rosen passed a basketball accounted for his nickname.[7]

Miami's recreation director, J. B. Lemon, was so impressed with Rosen, he arranged for the boy to attend Florida Military Academy on scholarship. Rosen spent the last two years of high school at the academy where he participated in football, basketball, baseball, and boxing. While in high school, Rosen won the middleweight boxing crown.[8]

Rosen always possessed a natural zest for combat, whether in the boxing ring or on the baseball diamond. Over the course of his years as an athlete, he broke his nose 11 times—twice in boxing, six times in football, and three times in baseball.[9]

Rosen experienced anti–Semitism again in high school when his football coach asked him why he was going out for football. When Rosen answered, "I love it," the coach replied,

"Well, I didn't know you Jewboys liked contact." Rosen never forgot that incident; he was determined to dispel the image the coach had of Jews. "I was proud, and when I was in the majors, uppermost in my mind was conducting myself in a way that would give Jewish people someone to be proud of, something to cheer about."[10]

After graduation, Rosen entered the University of Florida. He had worked out an arrangement to meet his expenses by waiting on tables in a fraternity house. Because of unpleasant conditions at the frat house, Al switched to the University of Miami. There he majored in business administration, graduating with a B average. He did not receive a degree until 1948 because both World War II and baseball interrupted his studies.[11]

"I always knew I wanted to play ball," said Rosen.[12] He got his opportunity in 1942 when he obtained a tryout with the Cleveland Indians' Class A farm team at Wilkes-Barre. At that time he lacked the talent to play at that level, but he did receive an offer from Thomasville, a Class D Club in the North Carolina State League. They paid him $90 a month. "It was a typical town," recalled Rosen. "I was barely eighteen years old." Rosen signed his contract, went directly to the ballpark, suited up as a professional baseball player for the first time, and played that same day. "I got a base hit the first time up," Rosen remembered. "I was off and running and that's how it all began. I played that season and then I went into the service."[13]

With his college education, Rosen was commissioned a lieutenant in the Navy. He went from Ft. Pierce, an amphibious school, up to Camp Shelton in the Norfolk area where he also played baseball with major league players such as Joe Beggs, a relief pitcher for the Cincinnati Reds, Mace Brown, who pitched for the Boston Red Sox, and Whitey Platt, who played for both Chicago teams as well as the St. Louis Browns.[14]

It was not all fun and games in the Navy. Rosen was sent to the South Pacific and was on the beach at Okinawa on D-Day. Once asked if Okinawa might have been responsible for the grayish streaks in his hair, he replied, "No siree, that's heredity. My family is all prematurely gray." Years later when he was with the Indians, the fans began calling him the Gray Eagle, the same name they had dubbed a past Indian, Hall of Famer Tris Speaker. "I won't mind," he said, "if I can hit like Speaker did."[15]

Rosen was discharged from the service in 1946 and went directly to the Indians' training camp. Beginning in 1946, the five-foot, 10-and-one-half inch, 180-pound third baseman launched an exceptional record in the minor leagues. Still a member of the Cleveland Indians organization, Rosen was assigned to Pittsfield, Massachusetts, in the Class C Canadian-American League where he was chosen the league's Most Valuable Rookie that year. He was MVP again in 1947 with Oklahoma City in the Texas League.[16] Rosen, described as the first Jewish star in the Texas League, also led the league in total bases and RBIs.[17]

Near the end of the 1947 season, the Indians called Rosen up to Cleveland. Bill Veeck and Hank Greenberg, one of Rosen's boyhood idols, had just purchased the Indians. When Rosen arrived in Cleveland, Bill Veeck asked the young third baseman to fly to Chicago to meet him personally. Rosen walked off the plane at 6 A.M. and was amazed to find Bill Veeck waiting for him. Veeck treated the rookie to breakfast and returned Rosen to his plane. Before the plane took off, Veeck handed Rosen a check for $1,000. The amazed Rosen stated, "I had never seen $1,000 before."[18]

Rosen, in seven games in 1947 for the Indians, went to the plate nine times and got one hit.[19] "I remember my first at-bat in the major leagues," recalled Rosen. It was at Yankee Stadium before a crowd of 74,000 fans. I was overwhelmed by everything—including

Joe Page, who was on the mound for the Yankees. Cleveland had runners at second and third. Page struck me out on three pitches."[20]

His first hit came in an important pinch-hitting role in the ninth inning of the second game of a doubleheader in Detroit, and allowed the Indians to rally to win the game, 7–6.

In 1948, Rosen once again went to spring training with the Indians. This time he went north with the team and started the season in the big leagues. After only five at-bats in the big leagues in 1948, Rosen, who needed to develop his fielding skills, was assigned to Kansas City in the American Association.[21] His batting was exceptional in Kansas City where he hit five consecutive home runs in two games. In addition to his hitting, Rosen worked hard to improve his fielding. Although not yet a finished product at the hot corner, his hustling play and his hitting prowess made Rosen one of the top stars in the American Association.[22] His .327 batting average also earned him the Rookie of the Year in that league.[23]

At the end of the year the Indians recalled Rosen in time to make him eligible for the 1948 World Series where he pinch hit against the Boston Braves. Rosen was hitless, but the Indians won the World Series in seven games.[24]

Part of the difficulty Rosen faced in staying with the big club was that veteran Ken Keltner had been the Indians' regular third baseman since 1938 and was still playing well ten years later. "He was popular with the fans," said Rosen, "and very popular with his teammates and I was not accepted because they knew why I was there. It had to happen; the writing was on the wall. Keltner was getting older, and I led every league I played for in the minor leagues.... Fortunately, as time went on I became very friendly with a lot of the players, including Keltner and Bob Lemon."[25]

Al Rosen, prominent Cleveland Indians third baseman, had two successful careers in professional baseball. As a major league player from 1947 through 1956, his achievements were many. In 1951 he tied a major-league record with four grand slam home runs; in 1953 he was unanimously voted the American League's Most Valuable Player and the following year, he was selected the All-Star game MVP. More than 20 years later, Rosen, who held a business degree, returned to baseball on the management side, serving in executive positions with the Yankees, the Astros, and the Giants (courtesy National Baseball Hall of Fame Library; Cooperstown, N.Y.).

The next year, 1949, was also a divided year for Rosen. He played only 23 games for the Indians and spent most of the year with the San Diego Padres in the Pacific Coast League.[26] It was also probably the most frustrating season for Al Rosen. He had proven that he was ready to become an everyday player, but Ken Keltner, although beginning to slow down, seemed entrenched at third. Indian manager Lou Boudreau, like many major league managers, was hesitant to play newcomers and was reluctant to take Keltner out of the lineup. However, Boudreau was well aware of Rosen's presence. "I am happy that with Rosen able to step in when needed, I won't have to lose sleep wondering what would happen if one of our veterans was hurt."[27]

In 1949 it was apparent that Keltner was having difficulties with his legs. He would never match his 1948 performance when he hit .297, drove in 119 runs, and clouted 31 home runs.[28]

Before the 1950 season, Keltner's continued fielding problems convinced the Indians to replace him at third with Al Rosen. Keltner was released and signed with the Boston Red Sox.[29] Boudreau told Rosen during spring training that the regular third base post was his.[30] He would never again be sent to the minors, but would remain a fixture at third until his retirement following the 1956 season.

The question of whether Al Rosen encountered anti–Semitism during his minor league career is a difficult one to answer. If anti–Semitism did exist against Rosen, it was probably "under the surface." Since he was an excellent player, this probably muted any overt anti–Semitism. He also had a reputation for being quick with his fists when taunted. Some teammates also supported him, spreading news to the rest of the club not to "fool around" with Al Rosen about his religion.[31]

Rosen encountered a few isolated instances of anti–Semitism in the major leagues. When he came to the Indians, an out-of-state writer claimed that Rosen and a pitcher named Salzman (who never made it to the big leagues) only got an opportunity to play because Hank Greenberg was a part-owner. Later when Rosen was an established player, he and Greenberg often spoke of Rosen's goals, but the two men never shared confidences about being Jewish or confronting anti–Semitism. "I felt they were personal experiences for both of us," said Rosen, "and neither of us wanted to discuss the topic."[32]

Some pitchers deliberately aimed their pitches at Rosen's ribs, but he refused to "rub it off." His attitude was simple: "Why give the pitchers any satisfaction? It would merely encourage them to do it again." He actually felt it was a compliment since major league pitchers never hit mediocre players.

On another occasion, one of the Red Sox reserves gave him what Rosen termed "the Jew stuff." Rosen ran toward the Boston dugout, but before any blows could be exchanged, two Red Sox veterans, Bobby Doerr and Johnny Pesky, grabbed their teammate and shut him up.[33]

Probably the most overt case of anti–Semitism Al Rosen encountered occurred in 1951 when the Indians were playing the White Sox. Chicago pitcher Saul Rogovin recalled that one of his teammates yelled at Rosen as he passed the Sox dugout after making an out, "'Well, we got you that time, you Jew bastard.' Al walked over to our dugout and said, 'That son of a bitch that called me a Jew bastard, would he care to say that again?' Everybody just sat there. I felt very funny, because I had mixed feelings over that. I felt good for Al, thinking, 'Thattaboy, Al, give it to them,' and I also felt sort of disloyal, because Al was an opposing player."[34]

Rosen's teammates on the Indians were also quick to defend him against insults. Once, while a rookie, he was sitting in a Boston bar and overheard someone talking about a big-nosed Jewboy. Before Rosen could move, Joe Gordon, a non–Jewish teammate and a veteran Cleveland infielder, got up and without making a comment, punched the offender in the mouth.

Another of his teammates, infielder George Strickland, also had occasion to come to Rosen's defense. In one game, a runner slid into third after Rosen slapped him with a sweeping tag, but the third base umpire signaled the runner safe. When Rosen accused him of "blowing the play," the umpire walked away from Rosen, approached Strickland at short and said to him, "I'll get that Jew bastard one of these days." Strickland quickly responded, "I'm telling him [what you said] and after he takes a belt at you, if he misses, I'm going to get you myself." Of course, there were no blows struck, but the umpire told the rest of the crew that Strickland was a Communist troublemaker.[35]

Rosen also credited his idol and now boss Hank Greenberg for making it a "little easier" for Jews in the big leagues.[36] He often said publicly, "For Jewish ballplayers, Greenberg was really a pathfinder. Hank paved the way for people like me."[37]

Nineteen-fifty was actually the fourth season Rosen played with Cleveland, but he had spent most of the first three seasons in the minors. By 1950, Hank Greenberg was not only a part-owner of the Indians, he had become general manager in charge of the entire baseball team. He was actually responsible for handing Keltner his release and putting Rosen into the Cleveland lineup, fully aware that replacing Keltner, a popular star, with a young Jewish ballplayer, would be controversial.[38] When a skeptic reminded Rosen that third baseman Kenny Keltner's shoes would be hard to fill, Rosen replied, "I have mighty big feet."[39]

Rosen never forgot the opening game of the 1950 season. Although it was not his first appearance in the major leagues, it was his first appearance as a regular in the Indian lineup. "They announced my name on opening day," Rosen recalled, "and I ran out to my position. I remember hearing 60,000 people yelling, 'We want Keltner.'" He understood why the fans were calling for the popular Keltner, but his best years were behind him, and the Indians felt that Rosen was the future. "The shouts didn't bother me," Rosen said. "I knew I had yet to prove in real games that I was a better ballplayer than the veteran Keltner, even with his declining skills. So it was just a chilling moment to run out of the dugout and to third base and know you were the starting third baseman. That was really the highlight of my career."[40]

Eventually, Rosen's prowess at the plate began to make the fans forget about Keltner. More significantly, the team was beginning to recognize his all-around potential and moved him from hitting second in the order to cleanup—the fourth-place slot. That truly indicated that he had won the approval of everyone—the players, the coaches, and the managers. Unlike Cal Abrams before him, his teammates and their families accepted Rosen, and his wife developed close relationships with the other team wives.[41]

Rosen, however, faced one major obstacle—his weakness as a fielder. No one ever doubted his ability to hit the baseball; he swung the bat with a slightly choked grip, but his fielding had always been a question mark, and opposing players took a ruthless delight in watching him at third base. Boudreau and Hank Greenberg had done Rosen a favor by letting Keltner go and getting Rosen out from under the shadow of the formerly great third baseman. The biggest help, however, came from one of Cleveland's coaches, Oscar Melillo, who had been a slick-fielding infielder for 12 years with the St. Louis Browns and Boston Red Sox.

Melillo liked Rosen's "gutsy" attitude and his desire to improve his play. Before and after games, Melillo hit ground balls to Rosen and rebuilt his fielding style. Rosen once said, "Oscar changed everything I had been doing. He changed my throwing from sidearm to overhand. He changed my fielding stance from an upright hunched-over posture to a crouch. He showed me how to get my hands in front of a ball and be ready to throw."[42]

The 1950 season was a breakout season for Rosen. As the regular third baseman for the Indians, he won the American League home-run title with 37, which set the rookie record, until Mark McGwire broke it 37 years later.[43] He scored 100 runs, walked 100 times, and topped the 100-mark in RBIs with 116, the first of five consecutive seasons of 100-plus RBIs. Rosen also led the American League in assists with 322.[44] Rosen was earning a reputation not only for his power, but also for his ability to hit in the clutch. The late Early Wynn, a 300-game winner and a member of Baseball's Hall of Fame, considered Yogi Berra and Al Rosen the two best clutch hitters he had ever seen. "Believe me," said Wynn, "most of us pitchers wish to hell they'd switch to golf. Fortunately, Rosen is my teammate."[45]

Rosen received the ultimate tribute a hitter would receive—a compliment from outfielder Ted Williams who told the Indian slugger, "You have a strong, quick pair of wrists. You're a natural hitter."[46] The only disappointment for Rosen in what otherwise was a banner year, was the snubbing he received from Casey Stengel who refused to place Rosen on the All-Star roster as backup to George Kell, who received the highest number of votes for third base. Indians' manager, Lou Boudreau, said. "Rosen definitely should have been selected. He's leading the majors in home runs and he tops our club in RBIs. I don't know what else a fellow has to do to get on." Hank Greenberg was even more incensed and called his omission a flaw in the selection system.[47]

Even though most hitters would have been elated to have a season similar to the one Rosen had in 1950, he continually tried to improve his long ball hitting. Ralph Kiner, the National League home run champ in 1950, advised Rosen to seek the advice of his general manager, Hank Greenberg, telling Rosen "Hank Greenberg was my instructor when we were roommates at Pittsburgh, and he helped me with my consistency. You're lucky that he's the general manager of the Indians. If I were you, I'd go to him for help." Greenberg, a perfectionist himself, was elated that Rosen sought his advice, and he made the third baseman his number one project at Tucson, the Indians' spring training site in 1951.[48]

Rosen obviously took some of Greenberg's advice, for in 1951, the slugging third sacker tied a record by hitting four grand slams.[49] However, his average slipped to .265 and even with the grand slams, his HR total for the season was only 24.[50] Despite the fact that his offensive numbers declined in 1951, no other third baseman supplied anywhere near the offense.[51]

During the 1951 season, the popular New York columnist and television star Ed Sullivan, wrote, "Al Rosen, Cleveland third baseman, is a native of Miami, Florida. Of Jewish parentage, he is Catholic. At the plate, you'll notice he makes the sign of the cross with his bat."

Rosen bitterly denied the story and said that ever since he was a kid, he would make an "x" mark on the plate before stepping into the batter's box. This was a superstitious gesture employed by many players. He asked Sullivan to retract his story and he insisted that he was a proud Jew. "I have belonged to a synagogue for most of my life," Rosen stated. Rosen also confessed that when he was working his way up the ladder in the minor leagues, he had often wished his name sounded less Jewish. "But once I was established as a star, I wished my name were more Jewish, perhaps Rosenthal or Rosenstein. I wanted to be sure there was no mistaking about what I was."[52] Rosen was always quick to point out that he did not play on the High Holy Days.[53]

Rosen had three sensational years from 1952 to 1954. After his off-year in 1951, Al resolved to improve. "I was just a lousy ballplayer last year," he said. I used to think if a fellow hit 24 home runs and drove in over 100 runs, he had a pretty good year. But I did that and now I know. It's the average that counts. It's fine to hit the homer and get the RBIs, but not if you hit only .265."[54]

In the spring of 1952 the Indians held a pre-season camp for rookies at Daytona Beach. The team's stars were not expected to attend, but one morning Indian manager Al Lopez and general manager Greenberg discovered Rosen in the batting cage. When told that he did not have to be there, Rosen agreed, and told Greenberg, "You're right. That can wait. There are some things I've got to do at third base first." He practiced his fielding with the coaches.[55]

His hard work paid off in 1952. He scored 101 runs, had 171 hits and drove in 105 runs with a .302 batting average.[56] The fans selected Rosen as the starting third baseman for the American League All-Star team, beating out George Kell, 1,163,632 votes to 1,112,114.[57] Nineteen fifty-two was also a banner year personally when Al married his long-time girl friend, Terry Blumberg, from Dothan, Alabama.[58]

Cleveland lost the 1952 pennant race to the Yankees by two games. The Indians fielded that year the most ethnically and racially mixed lineup in the majors. Besides Larry Doby, the Indians' African-American regulars included Harry Simpson, and Luke Easter, formerly of the Homestead Grays. Third baseman Al Rosen, whose 105 RBIs led the league, was the most prominent Jewish player since Hank Greenberg. Roberto Avila, a Mexican citizen, starred at second base, and Mike Garcia, a California Mexican-American, won 22 games, the same number as Bob Lemon and 23 by Early Wynn.[59]

Al Rosen had his most productive year in the majors in 1953. An All-Star for the second straight year, he led the league in games played (155), runs scored (115), home runs (43), RBIs (145), and slugging percentage, (.613).[60] He lost the batting title to Mickey Vernon, Washington Senator first baseman by .001. Rosen needed one hit in his final at-bat in 1953 to win baseball's Triple Crown. He chopped a slow roller to third base, and umpire Hank Soar called him out by half a step. Despite the furor, Rosen defended the umpire saying, "Soar called it right, and I'm glad he did," Rosen firmly stated. "I don't want any gifts. Why, I wouldn't sleep at night all winter if I won the batting championship on a call I knew was wrong."[61]

In addition to his offensive records, Rosen demonstrated a greatly improved defense. He led American League third basemen in assists, double plays, and total chances per game.[62] His defensive achievements were all the more remarkable when as recently as two years earlier, Rogers Hornsby, then manager of the St. Louis Browns, dismissed the Cleveland third baseman's ability saying, "He'll help you with his bat, but, with that glove, he'll kill you."[63]

To cap Rosen's outstanding 1953 season, he was the unanimous choice for the American League Most Valuable Player, the first person ever to be chosen without any dissenting votes.[64] Milton Gross of the New York Post wrote, "Against the backdrop of provincialism usually shown in this voting, the landslide not only is unprecedented, but the most sincere sort of testimonial to the prematurely graying twenty-eight year old after only four (full) seasons of big league baseball."[65]

During the 1953 season, almost all of baseball was singing his praises. His manager, Al Lopez, talked about his great attitude. "What I like about Al most of all is his determination. After a pitcher gets him out he'll come back to the bench and say, 'I'll get him next time.' And by golly, he does. To him, each pitcher is a personal challenge."[66]

After losing all five games in a series to the Indians, Harry Brecheen, coach and pitcher for the St. Louis Browns unequivocally called Rosen "the best hitter in the American League." After a pause Brecheen, who had spent most of his major league career in the National League, added, "And there's none better in the other league." Buddy Blattner, former major leaguer and the Browns' radio broadcaster, said, "If I wanted to try to teach a youngster how to hit I'd tell him to watch Rosen day after day. He is a picture book hitter."[67]

One of the major reasons for Rosen's success in the majors was his willingness to always try to improve his play by maintaining a regimen of hard work, study, and seeking out the advice of successful people. "This has enabled me," said Rosen, "to help transform from a run-of-the mill player to an established star."[68]

Al Rosen did not win the praise and honor that came his way merely by putting his natural gifts to work. Many baseball men feel that probably no other ballplayer of his day worked harder to perfect himself, not only in the things he was naturally good at, but in the things in which he seemed to have no real aptitude.[69]

In the middle of April in 1954, Al Lopez decided to move Rosen from third base to first base and start the flashy, hard-hitting Rudy Regalado at third. Rosen had played some first base at San Diego, and when his manager asked him to make the move, Rosen agreed.[70]

After playing first base for two weeks, Rosen seemed to enjoy the switch and adjusted to the new position quickly. His manager seemed impressed and commented, "From what I've seen so far, I have every reason to think that Al will become one of the better first basemen in the league."[71]

Between 1954 and 1956, Rosen was often hindered by injuries. On May 13, 1954, while Rosen was playing first base, a runner on first blocked his view of the batter who hit a line drive that crumpled the index finger of Rosen's right hand. Rosen left the game but remained out of the lineup for only a few days, not long enough to allow the finger adequate time to heal. After he returned, pitchers continually threw him fastballs inside, so that every time he connected, he further damaged the index finger. He was able to retain only half of that finger. Rosen played first base until early July when Lopez, unhappy that Regalado had not measured up to expectations, benched the rookie and returned Rosen to third base, while playing ex–Oriole Vic Wertz at first.[72]

The fans' attitude in Cleveland changed for some reason in 1954. Much to Rosen's displeasure, whenever he missed a play at third, the fans for the first time in his career began to boo their All-Star third baseman. Despite his injuries, Rosen still was able to appear in 137 games. He finished the year with a batting average of .300, hit 24 home runs, and drove in 102 runs, the fourth consecutive year of more than 100 RBIs.[73]

There were two highlights to the Indians' 1954 season. For the third consecutive year, the fans chose Al Rosen to start the All-Star Game at third base for the American League. Even though elected, Rosen wasn't sure his injured finger would allow him to play the game. As late as the day of the game, Rosen was not sure what he should do. He later admitted that if it had not been the All Star game, he would definitely have sat it out but he felt he had an obligation to play, especially since the game was being held in Cleveland.

American League manager Casey Stengel suggested he take at least one turn at bat and make a final decision. He struck out against Robin Roberts his first at-bat. He was scheduled to come up again to hit in the third inning, and saw that Mickey Vernon was going to pinch-hit for him. "I want to stay in," I told Casey, and then hit a Roberts fastball that cleared the fence by 15 to 20 feet for a three-run homer. When he came to the plate a third time with a runner on first, Johnny Antonelli was pitching. This time, Rosen hit the ball 400 feet into the left field stands. In his next two at-bats, Rosen singled off Warren Spahn in the sixth inning, and walked in the eighth, courtesy of Carl Erskine. In summary, as a 1954 American League All-Star, after a strike out, Rosen got on base four straight times, hit two homers, and a single, walked once and drove in five runs.[74] Not surprisingly, Rosen won the MVP award in the 1954 All-Star Game.[75]

The second highlight for Rosen in 1954 was the Indians' winning the American League pennant that year with the best record in baseball—111–43. Their 111 regular-season wins was the major league record until the New York Yankees, playing a 162-game schedule in 1998, won 114 games.[76]

The Indians opposed the New York Giants in the 1954 World Series, and for the Indians it was not really much of a Series. Rosen entered the World Series injured again. Towards the end of the season, he had had a hamstring pull that caused him to sit out a number of the team's final games. When he did play, he felt "tentative." Just hours before the Indians boarded the evening train for New York City, Rosen took extra batting practice and complained, "I can't seem to get the ball up in the air."[77]

The Giants swept the Indians in four games, outscoring them 20–9. Rosen came to the plate 12 times in the Series, and managed just three hits, all singles.[78] He did not drive in any runs.[79] The Cleveland sportswriters argued that the team had collapsed in the most critical games, but they were always careful to omit Rosen's name from the list of culprits. The sportswriters liked Rosen; to most of them, he was simply "Flip."[80]

Between the 1954 and the 1955 seasons, Al spent part of his time in the hospital suffering from whiplash from an automobile accident. The injury continued to bother him throughout the entire 1955 season, but it was his injured finger that caused the most concern. When Rosen reported to spring training, many observers wondered if his broken finger would permanently hinder his hitting. Although Rosen's manager asserted that Rosen really did not need full use of his right index finger to bat well, there was no denying that since the injury, his performance had not been up to par.

Rosen was in a horrible batting slump during Cleveland's exhibition games, and his trainer admitted that the third base slugger might never be able to bend his right index finger completely. "He's over the worst effects of that break. I suppose there will be a certain amount of pain for a while if the finger is shocked. It's just one of those things you've got to learn to live with."[81]

Rosen's injuries in 1955 took a toll on him physically, and his statistics took a nosedive. He played in only 139 games, batted a lowly .244, drove in 81 runs, his lowest output in six years, and hit only 21 home runs.[82]

The boo-birds continued to taunt him, but Rosen took this in stride. "Those who are booing me now, I'll make them cheer me before I'm through." Rosen emphasized that he was not seeking sympathy. "I'm a professional and it's part of my job to take it," he said. "But if those who boo—whether they boo at me or somebody else—knew how they were eating our insides out, I' m sure they wouldn't feel very proud of themselves."

Rosen's teammates admitted they found it difficult to understand why the fans were so antagonistic. The players around the league were also amazed. Ex–Yankee outfielder Gene Woodling, new to the Indians, said that he had played in both leagues and that "The fans in Cleveland are the worst." Ray Boone, a former teammate of Rosen and also once a target of the Tribe fans, sympathized with him. "I certainly feel sorry for old Rosey," Boone observed near the end of the season. "Cleveland is a poor town. I thought I used to get it pretty good in Cleveland and I probably deserved it because I couldn't get the job done. But I'll say one thing—it never got so bad as Rosen got."[83] It certainly did not help Rosen's cause when the Cleveland press implied that the only reason he, a Jewish player, was allowed to play though such a horrific slump, was that one of the owners of the Indians also was Jewish.[84]

If Hank Greenberg was showing partiality to Rosen because he was Jewish, he surely did not indicate it at the bargaining table. After conferring with Hank Greenberg briefly, Al Rosen signed his 1956 contract, which called for a cut of approximately 20 percent. This was the first time in his career that he was forced to take a reduction in salary, and Rosen stated simply, "Oh, it hurts. It hurts plenty, but I had it coming. I had an awful season." He blamed only himself for the team's second-place finish in 1955 and said that if he had only had an ordinary year the Indians would have captured the pennant. "I'm determined to make the same fans who booed me last season cheer me this year."[85]

Not only was Greenberg not showing favoritism towards Al Rosen, by 1956 their relationship was strained. Greenberg resented Rosen's popularity in Cleveland, while at the same time he felt the fans and reporters seemed to pick on him. When Oakwood Country Club, a posh Jewish establishment, admitted Rosen as a member, Greenberg once curtly remarked, "How can you get into Oakwood and I can't?" At a luncheon in Cleveland, Greenberg suggested that Rosen had "lost his confidence and needed a change of scenery." Greenberg did not say so publicly, but he already had a location in mind—Boston. He planned to send his star third baseman to the Red Sox.[86]

Al Rosen reported to the Indians' spring training camp at Tucson hoping to have a good year in 1956. Al Lopez decided to make it easy for Rosen and declared, "Rosen's best position is third base and I hope we keep him there unless we cannot find an answer at first base. Rosen's only reply to Lopez was, "I'm aiming at another '53, and I'm in shape to make it."[87]

Despite the fact that he probably worked harder than any other Indian in camp, and he reported earlier at his own expense, during the first week in camp Rosen fought off a sore toe, a sore shoulder, and a sore thigh. He indicated that only the shoulder trouble remained from his automobile accident the previous year. When one writer charged that Rosen was all washed up, he was infuriated and responded, "I have no intention of quitting baseball. I have put a lot of effort into this game—it's my profession, and I intend to stay in it as long as I can, three or four more years, I hope. When I can no longer help the team I'll quit. I have no intentions of going back to the minors. But I firmly believe I can do the job up here for several more seasons."[88]

Rosen was plagued by injuries again during the 1956 season. His back, still sore from the auto accident, continued to give him problems. He was hooted by the fans for exiting a game when he broke his nose. On another occasion, Rosen attempted to make a play on a difficult infield grounder, stumbled and hurt himself. As he lay on the ground, in obvious agony, the fans cheered his misfortune.[89]

At the end of May, Rosen was hospitalized with an injury to his right knee after Washington Senator infielder Pete Runnels crashed into him while Rosen attempted to block the base. He had been hearing catcalls before, during, and after the incident at third base. As he was helped off the field, the anti–Rosen fans, although in the minority, cheered his pain and roundly booed him. From his hospital bed, Rosen said, "I have never complained and I don't intend to start now. I have a job to do, and I'll continue to try to do it to the best of my ability."[90]

Even before the season ended, Greenberg indicated Rosen would probably not be back with the Indians in 1957. He told the Sigma Delta Chi journalism fraternity that Rosen had reached "the mental state where he can't play in Cleveland any longer, and would probably be better off with another team." When asked to comment on Greenberg's remarks, Rosen said he did not wish to become involved in an employee-employer controversy while he still had a job to do.[91]

Rosen did indicate, however, that if the pain he was suffering did not subside, he would be forced to retire. Al Lopez, his manager, said Rosen was far from through as a player and added, "He would be making a great mistake if he retired at the end of the current season as he hinted."[92]

Rosen finished the 1956 season with what for him was a subpar performance. His batting average was .267, a little better than in 1955, but still below his norm, and his offensive production fell off considerably—only 15 home runs and 61 RBIs. He played in 121 games, the lowest number since he became the regular Indian third baseman.[93]

Hank Greenberg offered Rosen $27,500 to play for the Indians in 1957. Rosen, furious about being offered a second consecutive pay cut, announced that he would retire. He planned to stay in Cleveland and work full time for the investment firm of Bache & Company, where he had been employed during the off-seasons. Rosen enjoyed living in Cleveland and was active in many civic and religious causes, including the Bellefaire Jewish Children's Home and the Jewish Community Center–YMHA building in Cleveland.[94]

By early 1957, it became obvious that the Indians did not have a third baseman to replace Rosen. Al Lopez had resigned as Indian manager, and his replacement, Kerby Farrell, pleaded with Rosen to change his mind. "I need someone like you to get me over the rough spots. If you don't come along with me, I don't think I can succeed here." Rosen told Farrell he would play, but it would cost the team more than $27,500.

Because Rosen and Greenberg were not on speaking terms, Bill Veeck offered to act as an intermediary. He drove to Rosen's home in Shaker Heights and asked him if he would accept $40,000 for 1957. When Rosen's boss at Bache assured him that his job would still be waiting once he left baseball, Rosen gave Veeck permission to speak with Greenberg. But Greenberg was adamant, telling Rosen, "You'll play for $27,500 or you won't play." Rosen refused the offer and told Greenberg he was finished. Al Lopez, who had taken the managerial post with the White Sox after he left Cleveland, called Greenberg and said, "Hank, if you'll let me talk to Rosen, he's willing to come back. I'd like to make a deal for him." Greenberg rejected Lopez's offer and bluntly told him, "If he doesn't play for me, Al, he doesn't play for anybody."[95]

In February 1957 Al Rosen officially retired from baseball. "I'm lucky I retired from baseball before it retired me. But you can't say the same thing about some players. They are just hanging on and they won't have a thing going for them when they are forced to leave the game." Rosen made it absolutely clear that "the Cleveland fans had nothing to do with my retiring."[96]

Before the start of a night game in 1957, his old friend, Bob Lemon, invited him to the stadium to take batting practice. Those around the batting cage quickly learned that Rosen's swing was as powerful as ever, as he drilled the first pitch on a line drive off the left field wall. "I came down to lend a rooting interest and couldn't resist the temptation to put on a uniform," Rosen said. But he had to admit that he really felt unwanted by his former teammates. He later confided that the summer of 1957 was the longest summer of his life. "Nobody will ever know how much I missed baseball," he said after the season.[97]

Rosen spent his entire baseball-playing career with the Cleveland Indians. He played in a total of 1,044 games, batted 3,725 times, scored 603 runs, pounded out 1,063 hits, and 192 home runs, drove in 717 runs, and had a career batting average of .285. He appeared in two World Series—1948 and 1954, but his statistics in the Fall Classic are not impressive—3 for 13. He retired at the age of 32.[98]

For the next seventeen years, he remained in Cleveland as a stockbroker for Bache and occasionally coached for the Indians.[99] He formed his own investment firm, but it never succeeded.

Caesar's Palace, at that time the glitziest hotel in Las Vegas, hired Rosen in 1977 as vice-president. The job involved press and public relations, but more importantly, he was asked to build the hotel's sports program to lure customers who were not interested in gambling, the hotel's show girls, or the pseudo–Roman statuary that towered over the hotel's lobby. Rosen was very successful at his job and gained an excellent reputation for attracting top flight fighters for championship matches, such as the Ken Norton–Jimmy Young heavyweight fight on November 14, 1977.[100] However, Rosen could not get baseball out of his blood.

On March 28, 1978, George Steinbrenner hired Al Rosen to replace Gabe Paul as president of the New York Yankees. Steinbrenner told the press, "In Al Rosen, we are fortunate to land a man, who in my opinion, will become one of the finest front office executives in baseball. I couldn't have found a finer man to assume the presidency."[101] Steinbrenner added that Rosen was "in command." "That's what being president of the New York Yankees means," added Steinbrenner. As a perk, he gave Rosen a few shares of Yankee stock, making him a limited partner. Rosen was president, but time would tell if Rosen would be "in command."[102]

Always known for his sartorial elegance, Rosen was still perfectly dressed and distinguished-looking although his gray hair was now completely white.[103] He became known as one of Steinbrenner's toughest player negotiators through one acquisition. In 1978 a scout tipped Rosen that he ought to take a look at a Texas farmhand, left-handed pitcher Dave Righetti. Al Rosen ultimately acquired Righetti but only after he had completed a ten-player-cash-swap.[104]

Al Rosen's one-year term as president of the New York Yankees was both rocky and very painful. He could not tolerate Steinbrenner's constant meddling. First, Rosen was unhappy that his baseball functions were diminishing while his role in the business end was increasing rapidly. Second, Steinbrenner replaced Rosen's long-time friend, Bob Lemon, as manager of the Yankees with Billy Martin. Martin and Rosen never got along. Martin refused to discuss baseball matters with Rosen, preferring to go to either Steinbrenner or Yankee general manager Cedric Tallis. Finally, Rosen, much to the wrath of Steinbrenner, allowed the American League to reschedule a night game in California to a 5:30 P.M. start to accommodate ABC television. The Yankees had to face hard thrower Nolan Ryan in the twilight. After the Yankees managed to get only one hit off Ryan, Steinbrenner blew his top. Rosen defended his decision and told Steinbrenner, "You were busy and Billy wouldn't return my calls so I approved the switch."[105]

In July 1979, midway through the baseball season, Al Rosen resigned as president of the New York Yankees. No official reason was given for his resignation, but many believed that Rosen's decision was prompted by the fact that he was little more than a figurehead in an organization where the owner makes most of the decisions. Rosen thanked Steinbrenner for bringing him back into baseball when he needed a job. Rosen said, "I've always told George: 'I love you as a friend. I just can't work for you.'"[106]

After Rosen left the Yankees he was hired as supervisor of credit operations at a Bally's Park Place Casino in Atlantic City. He remained there for only one year, getting into trouble when he authorized a $2.5 million loan to four casinos that had been defrauded in a scam. Five people were arrested in the probe, and while Rosen was not one of them, he did admit that he had shown poor judgment in authorizing the loans.[107]

He also displayed questionable judgment when he hired Willie Mays as a greeter and public relations man at the casino. Commissioner Bowie Kuhn quickly informed Mays that he could not work as a scout and coach for the Mets if a casino also employed him. Four years later, Kuhn applied the same restriction to Mickey Mantle. Many considered Kuhn's actions among his least popular moves.[108] Rosen resigned from his casino job in October 1980.[109]

That same year, John McMullen, the volatile owner of the Houston Astros, fired Tal Smith after the Astros lost a playoff series to the Philadelphia Phillies. The firing came about even though Smith had led his team to the National League Western title and was named by United Press International as Executive of the Year for 1980. McMullen replaced him with Al Rosen.[110]

Because of the incident at Bally's in Atlantic City where Rosen was employed, Bowie Kuhn, commissioner of baseball, felt he was obligated to investigate the situation before he allowed McMullen to hire Al Rosen. This infuriated McMullen, but Kuhn stuck to his guns in order to ensure that Rosen had not broken any laws. Fortunately, Kuhn fully cleared Rosen and Rosen bore no grudge against the commissioner.[111]

Rosen faced a hostile press when he succeeded Tal Smith. John McMullen was not a popular owner in Houston, and the team's 20 limited owners were upset that he had fired Smith. McMullen decided to give Rosen complete authority for the club, which put him "on the hot seat." One of Smith's assistants, Tony Siegle, said of the situation, "General Santa Ana received a friendlier welcome from the state of Texas than Al did."[112]

Rosen knew he had inherited a difficult situation, and he attempted to ward off some criticism when he declared his support of the Houston farm system. He also stated that the Astros already were positioned well and had talent. "We won't be changing a lot."[113]

In January 1981, Al Rosen underwent a single bypass heart surgery. His condition was described as "great" and he made a full recovery.[114] According to newspaper accounts, he was back in command in time for spring training.[115]

In 1981 the Astros won the second half of the split-season but lost the first round of postseason play to the Los Angeles Dodgers. As a reward for the fine showing in 1981, the Astros signed Rosen as president and general-manager.[116]

He remained with Houston for a total of five years but the Astros tumbled to fifth place in 1982 and never finished higher than second in 1985. Despite the infighting on the team during those five years, the Astros managed to sign some relatively successful players such as Dickie Thon, Ray Knight, and Mike La Coss, and they traded Danny Heep to the Mets for Mike Scott. The Astros' record during Rosen's five-year stay was 386 wins and 371 losses.[117]

Astros owner John McMullen, calling baseball a "cruel sport," fired Al Rosen as the team's president and general-manager near the end of the 1985 season and replaced him with former Cincinnati Reds official Dick Wagner. It was rumored that Rosen would become general manager of the San Francisco Giants. "Al is a true friend of mine," noted McMullen, "and he's obviously going to continue his career. We're not at liberty to discuss it."[118]

In one of baseball's worst kept secrets, the San Francisco Giants announced just a few days later that Al Rosen would be the team's president and general manager, replacing Tom Haller, and that Roger Craig, the Tigers' pitching coach, would replace Jim Davenport as field manager. Giants owner Bob Lurie gave Rosen financial responsibilities that Haller had not had and more authority to shape the Giants. One of the first tasks Rosen undertook was to seek another site for a ballpark, noting that Candlestick Park was a cold, windy stadium, not conducive to playing baseball.[119]

Rosen told the fans that the Giants would have new vitality and energy in 1986 to be a competitive club on the field. "I will put together the best front office, the best minor league system, and the best coaching staff," promised Rosen.[120]

The Giants went from last place in the National West in 1985 to third place in 1986. Before the 1987 season, Rosen had traded for pitchers Dave Dravecky, Craig Lefferts, Don Robinson and Rick Reuschel and had also acquired third baseman Kevin Mitchell.[121] As a result, the Giants captured the West Division title in 1987 for the first time in 16 years. For his efforts, Rosen was named United Press International's baseball executive of the year.[122]

In 1988 the Giants dropped to fourth place in the NL West, but the following year they won the pennant again and this time faced the Oakland Athletics in the World Series. The A's swept the Giants in four games, but it was one of the most memorable series in the history of baseball. On October 17, 1989, just before World Series Game 3 was scheduled to begin in Candlestick Park, a major earthquake, nicknamed the World Series quake, struck the San Francisco Bay. Millions of people witnessed the motion of the quake on television. Game 3 did not begin until ten days after the earthquake.[123]

Rosen remained with the Giants as general manager through the 1992 season. Shortly after the season ended, Bob Lurie sold the Giants to a group headed by Safeway Inc. chairman Peter Magowan. Rosen resigned, stating that the new owners should pick their own management. "It's been a great seven years," said Rosen, who led the Giants to two National League West titles and the league's pennant in 1989. The 68-year-old Rosen indicated that he would not be very far from the game. "I'll be available," he said.[124]

In 1994 the Indians held a special celebration honoring Rosen's unanimous MVP Award, which he had received in 1953, and in 2006 Rosen was inducted into Cleveland's Hall of Fame. Rosen is also a member of the Jewish Sports Hall of Fame and the Texas League Hall of Fame.[125]

After his time with the Giants, Al Rosen completely retired from baseball.[126] But he never forgot two vital elements that had a major influence on his life. One is the game of baseball. "There is a whole new aura that has been built up and it all has to do with dreams, it has to do with wants, desires, and love. Think of the weddings that take place on home plate, the children who are named after heroes. Why? I don't know why, except what better thing is there to talk about? What common denominator do we have in this country that is better than baseball?"[127]

The other is his Jewish heritage. When he was inducted in 1980 into the Jewish Sports Hall of Fame in Beverly Hills, he observed, "At no time have I been so deeply moved as I have been this evening to be recognized a Jew by Jews."[128] "When I was there in the majors," Al Rosen often said, "I always knew how I wanted it to be about me. I wanted it to be, *Here comes one Jewish kid that every Jew in the world can be proud of.*"[129]

4. Spanning the Decades

In the last half of the 1950s, another group of Jewish players, who differed in several ways from those who preceded them, broke into the major leagues. First, they were all second-generation Jews who did not have to overcome parental objections to playing baseball. On the contrary, like Al Rosen, they were encouraged and supported in their dreams of making baseball their careers. In an interesting parallel to the expansion of major league baseball to the West Coast, a majority of the Jewish players who debuted in the late 1950s were born and grew up in California. Several of these players lasted a number of years in the majors, playing into the mid-sixties. They encountered very few instances of anti–Semitism.

Ed Mayer

One of the last Jewish major leaguers to play ball at the end of the 1950s was Ed Mayer, who had a two-year career with the Chicago Cubs. He was the third Jewish Mayer to play in the major leagues, but he was not related to the first two, brothers Erskine and Sam Mayer.

The bespectacled, lanky Ed Mayer, was born in San Francisco on November 30, 1931, the son of Ned and Sylvia Mayer. His father was a native of Hong Kong, the son of Romanian Jews, and his mother was born in Pennsylvania and had moved to San Francisco where she met Ed's father. Ned Mayer played semipro ball during the 1920s in San Francisco, but with the onset of the Depression, he abandoned baseball and became a plumber to support his family.[1]

According to Ed Mayer, his father, who played high school ball in San Francisco on the same team as Joe DiMaggio, was more than an adequate player, and he might have made it in the big leagues had he not had to give up baseball. "My father had a chance to sign with the Oakland Oaks," said Mayer. "Even though he never played professional baseball, my father continued to encourage me to play ball and was very supportive."[2]

No matter how much Mayer's father supported his son's interest in baseball, the family did not neglect Ed's education—both secular and religious. The Mayers attended Congregation Beth Israel on Fillmore Street where Ed had his bar mitzvah. Unfortunately, the building burned down, but its stained-glass windows still exist at Temple Beth El in Aptos.[3]

Mayer attended Lowell High in San Francisco, the alma mater of former big leaguers Mark Koenig and Jerry Coleman. In his senior year, the southpaw pitcher was named All-City. He also played American Legion ball and experienced one of his biggest thrills when he was voted Most Valuable Player in 1947. His team's sponsor had hired Babe Ruth to present the MVP trophy. "I still have that trophy, and that's one of my wonderful memories about baseball," Mayer recalled.[4]

Mayer graduated high school in 1950 and attended the University of California–Berkeley where he played baseball for two seasons.[5] While at college, Mayer got his first real taste of anti–Semitism. Because it was unclear whether the name Mayer was actually a "Jewish name," he was pledged into a fraternity whose bylaws barred Jews from membership. When the fraternity learned that he actually was Jewish, the fraternity "politely" asked him to leave. He immediately joined the Jewish fraternity, Sigma Alpha Mu.[6]

Mayer later recalled that although he had no scholastic problems in college, he was not happy with his business administration major. After taking a battery of tests, it seemed that he had no aptitude for anything besides baseball, which suited Ed just fine. As he told his counselor, "I want to go play professional baseball. That's my dream." She suggested that Mayer do exactly as he wished.[7] Mayer left Berkeley in 1952 during his junior year to play baseball for the Boston Red Sox organization. The Red Sox were impressed that the six-foot, two-inch Mayer was a lefthander with a variety of pitches and tremendous poise on the mound.[8]

Ed Mayer spent two years in the major leagues, both with the Chicago Cubs. After pitching in three games in 1957, he had a solid season the following year, appearing in 19 games with a 3.80 ERA. He played two more seasons of professional ball in the minors before retiring in 1960 to become an elementary school teacher (courtesy National Baseball Hall of Fame Library; Cooperstown, N.Y.).

He toiled in the minors for nearly six years. During this time, the Red Sox recognized that Mayer could not only pitch, he could also hit. When he was not on the mound, he often played either first base or the outfield. On quite a few occasions, Ed was named to the minor league all-star teams.[9]

In the winter of 1955, the St. Louis Cardinals organization acquired Mayer, and the following spring he pitched for their AAA teams in Rochester and Omaha. Mayer believes that he did his best pitching at Omaha under the tutelage of their manager, Johnny Keane, who later managed the Cardinals and then the Yankees.[10]

In 1957 Mayer went to spring training in Florida, but before the start of the 1957 season, the Cardinals and Chicago Cubs made a three-player swap. The Cubs shipped Jim King to the Cardinals in exchange for outfielder Bobby Del Greco and pitcher Ed Mayer. Del Greco remained with the Cubs (he was traded to the New York Yankees later in the season), but Chicago assigned Mayer to its Fort Worth farm club in the AA Texas League. It was at Fort Worth where the Cubs converted Mayer from a starter to a relief pitcher.[11]

The Chicago Cubs purchased Mayer's contract from Fort Worth in September 1957.[12] He made his debut with the Cubs on September 15 at Wrigley Field in a game against the Giants. It was certainly not an auspicious beginning. Mayer was tagged for five runs in five innings, including a home run by Willie Mays. The Cubs, nevertheless, managed to win the game, 7–6, although Mayer did not get credit for the win. He appeared in two other games for the Cubs that year and ended the 1957 season with no decisions and an ERA of 5.87.[13]

Mayer inked his 1958 contract for the Cubs in January and headed for spring training.[14] He had such a successful spring, that the Cubs decided to sell one of their veteran pitchers, Dick Littlefield, to the Milwaukee Braves for an amount reported to be more than the $25,000 waiver price.[15]

The Cubs began the 1958 season on a high note and were among the league leaders for the first month of the season. Mayer got his first and only career save the first month of the season at Busch Stadium against the St. Louis Cardinals. He entered the game in the eighth inning with one out and a runner on first. He threw a double-play ball to pinch-hitter Hal Smith and pitched out of another jam in the ninth to preserve the victory for Cub starting pitcher Glenn Hobbie.[16]

Mayer defeated the St. Louis Cardinals that same month for his first win and won his second and last game on May 30 against the Los Angeles Dodgers. The losing pitcher in that game was Sandy Koufax. Mayer often refers to that victory as his "fifteen minutes of fame."[17] For the first month of the 1958 season, the Cubs were in second place in the National League with a mark of 13–8. Mayer, who had pitched 17 innings for the Cubs during April, ranked second in the league with an ERA of 1.50.[18]

During the 1958 season his arm began to feel progressively weaker and doctors told him that all of his years of pitching had worn out the muscles in his left arm and his career was over. Mayer was philosophical about his brief career in baseball. "I have no regrets," he stated. "I had a really good time."[19]

Mayer ended the 1958 season and his major league career with a record of 2–2 and an ERA of 3.80. His lifetime ERA was 4.31, compiled in a total of just 22 games in the big leagues.[20]

Mayer encountered anti–Semitism a few times during his baseball career, but he felt he had it easy compared with the effects of segregation on the African-American players. During spring training in Phoenix one year, the Cubs were invited to a country club, but Mayer could not attend because the club prohibited Jews. (Mayer's favorite teammate, Ernie Banks, also was not invited because of his color.)[21]

The most serious incident occurred in Montgomery, Alabama. Mayer's team bus, on the way to Georgia, stopped at a service station to purchase soda from the machine. One of Mayer's African-American teammates, Earl Wilson, who passed away in 1955, began to put his nickel in the machine. The station attendant pointed a gun at Wilson and said, "No n----- is going to buy a Coke out of my machine." Mayer got in front of Wilson, pushed him back on the bus and bought the Coke for him.[22]

After he left the Cubs in 1958, Mayer returned to the minors. He retired from baseball in 1960 and returned to his San Francisco home where he completed his undergraduate degree and taught school from 1967 until he retired in 1992. He retained his interest in baseball and once commented on how the game has changed. "In every way," he says, "the players of today are bigger, faster and stronger than we were. On the other hand, today's players don't know all of the basics of the game because many didn't have time to learn them in the minors. One thing I am sure of—if I were pitching today, I would see myself as a long reliever. I'm not really sure I had enough stuff to be a starter."[23]

Don Taussig

Like Ed Mayer, outfielder Don Taussig spent many years in the minor leagues and only a few in the majors.

Donald Franklin Taussig was born in New York City, February 19, 1932. His family later moved to Long Beach, New York, where Don graduated from Long Beach High School. He attended Rutgers University, Columbia University, and graduated from Hofstra College. The six-foot, 180-pound outfielder played for three major league teams, the San Francisco Giants in 1958, the St. Louis Cardinals in 1961, and the Houston Colt .45s in 1962.[24]

Taussig spent eight years in the minors before he made it to the big leagues. He signed his first professional contract in 1950 with the Yankees, who assigned him to La Grange in the Class D Georgia-Alabama League. After advancing to higher-level ball each season, Taussig's baseball career was interrupted in 1953 with a 21-month stint in the Army.[25]

When Taussig went back to professional baseball in 1955, he returned to the Yankee farm system and continued his slow climb toward the majors. In 1956 and in 1957, Taussig was playing AA ball for Dallas in the Texas League. His 445 putouts in 1957 led the Texas League, and Taussig was named the league's All-Star centerfielder.[26]

In January 1958, the San Francisco Giants, in their first year on the West Coast, signed four players from the Dallas team. One was outfielder Don Taussig.[27] When he appeared at the Giants' training camp in Phoenix, Giants owner Horace Stoneham greeted him, extended his hand, and said to the rookie, "Hi, I'm Horace Stoneham." Rookie Don Taussig smiled back and replied, "I'm Don Taussig," and proceeded to slap his boss on the back as if the gathering were a fraternity smoker. Veteran Giant outfielder Hank Sauer was absolutely amazed at how things had changed since he entered his rookie camp. "When I came up with Cincinnati in 1941," recalled Sauer, "nobody would talk to me."[28]

Taussig went north with the club, but as a center fielder, he had to compete against the legendary Willie Mays. A disturbed Taussig asked, "You want to know the main thing that is frustrating to a rookie? It's when you think you have the ability and you're not given a chance to show it."[29]

Taussig made his major league debut with

Don Taussig was 26 years old when he broke into the major leagues with the San Francisco Giants. The Hofstra University graduate played three years in the majors with three different teams, the Giants, Cardinals, and Astros. His lifetime batting average was .262 in 153 major league games (courtesy National Baseball Hall of Fame Library; Cooperstown, N.Y.).

the Giants on April 23, 1958. Six days later he got his first major league hit off Philadelphia Phillies veteran hurler Curt Simmons, and on June 6, Taussig hit the first of his four major league home runs against Cincinnati Reds pitcher Harvey Haddix. Taussig appeared in 39 games for the Giants in 1958 before he was optioned to Phoenix in the Pacific Coast League along with outfielder Jim King, while the Giants announced the recall of outfielder Willie Kirkland.[30] At the time of his release, Taussig was hitting .200, although he was displaying stellar defense. The Giant manager stated he simply had a surplus of outfielders. After September 1, when teams were allowed to expand their rosters, the Giants recalled Don Taussig and he completed the 1958 season in the big leagues.[31]

Taussig spent 1959 and 1960 back in the minor leagues, but he returned to the majors in 1961 with the St. Louis Cardinals.[32] The Cardinals used Taussig primarily as a pinch-hitter and utility outfielder. He appeared in 98 games for the Cardinals and hit .287. Again his defensive play was superb. He finished the 1961 season with a .992 fielding percentage.[33]

In 1962 the Houston Colt .45s (the forerunners of the Houston Astros), made their debut in the National League. One of the players they selected in the expansion draft was Don Taussig.[34] Unfortunately for both Taussig and Houston, Taussig was placed on the disabled list for the first three months of the season due to surgery for torn ligaments in his left knee. When he finally returned to duty, he could only muster a .200 batting average in 16 games and was sent down to Oklahoma City in the American Association before the completion of the 1962 season.[35] He got one more chance at the end of July. Houston, looking for a clutch hitter, recalled Taussig from the minors. However, less than one month later, Houston returned him to their Oklahoma City farm club.[36]

In his three-year major league career, Don Taussig played for three teams and appeared in 153 games. He hit safely 69 times in 263 at-bats, hit four home runs, drove in 30 runs and had a life time batting average of .262.[37] After he left baseball, Taussig moved back to the city of his birth, Long Beach, New York.

Barry Latman

In his eleven-year major league career, pitcher Arnold Barry Latman won 59 games for four teams. His best season was 1961 when he compiled a 13–5 record for the Chicago White Sox.[38]

Born in Los Angeles, May 21, 1936, the six-foot, three-inch, 220-pound Latman was an outstanding pitcher at Fairfax High in Los Angeles and teammate of another future Jewish major leaguer, Larry Sherry.[39] Fairfax High School always had winning baseball teams. Latman began playing baseball in the Cub Scouts, but put baseball aside while he prepared for his bar mitzvah.[40] After high school, he turned down a major league contract and opted to attend the University of Southern California on a baseball scholarship.[41] When Latman gave up the scholarship later to play pro ball, he displeased his grandfather, an immigrant from Eastern Europe, who refused to speak with his grandson for three years. "However," said Latman, "after he saw me pitch against one of the New York teams on television, he forgave me and everything was okay after that."[42]

Unlike Jewish parents of previous generations, Barry Latman's father had meticulously charted his son's course for a career in the big leagues. Because he felt his son was a little too cocky in his desire to be a pro, in 1953, Latman's father came up with an unusual way to improve Barry's attitude. He asked his son, "Barry, how would you like to meet a man who *really* was a great ballplayer?" When Barry emphatically answered, "Yes," his father told him that the illustrious player was Ty Cobb.

The Latmans spent an entire day visiting with Cobb in his home in Palo Alto as he watched Barry throw the ball.[43] Cobb gave Latman some pointers and then told him, "It's easy to say you deserve to be in the major leagues, it's another, harder thing to prove it." Before the Latmans left, Cobb agreed that he and Barry would write each other from time to time and that Cobb would offer advice whenever Barry asked. "Every time I saw him, every time I received a letter from him," said Latman, "I moved close to big-league success."[44]

The correspondence between Cobb and Latman took place over approximately five years and covered basically three categories: conditioning, concentration, and overall mental attitude. Latman published the letters shortly after Cobb died as a tribute to the "Georgia Peach" and as his personal way of saying thank you to Cobb.[45]

There are two interesting aspects about the relationship between Cobb and Latman. The first is that Latman, a pitcher, would find advice from Cobb, an outfielder, so useful.[46] More interesting, however, is that Cobb had a reputation as being one of baseball's most notorious bigots—both anti–Semitic and anti-black. It is not clear whether Cobb was aware that Latman was Jewish, and that question remains unanswered to this day.[47]

Latman signed a contract with the White Sox organization while still on the campus of USC, and began his professional career with Waterloo in the 3-I League in 1955 where he compiled an excellent record of 18–4 with an ERA of 4.12.[48] Los Angeles baseball writers selected Latman as the best first-year pro from California for his record with Waterloo. The writers were impressed with his 114 strikeouts in 203 innings and with his hurling 14 complete games.[49]

Latman continued pitching in the minors in 1956 and 1957. With Indianapolis in 1957, he impressed the White Sox with an ERA of 3.95, and on September 10 of that year, he made his major league debut.[50] "It was the fifth inning and the White Sox were losing, 16–1, to the New York Yankees, and manager Lopez was running out of relief pitchers. He sent a call to the bullpen, and I finally realized he was calling for me to come in and pitch. When I reached the mound, Al handed me the ball and patted me on the rumble seat and said, 'Good Luck.' I felt like following him off the mound when I saw the batter I had to face with the bases loaded—No. 7—Mickey Mantle. On the third pitch, I threw a fast ball like 180 miles an hour and he hit it and it takes off ... 360 miles an hour. The second baseman caught it to retire the side. When I got back to the dugout, Lopez looked at me funny and asked what the first and second pitches were. I told him and he asked me about the third pitch, the one Mantle hit. I told him, and he says to me, 'Son, please learn another pitch.'"[51]

Five days later, Latman won his first major league game, pitching two scoreless innings against the Washington Senators. During his stay with the White Sox in 1957, Latman appeared in seven games, pitched 12.1 innings, had a record of 1–2, and an ERA of 8.03.[52]

In 1958 the White Sox took Latman to spring training, but they were forced to trim their roster, and despite his being named top rookie in camp, they sent Latman back to Indianapolis.[53] Pitching the opening game for Indianapolis against the Denver Bears, Latman allowed only two hits, shutting out the Bears, 2–0. Denver manager and former New York Giants infielder Andy Cohen said Latman's strength and ball control did not surprise him, for Cohen had coached Latman the previous year.[54] "Andy Cohen was one of the earliest coaches to predict that one day I would be pitching in the major leagues," said Latman.[55]

He pitched at Indianapolis until the end of July when the White Sox brought him back to the major leagues.[56] In 1958 Latman appeared in 13 games for the Sox and had a record of 3–0, with an outstanding ERA of 0.76, giving up only four earned runs in 47.2 innings.[57]

Latman started 21 games in 1959, his first full season in the majors. After he tossed 18 consecutive scoreless innings in relief, he was given his first start on June 25 and defeated the Senators, 4–1, on a five-hitter. He tossed a four-hitter in July against Kansas City and, in the era before the designated hitter, Latman hit safely three times. On September 11, Latman pitched 9.1 innings against the Orioles, retiring 21 batters in a row. He helped the White Sox to the pennant in 1959 but did not pitch in the Series, which the Dodgers won four games to two.[58] The pitching star in the Series was Latman's teammate at Fairfax High, Larry Sherry.[59]

Barry Latman was having his hair cut in April 1960 when he heard the news that the

Pitcher Barry Latman had an eleven-year career in the major leagues with four teams, and he credits baseball legend Ty Cobb with playing a major role in encouraging him in his career. Cobb's interest in Latman seems unusual given that Cobb was not a pitcher and was considered notoriously anti–Semitic, but the two men kept up a five-year correspondence discussing Latman's progress in baseball (courtesy National Baseball Hall of Fame Library; Cooperstown, N.Y.).

White Sox had traded him to the Cleveland Indians in return for pitcher Herb Score. "I sort of jumped up and nearly got nicked," Latman said. "I was shocked, but ... it's an honor just to be traded in a deal with a great pitcher like Herb Score. I know I was wild this spring but I felt that in the last couple of days I was getting my control back."[60]

With the Indians in 1960, Latman had a .500 season—seven wins and seven losses, and an ERA of 4.03.[61] At the end of the 1960 season, Cleveland manager Jimmy Dykes stated he was pleased with Latman's performance in 1960 and had already penned him into the starting rotation for next year. "Latman deserves to be one of my starters," declared Dykes. "Every time I'd call on him for relief he showed so much stuff I made a mental note to put him into the starting rotation."[62] Even Indian general manager "Trader" Frank Lane was pleased with the deal he had made with the White Sox for Latman. "Latman has been steadily improving. I'd like to make about five Latman deals."[63]

Both Dykes and Lane were correct in their assessment of Latman. He had his best year in the majors in 1961. After he won his first nine starts, Dykes summed up Latman's success. "He stopped being cute. That's his secret.

He fires the fastball high and keeps the curve low. I wish some of the others would follow his example." Latman agreed, adding, "I have so much more confidence. I have a third pitch, I have a slider and I'm getting all three pitches over. I've worked hard and it's paying off."[64]

Latman also credited a romance with Lynne Schwab as a reason for his improvement. "Finding the right girl and becoming engaged has been the major influence," he said.[65] Latman ended the season with a 13 and 5 record and a 4.02 ERA. Although he was chosen to represent the American League in the year's second All-Star Game, it was rained out before he had a chance to pitch, the first All-Star Game to end as a tie, 1–1.[66]

The Indians expected Latman to have another outstanding year in 1962, but that year proved disappointing. He was both a starter and a relief pitcher for the Indians and finished the season with a record of 8–13 and an ERA of 4.17. His teammates thought he pitched much better than his record indicated. They were convinced he was "snake bit," baseball lingo for pitching in bad luck.[67]

Latman's last year with Cleveland was 1963. Early in the season he told the press, "If you're going to write about me, it's going to be a mystery story. I haven't reached my goals and I don't know why. In the past I've always popped off, predicted big things for myself. Last year was my first losing one. You're looking at the new Latman. I'm not saying anything."[68]

His record for 1963 was worse than the previous year. His won–loss record fell to 7–12 and his ERA jumped to 4.94. At the 1963 winter meeting, the Cleveland Indians traded Barry Latman to the Los Angeles Angels for slugger Leon Wagner, who had hit 26 home runs and driven in 90 runs for the Angels in 1963. Angels General Manager Fred Haney was not impressed with Wagner's home run total because only two of his 26 were hit at the Angels home park, Chavez Ravine. "We must tailor our club," said Haney, "for pitching and speed rather than power."[69]

Latman was thrilled about the trade to his hometown.[70] "Being a member of the White Sox when they made the World Series in 1959 and also making the All-Star team used to be my biggest thrills," said Latman. "But not any more. The best thrill is being traded to the Angels. I doubt if there are half a dozen pitchers in the majors who get to play in their hometown.[71] He added, "I know one thing, I'm happier now than I've ever been in baseball so that ought to help me become a better pitcher."[72]

In his first year in Los Angeles, Latman won 6 and lost 10, but finished the season with a respectable ERA of 3.85. He appeared in 40 games, 18 as a starter. In 1965, the year the Los Angeles Angels became the California Angels, Latman was plagued by physical problems which would haunt him for the rest of his professional career. He pitched only 31.2 innings in 18 games and finished the season with Seattle in the Pacific Coast League.[73]

On December 16, 1965, the Houston Astros announced their purchase of Latman's contract.[74] Latman pitched in 31 games and had the best ERA of any righthander on the Astros staff—2.71. However, his won–loss record for Houston in 1966 was a dismal 2–7. The following year, 1967, was Latman's final year in the major leagues. Still with the Astros, he won 3 games and lost 6, with an ERA of 4.52. In August, Houston asked waivers on him.[75]

Latman had pitched 11 years in the major leagues and finished his career with a record of 59–68, appearing in 344 games with a lifetime ERA of 3.91. He pitched 28 complete games, including 10 shutouts. Although his overall record was below .500, his record as a relief pitcher was 20–16 with 16 saves.[76]

After he left the major leagues, Latman coached in the minor leagues before retiring completely to provide a "real home" for his wife and his children who were beginning school.

He admits that it took ten years before he could watch baseball on television without feeling he should still be playing. Latman worked as a general contractor and then retired to Mexico.[77]

Larry Sherry

Larry Sherry was the younger half of the last set of six Jewish brothers to play in the major leagues; he and Norm were the only brothers to play on the same team at the same time. Larry, the youngest of four boys, was born in Los Angeles, July 25, 1935, in Fairfax, a large Jewish area of the city. His father was a dry cleaner. While Larry's mother was pregnant with him, she had a fall, and members of the Sherry family believed that the accident caused Larry to be born with two clubfeet, a condition that causes feet to turn inward.[78]

Larry had to wear braces until he was twelve years old and special shoes even after the braces were off. Despite his physical problems, Sherry was determined to play baseball like his brothers Stan, Norm, and George, all of whom were stars on the Fairfax High School baseball team. Although many people encouraged him to play baseball, Sherry often commented, "I don't want to slight my mom and dad. Dad always encouraged me and mom never said anything when I came home late for dinner as a kid."[79]

From the moment Larry began to play ball and up to the time he reached the majors, his brother Norm was always there to coach him. He was also fortunate in having a baseball coach at Fairfax High School, Frank Shaffer, who provided him with special shoes to help him participate in sports. When he entered high school, Larry was five-feet, one-inch, and 110 pounds, but by his senior year he had shot up to six-feet, one-inch and weighed 135 pounds.[80]

Sherry made the junior varsity team in basketball and the varsity team in baseball where he played second base for two years. During his junior year he alternated between first and pitching. When Sherry broke his right ankle preparing for his senior season, his coach encouraged him to concentrate on pitching. He told Sherry that even before the accident he had been too slow to make it as a professional infielder.[81] (The star pitcher for Fairfax High School at that time was future major leaguer Barry Latman.)

It was Dodgers scout and coach Harold "Lefty" Phillips who discovered Larry Sherry pitching in an all-star high school game. "His pitching rhythm wasn't good," said Phillips. "He was sort of herky-jerky but one out of every six or seven fast balls he threw was a good one. I could see he had a good arm. I figured that with the proper attention, he might develop."[82]

Larry signed a contract with Santa Barbara, a Dodgers farm club, on July 24, 1953, six weeks after he graduated high school, and a day before his 18th birthday. He received a $2,200 bonus plus a salary of $250 a month. Two days after he signed the contract he pitched in his first professional game.[83]

From 1953 until he reached the major leagues in 1958, Larry Sherry climbed up the farm club ladder, playing for eight teams in six seasons.[84]

Despite his many stops in the minor leagues, Sherry almost quit baseball during his third season in professional ball. Pitching for Class B in Newport News, Sherry finished the year with a record of 5–10 and an ERA of 4.90 and he began to talk about retiring. "Thank goodness," said Sherry, "my brother Norm, who had been working with me, and Harold "Lefty" Phillips," who had signed me, talked me out of it."[85]

In 1957, the last year the Dodgers played in Brooklyn, Sherry pitched for both the Dodgers farm club in Los Angeles and their AAA farm club in Fort Worth, notching an excellent ERA of 3.07.[86]

Sherry had a stroke of good luck in 1958 when the Dodgers pitching staff was in complete disarray. Their stalwarts, Roger Craig, Don Newcombe, Carl Erskine, and Ed Roebuck, all showed up with sore arms during their inaugural season in Los Angeles, and both Don Drysdale and Sandy Koufax were on active duty with the military for six months.

The six-foot, two-inch, 204-pound right-hander debuted with the Dodgers on April 17, 1958. In his first stint in the majors it was apparent that Sherry needed more seasoning. In five innings, he allowed 10 hits and 7 walks for an ERA of 12.46. Despite the statistics, Dodger manager Walter Alston thought Sherry had "good stuff," but needed more work; in May, the Dodgers dispatched him to Spokane in the Pacific Coast League, where his brother Norm was a catcher.[87] For the only time in their minor league careers, Norman and Larry Sherry played on the same team. Larry noted that being united with his

Each year, one player is generally the hero of the World Series. In 1959, that hero was relief pitcher Larry Sherry, who completed all four victories for the Dodgers over the White Sox. Used only in relief, Sherry had two victories and two saves. He was also one half of the last all–Jewish battery in the major leagues (courtesy National Baseball Hall of Fame Library; Cooperstown, N.Y.).

brother and the birth of his daughter were the only good things that happened in 1958.[88]

During the 1958-1959 off-season, Larry Sherry worked with his brother Norm to develop a slider, and he felt confident that this new pitch, along with his fastball and curve, would help him succeed in the big leagues. "Norm was very instrumental in my career," admitted Sherry. "You couldn't ask for a better teacher."[89]

Larry Sherry began to rely more and more on the slider. The more faith he had in that pitch, the more his confidence increased. "It was a revelation to me," said Sherry. "I suddenly found out how to pitch."[90]

Sherry went to spring training with the Dodgers in 1959, but when camp broke, he was sent, along with pitcher Don Bessent, to St. Paul in the American Association.[91] By mid-season he was leading the American Association in strikeouts and had won six games. In July, the Dodgers recalled Sherry from their St. Paul team.[92]

While Sherry was at best, a .500 pitcher in the minor leagues, and lost his first start with LA by a score of 2–1, he finished 1959 in an amazing fashion. As both a starter and reliever, he was one of the hardest pitchers to hit in the National League. He gave up only 75 hits in 94.1 innings with an ERA of just 2.19, and he ended the regular season with a record of 7–2, winning seven straight decisions after losing his first two.[93]

Sherry considered one particular game against the St. Louis Cardinals his turning point in the season. He relieved Johnny Podres in the first inning and pitched the remaining 8.2

innings. At the plate, Sherry was three-for-three with a home run and three RBIs. He struck out the side in the ninth—Stan Musial, Bill White, and Ken Boyer—to end the game. Manager Walt Alston stated that it was "the best one-man performance in the history of the game."[94]

The regular 1959 season ended with a tie for first place between the Los Angeles Dodgers and the Milwaukee Braves that had to be resolved in a best two-out-of-three playoff series. Danny McDevitt started for the Dodgers in Game One, but Alston lifted him after he pitched only 1.1 innings and brought in Sherry to protect LA's 2–1 lead. Sherry gave up only four hits the rest of the game, and his relief work won Game One in Milwaukee. Furillo's key hit along with the contributions of six Dodger pitchers, won Game Two in the Coliseum. The Dodgers had clinched their first pennant in Los Angeles.[95]

In 1959 the Dodgers faced the Chicago White Sox in the World Series. Each team in the 1959 World Series had a Jewish relief pitcher on its roster. Barry Latman, the Chicago White Sox right-handed hurler and Sherry's high school teammate, had helped his team win the pennant, but he would not make a single appearance in the World Series. Larry Sherry had not only helped the Dodgers reach the World Series, but he also would play a significant role in their winning it.

Numerous relief pitchers had such great success in 1959, that many baseball *mavens* dubbed it "The Year of Relief." It is not surprising, therefore, that in all six games of the 1959 World Series, no starting pitcher on either team hurled a complete game. During its fifty-six year history, the World Series had always had its share of relief heroics but the accomplishments of Los Angeles Dodger Larry Sherry far surpassed any previous efforts.[96]

Bill Veeck's White Sox were heavily favored to defeat whichever team won the National League title. They had broken the Yankees' streak of four consecutive pennant victories; Early Wynn was their ace pitcher; and they fielded a dazzling combination of Nellie Fox at second base and Luis Aparicio at shortstop. In addition, the Sox were able to rest their players while the Dodgers battled the Braves for the National League flag. What the White Sox did not anticipate was Larry Sherry. What he accomplished in the 1959 World Series put him in the record books and made him one of the bona fide heroes of World Series history.[97]

The White Sox took the first game of the Series, 11–0. Sherry relieved Johnny Podres in the second game, got out of a jam in the eighth, and set the White Sox down in order in the ninth to get a save. In the third game, which the Dodgers won, 3–1, Sherry got Al Smith to hit into a double play with the bases loaded in the eighth. He then struck out all three men he faced in the ninth for his second save in the Series. Sherry got the victory in Game Four when he held the White Sox hitless in both the eighth and ninth innings, allowing the Dodgers to score the winning run. The White Sox shut the Dodgers out, 1–0, in the fifth game. In the sixth game, Johnny Podres took an 8–0 lead into the fourth inning. He then hit Jim Landis, walked Sherman Lollar, and gave up a powerful drive for a three-run homer to first baseman Ted Kluzewski. With the game getting close, Alston once again called on Larry Sherry who proceeded to shut out the White Sox the rest of the way. The Dodgers won the sixth game, 9–3. Larry Sherry received his second win, and the Dodgers had won the World Series, four games to two.[98]

Sherry had given up one run in 12.2 innings and only eight hits. He had won or saved all four of the Dodger victories. After the Series concluded, Al Lopez, White Sox manager admitted, "He's the guy who killed us. He was the guy we couldn't touch." Walt Alston's reaction was simple. He called 1959 Sherry's year of immortality and said, "I've never had a pitcher with so little experience who was thrown into so many situations as Sherry was. As a matter of fact, I can't think of a pitcher like him that anybody ever had."

Larry Sherry was humble in accepting the praise others heaped on him. He insisted that his brother be given some of the credit. "My older brother Norm didn't even get his name in the box score, but if it wasn't for him, my name wouldn't have been in it either during the World Series. No one worked harder with me than he did. Even when we were kids, we'd spend hours working together. For me—and for Norm, too—this series is a dream come true."[99]

For his work in the World Series, Larry Sherry received a number of awards and honors. *Sport Magazine* named Larry Sherry the outstanding player of the World Series and awarded him a Chevrolet Corvette.[100] In February 1960, the Baseball Writers Association, by unanimous vote, awarded Sherry the Babe Ruth award as the outstanding player in the 1959 World Series. The following month, Sherry won the Times National Sports Award. When he accepted the award, he again praised his brother for his continuing words of encouragement. "If not for my brother I would not today be the toast of the baseball world."[101]

Larry Sherry was the hero of the 1959 World Series, but he could not afford to go home. He needed all the money he could get from endorsements to supplement his total player salary of $6,600. Now, in addition to his World Series share, he had an opportunity to make a profitable appearance tour for a clothing firm that required his visiting fifteen cities in seventeen days. "I'd come into a city the night before and the next morning there would be a press conference waiting for me. Then I'd make appearances at a few stores in the afternoon and go to dinner and then fly on to the next city," bemoaned Sherry.[102]

In January 1960, Sherry also did the banquet circuit. "You're on the go the whole month," said Sherry, "and it's rough. You get expenses, but no money. But I felt it was something I *should* do. If it hadn't been for baseball, I wouldn't have been a World Series hero. By appearing at the big banquets, I was able to give back something of what I owed to baseball."[103] Sherry figured out that he was the guest of honor at more than 25 banquets and appeared on 78 radio and television shows, including the *Ed Sullivan Show*. "For the *Ed Sullivan Show* I had to go out and buy a suit," Sherry noted. "I didn't own one. I didn't even make the minimum salary that year. Hell, my World Series check was double my salary."[104]

Larry Sherry insisted that he be given a chance as a starter in 1960. He appeared in 57 games, started three and completed one. In June he suffered a sprained ankle in a game with the Cubs when he stepped on a bat while running to cover home plate.[105] Although Sherry finished 1960 with a record of 14 wins, 10 losses, and seven saves, it would be the only year he would have double digit wins. He never again regained the brilliance of his 1959 form.[106]

One of the highlights for Larry Sherry during the 1960 season was the game on May 7 when Larry teamed for the first time in the majors with his brother to make up the battery. The two Sherrys were the only battery of Jewish brothers in major league history, and in 1960, only the tenth brother battery in the major leagues. On the day Norman Sherry caught his brother, Larry won the game and Norman hit a home run. The Sherrys were both with the Dodgers until 1962 when Norman was traded to the New York Mets. Larry Sherry pitched for the Dodgers through 1963. His career record with Los Angeles was 34–25 with 39 saves.[107]

On April 10, 1964, Larry Sherry was sold to the Detroit Tigers where he was reunited with his former Los Angeles manager, Charley Dressen.[108] In his first year with the Tigers,

Sherry had a 7–5 record despite breaking a bone in his foot in August and missing the remainder of the year.[109] His record in 1965 fell to 3–6, with 5 saves and an ERA of 3.10, and the following year he won eight games while losing five and posted a career-high 20 saves and a 3.82 ERA.[110]

At the end of June 1967, the Detroit Tigers traded Larry Sherry to the Houston Astros for veteran outfielder Jim Landis. Astros manager Grady Hatton was hopeful that Sherry would regain his old form and help the Astros in the bullpen.[111] In Houston, Sherry had another reunion, this time with his Fairfax High School classmate, Barry Latman. He did not remain very long with the Astros, who put Sherry on waivers in March 1968. Four months later, the California Angels picked him up, but he pitched in only three games before the Angels sent him to the minors on 24-hour recall.[112]

Those were his last games in the majors. In his 11-year career, Larry Sherry won 53 games and lost 44. He had a respectable lifetime ERA of 3.67 and had saved 82 games.[113]

Sherry went to the Royals spring training camp in 1969 but did not catch on with Kansas City.[114] In 1970, Sherry coached for the Mobile White Sox; the following year he managed the Asheville Tourists in the Dixie Association. In 1971 the White Sox announced that Sherry would manage their Pacific Coast League team at Tucson, Arizona.[115]

He finally returned to the major leagues in 1977, serving as pitching coach at various times for the Pittsburgh Pirates, the California Angels, the Dodgers and the Padres.[116]

Years later as Sherry looked back on his career, he admitted he had encountered some anti–Semitism when he played in the minor leagues, but not in the majors. "If I let those people bother me," he said, "I'd be getting down on their level."[117] After a long bout with cancer, Larry Sherry died on December 17, 2006.[118]

Baseball pundits still believe that Sherry's performance in the 1959 World Series has never been equaled. Two pitchers have performed similar outstanding feats in relief—John Wetteland saved all four Yankee victories against the Braves in 1996, and Keith Foulke closed out all four Red Sox wins when they swept the Cardinals in 2004. These analysts also point out that relief pitching in 1959 differed from relief pitching in 2008. When Sherry pitched in the 1959 World Series, there was no closer, no set-up man, nor any middle reliever; relievers of his day were often summoned into the ball game in pressure situations at any time in the game, making his achievements even more remarkable.[119]

Norman Sherry

Norman Burt "Norm" Sherry was born in upper Manhattan, July 16, 1931. The family moved to the West Hollywood section of Los Angeles when Norm was two years old. He was the oldest of four brothers, all of whom played baseball at Fairfax Senior High in Los Angeles. Norm and Larry played in the major leagues while a third Sherry, George, played pro ball in the Far West League for one year before he hurt his arm.[120]

"I knew I was going to be a baseball player," Sherry recalled. "I loved it. We played all day long. My mother used to threaten us—'I'm going to burn your bats, I'm going to throw away your gloves'—because we would never come home. We lived three houses from the high school and we'd jump the fence and play ball in the field there. We wouldn't come home until it was pitch dark."[121]

Like his brother Larry, Norman Sherry credits his coach at Fairfax, Frank Shaffer, for helping him find his best position—catcher. He had pitched and played first base up to then,

but his coach saw that he had more potential behind the plate.[122] Shaffer obviously
picked the right spot for Norm for when
he went to spring training with the
Dodgers in 1958, Manager Walt Alston
said of Sherry, "There's never been any
doubt about his ability to handle the
assignment back of the plate.[123]

For his entire baseball career, Sherry,
always described as a mild man, was considered diminutive by today's athletic stan-
dards. In addition, his face was sun-dried
and freckled and his hands were gnarled
and twisted. One of his teammates, Don
Drysdale, once told Sherry, "You have the
face and hands of a catcher," and he continued to refer to Sherry as "Catcher
Face."[124]

After he graduated from high school,
a Dodgers farm team, the Hollywood Stars,
signed Norm into their organization for
the 1950 season. He got a $6,000 bonus in
addition to his salary.[125] Norman Sherry
spent 10 years in the minors interrupted by
2 years in the United States Army before
he had an opportunity to play in the major
leagues.[126]

During his minor league days, Sherry
went through a number of physical prob-

Catcher Norman Sherry, who caught his brother
Larry for four years, not only helped form the
last Jewish brother battery in baseball, but he
was a major influence on his brother's pitching
career. He is also credited with giving Sandy Koufax advice that immensely aided his climb to
greatness. Thirteen years after he retired from
major league baseball, Norman Sherry managed
the California Angels in 1976 and 1977 (courtesy
National Baseball Hall of Fame Library; Cooperstown, N.Y.).

lems, including an elbow operation, a broken thumb, and an operation for a ruptured disc.
He could barely walk by the time he reported for spring training in 1956, but he was still
able to catch 66 games that year for Fort Worth and Buffalo, two teams in the International
League.[127]

Sherry had a successful spring training in 1957, and until two days prior to the start
of the season, his name was on the Dodgers roster. He was sent instead to St. Paul in the
American Association where on May 20, a foul ball shattered his right wrist. Injury notwith-
standing, Norm Sherry got married two days later with a cast on his hand. Larry Sherry was
his best man.[128]

Sherry spent the 1958 season with Spokane in the Pacific Coast League.[129] He had a
good season there, hitting .278 with 27 doubles and 41 RBIs. His brother Larry played part
of the season in Spokane with him. On June 14, 1958, Norm's wife had their first child on
the same day Larry's wife gave birth to a daughter. The same doctor delivered both girls.[130]
In other good news, the Dodgers announced that they were bringing Norman up to the
major leagues for spring training in 1959.[131]

During the winter of 1958-1959, Norm and Larry Sherry played winter ball in Venezuela,
and it was there that Norm helped his brother develop his slider, the pitch that was to prove
quite helpful to the younger sibling. The two brothers began the 1959 season together with

the Dodgers where team brass hoped the brother battery of Larry and Norm Sherry would follow in the successful footsteps of two other brother batteries, Mort and Walker Cooper and Wes and Rick Ferrell.[132] The Sherry brothers were not the first pair of Dodger brothers, but they were the only brother battery in Dodgers history.[133]

Unfortunately for Norm, he was unable to stay in Los Angeles in 1959, although in the second game of the season, and Norm's first, he got a base hit, drove in two runs and won the game in Wrigley Field for his brother.[134] Norm was the victim of baseball's rules. The Dodgers needed to get one catcher off their roster, but their other catcher, Joe Pignatano, had no options remaining. If the Dodgers sent him to the minors, they would not have been able to get him back. Norm Sherry, on the other hand, had many options remaining and could always be recalled.[135] While Norm Sherry was always happy for Larry's success, he could not help but wonder when his own big break would come.[136]

From 1960 to 1962, Sherry did stay on the Dodger roster permanently as third-string catcher. He hit eight home runs in 1960, but the one he most remembered was the home run he hit on May 7 when he and his brother Larry became the first Jewish battery in major league history. It was an 11th inning, game-winning blast that gave the Dodgers a 3–2 victory over the Phillies and gave his brother the win.[137]

Sherry's 1960 season was cut short when, on August 22, in a game against the San Francisco Giants, he was struck on the wrist by a Stu Miller pitch. It was the same wrist he had fractured in 1957. In the 47 games he caught for the Dodgers that year, he had a .283 batting average, the Dodgers' highest against left-handed pitchers.[138]

Norm Sherry also played in 47 games in 1961, and this year he was injured twice. On April 20, he was on the third base side of home plate waiting to take a wide throw from Frank Howard. The ball and Cardinal pitcher Curt Simmons arrived at the same time, and after a bone-crushing collision, Sherry was hospitalized with a badly ulcerated kidney. He was unable to play for a month.[139] Then on July 7 the Dodgers announced that the injury-prone Sherry had suffered a broken rib from being hit with a batted ball when he was warming up a pitcher in the bullpen; he was placed on the disabled list until mid–August.[140]

Norman Sherry may have had a limited season in 1961, but he made his most important contribution to the Dodgers and the game of baseball that year. Pitcher Sandy Koufax had been a member of the Dodgers since 1955. A pitcher with great potential, Koufax had won only 36 games in six years with the Dodgers. Many credit Norman Sherry for providing the biggest factor in Koufax's career turnaround in 1961.

In 1959, Sherry thought Koufax was just another pitcher with a good arm who pitched well at times, but had frequent control problems. Sherry also knew he was quiet, a hard worker, and a perfectionist.

During spring training in 1961, Sherry and Koufax were roommates. Sherry was scheduled to catch Koufax in an exhibition game for the B squad in Orlando against the Minnesota Twins. On the bus ride to the game, the two went over their signals, discussing which pitches Koufax was going to throw. There was a special bond between the two because they were "roomies" on the road, they had their catcher-pitcher relationship, and they were both Jewish.

As soon as the game began, Koufax had problems finding the plate. He threw a lot of fastballs up and out of the strike zone. Sherry noticed immediately that the hitters would not swing at these pitches. "I went out to the mound," recalled Sherry, "and said 'Sandy, why don't you take something off the ball and just let them hit it? We can get the outs and get out of this inning, because nobody's going to swing at the rate you're throwing.'"

Koufax went back to the mound, took his catcher's advice and struck out the side. When Koufax walked off the field, Sherry told his pitcher, "You just threw harder trying not to than when you tried to."

Sherry had offered the same advice to Koufax before, but he had tuned him out. This time he seemed to listen and pitched without pressing. "Think about what you're doing. Pick me up. Watch my glove. Be a pitcher. Make them swing the bat," Sherry reminded him. Later Koufax told his catcher that there was nothing like instantaneous success to let you know you are on the right track. And he credited Sherry with helping him find it.[141] "He convinced me I could throw just as fast without trying so hard," Koufax said. "That, I think, is when I became a pitcher."[142]

Sherry's injuries and lack of playing time made it difficult for him to get in shape. "It was like going through three spring trainings for me in 1961," recalled Sherry. "No wonder my arm went sour. I never did get in good condition after the first injury."[143] Sherry's injuries indirectly kept him on the Dodgers roster for the 1962 season. Two expansion teams for 1962, the New York Mets and the Houston Colt .45s, were both seeking to draft players to fill their roster spots. Both had considered drafting Norman Sherry, but the concern over his ability to throw assured that for the 1962 season the Sherry brothers would be with the same team.[144]

But 1962 was Norm's final year with the Dodgers. He caught only 35 games and hit just .182. During the season he did accomplish a rare feat—an unassisted double play.[145] In the fall of 1962, the New York Mets purchased Sherry's contract along with that of outfielder Dick Smith. It was a straight cash transaction.[146]

In 1963, Sherry's last year in the majors, he caught 63 games for the Mets, and hit a career low .136. Sherry, in his five-year big league career, had a .215 lifetime batting average and 107 hits, including 18 home runs. His real value to his team was not his offense, but his defense. His lifetime fielding average as a catcher was .989. His two fellow Dodger catchers, Roy Campanella and Johnny Roseboro, recognized as two of the greatest catchers of all time, were no better defensively than Sherry. Roseboro's percentage was the same as Norm's, .989, and Campanella finished his career with a fielding percentage of .988.[147]

Sherry's last year as a catcher in professional baseball was 1964. The New York Mets released Sherry outright to Buffalo in the International League.[148] "I played ball because I loved it. It was my life. I can't understand anybody who puts this uniform on and doesn't love it."[149]

Norman Sherry, like many players who went into professional baseball straight out of high school, really had no training in any career other than baseball. Dodger executives offered him a job as manager of the Santa Barbara club in the Cal State League. He was there for three years before he became a scout for the New York Yankees, then left the Yankees to scout for the California Angels. He held that position for a year and in 1970 and 1971 was a member of the Angel coaching staff. "After the '71 season," said Sherry, "General Manager Dick Walsh got fired, Lefty Phillips the manager, got fired, and I got fired. Everybody got fired."

Sherry rejoined the Angels the following spring as a minor league manager, serving two years in the Texas League and then two at Salt Lake City in the Pacific Coast League. He felt good about his team in Salt Lake City. "We will have an interesting, young and speedy club this season," promised Sherry.[150] He won the PCL Eastern Division title and as a reward for directing Salt Lake City to a league title, he returned to the Angels as their third base coach.[151]

On July 23, 1976, the Angels fired their manager Dick Williams, the fifth manager to get the ax in eight years. Norman Sherry replaced Williams. Sherry was ecstatic when he heard the news. It had always been his dream to become a major league manager.[152]

Sherry and Williams differed greatly in their approach to young players. Williams, a manager from the old school, could not communicate with the players and demanded perfection. Sherry, on the other hand, seemed easier to get along with, although he always denied it.[153]

Red Patterson, a former Dodger executive, who had become president of the Angels, was happy to have Sherry as his big league manager. "In the old days," he noted, "the managers were almost always players of renown such as Frisch, McGraw, and Dykes. The best managers now are guys who work in the majors, go to the minors and come back."[154]

Sherry's proclivity to injury followed him to his job as manager. During a game he was hit above the eye by a wild throw. "My head was exploding and I thought I was going to die," said Sherry. "I kept moaning, my temple, my temple." A concerned Angels pitching coach, Billy Muffett, leaned over Sherry, and whispered comfortingly, "Norm, today is Sunday. Temple is on Saturday."[155]

Sherry managed 66 games for the Angels in 1976 and ended the season with a record of 37–29, a .561 percentage.[156] The *Los Angeles Times* urged that the Angels rehire Sherry for the 1977 season. "The fact is that Sherry, in the limited time given him, has done a good job with an ordinary team. When [Angels owner] Gene Autry finally gives his order, he could do worse than say 'Make mine Sherry.'"[157] The following month, Harry Dalton, Angel general manager, signed Norman Sherry to manage the Angels in 1977.[158]

By the sixth week of the 1977 season the Angels were in sixth place in the American League West. Their record was 10–17, and the team was 7½ games out of first place.[159] At the end of the first half of the 1977 season, the Angels were barely below .500 at 39–42, but the team fired Sherry as their manager and replaced him with third base coach Dave Garcia. Gene Autry had spent $4.5 million on free agents to help bolster their offense, and he was not pleased with the returns he received for the money spent.[160]

Sherry was shocked when he heard that he had been let go. "I know we played bad in the last road trip," he said, "but what can I do? I couldn't field the balls they missed."[161]

The fans were firmly behind Sherry, and on the night he was fired, banners appeared demanding Dalton be fired and Sherry rehired. Before the first pitch, fans on the third base side of Anaheim Stadium began to chant "Norm ... Norm ... Norm...." The players were as upset as the fans and feeling guilty. They knew that Sherry had treated them like grown men but they had responded by playing like petulant adolescents. Jerry Remy, appointed team captain two weeks earlier by Sherry, said, "There was a feeling a change had to be made. Norm is a helluva nice guy."[162]

Like a gentleman, Sherry tried to sound a positive note about his firing. "I was disappointed that we hadn't played better and that we didn't have a better record, but a lot of things had happened. I hope someone does better just for Mr. Autry's sake. He really deserves a winner."[163]

In 1978, Dick Williams, who had become manager of the Montreal Expos, hired Sherry as his bullpen coach. Sherry remained with Williams at Montreal from 1978 to 1981.[164] After the 1981 season, Williams took the managerial job with the San Diego Padres and asked Sherry to come with him.[165]

Sherry was the Padres pitching coach from 1982 to 1984. In 1984 the Padres lost the World Series to the Detroit Tigers in five games. And, in a surprise move, General Manager Jack McKeon fired Sherry when the Series ended. Rumors said that the firing followed complaints by several Padres pitchers that Sherry was too critical.[166] Sherry's only comment was "I thought I did a good job. Evidently it wasn't good enough."[167]

Dick Williams was incensed when he heard his long-time friend Sherry had been fired. "When I demanded a reason," he said, "McKeon told me Sherry had won a workman's compensation decision from his former employers, the Montreal Expos, something about an untreated heart problem." Williams never did believe that was the real reason for the firing.[168]

A year later, Sherry's former Dodger teammate, Roger Craig, who was now the Giants' manager, approached Sherry about becoming the Giants' pitching coach. "Roger and I had played together in 1951 and 1954, then played together in Spokane in 1959 and in the sixties in the major leagues," said Sherry. "We were always good friends; his kids called me Uncle Norm and my kids called him Uncle Roger. It's great for me to say, "I'm a coach for Roger Craig."[169] At the end of 1991, the Giants announced that Carlos Alfonso had replaced Sherry as San Francisco's pitching coach.[170]

Norman Sherry left organized baseball in 1991. He had spent five years as a major league player and many more years coaching and managing. He is probably remembered best, however, as supplying the critical ingredient for producing one of baseball's greatest pitchers, Sandy Koufax.

5. Sandy Koufax— "Super Jew"

The decade of the 1960s marked a number of changes in the country, the American Jewish community, and baseball. The youthful John F. Kennedy became the country's first Roman Catholic president, running on a platform that upheld the right of African-Americans to conduct "peaceful demonstrations for first-class citizenship."[1]

In 1960 Jews, including those of eastern European descent, comprised less than three percent of the population, but they cast at least five percent of the votes helping elect Kennedy and then played an important role in his presidential administration.[2]

Jews in the early 1960s were also prominent in efforts on behalf of civil rights for African-Americans. In fact, Jews were pushing for civil rights in larger numbers than any other white group.[3] One black leader in Mississippi estimated that in the 1960s, as many as ninety percent of the civil rights lawyers in Mississippi were Jewish, and at least 30 percent of the white volunteers who rode freedom buses to the South to register blacks were Jewish.[4]

The 1960 baseball season ended a period of 56 years in which the National and American Leagues consisted of eight teams each, and except for 1919, scheduled a 154-game season.[5] Between 1960 and 1965, four new franchises in baseball were added in Houston, Los Angeles, New York, and Washington, D.C.[6] The first domed stadium was built in Houston, and new parks were under construction in several other cities. In 1964 major league baseball instituted a universal draft for those players not under contract within organized baseball. Finally, with the refusal of Fidel Castro to allow Cubans to participate in major league baseball, large numbers of African-Americans and racially mixed Hispanic Americans entered organized baseball.[7]

Finally, the decade of the 1960s saw the unbelievable metamorphosis of a remarkable pitcher. For the first six years of his career, this pitcher had a record below .500.[8] However, during the next six years, he would dominate the National League and make his mark as one of the greatest pitchers in the history of major league baseball. He would become the second truly undisputed Jewish superstar and only the second Jew to be inducted into Baseball's Hall of Fame. His name was Sandy Koufax.

Sandy Koufax was born Sanford Braun on December 30, 1935, in the Borough Park section of Brooklyn, a middle-class neighborhood which Koufax called "Sort of on the borderline between where the Jewish and Italian neighborhoods came together." When Koufax was three years old, his parents, Jack and Evelyn Braun, divorced. Six years later his mother, an accountant, married attorney Irving Koufax, and Sandy took his stepfather's name. The family then moved to Long Island, and his birth father dropped out of Sandy's life. "When I speak of my father," Koufax wrote in his autobiography, "I speak of Irving Koufax, for he has been to me everything a father could be."[9]

Sandy Koufax had a great pitching arm even growing up. During his early years in Brooklyn, he could engage in snowball fights with other neighborhood kids, stand further back, and be able to hit them without getting hit himself. On the sandlots he could make long throws from the outfield although he often admitted he had no desire to play the outfield. He played baseball first on the playgrounds of New York and then at the Jewish Community House on Bay Parkway. Often referred to simply as the "JCH," the Community House was, in some ways, Koufax's second home.[10]

Koufax's friends always thought Sandy was a nice guy who liked to have fun but never took chances by doing crazy things. He was reserved, but liked to laugh a lot. One of Koufax's childhood friends was talk show host Larry King, who grew up in the same neighborhood as Sandy. King told author Peter Golenbock that what he most remembered about Koufax was what the whole neighborhood knew—he was a *mensch*. He recalled that Koufax was as close to being an Orthodox Jew as any of the neighborhood kids. While most of the kids in the neighborhood observed the dietary laws, Koufax would not even drive a car on the Jewish Sabbath. "He always observed the High Holidays," said King. On the day prior to Rosh Hashanah one year, King interviewed Koufax. At the interview to be aired the next day, Koufax cautioned him, "'Don't forget to remind everybody we taped this the day before.' He didn't want people to think that he would do an interview on Rosh Hashanah."[11]

Koufax returned to the Bensonhurst section of Brooklyn to attend Lafayette High School where he played on the basketball squad and was the captain his senior year. He finished the basketball season as the second-highest scorer in his division and was named All-City.[12]

Koufax did not make the baseball team at Lafayette until his senior year, and he was primarily a first baseman who occasionally would pitch in relief of teammate Fred Wilpon, who, in later years, would become President and CEO of the New York Mets.[13]

According to his high school friends, Koufax played baseball in high school merely to occupy his time. Larry Merchant, who would later cover Koufax as a sportswriter in Philadelphia, recalled, "He just wanted to be one of the guys in high school; he was not a strutting person, but he was very competitive and wanted to win." Merchant also noted that Koufax was low-key even at the height of his fame. "Even though he was a superstar, he didn't want to be considered a star among his teammates. He was very sensitive to that."[14]

Koufax never pitched at all until he was 15 years old, and he did not pitch regularly until he was 17. He never gave any thought to pitching until Milt Laurie, former minor league pitcher, and at that time manager of the Parkviews in the amateur Coney Island League, saw Koufax throw and convinced him to pitch for the Parkviews.[15]

Scouts from the Red Sox and the Phillies began to turn out to watch Koufax pitch, but Koufax opted for an athletic scholarship to the University of Cincinnati where he planned to study architecture and play basketball.

Ed Jucker was both the Cincinnati Bearcats' freshman basketball coach and head baseball coach. Koufax averaged ten points a game for the basketball Bearcats during his freshman year.[16] He also joined a Jewish fraternity, made many friends, but was a quiet person.[17] In the spring he went out for baseball when he learned that the team planned a spring trip to New Orleans.[18] Coach Jucker watched as he held a tryout for pitchers and catchers in the poorly lit university gym. As Koufax's fastball continued to blast out of the shadows, his traumatized catcher told the coach, "Get somebody else. I don't want any part of this guy." In his first two starts, the six-foot, two-inch, 190-pound southpaw struck out 34 hitters.[19] Coach Jucker realized that Koufax was wild and had to improve his control. He would walk three and strike out three. Still, the coach was surprised that Koufax had not gained more attention from major league scouts. "I just wondered," Jucker thought, "how could they overlook this guy?"[20]

It seemed that Jucker had spoken too soon. Scouts from the New York Giants were sent to watch Koufax pitch, and he was given a tryout at the Polo Grounds. Unfortunately, he threw several pitches over the catcher's head. He then had a tryout with the Pittsburgh Pirates at Forbes Field. During the tryout, Koufax threw so hard that he broke the thumb of his catcher, Sam Narron, the bullpen coach for the Pirates. Branch Rickey, then general manager for the Pirates, told his scout Clyde Sukeforth that Koufax had the "greatest arm I'd ever seen." The Pirates offered Koufax $15,000, but he turned them down.[21]

Eventually Brooklyn sportswriter Jimmy Murphy tipped the Dodgers that Brooklyn-born Koufax was the fastest amateur pitcher he had ever seen. The Dodgers immediately sent Murphy to check him out, but soon eleven other big league scouts joined him. Koufax was stunned by all the attention. "The last thing that entered my mind," recalled Sandy, "was becoming a professional athlete. Some kids dream of becoming a professional ballplayer. I wanted to be an architect."

Dodger scout Al Campanis arranged for a tryout at Ebbets Field where Walt Alston, Vice President Fresco Thompson, and second-string catcher Rube Walker joined him. For the next fifteen minutes, Sandy threw fastballs into the mitt of Rube Walker. Every time Sandy released the ball it seemed to explode in Walker's glove. Even though not every pitch Koufax threw was a strike, the Dodgers did not seem concerned with his lack of control. They wanted to find out how long Sandy could keep throwing before he tired. After an hour, the workout ended, and the four men went into a conference, leaving Koufax by himself. When Campanis asked Walker for his opinion, the catcher replied, "You're crazy if you let him get out of the park without signing him."[22]

The Dodgers did allow Koufax to leave the park, but they went to his home to talk with his parents. Al Campanis convinced Koufax's parents two weeks before his nineteenth birthday in 1954 that their boy should sign with Brooklyn. As Campanis told the story, "First, we agreed to beat all bonuses tendered to date. We offered $14,000. And second, we told the parents the boy should play in Brooklyn where he could live with his family. Sandy's father and I closed the deal on a handshake."

A few days later, Milwaukee, unaware of Sandy's agreement with Brooklyn, came forward with a bonus offer of $30,000. Campanis later commented that he had always felt a little guilty about the transaction with Koufax's parents. "Signing with us not only cost them money, but not long afterward we left Brooklyn for Los Angeles, taking Sandy away from home."[23]

The Dodgers signed Koufax for $20,000—a $14,000 signing bonus and a $6,000 salary. Koufax left the University of Cincinnati after his freshman year and accepted the offer, planning to use the signing bonus as tuition for architectural school just in case baseball did not work out.[24]

Brooklyn ownership regarded the signing of a Jewish ballplayer as a dream come true. The Dodgers had been desperate for a Jewish player to replace former Dodgers Harry Eisenstat, Sid Gordon and Cal Abrams who were all gone—traded, retired, or spent out. Koufax was a marketing gift. The *Brooklyn Eagle* proclaimed, "Jewish Southpaw from Boro a Natural for Ebbets Field." Walter O'Malley told a reporter: "We hope he'll be as great as Hank Greenberg or Sid Gordon."[25]

Sandy Koufax never spent a single day in the minors. He was signed under a rule that was then in effect that said bonus players had to stay two years on the parent club.[26] As a result, Koufax came to the major leagues knowing next to nothing about pitching simply because he had pitched so little. When runners were on base, he had no idea how to stretch properly or how to pivot when attempting a pickoff move. Pitching coach Joe Becker worked diligently with Koufax, studying his special problems and attempting to correct them. Koufax and Becker formed a solid relationship over the next several years.[27]

"I'll never forget my first year," reminisced Koufax. "I didn't know what I was doing. I was scared to death. I had just turned 19 and there I was in spring training with the greatest names in baseball—Reese, Robinson, Snider. I had no right being there. They gave me the money and now, every time I threw, I could feel someone watching me. So I tried to throw a little harder just to prove that I was worth the money. I ended up hurting my arm. For two weeks I was combing my hair and brushing my teeth right-handed."

From 1963 to 1966, Hall of Famer Sandy Koufax was the major league's most dominant pitcher. The Los Angeles Dodger southpaw pitched four no-hitters, his last one a perfect game, and received three unanimous Cy Young Awards. He was also an observant Jew who was modest in demeanor but proud to be a hero to the Jewish community (courtesy National Baseball Hall of Fame Library; Cooperstown, N.Y.).

Koufax's manager, Walt Alston, remembered those days with uncomfortable clarity. "I couldn't believe my eyes," said Alston. "Playing pepper and tossing the ball back and forth, he was so wild the other fellow couldn't catch it, and when he was just lobbing them to a catcher, three or four out of every 20 pitches would be over the catcher's head."[28]

Koufax did very little for the Dodgers during the 1955 season. He had either a strained or stiff neck so he was placed on the 30-day disabled list on May 9 to preserve a roster spot. Since bonus rules prevented his reassignment to the minors, when he returned from the disabled list, the Dodgers were forced to demote another southpaw to the minors, Tommy Lasorda. Lasorda, who would someday manage the Dodgers, later quipped, "It took the greatest lefthanded pitcher in the history of baseball to get me out of the majors."[29]

The Dodgers were leading the league in 1955, but most of their starting pitchers were complaining of sore arms. Alston decided to give Koufax an opportunity to pitch. He debuted in the major leagues on June 24, 1955, in relief of Carl Erskine in the fifth inning. In his first start on July 6, he walked eight men in 4.2 innings. In his second start, however, he tossed a two-hit, complete game shutout with 14 strikeouts.[30]

Koufax appeared in only 12 games in 1955, winning two and losing two with an ERA of 3.02. He walked 29 men and struck out 30.[31] The Dodgers not only won the National League pennant that year, they also won their first and their only World Series victory in Brooklyn. Koufax sat on the bench for the entire series.[32]

It rankled Koufax that he had so little playing time when he first joined the Dodgers. At one time he went 49 days with only two widely spaced relief assignments. Years later, after he had become the league's premier pitcher, Koufax told his biographer, Ed Linn, that he knew the reason why. "He [Alston] didn't think I had any guts. That's another trouble with us Jews, you know, no guts."[33]

Koufax remembered that he had encountered his first examples of anti–Semitism in 1955 when he arrived in segregated Florida where blacks and Jews could identify each other as persecuted minorities. Sandy Koufax neither proclaimed nor hid his Jewishness. One of the broadcast coordinators who traveled with the Dodgers said, "It wasn't as though Sandy had a Star of David on his sleeve." In one incident, Koufax and the Dodgers were stuck on a bus in Miami without air conditioning. Carl Erskine remembered the occasion when the players were "moaning and mumbling," and Dodger coach Billy Herman yelled out quite loudly, "You can give this damn town back to the Jews." Koufax was sitting right across the aisle from Herman and after a minute or two of silence, Sandy in a very quiet voice said, "Now, Billy, you know we've already got it."[34]

Some of the African-American Dodger players remembered how supportive Hank Greenberg had been of Jackie Robinson when he first broke into major league baseball. One of them, pitcher Don Newcombe, admitted that some of the Dodgers did not like Koufax because he was Jewish and because he was a bonus baby who had to remain on the roster. "He wanted to go to the minors," said Newcombe. "I couldn't understand the narrow-mindedness of these players when they would come to us and talk about Sandy as 'this kike' and this 'Jew bastard' or 'Jew sonofabitch that's gonna take my job.' They said that right in front of us about Sandy. They hated Jews as much as they hated blacks. I don't know if Sandy ever knew, but that's why we took care of Sandy."[35]

Joe Torre's brother, Frank, a first baseman who played half his seven years of baseball during the 1950s, analyzed the general feeling about Jews at that time: "Around the league there was definitely some of that: the spoiled Jewish kid with a lot of money. You talk to some of the old-timers, I don't care what they tell you today, and they used to grumble like hell. Two things were happening. They had a good team. They felt it could have been better without him. Then there would have somebody legitimate in his spot that was really going to help the team. Down deep most of them resented the fact that that he earned more money than them."[36]

The Dodgers remained in Brooklyn for the 1956 and 1957 seasons. In 1956, Koufax's second season with the Dodgers, he won two games and lost four. His third year he was five and four. His control in 1956 was better than the previous year, but he allowed more hits. In 1956 the Dodgers once again appeared in the World Series, and they again faced the New York Yankees. The results were a complete reversal from the previous year. This time the Yankees defeated the Dodgers in seven games. However, for the second consecutive year, Koufax did not participate in the World Series.[37]

In the spring of 1957, Koufax's bonus time expired and the Dodgers announced they were sending him down to the minor leagues. However, the National League office informed the Dodgers that his bonus time actually extended 30 days into 1957 because of the 30 days he had spent on the disabled list in 1955.

Koufax ended up spending the entire 1957 season with Brooklyn. The 1957 Dodger pitching staff was in disarray. Don Newcombe, Carl Erskine and Sal Maglie had combined to win 53 games in 1956—in 1957 they won only 22. Koufax was one of seven Dodger pitchers to start 13 or more games. He had an interesting season. He pitched 104.1 innings and struck out 122 batters; his ERA was 3.88; his record as a starter was four and four, and he won another game in relief.[38] On September 28, 1957, Koufax had the distinction of being the last Dodgers hurler to throw a pitch for the Brooklyn Dodgers before the team moved west to Los Angeles.[39] The Dodgers, who had won consecutive pennants in 1955 and 1956, finished the 1957 season in third place, 11 games behind first-place Milwaukee, and three games behind the second-place Cardinals.[40]

Koufax's statistics in 1957 encouraged Al Campanis, the scout who had signed him. He knew exactly what the problem was. "All he needed was innings," said Campanis. Joe L. Brown, then general manager of the Pittsburgh Pirates agreed. "Without the bonus," he said, "the innings may have come sooner. It took Koufax a long time before he achieved stardom. Had Koufax gone where he could've gotten in 150 to 200 innings in minor league competition, he probably would've been ready at least three years before he was."[41]

Koufax spent the winter of 1957 in the Army before he rejoined the Dodgers in their new location—Los Angeles. Koufax's record in 1958, the first year he pitched in Los Angeles, was 11–11. The following year, 1959, was a milestone for him. In June he started a game against the Phillies and fanned 16 hitters to set a record for a night game. Two months later, he broke that record in Los Angeles against the San Francisco Giants, tying the major league record of 18 strikeouts set by Bob Feller in 1938.[42] The Dodgers won the pennant that year and Koufax pitched Game Five, which the Dodgers lost, 1–0, when White Sox second baseman Nellie Fox scored on a double play.[43]

In 1960, Koufax's record fell to 8–13. He became so frustrated that he nearly quit baseball to sell lighting fixtures, a business he had gone into as a manufacturer's representative for electrical lines.[44] "I began to think," said Koufax, "that maybe putting ten years into something else might be better. At the end of 10 years I wouldn't be through, I'd just be starting. Quitting seemed like a possibility."[45] Koufax's manager, Walter Alston, was not very helpful. He announced at several confidential Dodger meetings that he doubted Koufax would ever make it.[46]

When the 1960 season ended, Koufax disgustedly threw his glove and spikes into the trash. Fortunately, clubhouse supervisor Nobe Kawano was wise enough to retrieve them, either to return them to Koufax the following year or to give them to someone else should Koufax actually quit the game.[47]

Before he made a final decision about his future in baseball, Koufax decided to talk to his general manager, Buzzy Bavasi. He told Bavasi that he wanted to pitch more often. Bavasi simply told Koufax, "How can you pitch? You can't get anybody out." Koufax retorted: "I don't know anybody else that can get anybody out once a month either."[48] Frustrated even more by his talk with Bavasi, Koufax asked to be traded, but the general manager paid no attention. "We stayed with you this long, we might as well keep you."[49]

At the conclusion of the 1960 season, Sandy Koufax had been in the major leagues six years—three in Brooklyn and three in Los Angeles. His record for those six years was 36–40. He had walked 405 batters in 691.2 innings.[50] Koufax finally decided to return to the Dodgers in 1961 and make one more attempt to salvage his baseball career. The thought of quitting baseball before achieving any amount of success bothered him, and he began to realize that perhaps he did not work as hard as he might have.

Beginning in 1961, Koufax was remarkably transformed from a thrower to a pitcher.

He attributes that transformation to three individuals—club statistician Allan Roth, pitching coach Joe Becker, and catcher Norman Sherry. It was not lost on the anti–Semites who favored the Jewish-conspiracy theory of history that two of those Koufax most credited with turning his pitching career around were Jews—Roth and Sherry.[51]

During the off-season, Koufax conferred with Roth who showed the young southpaw data that proved he was less effective against left-handed hitters than right-handers. Normally the opposite is true. Southpaw pitchers traditionally fare better against lefty hitters chiefly because of the way a southpaw's curve breaks in on the hitter. Roth pointed out that Sandy's curve was breaking in a way that prevented him from exploiting what should have been a natural advantage against lefties.[52]

Koufax asked Roth to show him his personal statistics every time he pitched. Over the years, Roth chartered 26,450 Koufax pitches and 313 of his 397 games. He tracked each at-bat and the count on which the decisive pitch was made. His numbers demonstrated an obvious but very important fact—it is to a pitcher's advantage to get ahead of the batter. Roth showed Koufax the difference in the batting average against him when he was ahead in the count (.146) and when he was behind (.286). Because of what Roth told Koufax, whenever anyone would ask him what his best pitch was, Koufax had a ready answer: "Strike one."[53]

Pitching coach Joe Becker was also instrumental in improving Koufax's pitching. He would take Sandy off to the side and work with him for extended periods of time developing his control and his curve. He showed Sandy how to throw with an easy, natural rhythm, and got Koufax to slow down his pitches rather than rush them as he had always done, especially when he was upset.[54]

Becker also convinced Koufax to tighten the windup on his delivery. Although this was a slight mechanical adjustment, it helped his control while hiding his pitches. Koufax's teammate, Wally Moon, had told Sandy that his former team, the Cardinals, could tell what he would throw by watching his delivery from the stretch, because he brought his hands up higher for the fastball than the curve. "You're tipping the pitch," Moon told Koufax. "You're giving the hitter a chance to gear up for either the fastball or the breaking ball."[55]

Becker emphasized control to Koufax. "If you shorten your stride on your front step, it will help your control," he told his pitcher. "Don't hurry and don't get upset. Nothing can start until you get damn good and ready to pitch. Whatever you do, don't rush. He advised Koufax to pick up the resin bag from time to time.

Koufax took his pitching coach's advice and suddenly discovered that he did not have to throw each pitch harder than the previous one. "There was no need for it," he confessed. "If I take it easy and throw naturally, the ball goes just as far."[56]

No man was more aware of the improvement than his manager, Walter Alston. He noticed how Coach Becker had advised Koufax to get snap in the ball at the position of release. "All at once Sandy got control," Alston said. "And I don't mean control in the sense of just throwing the ball over the plate. He could throw the fastball where he wanted to—to spots. When you have that kind of stuff and that kind of control, well, they just stopped hitting him. And it all happened in one year. It made me a much smarter manager."[57]

Without minimizing Roth's and Becker's help in bringing about Koufax's turnaround, it was actually Norman Sherry whom Koufax credited most for his success. Koufax, Norman Sherry, and his brother Larry were Dodger teammates in 1961. Sandy and Norm roomed together during the 1961 spring training camp and were very close. On the bus to Orlando for a B-squad game, the pitcher and catcher went over the signs and pitches Koufax would work on. Sherry, who came to the Dodgers in 1959, always knew that Koufax possessed a good arm but had control problems. On the ride to Orlando, Koufax told his catcher that he wanted to work on his changeup and curveball.

Early in the game, Koufax got into trouble when he quickly loaded the bases. Sherry trotted to the mound and told his pitcher to "take a little something off the ball and let the batters hit it. I reminded him," said Sherry, "that we didn't bring too many pitchers to Orlando, and we were short-handed in the bullpen." Obviously, Sherry gave good advice to Koufax, for at the end of the seven-inning game, Koufax had struck out eight and walked five without allowing a hit. A few years later Koufax still remembered that game. "Every time I just reared back and threw, Sherry walked out and made me use changeups and control. I pitched a no-hitter."[58]

In the privacy of the Dodger clubhouse, Norman Sherry, aka "Catcher Face," was also known as "the Jolly Jew." His brother, Larry, was "the Rude Jew," and Koufax was on his way to becoming "Super Jew." Why was he able to listen to Norm when so many others had failed to get through? "Catcher Face" grinned, "*Landsmen*, eh?" It also helped that Koufax was pitching regularly as a member of the starting rotation.[59]

It was obvious that Koufax strictly adhered to the counsel both Sherry and Becker had given him. In 1961 Koufax won six of his first seven starts. He went on to pitch 256 innings, the first time he had thrown more than 200 innings in a single year. His record was 18–13, and he finished the year with an ERA of 3.25. He also fanned 269 batters, breaking Christy Mathewson's record set 57 years earlier. Koufax said, "I finally began to learn to concentrate on the next pitch and forget about the last one."[60]

In 1961 Koufax was named to the first of six consecutive All-Star teams. He also closed his second Dodgers ballpark, the Los Angeles Coliseum, with a 13-inning, 205-pitch, seven-hit complete game, striking out 15 in a 3–2 victory over the Chicago Cubs.[61]

In 1962 the Dodgers moved to their new stadium in Chavez Ravine, which was designed to be a pitcher-friendly park. It had a large foul territory and a poor hitting background. On June 30, Koufax tossed the first no-hitter of his career as the Dodgers defeated the Mets, 5–0. No Met hitter reached second base, and only five reached first, all via bases on balls.[62] He struck out 13 men in the game, and Richie Ashburn, a former Phillie and Cub, and playing for the Mets in what would be his last year in the majors, exclaimed, "Either he throws the fastest ball I've ever seen, or I'm going blind."[63]

Earlier in the year Koufax had struck out 18 batters, the same feat he had accomplished in 1959, making him the only major league pitcher at that time to strike out 18 batters in two different games.[64] He finished the month of June with an ERA of 1.23 and was named Player of the Month.[65]

By mid–July, Koufax was leading the National League in earned run average (2.06), in strikeouts (209) and in wins, 14, against only four losses, but something was wrong with the index finger of his pitching hand. The hand had turned numb and white and the skin had begun peeling off. It was extremely painful for him to even touch anything, much less to try and hold a baseball. The doctors treated his finger with antibiotics and although they were able to reduce the soreness, at first they were not able to locate the cause of the trouble.[66]

Finally, his condition was diagnosed as "Reynaud's Phenomenon," a circulatory ailment that affects the blood vessels in the extremities—generally the fingers and toes.[67] Once the doctors knew they had his ailment under control, they told Koufax, "If you hadn't come to us when you did, we might have had to amputate your finger."[68]

The doctors thought Koufax would not be able to pitch any more in 1962, but after they successfully opened the artery, he came back in September when the Dodgers were locked in a tight pennant race with the San Francisco Giants. But Koufax was unable to get back into shape after the long layoff, as the Giants caught up with the Dodgers at the end of the season. Alston was forced to use Koufax as his starting pitcher in the first game of a best-of-three playoff. As Koufax later admitted, "I had nothing at all." The Giants knocked him out in the second inning after he surrendered home runs to Willie Mays and Jim Davenport. The Dodgers lost that game, won the second game of the series, and then blew a 4–2 lead in the ninth inning of the third game, losing the pennant.[69]

Despite the shortened season for Koufax, he ended 1962 with a record of 14 wins and seven losses. His 2.54 ERA was good enough to win the 1962 ERA Title.[70]

Sandy Koufax and his tinplate finger were the talk of the spring training camps in 1963. He was examined by a doctor before leaving for Vero Beach and reported, "The finger feels good. As good as new. I'm not going to rush my pitching this spring, just take it natural, and maybe even a little slower than usual. I'll know soon enough how it stands up under real pitching."[71]

It stood up very well. Sandy Koufax was the most dominant pitcher in major league baseball in 1963. He won his first three starts and on May 11, 1963, he hurled his second no-hitter, this time against a good-hitting San Francisco Giant team with sluggers such as Willie Mays, Willie McCovey and Orlando Cepeda. He was pitching a perfect game until Ed Bailey walked on a full count with one out in the eighth inning. The only other Giant to reach base was pinch-hitter Willie McCovey who drew a pass in the ninth inning.

After the game Koufax admitted, "To pitch a perfect game would have been the greatest thrill. It's too bad I walked those two guys, but it still is my greatest thrill." He paid a special compliment to his catcher John Roseboro, saying, "John fought all the way; I have to give him a lot of credit."[72]

What made the no-hitter more impressive was the fact that the Dodgers offense in 1963 was generally anemic, which allowed Koufax little room for error. When fellow hurler Don Drysdale learned that his teammate had tossed a no-hitter, he caustically asked, "Did he win?"[73]

After he pitched his second no-hitter, Koufax received a call from Dodgers vice-president Buzzy Bavasi. Bavasi informed Koufax that the club was going to give him something extra as a reward. Koufax told Bavasi, "You don't owe me a thing. You've been too good to me already." Later Koufax elaborated. "They paid me for 1963 just like I had pitched great ball all season long last year. My contract never reflected the fact that I was hurt from July on. I won't forget what the club has done for me."[74]

At the end of August, Koufax won his twentieth game by defeating the Giants, 11–1. He considered that a bigger thrill than pitching a no-hitter. "It took me nine years to win 20—and it took me three tries before I finally made it." Koufax not only reached the 20-game class for the first time in his career, but also became the first hurler in the majors to turn the trick in 1963.[75]

Two weeks later, Koufax struck out nine Pirates en route to his twenty-third victory, which made him the top winner in the National League for 1963 and the winningest left-hander in Dodger club history.[76]

In his next start, Koufax held the St. Louis Cardinals scoreless and permitted only 4 singles in a 4–0 victory. It was his twenty-fourth win and set a major league record for a southpaw of 11 shutouts in a single season, the most in the majors since Grover Cleveland Alexander's 16 in 1916. He threw only 87 pitches in the game.[77]

Koufax's statistics for the 1963 season were amazing. His won–lost record was 25–5 with an ERA of 1.88, the lowest in the National League since Howard Pollet's 1.75 in 1943. His 25 victories led the National League. He fanned 306 batters, a figure topped by only three other pitchers since 1900, and his 311 innings pitched were the most by a National League left-hander since 1921. His wins, ERA and strikeouts earned for Koufax the pitcher's Triple Crown. Koufax unanimously won the Cy Young Award and was named the NL's Most Valuable Player.[78]

In 1963 the Dodgers were considered the underdogs against the Yankees in the World Series, their first match-up since the Dodgers moved to Los Angeles. Koufax opposed Whitey Ford in the first game of the Series, fanning the first five batters he faced. One Yankee admitted, "After I saw him strike out Bobby Richardson, I knew we were in trouble." Koufax struck out 15 Yankees that day, breaking the World Series record set by teammate Carl Erskine 10 years earlier to the day, and he pitched a complete-game victory, allowing only six hits.[79]

After Yogi Berra witnessed Koufax's performance in Game One of the Series, he was quoted as saying, "I can see how he won twenty-five games. What I don't understand is how he lost five."[80]

Four days later Koufax threw another six-hitter with eight strikeouts, again defeating Whitey Ford. Koufax's victory in Game Four gave the Dodgers the sweep in the Series and Koufax was voted MVP of the World Series.[81]

After the Series ended, Koufax stated that the picture of him surrounded by his teammates after he had clinched the World Series gave him more satisfaction than the wins themselves. Jackie Robinson, who was with the Dodgers in 1955, the first year Koufax joined the team, expressed the team's feelings best. "We all knew the boy was going to be good, but never in our wildest dreams did we imagine he would grow into the most outstanding pitcher of his time."[82]

Once the World Series ended, Koufax began to win additional awards. *Sport* Magazine chose Koufax as "Man of the Year" and "Top Performer in Baseball," and he received two plaques in recognition of his achievement in the World Series. He was also voted "Male Athlete of the Year" by the Associated Press, outdistancing two top quarterbacks, Y.A. Tittle and Roger Staubach. The New York Chapter of the Baseball Writers Association named Koufax Player of the Year. Koufax was also the landslide winner of the fourteenth annual S. Rae Hickock "Professional Athlete of the Year" by an unprecedented margin. Finally, the St. Louis Chapter of the Baseball Writers' Association gave Koufax the J. Roy Stockton award for outstanding baseball achievement. The award was named in honor of the retired sports editor of the *St. Louis Post-Dispatch*.[83]

With all the attention Koufax was receiving for his extraordinary achievements on the field, fans and press clamored to learn more about him off the field. Despite his ability to perform in front of millions and to articulately accept the awards and honors he was given, Sandy Koufax was very shy and reserved, especially when talking to reporters. To many he seemed aloof, but Koufax was basically just a private person. He never spoke ill of others although he was fond of "kidding around" with his teammates. His roommate on the road, Norman Sherry, said of Koufax, "He was a good guy. He was easy to room with. For the most part he kept to himself. Everybody liked him."[84]

On road trips he could be found in his hotel room listening to one of several dozen musical comedy scores he carried with him on tape. Reports circulated that he listened only to Beethoven or Mendelssohn and would read only Thomas Wolfe or Aldous Huxley. He admitted that he might have read Wolfe in school, but denied ever reading Huxley. As far as music was concerned, he once said, "I don't know what's so highbrow about Men-delssohn."[85]

When the Dodgers played home games, Koufax lived in his two-bedroom home in Studio City and had several business interests. He also had a rich speaking voice, com-pletely devoid of any trace of his years in Brooklyn. Furthermore, he knew that he was a role model for many youngsters, and he refused to be photographed smoking or to endorse cigarettes.[86]

After 1963 Koufax seemed even more reserved and insisted that while he enjoyed the attention, he also wanted some privacy. "I'm the same as I was before," insisted Koufax, but it was very difficult for him to be exactly the same after he had been exposed to all the pub-licity and celebrity. He voiced his frustration publicly to Milton Gross, a sports columnist for the New York Post: "I'm just a normal twenty-seven-year-old bachelor who happens to be of the Jewish faith. I like nice clothes, I like comfort. I like to read a book and listen to music and I'd like to meet a girl I'd want to marry. That's normal, isn't it?"[87]

Prior to the beginning of spring training in 1964, Sandy Koufax signed for a reported $70,000, double his 1963 salary. "I'm very happy I got what I did." Koufax stated. "This is pretty big business for me."[88]

In 1964 the Dodgers gave Koufax the honor of starting on opening day for the first time in his career; he whitewashed the Cardinals on six hits. On June 4, against the Phillies, Koufax threw his third no-hitter in three years, tying Bob Feller's modern record.[89] It was almost, but not quite, a perfect game. He faced the minimum 27 batters, but walked Richie Allen who promptly was thrown out attempting to steal second. "That was it—the best of 'em all—the best of the no-hitters." Those were the first words of Sandy Koufax as he entered the Dodger clubhouse following the final out. "I had everything I needed and I controlled it," he said. "It was my best game ever."[90]

More records followed in 1964. Three weeks later, Koufax set a major league mark by striking out 10 batters for the fifty-fifth time and on August 8, Koufax struck out nine Mil-waukee Braves to run his season total to 200. He became the first pitcher in National League history to strike out 200 or more batters in four consecutive seasons. Christy Mathewson had recorded five 200-strikeout years, but only three were consecutive.[91]

But that August 8, 1964, game was to also have far reaching consequences. In that game, Koufax jammed his pitching arm while diving back to second base to beat a pick-off throw. He managed to win two more games in 1964. The morning after his nineteenth win, a shutout in which he fanned 13 batters, he could not straighten his left arm. The Dodgers' team physician diagnosed his ailment as traumatic arthritis, and Koufax did not pitch the rest of the year.[92] He ended the 1964 season with a record of 19–5 and an ERA of 1.74, which tied a a 47-year-old record held by Grover Cleveland Alexander.[93]

The 1965 baseball season started out painfully for Koufax. After pitching a spring train-ing game, he found his entire left arm black and blue from internal hemorrhaging. The team physician warned him that he could eventually lose full use of his arm if he did not take drastic steps. Together the two mapped out a schedule for Koufax to pitch every fifth day, rather than every fourth. Prior to each pitching appearance, he was given cortisone shots in his elbow, codeine for the pain, and capsoline ointment, which players called "atomic balm." The team physician, Robert Kerlan, instructed Koufax to soak his arm in a tub of ice after every game he pitched. He left three bottles of beer for Koufax next to the ice and instructed Koufax not to take his arm out until he had drunk all three.[94]

Despite his constant pain, Koufax had the best year of any pitcher in baseball history.

He led the major leagues in victories with 26 and in strikeouts with 382, breaking Bob Feller's single-season record. This record lasted until Nolan Ryan struck out 383 batters in 1973.[95] Koufax led the majors in complete games (27), innings pitched (336), and ERA (2.04). He also became the first pitcher ever to throw four no-hitters in a career.[96]

The highlight of Koufax's 1965 season, and perhaps of his entire career, took place on September 9, 1965, when he not only pitched his fourth no-hitter, but also his only perfect game. It was in the middle of the pennant race and the Dodgers were facing the Cubs. Koufax fanned 14 men that game, and the weak-hitting Dodgers scored their only run without benefit of a hit. Lou Johnson walked, was sacrificed to second, stole third, and continued home on a wild throw. Cub pitcher Bob Hendley gave up only one hit and Koufax won the game by the final score of 1–0. He clinched the pennant for the Dodgers with a four-hit, 13-strikeout complete game over the Braves on the next-to-last day of the season.[97]

The Dodgers faced the Minnesota Twins in the 1965 World Series. Sandy Koufax was scheduled to pitch Game One of the World Series, but that game was to be played on Yom Kippur, and Koufax had always been excused on the Jewish holy days. It was written into his contract that he did not have to "suit up" on those days and Dodger owner Walter O'Malley said he would not let Koufax pitch "under any circumstances."[98]

Twice in the fall of 1960 and 1961, manager Walter Alston had scheduled Koufax on Jewish holidays, not realizing which days Koufax would not pitch. In 1962 a Dodger fan sent Alston a Hebrew calendar marked with all the Jewish holidays. From then on, Alston made sure to consult Danny Goodman, director of advertising and novelties, who was Jewish, before making out his starting rotation.[99] He told Goodman, "There'll be no slipups this time."[100] Koufax downplayed the 1962 incident. "I don't know why people insist upon making something big out of that. I am not devout, but I have religious principles by which I've lived and by which I intend to keep living."[101]

In 1965, while Koufax attended Yom Kippur services, Don Drysdale opened the World Series against the Twins, losing the game, 8–2. Drysdale was knocked out of the box in the third inning after he yielded 6 runs. As Alston came to the mound to take him out, Drysdale handed the ball to his manager and said, "I bet right now you wish I was Jewish, too."[102] Before the beginning of the second game, a Minnesota Twin was quoted, "What this country needs is more Jewish holidays."[103]

But even in the mid–1960s vestiges of anti–Semitism remained. The morning after the Minnesota victory, the *St. Paul Pioneer Press* carried a sports column entitled, "An Open Letter to Sandy Koufax." It contained a number of veiled and uncomplimentary references to Koufax's religion, concluding, "The Twins love matza balls on Thursdays." Later, Sandy commented," I couldn't believe it. I thought that kind of thing went out with dialect comics." Koufax pitched the second game later that day and lost, 5–1. But he won the seventh and deciding game, and the Dodgers won the World Series.[104]

After the Series ended, Sandy said, "I clipped the column so that I could send it back to him (the author of the column) after we won the Series with a friendly little notation that I hoped his words were as easy to eat as my matza balls. I didn't of course [send it]. We were winners."[105]

Although Koufax's 1965 observance of Yom Kippur was a powerful symbol for Jews, Hank Greenberg took more of a risk in his refusal to play ball on Yom Kippur than did Sandy Koufax. When Greenberg abstained from playing on Yom Kippur, he faced a real dilemma—how to be a loyal Jew and a responsible American at the same time in a society where Jews were still struggling for acceptance. In contrast, by the time Koufax chose not to play, Greenberg's dilemma no longer existed for most American Jews. Fans could proudly proclaim their devotion to a Jewish baseball player without causing a furor.[106]

Rabbi Bruce Lustig, who became senior rabbi at the Washington Hebrew Congregation in Washington, D.C., was seven years old and attending Yom Kippur services in Tennessee with his parents the day Koufax was supposed to pitch. Years later he pointed to Koufax's decision not to pitch as a revolutionary event that provided the catalyst for many Jews to honor their religion as Koufax had done. Lustig believed that by refusing to pitch, Koufax both reinforced Jewish pride and enhanced the sense of belonging—a feat as extraordinary as any he accomplished on the baseball diamond.[107]

Jack Epstein, editor of the San Francisco Chronicle Foreign Service, felt that connection. "I am by no means an observant Jew," wrote Epstein, "but I never work on Yom Kippur. Perhaps, like Koufax, I see it as a cultural statement, a reinforcement of Jewish pride."[108]

Sandy Koufax also captivated Jewish mothers with sons, but none had as much a problem as Kenny Holtzman's mother. When Kenny was pitching against Sandy, for whom should she root? Holtzman told everyone, "Clearly, my mother did not want anyone to lose." When he told his mother that one of them had to lose, she replied, "Maybe you can get a no-decision."[109]

Ironically, Koufax's courteous reluctance to open up to the press often worked against him, allowing journalists to create their own version of Koufax the man. Columnist Jim Murray wrote that as a nice Jewish boy, he was a "tortured" unhappy soul on the mound who would have been much happier as a doctor or a lawyer. He was—in a word "different." Writer E. L. Doctorow, himself a Jew, considered characterizing a Jew as "different" the most discreetly structural variety of anti–Semitism.[110] Many believe, however, that Sandy Koufax was the last player whose Jewish identity drew substantial attention, for by the 1960s, anti–Semitism was not a major threat to American Jewry.[111]

After the 1965 Series ended, Koufax was again deluged with numerous awards. He won a sports car as Sport Magazine's outstanding player of the 1965 World Series, becoming the first player to win the award twice. Sports Illustrated chose him Sportsman of the Year for overcoming a physical disability to lead his team to the world championship. Other honors he won for the second time included Top Male Athlete of the Year from the Associated Press, and the Hitchcock Award as Professional Athlete of the Year for 1965, again becoming the first man in the 16-year history of the award to repeat as champion. Most impressively, Sandy Koufax was the unanimous Cy Young Award winner for the second time.[112]

In 1965, Don Drysdale and Sandy Koufax had together won 49 games and Walter O'Malley realized that he would have to reward each of them with a pay raise. He was not prepared for what ensued. Koufax and Drysdale broke new ground in contract negotiations in three ways: they acted together in their demands, they hired an agent to do their bargaining and they sought multi-year contracts.[113] Their agent, attorney William Hayes, informed O'Malley that his two clients were asking for a three-year contract which would pay each of the two hurlers $167,000 per year.[114]

Koufax defended this revolutionary move. "Don and I went into this thing with the realization we were serious about it. We teamed up, because as long as I could remember, we were played off against each other." Koufax also made no apologies about hiring an attorney. "Even the worst criminal is entitled to a lawyer."[115]

Walter O'Malley left the negotiation to his general manager, Buzzy Bavasi. When the two hurlers threatened to tour Japan and maybe even play there, Bavasi just laughed. He knew that the reserve clause extended even into Asia and the duo could not have made good with their threat.[116] Koufax and Drysdale even hinted that they would leave baseball and appear together in a movie in which Koufax would play an Italian waiter.[117]

Bavasi may have taken the other threats as merely ploys, but he was shocked when his two star pitchers actually stayed away from spring training camp in 1966. They proved how much the team needed them when the Dodgers' Grapefruit League record was 6–12, ranking them eighteenth out of the league's 20 teams. O'Malley begrudgingly told Bavasi to raise the total offer to $210,000, the "final figure." Koufax and Drysdale began to look elsewhere for work, signing movie and television contracts and showing up for rehearsal of a thriller called *Warning Shot.*[118]

Koufax was definitely negotiating from a position of strength. Attendance figures indicated that when Koufax took the mound, he brought 10,000 extra people into the stadium. Counting the concessions and the parking, each fan was worth five dollars or $50,000 per game to the ball clubs involved. And this figure did not include revenues Koufax brought to the box office indirectly by keeping the Dodgers in the pennant race.[119]

But Bavasi refused to budge and told the press, "No amount of pressure will make me meet their demands. If I did, I would have to tear up the contracts of every player and give new ones to make things equitable." He also indicated that he was going to stick to the club's policy of one-year contracts.[120]

Koufax saw his and Drysdale's battle as a fight for basic principles. "The ball club is defending the principle that it doesn't really have to negotiate with a ballplayer because we have no place to go. You might say Don and I are fighting for an anti-principle—that ballplayers aren't slaves, that we have a right to negotiate."[121]

With the opening of the 1966 season only 13 days away, O'Malley finally capitulated. One reason for this change of heart was the rumor that Koufax and Drysdale were prepared to sue the Dodgers, challenging baseball's reserve clause. O'Malley's Hollywood friends reminded him that in California, the movie industry's reserve clause for employees had been overturned. O'Malley feared that this could occur in baseball.[122] While the pitchers did not get the three-year contracts they asked for, they did get one-year contracts at significantly higher salaries than offered previously. Koufax's reported pay range was between $115,000 and $135,000; Drysdale's between $105,000 and $115,000.[123] Regardless of the exact amount, the sum was considerably below their initial request of $1 million over three years. "Our fight," Koufax said later, "was to establish ourselves at a certain plateau salary-wise. That's the battle of every ball player. We accomplished what we set out to accomplish and that is the right of a baseball player to bargain."[124]

Their action served as a preview of Marvin Miller's later challenge of baseball's reserve clause and the onset of free agency. Drysdale and Koufax double-handedly had made baseball economic history.[125] Other players watched carefully in the spring of 1966 as these two stars banded together to stage baseball's first successful collective holdout.[126]

With his contract settled, Koufax could concentrate on preparing for the 1966 season. His injuries remained problematic, and he made an agreement with Dr. Kerlan, the Dodger team physician, to "Let me know when I run the risk of permanent damage." Dr. Kerlan wanted Koufax to quit at the beginning of the season, feeling that his arm could not tolerate another year of pitching.[127]

Koufax, however, ignored Kerlan's advice and went to the mound every fourth day to pitch. To endure the pain, Koufax took butazoladine, a drug administered to sore-legged horses. Its effect on the stomach was so upsetting that to counter it, Sandy had to eat five or six small meals a day rather than the "normal ones."

He also took a codeine tablet for pain every time he took the mound and swallowed another around the sixth or seventh inning. This drug slowed his reactions to such an extent that he was always fearful that he might be beaned by a pitch or struck by a line drive.[128]

On the final Sunday of the season, the Giants trailed the Dodgers by two games, making it necessary for the Dodgers to win one of their two remaining games with the Phillies. The Phillies defeated Don Drysdale and the Dodgers in the first game, 4–3. Alston came back with Koufax in game two on just two days of rest. His mound opponent was Jim Bunning in the first-ever match-up between perfect game winners. Koufax was weary and pitching in pain. Luckily, his teammates had given him an early six-run lead. In the fifth inning, Koufax reared back to pitch, threw and felt a crack and pain in his back. He managed to complete the inning and asked his trainers to accompany him into the clubhouse.

Koufax lay on the dressing room table on his stomach, while one trainer rubbed his back just under the shoulder and to the left of his spine with capsoline while the other diagnosed that a disc had slipped. He tried to crack it back into place. One of Koufax's old Dodger teammates, Don Newcombe, held his friend while the trainer slipped the disc into place. Koufax quickly put on his flannel undershirt and uniform and ran out of the dugout, buttoning the shirt as he ran. He managed to complete the game, hanging onto a 6–3 lead.[129]

Koufax finished 1966 with an impressive 27–9 record. He turned in the third lowest ERA of any pitcher up to that time—1.73. He led the National League in complete games (25) and in strikeouts (317).[130]

Koufax also won his second Triple Crown in 1966, his third unanimous Cy Young Award, and he finished second in the MVP voting. His 27 wins set a National League record for southpaws, matched in 1972 by Steve Carlton. He also added 16 more 10-strikeout games for a career mark of 98, surpassed only by Nolan Ryan.[131]

Koufax made his last appearance in the World Series in 1966 against the Baltimore Orioles.[132] He opposed Jim Palmer in the second game of the Series, which remained scoreless until the fifth when Dodger outfielder Willie Davis unexpectedly lost a fly ball that ended up dropping to the ground. Later in the inning, Davis lost another fly ball and before the inning was over, Davis had committed three errors and the Orioles had scored three runs. The Orioles won the game, 6–0, and went on to sweep the Series.

Davis' teammates tried to avoid him after the fatal inning was finally over, but Koufax rushed to find the young outfielder hiding in the shadows of the dugout. He threw both his arms around Davis and said, "It's okay, Willie. Don't let it get you down."[133]

That World Series game was the finale of Sandy Koufax's career as a professional player. Six weeks after the Series had concluded, Koufax called a press conference in the Beverly Hills Hotel and stunned the sports world with the announcement that he was retiring from baseball. Koufax confirmed what many had suspected—he would permanently injure his arthritic left arm if he continued to pitch. He informed the press that he would like to live his years after baseball with the complete use of his body.

In the long history of professional baseball, Koufax's retirement stood as an unprecedented event. No other star in the history of the game had ever stepped down at the pinnacle of his career and only a handful of other professional athletes—heavyweight champions Gene Tunney and Rocky Marciano, and Cleveland Browns fullback Jim Brown—had retired while still dominating the sport.[134] The Dodgers brass had hoped to persuade Koufax to pitch one more year, but he was adamant. "I felt," he said, "that I was being too devious when my friends kept asking me what I was going to do. I didn't want to lie and I didn't want to keep on being devious."[135] He easily could have taken $135,000 from the Dodgers for another season and given them nothing in return, but that was not Koufax's way.[136]

Koufax had outstanding career statistics. His won–lost record was 165–87—a .655 percentage—a 2.76 ERA, 2,396 strikeouts in 2,324 innings, 167 complete games, and 40 shutouts. He was on the very short list of pitchers who retired with more career strikeouts than innings pitched. He was the first pitcher to win multiple Cy Young Awards and the first pitcher to win that award unanimously. In fact, he was elected unanimously all three times—in 1963, 1965, and in 1966. At the time Koufax won his three Cy Young Awards, only one was given for both leagues. The rule was changed in 1967, the year after Sandy retired, to elect a Cy Young Award winner for each league.[137] He was also the first pitcher in the twentieth century to record three 300-plus strikeout seasons.[138]

After he officially retired from baseball, the *New York Times* ran a brief tribute to Koufax, calling him a man who had retired with honor and dignity. It asked the fans to remember Koufax as a gentle, quiet individual, but a fierce competitor who pitched every game in pain his last years in baseball. "He has retired from the diamond; but he will be long remembered as a great player and a great human being."[139]

As 1967 spring training approached, Koufax admitted that he missed baseball. He had been going to spring training every year since 1955, and he found that old habits were difficult to break. "The first week of spring training hurts no matter what age you are," he admitted, "but after that it can be fun. That first spring of my retirement was tough to get used to."[140]

And like many retired players, he stayed connected with the game. In 1967 Koufax signed a 10-year, one million dollar contract with NBC to be a broadcaster on the "Saturday Game of the Week."[141] Dodgers owner O'Malley, who could be petty, was still angry with Koufax for retiring and tried to get even when he made a triumphant return to Dodger Stadium as part of the NBC broadcasting team. O'Malley spitefully refused to allow NBC to use the two front seats behind home plate for their cameras, a courtesy given in every other ballpark in baseball.[142]

After two years on the job, NBC shook up the broadcasting team by dismissing Pee Wee Reese and demoting Sandy Koufax to the backup team, which broadcast only in the two cities with teams participating in the national telecast. The second team would have the number one contest only in the event of rain. Chet Simmons, NBC's Director of Sports, indicated that this arrangement would allow Koufax to gain more experience.[143] Koufax, who had never felt comfortable in front of the cameras and was tired of traveling, resigned as a broadcaster just prior to the 1973 season.[144] He was also so sensitive to the feelings of others that it was difficult for him to offer even the mildest criticism of a player. NBC replaced him with former Dodger teammate, Maury Wills.[145]

Few were surprised that he had resigned; they had been amazed that he had accepted the job in the first place. His friend, Larry Merchant, noted, "When you look back at it, it seems a little nuts that a guy who didn't talk much would become an analyst. He was not a striking personality on the air, but the thing that helped him was his knowledge of baseball."[146]

During his early years as a broadcaster, Sandy Koufax had married Ann Widmark, daughter of movie actor Richard Widmark. They lived a quiet life, splitting their time between homes in Maine and California. Their marriage lasted until 1982 when the couple divorced, a breakup their neighbor in Maine recalled as "very congenial."[147] Koufax remarried and divorced again in the 1990s.[148]

In January 1970, Sandy Koufax received another honor when he was voted the top baseball player of the decade by the Associated Press, finishing ahead of sluggers Mantle, Mays, and Aaron. Frank Shaughnessy, the late president of the International League, who watched many great pitchers including Christy Mathewson, Grover Cleveland Alexander, and Walter Johnson, said of Koufax, "He comes closer to being unhittable than any other pitcher I ever saw."[149]

On January 19, 1972, Sandy Koufax, at the age of 36, became the youngest man voted into Baseball's Hall of Fame and only the fifth player selected in his first year of eligibility.[150] He received 344 votes from members of the Baseball Writers Association of America, the most in the 40-year history of the Hall. Koufax felt that this overwhelming vote was the highest accolade he had received as a ballplayer. "I'm a little surprised I got as many votes as I did," said Koufax. "I didn't have as many good years as some others in the Hall and I thought that might count against me." Also voted into the Hall along with Koufax were pitcher Early Wynn and catcher Larry "Yogi" Berra.[151]

Koufax's selection to the Hall of Fame elicited tributes from some of baseball's greatest hitters who had faced Koufax many times. Willie Stargell once said of Koufax, "Hitting against him is like eating soup with a fork." According to Willie Mays, "Sandy would strike me out two or three times a game. And I knew every pitch he was going to throw—fastball, breaking ball or whatever. Actually, he would let you look at it. And you still couldn't hit it."[152]

The day following Koufax's election to the Hall of Fame, the Los Angeles Times ran a brief but compelling editorial about Koufax's recent honor. It mentioned all of his accomplishments, but added that there was more to Koufax than statistics—there was style. The editorial lauded Koufax for the competence and grace of the true professional that always gave satisfaction to those who watched him work. "Baseball's honor to Sandy Koufax," concluded the editorial, "is only fitting, because Sandy Koufax honored the game."[153]

On June 4, 1970, Koufax's uniform number (32) was retired alongside Dodger greats Roy Campanella (39) and Jackie Robinson (42).[154]

Even before Koufax retired as an active player he had said, "I'm not sure I want to stay in baseball all my life. I have no managerial ambitions, but maybe I'd like to coach."[155] In early 1979, Sandy Koufax went to spring training with the Dodgers as a pitching instructor. O'Malley, who had now forgiven Sandy, announced that his former pitcher was rejoining the Dodgers and would be an asset to the organization. Koufax had found it difficult to stay away from the one thing he had done so well in his life, and that, given the economy of the times, he found it tough to "make ends meet."[156]

Koufax remained with the Dodgers until 1990. Some say he left then because the Dodgers had reduced his workload and he no longer felt he was earning the money the club was paying him. Others blame the departure on an "uneasy" working relationship with manager Tommy Lasorda. Four years later, Koufax completely severed all relationship with the team, which was then owned by Rupert Murdoch, when the Murdoch-owned New York Post implied that Koufax was gay. When the Dodgers were sold to Frank McCourt in 2004, Koufax returned to the Dodgers organization.[157]

Sandy Koufax was inducted into the Jewish Sports Hall of Fame on March 21, 1993.[158] In 2005 the Professional Baseball Scouts Foundation, an organization that helps former scouts who need financial assistance, honored Koufax.[159] Koufax was also an active board member of the Baseball Assistance Team, which performs a similar function for major leaguers.[160]

Although Hank Greenberg was actually the first of the great Jewish players and truly smoothed the path for all Jewish ballplayers that followed him, more Jews today admire Sandy Koufax. Why? One obvious answer is that Hank Greenberg, who played in the 1930s and 1940s, seems very remote to Jewish fans born or coming of age after World War II. But even though Koufax retired more than forty years ago, he continues to be an icon.[161] Koufax benefited from being not only a sport star but also a television personality, ideally suited for the post-war television age with his intensity of expression, his force of delivery, and his unbelievable accomplishments. By leaving at the top of his game, he was able to remain, as Gruver wrote, "a model—standard of excellence, the measuring stick for greatness, outside of baseball as well as inside the game."[162]

6. Baseball's Master Statistician

One of the people Sandy Koufax credits for his turnaround as a pitcher was Allan Roth, a man who never played a day of professional baseball in his life. But Roth knew everything there was to know about Koufax's pitching—what he threw against every hitter he faced in every situation, and most importantly, the exact extent of what worked and what didn't work. Allan Roth was the Dodgers' statistician. In fact, he was baseball's first full-time team statistician and is recognized for developing much of the data system that continues to shape our perceptions of baseball today.[1] The late noted sports writer and author Leonard Koppett called Allan Roth "The real developer of detailed, beyond-standard stats."[2]

Allan Roth was born Abraham Roth in Montreal, Quebec, Canada, May 10, 1917. He was considered something of a child prodigy; at the age of three he was able to count backwards from 100 by twos. As a teenager he played both football and baseball on the sandlots, but he always was more interested in the statistical side of baseball, keeping his own numbers for the International League, which included his hometown Montreal Royals, a Dodgers farm club.[3] The prestigious McGill University, where his brother Max was already attending, offered Roth a scholarship, but he turned it down in order to support his family by working as a salesman for a neckwear and suspenders company.[4]

While he was employed as a salesman, Roth began to write to *The Sporting News* and to Dodgers president Larry MacPhail about the results of his statistical studies. In September 1941 he sent the Dodgers a pitch-by-pitch analysis of the upcoming World Series. When MacPhail did not reply, Roth accepted a job with Frank Calder, President of the National Hockey League, gathering statistical analysis for the league. Roth began to invent his own system of charting every pass in every game.[5]

World War II had intensified and Roth spent the next three years in the Canadian army. Upon his release from the military, Roth went back to the National Hockey League, but he really preferred baseball. "I had always thought that baseball was a better field than hockey," he once stated. "Basically, baseball is a percentage game. I thought that everything in the game should be tabulated."[6] Roth became a man with a mission: to substitute facts for opinions in the management of baseball teams. From the moment he conceived this undertaking he was earmarked a "dangerous revolutionary."[7]

By 1944 Branch Rickey had replaced Larry MacPhail as Brooklyn's president. He had the reputation of having the most progressive mind in an industry not generally known for its forward thinking. Rickey's approach to statistics was very similar to Roth's. Unlike old-timers who had little or no use for the value of statistics, Rickey wanted to know much, much more. For example, while he ran the St. Louis Cardinals in the 1920s and 1930s, Rickey had employed Travis Hoke, who rated players by counting the number of bases their hits accounted for and the frequency with which they were able to advance base runners.[8]

Roth was aware of Rickey's philosophy and Rickey knew of Roth's compulsion for statistics. In 1944 Roth showed up at spring training and showed Rickey some of his statistical data on RBI percentages and Dodgers' batting averages against both righty and southpaw pitchers. These were numbers Rickey had never seen.

Rickey hired Roth primarily for two reasons. First, Roth presented Rickey with a whole series of new statistics, recording everything from bunts to possible RBIs—all exclusively for the use of the Brooklyn Dodgers. Second, Rickey was a well-known tightwad. When Roth offered his services using only a pencil and paper, never mentioning buying expensive machines, Rickey was more than interested. And when Roth never quibbled over salary, Rickey quickly realized that Roth was the man he wanted.[9]

Allan Roth was the first fulltime team statistician in baseball history. After keeping statistics for the minor-league Montreal Royals, Roth was hired by Branch Rickey where he pioneered the tracking of new, useful data for the Dodgers in Brooklyn and then in Los Angeles. In 1964, NBC and ABC hired Roth as their baseball statistician. One of Roth's statistical obsessions was his insistence that a player's on-base percentage was more important that his batting average (courtesy of Los Angeles Dodgers).

Allan Roth was a fanatic where baseball's numerology was concerned, but he was also very passionate about racism and anti–Semitism. The Jewish statistician was thirty years old when he joined the Dodgers—a rookie and an outsider. He had arrived in Brooklyn from Montreal within hours of another outsider—Jackie Robinson, who also had come in from the Montreal farm team just before Opening Day, 1947. Years later, Roth would tell his family about his encounters with Robinson that year. He kept no personal diaries—the only thing he ever recorded were baseball statistics, but his family could gather that Roth's friendship with Robinson in 1947 was very pleasant but not very intimate.[10]

Soon after Rickey hired Roth, the statistician introduced a practice used universally today in major league baseball—the pitch count. He began to count every pitch a man threw. Another of his innovations which is now widely popular, was to chart every pitch thrown during the game. This meant that in addition to counting the pitches, Roth marked down what type of pitch it was, curve, slider, screwball, or knuckler. From all this information, Roth was able to determine important patterns.[11]

Roth attended every Dodger game in 1947 both home and away. The stocky "old" statistician with thinning hair, who was quiet and personable with a wry sense of humor, could always be found sitting behind home plate, smoking his Sherlock Holmes–type pipe, clad in a jacket and tie, charting every pitch. He noted in his ledgers whether each pitch was high and inside, low and outside, or down the middle, where it was hit and who hit it. Roth always avoided liquids before games so he would not have to leave his seat to visit the rest room.[12]

Roth also kept a 200-page notebook tracking how all Dodgers hitters performed against all opposing pitchers and how all opposing pitchers fared against every Dodgers hitter. Over the years, Dodgers managers used this information to make dozens of decisions, including filling out their lineup cards, selecting relievers and pinch hitters, determining whether to have a runner steal, and whether to walk or pitch to a batter.

Roth told his managers that the statistics he gave them were reliable and useful, but he always cautioned that percentages were only probabilities, not foolproof predictions. "Statistics are scientific," he once told a reporter, "but baseball is a human game. In spite of all the figures in the world, it's the men who count—it's the managers and the players that win ball games."[13]

Despite Roth's claims, most of the Dodgers managers placed great faith in his statistics. He was once asked what would happen to his recordkeeping if he were stricken with appendicitis during the baseball season. Allan deliberated for a moment and then replied, "I guess I'd have to wait until the winter to have it removed."[14]

Rickey depended on Roth, and he would seldom make a move without consulting his statistician. He often commented that most baseball men like to call baseball a percentage game, but, said Rickey, "Quite often they have no idea what the percentage is." Eventually the press realized that something peculiar was taking place in the Dodgers' front office, but they could not figure out what. One article even noted, "Roth is a spy. He constitutes Branch Rickey's intelligence department."[15]

During his tenure as president of the Brooklyn Dodgers, Branch Rickey made some seemingly bizarre, but usually successful decisions. Right fielder Dixie Walker had hit .306 in 1947 but was shipped off to Pittsburgh the following year. In 1949 Jackie Robinson, a .296 hitter with only 12 home runs the previous year, was moved into the cleanup spot. In May 1952, catcher Roy Campanella who was hitting .325, was benched against the Cincinnati Reds in favor of second-string catcher Rube Walker who was hitting in the low .200s. Baseball scribes wondered why these moves had been made. Only one man knew—Allan Roth.

Dixie Walker was traded because Roth's hit-location diagram showed he was no longer pulling the ball, a sign of an aging hitter. Even though he had not been a power hitter, Robinson was moved to cleanup because he had batted .350 with men on base. Campanella rode the bench against the Reds because he owned a low lifetime batting average against Ewell Blackwell, who was the starting pitcher against the Dodgers that day. Campanella's inability to hit Blackwell was a piece of information that only Allan Roth had known. "Baseball is a game of percentages," Roth maintained. "I try to find the actual percentage which is constantly shifting and apply it to the situation where it will do the most good."[16]

Roth's success rate was remarkable considering that he never liked math very much, detested numbers outside baseball, and never did his own taxes. He had no statistical background other than ordinary math classes he had taken in school. He had once confessed that he could never remember his own phone number.[17]

One of the most important statistics devised by Allan Roth exclusively for the Brooklyn Dodgers, but used today by all major league teams, was the concept of on-base percentage (OBP). Roth claimed, and Rickey agreed, that this figure was the single most accurate definition of a batter's productivity and his offensive value to the team.[18]

The idea behind on-base percentage was to take into account how a player reached base by means other than getting a base hit. While batting average was very important, OBP calculated a long neglected factor in baseball—the base on balls. One of the baseball's most astute students of batting values, Ted Williams, once bragged more about his 162 walks in 1947 than his .343 batting average.[19]

Roth devised the concept of OBP in the 1950s. To compile it, he simply took the number of at-bats and added it to the number of times the batter reached base on a walk or by being hit by the pitch. He then added those totals to the batter's total hits. Peter Palmer, a statistician for the American League, tried to introduce the concept to a wider audience by writing an article in the 1974 *Baseball Research Journal*, but OBP was not accepted as an official statistic until 1984 when computers allowed researchers to prove just how meaningful the statistic actually was.[20] By that time, Ted Williams, who had been preaching the value of getting on base by any means for forty years said, "I first heard that there was such a statistic sometime back in the middle forties."[21]

The first two Dodgers managers Roth worked with from 1948 to 1950 were not fans of these findings. Leo Durocher considered Roth a "harmless nuisance" but made it quite clear that he was not impressed with baseball figures. Burt Shotton, while not hostile to Roth, did not make use of his statistics. Like Roth, he felt the human factor was much more important and did not believe that the past could actually predict the future.[22]

But Rickey welcomed every new piece of information Roth gave him. In addition to individual statistics, Roth turned over to management an overall detailed study of the Dodgers every two weeks. His information was presumably for the exclusive and very secret use of the Dodgers, but a landmark article appeared in *Life* magazine in 1954, which detailed Roth's theories. Included in the magazine was an article by Branch Rickey headlined "A New Formula Explodes Baseball's Myths." Rickey had attempted to keep Roth's work secret, but as newspapers and magazines began to feature "the demon statistician" of baseball, Rickey, always a man who demanded the spotlight, took much credit for the new theories. He did confess, "Roth, in my opinion, is the top statistics specialist in baseball."[23]

The *Life* article focused on a complicated Roth equation billed as "The Unifying Theory of Baseball." Roth's concepts, which looked ridiculous to the average person, were actually some forty years ahead of their time. They dealt with topics such as on-base percentage, a hitter's slugging percentage without the singles, and a quantification of a base runner's ability by determining how often a runner scored per times on base. Roth also ran statistics relating to the abilities of pitchers and fielders.[24]

Rickey left the Dodgers in 1950 to become general manager of the Pittsburgh Pirates, and E. J. "Buzzy" Bavasi, was named general manager in his place. He was the first member of Dodgers management with that title and served as GM until 1968.[25]

Burt Shotton retired as manager after the 1950 season, and the Dodgers hired Charlie Dressen to succeed him. Dressen, who ran the team on the field from 1951 to 1953, was in his early 50s and was known for his stubbornness. He had his own brand of baseball, gambling on hunches and stealing opponents' signs. He scoffed at Roth's statistics and openly admitted he had little use for the scraps of paper Roth would deliver to his office at Ebbets Field. He kindly accepted them, and when Roth left, he would simply file them in the trash can.

Dressen asked Roth to leave his post behind home plate and take a seat in the press box where he could create stats for the writers and club broadcasters. While Dressen might not have appreciated the statistics formulated by Roth, the broadcasters certainly did, especially young Dodgers broadcaster Vin Scully. Scully had been hired by Rickey after the 1949 season when he was only 22 years old. Roth and Scully became good friends and "hung out" outside Ebbets Field, going to the movies, having a few beers, and talking about all the possibilities of baseball. Roth considered his ouster from his seat behind home plate a demo-tion, but he found that the friendship that he developed with Scully helped him to ease the pain.[26]

Roth jokingly told everyone that he would guarantee the 100 percent accuracy of his statistics except for 1949, "the year Scully helped me." Roth would bolster the young broad-caster by arming him with all sorts of statistics he could use to make his broadcasts more interesting and informative, including such items as batter-versus-pitcher stats that made Scully appear to be a wizard. For example, when Gil Hodges came to the plate against Johnny Antonelli, Scully would state, "Hodges is 0-for-20 lifetime against the southpaw." If Hodges managed to get a hit off Antonelli, Scully would bring the statistics up-to-date by saying, "Now he's 1-for-21." Scully never forgot what Roth did for him during his formative years. "Long before there was Mary Poppins, there was Allan Roth," Scully fondly remembered. "If you had some question that came to you in the middle of a game, he would reach down into this bag, and next thing you knew you'd have your answer. It was marvelous."[27]

Roth was fortunate to have arrived on the scene at a time when baseball journalism was beginning to change. A newer breed of baseball scribes was emerging that used more realism and less creative prose. They were interested in actual information, exactly Roth's forte. The New York Daily News ran a daily column called "Diamond Dust" with all sorts of baseball trivia, primarily statistics. Baseball writers covering the Dodgers weaved Roth's information into their own notes columns primarily to fill space, but the fan reaction was unbelievable. Readers began to shout for more and more numbers; they could not get enough and baseball statistics began to attain the status of "cultural phenomenon."[28]

While Durocher, Shotton and Dressen were either lukewarm or completely unim-pressed with Roth's use of statistics, Dodgers manager Walter Alston was a completely dif-ferent story. Alston, who managed the team in both Brooklyn and Los Angeles from 1954 to 1976, believed in Roth's work and made extensive use of it. Vin Scully noted, "It was rumored that Alston never made a move without checking with Allan Roth first."[29] Alston considered Roth an extra coach and appreciated receiving complete reports on each Dodgers player, reports which contained little known facts such as how many times a batter pulled the ball and how often he hit to the opposite field.[30]

Roth continued supplying esoteric statistics to announcer Vin Scully and his partner Jerry Doggett, among the first broadcasters to pay attention to the pitch count of starting pitchers. Roth was the first to provide statistical evidence that right-handed batters hit better against left-handed pitchers than against right-handed pitchers.[31] Roth also pointed out how important it was to win on the road. By researching the records between 1946 and 1956, Roth discovered during that period, 14 pennant winners led their league in road play.[32]

In addition to the Dodgers announcers, Alston's players were uniformly receptive to Roth's data. One player who used Roth's data to greatly improve his performance was pitcher Sandy Koufax. Roth proved to Koufax that the key to becoming a successful pitcher was to get ahead of the batter. Roth charted over 26,000 of Koufax's pitches in 313 of his 397 games, tracking each at-bat and the count on which Koufax's decisive pitches were made. He then showed Koufax the conclusive results. When Koufax was ahead in the count, the opponents hit .146 against him; when he was behind, the average jumped to .286. It was no wonder that from then on, Koufax knew that his best pitch was "Strike One."[33]

Roth put his figures to four principal uses: as coaching aids during winter training; as tactical guides during the season; as material for the daily background sheets for reporters;

and as background material for the two Dodgers announcers Scully and Doggett through pieces of paper he passed to them as each game proceeded.[34]

When the Dodgers' new ball park, Dodger Stadium, opened in 1962, the park contained a huge twin scoreboard in left field. Dodgers owner Walter O'Malley wanted fans attending the game to have as much information as those listening on radio. He gave Allan Roth an added duty—feed as much information to Scully and Doggett as the fans could see on the new scoreboard. Roth had long ago convinced O'Malley that despite the opinion of some fans, the statistical part of baseball could never be overdone. "Baseball is a statistical game," insisted Roth. "One of the reasons is that fans talk baseball the year around and the statistics will figure in all the talk. I don't think baseball itself is overdoing it. It's the fans who insist on this information."[35]

Near the end of the 1964 season, Roth resigned as statistician of the Los Angeles Dodgers. A Dodgers spokesman said that Roth no longer wished to spend half of each baseball season traveling—a requirement of the job. The 47-year-old Roth had been with the Dodgers since the beginning of the 1947 season.[36]

After Roth left the Dodgers, he became statistician for NBC's *Game of the Week*, where he re-united with his friend Vin Scully. Roth also continued to publish material, which he made available to all major league clubs. Roth stayed with NBC until the early 1980s when he left to handle baseball analysis for ABC. He also was editor of *Who's Who in Baseball* for many years.[37]

Roth's health had been in decline for some time, and he died on March 4, 1992, after suffering a heart attack. Roth was divorced and was survived by a son, Michael, a daughter, Andrea Western, and one grandchild. He was 74 years old.[38]

The Los Angeles chapter of the Society for American Baseball Research was named in Roth's honor and his papers may be found in the Amateur Athletic Foundation archives in Los Angeles. Copies of Roth's 2,700 actual Dodger score sheets are in the collection of Retrosheet, Inc., a nonprofit organization dedicated to making play-by-play information publicly available to all interested researchers.[39]

New York Post sportswriter Paul Fisher once wrote, "A passion for statistics is the earmark of a literate people." In the first half of the twentieth century, three Jews, Louis Heilbroner and brothers Al and Walter Elias, pioneered baseball statistics. But the depth and value of baseball statistics that exist today owe much to Jewish statistician Allan Roth. Using either his head or a simple calculator, and without the aid of a computer, Roth explored and expanded the use of statistical analysis in a broader sense than had been done before his time and served as an inspiration to the baseball mathematicians who came after him.[40]

7. The Voice of Baseball

Following World War II, the baseball press included more and more broadcasters. Like their predecessors, the sportswriters and columnists, they became an important component in major league baseball, providing interviews, analyses, backgrounds, overviews, and opinions on particular games, players, and teams as well as on larger issues that affected the game as a whole.

Members of the electronic media differed from the writers, however, in two important ways. First, the writers, whether staff or free-lance, were paid by the newspapers and magazines in which their material was published, and most tried to be unbiased in their comments, regardless of their personal loyalties. In contrast, during the middle decades of the twentieth century, baseball teams hired most of the broadcasters; they were paid by the team's corporate sponsors who often determined who was hired and fired. Broadcasters were expected not only to describe the action on the field, but also to comment on the game, supporting for the most part, the performance of their teams' players, coaches, and management. Announcers who became "too critical" usually had to answer for their remarks to the team owner or executive.[1]

But the broadcasters brought to the game a dimension beyond the capability of the print journalist—instantaneous play-by-play descriptions of each game as it was happening.[2] More and more fans began to rely on baseball's radio and television announcers to enhance their enjoyment and understanding of major league baseball. And a few broadcasters developed such a large following of devoted fans that they became stars in their own right.

One of the earliest was Bill Stern, who in 1935 was NBC's first sports announcer.[3] Stern was described by many as self-confident, brash and sometimes arrogant, but he possessed a rich, baritone voice that tended to turn every player into a hero and brought drama to whatever game he was calling—even if none existed.[4] The *Sports Newsreel* program made him America's most popular radio announcer from 1940 to 1952 according to *Radio Daily Magazine*.[5] Despite "narrating" the first baseball game ever telecast (Princeton vs. Columbia on May 17, 1939), Stern was more identified with football than any other single sport.[6]

Mel Allen was the first sports broadcaster who employed both radio and television to bring thousands of baseball games to millions of fans nationwide. Although he occasionally broadcast a football game, he was associated throughout his life with baseball. To many, he was called simply "The Voice" but to many more, he was the Voice of Baseball and the most prominent sports announcer in America.

William Israel, a Russian Jew, came to the United States at the age of 35 and settled in West Brockton, Alabama, where he ran a dry goods store and raised seven children. One of his sons, Julius, worked in his father's store and remembers him as "a stern patriarch unfavorably disposed toward boyhood idleness and particularly inimical to baseball."[7]

Anna Leibovitz, the daughter of a cantor, was born in Russia and came to the United States at the age of nine. In 1912, Anna and Julius were married, and on February 14, 1913, their first child, Melvin, was born in Birmingham.[8] Julius was well established in the dry goods business in Johns, Alabama. As Julius prospered, he began to move his business and family around the state, always hoping to improve things—first to Sylacauga and then to Bessemer, a large steel-producing center where he opened a ladies' ready-to-wear shop. Bessemer's economy collapsed after World War I, and in 1922 the Israels made another move, this time to the small town of Cordova, Alabama, where Julius soon lost all of his money.[9]

In the early 1920s, Jews made up less than one percent of Alabama's 2.35 million people. The Israels were part of a distinct minority in Cordova. Anna had been raised as an Orthodox Jew, while Julius, who had grown up among non–Jewish

Mel Allen was one of major league baseball's most prominent sportscasters. From 1946 until 1964 he was the "Voice of the New York Yankees" on radio. Beginning in 1977, Allen gained nationwide recognition in his second career as the host of TV's popular *This Week in Baseball* (courtesy National Baseball Hall of Fame Library; Cooperstown, N.Y.).

friends, had spent little time in a synagogue and, unlike his wife, could not even read Hebrew. He called himself a "patriotic" Jew and was proud of his heritage. His wife was determined to keep a kosher home so Julius brought home kosher meat from Birmingham.[10] Melvin remembered his strictly kosher home and that his parents attended an orthodox synagogue regularly and celebrated all the Jewish holidays.[11]

In 1922 the Ku Klux Klan was re-emerging and because Julius and Anna were Jewish, Cordova's citizens began to boycott the Israel store. Julius was forced to close his store and took a job selling shirts on the road. The Cordova years were the only periods of Mel's life when anti–Semitism directly affected his family.[12]

Eventually, the family moved again, this time to Greensboro, North Carolina. Mel took Hebrew lessons in Greensboro from a man named Mr. Sinai, who also prepared Allen for his bar mitzvah where he delivered his speech completely in Hebrew. The Jewish community in Greensboro was so impressed with Allen's ability that it offered to pay Mel's way to study and become a rabbi.[13]

Before he moved to Greensboro, the very young boy would astonish his parents by reading the newspapers, especially the sports pages. He could recite current batting averages, RBIs and ERAs of all the prominent major league baseball players.[14]

It was in Greensboro, however, that baseball became an integral part of his young life.

At the age of 11 he obtained a job as batboy with the Greensboro Patriots, the town's minor league club.[15] One of the team's pitchers, Jim Turner, eventually made it to the big leagues, and when he was reunited with Melvin, he told him he remembered him from his days as a batboy in Greensboro.[16]

His mother was unhappy about her son's interest in baseball because she wanted him to become a concert violinist. "Always it was baseball this or that. Sometimes I think Mel was born with a baseball in his mouth."[17]

The Israels were facing financial hardship in Greensboro, so the family moved again, this time to Detroit where Mel spent his junior year in high school. The family lived with Anna's parents until they were able to get back on their feet. Mel attended Central High School in Detroit and spent most of his spare time at Navin Field, home of the Detroit Tigers. He had grown up a Tigers fan because he had visited his Detroit relatives so often. When he wasn't watching the Tigers in Navin Field, he would listen to the games on radio station WWJ. The voice of the Tigers was Ty Tyson, whose very pleasant style made it easy for fans to follow the game. Mel Israel would often comment about Tyson, "He's the one who got me hooked on broadcasting."[18] Years later, Israel told *The Sporting News*, "Now there is the ideal life. You talk and talk and folks listen and you get paid. In addition, you are in and out of baseball."[19]

Julius moved the family back to Birmingham after he was unsuccessful in finding work in Detroit. Back in Alabama, he got a job as a traveling salesman, selling men's clothing, mainly shirts, ties, and caps. He was so good at sales that he often made a generous commission. Mel attended Birmingham's Phillips High his senior year, his fourth high school in four years, and he once more made excellent grades. During his senior year at high school, Mel played baseball, basketball and football, but enjoyed baseball best. He completed high school in Birmingham at the age of 15 and entered the University of Alabama at Tuscaloosa, where he remained for eight years, earning his B.A. in 1932 and his law degree in 1936. During his years at the University, his father moved the family from Birmingham to Tuscaloosa because Mel could not afford to live in a dormitory.[20] "All I could do," said his father "was to put a roof over his head."[21]

Mel tried out for the Alabama football team, but he was too skinny, so he settled for the job of student manager, which also included announcing the tackles and downs over the public address system. Alabama football coach Frank Thomas was impressed with the way Israel handled himself on the microphone and he recommended him to a Birmingham radio station. In 1935, Mel was hired to broadcast Alabama and Auburn games for $5 a game.[22]

"From then on," said one sportswriter, "the stage was set for the entrance of one of the best sportscasters in the field." When Alabama played Tulane that fall, a Columbia Broadcasting System executive heard Israel's commentary, and in January 1936, Mel was hired to join the network as an announcer in New York.[23] Even though he was under contract to CBS, the network allowed him to remain in school and complete his law degree. In 1937 Mel went to New York as a CBS staff announcer for $45 a week.[24]

Mel's father, thinking his son was wasting a good education, was not pleased at this turn of events. He was even less pleased when his son explained to him that CBS wanted to change his surname which sounded too Jewish. "What's so bad about Mel Israel?" his father wanted to know.[25] In order to mollify his father, Mel took Julius's middle name as his new last name. Mel Israel now became Mel Allen. He told his father that the job was only for one year and that the experience would do him a world of good. His mother, sid-ing with her son, told Julius, "Oh, let the boy go. What did it matter what he did for one year, and what did it matter what he called himself for that time?"

Mel Allen's father correctly predicted that if his son were to go to New York, it certainly would be for longer than one year. "You'll never come back," he declared, and was right. Allen never went back to Alabama except to visit relatives, but his parents, brother, and sister all were willing eventually to move to New York.[26]

When he first began broadcasting, Allen took on a myriad of tasks. He interrupted Kate Smith to report the *Hindenburg* crash, he first introduced Perry Como on the radio, and with his rapid voice, he described the Kentucky Derby and the International Polo Game. He particularly impressed the brass at CBS with a long description of the Vanderbilt Cup yacht race, broadcast from an airplane overhead.[27] As Allen circled the course, he was compelled to ad-lib more than 50 minutes, unable to describe anything in the race because rain had delayed its running. Although the race never got started, Allen's career in sports announcing was off and running.[28]

All of Allen's hard work was paying off for him. He had long maintained that his ultimate goal was to broadcast baseball games, and in 1938 he had the opportunity to fulfill his dream. That year CBS was one of four networks to broadcast the World Series, and Allen's first major league baseball assignment was to provide color commentary for France Laux, the veteran announcer. In addition to his work in the World Series, Allen also broadcast some college football games. "They said I should do football to keep from getting rusty," quipped Allen.[29]

When Allen first arrived in New York, the New York teams—the Yankees, Giants, and Dodgers—refused to broadcast their home games. Even though it had been proven that broadcasting home games did not reduce a team's home attendance, the New York teams agreed that, since one of their teams was always at home, there would be a blackout to avoid competition with each other. Only opening games and major series were broadcast.

In 1939 Larry MacPhail, known as a pioneering executive, became Brooklyn's general manager. He notified the other teams that the Dodgers were going to air their home games, and he brought Red Barber with him from Cincinnati as the announcer. The Yankees and Giants also decided to broadcast their home games, and since they never played at home at the same time, both teams hired Washington Senators broadcaster, Arch McDonald, to be their principal announcer. When McDonald's assistant was axed for a blooper he made doing a commercial, Allen replaced him. McDonald, a native of Arkansas, coined two phrases which announcers still employ today: "ducks on the pond" and "right down Broadway for a strike." However, McDonald's Arkansas twang did "not play well in New York," and he returned to Washington the following season.[30]

In 1940 Mel Allen began his long association with the Yankees.[31] He won the job against the competition of most of the country's outstanding baseball announcers. Only 27 years old, Allen, according to the *New York Times*, was the nation's youngest big-league baseball reporter and ranked among the 13 most successful under-thirty men in the country.[32]

In 1940 Allen broadcast home games for both the Yankees and Giants. In 1941 neither team could find sponsors for their broadcasts, so there were none. Unfortunately for Allen, this "blackout" prevented him from calling Joe DiMaggio's 56-game hitting streak although he recorded a re-creation when it finally ended. In 1942 he was back on the air with both teams.[33]

Allen had convinced his family to move to New York in 1940. His sister had already married and had her own home; but his brother Larry and his parents lived together in

Westchester County. Larry worked for Mel as a statistician and a gofer.[34] The family remained very close-knit and everyone seemed happy except for his mother who lamented that her "son never married anybody except the New York Yankees." For the remainder of her life when she was asked whether she wished her son were anything less than the success he was, Anna Israel answered, "I wish he was a shoemaker. A married shoemaker."[35]

Allen had a ready reply to his mother's lament about his marital status. A bachelor his entire life, Mel said his career was his family. "I am a bachelor," he said, "by circumstances rather than design. I was engaged when I went into the Army, but with all my income cut off, I let my head rule my heart. She got tired of waiting, I suppose."[36]

Allen entered the Army in 1943 as a private in the infantry and was stationed at Fort Benning, Georgia. Two years later he made it to the rank of staff sergeant and was transferred to the Armed Forces radio service where he announced the *Army Hour* program. He also hosted a sports trivia show, recreated broadcasts of college football and the 1944 World Series between the St. Louis Cardinals and the St. Louis Browns.[37] While he was in the Army he legally changed his name to Melvin Israel Allen. The Army discharged him in 1946.[38]

After his release, both the New York Giants and the New York Yankees wanted Allen, but the Yankees had the advantage. Larry MacPhail was heading up the Yankees by then, along with co-owners Dan Topping and Del Webb.[39] They needed an announcer to travel with the team and actually call road games. Prior to 1946, Yankee road games were "recreated" or "simulated" in the studio based on telegraphed play-by-play summary. Allen chose the Yankees and Red Barber remained with the Dodgers.[40]

Mel Allen would be the Yankees announcer from 1946 until 1964. During that time, the Yankees would win fifteen pennants and only twice during that span would a World Series broadcast not be covered by Allen.[41] Because Allen fraternized with team members, he had his share of critics who complained that he was cheerful when the Yankees won but dull when they were behind. He answered his critics, "Any fair minded individual would know there is no prejudice, just partisanship. What's prejudice? Seeing only one side."[42]

Stephen Gould, writing in the *New York Times*, idolized Allen as a "voice of heart." But his critics argued that Allen was simply a salesman, pushing the sponsors' products—Ballantine Beer or White Owl Cigars. He was known for his "Ballantine Blast," or "White Owl Wallop," and for coining the expressions, "Going, going, gone," or "How about that." He got so carried away at times, that Baseball Commissioner Ford Frick often stepped in and asked Allen to "tone it down."[43]

Allen's partner for the first two years that he broadcast exclusively for the Yankees was Russ Hodges. Allen had asked for Hodges after hearing him in 1945, liking Hodges' warm and pleasant sound. Like Allen, Hodges was vibrant, effervescent and he also had a law degree. The Yankees became the only team in sports history to have an "all-lawyer booth."

Hodges and Allen made baseball history in 1946 by announcing the first live broadcasts of major league road games. As the Yankees' number one announcer, Mel determined which innings he would call and which would be Hodges' play-by-play innings. They worked together until the conclusion of the 1948 season when Hodges left the Bronx and headed to Manhattan's Polo Grounds to broadcast games for the New York Giants.[44] Allen's rival at Ebbets Field was still Red Barber, "the Old Redhead," who was the voice of the Dodgers from 1939 through 1953.[45]

Mel Allen's intimate knowledge of the game and his charm helped account for his popularity, especially between 1949 and 1964.[46] His exuberant style, his extreme loquaciousness, and his deep, full Southern voice, made him perfect for his profession. He never seemed to lose his enthusiasm for calling the games. He also never seemed to lack for words, but he never entered the radio booth without preparing for every game he announced. Some listeners thought he was corny and garrulous, but he was a skilled professional with a remarkable eye for detail, an amazing memory, and a thorough knowledge of baseball.[47] Throughout his career with the Yankees, Allen began most games with the simple greeting that would become one of his signature phrases, "Hello, everybody, this is Mel Allen."[48]

Allen always admitted that he could never pick his favorite milestone as Yankees announcer. Among the choices were Bill Mazeroski's homer which enabled the Pirates to defeat the Yankees in the World Series, Roger Maris' sixty-first homer for the Yankees which broke Babe Ruth's record, Ralph Terry's winning twenty-three games, Bobby Richardson's 209 hits, Mickey Mantle's winning his third Most Valuable Player Award, and the Yankees winning the 1962 pennant.[49]

Allen recalled heartbreaking moments as well. "I remember when the public address announcer told the Yankee home crowd that Lou Gehrig, after appearing in 2,130 consecutive games, would be out of the lineup that day. I can still see Lou's pal, Lefty Gomez, get up and walk over to Gehrig and sit down beside him and console him. As tears came down Lou's face, Gomez told him, "C'mon, Lou, cut it out. It took 'em 15 years to get you out of the lineup. When I pitch, a lot of times it only takes the other team 15 minutes."[50]

A related poignant event took place not long after. On July 4, 1939, when Lou Gehrig made his farewell speech to the fans of New York, it was Mel Allen who introduced Gehrig to a packed Yankee Stadium.[51] Gehrig also paid tribute to Allen when he visited him in 1940 to tell him that although he never had the opportunity before to listen to his broadcasts since he was playing, he wanted Allen to know that his broadcasts were the only thing that kept him going since his retirement.[52] Allen was so moved he had to go into another room where he burst into tears. The Iron Horse died the following year.[53]

Allen once declared that the most touching moment in his long career occurred in 1948 when the Yankees, realizing the Bambino was dying, held "Babe Ruth Day," and Allen had the honor of introducing him to the crowd. "I could never forget the hoarse whisper due to his cancer. There wasn't a dry eye in the house including mine." Ruth died two months later.[54]

Mel had a good relationship with the Yankees ball players. He nicknamed Joe DiMaggio "Joltin Joe," Phil Rizzuto, "The Scooter," and Tommy Henrich "Old Reliable."[55] Henrich's nickname harked back to Allen's boyhood in Alabama. Henrich usually could be counted on to get important hits late in the game and Mel compared him with a train that used to run through his hometown back in Alabama. His town folks knew that a person could set his watch by the time that train came through town, and they called it "Old Reliable."[56]

Allen was always capable of filling air space, and he liked to liven up the coverage of a game with a more elaborate version of English than was the norm from sportscasters. The World Series was not only the "Series" but also the "Fall Classic." DiMaggio's swing was not just "good" but it was "poetry in motion." On occasions, however, his capability for filling air space could become a little embarrassing. For example he told his audience "International Falls was the coldest place in the United States," he quickly added, "temperature-wise, that is."[57]

By 1948 three million people owned television sets.[58] In 1951 Allen covered the World Series, the first time it was televised coast-to-coast. Some accounts maintain that Allen was the first to suggest the center-field camera shot that is now standard on baseball telecasts.

However, General Manager George Weiss limited that use because he feared that the Yankees might be accused of stealing the catcher's signs.[59]

Fans who listened to Allen's broadcasts of the Yankee games somehow felt he was smaller than he actually was. He was six-foot-one, slim and dark-haired in his youth. Like his father, he began balding at an early age, but unlike his father, he wore a hairpiece, although he generally wore a hat during his broadcasts. His standard attire was a pair of loose-fitting casual slacks and a sports jacket. Although he never married, he never wanted for a date. Broadcaster Red Barber wrote of Allen, "His job was his life ... the wife and children he never had."[60]

Allen was considered a very humble person and not always filled with self-confidence. No one ever accused him of having an ego problem. Indeed, he constantly seemed concerned with his job security. Even at the peak of his career in 1957, he stated, "I have as much security in this business as a light switch going on and off."[61]

Sometimes Mel's work ethic conflicted with the Jewish holy day, Yom Kippur. Long before the public stir about Sandy Koufax pitching in the World Series on Yom Kippur, Allen had to face the prospect of announcing a World Series game on the Day of Atonement. He met with a rabbi, who agreed that broadcasting the World Series was an opportunity for Allen and he should not give it up. Though Allen tried not to work on Yom Kippur, he decided to call the Series a couple of times on the High Holy Days, but only after he spent many hours reflecting on the importance of the day with his prayer book.[62]

Mel Allen was never considered the easiest person to work with. He unilaterally assigned which innings his assistants would call, decided who would read the commercials, and distributed both the pre-game and the post-game duties. Nevertheless, his co-workers agreed, "It wasn't very easy to work for him, but when it was all over, you were glad you did."[63] Another associate added, "He made betters announcers out of all of us."[64]

Allen teamed with a number of partners for the Yankee broadcasts. After Russ Hodges left in 1948, Mel and Jack Slocum, who had helped the Yankees obtain Russ Hodges, were searching for a replacement. Slocum suggested that they listen to a radio broadcaster in Oklahoma City with a "relaxed style; his name was Curt Gowdy

In 1949 Curt Gowdy became Allen's second partner.[65] "I was scared to death," he said. "I was nervous and tense, but every one on the Yankees was wonderful. They had class, real class." Gowdy credited Allen with teaching him much, especially about paying attention to detail.[66]

Although Curt Gowdy admired Allen, he realized that his future would be limited as long as he remained second string to Allen. The Boston Red Sox, who had been broadcasting jointly with the Braves, went out on their own, and they hired Gowdy as their lead announcer in 1951. For the third time, Allen had to look for another assistant in the radio booth. The new Yankee manager, Casey Stengel, recommended to Yankee General Manager George Weiss, that the team hire west coast broadcaster Art Gleeson as Gowdy's replacement.

Gleeson, like Allen, was a bachelor. They were a twosome for a year until the Yankees added Bill Crowley to the booth. By the end of the 1952 season, both Crowley and Gleeson were gone and in 1953 the Yankees once again were looking for an assistant for Allen. This time they hired a Kansas City native named Jim Woods.[67]

In 1954, Red Barber quit as the announcer for the Brooklyn Dodgers because of a dispute with team owner Walter O'Malley. Barber accepted a job with the Yankees although he considered his new job a comedown from having been the Dodgers' chief announcer for

20 years. Since he disliked travel, Barber began by working only on television home games, handling pre-game and post-game shows and two and one-half innings of TV play-by-play.[68]

For the next three years Allen, Woods, and Barber anchored the Yankees' booth. Barber considered the trio of Barber, Woods and Allen, "the best baseball broadcasting trio in history."[69] Dan Topping, Yankee executive, had hired Barber for his talent and image. Many considered Barber and Allen the greatest ticket salesmen in town.[70]

In the fall of 1956, in what later could have been said was "handwriting on the wall for Mel Allen," George Weiss called Woods into his office and told him that Ballantine Beer, one of the team's sponsors, had ordered him to replace Woods with Phil Rizzuto, who was expected to be a big plus to their marketing efforts in the community. Shortly after his firing, Woods said, "It was a political thing, somebody had to go. It's a family business and these things happen. Ballantine, it is said, also didn't want to lose the popular Rizzuto to Baltimore and a competitive beer."[71]

Allen and Barber had little in common but they were united in their utter dislike for what they called the "jock in the booth." Although Allen had admired Rizzuto as a player, he had little regard for his work as a broadcaster. Rizzuto had the habit of leaving the games early without informing either Barber or Allen. On one occasion, the game had gone into extra innings, and Allen announced, "'And now to take you into the tenth inning, here is...' And I look around, and no Phil. At that moment, the Scooter was listening to the game halfway across the George Washington Bridge going home. He thought he didn't have to tell anybody he was going to leave early," said Allen.[72] Despite Barber's and Allen's feelings towards Rizzuto, the former Yankee shortstop connected well with the fans, who liked his warm personality and infectious enthusiasm.[73]

Through it all, Allen and Barber maintained a close, cordial relationship. Their styles differed greatly—Allen was radiant, extroverted, and a perfectionist. Barber was reserved and arcane, but they never got in each other's way in the booth. Announcer Vin Scully best summarized the differences between Barber and Allen. "Barber was white wine, crepes suzette, Allen was hot dogs and beer. Barber was detached while Allen was involved. Red always believed the professional should not root, while Allen maintained that he wanted the Yankees to win."[74] Despite their differences, they were close. When Barber died in 1992, Allen, nearly 80 years old, traveled from New York to Florida to attend his funeral.[75]

In 1956 former Yankee infielder Jerry Coleman became the fourth member of the Yankee broadcasting team. Barber and Rizzuto, who did not enjoy traveling, remained in New York, while Coleman and Allen broadcast the Yankees road games. The fans took to Coleman, despite his spoonerisms and malapropisms, such as "He's throwing up in the bullpen."[76]

Giants and Dodgers fans, who occasionally listened to Yankee broadcasts, accused Allen of talking too much. Practically every day he received letters from listeners claiming, "Your idle chatter is thoroughly disgusting," or from a lady in Yonkers who complained, "All I have to do is listen to the tone of your voice when I tune in, and I know instantly whether the Yankees are winning or losing."

He became more and more known for his talkativeness and even Yankee Yogi Berra, when asked what he thought of Allen as a sportscaster, simply replied, "Too many woids."[77] The same qualities which had won him so many fans earlier, seemed to be working against him. In the early 1960s, fans' attention spans were becoming short and Allen's narrative with its heavy description began to wear on their ears and displeased his sponsors and colleagues. They began to feel that Allen simply talked too much.[78]

The 1963 season ended roughly. Although the Yankees had again won the American League pennant, the Los Angeles Dodgers swept them in the World Series. During the season, Allen had had a recurrent bout with the flu and while broadcasting the 1963 World Series, Allen lost his voice—he was simply unable to speak. It was never discovered what the actual cause was (Allen insisted it was a "nasal condition"), but many commentators said he was struck speechless by the Yanks' humiliation. Sportswriter Dick Young of the *New York Daily News* reported that Allen had an "emotional crackup" on the air. It was true that Allen was losing his good nature because of what he perceived as a loss of support from the front office, which no longer included the three high-powered Allen supporters, Ed Barrow, George Weiss, and Larry MacPhail. The 1963 World Series was to be the last Mel Allen would call.[79]

Allen had announced every World Series from 1955 through 1963 in addition to All-Star Games from 1952 through 1961. One year *Variety* ran a list of the most recognizable voices in the world. Allen said, "I was the only sports announcer on the list. I guess I had a special voice."[80]

In 1964 the Yankees won the American League pennant again, but for the first time, the last-place Mets outdrew the Yankees at the gate. Sales of Ballantine Beer were slumping, and western breweries like Coors and Miller were beginning to enter Ballantine's regional markets at discounted prices. The brewery and the Yankees attempted to lay the blame and find a quick fix for their problems, and they decided it was Mel Allen.[81]

On September 21, 1964, Yankee co-owner Dan Topping called Allen to his Fifth Avenue office. Allen thought the meeting was to discuss a renewal of his contract, but Topping informed Mel that he would not be hired for the following year. Topping implied that Ballantine Beer had been behind the decision, but whoever was responsible, the termination was immediate. The Yankees did not even allow him to broadcast the 1964 World Series, assigning that task to former Yankee shortstop Phil Rizzuto.[82] Joe Garagiola replaced Allen on the radio broadcasts.[83] Gracious even in these circumstances, Mel congratulated his successor. "Hope you stay on the job as long as I did," read the first line of the telegram that Garagiola received.[84] Garagiola had only one answer—"I didn't know there were still guys like him around."[85]

Allen was stunned. "The Yankees never even held a press conference to announce my leaving," he remembered. "They just let it leak out. So there were all sort of lies spread around.... They said I was a lush or that I beat my relatives or that I had a breakdown or that I was taking so many medicines for my voice that I turned numb."[86]

Barber remembered Allen coming to Yankee Stadium before airtime the day following his firing. "When I got to the booth, Mel was already there. He was sitting in his place. He was staring across the ball field. He didn't speak. I don't think he knew where he was. He was the saddest-looking man I have ever seen. He was desolate, stricken."[87] Years later Barber, still saddened by the way Allen had been kicked out of the broadcasting booth, said "He gave the Yankees his life and they broke his heart."[88]

Literally thousands of letters were sent to Yankee Stadium supporting Mel Allen. One fan from Ithaca addressed his letter "Dear Mel" because he felt that "Mr. Allen seemed too detached for someone I think of as a friend." A woman from Madison, New Jersey, wrote "I became a Yankee fan first because of you and second because of the team." A man from Asbury Park, New Jersey, wrote that the winter would never end if Allen was not in Florida with the Yanks to say 'This is Mel Allen from Fort Lauderdale, Florida,'" A fan from New Haven, Connecticut, called the firing of Allen "completely unjustified and nothing short of a disgrace." And on and on the letters went, all echoing the thought of one fan who believed any team that would drop Allen from the broadcast booth must be crazy.

Even fans that were sick and tired of the Yankees winning year after year were distressed when they heard about Allen's fate. A Giant fan wrote, "I loved hating you win. I enjoyed your comments and loved talking back to you." Many wrote letters to Dan Topping demanding an explanation for letting Allen go.[89]

Mel Allen was not out of work very long. Before the 1965 season began, the Milwaukee Braves hired Allen to head a team that included Hank Morgan and Ernie Johnson broadcasting both radio and television over Atlanta station WSB.[90] When the Milwaukee Braves became the Atlanta Braves, it was expected that Allen would go south with the team as one of their announcers. For their first season in Atlanta, however, the Braves opted for Milo Hamilton, who was well known in the South for his broadcasts on the White Sox network. More importantly, Hamilton was also well known to the Braves' owners, who were mostly Chicago businessmen. Hamilton teamed with Larry Munson, a Nashville broadcaster, to air Atlanta's games.[91] Allen officially resigned as the Braves' announcer during the autumn of 1965.[92] In his letter of resignation, Allen said, "Deeply rooted professional and business commitments, complicated by the recent loss of my mother and the current serious illness of my father, make accepting an assignment outside the New York area most difficult at this time."[93]

In 1966 Allen was named play-by-play announcer for the Miami Dolphins of the American Football League.[94] That same year Mel Allen visited troops in Vietnam with five major league stars: Stan Musial of the St. Louis Cardinals, Hank Aaron and Joe Torre of the Atlanta Braves, Brooks Robinson of the American League champion Baltimore Orioles, and Harmon Killebrew of the Minnesota Twins.[95]

Charlie Finley asked Allen to broadcast the Athletics' games when the team moved to Oakland in 1968, but Allen's business interests, which included a Canada Dry soft-drink dealership, kept him busy on the East Coast. He made public appearances for Canada Dry, broadcast University of Miami football, and hosted several local and network radio sports shows.[96]

In 1968 Mel Allen was back in the television booth broadcasting major league baseball for the Cleveland Indians with Harry Jones. He had replaced former pitcher Herb Score who left the television job to handle the Indians' radio broadcasts. The 1968 season was not a very good one for the Indians, and one dull evening Allen shocked his listeners and viewers by reciting Longfellow's "Song of Hiawatha" to fill time during the game. It was his last big-time sports job for eight years.[97]

Ever since he had left the New York Yankees in 1964, Mel Allen had returned occasionally to Yankee Stadium. On June 8, 1969, he served as master of ceremonies on Mickey Mantle Day. In 1976, the Yankees' flagship TV station, WPIX, hired Allen to narrate a special program commemorating the opening of the refurbished ballpark. By then, the people who had fired Allen were no longer associated with the Yankees; George Steinbrenner owned the franchise. Allen returned to Yankee broadcasts in 1977, calling a selected few dozen games for Sports Channel cable network. He continued in that role until 1985.[98]

When the Yankees hired Allen to work their cablecasts, *Sports Illustrated* wrote, "The Voice is back where it belongs, an old campaigner, a keeper of tradition. If baseball is back, then Mel Allen must be too.... When you hear it, it's summer again, a lazy July or August afternoon with sunlight creeping across the infield.... Like the game itself. Allen is timeless."[99]

By 1977 football was growing in popularity and running a weekly promotional TV series *This Week in the NFL*; baseball on television was still in its infancy. Geoff Belinfante was an executive with an advertising agency whose number one client was the Major League Baseball Corporation, which wanted a weekly half-hour vehicle of lowlight/highlight, features. "Baseball," noted Belinfante, "wanted to combat football, but did not have much credibility. Sooner rather than later, it needed someone who did."

For the show itself, called *This Week in Baseball,* the producers decided to record 70 baseball games by paying someone to tape off the local TV feed, and copy to standard two-inch format. For credibility, they hired Mel Allen. "What better name, what better personality to give a new baseball show legitimacy than the man who had done so many World Series for so many years," asked Belinfante. "Mel was a big star and he gave us the legitimacy we needed to make a go with *This Week in Baseball* in the world of syndication that was tough for us to break into."[100]

Belinfante was correct. The show was tailor-made for Allen. With his voice providing the narration, the series highlighted summaries of the National and American Leagues games of the past week. It was a show frankly designed to boost baseball and to attract prospective fans. There was no doubt that Allen gave unqualified gusto to the show.[101]

On June 12, 1977, baseball's first highlight series began on fifty outlets. Each week tape was flown to New York, taken to a studio across the Hudson River and logged, viewed, and edited. In the early years, when Allen narrated newsreel footage, he had done all his own writing. On *TWIB* Allen wrote none of it. The show featured odd plays such as players running into each other and other bloopers. Soon the odd plays were as funny as the game. But the key was Allen's narration. Many listeners were shocked to hear his voice. A woman wrote that when her mother heard Allen's voice she exclaimed, "I can't believe it. Is that Mel Allen?"

Eventually, nuance, inflection and drama came back. Belinfante said, "Part was his wonderful newsreel background, part dramatic training." Every year Belinfante told Allen what his salary would be and Allen merely shook his hand. He never had a contract.[102]

By 1979 the show had soared to become sports' highest-rated syndicated series.[103] Up until 1989, *TWIB* ran right before *Game of the Week* on nearly every NBC affiliate. Episodes of *TWIB* made Mel Allen known to a new generation of fans and episodes routinely played in stadiums across the major leagues and on television sets at Baseball's Hall of Fame in Cooperstown, New York.[104]

Creator of *TWIB*, Joe Reichler, stated that the show made Mel Allen a Grand Old Man of Broadcasting. "Everywhere I go," he said, "players tell me, 'Jesus, wait till Mel gets hold of *that* play.'" *Sports Illustrated* wrote that Allen was "back where he belongs, an old campaigner, a keeper of tradition. For years he was the forgotten man, but it has all come back to him in abundance. The taste must be sweet."[105]

This Week in Baseball turned Mel Allen from the Voice of the Yankees into the Voice of Baseball. Critics hailed him finally as "everything a sportscaster should be."[106] Merle Harmon, sportscaster for five major league teams, spoke for many when he said, "I've never seen a show like it so closely synonymous with one person."[107] *The Sporting News* summarized Allen's importance to *TWIB* when it wrote in 1990, "Mel Allen may be 78, but his voice is resonant, mellifluous, and invigorating as ever. His vibrant voice was the show's signature. To many too young to have experienced his play-by-play, Allen will be remembered as the narrator who gave baseball life and a few nonscripted rings of 'How About That! On *This Week in Baseball*.'"[108]

In 1978 the Baseball Hall of Fame established the Ford C. Frick Award to honor broadcasters for "major contributions to baseball." The first two recipients of this award were Red Barber and Mel Allen. While broadcasters are not considered members of the Hall of Fame per se, and although there is no "broadcasters' wing" in the Hall, the winners are honored in an exhibit near the Hall's library.[109] Allen considered this the greatest honor of his life. Mel Allen was also inducted into the Jewish Sports Hall of Fame in Israel, and in 1991 into B'nai Brith's Sports Hall of Fame.[110]

Throughout his lifetime, Allen received many other awards and honors. In 1950 the people of New York held a Mel Allen Day at Yankee Stadium. He inundated him with gifts plus $14,000, a rather large sum of money at that time. Allen used the money to establish two scholarship funds, one at his alma mater, the University of Alabama, and the other at Columbia University. Any money Allen received from speaking engagements was immediately added to the scholarship funds, which he named in honor of Babe Ruth and Lou Gehrig.[111] In 1984 Allen's alma mater, Alabama's Farrah Law School, named a chair in his honor and in 1990 the State University of New York at Geneseo, celebrated the first annual Mel Allen Scholarship. Later, Allen called that night "among the most emotional of my life."[112]

Mel Allen gave much more than he received. He founded the ALS (Lou Gehrig Disease) Foundation. At various times he chaired fundraising drives for the American Legion, Boy Scouts of America, Cancer Fund, Children to Palestine Drive, Fight for Sight, Mickey Mantle Hodgkin's Foundation, Multiple Sclerosis, Muscular Dystrophy, the Police Athletic League, as well as Cerebral Palsy, and the United Jewish Appeal.[113] Most of his charity work was done without fanfare. He quietly visited orphanages, veterans' hospitals and even a yard full of inmates at the Indiana State Prison.[114]

Allen was also known for his efforts to promote harmony between Jews and Catholics. He developed a close friendship with Cardinal Francis Spellman, the Archbishop of New York. Spellman was an ardent baseball fan and he asked Mel to visit the homesick seminarians at the North American College in the Vatican. Mel turned the cardinal's request into an annual visit, often bringing highlight reels of the previous year's World Series to show the young men studying for the priesthood.[115]

By the mid–1990s Mel Allen's health began to decline. He was hospitalized in 1995, the same year Mickey Mantle died. Saddened by the loss of one of his favorite Yankees, he narrated a tribute to Mantle on *TWIB* August 18, 1995.[116] Allen intended to continue his show for the 1996 season, but he returned to the hospital that spring due to a heart condition. He had turned 83 on February 14, 1996, and by early June, he seemed to be doing well. He died, however, on June 16 at his home in Greenwich, Connecticut, apparently from his heart condition.[117]

The day following Allen's death, flags flew at half-staff at Yankee Stadium. Yankee players wore black armbands, lined up near their dugout, and placed their hats over their hearts. The scoreboard read, "So long, Mel, we'll miss you."[118]

Joe Torre, who had recently become Yankee skipper, recalled that in 1966 Mel Allen's voice was familiar to all the American troops in Vietnam. Yankee field announcer Bob Sheppard told the crowd at Yankee Stadium prior to the game, "May we ask you to spend a few moments in silent prayer as we remember Mel Allen, in his time the best-known announcer in America."

Services were held for Allen on June 19, 1996, at Temple Beth-El in Stamford, Connecticut. Rabbi Joshua Hammerman told the more than 600 mourners, "Mel Allen's life was one long, extended, exhaustive, triumphant prayer, a call to us to see the sublimities of the stolen sign or the first seasonal shifts of the wind." Rabbi Hammerman said that Mel Allen was a good, humble and sensitive man, a loving son who took care of his parents in their old age. He also noted, "Mel Allen is a resident of several Halls of Fame, but it didn't change him one bit.... May his voice continue to resonate through the heavens and through our souls, and may his gentle spirit be bound up in the web of life."[119]

Allen often referred to St. Patrick's Cathedral as "the Yankee Stadium of Churches." In November 1996, Cardinal John O'Connor, Archbishop of New York, honored Allen with a memorial at St. Patrick's Cathedral—a rare honor for a Jew.[120]

Sportscaster Suzyn Waldman, a female pioneer in a field dominated by men, sang both the national anthem and "America the Beautiful." She once introduced herself to Allen at a press conference, but Mel interrupted her and said, "I know who you are." After they chatted for a while, Allen told her that she had an intrinsic love for baseball and that she should not allow anyone to stop her. "He was a lovely man," said Waldman, "and I never forgot that he was so kind to me when most people weren't."[121]

On June 25, 1998, a commemorative plaque was placed in Monument Park in Yankee Stadium's center field, along with those of the greatest Yankee players and was moved to the Yankees' new ballpark when it opened in 2009.[122]

Mel Allen always modestly claimed that his fame was merely the result of good timing. Baseball was the most popular sport during his era and he was fortunate to have been associated with the Yankees in their heyday. He would never acknowledge that his success was a combination of his unique voice and the work he put into every situation.[123] Curt Gowdy, who probably knew Allen as well as anyone, summed up how people felt about Allen. "This was Mel Allen—a giant in our business and one of the most decent men you'll ever meet in your lifetime."[124]

8. The Class of 1965-66

The latter half of the decade of the 1960s continued many of the trends begun earlier. The United States became even more embroiled in the Vietnam War, and many college students began to protest American involvement in that conflict. Other groups were standing up for equal rights for both women and African-Americans.

Officially, anti–Semitism and acceptance of discrimination was declining, although traces of anti–Semitism could still be found in places, especially where Northern Jews had been active in civil rights action in the South.[1]

Some Jews in the United States became concerned about the rise in intermarriages involving Jews, fearful that this trend would weaken Jewish cultural ties. Others felt intermarriage showed the acceptance of Jews by non–Jews.[2] Until the 1960s, there had been just a handful of ballplayers with only one Jewish parent, but more children of mixed marriages entered the game in the 1960s and 1970s.[3]

Baseball in the 1960s was only peripherally affected by events in the country.[4] Art Shamsky, who starred for the New York Mets in 1969, noted, "I was caught up in my own world then, as a ballplayer. I was amazed at all the things that I didn't realize were going on, such as teachers' strikes, Vietnam War protests, and the killings of four student antiwar demonstrators at Kent State And I was here—New York was the Mecca—but I didn't realize the extent of what was going on."[5]

Only a handful of Jewish players entered the major leagues during the first half of the 1960s, and none of them made much of an impact on the game. They included Alan Koch, Conrad "Randy" Cardinal, Larry Yellen, and Steve Hertz.

Alan Koch

Alan Goodman Koch, a native of Alabama, was a big right-handed pitcher who appeared in a total of 10 games for the Detroit Tigers during the 1963 and 1964 seasons, finishing with the Washington Senators in 1964. He had been an excellent pitcher for his alma mater, Auburn University, and he spent three years in the minors pitching for Birmingham, Denver and Syracuse.[6] His record in Syracuse was outstanding: 11 wins and two losses with 131 strikeouts and an ERA of 3.36 in 126 innings. His major league stats are a 4–11 record and an ERA of 5.41.[7] After baseball, Koch returned to Alabama and became an attorney.

A native of Alabama and a graduate of Auburn University, Alan Koch was a big right-hander who played only two years in the majors, appearing in 42 games for the Tigers and Senators. Used mostly in relief, Koch finished his professional career with a record of 4 wins and 11 losses. His pitching percentage was .267 but his lifetime batting average was a respectable .286 (courtesy National Baseball Hall of Fame Library; Cooperstown, N.Y.).

Conrad Cardinal

All three of the other Jewish players who debuted in the first half of the 1960s played on Houston's new expansion club.

Conrad Seth "Randy" Cardinal was born in Brooklyn, March 30, 1942. He originally signed with the Detroit Tigers in 1962 after he graduated from high school in Long Island. Pitching in Class D ball at Jamestown of the New York–Pennsylvania League, he compiled a record of 14–7 before being sent to the Houston Colt .45s in 1963.[8] Cardinal arrived at the Colts' spring site fully expecting to return to the minor leagues, but he impressed Houston so much (his ERA during spring training was 1.69) that when the Colts broke camp, Cardinal stayed with the team. One local newspaper claimed, "Randy looked like the greatest find since uranium."[9]

Despite his showing in spring training, Cardinal appeared in only six games for Houston in 1963. He had a record of 0–1, with one save and his ERA was 6.08. He was sent back to the minors where he hurled for the Durham Bulls in 1964 and 1965. Following the 1965 season, Cardinal retired from baseball.[10]

Larry Yellen

Like Conrad Cardinal, Larry Yellen was a native of Brooklyn. Born January 4, 1943, he graduated from Lafayette High School, the same school that Sandy Koufax attended. Yellen often joked that he and Koufax had two things in common—they both graduated from the same high school and they were both Jewish.[11] Yellen attended Hunter College, pitching on its baseball team where he was named Most Valuable Player twice.[12]

He had a phenomenal senior year—in 61 innings he fanned 101 hitters and did not allow a single run. The Houston Colt .45s immediately signed him, and in 1963 they sent him to their San Antonio farm club.[13] His outstanding pitching at San Antonio (a 2.82 ERA in 18 games) earned him a promotion to the big leagues late in September. On September 27, 1963, Yellen was slated to make his major league debut against the New York Mets. "When my mom read in the *New York* Times," recalled Yellen, "that I was going to pitch on Yom Kippur, she called to ask me how I could disgrace the family."[14]

Out of respect for his family and Judaism, Yellen informed his manager, Harry Craft and his general manager, Paul Richards, that he could not pitch that day. In fact, he told them he would not even show up at the ballpark. Richards apologized to Yellen for sched-

uling him to pitch on the Day of Atonement, and his debut was moved up a day to
September 26. Yellen faced the Pirates in
his first and only game that year and pitched
five innings. The Colts won the game in 11
innings, 5–4, so Yellen did not figure in the
win.[15] His ERA for that game and for the
season was a solid 3.60.[16]

Yellen returned to the Houston lineup
in 1964 and pitched 13 games for the Colts,
including one start. That year, he also toiled
for Oklahoma City in the Pacific Coast
League. His lifetime major league ERA was
6.23.[17]

Before baseball, Yellen had attended
Hunter College, but he never received a
degree. In 1987 he enrolled at the State University of New York at Fredonia. He was
proud that he not only received his degree,
but also graduated with a 3.87 average,
summa cum laude.[18]

Steve Hertz

A teammate of Larry Yellen during
Yellen's second and final year in the majors,
Stephen Allan Hertz's entire major league

Pitcher Larry Yellen made 14 appearances in
the major leagues, all with Houston. He made
one appearance for the Houston Colt .45s in
1962 and thirteen appearances for the Houston
Astros in 1963. His entire major league career
consisted of 26 innings before he returned to
the minors (courtesy National Baseball Hall of
Fame Library; Cooperstown, N.Y.).

career consisted of five games in 1964 for the Houston Colt .45's. Born February 26, 1945,
at Wright Patterson Air Force Base in Fairfield, Ohio, Hertz moved to Miami with his family when he was a child. His father was not very religious, but his mother came from an
Orthodox Jewish family and pushed him into attending Hebrew School. This made it impossible for him to play little league ball until he was eleven years old. Hertz celebrated his bar
mitzvah in Miami.[19] The six-foot, one-inch bonus-baby third baseman was only 19 when he
debuted with Houston on April 21, 1964, replacing Bob Aspromonte. He struck out his first
time at bat. After one more game, Houston sent Hertz to the Durham Bulls in the Carolina
League. He did return to the majors later that year, but appeared in only three more games.
In the five games he played in the big leagues, Hertz scored two runs, but had no hits or
runs batted in.[20]

He spent the next five years playing in the minor leagues for Houston's and the Dodgers'
farm systems. He was surprised that in all the places he played, he found the strongest examples of both anti-black and anti–Semitism in Dubuque, Iowa.[21] In 1969 he was traded to
the Mets organization and played in the Florida State League.[22]

In 1969 Hertz also received his B.A. in physical education from the University of Miami,
and in 1978 earned a master's degree in administration and supervision. From 1970 through
1985, Hertz coached high school baseball, helping his teams win several state championships.
He began another highly successful coaching career in 1986 for Miami-Dade Community

College.[23] A number of the players he coached reached the major leagues, including Placido Polanco, Jamie Navarro, Omar Oliveras, Orestes Destrade, Orlando Palmeiro, Alex Sanchez, Edward Guzman, and Andres Torres.[24]

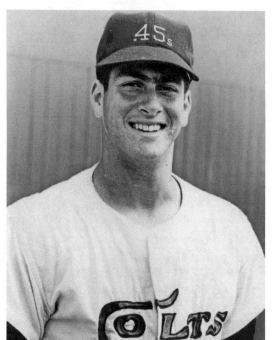

In 2007 Hertz was selected manager of the Tel-Aviv Lightning in the newly launched Israel Baseball League.[25] He considered the year he spent coaching in Israel "a phenomenal experience." The players ranged in age from high school to college age. It was a six-team league with players from nine countries including the United States, Canada, the Dominican Republic, Australia, and Israel. In addition to Hertz, the league also attracted former Jewish major leaguers Art Shamsky, Ken Holtzman and Ron Blomberg. Hertz called his time as coach one of the most exciting years of his life.

During the 1965 and 1966 seasons, several players made their major league debuts; some of them would play for a number of years and achieve a measure of success.

Steve Hertz's major league career consisted of five games at third base for the Houston Colt .45s in 1964. He was much more successful as head baseball coach, first at the high school level and for more than 20 years at Miami Dade College. The list of major league players he coached at Miami Dade include Placido Polanco, Orlando Palmeiro, Orestes Destrade, Jamie Navarro, and Omar Olivares (courtesy National Baseball Hall of Fame Library; Cooperstown, N.Y.).

Art Shamsky

Although Art Shamsky was a hero in New York, he was born in St. Louis where he lived for many years. The six-foot, one-inch outfielder possessed a loose-jointed walk and unbelievably powerful wrists. He began his professional baseball career in the minors in 1960; his home run totals in the AAA Pacific Coast League in both 1963 and 1964 caused the Cincinnati Reds to invite him to spring training in 1965.[26]

The gregarious, good-looking, and quick-witted outfielder made his team debut on April 17, 1965, and quickly established him as a very good left-handed pinch hitter.[27] The following year, platooning against right-handed pitchers, Shamsky clouted 21 home runs in 96 games, but could not get into the Reds regular lineup. His manager, Dave Bristol, noted, "You send him in to pinch hit and he hits. He hits home runs. You put him in the lineup regularly and he doesn't do anything."[28]

In 1966 Art Shamsky equaled a major league record when he smacked four home runs in four consecutive trips to the plate from August 12 through 14. The homer streak ended at four; Shamsky managed only a single in his fifth at-bat.[29] A few days later, the Hall of Fame asked the outfielder to send his bat to be enshrined in the Hall.[30] He was also honored by sharing the St. Louis Baseball Man-of-the-Year Award with Sonny Siebert, Cleveland Indians pitcher, who hurled the only no-hitter in 1966.[31]

The Cincinnati Reds, however, did nothing to commemorate his feat. Shamsky complained publicly about this omission. "Jim Maloney received a bonus for his no-hitter in 1965," Shamsky said, "and I think I deserve one for what I did."[32]

Shamsky had a poor year in 1967. He appeared in 76 games, hit only three home runs and batted .197.[33] Before the start of the 1968 season, Cincinnati traded the 25-year-old Shamsky to the New York Mets for infielder-outfielder Bob Johnson.[34] Shamsky called the trade a break. "I'm excited about going to the Mets," he said.[35] He was also pleased that the Mets intended to give him a tryout at first base in addition to the outfield. He had played both positions previously with the Reds.[36]

The 1968 season began with Shamsky on the disabled list and later optioned to Tidewater of the International League.[37] He did manage, however, to appear in 116 games for the Mets in 1968, hitting 12 home runs and ending the season with a .238 batting average.[38]

Shamsky began 1969 also on the disabled list with a back injury, but he finished the season with a .300 batting average. He had 91 hits, including 14 home runs, 9 doubles and 47 runs batted in. This was the year

Although Art Shamsky played with four teams during his eight-year major league career, he is best remembered for being a member of the "Amazing Mets" team of 1969 that won the World Series. When Shamsky joined the Mets, he became an instant hero to the Jewish community in New York; his .300 season batting average and his refusal to play on Yom Kippur merely added to his popularity (courtesy National Baseball Hall of Fame Library; Cooperstown, N.Y.).

of the Amazing Mets. They faced the Atlanta Braves in the National League Championship Series and Shamsky was outstanding at the plate—going 7–13 for a .538 average and helping boost the Mets to the National League pennant. They then defeated the heavily favored Baltimore Orioles, four games to one, to win the 1969 World Series.[39]

The New York Jewish community idolized Shamsky for his accomplishments. They also lauded his refusal to play on Yom Kippur during the pennant drive, taking abuse for missing a road trip to Pittsburgh that coincided with the Jewish High Holy Days. He recalled that the Mets won a doubleheader that day despite his absence.[40] Early in 1970, Shamsky was one of four Mets cited by the Sports Lodge of B'nai B'rith, for "high principle and achievement in sports in 1969."

Shamsky enjoyed his tenure with the New York Mets. "We had a terrific clubhouse," he recalled. "There were never any black-white problems. Nor did I ever have a problem because of my religion." He noted that when he was first traded to the Mets he was unhappy. "I was daunted by my new surroundings, New York City. Eventually, I fell in love with the energy, and I got to know the city a bit. My life changed."[41]

Nineteen seventy-one was another low point for Shamsky; his batting average dipped to .185 and he played in only 68 games. That fall, the Mets dealt Shamsky to his hometown team, the St. Louis Cardinals, in an eight-player deal. Shamsky went to spring training with the Cardinals in 1972, but before the season even got under way, the Cardinals released him.[42]

The Chicago Cubs had been searching for a left-handed pinch hitter for a long time and felt that they had found their man in Shamsky. In April 1972, the Cubs acquired Shamsky as a free agent and announced that they would option one of their pitchers to make room for him.[43]

Unfortunately, Shamsky was still suffering from back problems. He appeared in only 15 games for the Cubs, batting .125. He got two singles, his last hits as a major league ballplayer. After these 15 games, he was traded to the Oakland Athletics and appeared in eight games for the A's, but made only seven plate appearances. He got no hits during his stay in Oakland, and he was soon given his outright release.[44] While he was a member of the Oakland Athletics, he joined Mike Epstein and Ken Holtzman, which caused some one to quip, "There is now a rumor that Finley is trading the team chaplain for a team rabbi."[45]

Art Shamsky was only 30 years old when he retired from baseball, and 31 when he participated in his first Old-Timer's Game. He retired because he could not envision a future for himself as a full-time player and he did not want to be "bench strength."[46]

Shamsky was well prepared for life after baseball. He owned a group of restaurants, which he later sold. He also went into television as a color commentator for the Mets cable channel. In addition, Shamsky founded a business designed to produce information on various sports activities. "We give out opinions," explained Shamsky, "and we charge for them. It's done strictly on the telephone. I have consultants working for me who help me evaluate facts and figures."[47]

On April 3, 1994, Art Shamsky was inducted into the Jewish Sports Hall of Fame.[48]

Norman Miller

Norman Calvin Miller was born on February 5, 1946, in Los Angeles. He learned baseball at an early age from his father, who owned a drugstore in the city, and was an ardent fan of the game. "He was so much a fan of the game," noted his son, "that he would attend the World Series every year."[49]

Norman also played baseball growing up. At the age of eleven, he was the subject of a TV sports special about "kid baseball" narrated by Leo Durocher, at that time a CBS vice-president working in the television sports field. He commented about Miller, "You're going to see that kid at third base in the major leagues some day." Miller reminded him of the prediction years later when Leo managed the Astros and Miller was one of his players.[50]

Miller idolized his hometown Dodgers and skipped school so he could see the 1962 playoff games between the Dodgers and the San Francisco Giants. After graduating from Van Nuys High School in 1964, Miller immediately signed with the Los Angeles Angels as a free agent. He was assigned to the Quad Cities in the Midwest League where he played second base and had a .301 batting average. Miller played just one season in the minor leagues before the Houston Astros drafted him and sent him to Amarillo where he led the AA Texas League with 89 bases on balls. He also had 20 homers and drove in 92 runs.

Late in the 1965 season he reported to Dodger Stadium where he debuted on September 11, 1965, with a pinch-hit single for the Astros. He appeared in 10 more games for Houston that year, hitting .200. Miller was back in the minors at the start of the 1966 season; he then rejoined Houston to play the outfield in 11 more games. Miller batted only .147, but got his first major league home run.[51]

Despite his lack of major league experience, the future for the five-foot, ten-inch Miller, looked bright. Not only was he very speedy, but the legendary Casey Stengel, who saw Miller early in his career, once described him as having "the sweetest swing in baseball."[52]

Miller began both 1967 and 1968 playing with AAA Oklahoma City. In 1967 he also spent some time in the military reserves. During his games with Houston in 1967, he platooned with outfielder Ron Davis in left field, and his manager Grady Hatton was impressed with his defensive improvement. Two of his teammates on the 1967 Astros were Jewish— pitchers Barry Latman and Larry Sherry.[53]

Miller was up and down again in the 1968 season but got an opportunity to make his mark on baseball history. On April 15, 1968, the Astros and the New York Mets played the longest night game and shutout in major league history. Norman Miller led off the bottom of the twenty-fourth inning with a single, his first hit in eight at bats; he went to second on a balk. When Bob Aspromonte's ground ball was misplayed by shortstop Al Weis, Miller scored, ending the six-hour-and-six-minute game with a win for the Astros, 1–0.[54]

Norman Miller had a ten-year major league career as a member of the Houston Astros and the Atlanta Braves between 1965 and 1974. As a native of Los Angeles, he had always dreamed of playing for his home town team, the Dodgers. That dream almost became a reality when the Dodgers signed him prior to the start of the 1975 season, but a back injury ended his career at the age of twenty-nine (courtesy of Norm Miller).

In October of that year, Miller was married just after breaking his ankle crashing into the wall at the Astrodome. His injury came at an inopportune time, as his hitting against major league pitching was better than it had ever been before. Despite his injury, the Astros still considered Miller a top prospect to fill one of the regular outfield jobs for 1969.[55]

Miller received the most playing time in his major league career in 1969 when he appeared in 119 games and hit .264. He made no trips to the minors that year and even was on the field when two Astro pitchers, Jim Maloney and Don Wilson, threw consecutive no-hitters.[56]

He also surprised his teammates that year by announcing he would never again play on a Jewish holiday. Miller, who had earlier stated that he did not participate in organized religion, explained that he had played on both days of Rosh Hashanah previously and had gone 0–9 in the two games.[57]

In 1970, Maury Wills picked Norman Miller as one of the National League's most underrated players. "I have to pick Norm Miller," stated Wills, "Houston's young right-fielder, even though he has had only one real good year. He hustles, he throws well, fields well, and he gets the bat on the ball most of the time. Walter Alston thinks he is Houston's toughest out."[58] Wills might also have mentioned that Norman Miller was one Houston's sports media favorites because he always cooperated with them.[59]

Despite Wills' endorsement and Miller's performance in 1969, from 1970 through 1972 Miller played in a total of just 202 games. In only one of those three years was his average above .250. However, as a pinch hitter, he hit .300 all three years.[60] Miller demanded that the Astros play him regularly or trade him. At the beginning of 1970, he stated, "I'm 24 and I can't see where I'm making progress if I'm not in the lineup."[61] Later that spring, Miller had a talk with Houston manager Harry Walker, and he changed his tune. "I'm a happy ball player again, and I even would be content to be platooned."[62] By the end of the 1970 season, Miller had decided to accept the situation with the Astros and try to do what he could to help himself. As one Astro official stated, "Norm has gone through the 'play-me-or-trade-me bit.'"[63]

During spring training in 1973, the Astro players selected Norman as their player representative. In those years, the head of the players' union, Marvin Miller, always toured the training camps. Houston's manager, Leo Durocher, who was anti-union and disliked Marvin Miller intensely, took only non-regular players to games where the meeting with Marvin Miller was to take place. Durocher wanted to make sure the regular players and the union head would not get together. Despite knowing Durocher as a child, Norman Miller was quick to state, "I never did care for Leo, and I was not sorry that the Astros traded me in the spring of 1973."[64]

Norman Miller and a player to be named later were sent to the Atlanta Braves for relief pitcher Cecil Upshaw.[65] Miller's back and shoulder injuries limited his playing time in 1973 to only twelve games, but as a pinch-hitter, he got ten hits and hit .323 in a Braves' uniform.[66]

In 1974, Miller appeared in only 42 games with the Braves and hit below .200. His one highlight for that year was his presence on the team when Hank Aaron broke Babe Ruth's lifetime home run record.[67] "My locker was next to Aaron's," recalled Miller. "He was a great guy, and although he received death threats as he got closer to breaking Ruth's record, he just accepted all the hate. It was a huge honor just being on the same team with him."[68]

Miller became a free agent following the 1974 campaign, and he signed with the Los Angeles Dodgers after the team sold outfielder Von Joshua to the San Francisco Giants. Manager Walt Alston, who had long been a fan of Norman Miller, had general manager Al Campanis call Miller early in 1975 to offer him a contract. After he passed his physical, Miller reported to the Dodgers' spring training camp. Miller had started to learn how to catch to improve his chances of receiving more playing time. When the Dodgers signed him, they intended to use him as a left-handed pinch-hitter, reserve outfielder, and third string catcher.[69]

"Unfortunately for me," said Miller, "my back injury recurred and this ended my playing career at the age of twenty-nine."[70] He had appeared in 540 games during his ten-season major league career, with a lifetime batting average of .238. Miller, however, was more valuable as a pinch-hitter; for his on-base percentage was .323.[71]

After he retired from baseball, Miller became Director of Advertising Sales and Promotions for the Houston Astros from 1987 to 1993. He also became active in the Greater Houston Sports Association. "The Braves and I discussed my managing in their minor league system, but I told them I was not interested in remaining in the game."[72] A few years later Miller became director of baseball operations at the University of Houston.

Greg Goossen

Although Gregory Bryan Goossen was one of the Jewish players who entered major league baseball in 1965, he only had a limited number of highlights in his six-year career in the majors. Goossen was another Los Angeles native, born December 13, 1945, the son of a Jewish father of Russian origin and a Christian mother. Goossen, a six-foot, one-inch, 210-pound athlete at Notre Dame High School, like Norman Miller, turned professional immediately after graduating from high school in 1964. He was offered four athletic scholarships but opted to sign with the Los Angeles Dodgers instead.[73]

The contract Goossen signed stipulated that if he did not make the Dodgers in one year, he would be placed on waivers. Goossen agreed, and the Dodgers assigned the young catcher to Pocatello where he led the Pioneer League in putouts with 316. The Dodgers then promoted him to St. Petersburg in the Florida State League, but he never made the Dodgers squad that year. LA placed him on waivers in the spring of 1965.[74]

The New York Mets quickly claimed Goossen and sent him to their Class A team at Auburn where his .305 batting average was fifth-highest in the New York–Penn League. He was voted the Most Valuable Player and a member of the All-Star team. The Mets rewarded his fine play at Auburn by bringing him to the majors near the end of the 1965 season. He debuted on September 3 and played in 11 games that year, hitting safely nine times in 31 at-bats for a .290 average.[75] Met manager Wes Westrum thought he had found the answer to his team's catching problems in young Greg Goossen.[76]

From 1966 through 1968, Goossen's career followed the same pattern. He would play briefly for the Mets, then be demoted to the minors, and brought back to the majors at the tail end of the season. One of the clubs he caught for in the Met's minor league system was Jacksonville in the International League. While at Jacksonville, Goossen caught a young pitcher, destined to be inducted into Baseball's Hall of Fame—Tom Seaver. That was Seaver's only stint in the minors.[77]

In his four-year tenure with the Mets, Goossen appeared in fewer than 100 games, catching 42, and playing first base in 30. He hit safely 48 times.[78]

In 1969 the Mets traded Goossen to the new Seattle Pilots where he had the best season of his career. He played 52 games, belted ten homers, and hit .309 with a slugging percentage of .597. Goossen holds the Pilots' records for the highest batting average, most pinch home runs (1), most total bases in a game (10), and most assists by a first baseman in a game (1). All of his home runs were hit in Seattle's Sick's Stadium.[79]

When the Pilots became the Milwaukee Brewers in 1970, Goossen moved with the team, but he appeared in only 21 games. Late in the season, the Washington Senators bought Goossen. In the District of Columbia, he again appeared in only 21 games for the Senators and his average was .222.[80]

In November, the Senators sent Goossen to the Philadelphia Phillies to complete the Curt Flood deal with Washington. The Phils had acquired three players from the Senators in exchange for Flood, and Goossen was one of the three selected. Despite the transaction, Goossen never appeared in a major league uniform after 1970.[81]

Goossen's life off the field was actually more unusual than on the diamond. During the off-season, he worked as a private detective and continued that profession when he retired from baseball. Goossen also had a minor acting career, appearing in bit parts in the movies *Get Shorty*, *Under Suspicion* (2000), and *The Royal Tenenbaums* (2001).[82]

Richie Scheinblum

Richard Alan Scheinblum was the only Jewish major league switch hitter to hit .300 in a season. He was also one of only a few players to star on three different continents.[83]

Scheinblum was born November 5, 1942, the second of five children, in a very poor section of the Bronx. His father was a CPA and his mother, who died when Richie was very young, had come to the United States from the Ukraine. Richie and his brother lived with their uncle for a few years after their mother's death, and Richie remembers that he and his brother regularly attended the shul at the end of their street. "Although my grandfather spoke only Yiddish, I just know a couple of words. I always attended synagogue on the High Holydays. I'm a good Jew, other than getting some of the formalities. Some day I even hope to get Bar Mitzvah."[84]

Although Scheinblum lived near Yankee Stadium, he never saw a big-league game until he played in one. "I never went when I lived in the Bronx," recalled Scheinblum. "We lived in the slum areas of the Bronx and I couldn't afford to attend the games. Admission price was three weeks' worth of food."[85]

When Richie was seven, his father remarried, and the family moved to Englewood, New Jersey. He began playing Little League baseball across the street from his home, and he admits that one of the greatest influences on his career was a woman—his coach Janet Murke. She advised Scheinblum, who was naturally a right-handed hitter, to become a switch-hitter. Scheinblum noted years later that statistically, he was much better hitting left-handed.[86] "She was a great coach, took good care of me, and she could hit, also," recalls Scheinblum.[87]

Richie Scheinblum is the only Jewish switch-hitter to hit .300 in a season. During his eight-year career in the majors, Scheinblum played for six different organizations, five in the American League and one in the National League. During the final two years of his career, Scheinblum played for the Hiroshima Carp of the Japanese Central League, making him the first Jew to play baseball in Japan. He was forced to retire in 1976 after he tore his Achilles tendon (courtesy of Richie Scheinblum; Hall of Fame disc, courtesy National Baseball Hall of Fame Library; Cooperstown, N.Y.).

Scheinblum was a three-sport athlete in high school and became an outfielder on his high school baseball team. He had a few conditional scholarships to college, but lost them because he scored low on his college boards, especially English. He graduated high school in 1960 and was determined to play professional baseball. His father had other ideas. "You're going to college," he insisted."[88]

Richie ultimately enrolled at C.W. Post College in Greenvale, New York. Scheinblum laughingly said, "In those days, I think all you had to do was fog a mirror and you got in." He graduated, however, with a degree in business administration in 1964, one year before the free agent draft was initiated. He even managed to complete a year of his MBA.[89]

A year before he graduated college, Scheinblum played semi-pro baseball for Bloomington in the Central Illinois Collegiate League where he batted .287 in 44 games. He caught the eye of scout and former American League star "Hoot" Evers, who was employed by the Cleveland Indians. Evers signed Scheinblum to a $12,000 minor league contract. Scheinblum played in Bloomington again in 1964. Although he hit .309 for the year, he did not hit with power, so he decided to spend the off-season swinging a sledgehammer to strengthen his hands.[90]

Scheinblum played on teams and in leagues where they never had seen a Jewish player. His roommate in his first year of organized ball, who came from the hills of North Carolina, called his parents to tell them that he had met a Jewish person who had neither horns nor a tail. "I just thought that was funny," recalled Scheinblum.[91]

Late in the 1965 season, Scheinblum was one of five players the Indians recalled from the minor leagues. He made his major league debut with Cleveland on September 1, 1965, in Kansas City as a pinch runner in the seventh inning. He appeared in three more games that year.[92]

Scheinblum spent the entire 1966 season in the minors. During the winter of 1966 and 1967 Scheinblum played in the Nicaraguan League in the midst of the revolution in Nicaragua. "My home run in the seventh and deciding game won the playoffs for the team of dictator Samoza," said Richie. "The revolution started that day and we heard shooting all night. Armed Forces Radio said it was a minor political demonstration, but it was a lot worse than that."[93]

In 1967 Scheinblum spent most of his playing time in the minors. He did manage to play 18 games for the Indians that year, and he hit .318.[94]

Indian officials hoped that 1968 would be the year Scheinblum would be ready to live up to his annual advance notices. Since 1964 he had been called "the apple of the farm system's eye," but he still had problems defensively; he especially seemed to have trouble getting a jump on fly balls.[95]

Scheinblum played in the farm system at Portland for the bulk of the 1968 season and he was again brought up by the Indians near the end of the year.[96]

In addition to his defense, Scheinblum was also aware of a second deficiency—notoriously slow starts. He would turn in poor to mediocre stats at the beginning of every season. On one occasion he noted, "Aprils kill me. I shouldn't show up until May." In 1968 at Portland, he batted below .200 for the first month, but came on to finish at .304.[97]

Indian manager Alvin Dark indicated that 1969 might be Scheinblum's last chance. "I'm going to play him in right field every day and find out just what he can do," said Dark. "It will be up to him."[98]

Dark kept his word. Nineteen-sixty-nine was Scheinblum's most complete year in the majors for the Indians. He appeared in 102 games, but managed to hit only .186. He got his first major league home run the same day the U.S. astronauts first landed on the moon, July 20, 1969.[99]

During the winters from 1969 to 1971, Scheinblum established himself in South America as one of the stars in the Venezuelan League. At the same time, in the winter of 1969, the Indians sent Scheinblum outright to Wichita in the American Association.[100]

Scheinblum spent the entire 1970 season at Wichita where he appeared to find himself by having an excellent year, batting .337 and leading the league in runs, hits, and total bases. Named to the league's All-Star team and the All-Star team of the Class AAA-East, he was also voted the league's Topps Player of the Year and his team's MVP.[101]

By the spring of 1971 he had been traded to the Washington Senators managed by Ted Williams. He spent spring training with the Senators and six weeks of the regular season. Scheinblum benefited from Williams' hitting tips. "He taught me how to think while I'm at bat."[102] Despite the tutelage, he got off to his usual slow start, hitting only .143. He spent most of that season with the Denver Bears in the American Association where he again compiled excellent stats. His .388 batting average was the highest since Harry Walker hit .391 for Columbus and 51 points higher than his nearest competitor. In the playoffs, Richie led Denver to victory with two home runs and made a sensational throw home from right field to cut down the tying run.[103]

After the completion of the 1971 season, Scheinblum's options had been all used up. This meant that Washington could not repurchase him unless he first passed through waivers or the major league draft in December.[104]

In 1972 the Kansas City Royals had long been searching for batting punch, and they purchased Scheinblum.[105] Richie Scheinblum finally found success. He appeared in 134 games, the most in his eight-year major league career. As one of the Royals' regular outfielders he led the American League in hitting for five months. Although he eventually lost the title to Rod Carew, his .300 batting average was sixth-highest in the American League that year.[106] He was selected to represent the Royals at the All-Star Game in Atlanta, and he also had career highs in home runs (8), runs batted in (66), and every other hitting category.[107]

The media loved to interview him because of his good-natured sense of humor and his reputation for being offbeat. When asked what he thought when he saw his name in the top 10, Scheinblum replied, "That maybe it's a misprint." A reporter wanted to know what happened the first time he was traded. He replied, "The Indians sent me to the Washington Senators for money and a player to be named later. A month and a half later I think they tried to make me the player to be named later." Finally, when asked what he planned to do when his playing days were over, he replied, "Why, have you heard something?"[108]

Despite Scheinblum's achievements in 1972, the Royals traded him to the Cincinnati Reds that winter. Reds manager Sparky Anderson stated, "Richie isn't walking into a regular job with us. We're simply going to wait and see how he fits in."[109]

Scheinblum was not elated when Anderson intimated that he was going to battle Cesar Geronimo for the starting job in right field. "I just hope I get a fair shot at it," he said. "I don't want to sit on the bench. If I sit and hit .210, my career will be down the drain."[110]

After appearing in 29 games with the Reds in 1973 and hitting only .222, Scheinblum was traded for the fifth time in four years. As he was packing his bags to go to the California Angels, he took a parting shot at the Reds. "I was given no chance at all. It was ridiculous. This is probably the best thing they've done for me."

Angels manager Bobby Winkles said Scheinblum would start as a pinch-hitter "and play some of the time. He'll have to work his way into the lineup."[111] The trade to the Angels had at least one benefit; it reunited Richie with Jewish first baseman Mike Epstein. The two had briefly been roommates with the Senators in 1971, and Epstein was the first Angel Scheinblum saw when he arrived at the park.[112]

Changing teams so often certainly did not affect Scheinblum's sense of humor. His second hit as an Angel was a home run off Yankee starter Pat Dobson. Maintaining his reputation as one of baseball's flakiest characters, he told his teammates in the dugout with a straight face, "I'm only 703 behind the Babe. I haven't been in a home run trot in so long I forgot to notice it."[113]

Scheinblum appeared in 77 games with the Angels in 1973, hitting .328. When he went to spring training in 1974 manager Bobby Winkles promised him, "I'm going to make a good outfielder out of you or kill you."[114] Scheinblum worked hard in spring training, but according to his usual pattern, he had a miserable April start with the Angels, hitting only .154.[115] At the end of April the Angels traded Scheinblum back to the Kansas City Royals for their third baseman, Paul Schaal.[116]

In his second stint with the Royals, Scheinblum played only 36 games before he was traded across the state to the St. Louis Cardinals late in the season. He was sent to the Cardinals' Tulsa farm club until he was recalled in September along with catcher Marc Hill, first baseman Keith Hernandez and two young outfielders, Larry Herndon and Jerry Mumphrey.[117] St. Louis was Scheinblum's last major league team. He hit .333 in the six games in which he appeared.[118]

The Cardinals traded him to the Los Angeles Dodgers, but he told St. Louis that he could not play for the Dodgers because he had hated them while he was growing up. He asked for his release to go to Japan and play ball there. Scheinblum joined the Hiroshima Carp of the Japanese Central League, making him the first Jew to play baseball in Japan.[119] He also was the first player in the Japanese leagues to hit home runs from both sides of the plate in a single game.[120]

Scheinblum played two seasons in Japan—1975 and 1976. He had hoped to return in 1977, but he tore an Achilles tendon playing basketball in the off-season and was incapacitated for eight months. Scheinblum finally retired from baseball.[121]

While playing in Japan, Scheinblum sat out a game on Yom Kippur for the first time in his baseball career. During his years in the majors, he never had had to make that choice, but he indicated he would not have played on Yom Kippur even if it had become an issue. In trying to explain Yom Kippur to the Japanese, he told reporters that Yom Kippur was the one day of the year he had his one-on-one with God and he atoned for his sins.[122]

In 1992, the last year before the Rockies became a major league team, Scheinblum was honored by Denver for the records he had set in 1971. He never lost his enthusiasm for the game. "I think I could have played in the era behind me and the era ahead of me. I had fun. I would have done it again," he said.[123]

Mike Epstein

Michael Peter Epstein, known for his home run prowess, was the last Jewish player in the Class of 1965-1966 to make his debut in the major leagues and the most aggressively Jewish of the group. The second of three children, Epstein was born April 4, 1943, in the Bronx, in a Jewish neighborhood, but moved to Long Island when he was five. When Mike was 15, his father Jack, a salesman, moved the family to Los Angeles for business reasons. Jack was a native of Toronto while Mike's mother, Evelyn, a stay-at-home mom, was a native New Yorker.[124]

Mike went to Fairfax High School in Los Angeles, the same school Barry Latman and

the Sherry brothers attended. He played both football and basketball at Fairfax and graduated in 1961. Growing up in the city's Jewish Fairfax section, Mike always felt different from
his peers who "didn't have the same desires that I had to excel in sports. They would end
up excelling in a lot of other things—business, medical professions; you know they were
professional people. Me, I wanted to be a ballplayer."[125]

Jack Epstein did not share his son's ambitions and, as a result, Mike enrolled at the
University of California at Berkeley where he played both football and baseball, majoring
in social psychology. The muscular, 230 pound, six-foot, three-and-one-half-inch star fullback for the football team and star first baseman chose baseball over football because baseball was more of an individual challenge.[126] As a junior, Epstein hit .375 and was offered a
contract by the Los Angeles Dodgers. Mike's father refused to sign it. "He wanted me to be
a lawyer rather than a bum like the rest of the ballplayers." At the least, Mr. Epstein
demanded that his son first complete his bachelor's degree so that he would have "something to fall back on."[127]

Mike won the argument and left school after three years of college, signing a bonus
contract with the Baltimore Orioles, estimated to be around $5,000.[128]

Epstein began his professional career at Stockton in the California League in 1965 and
got off to an auspicious start. He led the league in both hitting and home runs, and was
selected the league's Most Valuable Player and Rookie of the Year. He hit .338 and clouted
30 homers.[129] In 1966 he was promoted to the Orioles' AAA team, Rochester, in the International League, where he was named that league's Most Valuable Player and Rookie of the
Year.[130]

While playing for Stockton, Epstein had penciled a Star of David on his glove, and
after he hit a home run, his manager, Rocky Bridges, dubbed him SuperJew, a nickname
suggestive of earlier sobriquets such as "The Yiddish Curver," Barney Pelty's nickname, or
"The Rabbi of Swat," a name given to Mose Solomon. Epstein was never offended by the
nickname and took pride in it. However, he felt, "I don't think there's a Super Jew or a
Super Christian or a Super Negro. If there was anybody, it had to be Sandy Koufax or Hank
Greenberg."[131]

Like many minor league stars, Epstein was called up to the parent club late in the 1966
season. He appeared in six games and had two hits in 11 at-bats for an average of .182.[132]
The *Baltimore Jewish Times'* headline trumpeted his arrival in a headline reading, "The Orioles Hank Greenberg." Earl Weaver, Oriole manager, said, "He's the best prospect I've ever
seen."[133] The Orioles played the Dodgers in the 1966 World Series, but Epstein was ineligi-
ble to play since he was not on the team by the September 1 deadline.

In 1966 Epstein won *The Sporting News* Minor League Player of the Year Award, the
ninth award Epstein had won in only two years of professional ball. American League
observers fully expected Epstein to "crack the big time" in 1967.[134]

The pressure was on Epstein to succeed in the major leagues. Oriole manager Hank
Bauer wanted one thing from Epstein—consistency with the bat. "I'm not about to take
Powell off first base," growled Bauer. "If Epstein is going to make this team, he's going to
have to beat out Curt Blefary for the third outfield spot."[135]

Because he resembled Mickey Mantle in coloring, facial expression and size, some began
to call him "The Jewish Mickey Mantle." Epstein felt that it was his stance that made him
resemble the Yankee slugger. "I grew up in the Bronx," said Epstein, "and I used to go to a
lot of Yankee games. I guess I subconsciously copied Mantle's stance. You do a lot of things
subconsciously, you know. I only hope that some day I can hit even a little bit like him."[136]

Epstein played nine games in 1967 before the Orioles realized he was not ready yet to play in the major leagues.[137] Baltimore ordered him to report to their AAA farm club, Rochester. However, Epstein refused. He informed the team that he intended to return to California, enroll at the University of the Pacific in Stockton where he would finish the two semesters he needed to obtain his degree in social psychology.[138]

General Manager Harry Dalton argued that Epstein needed to play every day and that he simply could not do this with the Orioles. "Our position is that he could further himself by playing at Rochester.... If he's playing there at a major league salary with a chance to come back, I don't think you could say he is stymied." Epstein claimed that all he wanted to do was to provide a means for him and his family to get ahead in the world.[139]

After unsuccessfully trying to get Epstein to accept a roster spot at Rochester, the Orioles announced in late May that Baltimore had traded him and pitcher Frank Bertaina to the Washington Senators for Pitcher Pete Richert.[140] Epstein said he was "stunned" at the trade. "Who wouldn't be? All I want is a chance to play, to prove or disprove myself. I'm elated it turned out this way."[141]

Few Jewish major leaguers took more pride in their Jewish heritage than Mike Epstein. Dubbed "SuperJew" by one of his minor league coaches, Epstein got a kick out of the title, and began marking it on his baseball equipment including his hat, his glove, and some of his bats. The name caught on and during his nine years in the majors, it was often used in a positive way by both fans and reporters (courtesy National Baseball Hall of Fame Library; Cooperstown, N.Y.).

Washington manager Gil Hodges said he contacted Epstein and indicated that he was "pleased" with his rookie's attitude. "Mike seemed real eager," noted Hodges, "and I want to install him as our regular first baseman as soon as he gets into shape."[142]

With his new team, Mike Epstein hit his first major league home run, a fly ball that skipped into the crazy angles alongside the stands in Yankee Stadium and ended up being an inside-the-park homer. [143] Epstein felt the most satisfying hit in 1967 was his first at-bat against his former club, the Baltimore Orioles. He hit a grand slam.[144]

Epstein was well liked by his teammates who were impressed by his intellect. Jim Murray, writing in the *Los Angeles Times*, noted tongue-in-cheek that Epstein's vocabulary was so extensive that he used some words not heard in general conversation since Chaucer. He considered his team a "peer group," referred to the curve ball as a "subterfuge," and when a pitcher threw a home run hitter a fastball right over the plate, Epstein would prefer to think "our pitcher behaved illogically with concomitant unrealized goals."[145]

Epstein's teammates were impressed by his ability to quote Socrates and Emerson and the fact that they were in the presence of a scholar with muscles. When he was asked whether "SuperJew" was spelled as one or two words, he answered, "Well, you spell Superman with one word." He was never offended when the press referred to him as a "SuperJew." In fact, he considered it a compliment. Except for one incident involving Billy Martin, Epstein could not recall experiencing any anti–Semitism during his baseball career.[146] He felt there was a reason for that. "I think the Jewish players in the 40s and 50s absorbed the brunt of it, blazed a trail for us. I really didn't notice anything," Epstein said. "Of course, I was a lot bigger than the average player, too, so they probably wouldn't have said anything to my face."[147]

Epstein also noted one other difference in the treatment of Jewish players of his era and those who preceded him. He remembered that in all the towns in which he played, Jewish organizations paid almost no attention to him. He never had a "night" at the ballpark, which was so common for journeymen Jewish players a generation earlier. When he and his teammate Ken Holtzman helped the Athletics win a pennant in 1972, there was no response at all from the local Jewish community.[148]

Still, Epstein always remembered the Jewish home in which he grew up where the tradition was alive. He also never forgot that he was a "survivor among a people of survivors." Concerned that it could happen again, Epstein admitted that he always stood ready to "fight you for who I am."[149]

Epstein played 96 games for the Senators in 1967 and in 284 plate appearances, he had 64 hits for an average of .226. The following year he played for a new manager, Jim Lemon, who looked to Epstein to help the Senators improve their sixth-place finish.[150] In June 1968, Epstein's batting average was .099, and the Senators decided to option him to their Buffalo farm club in the International League. Lemon promised that Epstein would be back with the parent club by June, and this time Epstein accepted the demotion. "I hope to get straightened out," he said. "I was not helping the club." Before he left for Buffalo, Lemon and Epstein had a heart-to-heart talk and agreed that his problem was a complete inability to hit left-handers.[151]

As promised, the Senators recalled Epstein from Buffalo in June. At the time, Epstein was hitting .400 at Buffalo, and Senator manager Lemon indicated that Frank Howard, home run leader in the American League, would be shifted to left field so that Epstein could take over at first base.[152] As the 1968 season progressed, Epstein altered both his attitude and his batting stance. He took Lemon's advice and moved back six inches from the plate. Washington general manager George Selkirk, who had played for the New York Yankees from 1934 to 1942, also noticed the change in Epstein and commented, "Epstein has every attribute of a fine hitter—fast arms, fast hands and good reflexes. I just wish I had been as strong."[153]

Epstein played 123 games for Washington in 1968, but despite the changes, he did not have a very good year offensively. He hit only .234 with 13 home runs and 33 RBIs.[154] Jim Lemon's Senators ended the season in tenth place, winning 65 games and losing 96.[155]

In 1969 the Senators replaced Lemon as their pilot with former Red Sox slugger Ted Williams. Williams managed Epstein for a little over two years, and he would constantly tell the press, "That's my prodigy. That Epstein ought to hit 40 home runs a year."[156] Although Epstein never had a 40-home run season for Williams, 1969 was definitely his best year in the majors. Williams tutored him throughout spring training and after he watched Epstein take a few cuts, Williams said Epstein's chief fault was that Mike was trying to hit a 450-foot home run every time he swung. "A 380-foot homer is just as good," Williams reasoned.[157]

Epstein finished the 1969 season with a batting average of .278, the highest he would hit in his nine-year major league career. He also clubbed 30 home runs, hitting three in one game on May 16.[158] Whenever the Senators played at Yankee Stadium, there was always trade gossip concerning Epstein. It seemed he was just what the Yankees needed to re-attract New York fans who were gravitating towards the Mets—a nice Jewish boy from the Bronx who could hit the ball into the bleachers. Epstein admitted that the thought of being traded to the Yankees was not completely distasteful. "I like it fine in Washington," he stated, "but there are worse places to be than in New York."[159]

Epstein had a relatively good season in 1970. Although his manager, Ted Williams, liked Epstein, he decided his first baseman had too much trouble hitting left-handed pitching and he platooned him, much to Epstein's dismay. Throughout the 1970 season, whispers that Epstein was "on the block" were heard everywhere.[160] Despite the trade rumors, Epstein remained with the Senators the entire 1970 season. He hit .256 in 140 games, clouted 20 home runs and drove in 56 runs.[161]

After he played in 24 games for the Senators in 1971, Washington finally traded Epstein to the Oakland Athletics in a five-player swap for A's first baseman Don Mincher, catcher Frank Fernandez, and pitcher Paul Lindblad. In addition to Epstein, Washington gave up relief pitcher Darold Knowles.[162] There was no ill feeling between Epstein and Washington's front office. Owner Bob Short put his arms around Epstein's huge shoulders and called him, "My son." At a news conference, Epstein said that Ted Williams "has helped me more than anybody I ever played for. And Bob Short is the greatest owner in baseball."[163]

Epstein might have had kind words for his former bosses, but he could not hide his elation at getting traded to a contending team. He played 104 games for the A's in 1971 and although he batted only .234, he drove in 51 runs and hit 18 home runs. In an amazing turnaround, he was so effective with the A's against lefty relievers that he played against both southpaws and right-handed pitchers. "You take more pride with a first-place club," he said. "You people have to remember that I was down for years with Washington. We just never had the chance to do things in Washington. Things are falling into place with me and all I know is that I'm helping the club."[164]

He was proud that he tied Shamsky's record for four consecutive home runs. Interestingly, he tied the record against his old club, the Senators.[165] The A's did manage to reach the American League Championship Series, but lost to the Orioles, 3–0. Epstein went 1-for-5 in the series.[166]

But Epstein could become sullen at times. He was unhappy when he was not hitting, ascribed his low average to mental fatigue, and felt he had the ability to make himself into a winning player.[167] He resented being asked repeatedly the question, "How come a nice Jewish boy like you plays games for a living?" He gave the same answer for a while until he tired of the question, "There's no such thing as a 'nice Jewish boy like you.'"[168]

In 1972 the Athletics' roster included two Jewish players in addition to Mike Epstein— Ken Holtzman and Art Shamsky. A third, Joe Horlen, later converted to Judaism. The year 1972 began with the first full players' strike, which lasted ten days.[169] Epstein got off to a slow start in 1972, but soon "got in the groove." It was an interesting year. It seemed that Epstein played better when angry and playing for owner Charles Finley and manager Dick Williams gave him numerous occasions to lose his temper.

In a game on June 17, Epstein hit an infield pop fly and failed to run to first base. Manager Williams immediately pulled Epstein out of the game. On the following day the humiliated Epstein homered to enable Vida Blue to win his first game of the season. The next day he went two-for-four and drove in four runs.

There was also bad feeling when Oakland obtained Orlando Cepeda and indicated

Cepeda might play first base against southpaws. Finally, Epstein and his manager got into a shouting match on a plane bound for Oakland. Epstein was upset with Williams for removing him for a pinch runner.[170]

Epstein's squabbles with his bosses did not deter him from having a relatively good year in 1972. In 138 games, he hit .270, with 26 home runs and 70 runs batted in.[171] The A's met the Detroit Tigers in the American League Championship Series and defeated them three games to two. Epstein hit only .166 in the series although he did walk four times and scored one run. The A's went on to defeat the Cincinnati Reds in seven games in the World Series. Epstein appeared in six of the seven games but went hitless in 16 trips to the plate.[172]

Very few Jewish players were more openly proud of their Jewish heritage than Mike Epstein. On September 5, 1972, eleven Israeli athletes were slaughtered at the Olympics in Munich by a group known as "Black September." Epstein convinced his Oakland teammate, Ken Holtzman, to wear a black armband on his A's uniform the remainder of the season in memory of the deceased athletes. Even Reggie Jackson who was not Jewish joined out of respect to the fallen Olympians. "It hit us like a ton of bricks last night," Epstein said. "Of course, Ken and I are Jewish, but I'd feel the same way if it was any other team. The Olympics are supposed to foster international brotherhood."[173]

Whether it was retaliation against Epstein's wearing an armband or whether Finley had no more patience with his continuous wrangling, the A's traded Epstein to the Texas Rangers at the end of the 1972 season. In return the A's obtained relief pitcher Horacio Pina. Epstein once more was playing for his friend from Washington, Bob Short, who now owned the Texas Rangers.[174]

Epstein's new manager at Texas was Whitey Herzog. Herzog had heard of the feuds Epstein had with management at Oakland, but this was of no concern to the Rangers skipper. "His reputation doesn't interest me," said Herzog. "I know what people say about him, but then I don't know the guy personally. I've never met him in my life. I do plan to stick him out there and hope that he does the same kind of job for us that he did for Oakland. We'll get along just fine."[175]

Herzog quickly found out. Epstein played 27 games with Texas and was hitting .188 when the Rangers traded him to the California Angels along with right-handed pitcher Rich Hand and catcher Rick Stelmaszek for pitcher Floyd Allen and left-hand hitting first baseman Jim Spencer. The Angels announced that Epstein would be used regularly, either at first base or as a pinch hitter. Short said of Epstein, "He was unhappy in Texas and there was nothing we could do to make him happy."[176]

Epstein started slowly with the Angels. He even discarded his contacts for glasses to improve his vision, and his hitting seemed to improve immediately, but he still ended the year with poor numbers—eight home runs and a .215 batting average for the Angels.[177]

Epstein continued into the 1974 season with the Angels, but after appearing in only 18 games, California asked waivers on the 31 year old for the purpose of giving him his unconditional release. Although he hit only .161 and drove in only six runs, Epstein claimed he was in manager Bobby Winkles' doghouse almost from the start. "I guess the old man couldn't handle me," said Epstein. "It was difficult playing here." Winkles retorted that the Angels had acquired Epstein for his power, but "He didn't give us what we wanted." After his release, Epstein declared, "I have a lot of productive years left. I felt I was right on the verge of breaking out of it. I'll try to hook on with another team." But Epstein was finished in the majors. He played his final big league game on April 28, 1974.[178]

Epstein's release brought him only one consolation. He became the first player to come under the new agreement between the owners and the Major League Players Association which required that the club pay a full season salary to any player released May 15 or later. Epstein had been placed on waivers May 5, but his release did not become official until after a six-day waiver period plus four days for notification through the mail. Had Epstein been released any earlier, he would have been paid his salary only to the date of his release plus 60 days' severance pay.[179]

In his nine-year major league career, Mike Epstein appeared in 907 games and had a lifetime batting average of .244. He walloped 130 home runs and drove in 380 runs. He had excellent defensive stats—.991 as a first baseman, the only position he ever played.[180]

Epstein admitted he never lived up to expectations because he felt they were set too high and he tried too hard. "When I was playing," he said, "nothing was ever good enough for me. I probably tried too hard for my own good. Now I finally have a perspective and I realize I was a bear-down guy. How much better could I have been?"[181]

After his retirement Epstein served as a hitting instructor in the minors, founded a precious metals company, and owned a ranch in Wyoming. He and his wife have two daughters and one son. The Epsteins maintain that they "have raised their children with a strong sense of tradition, born out of their own convictions as practicing Jews."[182]

On March 28, 2004, Mike Epstein was inducted into the Jewish Sports Hall of Fame.[183]

9. The Winningest Jewish Pitcher

Of all the Jewish baseball players in the class of 1965-1966, Kenneth Dale Holtzman had the most successful major league career. Although he was never as dominant a pitcher as Sandy Koufax with whom he was constantly compared, Holtzman actually notched more wins in the majors than any other Jewish pitcher before or since.

Ken Holtzman was born in St. Louis, November 3, 1945, the son of two native St. Louisans, Henry and Jacqueline Holtzman. Holtzman grew up in the St. Louis suburb of University City, at that time a predominately Jewish area, and graduated from University City High School in 1963, a few years after fellow St. Louisan Art Shamsky. He then attended the University of Illinois, graduating with a B.A. in business administration in 1967.[1]

Ken was raised in a conservative Jewish home in St. Louis, but had his bar mitzvah in an Orthodox synagogue. He was always very serious about his Jewish background and proud of his heritage. When he traveled with his various teams, he tried to observe the Jewish dietary laws as well as he could, and when he married, he always maintained a kosher home.[2]

The Chicago Cubs selected the six-foot, two-inch southpaw pitcher in the fourth round of the 1965 free agent draft, giving him a small bonus for signing. They sent Holtzman to the rookie Pioneer League, and after only four games promoted him to the Class A Northwest League.[3] Holtzman pitched just eight games in Class A before his record earned him a call-up by the parent club in the fall of 1965.[4] Holtzman appeared in three games for the Cubs and had an ERA of 2.25.[5]

Holtzman's first full season with the Cubs was 1966, but his time on the team was limited. The 19-year-old was actually a part-time pitcher and a full-time college student at the University of Illinois, Chicago branch. He had worked out a deal with the Cubs to pitch only home games and weekend road games when classes were in session.[6] His Cub manager, Leo Durocher, lamented, "I just wish it were possible for the boy to be with us for the entire season, but a half loaf is better than no loaf at all."[7]

Holtzman's record in 1966 was an unimpressive 11 wins and 16 losses, but there were at least two games in which the rookie caught the public eye; both were against the Los Angeles Dodgers. The first game, which was also his first major league victory, made an impact on baseball fans because his pitching opponent was Dodgers ace Don Drysdale. Holtzman pitched six innings, allowing only three hits, walking three and shutting out the hard-hitting Dodgers.

Holtzman's second impressive win in 1966 was important because he was facing his boyhood hero, Sandy Koufax. One of Holtzman's major concerns was that he was constantly being compared with veteran hurler, Sandy Koufax. He once told a Chicago reporter, "We're both Jewish and we're left-handed pitchers. But that's all we have in common. He's a super star and I'm a kid trying to make a ball club."[8]

Koufax was actually scheduled to pitch a day earlier, but September 24 was Yom Kippur and he would never play on the Jewish High Holy Days. On September 25, Holtzman faced Sandy Koufax for the first and only time in his major league career. The Cubs were leading after eight innings by the score of 2–0, and Holtzman had not allowed a single hit. In fact, he had faced the minimum 24 batters. The only Dodgers base runner, Dick Schofield, had walked, but he had been erased in a double play. With no outs in the ninth inning, Schofield broke up Holtzman's no-hitter with a single up the middle, and one out later, the Dodgers got their second and last hit, a ground single by Maury Wills. Holtzman defeated Koufax and the Dodgers, 2–1.[9] This was Koufax's penultimate start and final loss in the last regular season of this career.[10]

After the game, reporters flocked around Holtzman's locker. One reporter, remembering that Koufax never pitched on Jewish holidays, asked Holtzman if he would have pitched on Yom Kippur. "No," replied Holtzman, "I told Leo [Durocher] that a couple of weeks ago. I keep the Holy Days. I went to temple on Yom Kippur." When the reporter asked whether he had gone with Koufax, Holtzman quipped, "No, that wouldn't have looked too good."[11] In the Dodgers dressing room, Koufax, when reminded how the press was now comparing Holtzman to the Dodgers star pitcher, simply stated, "He's not the 'new Sandy Koufax,' he's the first Kenny Holtzman."[12]

Holtzman could not understand the constant comparison between him and Koufax. On one of his first road trips when the Cubs were to face Koufax, Holtzman was asked to pitch batting practice to give the hitters a preview of what they would see facing Koufax. "I threw pretty hard," said Holtzman. "That was the game Koufax threw a perfect game. I'm watching this, 27 up and 27 down. Guys are coming back to the dugout talking to themselves. 'I didn't see that pitch.' He was the best I ever saw."[13]

After Koufax retired, he and Holtzman became very good friends. In fact, Holtzman emphatically credited the former Dodgers star for his fine showing in 1967. "Sandy gave me many valuable tips on how to pitch to certain hitters and what to throw in given situations," said Holtzman.[14]

Holtzman appeared in only 12 games for the Cubs in 1967 because he was called into active Army service with his National Guard unit. He was being trained as a "combat medic" in the 108th Medical Battalion. Despite his restricted playing time, Holtzman won nine and lost none, with an earned average of 2.52. He set a National League record for the most wins in an undefeated season.[15] His pitching was so good that Leo Durocher made him the Cubs strong second starter behind Ferguson Jenkins.[16]

From 1968 through 1971, the Chicago Cubs had winning seasons.[17] The sensitive Holtzman continued to be compared with Sandy Koufax, but he worked diligently to be evaluated for himself.[18] In 1968 Holtzman posted a record of 11–14, but won 17 games and lost 13 in 1969. On August 19, 1969, he pitched a no-hitter against the Atlanta Braves. It was Holtzman's first no-hitter, and the first one ever thrown by a southpaw at Wrigley Field. While Holtzman did not allow any hits, he also did not strike out any Braves batters.[19] The last time this feat occurred was 1892.[20] Holtzman also worked with two different catchers during the game, Bill Heath and Gene Oliver. Heath broke his hand during the game and Oliver had to replace him.[21]

Holtzman had his best season with the Cubs in 1970. He again won 17 games, but this time he lost only 11. His ERA was 3.38; he finished fifth in the National League in both innings pitched (287.2) and in strikeouts (202).[22]

Despite his successive 17-win seasons, Holtzman was becoming disenchanted with his stay in Chicago, and his 9–15 record in 1971 reflected this. But 1971 had at least one high point. Even though he was unhappy in Chicago and expressed a desire to be traded, Holtzman pitched his second no-hitter as a Cub on June 3. When he stopped the Cincinnati Reds, 1–0, Holtzman became the first Cub hurler in the modern history of the team to pitch two no-hit games. While he had no strikeouts in his previous no-hitter, he fanned six batters this time. After the game, Cubs vice-president and general manager John Holland presented Holtzman with a new contract, that called for a $1,500 raise.[23]

Leo Durocher had become manager of the Chicago Cubs in 1966, the second year Ken Holtzman was on the team roster. The relationship between manager and pitcher had been good for a few years, but Holtzman quickly fell out of Durocher's favor. Leo began to criticize everything about Holtzman. He accused the southpaw of not working hard enough and not throwing enough fastballs. Most observers felt that the real reason behind this animosity was that Durocher found his pitcher too intellectual, and he was particularly displeased with Holtzman's unembarrassed observance of Jewish traditions.[24]

Durocher's anti–Semitism could be traced back to the time he was a player. In the first game of the 1934 World Series, which pit the Detroit Tigers against the St. Louis Cardinals, Leo Durocher was the Cardinals shortstop and Dizzy Dean was on the mound. When Hank Greenberg came to the plate against Dean with two runners on base, Durocher supposedly yelled to his pitcher, "Don't waste your fastball. Throw the son of a bitch a ham sandwich. He won't touch it."[25]

Durocher had begun his unrelentless "needling" of Holtzman in 1969 and he never let up. In an article in *Look* magazine, William Furlong wrote that Durocher would constantly call out to Holtzman in the clubhouse, "Hey, Jew," or "C'mon, kike." Furlong added that Durocher often called Ron Santo "wop," or college-grad Don Kessinger, "dumb hillbilly," but Durocher completely alienated Holtzman when he continually referred to his pitcher as a "gutless Jew" in front of his teammates.[26]

One of Holtzman's former teammates, outfielder Richard Bladt, wrote that Holtzman's normal reaction to Durocher's taunting when he was on the mound was simply to pay no attention and concentrate on the game. "I remember the time Holtzman was working on a no-hitter and gave up a walk and a hit, and was called a 'gutless Jew,'" wrote Bladt. "Frankly I hope my generation and the newer ones are past that behavior."[27]

Holtzman never publicly commented about Leo Durocher's anti–Semitism. His only complaint was that Durocher removed him from games too soon, a complete reversal of Durocher's reputation for leaving his starting pitchers in the game too long. Holtzman was also concerned that Durocher was hindering his development as a pitcher.[28]

Even after he left Chicago, Holtzman refused to "badmouth" his former manager. "Those stories about Durocher and me were blown out of proportion," said Holtzman. "I was angry because he was taking me out of games too early and maybe he misunderstood me. I guess it was all a matter of communication."[29]

After the 1971 season ended, the Cubs granted Holtzman his request and traded him to the Oakland Athletics for outfielder Rick Monday. Holtzman responded to the trade, "The air is clear now. I wouldn't have cared if the Cubs had traded me for two dozen eggs."[30]

Holtzman pitched for the A's from 1972 through 1975. In Oakland, he joined a staff of outstanding pitchers, including Vida Blue, Rollie Fingers, "Blue Moon" Odom, and Catfish Hunter. He also had three Jewish teammates, Joe Horlen, a convert to Judaism, Mike Epstein, and Art Shamsky, who joined the A's late in the season. Manager Dick Williams was especially delighted with the acquisition of Holtzman. "He immediately impressed me," said Williams, "not just on the field but in the clubhouse, where he became Fingers' guardian and helped him grow up."[31]

One of the reasons Holtzman was elated to pitch for the Athletics was that with the A's, he could rely more and more on his fastball. Wes Stock, the pitching coach, stated, "I've never seen a pitcher who throws as fast as he does who has his control. He's amazing. He gets the ball exactly where he wants to time after time." Ray Fosse, Holtzman's catcher on the A's, observed that it was the hurler's control that made him effective. "He's got good stuff too," noted Fosse, "but the main thing is he can get the ball where he wants it."[32]

Ken Holtzman was Oakland's most effective pitcher during the entire 1972 season. He was selected as one of the American League pitchers to compete in the All-Star Game, and his 19–11 record was instrumental in leading his team into

With 174 wins, southpaw Ken Holtzman won more major-league games than any other Jewish pitcher. Holtzman also tossed two no-hitters during his 15-year career while pitching for five teams. In addition to his prowess on the mound, Holtzman was known for his strong religious convictions; he never pitched on a Jewish high holiday (courtesy National Baseball Hall of Fame Library; Cooperstown, N.Y.).

the American League playoffs. In the American League Championship Series, the A's eliminated the Detroit Tigers, three games to two, although Holtzman lost the one game in which he appeared. When the A's defeated the Cincinnati Reds and their "Big Red Machine" in seven games, it marked the team's first World Series victory since 1930 when the team was the Philadelphia Athletics.[33] Holtzman appeared in three of the seven games, pitched 12.2 innings, and had a record of 1–0 with an ERA of 2.13.[34]

Ken Holtzman enjoyed his finest season in the major leagues in 1973 when he became a 20-game winner for the first and only time in his professional career. He compiled a record of 21–13, and represented the A's in the All-Star Game for the second consecutive season. His only complaint about the 1973 season was that with the new designated hitter rule in the American League, he did not have the opportunity to demonstrate his hitting ability. Holtzman, a good hitter, lamented, "There's a good chance I might never get a major league at-bat again." He felt the rule, however, might give him the opportunity to get more decisions.[35]

The A's once again made the playoffs in 1973, and this year they defeated the Baltimore Orioles three games to two. Holtzman started Game Three against Baltimore's Mike Cuellar. The A's won in eleven innings, 2–1, when Bert Campaneris homered to get the win for Holtzman, who pitched the entire game.

Oakland faced the New York Mets in the World Series and again won the Series in seven games. Holtzman started three of the seven games and won two of Oakland's four victories. In the Series, for the first time in 1973, Holtzman was allowed to hit, and he doubled and scored one of the two runs in his 2–1 victory.[36] After the A's had won their second successive World Series, A's owner Charlie Finley told Holtzman, "Without you, we couldn't have won two World Series in a row. With you, we're going to make it three in a row."[37] *The Sporting News* named Holtzman the American League's best left-handed pitcher in 1973.[38]

Holtzman played a major role in getting the A's to the 1974 World Series, winning 19 games during the season. He also suffered 17 losses despite a respectable ERA of 3.07.[39] In the ALCS, the A's were again up against the Baltimore Orioles, their opponents a year earlier. In the playoff opener at Oakland, the Orioles defeated Catfish Hunter and the A's, 6–3. Holtzman halted their momentum in Game Two by shutting out the Orioles, 5–0. In Game Three, Vida Blue bested Jim Palmer, 1–0, and in the final game, Catfish Hunter pitched eight shutout innings, defeating the Orioles, 2–1.[40]

The 1974 A's had the reputation of disliking each other almost as much as they disliked Finley, their owner. They also had a new manager—Alvin Dark. But they still played well enough together to win their third consecutive World Series, defeating the Los Angeles Dodgers in five games. The A's may have had a new manager, but they employed the same strategy in the World Series as they had the two previous years—pitch Ken Holtzman in the opener. For the third consecutive year Holtzman faced a different team in the World Series opener. He left the game during the fifth inning, and although Oakland won the game, Rollie Fingers received the victory. Los Angeles won the second game by the identical score, 3–2. (The final score in four of the five games was 3–2). The A's then won three consecutive games and the World Series. They were the first team to win three consecutive World Series since the Yankees had won five from 1949 through 1953.[41] Holtzman had a remarkable 1.50 ERA in the World Series, but he was as proud of his hitting as his pitching. In the 1974 Series, he had a double and a home run.[42]

The A's were in disarray after their third consecutive World Series win. One of their ace pitchers, Catfish Hunter, had left for "greener pastures" in New York, and many of his teammates were also threatening to quit, play out their options, or demand trades. Holtzman, too, was having his run-ins with Finley, but he continued to maintain his professionalism. "I have to say that Finley's knowledge of baseball is limited," Holtzman said, "but he has contact with his players. He wants to win. And he has influenced some good ideas, like the designated hitter rule and the color he's added."[43]

Holtzman still managed to have a formidable 1975 season—winning 18 and losing 14 games.[44] He helped Oakland win its fourth consecutive Division title, but the Boston Red Sox defeated the A's in the ALCS, winning three consecutive games. Holtzman lost two of the three games in that series.[45]

By 1976 Ken Holtzman was no longer the wide-eyed naïve pitcher he had been when he first made it to the big leagues in 1965 and who had considered baseball a game for thrills. It was now a business. He had married Michelle Collons in 1971, and the couple had a family. He began to dislike the travel baseball demanded; he wanted to be home more with his family.[46]

Holtzman told his agent, attorney Jerry Kapstein, that he wanted A's owner Charlie Finley to give him a multi-year contract at $480,000 for three years. Finley's reply to Kapstein was quite succinct, "I don't give multi-year contracts."[47]

Despite the success of the Oakland Athletics, the parsimonious Charlie O. never believed in rewarding his players financially. He was, however, a realist. Anticipating free agency and unable to come to terms with either Kenny Holtzman or Reggie Jackson, Finley traded both of them plus minor league pitcher Bill Van Bommell to the Baltimore Orioles for outfielder Don Baylor and pitchers Mike Torrez and Paul Mitchell at the start of the 1976 season.[48] When he heard the trade announced, Holtzman called it "the greatest thing that ever happened to me." He pointed out that he had been traded before so he was not shocked. "I just thought I'd never get away from Charlie Finley that easily," he added.[49]

While Holtzman announced that he was happy to leave Oakland, he made it clear to Orioles' management he was still going to let his agent negotiate his contract. "If the Orioles will not deal with me fairly," stated Holtzman, "I'll play out my option, and as far as I'm concerned, I'll be a free agent at the end of the year. Then I'll have 22 clubs I can deal with instead of 23. But I don't want to be a free agent. If they offer me a fair contract, I'll sign it right now."[50]

Holtzman remained an Oriole for only part of the 1976 season, appearing in 13 games and posting a record of five wins and four losses.[51]

In June the Yankees and the Orioles completed a 10-player deal. The Yankees acquired unsigned pitchers Ken Holtzman and Doyle Alexander and sent unsigned catcher Rick Dempsey to the Orioles. In addition, the Yankees received reliever Grant Jackson and catcher Elrod Hendricks. Baltimore also received southpaw pitchers Rudy May and Tippy Martinez, right-hander Dave Pagan and minor league pitcher Scott McGregor. Finally, the Orioles sent pitcher Jim Freeman to the Yankees' Syracuse farm club.[52]

Holtzman appeared in 21 games with the Yankees in 1976; his record was 9–7 with an ERA of 4.17. He re-signed with the Yankees for the 1977 and 1978 seasons, but worked fewer than 90 innings those two years, pitching in only 23 games, winning three and losing three.[53]

During his tenure with the Yankees, Holtzman found himself in conflict with his manager, Billy Martin. Martin showed almost no confidence in Holtzman, which kept him from reaching his potential as a Yankees hurler. Throughout both the 1976 playoffs and the World Series, Holtzman remained on the bench—he did not pitch a single inning in postseason play even though he was known for his clutch performances. Even when the Cincinnati Reds swept the Yankees in the 1976 World Series, Holtzman understood the business aspects of the game and refused to criticize Martin or any other member of the Yankees management. He replied to the constant probing questions about his use or nonuse with the same reply: "I'm a professional ballplayer," he said, "and I am being paid a lot of money. I'll do whatever I'm asked to do."[54] He did admit however, "I am not bitter, but I am frustrated."[55]

A number of reasons have been given to explain why Holtzman got so little playing time. Some insist that Holtzman and his manager simply did not get along. Others claim that Holtzman, the Yankees player who represented the ball players' union on the team, was a natural target for management's acrimony. Some of Holtzman's defenders place the blame on George Steinbrenner who tried unsuccessfully to force Holtzman to waive his no-trade clause. When that ploy failed, he relegated him to the bullpen to punish him for defying management.[56]

Reggie Jackson, Holtzman's teammate on both the A's and the Yankees, saw the situation a little differently. In his 1984 autobiography, Jackson accused several former Yankees of making comments that were anti-black and anti–Semitic. Although he denied the accusation, Billy Martin was among those on Jackson's list.[57]

In 1977 Holtzman tied Koufax's record for the most wins by a Jewish pitcher. The following year, his only win with the Yankees earned him the record. In June 1978 he also passed Larry Sherry for the most appearances by a Jewish pitcher in the major leagues, a mark he held until in 1998, when Scott Radinsky passed him.[58]

Holtzman suggested that Steinbrenner trade him for a productive hitter rather than have him sit on the bench all season. But there was no trade during the 1977 season, and the following year Holtzman made the same request. On June 10, 1978, Steinbrenner acquiesced, and sent Holtzman back to his first team, the Chicago Cubs, for a minor league player to be named later. Holtzman was at home watching the Cubs play the Padres on TV when he was told about the move. "I feel super about it," he said. "I talked to Herman [Franks, the Cubs manager] and he understands I haven't done any serious pitching in a year-and-a-half. We feel I might have to be used in relief for a while. I think the Cubs have an excellent young team and maybe my experience can help them."[59]

At the age of 32, Kenny Holtzman was starting a new phase in his baseball career when he returned to the Cubs. Unfortunately, in 1978 Holtzman did not win a game, although he made 23 appearances. He finished the year with a record of 0–3 and a 6.11 ERA.[60]

In 1979 Franks agreed to Holtzman's request to pitch his last game in the major leagues in St. Louis so his mother and father could attend. Holtzman left the game in the seventh, leading, 1–0. The Cubs won, 3–1, but Bruce Sutter was credited with the victory. The 33-year-old Holtzman retired from baseball at the end of the season.[61]

After his days as a player, Holtzman, his wife, and three daughters lived in a northern Chicago suburb. He worked as a stockbroker and sold insurance before moving to the St. Louis area where he did substitute teaching and coached children for the Jewish Community Center. "I could afford [to do] this," said Holtzman, "because of the pension I received from playing in the big leagues."[62]

In his 15-year career in the majors, Holtzman won 174 games and lost 150, with a lifetime ERA of 3.49. Among his 174 victories were 30 shutouts, two no-hitters, and more than 1,600 strikeouts. In 1995 he was inducted into the International Jewish Sports Hall of Fame, and in 1999, into the National Jewish Sports Hall of Fame.[63]

Holtzman was one of four former major leaguers who managed an Israeli baseball team in 2007. He was originally surprised when he was offered the job, but accepted because he felt it would be an excellent way to visit Israel for the first time. He also enjoyed the challenge of starting a new league in a country lacking a baseball tradition.[64]

Along with his family and his high school baseball coach, Holtzman attended the Hall of Fame gathering of Jewish players in 2004. He echoed feelings similar to many of his contemporaries when he stated," You're proud to be Jewish and represent a group that historically hasn't been in great numbers in Major League sports, but all of us here finally made it to the major leagues. It's good to go back and reflect once in a while."[65]

Ron Bergman, sports writer for the *Oakland Tribune*, said that Holtzman was one of the few close friends he had made in baseball. He spoke for many when he said, "He was by far the most intelligent single individual I ever met in the game."[66]

10. The Man Who Revolutionized Baseball

Marvin Miller was the first union professional to head a baseball players' association, and during his more than two decades of leadership, that association would become a major force in the operation of the game.

Marvin Julian Miller was born April 4, 1917, the son of an Orthodox Jewish garment salesman, Alexander Miller, and a school teacher, Gertrude Wald Miller. He grew up in Brooklyn during the Depression and became an avid Dodgers fan, although his father favored the Giants. "Much of what I learned about baseball," claimed Miller, "came from my father."[1] As a child Marvin was athletic even though he had limited range of motion in his right shoulder because of an injury at birth.[2]

Until his tenth birthday, Miller, in deference to his father's religious beliefs, attended Hebrew School four days a week after a full day of public school. As his thirteenth birthday approached, his mother hired a private tutor three nights a week to prepare him for his bar mitzvah, which he celebrated.[3]

Always a bright child, Miller entered his freshman year at James Madison High School in 1929 when he was only eleven. After his high school graduation, Miller worked his way through New York University studying education and economics, receiving his undergraduate degree in 1938. He then took graduate courses at the New School for Social Research.[4]

In 1938 he also met his future wife, Theresa (Terry) Morganstern, at NYU, and the couple married the following year. The marriage produced two children. Terry later went back to school and earned her doctorate.[5]

Miller first learned about labor unions at the age of ten or eleven when his father and other employees of a retail store in Manhattan, which sold expensive women's coats, organized all the sales people and held a strike. "When my father walked the picket line," said Miller, "I went with him." Miller also said that as a child he "enjoyed the regular paid vacations, paid holidays and so on, the union had won for those people."[6]

Miller became a staunch union member himself on his first job, working with the unemployed for the New York City Department of Welfare. He became involved in labor relations when World War II broke out. Disqualified from active duty because he could not raise his arm above his shoulder, Miller joined the National War Labor Board. Congress had created this federal agency to arbitrate labor disputes during the war and ensure that vital factory production was not impaired by strikes or lockouts. Miller's role as a hearing officer gave him a practical education in labor-management problems and dispute resolution. For a little more than a year following the end of World War II, he trained personnel for the United States Conciliation Service. In 1947 Miller left government work permanently to begin his long and impressive career in the labor movement. The most enduring lesson Miller learned during those years was the importance of studying both sides in labor disputes.[7]

Miller spent three years as an organizer, researcher, and negotiator for the International Association of Machinists, and for a brief period, he did the same work for the New York region of the United Auto Workers.[8] For the next 16 years, Miller was associated with the United States Steelworkers of America; it was here that his genius in the field of labor relations was first recognized. Miller started with the Steelworkers as a researcher, economist, and legal consultant. He was later promoted to assistant to president David McDonald and took part in all top-level negotiations with industry. In that capacity, he was credited with several creative labor-management projects including the Kaiser Aluminum productivity-sharing plan and the industry-wide human relations committee designed to prevent strikes and increase efficiency. His brilliance in labor matters in general, and bargaining in particular, was becoming evident.[9]

Even business publications such as *Fortune* and the *Wall Street Journal* singled Miller out for praise. Both Presidents John F. Kennedy and Lyndon Johnson named him to presidential commissions.[10]

In 1965, I. W. Abel, secretary-treasurer of the Steelworkers Union, defeated McDonald for the union presidency. The change in the leadership hierarchy brought about numerous staff reshufflings, and Miller left the union. Both Carnegie-Mellon and Harvard asked Miller to accept a visiting professorship, but he refused their offers because he preferred what he called "the stimulating atmosphere of labor relations battles" rather than the "dusty, quiet halls of academia."[11]

In a very short time Marvin Miller would have his opportunity to participate in an area where labor relations were virtually unknown—major league baseball.

On five occasions prior to 1960, baseball players had attempted to organize themselves against team owners. In 1885 John Montgomery Ward and eight associates formed the first players' union—the Brotherhood of Professional Baseball Players. This union was opposed to the reserve clause and a growing movement to establish a cap on players' salaries. Players were so frustrated by owners' opposition that they formed a new league—the Players League that lasted only one year.

Players tried for a second time when the Players' Protective Association was formed. Founded by Clark Griffith, a pitcher at that time, and Hugh Jennings, this organization also wanted to modify the reserve clause. This group was dissolved after a few years when it could not prevent some of its members from jumping to the newly formed American League.

The next group, the Fraternity of Professional Baseball Players, was established in 1912 as a result of the American League's attempt to discipline Ty Cobb for trying to beat up a fan who had been heckling him. This union also sought higher salaries for its members, but the reserve clause limited its bargaining power.

The fourth union, the American Baseball Guild, was founded in 1946 as a result of the Mexican League incident. Several major leaguers who felt they had been underpaid, went to Mexico to play for more money. This prompted Commissioner Albert "Happy" Chandler to blacklist them from the major leagues for five years. Litigation eventually rescinded Chandler's decision, and eventually the Guild disbanded. None of these four unions was successful in removing the reserve clause which bound a player to his respective club.[12]

A fifth attempt to establish a baseball union—the Major League Baseball Players Association—occurred in 1954 in reaction to the owners' efforts to abolish players' pensions. Its first president was future Hall of Fame pitcher Bob Feller. Founded by the players but funded by the owners, this union was not only relatively powerless, it was also in direct violation of the Taft-Hartley Act which forbade the financing of a union with management money. Its one achievement was that it did save the pension plan by getting owners to agree to contribute 60 percent of television revenues from the All-Star Game and the World Series.[13]

The baseball owners seemed quite content to think of themselves as benevolent dictators. In late 1965, however, forward-thinking players like future Hall of Fame pitchers Robin Roberts and Jim Bunning and former American League batting champ Harvey Kuenn began to view their roles as baseball players from a business perspective.[14]

At that time, the primary concern of major league ballplayers was to improve their pension system. They knew that the owners had received large amounts of TV revenues and had not shared them with the pension fund. The progressive group felt that the only way for them to negotiate effectively with the owners was to strengthen the Players Association by establishing a permanent association office in New York and, most importantly, by hiring a strong, full-time executive director. Despite some opposition from more conservative players like Pittsburgh Pirates hurler Bob Friend, the progressives prevailed.[15]

To pick a nominee for executive director, the MLBPA's executive board selected a four-person search committee made up of Robin Roberts, Jim Bunning, Bob Friend, and Harvey Kuenn. Roberts, who lived in the Philadelphia area, contacted Professor George Taylor, a Philadelphia-based labor expert and professor at the Wharton School of Finance, for his recommendations. Taylor suggested Marvin Miller. Miller had been Taylor's colleague at the War Labor Board and on the Kaiser Commission. He also knew that Marvin had served the Steelworkers of America with distinction for many years.[16]

When Taylor contacted him, Miller was living in Pittsburgh and indicated he would be willing to meet with the search committee. As a lifelong baseball fan, the potential of an untapped baseball union intrigued him. He considered labor relations for baseball the same as for any other industry or product. He would soon find out there were differences.[17]

Before he was even interviewed by the committee, Miller learned that others were also interested in the position. The candidates included Chub Feeney, vice-president of the San Francisco Giants, former Tiger slugger Hank Greenberg, and the one-time association president, Bob Feller. His most serious rival, however, was Judge Robert Cannon of the Circuit Court of Wisconsin, who had served as legal counsel of the MLBPA for six years. During this time, he had accomplished virtually nothing for the players, but got along so well with the owners that many believed his ultimate ambition was to become baseball commissioner.[18]

On the whole, Miller felt that his meeting with the search committee did not go very well. His first concern was that all of the players would have to approve his selection and this concerned Miller. He was also worried when he discovered that many, if not most, of the major league players at that time not only had very little experience with unions, but were fairly hostile to them. A number of these players were quite conservative, hailing from either the south or from rural areas.

During the course of the meeting, Robin Roberts suggested that Miller hire Richard Nixon as general counsel to the union in order to mollify the conservative players who feared and mistrusted unions in general. Despite the possibility of risking his candidacy,

Miller explained that he could not go along with that suggestion. Miller cited Nixon's conservative bent and the likelihood he would be distracted by a presidential run in 1968. Miller told the search committee that the association needed one clear leader. As he was about to leave the meeting, he told the committee, "I'm going to offer you some advice. Whoever gets elected executive director, let him pick the general counsel. It's got to be someone he's totally compatible with. Otherwise you're going to create chaos and undermine your situation."[19]

Marvin Miller began actively campaigning for the job prior to the 1966 baseball season. The baseball owners, however, were very much opposed to him for a number of reasons. First, they favored Judge Cannon as they knew him well and felt that they could deal with him effectively. Second, the owners quickly realized that the hiring of Miller would signal turning the MLBPA into a functioning labor union, an action utterly abhorrent to baseball's moguls and their unilateral decision-making powers. Finally, Miller was an experienced labor negotiator for whom organized baseball had no counterpart, no one who could effectively deal with Miller and the players.[20]

The players had every reason not to favor the hiring of Judge Cannon as the full-time executive director of the MLBPA. While president of the MLBPA, Bob Feller had recognized his ineffectiveness in winning player rights and admitted, "Before employing Cannon the state of collective bargaining was "pathetic," and under Cannon it remained so."[21]

However, the players were still intimidated by the owners' opposition to Miller, and the search committee originally offered the job to Cannon.[22] The judge insisted on a number of concessions before he would agree to accept the offer. He demanded that the union match his judicial pension in addition to giving him a $50,000 salary and a $100,000 office account. He also insisted that the association office be transferred to his home city of Milwaukee rather than remaining near the teams' management offices in New York. The players tried to compromise, but Cannon was adamant. Angered and frustrated, the committee decided to look elsewhere.[23]

The search committee met once more and offered the job of executive director to Marvin Miller for two years at an annual salary of $50,000 plus $20,000 for expenses. At the time Miller accepted the post, the average salary of a major league player was $19,000. Before Miller could formally accept the position, the ball players, who were at spring training camps, had to ratify his appointment.[24]

Jim Bunning quickly became one of Miller's strongest advocates. The Phillies pitcher had been one of the earliest to speak out in favor of the need to create a permanent office and to hire a full-time director. He was aware that Miller's background with the steelworkers frightened many of baseball's moguls, but he also realized that Miller's knowledge of labor-management law would prove advantageous to the players. He fully understood that even in 1966, most major leaguers had long been brainwashed by two of management's pet phrases—"We'll take care of you," and "For the good of the game."[25]

Interestingly, years later, Jim Bunning, as a conservative Republican Congressman and Senator from Kentucky, compiled a voting record considered unfriendly to labor. But as a member of the screening committee, his philosophy was different. He remarked, "Some of the players' representatives were leery about picking a union man. We were impressed with Marvin's credentials and the way he handled himself. He was very articulate—not the cigar-chewing type some of us guys expected. What he said about standing on our own made sense."[26]

Miller's selection coincided with the joint holdout of Dodgers pitchers Sandy Koufax and Don Drysdale. The owners now had a dual reason to become alarmed and attempted to thwart Miller's election. They began spreading rumors that Miller was a mob-tied "labor boss" who would hire "goon squads" against opposing players. Robin Roberts, a Miller supporter, gently advised Miller that perhaps he should shave off his moustache because of being caricatured by management as a shiny-suited Jewish hireling of gangsters.[27]

Miller kept the moustache. The owners' next tactic to demonstrate their discontent with Miller was to renege on their pledge to allocate $150,000 in All-Star Game proceeds to the players' pension fund. They also blacklisted Roberts for his fervent support of Miller. After 1966, Roberts never found permanent employment in organized baseball.[28]

Miller traveled to the 1966 spring training camps of both the Grapefruit League in Florida and the Cactus League in Arizona to meet with the players and explain the ratification process. On his first trip, he met with organized harassment from coaches, managers, and even some players in the west. The Los Angeles Angels, spearheaded by veteran stars Jim Piersall, Joe Adcock, Jack Sanford, and Lew Burdette, signed petitions opposing Miller's appointment, and insisting that Cannon be retained. One of the Angels said, "The selection of Miller was a railroad job. Only a few such as Robin Roberts and Bob Allison are trying to push him off on us." The Angels feared that Miller's appointment could damage their relationship with the major league owners.[29]

Birdie Tebbetts, manager of the Cleveland Indians, a team that trained out west, insinuated that Miller was a Communist. The managers, rather than the player reps, ran the team meetings and verbally attacked Miller with hostile questions. Anti-Miller petitions, paid for by the owners, were sent to all the players. The five teams training out west voted, 102 to 17, against hiring Miller.[30]

In Florida, management attempted similar tactics. Joe Reichler, former sportswriter turned flunky for the commissioner's office, circulated among the players and warned them to be "very, very, *very* careful before they even considered voting for Miller." Houston manager Leo Durocher hit fungoes into an outdoors Houston team meeting in an effort to disrupt it. However, in Florida, unlike in Arizona, player representatives led by Robin Roberts worked hard to shore up support for their candidate. Miller, realizing that he had been too tense out west, seemed more at ease at the second group of meetings and demonstrated that he was willing to listen to the players and offer a realistic approach to their problems.

Jim Lefebvre's story clearly explains one of the ways Miller was able to win over many of the players. When Miller visited Dodgers headquarters in Vero Beach, Dodgers executive Buzzie Bavasi grimly informed his players, "We can't have this guy." "That meant Miller was in," said Lefebvre. "Anybody Buzzie was that scared of had to be good for you."

St. Louis Cardinal Curt Flood was greatly impressed with Miller's calm demeanor and his broad grasp of the problems facing the major leaguers in 1966. "We had been sent our share of anti–Miller propaganda but, as I recall at the time saying, if the owners are so vehemently opposed to the guy, he can't be too bad."[31]

Marvin Miller could not argue with that assessment. "Our biggest ally," Miller had long said, "has been the owners. In every crisis situation they have pushed us into taking positions that didn't come naturally to us."[32]

Miller won over the Grapefruit League players, who gave him 472 out of 506 votes cast.[33] Five of the 16 teams training in Florida accepted Miller unanimously. Three others cast only one negative vote each. Miller had passed his first and possibly most crucial test by a total 489–136 margin.[34] Although the owners were stung by the outcome of the vote, they were determined to place roadblocks for Miller in the weeks to come. On April 14, 1966, his forty-ninth birthday, Miller was officially named executive director of the MLBPA.[35]

When Miller took office, he had to face a baseball ownership with 100 years of absolute power and control that they were determined to keep. The shrewd Miller, however, was to turn the owners' arrogance back upon them to an overwhelming degree.

Brooks Robinson, Baltimore Orioles star third baseman for 23 years and a member of Baseball's Hall of Fame, was acutely aware of Miller's amazing ability to take a traditionally anti-union work force and rally it behind him. "He was able to do it because he was honest and everything he said was the actual truth. Miller was also among the smartest men in baseball. He combined a brilliant mind with an uncanny ability to lay out his position in such a logical manner that it seemed impossible to disagree with him."[36]

Miller's strategy in his new post was simple—reshape the Association into a union able to negotiate as an equal with the owners to secure benefits for its members. He had two immediate goals in mind: money (he felt the players were underpaid) and justice (he felt the players lacked the right to choose where they worked and under what conditions).

Miller admitted that before he could accomplish any of his goals he had to educate the players. Many were youngsters who knew nothing about workers' rights and safety. They had accepted the *status quo* because that was all they knew. They wanted to talk about pensions but they had little idea how their pension plan operated or how it compared with industry pensions. "Education became a part of every agenda with the players," said Miller. "I held regular and special sessions with both player reps and individual players. We started from a low understanding of what a union could do. It was surprising for the players and I taught them how to work together. To many, that was a foreign concept."[37]

Tim McCarver said of Miller: "The most remarkable thing to me looking back was that how disparate his knowledge of negotiating and contracts was from ours. He educated the player reps and they educated the rest. It was a very methodical process. He never let the cart get before the horse."[38]

Miller was union in every sense, but he defined the union in a very non-threatening manner for those players who seemed hesitant to belong to one—hearing that all unions did was to go out on strike. A strike, Miller stressed to the nervous players, was simply "a unified holdout of services."[39]

The ease with which the players accepted Miller's advice and the success he had with the players terrified the owners. They tried another tactic—this time they announced that they would no longer fund the Players' Association. Miller again turned the tables by getting them to take over the players' contribution to the pension fund so that the players could voluntarily use those funds for their Association dues.[40]

To provide money until the dues came in, Miller

Few men have affected baseball's history as much as Marvin Miller. As the first fulltime executive director of the Major League Baseball Players Association, Miller brought about a more equal relationship between players and owners by taking a work force that was unaware of its fundamental rights and turning it into what many deemed one of the country's most powerful unions (photograph: Transcendental Graphics).

had the MLBPA renegotiate what amounted to a "reserve clause" contract with Topps for the player pictures in the bubble gum card packs. He changed the agreement from a ridiculously low flat fee per player with no percentage of sales into a lucrative royalty arrangement that brought the players far more revenue. He also made a deal with Coca Cola for promotional rights. It seemed that the owners were turning out to be Marvin Miller's best allies. Their actions only solidified Marvin Miller's position with the players and made the association stronger.[41]

Marvin Miller insisted it was most important to formalize the results obtained through collective bargaining into written contracts, which came to be known as Basic Agreements. The term "Basic Agreement" was applied to each formal contract hammered out between the owners and the MLBPA.[42]

The first Basic Agreement was worked out in 1967 and in 1968. At first, the owners refused to bargain with the association, basically ignoring Miller and the player reps as much as possible. The owners hoped that by this non-action, the players would become passive again and accept any crumbs the owners might throw them. American League president Joe Cronin spoke for management when he reminded Miller in a very friendly manner, "I've got some advice for you, young man. The players come and go, but the owners stay on forever."[43]

When Miller and Dick Moss, the legal counsel he had hired, finally were able to get management talking enough to negotiate, he employed one of his other keys to success with his members—full communications. Through direct memos and the media, Miller kept his members informed of every action taken by both sides.

The owners then formed their own bargaining committee, the Player Relations Committee (PRC), and hired John Gaherin, a pragmatic, streetwise veteran of labor negotiations, as their chief negotiator. Gaherin respected Miller's position and understood the situation better than the owners, who did not want to recognize that the MLBPA was a union. Gaherin and Miller developed a relationship of mutual respect and admiration as fellow professionals, although Gaherin was convinced that "Miller intended to destroy the whole goddamned temple that I was paid to hold up [since he thought] the whole structure of baseball was evil."[44]

With Gaherin and Miller representing them, the two sides began their negotiations in November 1967 and ended in February 1968 with the first written agreement between the association and the owners. The player's minimum salary was raised to $10,000—the first increase in two decades. On-the-road food allowances were increased. First-class hotel and travel accommodations became contractual requirements. Management increased its contribution to the pension fund. For the first time in the history of baseball, a procedure for the orderly resolution of grievances was established.[45]

It was really not much of a grievance procedure, because its final stage was arbitration by the commissioner of baseball. Dick Moss told the Federal Bar Association, "The Commissioner is hired by, paid by and can be fired by the club owners. I know [the grievance procedure] sounds shameful, but that was the best we could do."[46]

This first Basic Agreement was important for many reasons. It was reached through collective bargaining—the first collective bargaining contract in any sport. It included a provision to review the reserve clause under which the major league franchise holders held players as property. Finally, Miller was able to obtain a provision common to almost every union contract—a formal procedure for grievances.[47]

Generally, Miller was satisfied with the provisions of the first Basic Agreement, but three months before its approval, he indicated that he had every intention of bringing forward at some later date the issue of the reserve clause. "When we call for a discussion of the reserve clause in a player's contract," said Miller, "we're not making threats. We just want to bring this subject into the open so baseball people won't throw up their hands and say the game will collapse if we even talk about it. There may be many ways to solve the problem." Miller fully understood that baseball officials regarded the reserve clause as the basic item that kept them in business. He did state, however, that he regarded its legality as doubtful.[48]

As the first Basic Agreement was about to expire, many players were still concerned about TV revenue going into the pension fund. Miller urged the players not to sign contracts for the 1969 season until an agreement could be reached.[49] According to Miller, the critical points in negotiations were what the players considered the "historic right" to a percentage of the radio–TV take and the guarantee of existing benefits.[50] Miller suggested that the players might stage an "informal strike" which would delay the opening of spring training camps in 1969.[51]

As the opening of the 1969 spring training neared, Miller reported that his members were solidly united. Many owners still believed the whole idea of a players' union was ridiculous and waited to see if Miller was bluffing. Some owners threatened to play their spring training games without the current players, but Miller doubted that anyone would pay to watch minor leaguers just because the owners stuck a "major league tag" on them.[52]

Many of baseball's executives were becoming agitated at Miller, his tactics, and his union. Paul Richards, Atlanta Braves vice-president, was one of Miller's most vocal adversaries. "Either Miller or baseball has to go," claimed Richards, "and I'm afraid right now baseball will go first."[53]

Richards continued his assault on Miller. "Everywhere I go, people ask me, 'are we going to play?' I answer in a simple three letter word—yes." Then lashing out at Miller, Richards added, "I have always been for the players. But, when they come up with a four-flushing, mustachioed union organizer by the name of Marvin Miller ... I don't know."[54]

Despite the rantings of Richards and his ilk, in February 1969, Miller insisted that the players would not panic nor desert as the pressure from the owners increased. He stated: "The players will stick together and I am confident they will hold out."[55]

Miller proved to be correct. The owners gave in and a new three-year agreement emerged before the month was over, although it was not ratified until May 1970. In the new contract, which became baseball's second Basic Agreement, baseball's pension dispute was finally settled.[56] The owners agreed to place $5.45 million in the pension fund, and the rules for qualifying for a pension and withdrawing benefits were made less restrictive. The agreement also established a dental program and improvements in life insurance, health care, and other benefits.[57]

Miller considered his role in the second Basic Agreement and what he had won for the players the most important victory of his early years: by bringing to arbitration multiple grievances against management and winning, Miller had been able to destroy the paternalistic relationship of the owners and the players.[58]

The owners finally recognized the MLBPA as the players' official bargaining agent on all matters except those dealing with "the integrity of the game" (which was left to the commissioner) and individual salaries.[59]

By including the owners' acceptance of negotiating players' salaries with their designated agents, the second Basic Agreement led to the arrival of professional agents—tough-minded individuals who worked for a maximum ten percent of whatever they got for their clients. Years later, Miller admitted he had had some reservations about bringing agents into the salary discussions, and he warned the players not to become employees of their own representatives.[60]

The decade of the 1970s began with a test of the long-standing reserve clause. In 1969 the St. Louis Cardinals had traded Curt Flood to the Philadelphia Phillies for the 1970 season, but Flood objected to the trade. He consulted with Marvin Miller who warned him that the courts still upheld the reserve clause, giving the Cardinals the right to make the trade. Miller, however, allowed Flood to explain the situation to player reps who agreed to fund all of his legal fees. Even though Flood ended up sitting out the entire 1970 baseball season and retiring in 1971, he continued to pursue the case.

Miller, along with Hank Greenberg, Jackie Robinson, former owner Bill Veeck, and Jim Brosnan, all testified on Flood's behalf. Miller even prevailed on his former colleague from the Steelworkers Union and former Supreme Court Justice, Arthur Goldberg, to serve as Flood's attorney.[61] Unfortunately Goldberg did not have a grasp of baseball practice and, in the case of *Flood v. Kuhn*, Flood lost his appeal in the United States Supreme Court. "I think he showed a tremendous amount of courage, no matter what," said Miller.[62]

The Flood case coincided with Miller's efforts to gain the trust of African-American and Hispanic players. Hispanics appreciated receiving copies of Basic Agreements in Spanish. African-Americans appreciated Miller's efforts to get owners to correct racial abuses in some of the smaller Florida cities during spring training. Once convinced of Miller's sincerity, African-Americans became enthusiastic supporters of the union. In many ways, Miller found it easier to convince the African-American players to unionize than the Caucasian players. Miller realized that the African-American players, with a legacy of slavery, segregation, and bigotry, found a union quite helpful in their fight against paternalistic attitudes. On the other hand, most of the white players came from families that had no union background and had been raised to be deferential to coaches and others in authority.[63]

When the 1970 Basic Agreement ran out in 1972, the MLPBA sought a 25 percent increase in the club owners' contributions to the pension fund as well as improvements in medical benefits. The owners balked and stood together. Miller's reaction was to issue the following statement: "The owners must be deliberately trying to provoke a strike. That's the only way I can explain that kind of negotiating." Within 72 hours of the statement, the Chicago White Sox and four other major league teams voted to strike over the pension issue.[64] Miller attempted at least ten times to warn the players of the effects of a strike. He emphasized that the players association had only limited resources to meet the charges that would come from the club owners.[65]

The players were well aware that they did not have the support of former baseball stars who were likely to speak out against them. Rip Sewell, who pitched for the Pirates in the 1940s, noted that he had stopped a possible strike in 1947 and commented, "If they're going to have a union in baseball, they might as well call it the Soviet Union." Johnny Vander Meer, who pitched two consecutive no-hit games for Cincinnati in the late 1930s, said, "I just feel that the game belongs to the fans more than anyone else. I don't believe that a strike in sports is a good idea." Red Schoendienst, Larry Jackson, and Gus Bell all spoke out against the strike. Bell added, "I just hope nothing happens to louse up my pension."[66]

Despite Miller's warnings, the players voted 663–10 to walk out of the spring training camps and delay the opening of the 1972 season.[67] This was the first general strike in the history of organized sports. Miller and baseball historians considered this strike the turning point in the history of baseball labor relations.[68] The strike demonstrated that the players were unified and were quickly learning Miller's strategies that had resulted in increased benefits for all players.

Miller was certainly on target when he warned the players that there might be hostile press coverage if they walked out. Noted sports writer Dick Young had been an outspoken foe of arrogant and powerful baseball owners, but after a strike against the New York newspapers, he also developed a deep distrust of labor unions and their leaders. For many years Young had also been one of the most ardent defenders of the values of American baseball. He abhorred the new generation of major league players who seemed to have no respect for the past. For him, the strike was the last straw and, of course, he blamed Marvin Miller. "Clearly the enemy [of the owners] is not the players whom the owners regard merely as ingrates. The enemy is Marvin Miller, general of the union." According to Young, "[Miller] has a steel trap wrapped in a melting butter voice. With few exceptions, they follow him blindly, like zombies."[69]

Both sides hurled accusations during the strike. Paul Richards was at it again, blasting Miller by saying the owners were not against the players but were "fed up" with Miller. He warned that the players should end the strike for their own good and if they didn't, they would have to pay the price.[70]

In turn, Miller directed an attack against the owners, accusing them of being out to break the union.[71] The strike delayed the season opening for 13 days and cancelled 86 games of the regular schedule.[72] As expected, the press and the fans blamed Miller and the Association for the strike, but the players remained firm. In answer to fan anger, Miller explained why the players, like movie stars, needed a union.[73]

The first general strike in baseball history ended in its thirteenth day when the players and owners agreed to begin the season without making up any of the 86 missed games. Soon after the strike ended, *The Sporting News* editorialized that Marvin Miller had emerged from the strike as the most powerful man in baseball. "He achieved such unity," wrote C. C. Johnson Spink, editor and publisher, "that he was able to speak for all major league players with a single voice. The players wisely kept their comments pretty much under control and let Miller fire the bullet.... We only hope that both sides will profit from the lamented strike to develop a degree of good will toward each other in meeting the problems of the game."[74]

A compromise was reached. The players won their demands on the pension fund plus achieved some success on salary and increased health care. There was no change, however, to the reserve clause. This third Basic Agreement was not finalized, however, until a lockout by the owners during the spring of 1973, which cancelled early spring training for 13 days and kept the players out of nine regularly scheduled games.[75]

The most long-standing result of the third Basic Agreement included arbitration on salaries by an independent arbitrator for players with two years or more of major league experience. Many considered this Miller's biggest prize of the Agreement. Helping players' salaries to escalate was the increasing flow of television revenue, which Miller was able to include in the Agreement.[76] This caused C. C. Johnson Spink to write, "Miller is so powerful that his authority knows no bounds. By leading the Association into the area of salary negotiations, he has even gone beyond the limits he imposed on himself."[77]

Miller had given the players a new tool—salary arbitration, and they were not hesitant to use it. In 1974, 29 players went to arbitration. Thirteen of the players won their hearings and the remaining sixteen lost. John Gaherin, labor counsel for the owners, claimed that the hearings proved that owners were playing fairly with the players. Miller, on the other hand, emphasized that a 16-to-13 score should not mislead the public. "The results ought not be interpreted in the manner of a box score," he warned. "The overall impact was good. The 16 players who lost in arbitration, in effect, didn't lose anything. They couldn't lose because they still got the club's best offer." Miller added that in almost all of the 29 cases, the clubs, immediately prior to arbitration, increased their offers. According to Miller, each of these players, in effect, was a winner.[78]

The most noteworthy case of arbitration was that of Jim "Catfish" Hunter of the Oakland Athletics, who had filed for free agency when Charlie Finley refused to honor the terms of his contract. Miller, owners' rep Gaherin, and a professional arbitrator, Peter Seitz, all ruled in Hunter's favor and, as a free agent, Hunter signed with the New York Yankees.[79] When other players learned that Hunter had inked a multi-year deal worth more than $3 million, it opened a lot of eyes, chiefly on the players' side. Many began to comprehend what they would be worth on the open market.[80]

The results of this case only increased management's hatred of Miller. They never called him by name; he was simply referred to as "that gimpy-armed Jew bastard." Fortunately, Miller was able to ignore the insults—and he was winning. "It was vitriolic," recalled Tim McCarver. "You talk about thick skin—this guy [Miller] was a rhinoceros."[81]

The fourth Basic Agreement, ratified in 1976, dealt with the reserve clause and free agency. Miller considered the reserve clause not only unjust, but also the greatest impediment to players earning fair salaries, since owners could dictate the amounts and the players had no option other than to accept. The actual clause said that the owner could automatically renew the contract of an unsigned player for one year, but the owners applied this one-year clause every year ad infinitum. Miller argued that one year was exactly one year, and then a player was a free agent.[82]

Miller needed a case to test the validity of the reserve clause and he got one in 1975. In March of that year, Dave McNally, a pitcher recently acquired by the Montreal Expos, and Andy Messersmith, pitching star of the Los Angeles Dodgers, refused to sign their contracts. Both teams invoked the reserve clause in order to force the two pitchers to report to their respective teams. The pitchers complied, but announced that for the entire 1975 season, they would play without signing their contracts.

Baseball owners were convinced that they had to take an immediate stand to preserve the reserve clause or they would lose their remaining hold over baseball's salary structure. Miller attempted to reach a compromise with the owners, but the owners refused to give any ground. The union then offered a plan to adjust the reserve clause but not abolish it. Again, the owners remained firm. The Players Association felt it had no alternative but to directly challenge the reserve clause. McNally was not a factor in this challenge because he had to quit baseball in the middle of the season due to arm problems. On November 21, 1975, MLBPA counsel Richard Moss presented the Messersmith case to a three-man panel chaired by independent arbitrator Peter Seitz, the same man who had served on the Catfish Hunter panel.

Before the group even met, Seitz urged both sides to negotiate a settlement, but Commissioner Bowie Kuhn and the attorneys for the owners refused. They felt that even if the arbitration board ruled against them, they could appeal that ruling successfully in the courts; they also were unhappy with Seitz for his decision in the Hunter case and felt that this would be an excellent opportunity to dismiss him.

The following month Seitz ruled that Messersmith was a free agent, agreeing with Marvin Miller and the MLBPA's position that the reserve clause bound a player to his team for only one year after his contract expired. Seitz's ruling stated that the option year in every contract was just that: one option year that could not be renewed perpetually.[83] This decision applied not just to Messersmith; the immediate impact was that every baseball player with a one-year contract could become a free agent simply by refusing to sign the next year's contract and then playing out the 1976 season. The owners took two immediate steps—they fired Seitz, claiming that he was "unable to understand the basic structure of organized baseball." Seitz's reply to this statement was, "I am not an Abraham Lincoln freeing slaves. I am just interpreting the renewal clause as a lawyer and arbitrator."[84] They also challenged his decision in court, declaring that the decision could have a disastrous effect on baseball.[85]

Charlie Finley was the only owner who really understood the situation. He advised the magnates to declare every player a free agent—an approach that Miller admitted would have been a logical countermove. Fortunately for the union, the other owners despised Finley and laughed off his advice, much to Miller's relief.[86] Miller told Jerry Reuss, a key member of the union's leadership during his days with the Dodgers, that he had always been afraid of all players becoming free agents at the same time. Miller knew that with the players competing against each other in a flooded market of talent, the bidding process would be limited and overall salaries would come down.[87]

At this time, Marvin Miller met Don Fehr, a Kansas City attorney, who helped him with the Association's defense as the owners, as expected, continued fighting the reserve clause decision. Miller admired Fehr's legal eloquence and the fact that the two men were on the same philosophical page. He eventually hired Fehr as the Association's legal counsel, replacing Dick Moss, who had left to become an agent.[88]

While waiting for a decision on the court tests of the free agency question, the owners stalled on negotiations to replace the basic agreement, which had expired in 1975. The federal court upheld Seitz's ruling, and in protest, the owners staged another lockout in 1976, which delayed spring training until March 17 when Bowie Kuhn ordered the camps opened.[89]

The union and the owners reached a settlement in 1976—the fourth Basic Agreement that contained several points. First, it established that a player could become a free agent after six years. This was another victory for Miller. Not only did this rule limit the supply of free agents, but a six-year player on the open market would likely command the most interest since he would probably be near or at the peak of his career.[90]

The owners demanded a way to obtain another player in return for the one lost through free agency. The source of replacement, an amateur draft choice, remained a contentious issue that was not completely resolved in the 1976 Basic Agreement.

The re-entry draft required that a club which signed a free agent had to lose a player to the draft. The problem was that the rule did not stipulate that the replacement had to be a proven player. That was the omission that would figure in renewed hostilities later.[91]

Miller was now widely regarded as the most potent figure in baseball. Employing his vast knowledge of labor laws and his charismatic leadership, he had built his Association into a powerful group, and he had been able to win concessions that had long seemed impossible. The minimum salary had climbed to $21,000 a year, while average salaries neared $100,000. He had engineered a pension plan that was the envy of every organized professional sport and inaugurated formal labor contracts arrived at by collective bargaining.[92] In addition, he had educated his members so well that the players were able to remain unruffled in the face of organized attempts to divide them.[93]

The ink had barely dried on the fourth Basic Agreement in 1976 when negotiations began on the next one. The owners complained that the plethora of free agents, combined with salary arbitration awards, escalated players' salaries. In retaliation, they demanded compensation in the form of an established major league player rather than an amateur for those players lost through free agency. Moreover, the owners demanded a "ranking" player to be drawn from what would be left after a team listed eighteen men on a "protected list."[94]

Miller and the MLBPA rejected the demand outright on the grounds that such upgraded compensation would not only inhibit the free-agent market, but also, according to Miller, "The owners are trying to force the players to force the owners to regulate themselves. That is not the players' responsibility."[95] Furthermore, he refuted the owners' claims that free agency was hurting the game by pointing out that major league attendance was on the rise.[96]

Negotiations were rancorous between Miller, Bowie Kuhn, and the new owners' representative, Ray Grebey. Grebey came to baseball from General Electric, and Miller's research found that he had a reputation as a tough bargainer with an enmity toward workers. The magnates, on the other hand, saw in Grebey the long-overdue solution to their past miscalculations. The general feeling was that the owners had finally brought in a guy to challenge Miller, a negotiator who could defeat both Marvin Miller and the union.[97]

One player-leader needed no introduction to Ray Grebey. Mark Belanger's mother had worked at a GE plant in Pittsfield, Massachusetts, for more than thirty years and in 1969 had gone through a 102-day strike there. When her son mentioned that an ex–GE negotiator named Grebey had been hired to represent the owners, her face whitened. "Oh, that's the guy who handled the [strike] at GE," she said.[98]

That there would be a showdown was evident. The late journalist Leonard Koppett aptly summed up the situation: "From Commissioner Bowie Kuhn on down, baseball authorities are obsessed with the craving for a victory, however pointless and symbolic, over the ogre, Marvin Miller." To the owners, Miller represented everything that had gone wrong in baseball during the past decade. The veteran owners never forgave him for breaking their power, and the newer owners considered him the force which was holding the union together.[99]

In 1980 and 1981, Miller faced one more battle with the owners who wanted to establish compensation for free agents. The players were obdurate in opposing this plan, which they felt would severely damage their influence in negotiations. They authorized a strike in 1980, but it was averted when the players decided before the start of the season to play without an agreement while continuing negotiations. Despite a series of proposals back and forth from both sides, the stalemate continued into 1981.[100]

The owners promised to unilaterally implement the "protected list" compensation plan in 1981, and the players announced they would strike on June 1 of that year if they still found the plan unacceptable.[101]

On February 25, 1981, the executive board of the MLBPA, meeting in Tampa, voted unanimously to strike on May 29 unless a compromise could be reached on the issue of free-agency compensation. The players felt that any form of compensation would restrict movement and salary growth, while the owners wanted assurances that they would be compensated for movement of players as a result of free agency.[102]

On May 28, one day before the strike was to take place, representatives of the players and the owners agreed to extend the deadline. Miller petitioned the National Labor Relations Board for an injunction to rescind for one year management's controversial plan. On

June 10, 1981, Federal Judge Henry Werker denied the injunction. Miller immediately sent out a memorandum to his membership for a walkout before games of June 12.[103]

The players struck on June 11, 1981, in what turned out to be baseball's most damaging labor-management conflict since the 1890 Brotherhood war.[104] Many players in the game had never gone through a strike before, and there was a large gap between the contracts of top stars and "ordinary" players. Miller hoped that both groups would support the strike. The owners figured that stars would not strike because their high salaries were too lucrative to lose. The owners were wrong. Based on the number of top players willing to risk their popularity and their pocket books, the union was unified.[105]

On July 16, management offered a new proposal to end the 35-day-old strike, but tied it to a demand that players surrender service time for the period of the strike. Miller rejected the proposal, replying that players would not surrender on the issue of credited service time.[106] On July 30, Miller held the first of his meetings with players who unanimously adopted a resolution endorsing Miller and the negotiating committee. The strike headed into its forty-ninth day.[107]

It ended on the fiftieth day and was settled on July 31. White Sox owner Jerry Reinsdorf called it "the most insane strike I've ever heard of."[108] The two basic provisions of the agreement were that a team losing a premium free-agent player could select a player from a pool to which all teams—with limited exceptions—would contribute. The other major provision was that the Basic Agreement would be extended one year or at least until the end of the 1984 season.[109]

Neither Miller nor Grebey made an effort to claim victory in the strike. "It's a victory for nobody and a loss for nobody," said Grebey. "It's a good collective bargaining agreement. There's something in it for both sides." Many players believed that the owners' motivation in the strike was to score a "victory" over Miller in his last battle, for he had previously stated he would retire once an agreement was reached on free-agent compensation.[110] According to Marvin Miller, the 50-day player strike was to defend the players' victories achieved in the previous agreements.[111] Miller felt that the 1981 strike was the Players Association's finest hour. Unlike the strike in 1972, this time the players knew the consequences and stood up for their rights regardless of the penalties.[112]

The 1981 baseball strike was the first completely in-season strike in the history of major league baseball and wiped more than 700 games off the regular schedule. It was estimated that the strike cost the players $30 million in salaries; the owners estimated their losses at $16 million since their financial suffering was assuaged by $50 million in strike insurance, which they collectively secured. Miller, who was now making $160,000 a year, did not accept his salary during the strike.[113]

The strike also had a devastating effect on big-league cities, which lamented lost tax revenue and hotel, restaurant, and other baseball-related income. Commissioner Bowie Kuhn did nothing about the strike, but basically sided with the owners and officially remained remote.[114] He was not too remote to accuse the players of being "prisoners" of Miller's ego and knee-jerk hatred of management.[115]

Throughout Miller's career, many owners and some of the press attacked him for causing "spiritual erosion" in baseball. Sports writers often claimed that Miller had brainwashed his players and would refer to Miller as "Comrade Miller," or "Marvin Millerinski" a quasi–Bolshevist who was trying to support a strike. To a majority of the baseball press, Miller was simply a dangerous annoyance who "must have thought that baseball was invented the same time he came onto the scene."[116]

Miller claimed that the press seemed to exaggerate the relationship he had with Bowie Kuhn. However, Miller believed that Kuhn, like most commissioners before him, felt that he was a neutral party who represented the interests of everyone—owners, league officials, umpires, and players. Not so, Miller asserted. "He [Kuhn] represents one narrow interest: the owners and their profits. He's an employee of the owners—they pick him, they pay him, they tell him their bidding, and when they're unhappy they fire him."[117] For his part, Bowie Kuhn considered Miller an "old-fashioned, 19th century trade unionist who hated management generally, and the management of baseball specifically."[118]

The players, however, revered Miller. Jim Bunning said, "We lacked direction, and that's what Marvin gave us. He focused on things that were important." Sal Bando said that Miller was so low-keyed that "I never saw him rattled."[119] Reggie Jackson commented, "Marvin Miller took on an establishment and whipped them. We never would have been free agents without him."[120] Hank Aaron called Marvin Miller "as important to the game of baseball as Jackie Robinson."[121] Former player Joe Morgan complimented Miller on the rights players won as a direct result of his leadership. "He set the tone and directed the strategies that brought about these landmark changes," wrote Morgan.[122] At Miller's retirement, players acclaimed him as their "Commissioner."[123]

Marvin Miller retired in 1982 and the executive committee selected Ken Moffett, the federal mediator during the 1981 baseball negotiations, to succeed him. However, they kept Marvin Miller in the Association's office as a consultant to bring Moffett up to speed.[124] Miller's mission had always been to obtain and then keep benefits for the players. Moffett, as a conciliator, wanted to take on the nearly impossible task of mending the gap between the players and the owners. Miller thought Moffett was undermining the players' positions.

Few players were aware that there was a rift between Miller and Moffett, but one unidentified player who did, remarked, "These guys on the executive board picked Moffett, but when it comes down to the rank and file, the players will do whatever Marvin says. He's the guy who built the union. Without him, we're still peons."[125] After ten months in office, Moffett was fired on November 23, 1983, thanks in no small part to Miller.[126] Dick Moss, the player agent who had served as the union's general counsel during part of Miller's tenure, said the players "felt it was time to admit they made a mistake." Marvin Miller agreed to lead the union until December 6, but announced that Don Fehr would then become acting director.[127]

The executive board of the MLBPA elected Donald Fehr interim executive director of the association in December 1983 and director in 1984. With the election of the 35-year-old Fehr, Miller stepped down for good.[128] Miller had every reason to be optimistic about Fehr's success as director, calling him capable and bright. His only disadvantage was that he had to work with people who never had to understand the struggle or the necessity of resisting owners' demands. "They have no history to fortify them," noted Miller.[129]

During his career, Miller received a number of honors. In 2000 The Sporting News ranked Miller fifth on its list of the "100 Most Powerful People in Sports for the 20th Century."[130] Three years later he was inducted into the Shrine of the Eternals, also known as the Baseball Reliquary—the so-called 'people's Hall of Fame" which annually salutes the game's rebels, radicals and reprobates.[131] In 2001 Miller was elected to the International Jewish Sports Hall of Fame.[132]

Besides formal recognitions, some of those who had opposed Miller during his tenure also paid tribute to him. Miller received a note conveying Birdie Tebbetts' thanks for the gains the association had made for the players and the increased benefits he received from the pension fund. Bob Hunter, an influential West Coast writer, who had opposed the actions of the union, found out that, "you more or less got to like him because he always gave you a straight answer." Buzzie Bavasi learned to appreciate Miller because "he never lied to me."[133]

Despite admiration many had for Miller, inclusion in Baseball's Hall of Fame at Cooperstown always eluded him. Yankees owner George Steinbrenner, former executive Buzzie Bavasi, and former hurler and United States Senator Jim Bunning, high-profile Republicans, have all touted Miller for enshrinement at Cooperstown. "The Hall of Fame is about players, and Marvin did more for the players than anyone else," they all agree. The argument against admitting Miller is that he fits no category—he was neither a player nor an executive. However, his supporters claim the reason that Miller has not been admitted to the Hall of Fame is that "The Hall of Fame is a private organization run by the owners of Major League Baseball. There are a great many men on those committees who have vivid memories of the stomping Marvin Miller gave them in every labor battle. Do you think those men are now going to roll out the red carpet and ask him into Cooperstown?"[134]

In June 2008, Miller formally asked Jack O'Connell of the Baseball Writers Association of America that he not be considered for the Hall again. "I find myself unwilling to contemplate one more rigged Veterans Committee whose members are handpicked to reach a particular outcome while offering the pretense of a democratic vote. It is an insult to baseball fans, historians, and sports writers and especially to those baseball players who sacrificed and brought the game into the 21st century. At the age of 91, I can do without farce."[135]

Marvin Miller might have been reviled for making baseball a business, but it had been one since 1876. He simply made the business pay off for the more than 600 men who play the game each year instead of merely their bosses.[136] His astute organization of the players served as a model for major league umpires and other groups, and his negotiating skills with owners led to success across the board.[137] Few labor unions ever matched the gains of the MLBPA under Miller.[138] He had created one of the most powerful unions in the United States.[139]

Miller and the association were successful because they worked hard, used imagination, took chances, communicated quickly and completely with the members, and had a position that was very difficult to assail. Miller used two fundamental issues to win his battles—money and justice. While the owners focused only on the former, Miller got both for his players.[140]

Bill Madden, *New York Daily News* sportswriter, echoed the feelings of many when he wrote in 1991, "Baseball officialdom would be hard-pressed to write the history of baseball without mentioning most prominently in it the man who did more to change the game in the last 25 years than anyone else."[141]

Baseball executive Roland Hemond, who was very active during the Miller years, agreed that Miller had done his job well and that he had brought positive change to baseball. "He enhanced the popularity of the game partly because of free agency." Hemond maintained that, "People wanted to go out and see these players who were worth millions." On a more personal note, Hemond praised Miller's integrity. "He never went for the jugular. It seemed at times that he was demanding, but nowadays he would be considered a man who merely wanted things to be fair."[142]

11. Baseball's First Designated Hitter

Most students of baseball are well aware that there are two Jewish major leaguers in Baseball's Hall of Fame. Many, however, do not know that a bat enshrined there represents a third, Ronald Mark Blomberg. Blomberg's bat, which bears a Star of David, was sent to Cooperstown shortly after Blomberg became the first designated hitter in major league baseball.[1]

Chronologically, Blomberg was the last Jewish major leaguer to debut in the 1960s. He was born August 23, 1948, in Atlanta, the only child of Sol and Goldie Blomberg. The family name was pronounced "Bloomberg" but the extra "o" was lost somewhere in earlier generations.[2]

As a child, Ron attended Hebrew School twice a week. He was not an Orthodox Jew, but he did observe the High Holy Days, wearing his *yarmulke* and *tallis*. His family adhered to Jewish traditions, and he remembers having a Seder every Passover. "I wasn't as religious a person as my parents were," recalls Blomberg, "but I was never ashamed of my religion."[3]

His parents never stood in the way of his wanting to play baseball as a child or later in life, but they would not allow him to play high school football. "Too many knee injuries," his dad would explain."[4] His father, who called his son Ronnie, would often tell the story about two well-worn spots in the backyard where he and his son stood to play catch. "When I wasn't around," related Sol, "Ronnie would swing a bat all by himself for hours. We have a holly berry bush near our driveway and Ronnie would throw berries from the bush to hit."[5]

Blomberg played Little League baseball at the age of 12, and in high school, lettered all four years in baseball, basketball and track. While he was growing up in Atlanta, he witnessed many disturbing incidents. The infamous bombing of the Jewish temple in Atlanta occurred just three blocks from his home. It made national headlines and was depicted in the movie, *Driving Miss Daisy*.[6]

"A lot of people I played in high school with, half my team, was in the Ku Klux Klan, and after the ballgames, they had their robes and they had their hoods and they went out and had cross burnings," Blomberg remembered. "Most people don't believe it, but it really does happen. I was very lucky that when I was in high school, I did not personally face any anti–Semitism towards me directly. At that time, few people in Georgia even knew what a Jew was. There were bombings and marching of the KKK. That was the environment."[7]

Blomberg turned down several college basketball scholarships to concentrate on baseball; he attended DeKalb Junior College for two years. While playing professional baseball, Blomberg also continued his college studies, majoring in psychology at Fairleigh Dickinson University in Teaneck, New Jersey.[8]

The blond, six-foot, one-inch, left-handed hitting outfielder/first baseman with a charming Southern drawl was the number one selection in the 1967 free agent draft. The Yankees, who had the first selection because of their last-place finish in 1966, signed Blomberg for "better than a $50,000 bonus."[9] When he signed, he told the Yankees that if the team had to play even a World Series game on either Rosh Hashanah or Yom Kippur, he would not take part. "Those are the days I have to worship God," he said.[10]

Savvy observers thought there was more to the Blomberg signing than met the eye. According to the prominent (and Jewish) sportswriter Shirley Povich, "Only the naïve would not suspect there is an ethnic angle in the Yankees' interest in Blomberg.... He had a proper bar mitzvah ten years ago in Atlanta and could, at last, spell success for the Yankees' long-unrewarded search for a Jewish ballplayer."[11]

Bob Fishel, the Yankee public relations director admitted that they signed the personable, enthusiastic, and good-looking Ron Blomberg not only because of his natural ability, but also because he was Jewish. "We made a conscious effort to find a Jewish player. We certainly didn't draft Blomberg for the reason that he was Jewish; we felt that he was the best player in the country." Nevertheless, Fishel admitted that if the muscular player attracted more Jewish fans to Yankee Stadium, the Yankees might reap rich dividends besides those on the scoreboard.[12]

Blomberg began his professional career in the Yankees organization in 1967 with Johnson City of the Appalachian League where he hit 10 home runs in 66 games with a .297 average. In 1968, playing for Kingston in the Class A Carolina League, he hit only .251 in 105 games with seven homers. Despite his two relatively mediocre years in the minors, both the newspapers and the Yankees were ready to proclaim Blomberg the "Jewish Mantle." His roommate at Kingston said, "I don't see how Ron can miss. The guy runs like a deer, has a good bat and the will to get where he's going." Even Yankees general manager Lee MacPhail touted Blomberg and boasted, "I feel that Ronnie is the best pro prospect to come along in several years."[13]

Blomberg admitted that he had encountered ridicule and derision during his tenure in the minor leagues, especially the years he spent in the south. "I heard plenty of catcalls in the minor leagues, 'Jew boy' and things like that. It does hurt you. But you know that you've got to prevail and come out of it and I feel like I did."[14]

Blomberg indicated that from time to time, a letter would arrive with no return address and a swastika or a Ku Klux Klan sign inside. A few pieces of mail were addressed to "Jew-boy" or at least had a swastika on the envelope. "I would occasionally hear abusive taunts from the crowd. I played ball in plenty of small coal mining or tobacco towns and the townspeople looked at a Jew almost as an alien. In their eyes, I was quite different from them. In Winston-Salem I hit a home run against Bill Lee and as I rounded the bases, I could hear someone shout from the stands, "Sit down, Jew-boy, you got horns." Blomberg admitted that in the majors, at no time did he hear any derogatory comments from fans in the stands."[15]

Blomberg played the 1969 season with Manchester, New Hampshire, in the Eastern League, and at the end of the season, the Yankees gave him a brief tryout. He made his debut on September 10, 1969, appeared in four games and had three hits in six at-bats that year.[16]

In 1970 he was with Syracuse in the AAA International League. A scouting report on International League prospects summarized Blomberg's abilities. "He has great physical assets, speed, a good arm, and a good batting eye. Platooned a lot this season, he'll probably get extensive instruction in winter ball. Blomberg should improve by playing and youth is on his side. He's 21."[17]

In 1971 Blomberg appeared in 46 games for Syracuse before being called up by the Yankees on June 25.[18] He played 64 games for the New York club in 1971, hit seven home runs and batted .322.[19]

From the moment Blomberg was promoted to the parent team, there was no question about his power. But his manager, Ralph Houk, who was quite fond of him, had a dilemma. Blomberg had been playing the outfield at the request of the Yankees organization, but the Yankees had a glut of outfielders and decided to make him a first baseman again, his original position. The team sent Blomberg to Florida to play winter ball during the 1971-72 off-season to give him some additional work at first base. "I don't want to wait until spring training to make the move," said Houk.[20]

Blomberg had another problem—he had difficulty hitting left-handed pitchers. Houk benched him most of the time when a southpaw was on the mound. "He was hitting right-handers so well," said Houk, "that I didn't want to hurt his confidence." Blomberg made it very clear that he did not like the idea of platooning. "I can hit any kind of pitching if they leave me in there long enough."[21]

During the early 1972 Grapefruit League season, Blomberg failed to get a single base hit against southpaws in 19 times at bat. On the other hand, against right-handed pitchers, he hit a solid .524, with 11 hits in 21 times at bat. He was beginning to feel comfortable at first base and had proven to be adept there after four seasons as a minor-league outfielder. But Houk indicated that if he did not begin to hit southpaws, he was going to platoon Blomberg at first base with either Felipe Alou or Danny Cater.[22]

In 1972 Blomberg played both first base and the outfield. Appearing in 107 games, he hit 14 homers and drove in 49 runs, but his average was only .268.[23]

Author and sportswriter Roger Kahn noted that the Yankees organization failed to help Blomberg overcome his inabilities to hit left-handers even though he spent a good part of the season in AAA. "Supposedly," wrote Kahn, "he was at Syracuse to learn. Instead, the manager platooned him, so Blomberg worked at his strength, powdering right-handers, something he did naturally, but he was given no chance to work at his weakness—the left-handed curveball. "Granted sensitive handling," concluded Kahn, "and he might have been a big-league star."[24]

Despite Blomberg's shortcomings, he seemed to be the answer to the Yankees' search for a good Jewish ballplayer to attract Jewish fans and counter the appeal of the New York Mets. By the time Blomberg arrived, many in the closely-knit Jewish neighborhoods had left the Bronx for the suburbs. Bob Fishel, who had boasted that Blomberg's presence wearing the Yankee pinstripes would increase the number of Jewish fans at Yankee Stadium, began to admit that he was not so sure how important the ethnic element was. When Blomberg was told that the Bronx's Jewish population had moved to the suburbs, he said, "That's all right. I'll bring them back." And Jewish fans, suburban or not, did respond to the "Yiddish Yankee."[25] Blomberg's boast that he "would bring them back" was partially true. While the Jews would leave their suburban life to attend Yankees games, once they had moved from the South Bronx, they never returned permanently.[26]

Bloomberg was invited to celebrate every bar mitzvah in the city. The Stage Deli named a sandwich for him. "It was a reuben, with corned beef, pastrami, cheese, and Russian dressing."[27] He received offers to do commercials for Hebrew National salami and was sent mezuzahs in the mail. Yankees fans began to call Blomberg the "Messiah." The day the Yankees put his name on the scoreboard after they had signed him, he was at the stadium with his parents to watch the game and a big cheer went up. "It must have been all those Jewish fans from Paramus to Riverdale, they all stood up to cheer me." The Yankees were especially pleased when he was contacted by several organizations wishing to sponsor Blomberg nights at the stadium.[28]

If Jews were delighted to have Blomberg, he was equally delighted to be in New York although he often stated that he was a Southern person at heart and did not think he could live there forever. "I'd like to have a house some day where I could see trees and grass."[29] He also pointed out that being raised Jewish in the South is different from being raised Jewish in New York. "No one kept kosher even though we attended a conservative congregation. When I first came to New York and saw Hasidic Jews, I thought they were Quakers. I was mobbed by the New York Jews who took to me as if I were a native New Yorker."[30]

Blomberg was elated to be playing in the major leagues and happy to demonstrate that he was a Jewish athlete. Whenever he took the field or came to bat, he always wore a Chai necklace and had a Jewish Star drawn under the brim of his hat, on his glove, and on his bat.[31]

Although Ron Blomberg had a respectable eight-year career in the major leagues, the Atlanta native will always be remembered for one plate appearance in Fenway Park on April 6, 1973, when he became the world's first designated hitter. The event was so historical that Blomberg's bat was immediately sent to Cooperstown where it is now preserved at the Baseball Hall of Fame (courtesy National Baseball Hall of Fame Library; Cooperstown, N.Y.).

For some time, a number of major league owners had been concerned about the lack of offense in the American League and the drop in attendance at the ballparks. Many of these owners felt that replacing the pitcher's slot in the lineup with a professional hitter would result in more scoring and more fan interest.[32]

Many baseball mavens actually felt the replacement was long overdue. Connie Mack had suggested the change as early as 1906.[33] A's owner Charlie Finley was one of its original backers. He suggested to Bowie Kuhn that a "designated hitter" replace the pitcher in the lineup because he felt that "Fans come to the park to see action, home runs. Let's have a permanent pinch-hitter for the pitcher."[34] Kuhn took Finley's advice, and as expected, the American League strongly endorsed the idea, but the National League was resolute in its opposition. Beginning with the 1973 season, Kuhn decided to allow the American League to adopt the rule change for three years on an experimental basis. Originally, the rule was called the DPH (designated pinch-hitter), but changed simply to DH.[35]

The rule went into effect at exhibition games in spring training camps in 1973. Blomberg gave little thought to the rule, and during the Yankee spring training games, he made no appearances as a "designated hitter." Houk used either Felipe Alou or Johnny Callison in that role, depending on who was pitching on a given day. During the spring, Blomberg played in the outfield and at first base against both right- and left-handed pitchers.

A week before the end of spring training, Blomberg pulled a hamstring while stretching to reach the first-base bag in an attempt to run out a ball. When the Yankees broke camp, he was swinging the bat just fine, but his leg was still taped up. On 1973's opening day, the Yankees were scheduled to play at Fenway Park against the Red Sox. While flying to Boston, Ralph Houk asked Blomberg what he thought about appearing as the DH. "What do I have to do?" asked Blomberg. Houk replied that he would just need to come to the plate, take four swings, drive in runs, come back to the bench and keep loose in the runway." As Houk explained, "You're basically pinch-hitting for the pitcher four times in the same game."[36]

Immediately before the game began, coach Elston Howard informed Blomberg that Houk did not want him to play first base and further hurt his hamstring, but that he would be the "designated hitter" that day and bat sixth. In the first inning, with two outs, Blomberg came to the plate with the bases loaded. Pitcher Luis Tiant had had difficulty finding home plate that cold, raw afternoon, and Blomberg worked him for a walk. Since the Yankees were the visiting team, they batted first. The Red Sox also employed a DH, Orlando Cepeda, but he hit in the bottom half of the inning. If Matty Alou, batting third for the Yankees, had not doubled with two out, the top of the first would have ended and Cepeda could have made the history books.[37] Other American League teams were employing the DH that day, too, but the Yankees–Red Sox game was the first to start. Therefore, on that winter-like day, April 7, 1973, at 12:50 P.M. Eastern Time, Ron Blomberg had the distinction of becoming baseball's first designated hitter.[38]

After the game, swarms of reporters surrounded Blomberg's locker waiting to speak with him. He finally understood the significance of being major league baseball's first DH. Marty Appel of the Yankees front office ran up to him and demanded Blomberg give him his bat so it could be sent to Cooperstown. Blomberg refused, but Appel was insistent. Later that evening, Blomberg told Appel that the rule would never last.[39]

Blomberg's bat was taken to the Hall of Fame in Cooperstown, and years later, Blomberg thinks the honor is far more special than he did in April 1973. "I may have made it into the Hall of Fame through the back door," he said, "but I'm still there." Sportswriter Dick Schaap reminded Blomberg that there were not too many "firsts" in the world of baseball, but they can never take away that you were the first DH. Blomberg replied, "Yeah—Designated Hebrew."[40] Several years later, Blomberg admitted, "I was quite happy to be the designated hitter. With Bobby Bonds in right field and three first basemen, I might as well have donated my glove to charity."[41]

Beginning with his history-making opening game, Blomberg's best year in major league baseball was 1973. He carried a .400 average into mid-season and became one of the "glamour boys" of the Yankees. In addition to making his mark as a hitter, he was also becoming known as one of the game's characters, driving teammates crazy with his frenetic energy, exuberance, and impulsiveness. He had the capacity to make people laugh and had a prodigious appetite. *Newsweek* called Blomberg a "kind of Jewish L'il Abner, who speaks in engaging malapropisms, plays first base the way he speaks, and bats only against right-handed pitchers." However, the magazine noted that Blomberg led the left-handed hitters of the world in batting.[42]

Despite an obvious fit as a platooned DH, Blomberg continued trying to hit lefties and play first base regularly. He split time, however, between first base and DH. He aggravated his hamstring again in the late summer and ended the 1973 season hitting .329 in 100 games. He had 12 homers and 57 RBIs.[43]

According to the *New York Times*, an anonymous member of the Yankees organization—someone who had coached and encouraged Blomberg—gave a serious assessment of him. "He's a helluva hitter, but he's never going to get any better. He won't listen. He nods and he nods and he nods, but he doesn't listen. He may end up being the greatest designated hitter in history—against right-handers—but that's all he'll be."[44]

In 1974 Blomberg played in 90 games for the Yankees, mostly as a DH, hitting .311 with ten homers. He had more opportunities to hit against southpaws, and his average against lefties was a respectable .276. He seemed satisfied with his role as a designated hitter. There's no doubt that the Yankees lineup was much more potent with Blomberg in it; rival managers tended to use their lefthanders to keep Blomberg on the bench. His own manager, Bill Virdon, thought he did rather well in 1974 as long as he waited for his pitch and did not try to hit it out of the park.[45]

After the 1974 season, just as Blomberg looked as if he might live up to his potential, the injury bug hit. In June 1975, he hit a double against the Brewers but when he swung, he fell down. A tendon had popped in his shoulder. That double would be his last hit in the majors for three years. He spent the remainder of the season on the disabled list. During the abbreviated year, he batted only 106 times and played in just 27 games. After surgery to repair his shoulder, Blomberg returned in 1976 but appeared in only two games. In 1977, seemingly recovered and with just three days remaining in spring training, Blomberg went back for a fly ball, crashed into the Winter Haven, Florida, fence, and demolished his left knee. He underwent surgery again, this time to reassemble his shattered knee. With this injury, Ron was out for the entire 1977 season.[46]

Some of Blomberg's teammates reproached him for not playing after his knee surgery, implying that he was faking. Blomberg's manager that year, Billy Martin, however, was very supportive. "I thought Billy was great to me," said Blomberg."[47] During his tenure with the Yankees, Blomberg played for three managers and had good things to say about them all. Ralph Houk—"a great manager," said Blomberg; Bill Virdon—"a brilliant baseball man"; and for three years, Billy Martin—"a fiery competitor."

In 1976 and 1977, one of Blomberg's teammates on the Yankees was another Jewish player, Ken Holtzman. The Yankees were in the World Series both years, but neither Holtzman nor Blomberg appeared in any game in either of those years. This led many to wonder if Billy Martin had ill feelings toward Jews. When baseball historian Roger Kahn questioned Al Rosen, also a Jew and president of the Yankees at that time, about Billy Martin, Rosen replied that Martin was not anti–Semitic and told Kahn, "I know how he [Martin] runs the club for us. Winning is everything. Losing is nothing. I don't think Billy would have a bit of trouble managing a ball player he thinks is a winner, whatever the guy's religion."[48]

The Yankees did not protect Blomberg the year he was out, and in November 1977, the Chicago White Sox selected him through the re-entry draft. Six teams had selected Blomberg, but the White Sox offered him the security of a four-year guaranteed contract for which he was to receive $600,000 over the life of the contract. Blomberg narrowed his choice of teams to the New York Mets and the Chicago White Sox, owned by Bill Veeck.

While Blomberg hated to leave New York, he weighed all the factors and chose the White Sox. "For one thing, even if my knee is a little sore, I could be the designated hitter. And Veeck is an outstanding person. He's one of the warmest people I've ever met in baseball."[49]

Just as in New York, Blomberg's religion was part of his appeal to Bill Veeck whose White Sox roster also included Steve Stone and Ross Baumgarten. "With your personality," Veeck told Blomberg, "and all the Jewish people in Chicago, you're going to be a perfect fit."

In Chicago, Blomberg found welcoming synagogues, but not a welcoming clubhouse. Blomberg's relationship with Steve Stone was not the friendliest. In addition, Blomberg found a number of born-again Christians on the team who held regular prayer meetings. "They didn't accept that I was Jewish and didn't want me to get involved," said Blomberg, "even though the meetings were supposed to be nondenominational."[50]

But he still had the highest regard for Bill Veeck. Prior to his signing, Veeck made it a point to invite Blomberg to come to Chicago where he told him about having his leg amputated, hoping to inspire Ron to feel that if Veeck could do it and succeed, Blomberg could, too. "The man cares about his ballplayers," said Blomberg. "He's around the clubhouse talking to guys who aren't playing, asking them if they need any help in moving their stuff into their new apartments, talking to pitchers who have been knocked out and telling them not to worry about it."[51]

Veeck had acquired Blomberg as a full-time designated hitter against right-handed pitching and a part-time first baseman and outfielder. Early in the season, Blomberg was only a part-time designated hitter, although on opening day, he did hit a home run to help his team defeat the Boston Red Sox. Many in the press box were skeptical about his ability to play after being out of the lineup with injuries for most of the previous two seasons.

The critics were soon proven right. By the end of May, both Blomberg and the White Sox were mired in a slump and Blomberg's playing time had greatly diminished. In August, injuries once again ruined his season. He pulled a groin muscle and played only 61 games the entire year. He managed to hit only .231 with five home runs. In March of 1979 the White Sox released him.[52]

Blomberg was disappointed by his release, for he had had a relatively good spring at the White Sox training camp in Sarasota. He refused to rap the White Sox or Bill Veeck. "They gave me the opportunity to prove I could come back. Frankly, I thought I was proving it. I was surprised."[53] Years later, he still had kind words for Veeck. "He was one of the most wonderful human beings I've ever met. But every day it was like a circus at the ballpark. You never knew whether he was going to have you wear shorts or what. Bill was an entertainer ... [and] just a super guy."[54]

In his eight-year career in the major leagues, Bloomberg appeared in 461 games. He had 391 hits, 224 runs batted in, 52 home runs and a lifetime batting average of .293.[55]

Blomberg retired to his hometown Atlanta with his wife Beth and their son Adam and daughter Chelsey in order to be near his aging parents. Blomberg became an insurance executive, founded a career-counseling firm that lasted a few years and then ran into business problems.[56] He also did motivational speaking, participated in fantasy camps, and scouted for the New York Yankees.[57] In 1995 he turned down an offer from the Yankees to become a coach, and chose instead to establish the Ron Blomberg Championship Baseball Program, a series of clinics for children between the ages of five and seventeen in Atlanta.[58]

In 2003 Blomberg was inducted into the National Jewish Sports Hall of Fame. One of the reasons he was chosen was for his outreach efforts to the Jewish community to share his experiences in major league baseball.[59] He was also one of the managers of the Israel Baseball League in 2007.[60]

"I was very lucky to live my fantasy and do something I want to do," said Blomberg. "There are so many people in this world that are not happy to do what they do. God gave me the ability to be an athlete. Why shouldn't I use all the ability that I had?"[61]

12. The Numbers Decline

In the 1970s and the 1980s, African-Americans, women, and Latinos were stepping up their efforts to attain equal opportunities in American society. American Jews as a group, however, considered themselves secure in America. Most were financially successful, proud of Israel's achievements, and speaking confidently about their Jewish identity. Some Jews had gained powerful positions in politics and the economy. For the most part, Jews were well accepted and integrated into American culture, as the upward trend of intermarriage with non–Jews demonstrated.

Interestingly, this very success held down the number of Jewish ball players from roughly 1969 through 1989. Athletically gifted Jewish boys of this third generation were now able to participate in more "upscale" sports such as golf and swimming. They still retained their interest in baseball, but they were not as encouraged or motivated to succeed in the game as previous generations had been. At the same time, there was no longer a stigma attached to "a nice Jewish boy" becoming a baseball player. And since baseball recruiters now looked primarily to colleges for prospects, Jewish ballplayers were able to combine an education with a chance at a professional baseball career. Nevertheless, during this period, only a handful of Jews became major league players, and many of them came from intermarried families.[1]

Dave Roberts

Dave Roberts was one of the players who had a Jewish father and a non–Jewish mother. Yet Roberts, who played for 13 seasons with eight different franchises, was baseball historian Martin Abramowitz's inspiration for the Dave Roberts Wandering Jew Award in recognition of his highly traveled career in the major leagues.[2]

David Arthur Roberts was born September 11, 1944, in Gallipolis, Ohio. He was actually raised by his stepfather with whom he was quite close.[3] After he graduated high school, fourteen teams approached Roberts, but he signed with the Philadelphia Phillies.[4] It was a nomadic existence for the six-foot, three-inch, 195-pound southpaw pitcher whose minor league record was excellent as he starred in the Phillies, A's, Pirates, and Padres farm systems from 1963 until 1969.[5] His last complete year in the minors, 1968, Roberts, hurling for the Columbus Jets, was the winningest pitcher in the International League with an 18–6 record.[6]

The San Diego Padres, one of baseball's newest franchises in 1969, selected Roberts in that year's expansion draft, despite his having a sore arm and an arthritic shoulder. The Padres were preparing for their first full season in the majors and were relying on all the pitching help they could obtain.[7] Roberts started with their Eastern Coast farm club but was called up by the Padres on July 3, 1969, becoming the first minor leaguer recalled by the Padres in their inaugural season.[8] Unfortunately, Roberts was back in the minors quickly without getting into a game because the team felt he still needed to work on his arm. He finally made his major league debut on September 6, 1969, just days shy of his twenty-fifth birthday. Roberts appeared in 22 games that first year with a 4.78 ERA. He started five games and his record was 0–3.[9] Roberts pitched the 1970 season with bursitis and won 8 and lost 14 games that year.[10]

His arm was treated during the winter of 1970 with a combination of ultra-sound and exercise. When Roberts came to spring camp in 1971, his pitching had improved so much, the Padres could hardly believe it was the same Dave Roberts.[11] During the season his team-

mates noticed the improvement, as he became one of the aces of the staff. His battery mate, Bob Barton, who had caught San Francisco pitchers Juan Marichal and Gaylord Perry before being dealt to the Padres, rated Roberts one of the best he had ever caught. Fellow pitcher Tom Phoebus, who came from the Orioles, called him fantastic and stated, "He's as good as any pitcher in either league."[12]

Although the Padres finished in last place in 1971, 26.5 games behind the first-place Giants, Roberts finished the season with an ERA of 2.10, second only to the Mets' Tom Seaver in the National League. He also finished sixth in the Cy Young voting in 1971.[13]

Despite his superb earned run average, Roberts lost 17 games for the Padres in 1971. *The Sporting News* noted that Roberts might be the best 17-game loser in baseball history. "If there was a hard luck player of the year award," noted the newspaper, "the Padres' David Roberts would be a shoo-in for it in 1971."[14]

Even though Roberts won 14 games in 1971, the Padres dealt him and three minor leaguers to the Houston Astros during the winter meetings in December in exchange for pitchers Bill Greif and Mark Schaeffer and switch-hitting infielder Darrel Thomas.[15]

Southpaw Dave Roberts played for the 1979 World Series champion Pittsburgh Pirates during a 13-year career in the majors. He played for eight teams beginning in 1969 with the San Diego Padres, and ending his major league career in 1981 with the New York Mets. Roberts developed lung cancer through working as a boilermaker during the off-seasons and died from the disease January 9, 2009, at the age of 64 (courtesy National Baseball Hall of Fame Library; Cooperstown, N.Y.).

Roberts promised Houston that he would do his part to make his new team a formidable contender for the National League West flag. He was not the typical Astros' overpowering pitcher, but was more of a control pitcher. "My best pitch," said Roberts, "is a strike."[16]

Roberts had winning seasons for the Astros in both 1972 and 1973, compiling a record of 29–18 those two years. In 1973 he set an Astros record with six shutouts, and his 2.85 ERA was tenth best in the National League.[17] Roberts remained with the Astros until the end of the 1975 season. He had an 18–26 record with the Astros his last two years.[18]

At the winter meetings in December 1975, the Houston Astros traded Roberts to the Detroit Tigers in a seven-player swap. The Tigers received, along with Roberts, Milt May, a catcher, and another left-handed pitcher, Jim Crawford. In return, Houston acquired out-fielder Leon Roberts, catcher Terry Humphrey, and pitchers Gene Pentz and Mark Lemongello.[19]

Roberts remained with the Tigers for the 1976 and part of the 1977 seasons. In 1976 he won 16 games while losing 17. Prior to the start of the 1976 season, he told the Tigers that he would be more than willing to pinch-hit for the Tigers if needed. No Tiger pitcher had gone to the plate since the American League had inaugurated the DH rule in 1973, but Roberts looked forward to both pitching and hitting. "If I could pick my spot and hit off right-handed pitchers," he told his bosses, "I think I could hit pretty close to .300. And it would be a solid .300 because I'm not very fast. I don't get as many leg hits."[20]

After the 1976 season, Roberts required surgery to repair an arthritic knee. The following year he appeared in 22 games with Detroit, winning four and losing 10, before being shipped to the Chicago Cubs who intended to use him both as a spot starter and in relief. The Cubs actually needed another southpaw, for they had only one until he joined the Cubs' staff.[21]

Roberts regretted the trade, indicating that he wanted to remain in Detroit where he had bought a home. "The trade caught me completely by surprise," he said. "I knew I hadn't been pitching well, but I never expected this." He rationalized that perhaps he had become too settled in Detroit, "relaxed and got fat and did not do his job."[22] Roberts remained in Chicago for the balance of 1977 and the entire 1978 season, where his record was 6–8. His hitting was much better—he came to the plate 50 times and hit .327.[23]

Roberts was not surprised when the Cubs did not re-sign him in 1979. He had fallen into disfavor with his manager, Herman Franks, in a key September game in 1977, when he criticized Franks for relieving him with a rookie.[24] The San Francisco Giants picked him up early in 1979, and he appeared in 26 games for them, going 0–2. At the end of June, Roberts was on the move again. The Giants traded him and second baseman Bill Madlock to the Pittsburgh Pirates for right-handed pitcher Ed Whitson and two minor league hurlers.[25]

Appearing in 21 games for the Pirates in 1979, Roberts compiled a record of 5–2 and an ERA of 3.26, which helped his team win the World Series that year. He did not appear in the Series, but did make one appearance in the NLCS, walking the only batter he faced. Roberts remained in the major leagues two more years. In 1980 he pitched for the Pirates and the Seattle Mariners. He completed his major league career with the New York Mets in 1981 where he went 0–3.[26]

Roberts had a lifetime 3.78 ERA and pitched in 445 games with eight major league teams. His lifetime record was 103–125. After he retired as a major leaguer, he managed the Eugene, Oregon, club in the Northwest League, which had a working agreement with the Kansas City Royals.[27] Roberts had a very philosophical summation of his baseball experience. "The way I look at it, either I'm a bum or everybody wants me."[28]

Dave Roberts died of lung cancer January 9, 2009, at the age of 64.[29] Tal Smith, Houston Astros president of baseball operations said of his former pitcher, "Dave was the consummate pro. He'll really be remembered and missed for the leadership he provided and for being such a good guy."[30]

Ross Baumgarten

In contrast to Dave Roberts who pitched for eight different teams, Ross Baumgarten spent four of his five years in the major leagues with one team—the Chicago White Sox.

Baumgarten was born in Highland Park, Illinois, May 27, 1955, and spent the first eight years of his life in Skokie, a neighboring suburb, which was home to a large Jewish population and a number of Jewish institutions. He then moved to another North Shore suburb, affluent Glencoe.[31]

His grandfather, Joseph, was an industrialist and philanthropist who, in 1960, gave $1 million to Michael Reese Hospital in Chicago, at that time the largest gift in the hospital's history.[32] His father, Robert, was a manufacturers' rep. His parents divorced during the 1960s. Baumgarten did not come from a family of athletes. In fact, his father rarely followed baseball and frankly admitted that everything his son learned about baseball, he did all on his own. "I didn't push him or coach the teams or anything. I wasn't much of a baseball fan, to tell the truth. As long as I can remember, my son wanted to be a major-league ball player. Most boys just *dream* about it. Ross was a very determined young man."[33]

As a youngster, Baumgarten, like most North Siders, grew up rooting for the Chicago Cubs. He idolized Cub pitcher Ken Holtzman and later wore his uniform number, 30.[34]

When he was eight years old, Baumgarten began his career in organized athletics as a wrong-handed shortstop in a 12-inch softball league. He then switched to pitching on a summer hardball team. "The first game I played, the pitcher did not show up. I had never pitched a hard ball," recalled Baumgarten, "but I pitched that first day and did well and I kept going."[35]

He graduated from New Trier East High School in 1973 and admitted he was not much of a student. "I liked to learn, but I didn't enjoy sitting there," he confessed. He played baseball at New Trier, and his coach, Ron Klein, recalled that when Ross was a freshman, he was just a little guy—five feet, 90 pounds. "He was probably kept on the team more because of his *desire* than his ability. Same in his sophomore year. His junior year he broke his arm and didn't play at all. By his senior year he grew to 6 feet, but was still slender at 150 pounds. He played on the junior varsity most of his senior year, but once he made varsity, he became a top pitcher."[36]

After he graduated from New Trier, Baumgarten enrolled at Palm Beach Junior College in Florida where he had little trouble fitting in as a student. "There was no adjustment to be made," he stated. "I might have expected some at college, but there was none. As far as being a Jew, I was never very religious, so that was not a problem."[37]

After two years at Palm Beach, the University of Florida in Gainesville recruited him and he pitched there for the nationally rated team. When he made All-Conference, the pros finally began to notice him.[38]

In 1977 Baumgarten was selected in the free agent draft by the Chicago White Sox in the twentieth round. According to long-time baseball executive Rollie Hemond, who spent many years with the White Sox organization, Baumgarten was signed on the "recommendation" of Marv Samuel, founder of the Chicago Baseball Charities. Baumgarten was sent to the White Sox Class A club in Appleton, Wisconsin.[39] He pitched 17 games that year with a 3–6 record and an ERA of 3.75. When he returned to Appleton in 1978, he amazed everyone with a 9–1 record and an ERA of 1.82. During the 1978 season, Baumgarten was promoted to Class AAA Iowa.[40]

In only his second AAA start, the young southpaw struck out nine batters and pitched a four-hitter against Indianapolis, the league's hardest hitting club. Baumgarten, who had moved up to Iowa in late June, said, "I like to move up, that's the name of the game. But it's made me a little uncomfortable, moving around, meeting new guys."[41]

After only nine games at Iowa, on August 14, 1978, Baumgarten was promoted to the White Sox. Two days later he made his debut as a starter— winning the game, 6–2, with help from reliever Lerrin LaGrow. "The kid has an idea of what to do with the ball," said La Grow. "It was a pleasure to bring in the victory for him."[42] The press hailed him as a "local boy" doing well. Both his father and his older brother, a film producer in Los Angeles, flew in to watch the game and surprise Ross.[43] Baumgarten appeared in six more games for the White Sox in 1978 and had a 2–2 record with a 5.87 ERA.[44]

In 1978 the Chicago White Sox had two other Jews on their roster— Ron Blomberg and Steve Stone. Although Blomberg found Stone cold at times, he acted as a mentor to

Ross Baumgarten was a native of Chicago's North Shore, but pitched four years in the majors for the Cubs' cross-town rivals, the Chicago White Sox. After ending his baseball career in 1982 with the Pittsburgh Pirates, Baumgarten became a successful account executive with a Chicago investment firm (courtesy National Baseball Hall of Fame Library; Cooperstown, N.Y.).

Baumgarten. "He [Stone] was very helpful. He taught me how to be a big leaguer on and off the field. He had an overhand curve he could throw at any speed. He taught me how to get away with high fastballs," said Baumgarten.[45]

Stone taught him well, but Baumgarten knew that he lacked the speed of a Nolan Ryan and instead had to rely on a deceptive motion—including little jerks of the head—to throw the hitters off stride "I have to think a little bit more than most pitchers."[46]

Many years after all three players retired, Baumgarten stated that he still sees Blomberg occasionally, but that he and Stone talk frequently. That same year, Baumgarten's idol, Ken Holtzman, was pitching for the Chicago White Sox's cross-town rivals, the Chicago Cubs. Holtzman and Baumgarten also became good friends after both had left the game.[47]

At the beginning of 1979, the White Sox front office had some anxious moments when Baumgarten had a sore left arm. The club quietly sent him to a specialist in Los Angeles.[48] In addition to a sore arm, Baumgarten suffered through more than a month of mysterious throat problems during the middle of the season.[49]

Ross was getting a reputation as the team philosopher as well as a team leader. After he won his fifth consecutive game in August, he announced his own job specifications. "My role as a starter is to keep it close. I don't think about a complete game," he said. "I just want to keep us in position where we can pop ahead."[50]

On the road, while his teammates headed for their favorite night spot, Baumgarten most likely would remain in his hotel room reading autobiographies and biographies—the Kennedys, Mahatma Gandhi, Martin Luther King, Lyndon Johnson. "I like to study their traits," he said. "I try to learn from them. Right now, I'm reading Christopher Lasch's *The Culture of Narcissism*."[51]

"Ross is mature beyond his years," said Manager Tony LaRussa, who, at 34, was only 10 years older than Baumgarten. One source close to the ball club said, "Ross is 24 going on 34." Baumgarten maintained that there was nothing spectacular about him. "I just want to keep us in there."[52]

Despite his sore arm and his month-long throat problems, 1979 was Baumgarten's best year in the majors. He finished with a record of 13–8 and a 3.53 ERA. He tossed a one-hitter on May 25, and hurled three shutouts. The Chicago baseball writers named him Chicago Co-Rookie of the Year.[53]

If 1979 was Baumgarten's best year, 1980 was his most frustrating. He appeared in 24 games that year and his teammates gave him practically no support at the plate. They scored a total of 25 runs during his games and in ten of them, the opposing pitchers shut out the White Sox. Baumgarten improved his control by issuing 31 fewer runs than the previous year, and his ERA was a respectable 3.44. He was pitching most of the year with a shoulder problem that turned out to be a torn muscle.[54] "This whole year has been a study in adversity for me, with the exception of getting engaged. Sometimes I take it well. Sometimes I don't. And always I ask, 'Why me?'"[55]

Baumgarten wed Nancy Newman November 8, 1980, and he credited his wife with helping him get ready for the new season. "She's helped me work out all winter," he said. "We run together, play tennis, and it's kept me in pretty good shape."[56]

Baumgarten went to Sarasota for spring training, his last with the White Sox, in the spring of 1981. He announced that he was throwing without pain for the first time in almost a year. "It couldn't be better," he said enthusiastically.[57] He had no discomfort in his shoulders, true, but by the middle of the 1981 season, he was pitching with a painful pinched nerve in his left foot. Despite the foot, he managed to pitch in 19 games that year, but his record fell to 5–9 and his ERA rose to 4.06. When the season ended, Baumgarten had surgery on his foot.[58]

The White Sox were under new ownership in 1981; Jerry Reinsdorf and Eddie Einhorn had purchased the team from Bill Veeck that year. Like many players, Baumgarten had felt very close to Veeck who, he felt, had taken a real interest in him. Baumgarten called Veeck one of the three top people he had ever known. He said he was always able to ask for advice or merely talk with Veeck. Despite the fact that both new owners were Jewish, Baumgarten had no personal relationship with them, nor did he ever have an occasion to talk to either of them.[59]

Baumgarten was not surprised when he learned that the White Sox had traded him to the Pittsburgh Pirates for infielder Vance Law before the '82 season began. "I'm not really disappointed," said Baumgarten when he learned of the trade. "I just want to go where someone will treat me as a human being, an adult and a good pitcher. I wasn't treated anywhere near those three with the White Sox. I'm talking about the ball club in general, from the owner, who thought I was too smart to be a successful pitcher, to the manager and general manager who didn't think I was a good pitcher. It's as simple as that."[60]

In 1982, Baumgarten pitched in 12 ball games for Pittsburgh and spent the remainder of the season on the disabled list. His record in the National League was 0–5 with an ERA of 6.55. He had a lifetime record of 22–36 and a 3.99 ERA.[61] In March 1983, the Pirates reduced their roster by requesting waivers on Baumgarten. He retired at the age of twenty-seven.[62]

Baumgarten had no regrets about retiring and he never looked back. He returned to Glencoe where he was raised. He and his wife would eventually have four children. Baumgarten began a successful career as a money manager at a large Chicago-based financial firm. Although he has had no part in professional baseball since his retirement, he coached summer league teams and volunteered as a pitching coach at his alma mater, New Trier High School.[63]

Steve Ratzer

Despite his very short career in the major leagues, pitcher Steve Ratzer holds two distinctions: he was the first Jewish player to debut in the 1980s, and the first Jewish player on a team based in Canada.

Steven Wayne Ratzer, a native of Paterson, New Jersey, was born September 9, 1953, to Florence and Aaron Ratzer. Steve and his two younger siblings were raised in New York, where he was selected for the All-City team in his senior year. The Montreal Expos signed the right-handed pitcher as a free agent after he graduated from St. John's University in 1975.

The Expos assigned Ratzer to Lethbridge, Alaska, in the Pioneer League. While he was waiting at the Calgary airport for a connecting flight to Lethbridge, Ratzer learned that his father had died of a heart attack. He flew back to New York to sit shiva for his late father before beginning his baseball career.

From 1975 through 1980, the six-foot, 192-pound Ratzer pitched in the minors. One of his best years was 1980 with the AAA Denver Bears, and he was selected the American Association Pitcher of the Year for his 15–4 record and 3.59 ERA.[64]

Ratzer made his debut in the major leagues in 1980 when the Expos brought him up at the end of the season. He started his only game in the majors on October 5, 1980, pitching four innings in a game Montreal won, 8–7.

During the 1981 season, Ratzer appeared in 12 games as a reliever for the Expos, winning one game and losing one game. His only major league victory came against the Phillies at Veterans Stadium. Ratzer pitched one inning of relief and got credit for the victory in a 6–3 win for Montreal.[65]

During his two-year stint in the majors, Ratzer appeared in 13 games with an ERA of 7.17.[66] He was

Steve Ratzer was the first Jewish player to play on a major league team in Canada. The right-hander pitched in 13 games for the Expos, starting one game in 1980, and relieving in 12 in 1981. In December 1981, the Expos traded Ratzer to the New York Mets for Frank Taveras, and although Ratzer played two more years in the minors, he never played in the majors after the trade (courtesy National Baseball Hall of Fame Library; Cooperstown, N.Y.).

traded to the Mets for Frank Taveras at the conclusion of the 1981 season and played the 1982 season for the Tidewater Tides in the International League. The following year the Mets traded Ratzer to the Chicago White Sox for a player to be named later.[67] He quit baseball in 1983 to spend more time with his family. He pitched nine seasons in both the majors and the minors as well as six winter seasons in Venezuela and the Dominican Republic. He and his wife, the former Janet Eifert, have three children.[68]

Steve Rosenberg

Another Jewish pitcher to debut during the 1980s was Steve Rosenberg, who pitched four years for the Chicago White Sox and the San Diego Padres. The left-handed pitcher and native of Brooklyn was born on Halloween, 1964. He was signed by the New York Yankees organization in 1986 from the University of Florida and was employed primarily as a reliever. A number-four pick in the June draft, Rosenberg was considered one of the Yankees' top pitching prospects. However, after finishing the 1987 season with their AAA team, the Yankees traded Steve, along with Mark Salas and Don Pasqua, to the Chicago White Sox organization for Scott Neilsen and Richard Dotson.[69]

Steve Rosenberg, a native of Brooklyn, pitched four years in the major leagues. Despite being considered a top prospect by the New York Yankees, he was traded to the Chicago White Sox organization, where he made 77 major league appearances during the 1988, '89 and '90 seasons. The following year, his last in the majors, he had a 1–1 record with the San Diego Padres (courtesy National Baseball Hall of Fame Library; Cooperstown, N.Y.).

Rosenberg began the 1988 season with Vancouver, where his ERA was 3.33; he had three saves in 20 games. He made his major league debut on June 4, 1988, for the Chisox at Comiskey Park against the Texas Rangers. Rosenberg finished the 1988 season with no wins, one loss, one save, and a 4.30 ERA.[70]

The following year, 1989, was even more discouraging. The White Sox attempted to use Rosenberg as a starter, and although he did win four games, he led the club with 13 losses and was sent down to the minors to begin the 1990 season. The White Sox put him back in the bullpen in 1990, but during the spring of 1991, traded him along with Adam Peterson to the San Diego Padres for Warren Newson, Kevin Garner, and Joey Cora.[71]

Rosenberg began the 1991 season pitching for Las Vegas in the AAA Pacific Coast League, but did manage to appear in 10 games for the Padres, and ended the year with a record of one and one. He finished his major league career that year with a lifetime record of 6–15 and an ERA of 4.94.[72]

Jose Bautista

The fifth Jewish player to debut in the major leagues between 1969 and 1989 was Jose Joaquin Bautista. Bautista was more memorable for his unusual background than for his career achievements as a player.

Bautista, an observant Jew, was born July 25, 1964, in Bani, the Dominican Republic, the son of a Russian-Jewish mother, Rachael Cohen, and a Dominican Catholic father.[73]

Bautista was one of six children who also lived with step-siblings in a predominantly Catholic nation. Jose and his family practiced Judaism privately along with the small number of other Jewish families in the Dominican. Bautista's family observed Shabbat, and Jose was able to have a bar mitzvah.[74] "Our friends really didn't know that we were Jewish," he said. "We grew up with all the Catholics and we looked the same to them."[75]

The six-foot, one-inch, 200-pound right-handed pitcher was signed by the Mets organization in 1981 when he was not quite 17 years old.

Bautista met his future wife, Lea Robicheck, when he was studying engineering in Venezuela after the Mets had signed him. Lea and her family had immigrated to Venezuela from Eastern Europe after World War II. "I was lucky to find my wife. She and her brother grew up very religious and she teaches me a lot about it," said Bautista.[76]

Bautista pitched seven years in the Mets system from 1981 through 1987. When he traveled in the minors, like Mike Epstein, he wore a Star of David drawn on his glove and also wore the gold star around his neck. "I never talked about being Jewish. I just went and played baseball and didn't get into religion."[77]

In 1987 the Baltimore Orioles drafted him as their first pick from the Mets' Class AAA team at Tidewater.[78] They promoted him to the majors the following season, when he made his major league debut on April 9, 1988. He was added to Baltimore's starting rotation after the Orioles lost the first 21 games of the 1988 season. In 25 starts that year, Bautista's record of 6–15 and a 4.30 ERA did not look too bad in comparison with Baltimore's overall record of 54–107.[79]

After his rookie debut in 1988, he found himself bouncing back and forth between the majors and the minors for the next three seasons. In 1989 he pitched the first half of the season for the Orioles before they sent him to Rochester on the same day he had defeated the Oakland Athletics. He had a 3–4 record that year before going to Rochester.[80] He attempted to resurrect his career by becoming a relief pitcher, but for the next two years, he managed to win only one game while losing one. After pitching 75 games for the Orioles from

Jose Bautista, the son of a Russian-Jewish mother and a Dominican-Catholic father, experienced a religious awakening while playing winter ball in Venezuela where he met his future wife. Bautista, who pitched for five teams during his nine years in the majors, and his wife, Lea, whose family lives in Israel, raised their two sons to be observant Jews (courtesy National Baseball Hall of Fame Library; Cooperstown, N.Y.).

1988 to 1991 and 75 for their minor league teams, Bautista was granted his free agency at the end of the 1991 season. He spent the entire 1992 season in the minors.[81]

In 1993 the Chicago Cubs signed Bautista and he had the best season of his career. His record was 10–3 with two saves and an ERA of 2.82 in 58 appearances.[82] Because Bautista was from the Dominican Republic, it took reporters a while before they discovered he was Jewish. He explained that he had taken his shirt off in the clubhouse and a reporter noticed that he was wearing a Star of David. When asked why he was wearing it, he explained that it was a gift from his mother. It took the reporter a while to get the point.[83]

Whenever possible, Bautista's family lighted Sabbath candles together on Friday evenings, and he tried to attend weekly synagogue services on Saturdays. When he was on the road, Bautista telephoned his family on Friday nights to recite the Sabbath prayers together. When Bautista was asked if he were Jewish, he quickly replied, "You bet I am."[84]

He pitched one more year for the Cubs in 1994 and posted a record of 4–5 in a strike-shortened season. He was the only Jewish player in the majors that year, and he might have been faced with the issue of playing on Rosh Hashanah and Yom Kippur had the season been extended. In 1993, the Cubs had been in Los Angeles on Yom Kippur. "I didn't go to the park on Yom Kippur. I stayed back in the hotel and the Cubs didn't have a problem with that," said Bautista. "There hasn't been any conflict yet. But if there were, I still wouldn't do it. I'd just say I was sorry."[85]

The Cubs released Bautista at the end of the 1994 season. He spent part of the off-season celebrating the bar mitzvah of his oldest son Leo and visiting his wife's family in Tel Aviv and Haifa, Israel. He also took classes in Hebrew, as he and Lea raised their sons to be observant Jews.[86] "My family and I go to the synagogue whenever we can," said Bautista.[87]

On April 6, 1995, Bautista signed with the San Francisco Giants and spent the next two seasons pitching mostly in middle relief and alternating between the Giants and their AAA club, the Phoenix Firebirds. In 1996 Bautista's season ended early because of an aneurysm in his right shoulder and a blood clot in his right index finger. In his two seasons with the Giants, Bautista appeared in 89 games, winning 6 and losing 12. Always known for his excellent control, in his two-year stint with the Giants he walked only 41 men in 170 innings.[88]

In 1997 the Giants traded Bautista to the Detroit Tigers. He got off to a rocky start, and in 21 games his ERA was 6.69 with a record of 2–2. The Tigers released him on July 21; he did not catch on with another major league team until the St. Louis Cardinals signed him in September. He pitched in 11 games for the Cardinals but had no record. The Cardinals were the last major league team to sign Bautista. He played for various minor league teams during the 1998 and the 1999 seasons.[89] He appeared in 312 games in his nine-year major league career. winning 32 and losing 42 for a .432 percentage. His lifetime ERA was 4.62.[90]

In 1994, a few years before he retired from baseball, Bautista told a reporter, "Even though there aren't many Jews in the Dominican Republic, I would like to go back home and build a synagogue in my native land. That way, they will forever have a house of God."[91]

Dick Sharon

Like Dave Roberts, Dick Sharon was a major leaguer with a Jewish father and a non–Jewish mother. Known as a promising outfielder, Sharon's good defensive abilities could not make up for his light hitting. A California native, Richard Louis Sharon was born in San Mateo, April 15, 1950. In high school, he was All-League in baseball, basketball and football.

When Sharon was eighteen, he was the number one pick of the Pittsburgh Pirates in the 1968 free agent draft. The self-confident six-foot, two-inch, 195-pound outfielder spent the next five years in the Pirates' farm system where he was valued for his excellent defense. His tours with the Pirates organization included stops at Bradenton in the Gulf Coast Rookie League, Gastonia in the Western Carolina League, Salem in the Carolina League, Waterbury in the Eastern League, and at the AAA level for the Charleston Charlies of the International League. He hit .268 for Charleston with 14 home runs.[92]

He never played for the parent club, for in November 1972, the Pirates traded Sharon and a to-be-named-later minor-leaguer to the Detroit Tigers for Jim Foor, a left-handed pitcher and Norm McRae, a right-handed pitcher.[93]

Sharon came to the Tigers in an unusual way. While he was in the minors, the Pirates were late in paying him. When Sharon finally received his paycheck in Mexico, it bounced when it reached the bank. He hired his brother, a lawyer, to solve the problem. Because the Pirates organization did not come up with his paycheck within the required ten days, the young outfielder insisted he was entitled to become a free agent. Embarrassed by the legal action, the Pirates agreed to trade or sell him if he had not been promoted to the parent club by 1973, and followed through with the trade with the Tigers at the 1972 winter meetings. "I had no idea I'd end up with a contender like the Tigers," said Sharon.[94]

Tiger manager Billy Martin had not seen Sharon play the outfield, but he had heard of his defensive abilities. "They tell me Sharon is one of the best center fielders in the minor leagues," he said. Even though Martin already had Mickey Stanley and Paul Blair, generally regarded as two of the best glove men in the American League, Martin nevertheless said, "It's nice to have one in reserve."[95]

Sharon spent spring training in 1973 with the Tigers at their camp in Lakeland, and Martin liked what he saw. "Dick Sharon has changed something around here," noted Martin. "We have real competition for outfield jobs. I like that. It's the kind of situation I grew up under with the Yankees."

Even Stanley admitted that Sharon was a little too good with the glove to suit him. Sharon also impressed Martin with two booming home runs. Martin liked the fact that Sharon was making the veteran outfielders push themselves harder; they realized they had to do the job or ride the bench. "I'd love to finish a tough game with Sharon in left field, Stanley in center, and Al Kaline in right. Our pitchers would certainly like that."

At the beginning of the 1973 season, the Tigers sent Sharon to Toledo in the International League where he hit .208 in the first 16 games. In the middle of May, Tiger left fielder Willie Horton was placed on the 15-day disabled list after he sprained his right wrist crashing into a wall while making a catch of a line drive by John Mayberry.[96] The Tigers recalled the 23-year-old Sharon from Toledo to replace Horton. Dick Sharon made his major league debut May 13, 1973, when he entered the game as a late defensive replacement, and on the following day at Yankee Stadium, Sharon made his first plate appearance. He drove in a run his first time at bat, and in the eighth inning he got his first major league hit, a double off Mike Kekich. On May 31, Sharon hit his first major league home run off White Sox pitcher Eddie Fisher. Two other highlights of his rookie season were a perfect 4-for-4 game against the Texas Rangers in July, including two home runs and a double, and on September 9 when he stole two bases on two attempts.[97]

In 1973 many considered the Tigers an "old club" and management hoped to turn Sharon into the successor to Hank Greenberg's protégé, Al Kaline, a player Sharon greatly admired. "Al Kaline is the greatest player I've ever seen," said Sharon. "I spent four spring trainings with the Pirates and he's better than Roberto Clemente was. That may not mean much coming from a 23-year-old, but that's how I feel." Billy Martin had been platooning Sharon against left-handed pitchers and using his ability to play any of the outfield positions to shore up the defense in the late innings.[98]

At the end of his first season in the majors, Sharon won the Tiger Rookie of the Year for 1973. He demonstrated his defensive skills by finishing the season with a .970 fielding percentage. His offensive skills were not as sharp. He hit only .242 in 60 games with two home runs and 10 runs batted in.[99]

Despite his offensive numbers, the Tigers seemed happy with Sharon's performance in 1973. Tiger general manager Jim Campbell said, "Last year nobody had heard of Sharon, but he has turned out to be a pretty good player. In fact, he's one of the most sought-after young players we have in our organization."[100]

Sharon's fielding average in 1974, .989, was even higher than the previous year, but his batting average dipped to .212. Several veteran Tiger outfielders went down with injuries, and new manager Ralph Houk, instead of giving Sharon more playing time, employed outfielders the Tigers would recall from their farm system.

"I came to spring training thinking I might possibly get a starting outfield job. Once I realized I wasn't going to get that, I sort of accepted it, knowing I'd be the fourth outfielder, ready to take over a spot if something happened," admitted Sharon with his typical outspokenness. "Then when something did happen, another outfielder was called up. It's nice to see the young guys come up and play. I thought I was one of them. But now I sometimes wonder."[101]

In November 1974, the Detroit Tigers traded Sharon, pitcher Bob Strampe and shortstop Ed Brinkman to the San Diego Padres for Nate Colbert, once regarded as one of the premier home run hitters in the National League.[102] Sharon was not unhappy with the deal which brought him to San Diego, much closer to where he had grown up in Northern California. He was still upset with his former manager, Houk, calling him "dishonest" for breaking his promise to play Sharon more in 1974. "In two years at Detroit," said Sharon, "I never started more than five games in a row."[103]

In 1975, the one season he played for the Padres, Sharon appeared in 91 games, hitting .191, with four home runs and 20 runs batted in.[104] It was his last year in the majors. On October 20, 1975, the Padres traded Sharon to the St. Louis Cardinals for veteran outfielder Willie Davis. Sharon did not play in St. Louis; the Cardinals assigned him to their AAA Tulsa farm club.[105] The following year, the Cardinals traded Sharon to the California Angels for minor league pitcher Bill Rothan.[106]

In his three-year tenure in the majors, Sharon played in 242 games, had 102 hits, including 20 doubles and 13 home runs, for a career batting average of .218.[107]

Mark Gilbert

Many Jewish ball players during the seventies and eighties were third-generation Americans. Mark Gilbert, one of the Jewish players to debut in the 1980s, was a third-generation Jewish baseball player. His father, Herbert, had advanced to AAA ball in the White Sox organization, but his grandfather, Joseph, was more thrilled than anyone when Mark made it to the majors. Joseph Gilbert had been a semi-pro pitcher offered a contract by no less a baseball maven than Connie Mack. But his father had told Joseph that "...ballplayers are bums" and that he would have to move out of the house if he wanted to play.[108]

Mark David Gilbert was born August 22, 1956, in Atlanta, but grew up in Florida where his father and grandfather owned a furniture store.[109] Mark and his grandfather shared a knowledge and love of the game. Unlike his own father, his grandfather encouraged Mark to play ball and hoped Mark would be the Gilbert who reached the major leagues.[110]

The six-foot, 175-pound outfielder played college ball at Florida State in the late 1970s and was signed by the Cubs in the summer of 1978 after graduating from Florida State University with a degree in finance. According to the scouting reports, Gilbert "has outstanding speed and is strong defensively. He is also a good contact hitter but lacks power."[111]

Mark Gilbert was born into a baseball family. His grandfather played semi-pro ball and his father had been a professional baseball player. Gilbert had played seven games for the Chicago White Sox in 1985 when a snapped knee forced him to retire from the game (courtesy Mark Gilbert).

The switch-hitting center fielder began his minor league career with Geneva, New York, in the rookie New York–Pennsylvania League, and advanced to Class A Quad City in the Midwest League. Gilbert played with 43 minor leaguers that year; he was the only one who made it to the majors. At the end of the 1978 season, Gilbert was traded to the Cincinnati Reds organization.[112]

From 1980 to 1982, Gilbert played for Waterbury, Connecticut. During 1982-83, Gilbert was a baseball instructor, got married, and played with the Indianapolis Indians. He moved up to Wichita in 1984 where he had a very good year—a .280 batting average with 136 hits, including six home runs, and 55 stolen bases. After 1984, since Mark had spent so much time in the minors, he was eligible for free agency. He signed with his father's old organization, the Chicago White Sox, and went to their spring training camp in 1985.[113] When the Sox broke camp, Gilbert was assigned to AAA Buffalo at the start of the 1985 season.[114]

In July 1985 the White Sox recalled Gilbert from Buffalo where he was hitting .265 with three home runs and 22 extra-base hits. He had only 13 stolen bases, however, compared with 55 the season before at Wichita.[115]

Gilbert made his major league debut on July 21, 1985, and played seven days with the

White Sox. During that time, he had 22 at-bats, six hits, three RBIs, and a .273 average. Two nights prior to what would be his final game, Gilbert dove for a ball and felt his right knee give way, but he got up and continued playing. Two nights later, however, when he made another dive for a ball, his knee snapped again, and this time he was unable to get up. This ended Gilbert's baseball career.[116] On August 1, the White Sox optioned Gilbert to their Buffalo farm club.[117]

After four knee operations, Gilbert quit baseball and returned to Florida. Like Ross Baumgarten, Mark Gilbert worked in financial services after he completed his baseball career, becoming a trader for a large New York Stock Exchange firm.[118]

Roger Samuels

Although Roger Samuels played in the major leagues for only two years, he holds the distinction of being the last Jewish major leaguer to debut during the decade of the 1980s.

Roger Howard Samuels was born in San Jose, California, on January 5, 1961.[119] The six-foot, five-inch, 210-pound southpaw began his professional career with the Columbus Astros in 1985, played there again in 1986, and was released in 1987. He then signed with the San Francisco Giants organization and played for Fresno and Shreveport. In 1988, he was promoted to the Giants' AAA club, the Phoenix Firebirds.[120] On July 20, 1988, he debuted with the Giants after his promotion to the majors.[121]

Samuels appeared in 15 games for the Giants in 1988, all in relief. His won–loss record that year was 1–2 with an earned run average of 3.47.[122] He returned to Phoenix in 1989 where he had a record of 0–3 and an ERA of 3.20. In May, the Giants traded Samuels to the Pittsburgh Pirates for infielder Ken Oberkfell, a 13-year veteran with a lifetime batting average of .282.[123]

Southpaw Roger Samuels' brief career in professional baseball lasted only from 1985 until 1990. During those six years, he appeared in a major league uniform in 1988 for the San Francisco Giants and in 1989 for the Pittsburgh Pirates. His major league statistics are 20 games played, a record of one win and one loss, and 27 total innings pitched (courtesy of Pittsburg Pirates).

Samuels debuted for his new team on May 30, 1989, and pitched one scoreless inning against the Cincinnati Reds. Between May 30 and July 8, Samuels made five relief appearances, and although he had no record, his ERA was an astronomical 9.82.[124] Pittsburgh optioned Samuels to Buffalo where he was placed on the disabled list twice because of shoulder problems.[125] He finished the season with Phoenix and was released at the end of the season. Samuels pitched for the Mets' AAA Tidewater Tides in 1990 and retired from professional baseball after the season.[126]

13. Another Cy Young Winner

Without question, one of the most successful Jewish players during the seventies and eighties was pitcher Steve Stone. He, Koufax, and Holtzman, are often named as the three best Jewish major league pitchers. Stone is also one of only two Jewish Cy Young Award winners. Unlike Koufax or Holtzman, Stone's Judaism, while never denied, was more secular and less religious.[1]

Steven Michael Stone was born July 14, 1947, in Euclid, Ohio, a Cleveland suburb. His father, Paul, fixed jukeboxes and coached his son's Little League team, while his mother, Dorothy, waited on tables. As a child, Steve was a good athlete, played excellent golf and won the Cleveland junior tennis title when he was 13 years old.

Baseball, however, was Steve's first love. He claimed that both his parents wanted him to become a baseball player. His mother went to a Cleveland Indians night game before she gave birth to her son. Indians owner Bill Veeck reassured her that if her baby was born in the stands, he would give her a lifetime pass to the Indians' games.[2]

Steve's introduction to baseball came early in life when he played on the South Euclid–Lyndhurst Little League team at the age of six. He was a catcher until he reached the age of eleven, when his father, who was the coach, asked him to fill in for the pitcher. Because he did such a good job, he continued playing in that position. Years later, when he reminisced about his earliest days playing baseball, Stone admitted that he had absolutely no fastball. "I didn't get any speed," he admitted, "until my second year in high school, when I grew three inches and gained 25 pounds. But I've had a curve since I was 11, and I pitched with my head. I learned how to pitch before I had any speed. Most guys playing in the majors had speed from the beginning, and then learned how to pitch somewhere along the way."[3]

He also learned the lesson of determination as a child. His grandfather, Edward Mannheim, had a serious heart condition, but he told the family he wanted to live long enough to attend Steve's bar mitzvah. Despite at least 14 heart attacks, some of them quite major, his grandfather fulfilled his dream. On September 3, 1960, Steve Stone celebrated his bar mitzvah; his grandfather passed away two months later.[4]

In 1963, Stone pitched victories in both halves of a doubleheader in the Class D City Playoffs, and at Bush High School, where he graduated in 1965. He won all-star honors as a junior and was team captain during his senior year. In 1965, when he was 18, he was the winning pitcher in the state high school All-Star game.[5]

Stone received an undergraduate teaching degree in history and government from Kent State University in Kent, Ohio, in 1970. He participated in golf, tennis and volleyball, and he excelled at baseball, which was his primary interest. His catcher at Kent State was future big leaguer Thurman Munson.

During his senior year, in May 1970, students protesting the bombings of Cambodia by U.S. military forces came to blows with Ohio National Guardsmen on the Kent State campus. Guardsmen shot and killed four students on May 4, and the Kent State shootings became the turning point for a nation deeply divided by the Vietnam War.[6]

Before he graduated college, Stone signed a contract with the San Francisco Giants and spent the summer of 1969 in their farm system at Fresno. When he wasn't pitching, he could be found in the Napa Valley, taking notes and learning all he could about the origins of wine. Years later Stone would become a recognized wine expert and part-owner of no fewer than nine restaurants.[7]

In 1969 at Fresno, Stone averaged one strikeout per inning, as he compiled a record of 12 and 13. Once that year he struck out 17 batters in a nine-inning game. He figured that with 22 other pitchers around, he had to impress the Giants organization.[8]

The following year Stone pitched at Amarillo and Phoenix where his combined record was 14–8 with an ERA of 1.02.[9] In 1971 the Giants called Stone to the big leagues and he made his debut at San Diego on April 8. His manager, Charlie Fox, removed Stone in the fourth inning after he had allowed six hits and four runs.[10]

On April 23, Stone pitched a five-hit shutout for his first major league victory and drove in a run with a bases-loaded walk, as the Giants defeated the Pittsburgh Pirates.[11] While pitching for the Giants his first year, Stone had a 5–9 record, with an ERA of 4.15 in 24 appearances.[12] Before the end of the season, he was sent back to Phoenix.

Even though Steve Stone was in the minors again at the end of the 1971 season, he had at last made it to the big leagues. Before he was sent down to Phoenix, a newspaper reporter reminded him that he had now joined an "illustrious list of Jewish ballplayers who had played for the Giants." Stone admitted that he did not remember Sid Gordon, Andy Cohen, Harry Danning, or Phil Weintraub. When it came to Jewish ballplayers, "A guy my age," he volunteered, "can only identify with Sandy Koufax."[13]

In 1972, the five-foot, ten-inch right-hander returned to the major leagues for good. Although his ERA that year was an excellent 2.98, his record was a mediocre 6–8 due to a sore arm. At the end of the season, Stone and Ken Henderson were traded to the Chicago White Sox for Tom Bradley.[14]

Stone left the Giants under friendly circumstances, but during his two years with the Giants he had had to contend with what he considered "outmoded but prevalent stereotypes." He told *Inside Sports* that Giants manager Charlie Fox felt the only way a ballplayer could perform was to chew tobacco, wear a sloppy uniform, "be ready to get a bloody nose and eat, drink and sleep baseball."[15] In contrast to this image, Steve Stone appeared to be a member of a growing group of intellectuals in baseball. He had had five of his poems published and usually packed a miniature chessboard when his team was on the road.[16]

Stone was far from upset about the trade that brought him to the White Sox and he looked forward to working with Chisox manager Chuck Tanner. "I've never played for Tanner, but I've played against him while I was with Phoenix and Chuck was managing Hawaii," said Stone. "With Tanner as manager, I believe the White Sox are going to be in the division fight all the way."[17]

The White Sox employed Stone both as a starter and reliever in 1973, but he was able to win only six games to go with 11 losses. His ERA rose to 4.24. But in the final game of the season, Steve Stone gave a preview of his capabilities—he threw a three-hit shutout against the pennant-winning Oakland Athletics. In that game, Stone recorded 12 strikeouts, the highest number he had reached up to that point.[18]

On December 11, 1973, the Chicago White Sox made a deal with their cross-town rivals, the Chicago Cubs. The Cubs traded their star third baseman, Ron Santo, to the Sox for Steve Stone, southpaw Ken Frailing, and catcher Steve Swisher.[19]

Many baseball observers were convinced that the White Sox had given up too soon on Stone and attributed his poor showing in 1973 to Stone's lack of playing time as the Sox overused both Wilbur Wood and Stan Bahnsen. Stone agreed, admitting that he had had a promising spring, but lost his rhythm due to a slew of open dates early in the season. Then he struggled later in the season, even though he had managed to put together a number of hot streaks when he would retire 10 to 15 batters in succession.[20]

Cubs manager Whitey Lockman penciled Steve Stone into the starting rotation for 1974, and Stone said he could not have been happier. He rewarded his manager by turning in his finest winning season to date in the major leagues—a record of 8–6 with a 4.14 ERA. He had an even better year in 1975, increasing his won–loss record to 12–5 and reducing his ERA to 3.95. He threw six complete games and another shutout and was one of only two pitchers on the Cubs' staff with an earned run average of less than four runs per game.[21]

The 28-year-old Stone came to spring training in 1976 eager to build on his excellent showing the previous year.[22] Although he admittedly was the best pitcher on the Cubs staff, the second-rate Cubs asked him to take a pay cut for the 1976 season. Stone refused and since the reserve clause had been overturned the previous year, he announced that he would become a free agent after the 1976 season.[23]

Stone's plans seemed to go awry when he tore the rotator cuff in his pitching arm. He believed that his injury was due to his trying to hurry his preparation for the season in the lockout-shortened spring training that year. The Cubs thought he was faking, and although the team physician was not sure of a diagnosis, he advised Stone to have surgery or take cortisone. Stone refused both and decided to obtain his own medical help.[24]

The help that Stone chose was extremely unusual. A professor of Kinesiology (therapy through corrective exercise) from the University of Illinois–Chicago, Tom Satler, froze the shoulder and employed weight rehabilitation to strengthen the arm. These measures, Satler advised, would increase blood circulation to the part of the body where the blood flow is normally reduced. Radical or not, the treatment worked. Although Stone was on the disabled list from April 25 to July 2, he was able to pitch well by the conclusion of the 1976 season and finished with a 3–6 record. The Cubs' first free agent, Stone claimed that the team had used him sparingly to prevent his getting offers from other clubs. Regardless, five teams bid on him despite the question of whether his recovery was permanent.[25]

Steve Stone returned to his former team, the Chicago White Sox, for the 1977 season. Roland Hemond, White Sox general manager, saw Stone in action at Wrigley Field at the end of the '76 season and convinced Bill Veeck, the Sox's new owner, to offer Stone $60,000 for the 1977 season. Unlike Ron Blomberg the following year, Stone, who had become primarily a curve ball rather than a fastball pitcher following his injury, more than justified Veeck's faith and salary. In 1977, Stone reached a 15–12 record, the best in his career to that point.[26] After the season, Steve Stone said of Veeck, "He saved my career."[27]

As a reward for his outstanding season in 1977, Bill Veeck more than doubled Stone's salary for 1978, signing the 31-year-old hurler for $125,000. Veeck, however, refused to give Stone more than a one-year contract, nor would he offer him a no-trade clause. Stone, who wanted a three-year deal, announced he would once again become a free agent at the end of the 1978 season.[28]

He finished the season with a record of 12–12, determined to become the first major leaguer in the re-entry draft for a second time. Again, Stone received five offers, including one from a team he felt had a chance to win the pennant—the Baltimore Orioles. In November, the Orioles gave Stone a four-year contract for $760,000, at that time a magnanimous sum.[29]

Stone was only the second player ever acquired by Baltimore in the re-entry draft. General Manager Hank Peters said of him, "Steve is the kind of pitcher you'd like to have on your staff. He's highly competitive, intelligent, and he has a good arm."

Stone gave credit to Veeck. "He gave me the ball and an opportunity—and I didn't miss a start in two years. I was hoping right up until the end that the White Sox would come up with something." He said he was probably one of the few free agents who loved the city of Chicago. "Mr. Veeck's decision was strictly business and I can respect him for that. He has some fine young pitchers, and he wants to use them. As for our relationship, it will always be a good one."[30]

For at least the first half of the 1979 season, Stone was the fifth starter on an Orioles four-man rotation. By the All-Star break he had a mediocre record of 6–7 with an ERA of 4.40. His manager, Earl Weaver, conceded, "His performance wasn't what we expected it to be. We got him as a veteran pitcher who would serve as insurance and who could be spotted. I was disappointed that he thought he couldn't do it."[31]

Stone decided to do something about his poor showings on the mound. He sought advice from other Baltimore pitchers—Jim Palmer, Mike Flanagan, and Scott McGregor. He also began to follow fixed routines, such as playing the same tape on the way to the ballpark, eating the same meals at the same restaurants. He even kept a good luck charm in the form of a toy elephant inside his locker. He meditated and tried positive thinking.[32]

He also had help from a self-described psychic (she also called herself a witch), Ruth Rezven, who Stone had been consulting for many years. Rezven, who termed herself a "nice Jewish girl," had also been helping Dodgers third baseman Ron Cey break a lengthy hitting slump in 1977 by giving him a potion she had concocted. She gave Stone a similar potion and told him, "Jewish magic is the strongest there is." She mixed in some African rituals for additional power.[33]

Another mind trick Stone tried was to psychically link himself with his boyhood idol,

Steve Stone pitched in the major leagues for eleven years—1971 through 1981—for four different teams. He had a breakout season in 1980 with the Baltimore Orioles, winning 25 games and the American League Cy Young Award. After his retirement as an active player, Stone spent a number of years in the broadcast booth as a color commentator with Chicago Cubs' broadcaster Harry Carey (courtesy National Baseball Hall of Fame Library; Cooperstown, N.Y.).

Sandy Koufax. Stone changed his uniform number from 21 to Koufax's 32, and read Koufax's autobiography five times. "I admire Sandy Koufax for the way he conducted himself," said Stone. "I want to emulate him."[34]

After the 1979 All-Star break, Stone got a chance to pitch regularly because injuries plagued the Orioles pitching staff. McGregor hurt his elbow, Palmer his back, Dennis Martinez his shoulder, and Flanagan suffered through a slump. Weaver was forced to use Stone on a regular basis and Stone responded to the challenge for the remainder of the '79 season. He won five consecutive games with an ERA of 2.94; his home record for the year was 8–1, with an ERA of 1.97. He ended the season with a record of 11–7. Stone did not appear in the any of the ALCS games against the Angels and pitched only two innings in the World Series against the Pirates. Both of these two innings were in one of the Orioles' victories over Pittsburgh.[35]

By 1980, Steve Stone had been pitching in the major leagues for nine years and his record was 78–79, a .497 percentage. When he signed with the Orioles, his contract provided for a $10,000 bonus should he win a Cy Young Award in any given season. For a pitcher with less than a .500 lifetime percentage, and one who had never won more than 15 games in a single season, the likelihood that the Orioles would have to make good on their bonus to Stone seemed very remote.

In the early days of the 1980 season, one of Earl Weaver's four starting pitchers, Dennis Martinez, complained of a sore shoulder. The official diagnosis was "torn fibers of the deltoid muscle." The doctors told Martinez he could begin throwing after a few days rest and then test his arm in an exhibition game. This program was shattered by the players' strike and then Martinez went on the disabled list. Stone took his spot in the starting rotation.[36]

By the middle of June, Stone was the Orioles' most effective starter and their biggest winner. He had won six games and had a 3.20 earned run average. "I've been able to throw for strikes consistently," he said. "Also, I'm more relaxed here this year. I think maybe last season I was trying to prove to everybody I was worth what the Orioles were paying me as a free agent."[37]

Near the end of August, Stone had won 14 consecutive games, running his overall record to 18–4. He attributed his pitching improvement to being on a good club and to improving the velocity of his pitches. He also accepted the advice his pitching coach had been giving him. "Ray [Miller] told me to take less time between pitches. I think when you take longer, maybe you're not confident and certainly it's tough on the fielders behind you. Certainly, it's helped me tremendously."[38]

On August 19, Stone became the first 20-game winner in the majors in 1980. In his twentieth win, he was within five outs of pitching a no-hitter. He was also the earliest 20-game winner in the history of the modern Orioles and was the leading contender for the Cy Young Award in the American League.[39]

Throughout the 1980 season, Stone continued his superstitions of always doing the same thing prior to and after a ball game, claiming they were just ways of bringing order to his life. "I finally pieced it together," he said. "I realized that if I wanted to be consistent on the field, I had to get some measure of consistency in my life, and I began to do the same things on the day I pitched."[40]

In September, Stone won his twenty-fourth game, tying Dave McNally and Mike Cuellar for single season wins by an Orioles pitcher. In his next start, Stone defeated the Boston Red Sox for his twenty-fifth win, gaining the distinction of the most by an Orioles pitcher in one season. Stone ended the season with twenty-five wins—more than any other pitcher in the major leagues that year—against only seven losses. He started more games than any other pitcher—37. He pitched 250 innings, gave up 224 hits and struck out 149 hitters, compiling an earned-run average of 3.23.[41] He also led the league with a .781 won–lost percentage.[42]

On November 12, Steve Stone won the Cy Young Award in the American League, the second consecutive Oriole to accomplish that feat. (Mike Flanagan won in 1979.) Only seven pitchers in the entire league received any votes at all; Stone was the only pitcher named on every ballot. He received 13 first-place votes, 10 second-place votes, and five for third place.[43] Like his idol, Sandy Koufax, Steve Stone became the second Jewish pitcher to win the Cy Young Award.[44]

Earl Weaver agreed that Stone had earned his status as the league's ace hurler. "I always thought Stone could be a winner," he insisted. "There was never any doubt in my mind that this guy could be a winning pitcher with the Baltimore Orioles because of his ability. It's the pitchers who make the club good. If it wasn't for him now, we'd be a losing team."[45]

Steve Stone was honored to have won the Cy Young Award in 1980, but the biggest thrill he had in his ten years in the majors occurred in a game that had no bearing on the pennant race—the 1980 All-Star game. Stone was the starting pitcher in the only All-Star game in which he would appear during his eleven-year major league career. He pitched three perfect innings against the National League, retiring all nine men he faced. "I remember coming off the mound just feeling as exuberant as I have ever felt. I had really accomplished something. It was the most gratifying game of my career, the one I will never forget," he said."[46]

When told that only one American League Cy Young winner in the 1970s had improved his won–lost percentage the year following his award, Stone said, "Put me down for 30 wins and a no-hitter. Now that I've won twenty-five games," he said, "it seems everybody is telling me I can't do it again. Well, I believe I will do it again and maybe do it a little better. I can't come out and pitch the same way I did last year," he added. "With a sinker I can vary how I pitch in certain situations."[47]

Stone was firm in his desire to improve on his Cy Young year, but 1981 was instead a year of reckoning for him due to stress on his pitching arm. He began the year with a painful arm and a sore elbow, and was able to throw only 34 innings before he was diagnosed with tendinitis and placed on the disabled list in May. The baseball strike suspended the season from June to August, and although Stone pitched toward the end of the year, he was unable to return to his previous effectiveness.[48]

There was no real improvement to his pitching arm in the spring of 1982. He reinjured his right elbow in a spring training game against the Texas Rangers. "I don't understand it. It didn't hurt all winter," Stone said.[49] He faced he possibility of a return to Baltimore for further examination for his sore elbow.[50] On March 14, Baltimore placed Stone on the 21-day disabled list. "I threw the ball fairly well," he said, "but I haven't thrown any breaking pitches."[51]

On June 1, 1982, Steve Stone decided to retire from baseball rather than have surgery on his elbow. "The decision probably wasn't as difficult as it would have been. Basically, my elbow determined my decision. It didn't come around after a series of cortisone injections and a number of other types of therapy that we tried. So, realizing that I couldn't perform the way I wanted to," said the 34-year-old Stone, "I felt it was time to start the second half of my life."[52]

Stone left the game a winning pitcher with a lifetime record of 107–93 and an earned run average of 3.97.[53]

Although he was no longer an active player, the satisfaction he derived from baseball kept him involved in another aspect of the game. He immediately went to work for ABC as part of the Monday Night Baseball broadcast team. Among his partners were Al Michaels, Howard Cosell, Keith Jackson, Bob Uecker, and Don Drysdale.[54] He became an instant success, not very surprising considering that Stone was smart, articulate, and "steeped in self-assurance."[55] Even though Stone had spent his last four years pitching for Baltimore, he always considered Chicago the place he would like to make his home. He had lived in the Windy City for six years while pitching for both of Chicago's major league teams. While he was in Chicago in August 1982 waiting to go to Milwaukee for a telecast, he was told that Harry Caray was looking for a partner for the 150 games carried on the WGN cable channel. Jim Dowdle, head of Tribune Company broadcasting, which owned WGN, told Stone that Caray wanted someone as the color guy while he did the play-by-play and that the job was his if he wanted it. "It would probably be the best situation you could be involved in," he emphasized. Stone took the offer.[56]

In 1983 Stone joined Harry Caray in the Cubs' broadcast booth and for the next fifteen years they formed a relationship that Stone described as "like a marriage." Stone got excellent marks for his analysis, but he was always grateful to Harry Caray for the opportunity given to him.[57] He also called Cubs' telecasts with Harry's grandson Chip until he resigned from the Tribune station in 2004 over the flak he created when he criticized the Cubs on the air.[58] After he left the Cubs' broadcast, Steve Stone continued as sportscaster for other media including ESPN and WSCR in Chicago.[59]

Steve Stone had been preparing for a life after baseball for a long time. He had real estate investments, had been a partner in a restaurant chain at one time and actually ran restaurants in Scottsdale, Arizona, and Chicago even while playing baseball. Many people often asked him for financial advice, and he published many poems, some for *Sports Illustrated* and the *National Jewish Monthly*.[60]

Like many of the Jewish ballplayers, Stone considers his Jewishness a cultural, ethic tradition more than a religion. "I'm proud of the fact that I'm a Jew, but I don't belong to a temple," Stone said. "I observe Judaism in my own way without the organized aspects."[61] He often admitted that his Jewishness never hampered his progress in baseball. "Being Jewish in this sport has never been a drawback," he said. "Those who claim that anti–Semitism has held them back are looking for an easy excuse."[62] "If you're a good enough pitcher, they don't care if you're a Martian."[63]

14. Jews by Choice

In the years before World War II, it was not uncommon for Jews who wished to play professional baseball to change their names for "business reasons." In fact, at least seven Jews who made it to the major leagues legally changed their birth names, such as Cohen, to more gentile-sounding ones.

After World War II, however, no Jewish player changed his name just to become accepted in baseball, and most were far from embarrassed when it became known that they were Jews. Some, in fact, were valued for their Jewish heritage. As the years passed, Jews became more and more part of the American mainstream and intermarriage between Jews and non–Jews increased. Probably the acceptance of Jews into the American culture reached its apex when non–Jews chose to adopt Judaism as their religion of choice. Seven of these converts played major league baseball from the early 1960s through the mid–1980s. Some became Jewish because they had a Jewish wife, one chose Judaism after actively seeking a religion that felt right for him, and no information was found on why or when others converted.

Joe Horlen

Most of the non–Jewish players who became Jews played during the 1970s and 1980s, but right-handed pitcher Joe Horlen's 12 seasons in the majors were primarily in the sixties. His conversion, however, did not take place until after he completed his major league career.

Joel Edward Horlen was born August 14, 1937, in San Antonio. He attended Oklahoma State University where he helped the Cowboys win the College World Series.[1] Horlen was signed by the White Sox in 1959 and sent to their minor league Class B team. By 1961, the Chisox had moved Horlen up to their AAA Pacific Coast League team at San Diego where he was tutored by the late Cleveland Indians pitcher, Herb Score, who was rehabbing there from an injury. Score helped Horlen with his technique and he also helped him increase his stamina. Horlen's pitching greatly improved.[2]

The White Sox promoted Horlen to the parent club in 1961; he made his major league pitching debut on September 4, 1961, in the second game of a doubleheader against the Minnesota Twins. Horlen wore the only available team uniform that day, one with no number on the back, and the Sox won the game for Horlen's only win in 1961.[3]

Horlen was named a starter for the 1962 season, a job he would hold through 1971.

Although he was known for his outstanding control, the six-foot, 170-pound Horlen always seemed to fall just short of excellence. In fact, this situation occurred so frequently that he became known as "Hard Luck Horlen."[4]

In 1963 Horlen took a no-hitter into the ninth inning against the Washington Senators with a 1–0 lead, but Chuck Hinton hit a double with one man out and Don Lock followed with a two-run homer, causing the hard luck hurler to lose his no-hitter, his shutout and the game.[5]

Horlen earned his nickname again in 1964 when he struck out 138 hitters, had an earned run average of 1.88, and a winning percentage of .591, but was not able to lead the American League in any of the three categories.[6] In addition, Horlen's ERA was below 3.00 every season for the five years from 1964 through 1968. He had winning records only two of those years because he was pitching for the White Sox, one of the worst hitting teams in the majors.[7]

Horlen's best year was 1967. Along with teammate Gary Peters, he was selected as one of the seven pitchers to represent the American League in the All-Star

While most of the players who converted to Judaism played during the 1970s and 1980s, pitcher Joe Horlen's twelve-year career in the majors began early in the 1960s. His conversion to Judaism, which came about because of his long-standing interest in Jews and Judaism, occurred long after he ended his pitching career (courtesy National Baseball Hall of Fame Library; Cooperstown, N.Y.).

Game and he finally got his no-hitter at Comiskey Park against the Tigers.[8] That same year, Horlen was the American League's earned run leader with a 2.03 ERA; his won–lost record was an outstanding 19–7, and his .731 percentage was the best among all pitchers who appeared in more than 167 innings.[9] He had six shutouts that year and led the American League with six complete games, but he could not get his twentieth win and would never again come that close.[10] Despite his excellent numbers, the coveted Cy Young Award also eluded him. Instead, Jim Lonborg, with 22 wins, but with a lower winning percentage, won the Cy Young.[11]

Besides his pitching prowess, Horlen gained publicity for his odd habit of wadding a couple of tissues in his mouth and chewing on them, as he would gum. When asked why, he simply said, "Well, I found that chewing gum had a tendency to bloat me and, if I chew tobacco, I get sick. There's no taste to it, the wad doesn't break up on you and it keeps saliva in your mouth. It tends to relax me better than anything else."[12]

From 1967 through 1969, Horlen started 35 games for the White Sox, and his seven 1–0 career victories tied the record of Hall of Famer Bob Feller.[13] Horlen was considered the ace of the White Sox pitching staff, and a key member, along with Gary Peters and Tommy John, of the most effective rotation for the team since the dead ball era.[14]

After his sensational 1967 season, Horlen pitched three more years for the White Sox, but he never repeated the success of 1967. In 1968 Horlen posted an ERA of 2.37, but his record was 12–14. Once again the White Sox bats could not support his great pitching. In 1969 his record was 13–16. The following year, Horlen became the third top-flight major league pitcher to undergo a knee cartilage operation, and his injury was a blow to the White Sox who were languishing in the cellar of the American League's West Division. Horlen finished the 1970 season with a miserable record of 6–16. He pitched sparingly the following year and ended the 1971 season with a record of 8–9.[15]

The Sox did not renew Horlen's contract in 1972, releasing him on March 27. The 34-year-old Horlen had had a poor spring and in his five appearances in the Grapefruit League, his earned run average was 7.36.[16]

The Oakland Athletics picked up Horlen on waivers. He had not yet converted to Judaism, but he did have two Jewish teammates, Ken Holtzman and Mike Epstein. The A's used Horlen chiefly in relief although he did make six starts. He appeared in 32 games, compiled a 3–4 record and had an ERA of 3.00.[17]

With the A's in 1972, for the first time in his baseball career, Horlen pitched in post-season play although he did not pitch very well. In the American League Championship Series, he was charged with the loss in the fourth game; and in the sixth game of the World Series, he allowed Cincinnati four runs in a losing effort. Fortunately for Horlen, Oakland was able to come back to win the seventh and deciding game. Horlen retired after the A's had won the World Series, allowing him to leave the major leagues on a high note.[18]

Most baseball experts agree that Horlen was a much better pitcher than his record of 116–117 would indicate. His career earned average was 3.11, pitching all but one year for a team that literally gave him no offensive support.[19] He also had the satisfaction of knowing that he contributed to the A's getting into the playoffs in 1972.[20]

After his retirement from the major leagues, Horlen moved back to his birthplace of San Antonio where he worked as a building contractor. He also became a member of the San Antonio Spurs in the Texas League, taking spot starting assignments and working with some of the younger members of the pitching staff.[21]

From 1977 through 1987, Horlen was a traveling pitching instructor for the Cleveland Indians farm system. In 1987 he gave up his contracting business completely and became the pitching coach for Kingsport, Tennessee, the Mets' farm club in the Appalachian League. At the end of the 1989 season, Horlen was hired as pitching coach of the New York Mets.[22] He left the Mets in 1992 to join the Kansas City Royals organization, and the following year he moved to the San Francisco organization.[23]

Horlen married the former Lois Eisenstein, who is Jewish, and he converted to Judaism shortly after the two were married. "I had always been interested in the history of the Jews and Judaism," he stated, adding that when he told his old A's teammate Mike Epstein about his conversion at an old-timers game, Epstein responded with a hearty, " Welcome to the tribe."[24]

Lloyd Allen

It was almost the end of the 1960s before the second Jew by choice made his major league debut.

Lloyd Allen was one of the first major leaguers born in the 1950s. A native of Merced, California, born May 8, 1950, Allen was of Irish descent, but later converted to Judaism.[25]

Like most future major leaguers, Allen played ball in Little League and in high school where he was only the second freshman ever to qualify for the team.[26]

In 1967 Allen graduated high school and briefly attended Fresno City College prior to being drafted in the 1968 amateur draft by the California Angels.[27] The six-foot, one-inch right-handed hurler spent the entire 1968 season and most of the 1969 season in the minors. Newlyweds David and Julie Nixon Eisenhower attended his major league debut in Washington, D.C., on September 1, 1969. In the first game of a doubleheader, he hurled one scoreless inning in relief.[28] In his four appearances in 1969, Allen's record was 0–1.[29]

He started the 1970 season with El Paso in the Texas League and made the All-Star team despite leading the league in hit batsmen. Allen returned to the Angels late in the season, and on September 30, 1970, won his first major league game, pitching seven innings in a 5–1 victory over the Chicago White Sox.[30]

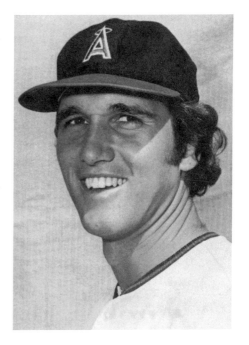

California native Lloyd Allen was one of the first major leaguers born in the 1950s. The 19-year-old made his major league pitching debut on September 1, 1969, and appeared in 159 major league games for three American League teams, 113 of them while wearing a California Angels uniform (courtesy National Baseball Hall of Fame Library; Cooperstown, N.Y.).

Allen's first full season in the big leagues was 1971. He appeared in fifty-four games, had an ERA of 2.49, and led the Angels pitchers with 15 saves. In a game on July 16, 1971, Allen combined a rare feat— he hit a home run and earned a save.[31]

He was on good terms with his manager, Lefty Phillips, and his pitching coach, Norman Sherry, both Jewish. He also became quite friendly with another Jewish Angels coach, Jimmie Reese, who called Allen "the right-handed Sandy Koufax," although the personalities of the outspoken Allen and the quiet Koufax were complete opposites.[32]

The colorful Allen quickly became a crowd pleaser, and manager Phillips now felt that calling the bullpen was "more like calling the Rescue Squad than like Dialing-a-Prayer."[33]

The Angels attempted to make Allen into a starter in 1972. New Angels manager Del Rice also ordered him to trim his long curly auburn hair. Allen had let his hair grow as part of his image as a "character," a role he truly enjoyed. His 1972 stats were not up to his previous year's marks. He pitched almost as many innings as he did in 1971, but his record was a disappointing 3–7 with only five saves, and his ERA was a run higher at 3.48.[34]

Allen made only five appearances for the Angels in 1973, and his earned average shot up above 11.00. He placed much of the blame for his high ERA on the new DH rule in the American League. "That new rule," lamented Allen, "is killing us out in the bullpen. It's a tough situation." Allen claimed that since pitchers were no longer removed for pinch hitters, they tended to last longer, and therefore inactivity afflicted those who were required to wait in the bullpen.[35]

On May 21, the Angels traded Lloyd Allen and pitcher Jim Spencer to the Rangers for left-handed slugger Mike Epstein and pitcher Rich Hand.[36] Allen appeared in 23 games for Texas in 1973, ending the season with a record of 0–6 and an ERA of 9.22.[37]

Allen began the 1974 season with Texas, pitching in 14 games before being traded to the Chicago White Sox organization in the middle of the season. Chicago optioned Allen to their AAA Iowa farm club, where he toiled for most of the year.[38]

Allen made three appearances for the White Sox in 1975, winning no games and losing two before he was shipped to the St. Louis Cardinals organization, but he never played in the major leagues again.[39] He played for Tulsa, a Cardinals AAA farm club. In 1977 after the Cardinals released Allen, the Toronto Blue Jays signed him as a free agent, but he never made it to the majors with Toronto either.[40]

Allen's career record was a rather dismal 8–25 with 22 saves and a 4.69 ERA. He lost his last 10 decisions between 1972 and 1975, including his final appearance. In his last game, Allen was taken out after less than an inning when he gave up a two-run home run to future Hall of Famer Reggie Jackson.[41]

Elliott Maddox

Elliott Maddox was probably the most unusual convert to Judaism. He was African-American and a non-practicing Baptist who chose Judaism after studying the religion for many years.

Maddox was born December 21, 1947, following the season when Jackie Robinson broke baseball's color line and Hank Greenberg played his last major league game. He grew up and attended high school in the black section of Union, New Jersey, known as Vaux Hall. Union is less than twenty miles from Manhattan where Maddox had a number of Jewish friends.[42]

According to Maddox, Union was so racist that the post office would be upset when mail to African-Americans was addressed "Union" instead of Vaux Hall. Known as an academic and baseball standout who graduated from high school with a 93 average, Maddox described himself as "an easy-going, fun-loving guy." He also had a reputation for "testing the limits," and was once expelled when an original poem he was required to write was very critical of the teacher.[43]

After Maddox completed high school, he entered the University of Michigan on an academic scholarship. He had rejected a baseball scholarship from the University of Southern California as well as a good financial offer from the Houston Astros.[44]

Maddox took a number of Judaic studies courses at Michigan and began to notice a very strong correlation between the black experience in America with that of the Jews. He felt that contrary to what the media continued to write, there was not that much dislike and distrust of Jews among blacks. "Blacks generally view Jews with a much closer bond than they do with any other white group," he said.[45]

Following his sophomore year, in which he hit .467 to lead the Big Ten and was named to a number of All-American teams, the Detroit Tigers drafted Maddox, but he remained in school until he graduated. After Maddox received his degree in political science and history at Ann Arbor, he spent the 1968 and 1969 seasons in Detroit's minor league farm system in Lakeland, Florida, and Rocky Mount, North Carolina, hitting over .300 with both clubs. On April 7, 1970, the five-foot, eleven-inch, 185-pound Maddox made his debut with the Tigers. He was a switch-hitting utility player able to play the infield or the outfield.[46]

Maddox played in 109 games and hit .248 in his first year with the Tigers. He was also voted Detroit's Rookie of the Year.[47] It did not, however, take Maddox very long to show that he possessed an independent streak. Tigers manager Billy Martin benched him for two weeks at one point during the year when he refused to cut his hair.[48]

Despite his relatively good year in 1970, Maddox was involved in an eight-man trade with the Washington Senators. Washington sent infielders Ed Brinkman and Auerilio Rodriguez along with pitchers Joe Coleman and Jim Hannan to the Tigers. The Tigers gave Washington pitchers Norm McRae and Denny McClain, infielder Don Wert, and utility man Elliott Maddox.[49]

Maddox played with the Senators for three years—one in Washington, D.C., and two with the team when they moved to Arlington and became the Texas Rangers.[50]

His manager with the Senators in 1971 and with the Rangers in 1972 was former Red Sox slugger Ted Williams. Williams, who knew a little something about hitting, predicted that Maddox would develop into one of the league's best right-handed hitters. Williams planned to use him primarily as an outfielder, since he felt the Senators had enough third basemen.[51]

Maddox respected Williams as a great left-handed slugger, but he also had a number of differences with him. Maddox, who had participated in a number of college sit-ins, was unhappy with Williams' political thinking. His manager was an outspoken admirer of President Richard Nixon, but Maddox did not hesitate to tell Williams exactly what he thought of the president.

The two men also disagreed about hitting. Williams, as he did with so many of his players, wanted Maddox to hit exactly as he had when he was an active player. "He would fly into a rage," remembered Maddox. "Ted Williams is a great hitting instructor for anyone who is 6'3", 200 pounds, left-handed and with great reflexes and eyesight."[52]

In 1971 Maddox played in 128 games for Williams at Washington, D.C., and hit a paltry .217. The following year in Arlington, he played in 98 games and hit .252.[53]

Nineteen seventy-three was another year of manager-player discord for Maddox. That year the Rangers replaced Williams with Whitey Herzog, a former third base coach for the New York Mets. Maddox was hitting over .300 through May when he injured his shoulder, but Herzog refused to believe Maddox's claim that he was hurt. In the middle of the year, Herzog was gone and the Rangers brought in another new manager—Billy Martin. This was the same Martin who had benched Maddox for his long hair in 1971 when the two of them were together at Detroit. Maddox decided to retire after the end of the 1973 season and go to law school. "I love baseball," said Maddox, "but I wouldn't have starved without it. I didn't go to college for four years to play baseball all my life."[54]

Elliot Maddox, who began taking Judaic study courses in his junior year at the University of Michigan, converted to Judaism in 1974 while a member of the New York Yankees. He spent eleven years in the major leagues and compiled a lifetime batting average of .261 for five American League clubs (courtesy National Baseball Hall of Fame Library; Cooperstown, N.Y.).

Maddox changed his plans when in March 1974 he learned that the New York Yankees had purchased his contract from the Rangers for $40,000. Yankees manager Bill Virdon planned to play Maddox primarily in defensive situations.[55] A few months later, Maddox decided to begin formal studies in Judaism with a rabbi in New York. "I've learned enough to know it's worth pursuing quite a bit further," he said. He had been wearing a large Star of David given to him by a friend. "In another year I'll be able to tell if that's it or not. I feel I can only benefit by studying it. It certainly isn't going to hurt me."[56]

Although he had been born a Baptist, he said he had never practiced that religion and that he had become very attracted to Judaism. Ever since he began wearing the Star of David, he had had to answer questions about why he was wearing it. His normal answer was, "I left my mezuzah at home."[57]

Maddox had his best major league season in 1974 when he proved to Bill Virdon that he could be an offensive as well as a defensive player. He became the regular centerfielder when he was hitting only .220, but he then hit safely in 21 of the next 22 games, raising his average above .300. After being inserted in the lineup full time, he hit in about 85 percent of the games the rest of the season. The first African-American player to be a regular center fielder for the Yankees, Maddox posted a season average in 1974 of .303, sixth in the American League.[58]

An injured knee the following year limited Maddox's playing time. He hurt his knee in the outfield at the Mets' Shea Stadium, which the Yankees were using while Yankee Stadium was being renovated. Maddox later sued the City of New York, claiming that the field was unplayable, but he lost the case. The court ruled that he knew of the risks and played anyway.[59] Although he hit .307 in 1975, he played in only 55 games.[60]

It took most of the 1976 season for him to return from his knee injury, and he managed to play in just 18 games, hitting only .217.[61] Although Maddox had an abbreviated season in 1976, he was able to return in time to participate in the World Series against the Cincinnati Reds. Despite the fact that Maddox walked and tripled in the two games he played, the Reds swept the World Series.[62]

In January 1977, the Yankees and Baltimore Orioles completed a three-player deal. The Yankees sent Maddox and minor league outfielder Rick Bladt from their Syracuse farm club to Baltimore for outfielder Paul Blair. The trade did not surprise Maddox because he realized that both general manager Gabe Paul and field manager Billy Martin considered him a "pain in the neck." "When I heard Gabe on the phone," Maddox related, "I knew I was traded because I hadn't talked to him since November 1 when he told me I didn't need another operation." Maddox's problems began with Martin, the manager with whom he did not get along when they both worked for the Texas Rangers. Maddox's problems multiplied when he clashed with Paul over various matters, particularly the disputed surgery.[63]

With the Orioles in 1977, Maddox hit .262, playing in only 69 games. At the end of the season, he announced his plans to go through the re-entry draft. On December 1, Maddox signed a five-year contract with the New York Mets, and their manager, Joe Torre, immediately indicated that Maddox would play right field for his team. "He gives us something we have not had," said Torre, "a good defensive right fielder."[64] By joining the Mets, Maddox became the twenty-first player to appear in the lineup for both the Mets and the Yankees.[65]

Maddox played three years for the Mets, from 1978 through 1980. On February 6, 1981, the Mets asked waivers on Maddox. If no team claimed him within the week, he would become a free agent. Maddox alleged that Frank Cashen, Mets general manager, viewed him as a troublemaker because he was the team's player rep and was involved in salary nego-tiations.[66]

Maddox completed his eleven-year stint in the major leagues with a career batting aver-age of .261 in 1,029 games. He had 18 career home runs, 235 runs batted in, and a fielding percentage of .989.[67]

Following his retirement as an active player, Maddox became an outfield and batting coach for the Yankees for ten years until 1991.[68] He was inducted into the National Jewish Sports Hall of Fame on March 28, 2004.[69] He joined other Jewish major leaguers that year when the Baseball Hall of Fame hosted a "Celebration of Jewish Players." Most of the play-ers there spoke of their Judaism and their feelings about being a Jewish baseball player. As a Jew by choice, Maddox stated, "I figured as far as being a minority, I was being a person persecuted anyway, I figured what the heck, throw one more thing on. It didn't matter. I felt comfortable within myself."[70]

After he retired from baseball, Maddox established a youth baseball program in Poland, and through his guidance, the Polish team flourished, winning the European Championship in 2004. The Israeli Ambassador to the United States recruited Maddox and another ex–major leaguer who had converted to Judaism, Bob Tufts, to take part in a camp and clinic in Israel to be held in 2006 for Israeli baseball players. The ambassador particularly wanted Maddox because of his success with the Polish team. Maddox agreed, saying it was a "no-brainer" to come and instruct the clinic. "I enjoy working with youth and I have time in which to do it," said Maddox. "I'm Jewish and being a person who loves history and loves to travel, why not take the opportunity to come to Israel? It seemed to make sense to me."[71]

Skip Jutze

Albert Henry "Skip" Jutze, born to Christian parents on May 28, 1946, in Bayside, New York, was another major league player who converted to Judaism. He had a six-year career in the major leagues, five in the National League and one in the American League.[72]

After he graduated from Clarke High School in Westbury, New York, Jutze attended Central Connecticut State College where he was the starting catcher on the college's base-ball team. In 1966 the Boston Red Sox selected Jutze in the fourth round of the overall ama-teur entry draft. The following year the Detroit Tigers selected Jutze in the third round of the amateur entry draft, but Jutze turned down both offers, preferring to remain in school until he obtained his degree in industrial education.[73] After he had received his degree in 1968, Jutze signed with the St. Louis Cardinals as an undrafted free agent.[74]

He spent nearly five years in the Cardinal organization, moving up in class steadily until 1972, when he spent the bulk of the season with the Tulsa Oilers in the American Associ-ation.[75] While at Tulsa, Jutze caught the attention of Oilers manager Jack Krol, who gave an honest appraisal of his catcher. "Skip isn't an exciting player, but he'll win for you. He doesn't do anything real well, but he does everything well. I think Skip has gotten the most out of his ability more than any player I've ever seen."

The five-foot, eleven-inch, 190-pound catcher also caught the attention of Hall of Famer Joe Medwick, hitting coach of the St. Louis farm system. "Skip did the same thing last year at Arkansas," boasted Medwick. "He must have carried the club for almost six weeks."[76]

Jutze was hitting .324 for Tulsa when the Cardinals brought him to the majors late in 1972. They regarded him as such a "hot property" that they considered moving their regular catcher, Ted Simmons, to first base, and placing Jutze behind the plate. Along with Jutze, the Cardinals also recalled another of their top minor league prospects, third baseman Ken Reitz. The Cardinals felt that neither of these two prospects would ever again be playing for Tulsa.[77]

Jutze made his debut with the parent club on September 2, 1972. He struck out three times in his first major league game, but got two hits and drove in two runs in his next game. He appeared in 21 games with the Redbirds in 1972 and had a .239 batting average.[78] During the off-season, Jutze tried teaching, but "That's not my bag any more," he said.[79]

On November 28, 1972, the Cardinals sent Jutze and infielder Milt Ramirez to the Houston Astros for infielders Bobby Fenwick and Ray Busse.[80] Jutze stated that he looked forward to becoming the starting catcher with the Astros and told the press, "I'm going to give it everything I have." After the Cardinals traded him to Houston, Astros general manager John Mullen informed Jutze that the team planned on giving Bob Watson the first crack at the catching job. If that did not work out, the Astros promised Jutze he would have a shot.[81]

In July 1973, Watson announced that he was through with catching and Astros manger Leo Durocher finally made Jutze the regular catcher.[82] He caught 90 games for the Astros in 1973 and hit .223 with no home runs and 18 runs batted in.[83] The Astros were not happy with his lack of hitting, and they optioned Jutze to their AAA team at Denver in April 1974.[84] He spent most of the 1974 season with the Denver farm team where he was elected to the American Association All-Star team, and then was recalled late in the year by the Astros, appearing in eight games and hitting .231.[85]

In 1975 and 1976, Jutze remained on the Astros' roster and platooned with left-handed hitting catcher Milt May. He played in 51 games in 1975, hitting .226, and 42 games in 1977, where his average took a nosedive to .152.[86] At the end of the season, the Astros traded Jutze to the Seattle Mariners for Alan Griffin and cash.[87] The trade elated Jutze who figured the change of scenery and more playing time were exactly what he needed.[88]

When Jutze played with the Mariners in their inaugural season in the major leagues, he fully expected to be Seattle's fulltime catcher. However, he soon found out that, as he had done with Houston the past two years, he would platoon with a catcher who hit from the left side. In Houston, that catcher was Milt May; in Seattle it was Bob Stinson. Jutze appeared in only 42 games for Seattle in 1977, and he hit a scant .220. However, he did hit the only three home runs of his major league career, one of them a grand slam clout, the first grand slam home run hit by a Mariner.[89]

Jutze retired at the end of the 1977 season. His lifetime batting average of .215 was very low,

Catcher Skip Jutze was a part-time player for three teams during his six years in the majors. With a lifetime batting average of only .215, his defensive abilities rather than his hitting kept him in the major leagues (courtesy National Baseball Hall of Fame Library; Cooperstown, N.Y.).

even for a catcher. It was his fine .983 lifetime fielding average that probably kept him in the major leagues for five years.[90]

Steve Yeager

Steve Yeager, a major league catcher from 1972 through 1986, was one of the game's finest defensive catchers and was described by Hall of Fame outfielder Lou Brock as "the best throwing catcher in the game." Steve Yeager's claim to fame included the invention of a throat protector for this vulnerable area.[91] Steve Wayne Yeager was not born Jewish but converted later in life after marrying the daughter of Holocaust survivors.[92]

Yeager, the nephew of test pilot Chuck Yeager, was born November 24, 1948, in Huntington, West Virginia.[93] The blond, six-foot, 195-pound Yeager was signed by the Dodgers organization in the June 1967 free agent draft and moved up rapidly in the minors based on his strong right throwing arm, intelligent pitch calling, and excellent defensive skills.[94]

During the five years Yeager played in the Dodgers farm system, he had always been the number two catcher. At the Dodgers' spring training camp in Vero Beach in 1972, Yeager admitted that he would gladly settle for making the team as the number three man for the Dodgers.

That year he was the only Dodgers rookie with a shot at being in Dodger Stadium on opening day. He was competing with Joe Ferguson who had divided his time between Spokane and Los Angeles in 1971. While Ferguson had a better bat, he had little experience catching; he was previously an outfielder. On the other hand, Yeager had been a catcher since he was a high school freshman in Dayton and was rated one of the best defensive catchers around.

Yeager impressed the Dodgers with his defensive abilities and his ruggedness behind the plate. When an opposing runner tried to score in an exhibition game, Yeager stood his ground to make a tag despite a bone-jarring collision. One of the Dodgers regular catchers, Chris Cannizzaro, dubbed the rookie "Raw Meat," his first baseball nickname. "I think my chances are very good now, which is quite the opposite of when I came down here. I always heard it took five years to make it as a major league catcher."[95]

When the Dodgers broke camp, Yea-

Catcher Steve Yeager played 15 years in the major leagues, including 14 with the Los Angeles Dodgers, where he was a back-up to catcher Joe Ferguson. Because he was hit by a broken bat, Yeager constructed a protective plastic shield which hung from the bottom of the catcher's mask. Named the "Steve Yeager Throat Guard," it is now used by almost all big league catchers (courtesy National Baseball Hall of Fame Library; Cooperstown, N.Y.).

ger was promoted to their AAA team at Albuquerque where he was determined to work on his hitting and correct any weakness. He was thrilled to have made the LA roster in the spring camp and said, "I'm here to stay—and I'll play in the majors. I know I'll make it."[96]

Yeager made his major league debut with the Dodgers on August 2, 1972, and caught 35 games before the end of the season. In those 35 games, his batting average was .274, a good mark for a light-hitting position and the highest he would ever attain in the major leagues.[97] As further evidence of his defensive skills, on August 8, Yeager tied a National League record for catchers with 22 of the 27 putouts in the game, and he set another record for 24 putouts in one game.[98]

For the 1973 and the 1974 seasons, Yeager was the Dodgers' second-string catcher with Joe Ferguson handling most of the chores behind the plate. "They're the best young catchers the Dodgers have had since Roy Campanella and Johnny Roseboro," said Walt Alston at Vero Beach in 1973.[99] Even though Alston handed Ferguson the catching job, Yeager still was confident that one day he would be behind the plate on a more regular basis. "I think I can give the Dodgers what they haven't had since Roseboro ... a defensive catcher who hits well enough to play regularly."[100]

During that year, he also tried wearing contact lenses. Since beginning in professional ball, Yeager had always worn glasses under his catcher's mask and had always worried that someday his glasses would be smashed into his face. Also, the glasses would usually wind up on the top of his head when he flipped his mask off. He began the 1973 season wearing contact lenses, but soon he abandoned them, explaining, "I lost about three of them." Since they were much smaller than glasses, they were more difficult to locate when dropped. He decided to forego contacts and went back to his glasses.[101] Yeager caught 54 games for the Dodgers in 1973 and hit .254. At the Dodger training camp in 1974, coach Tommy Lasorda extolled the defensive virtues of Steve Yeager, but unfortunately for him, first-string catcher Ferguson had set offensive records in 1973 with 25 home runs and 88 RBIs. He was pretty good defensively, too, setting a major league record by making only three errors. Yeager knew immediately that he would remain the Dodgers No. 2 catcher, at least for 1974.[102]

Other teams were making note of Steve Yeager's defensive skills. Ken Silvestri, coach of the Braves, and manager Red Schoendienst and coach George Kissell of the St. Louis Cardinals all agreed that Yeager had the quickest, shortest, release when throwing to second base. "He's as good as I've ever seen," Kissell said.[103] The Dodgers had a number of opportunities to trade Yeager during the winter, but wanted to keep him as a replacement for Ferguson if he were to be injured.[104]

All Yeager could do was sit and wait. "You've heard it said by other players," said Yeager, "but the fact remains that you can't maintain an average unless you're playing regularly. That's the only way to develop consistency and timing."[105]

On August 6, 1974, Joe Ferguson was forced to leave the lineup after suffering a painful torn muscle in his rib cage. Yeager replaced Ferguson behind the plate, and Steve's hitting picked up. After he hit a grand slam, Ferguson complimented him, saying, "Steve is doing a fine job behind the plate." Yeager had suffered a pulled groin muscle the same week Ferguson went down, but he played anyway. When the Dodgers vice-president, Al Campanis, wondered if he should bring in another catcher, Yeager told him "Forget it. I'm fine. Don't worry about me." Later Yeager admitted that it hurt him, but he said that there was no way he would allow anyone else to take his job. "I'm going to catch even with a cast."[106] Filling in for the injured Ferguson, Yeager hit .266 in 94 games.[107] In 1974, the Los Angeles Dodgers opposed the Oakland A's in the World Series and lost in five games. Yeager played in four of the games and hit a robust .364.[108]

Ferguson resumed his role of No. 1 catcher in 1975, but when he broke his arm in a brawl against the San Diego Padres on July 1, Yaeger moved up to his spot again and led the league in putouts with 806.[109] He would be the starting catcher for the Dodgers through 1983.[110]

On September 6, 1976, in a game at San Diego, Yeager suffered a freak but extremely frightening injury. While he was in the on-deck circle waiting for his turn to bat, the Dodgers hitter, Bill Russell, had his bat shattered, and the sharp, jagged end of the bat went flying right at Yeager's throat, seemingly piercing his esophagus. He was rushed to the hospital where the Padres physician, Dr. Paul Bauer, performed a 98-minute surgery. Dr. Bauer found that the esophagus was not punctured as first believed; the bat had narrowly missed not only the esophagus but also many arteries in that area. Dr. Bauer made a four-inch lateral incision so that nine splinters could be removed from the cut. Several were resting against the nerves which controlled the arm. According to medical reports, Yeager "was within one inch of being a dead man."[111]

As a result of his accident, Yeager, realizing how serious the injury could have been, introduced the catcher's throat protector, the small flap that hangs from his mask and protects that area. Ironically, it probably would not have prevented his injury since he would not have been wearing his mask in the on-deck circle.[112]

In 1977 Yeager was again the starting catcher for the Dodgers and his backup catcher was Johnny Oates, recently acquired from the Philadelphia Phillies for Dodgers infielder Ted Sizemore. Joe Ferguson, who had spent the previous season with the Dodgers before going to the St. Louis Cardinals, was now a member of the Houston Astros.[113]

Yeager had his breakout year for the Dodgers in 1977. He appeared in 125 games, the second highest of his career. He hit 16 home runs, including another grand slam. His average was .256, and he had a career high of 55 runs batted in.[114] The Dodgers won the National League pennant again that year, and Yeager once again hit at an out-of-character pace of .316 in the series. Unfortunately, the Dodgers were still unable to become World Champions, losing to the New York Yankees in six games.[115]

By 1978 the press was referring to Yeager as the "premier catcher in baseball, aggressive, somewhat smug and mercilessly needling the opposition with salty language and able to withstand numerous home plate crashes as evidenced by his bruises, nosebleeds and sore knees."[116]

For the second consecutive year, the Dodgers won the NL pennant, and once again they faced the New York Yankees, who, like the year before, won the Series in six games. Yeager caught in five of the six games and hit .231.[117]

Yeager distinguished himself again in the 1981 World Series, which marked the fourth Los Angeles Dodgers matchup against the New York Yankees. This year Yeager had two home runs including a game winner in Game Five, drove in four runs, and hit .285, bringing his cumulative World Series average to a very respectable .298. The Dodgers defeated the Yankees in the 1981 World Series.[118]

Yeager was named tri–MVP in the Series after he connected for his game-winning round-tripper against Yankees southpaw Ron Guidry. He shared the MVP award with teammates Ron Cey and Pedro Guerrero, the first time in the 27-year history of the award that it went to three members of the winning team.[119] Calling the World Championship a "win for the veterans," Yeager said, "We figured we might as well win it this time because it might be the last time we could do anything together."[120] At the conclusion of the 1981 World Series, Steve Yeager signed a two-year contract to remain with the Dodgers.[121]

Yeager predicted accurately. The year 1981 marked the last time he took part in a World Series. He got 18 hits in World Series play, four home runs and four doubles. In comparison, in his four World Series, Willie Mays got only 17 hits, three doubles and no homers.[122]

After the 1983 season ended, Yeager signed his last two-year contract with the Dodgers.[123] During 1984 and 1985, Yeager gave up his top spot and played back-up catcher behind Mike Sciosia.[124] In his final four seasons with the Dodgers, Yeager helped lead the team to two more division titles, but they lost the NL Championship Series both times (1983 to the Philadelphia Phillies and 1985 to the St. Louis Cardinals).[125]

At the winter meetings in December 1985, the Dodgers traded their longtime catcher, Steve Yeager, to the Seattle Mariners. Seattle sent left-handed relief pitcher Ed Vande Berg to the Dodgers. The 37-year-old Yeager had caught more games (1,181) than any other L.A. Dodgers catcher except John Roseboro (1,199).[126]

He played 50 games for the Mariners in 1986 but was on the disabled list for most of the season, hitting only .208 with two home runs but a fielding average of 1.000. He retired after the 1986 season when the Mariners did not pick up his option year.[127]

In his 15-year major league career, Yeager played in 1,269 games, had 816 hits, including 118 doubles, 16 triples, and 102 home runs. He walked 342 times. His career batting average was .228, but his on-base percentage was .300. He scored 357 runs and had 410 RBIs.[128]

After he ended his playing days, Yeager became a minor league coach and a manager in the Dodgers organization, including stints at Long Beach, a new team in the independent Western Baseball League.[129] He also coached for the California League's Class A affiliate of the Anaheim Angels.[130] Yeager was instrumental in tutoring the fine Los Angeles Dodgers catcher, Russell Martin, who was a star rookie in 2007.[131]

Yeager also acted in three movies, playing the role of Duke Temple in *Major League* and its two sequels. He also appeared in a television show with former major leaguer, Ken Brett, and posed for a *Playgirl* centerfold.[132] One of the most popular members of the L.A. Dodgers, Yeager spoke at various venues when he was an active player, including at least one appearance before a Jewish youth group. He married his wife on the steps of City Hall with the mayor as his best man.[133]

Jeff Newman

Jeffrey Lynn Newman was another major leaguer who was not born a Jew but converted later in life. A catcher who also played the infield, Newman was born in Fort Worth, September 11, 1948. He played baseball in high school and at Texas Christian University where he studied history and received his degree in education. After college, Newman played semipro ball in Fort Worth.[134]

The Cleveland Indians selected Newman in the twentieth round of the 1970 amateur entry draft. He played in the minors from 1970 to 1976, beginning his professional career as a third baseman, but while in the California League in 1972, he began catching for the first time in his career. He obviously found the transition a challenge since he led the league in passed balls with 51.[135]

The following year Newman was promoted to San Antonio in the Texas League where he greatly improved his catching skills. The six-foot, two-inch, 215-pound, right-handed hitter continued moving up the ladder in the minors.[136] For the next two years, Newman played in both the American Association and the Pacific Coast League.[137]

The Indians originally drafted Newman, but he never appeared in a single game for the parent club. The Oakland Athletics purchased his contract on October 24, 1975, and he remained in their organization until 1983.[138]

He debuted for the A's on June 30, 1976, at the age of 27.[139] In his first season in the majors, Newman appeared in 43 games, all behind the plate. He hit only .195, with 15 hits, four of them for extra bases.[140] The following year, Newman made 94 appearances, one of them as a pitcher. On September 17, 1977, he was asked to make a mound appearance in the eighth inning in the second game of a twi-night doubleheader. He tossed one scoreless inning, allowed one hit and hit one batter. The A's lost the game to Kansas City, 6–0.[141]

Newman was used more frequently in 1978, 1979, and 1980. In 1979, Newman played in the most games of his major league career—143—and made the All-Star team. Although he hit only .238 that year, he led the Athletics in home runs with 22.[142]

Between 1980 and 1982, Newman, who had never been a strong hitter, began to slump. He hit

Jeff Newman was 27 years old when he broke into the major leagues in 1976 with the Oakland Athletics. He remained with the A's for seven years before spending his last two major-league years as an active player with the Boston Red Sox. When Oakland fired manager Jackie Moore during the 1986 season, the A's organization chose Newman as interim manager for ten games until Tony La Russa could take over the managerial reins on a regular basis (courtesy National Baseball Hall of Fame Library; Cooperstown, N.Y.).

.233 in 1980 and .231 in 1981. In 1982, Newman's average fell below .200.

Although Newman was not the strongest hitter on the A's, he was one of the most popular players. He began to devote much of his time to charity work for his community, and he made a number of public appearances on behalf of the Athletics. He would often visit local hospitals, and he hosted golf tournaments to raise money for a school for mentally challenged children. "I'll do charity work for as much time as I have," said Newman.[143]

In the strike-shortened season of 1981, the first-half winner, Oakland, with the best won–lost record over the full-season, swept the division title from second-half champ Kansas City. The Royals, with a full season record of 50–53, had become the only club in major league history to qualify for post-season play with a losing record. Newman had no hits in three at-bats in the series.

The A's then lost the ALCS to the New York Yankees in three games. Newman went to the plate five times in that series, and once again, he took the collar for the entire post-season.[144]

Following the 1982 season, the A's traded pitcher Jerry King, outfielder and designated hitter Tony Armas, and Jeff Newman to the Boston Red Sox for third-baseman Carney Lansford and utility man Garry Hancock.[145]

Newman played sparingly for the Red Sox in 1983 and 1984—a total of only 83 games in the two years. He hit .189 in 1983 and .222 in 1984 and retired at the conclusion of the 1984 season with a lifetime batting average of .224 in 735 games. His lifetime fielding percentage as a catcher was .981, a better indicator of his value as a player.[146]

In November 1985, the A's rehired Newman, not as a player, but as a bullpen coach.[147] In the summer of 1986, the A's dismissed their manager, Jackie Moore, and named Jeff Newman to that post on an interim basis. He managed for ten games and posted a record of 2–8 before Tony La Russa took over as the permanent manager. Newman remained with the A's the rest of the season as a coach, and then continued his managing career in the minors until the end of the 1991 season.[148]

In 1992 Newman accepted an offer to coach third base for the Cleveland Indians; he held that position until the end of the 1997 season. He coached for the Baltimore Orioles in 2000 and the Mariners in 2005. In between coaching assignments, Newman and two other former players, Bill Madlock and Tom Lawless, worked as field assistants for the commissioner's office.[149]

Newman retired completely from baseball, but he could boast a full cycle in the game— minor league player, major leaguer, coach and manager.

Bob Tufts

Robert Malcolm Tufts was a left-handed reliever and the second player known to have converted to Judaism during his playing career. He was born November 2, 1955, in Medford, Massachusetts, just outside Boston. The son of a bank vice-president, Tufts graduated from Princeton University with a degree in economics and was drafted by the San Francisco Giants. He was the second in his family to go into pro ball. His older brother had pitched in the Cubs' organization, but never made it to the majors.[150]

Tufts was a starting pitcher during his first three years in the minors, but his minor league general manager, Tom Haller, told Tufts during spring training in 1980 that he would now be used as a relief pitcher. It was not Tufts' choice. He had been successful and he wanted to continue as a starter. "I was not prepared for the role and did not have the immediate success I needed to be confident with my change and I was changed back to a starter in late July," wrote Tufts.[151]

On August 5, 1981, the Giants continued their post-strike roster shake-up by placing outfielder Bill North and relief pitcher Randy Moffitt on waivers. As replacements, the Giants called up outfielder Jeff Leonard and left-handed pitcher Bob Tufts from Phoenix of the Pacific Coast League.[152]

Tufts did not delude himself as to why he had been recalled from Phoenix. "I knew I was playing only because I was left-handed. I took what was available and pitched well. Eventually when our closer [in Phoenix] had a bad spell in June, I took his position and within a month I was in the majors."[153]

The six foot, five-inch, 215-pound Tufts made eleven mound appearances for the Giants in 1981, but he had no won–loss record. He did, however, have a respectable 3.51 earned run average.[154]

In March 1982, the Giants traded Vida Blue and Bob Tufts to the Kansas City Royals for pitchers Renie Martin, Craig Chamberlain, Atlee Hammaker, and a player to be designated.[155] Tufts appeared in ten games for the Royals that year and spent most of the season with their AAA farm club, the Omaha Royals. It was there that Tufts employed a "herky jerky "delivery and discovered a sinkerball as his out pitch. Royals manager Dick Howser was impressed by Tufts' pitching. "He gets you on the ground ball and doesn't walk many," said Howser. "And I like his makeup, he's not afraid. We're not going to create opportunities for him, but I have the confidence in him."[156]

Despite the fact that he was on the Royals' roster for only a brief period of time, Tufts won two games in 1982, both in relief. He made a total of 10 appearances in the major leagues that season.[157] Tufts realized that he would have to use his education to help him. "I have to pitch smart," he said. "Like not trying to throw a 90-mile-an-hour fastball when I can't. There are a lot of guys with good bodies and good arms that don't make it because they don't use their heads."[158]

In addition to pitching for the Kansas City Royals in 1982, Tufts was undergoing a major change in his personal life. He had wed Suzanne Israel who he met as an undergraduate at Princeton, and was completing his conversion to Judaism. Tufts had been raised in the United Church of Christ, but his family had no objection to his decision to convert. "They were upset with the way the Protestant church was going," he said.

During the 1980 off-season, Tufts was working at the University of Virginia where Suzanne was enrolled in law school. He began his conversion by

Bob Tufts, a Princeton graduate, converted to Judaism during his playing days. A left-handed reliefer for both the San Francisco Giants and the Kansas City Royals, he appeared in 27 games from 1981 to 1983. Shortly after his retirement, Tufts and another convert to Judaism, Elliott Maddox, spent two weeks in Israel teaching the fundamentals of baseball to aspiring Israeli athletes (courtesy National Baseball Hall of Fame Library; Cooperstown, N.Y.).

studying with Hillel Rabbi Sheldon Ezring. Two of his teammates, Gary Lavelle of the Giants, and the late Dan Quisenberry with the Royals, were aware of Tuft's conversion. Although both were religious evangelical Christians, they supported Tufts. Besides studying with Rabbi Ezring, Tufts continued on his own privately because he felt it ought to be a personal matter.[159]

Tufts admitted that he kept his intentions to convert to Judaism quiet while he was in the Giants' farm system because not all players were as understanding as Lavelle and Quisenberry. "Baseball was a southern game for a long time," said Tufts, "and many managers came from that region and some minority players suffered for it. There were huge problems for urban blacks and Jews who openly held their faith. Even some of my minor league teammates who found out about my conversion were absolutely convinced that unless I accepted Jesus as my savior, I would be going to hell."[160]

After a non–Jew converts to Judaism, it is traditional for that person to adopt a Jewish name. The rabbi who performed Tufts' ceremony asked him if he wished to choose a Jewish name. "Yes," Tufts quickly replied. "Sandy Koufax."[161] After Tufts' conversion, his wife quipped, "My mother might be the only woman to have a life membership in Hadassah and a subscription to *The Sporting News*."[162]

Tufts began the 1983 season with the Royals, and after he made only six appearances with no decisions, the Royals optioned him to Omaha.[163] A few weeks later Tufts was traded to the Cincinnati Reds for pitcher Charlie Leibrandt. The Reds assigned Tufts to the minors, and he never pitched another inning in the major leagues.[164] He retired from baseball in 1983 and completed his MBA from Columbia University, finding employment in the financial district in New York where his wife practiced law.[165]

In August 2004, Tufts and several other Jewish ballplayers took part in a symposium at the Baseball Hall of Fame. Two years later, Tufts participated in a program on the contribution of Jews to baseball at the Yogi Berra Museum and Education Center at Montclair State University, where he was accompanied by his wife and daughter Abigail, who was a junior at the Berkshire School in Sheffield, Massachusetts. Tufts stated that he was very proud and "comforted" that she was involved in Jewish activities at her school.[166]

Also in 2006, Tufts and fellow-convert Elliott Maddox taught baseball to would-be athletes in a program sponsored by the Israel Association of Baseball. "It was the ten days in between the soldiers being kidnapped and the war in Lebanon," said Tufts. "The Phantom jets were flying overhead when we were out in Kibbutz Gezer doing the clinics."[167]

Although he pitched only 42 innings in the major leagues, Tufts said he was happy with all the decisions he had made. Tufts endorsed what Tigers hurler Mark Fydrych had once said about the game, "Baseball is a great job. You can wake up at three o'clock and [still] show up early to work."[168]

15. Two Jewish Managers

Andy Cohen, Norm Sherry, and Jeff Newman all managed briefly in the major leagues, but they are much better known as players. Two other Jews, one who appeared in only seven major league games, and the other, who never played a single game in the majors, also became major league managers.

Lefty Phillips

Harold Ross Phillips, always known as Lefty, was never a major league player, but he was responsible for signing and developing a number of major leaguers and for managing the California Angels from 1969 through 1971.[1]

Phillips was born June 16, 1919, in Los Angeles, and lived all of his early life in the Highland Park neighborhood. Phillips described the area as "tough" and one where the fist was the surest sign of a boy's superiority. "Baseball helped a lot of us," he said. "I remember the first time I ever picked up a glove and put it on. What a great thrill it was. It was a badge that said you were something special. I wanted to be a baseball player and it was all I ever thought about."[2]

He played first base and outfield at Franklin High School, but he was primarily a pitcher. While he was still in his junior year at Franklin, a baseball scout offered him $1,500 to sign with the Indians. He decided to wait until he finished school but, unfortunately, when he graduated, he did not see the scout again. Phillips began his professional career by pitching for Bisbee in the Arizona League when he was 20. After only five minor league games he had to stop pitching because he hurt his arm; the injury put an end to his professional playing career.[3]

Phillips did manage to play semipro ball while working in Los Angeles for the Pacific Electric Railroad in 1940. The next year he was able to return to pro ball when the St. Louis Browns hired him as a "bird dog scout." "A bird dog scout,'" explained Phillips, "meant that I'd go out and watch kids and then come back to the main scout who'd then look at the kid himself. I did that with the Browns for four years."[4]

Phillips switched to the Cincinnati Reds in 1946, and for the next five years continued to check boxcars by night and baseball players by day. "I said goodbye to the railroad in 1950," said Phillips, "and joined the Dodgers the following year. They offered me $4,200 a year to be one of their full-time West Coast scouts. That was a big day for me."[5]

During the 1950s and 1960s, Phillips was credited with either signing or scouting Don

Drysdale, Ron Fairly, Larry Sherry, Jim Lefebvre, Ken McMullen, Phil Ortega, and John Werhas.[6]

"By 1962," said Phillips, "I was sort of assistant to Buzzie Bavasi (then the general manager) and I'd do all kinds of special assignments for him, from scouting to traveling with the team and watching from the stands." When the Dodgers defeated the Yankees in the 1963 World Series in four games, many in the Dodger organization gave Phillips much credit for his excellent scouting reports.[7]

In the fall of 1964, the Dodgers fired all their coaches after finishing in the second division. Manager Walter Alston, who had been greatly impressed with the ability of Lefty Phillips, asked him to be his pitching coach for the 1965 season.[8]

Phillips was considered the quietest of the Dodger coaches and an expert student of the game. He was also considered such an astute handler of players that Alston handed Phillips the managerial reins while he had emergency surgery in the spring of 1968. "It's a challenge to sit in for Alston," said Phillips. "I've been with him so long, I believe I know how he thinks and what he wants done." Phillips revealed that while he was filling in for Alston during his recuperation, the two men talked over the strategy and lineups frequently.[9] "I've coached with the team," said Phillips, "I've traveled with it and managed many of the players in the Arizona Instructional League. That's the big thing in running a club. You must know your men. Most pitchers, for instance, give a tipoff when they're losing their stuff or tiring, and if you know them, it certainly helps."[10] When Alston returned to his managerial duties on April 29, he thanked Phillips for running the team so well. "The job Lefty did with the club is the most distinguished I've ever seen in a situation of this kind," said Alston.[11]

Harold "Lefty" Phillips never played a single inning in the major league games. In fact, he appeared in only five minor leagues as a pitcher with Bisbee of the Arizona-Texas League but retired because of arm problems. Never far from baseball, Phillips worked as a scout, a coach, and director of player personnel before becoming manager of the California Angels from 1969 until the end of the 1971 season. He died in the summer of 1972 a few days before his fifty-third birthday (courtesy National Baseball Hall of Fame Library; Cooperstown, N.Y.).

Phillips left the Dodgers organization at the end of September 1968 to become director of player personnel for the California Angels and to work with Angels general manager Dick Walsh. The following spring, Phillips was given the additional duty of coach as well.[12] The Angels got off to a miserable season losing 28 of their first 39 games.[13] In May, Angels manager Bill Rigney had an ulcer flare-up, and Phillips was assigned to manage the team in Rigney's absence.[14]

Shortly after, on May 28, 1969, the Angels fired Rigney, and Phillips was named to replace him. The firing came after the Angels had returned from a road trip on which they lost all ten of their games. Rigney had been California's only manager since the team had first entered the big leagues in 1961.[15]

Phillips insisted that his players remember they made their living from baseball and that learning the fundamentals was part of the game.[16] He quickly had his players repeating basic drills and working on skills such as pickoffs and taking leads on the base paths. "It's one thing to talk about basics," said Phillips, "it's another to take action." Phillips demanded that regardless of the situation, his players must always know three things: "They must know the score, what inning it is, and how many outs there are; two, they must know the strengths and weaknesses of the opposition; three, they must know their own strengths and weaknesses."[17]

By the middle of July, the Angels were still floundering in the basement of the American League West. There was dissension on the team and dissatisfaction with the manager. After pitcher Bob Priddy was critical of Phillips, the Angels shipped him to their minor league club in Hawaii. Another Angel told the press that Phillips was conducting a reign of terror. Phillips discounted the unhappiness among his players. "Every ball club has two or three similar to Priddy," the manager said. "Priddy has been on five clubs and he couldn't stay with any of them. The same troubles followed him wherever he was—popping off all the time. And curfews meant nothing to him."[18]

Despite the bickering among the players, Phillips was able to take the cellar-dwelling Angels from last place under Rigney to a third-place finish in the AL West in 1969.[19] Much to the chagrin of many of the Angels' players, especially the veterans, management announced that Phillips would return to manage the team in 1970.[20]

To many, Lefty Phillips simply did not look like a manager, but instead resembled an old time, small town store owner. He was paunchy, wore baggy uniform pants, always had a chaw of tobacco or an unlit cigar in his mouth, and mumbled when he spoke. But he was noted for his candor. His manager on the Dodgers emphatically stated that Phillips was not a "yes-man." "He talked the same way to Walter O'Malley as he would talk to me, and he'd talk the same way to me as to a relief pitcher. Of course, it wasn't always easy to understand. I had to ask him to repeat himself a lot."[21]

Many of his expressions resembled those of Casey Stengel. When the Angels were hit hard by injuries, and the team was struggling with young players, Lefty memorably said of his squad, "Our phenoms ain't phenominating."[22]

After he had signed to manage the Angels in 1970, Phillips told the press that his number one objective was "to come up with a good hitter."[23] Alex Johnson, who was acquired from the Reds during the off-season, seemed to be that hitter.[24] The Angels posted a winning record of 86–76 in 1970 and once again ended the season in third place, 12 games behind the division champion Minnesota Twins.[25]

Even though there were rumors that Jim Fregosi was going to replace Phillips as manager for the 1971 season, the Angels rehired Phillips for a third year as team manager. Team president Robert Reynolds announced the rehiring of Phillips, stating, "We owe Lefty our gratitude for pulling us up out of the dirt. He's done a superb job and we've felt that way all year."[26]

Phillips credited his managerial skills to Walter Alston. "Alston always put me in the stands," remarked Phillips. "He always felt you could see more up high than you could from the bench. Those years around Alston taught me to have patience with the young players."[27]

Prior to spring training in 1971, the Pasadena Sports Ambassadors honored Phillips for his accomplishments both as the Angels manager and for his lifelong devotion to baseball. Padres manager Preston Gomez pointed to Phillips and said, "Lefty has devoted his life to just three things. They are baseball, his family and his cigar." Former Dodger Ron Fairly praised Phillips. "Dollar for dollar," said Fairly, "no ball club gets more out of an employee than it does out of Lefty Phillips."[28]

Phillips went into the 1971 season feeling his team had an opportunity to win the pennant. "If this club plays to its potential it can win," said Phillips. "In my own mind we have the best balanced club in the Western Division."[29] Unfortunately, Phillips was forced to spend much of his time and energy dealing with player problems. Angels outfielder Alex Johnson had been the 1970 American League batting champion with a .329 average.[30] Despite his having won the title, the moody Johnson had been criticized by some of his teammates for not putting out enough effort. Phillips defended his outfielder, in turn blaming the critics for attempting to make Johnson the scapegoat for all the team's shortcomings.[31] But Phillips knew the other players were not completely wrong.

In 1971 Johnson again began what Phillips called "indifferent play." Phillips benched him and tried to talk to him about his attitude, but the problem continued to recur. "He's sitting down," said Phillips, "because his all-around play and practice have not satisfied me. If he does not satisfy me in his actions, I will not play the man. He's nonchalant about everything."[32]

Johnson's lackadaisical attitude became more pronounced. Phillips removed him from the lineup for failure to leave the batter's box after he had hit a ball that had fallen in foul territory by inches. "There comes a point," said Phillips, "when you can't stand it any more. I'm just about at my wit's end. In order to gain the respect of the other ballplayers, I had to take him out."[33]

Gene Autry, Angels majority stockholder and chairman of the board, announced that Phillips had his complete backing and stated he intended to make two immediate moves—hire a special counselor to general manager Dick Walsh on the subject of instant improvement of morale, and elect a team captain who could supply added leadership on the field.[34]

Meanwhile, another Angels player, Tony Conigliaro, was having almost as many problems with teammates as Alex Johnson. Even though Autry said he supported Phillips, there were rumors that the manager had lost the backing of the front office. There were also rumors, which were vigorously denied by Phillips, that weapons were being carried by the California Angels. Most of these reports pointed squarely at leftfielder Alex Johnson as the alleged cause of internal strife on the club. A Los Angeles columnist described the state of the clubhouse as "serious, ugly, approaching tragedy."[35]

Although Johnson had been diagnosed with mental problems, the Angels finally suspended him indefinitely without pay for "failure to give his best efforts to the winning of games with which he is concerned."[36] The Major League Baseball Players Association demanded an arbitration hearing to discuss Johnson's suspension.[37] In the meantime, Gene Autry gave a vote of confidence to both his manager and general manager, affirming that their positions were secure.[38]

On September 29, 1971, an arbitration panel ruled that Johnson had improperly been placed on the restricted list back in June and that as a result, the club was obligated to pay his salary to the end of the season, an amount totaling $29,832.[39] Marvin Miller said the finding was an historic one. "It means that a man who is emotionally disturbed is just as ill as one who has sustained an injury or has an ailment. He should not be suspended or disciplined. He should be placed on the disabled list."[40]

The editor of *Baseball Digest* took Phillips's side. "We think Phillips was extremely patient in his dealing with Johnson. We know of some managers who wouldn't have left spring training camp with him on their roster—despite the man's outstanding talent as a hitter and despite the fact he was the American League batting champion in 1970."[41]

Needless to say, all the distraction the Angels had to contend with in 1971 did not help them in the standings. They ended the season with a losing record of 76–86, finishing in fourth place, 25.5 games behind the division winners, Oakland.[42]

On October 6, the Angels traded Alex Johnson and another disgruntled player, catcher Jerry Moses, to the Cleveland Indians for outfielder Vada Pinson, infielder-outfielder Frank Baker, and pitcher Alan Foster, a former Dodger. Angels co-owner Robert Reynolds announced that the status of Lefty Phillips would be disclosed prior to the start of the 1971 World Series.[43]

Not surprisingly, two days later, the Angels announced the dismissal of general manager Dick Walsh, Phillips, and all four of his coaches, Rocky Bridges, Carl Koenig, Pete Reiser, and Norm Sherry.[44] Phillips was offered and accepted a job as a scout in the Angels organization. He received some offers to coach in the major leagues, but he turned them down, indicating that he had no desire to accept any managerial job in the minor leagues.[45]

Under their new manager, Del Rice, the Angels continued to struggle, finishing in fifth place in 1972 with a record of 75–80. Rice managed the Angels for one year before Bobby Winkles replaced him.[46]

On June 12, 1972, Lefty Phillips died of a severe asthmatic attack at his home in Fullerton, California, just days shy of his fifty-third birthday. A son, a daughter, and four grandchildren survived him.[47]

When Phillips was fired as Angels manager, he wasn't bitter. "I always knew I'd get fired," he said. "I didn't think it would be exactly like this." Buzzie Bavasi, former president of the Padres and former general manager of the Dodgers, called Lefty the "most dedicated man in baseball since Branch Rickey."[48]

Larry Rothschild

Larry Rothschild, like Lefty Phillips, a pitcher, appeared in seven major league games during two years with the Detroit Tigers, but made his mark in baseball history nearly 20 years later as the first Jew to be named the inaugural manager of a major league baseball team.[49]

Lawrence Lee Rothschild was born March 12, 1954, on the South Side of Chicago, to a Jewish father and a gentile mother. Even though he grew up in White Sox territory, he loved the Cubs. His German-born father rooted for the Yankees because it was the first team he had ever seen.[50]

Larry first attended Bradley University, but like so many hopeful baseball players, he transferred to Florida State where he graduated with a degree in business management and pitched for the school's NCAA regional championship team in 1955.[51]

That same year, the Cincinnati Reds signed Rothschild and assigned him to their Billings team in the Pioneer League as a non-drafted free agent. He spent 1975 through 1980 in the Reds' organization. His best year in the minors was 1976 when he played for the Three Rivers Eagles in the Eastern League, posting an 11–3 record with an ERA of 2.05. He eventually worked his way up to the Reds' American Association team in Indianapolis and also played winter ball in the Venezuelan League one year between seasons.[52]

The Detroit Tigers picked up his contract in 1981 and assigned him to their Evansville farm club in the American Association. When the AAA season ended, the Tigers called Rothschild up to the parent club, where he debuted on September 11, 1981. Entering the game with the bases loaded, Rothschild got the first batter he faced to hit a sure double play ball back to the mound, but he was able to get only one out because his new hat fell into his eyes when he fielded the ball. Larry pitched in five games in 1981, getting one save and notching a sterling 1.59 earned run average.[53]

In 1982 Rothschild spent most of the year with the Evansville Triplets, and rejoined the Tigers at the end of the season, as he had done the year before. He appeared in only two games in 1982 and his ERA was an atrocious 13.50, because in one of his appearances, he allowed four runs in just 2.2 innings. Rothschild's very brief pitching career in the major leagues ended after these seven appearances; he pitched a total of 8.1 innings for a lifetime earned run average of 5.40.[54]

Rothschild played two more years in the minors at the Chicago Cubs' Iowa (AAA) affiliate before he retired as an active player in 1985. He then became a coach for the organization that had first hired him—the Cincinnati Reds. Rothschild spent five years as a coach in Cincinnati's organization, beginning as a batting coach for the Reds' A and AA teams in 1986 and 1987, then becoming a roving pitching instructor for all the Reds' affiliates for the next two years.[55]

Larry Rothschild pitched only 8.1 innings in the major leagues in the early 1980s, but he can show off two World Series rings. In 1998, he also gained the distinction of being the only Jew to manage an expansion team, the Tampa Bay Devil Rays, in its inaugural season in the majors. Since 2002, Rothschild has been pitching coach for his hometown Chicago Cubs (courtesy National Baseball Hall of Fame Library; Cooperstown, N.Y.).

Late in 1989, Cincinnati Reds manager Lou Piniella completed his coaching staff for 1990 by hiring Larry Rothschild as his bullpen coach.[56] Rothschild remained with the Reds until 1993, winning a World Series ring in 1990 when the Reds defeated the Oakland Athletics in four games.[57] In May 1993, manager Tony Perez and the entire coaching staff, including Rothschild, were fired. Larry then spent a year as the Atlanta Braves' roving minor league pitching coach.[58]

In 1994, the Florida Marlins hired Rothschild as their pitching coach, replacing Marcel Lachemann, who had left at midseason to manage the Angels.[59] Three years later, Rothschild's young pitching staff led the Marlins, a wildcard team, to an unexpected 1997 World Championship over the Cleveland Indians, winning for Rothschild his second World Series ring.[60]

The Marlins' victory in the World Series was particularly impressive because the team had been in existence for only five years. Rothschild received much credit for that victory, having developed a solid staff that included Cuban hurler Livan Hernandez, who played a key role in Florida's winning both the NLCS and the Series.[61]

In 1997 Chuck LaMar, an old friend of Rothschild from their time together in the Reds' organization, was the general manager of the expansion team, the Tampa Bay Devil Rays. LaMar, who was building a team to begin play in 1998, asked Rothschild to become the Devil Rays' manager. Although Rothschild had no previous managerial experience, LaMar felt that his great communication skills and vast baseball knowledge would help him in his new role. Rothschild accepted LaMar's offer of his first managerial position at any level, becoming Tampa Bay's first manager.[62]

Rothschild managed Tampa Bay from 1998 through 2000 and 14 games into the 2001 season. In 1998, his team finished in fifth place with a record of 63–99, but with the best league finish for an expansion team in both ERA and fielding percentage. Despite his 99 losses, he had a relatively smooth rookie managerial season. Considered an intense and intelligent individual both on and off the field, Rothschild was serious and demanding of his players and coaches, insisting that they work as hard as he did.[63]

The following year, Rothschild's Devil Rays ended the season with a slightly better record of 69–93, but were hampered by a lack of speed and a weak bench.[64]

In 2000, Rothschild's last full season as Tampa's manager, the Devil Rays finished the year with an almost identical record of 69–92. After only 14 games in 2001, La Mar fired him and replaced him with bench coach Hal McRae. Tampa Bay's record was 4–10 at the time of Rothschild's firing. His dismissal was the sixth quickest managerial change in major league history.[65] Rothschild's total record as manager of the Devil Rays was 205–294.

After he left Tampa Bay, Rothschild finished the 2001 season as a consultant to the Florida Marlins.[66] In 2002 Rothschild returned to his hometown, Chicago, and became the pitching coach for the Chicago Cubs.[67]

16. The Resurgence of Jewish Players

The 1990s showed a marked increase in the number of Jewish players in the major leagues. Approximately twice as many Jewish-born players debuted in the big leagues in the 1990s as in the previous two decades combined. These were the children of baby boomers, and even more were from intermarried families. Of those who debuted in the 1990s, close to half of them played only during this decade, and with one exception, had very brief playing careers.[1] Several, however, continued to be active players into the first decade of the next century. Of the eighteen major leaguers of the 1990s, eight were pitchers, and ten played in the field—the infield, the outfield, or behind the plate.

IN THE FIELD

Brian Kowitz

Ten games was the extent of Brian Kowitz's major league career, but he played them in the right year with the right team and attained a highly valued reward.

Born in Baltimore, August 7, 1969, Kowitz was a star outfielder for Clemson University from 1988 through 1990. In 1990 he was the Atlantic Coast Conference Player of the Year, hitting safely in 38 consecutive games with a .403 batting average.[2]

The Atlanta Braves drafted him that year and like many eventual major leaguers, he worked his way up the farm system. His outstanding year with the Braves AAA team in Richmond was no doubt much of the rea-

Brian Kowitz appeared in ten games for the Atlanta Braves in 1995, filling in for the Braves' regular outfielder Dave Justice who was on the disabled list. Kowitz had three RBIs and scored three runs before returning to the minors when Justice came back. The Braves acknowledged Kowitz's brief, but productive stint in the majors by awarding him a World Series ring when the Braves won the World Championship that fall (courtesy of Gwinnett Braves).

son Atlanta chose the five-foot, ten-inch, 180-pound Kowitz in June 1995 to replace All-Star outfielder Dave Justice who had been placed on the disabled list.[3]

Kowitz debuted with the Braves June 4, 1995, against the Houston Astros with a pinch-hit double in the fifth inning. In the ten games in which he appeared, Kowitz went to the plate 24 times and hit safely four times for a batting average of .167. He had three runs batted in and also scored three runs.[4]

When Justice returned to the Braves, Kowitz returned to Richmond.[5] The Braves did not forget Kowitz's contribution during Justice's absence. Atlanta became World Series champions that fall, and the team rewarded Kowitz with a World Series ring.[6]

The Tigers signed Kowitz in 1996 and took him to their spring training camp. Before the season started, Detroit optioned him to their AAA farm club in Toledo where he played until his release in May. Toronto signed him and sent him to the Syracuse Chiefs.[7]

Kowitz played one more year of organized baseball when he resurfaced in 2000 to play for the Aberdeen Arsenal, the first professional baseball team in the history of Aberdeen, Maryland.[8]

Eric Helfand

Eric Helfand, a native of Erie, Pennsylvania, who grew up in San Diego, was drafted three times by three different teams, but played all 53 of his major league games with the Oakland A's during the 1990s.[9]

Born on March 26, 1969, Helfand's first chance to play professional baseball was in 1987 when the Seattle Mariners drafted the 18-year-old, right-handed hitting catcher. He turned down Seattle's offer and instead attended first Nebraska State University and then Arizona State where he played baseball at both schools.[10]

Drafted again in 1990 by the Oakland Athletics, the six-foot, one-inch, 195-pound Helfand signed with the A's and played in their minor league system, working his way up to AAA by 1992.[11]

After the 1992 season, the Florida Marlins in the expansion draft took Helfand, but he never played for Florida. As part of a complicated transaction designed to protect some additional Oakland players, the Marlins immediately traded Helfand back to the A's for shortstop Walt Weiss.[12]

Helfand debuted with the A's on September 4, 1993, played seven games and went back to the minors to begin the 1994 season. The A's brought him back up for seven more games in 1994 and kept him in Oakland in 1995, chiefly as a back-up catcher to Terry Steinbach. That year, he hit just .163 and appeared in only 38 games. At the end of the season he was granted free agency.[13]

After leaving the big leagues, Helfand played for

Eric Helfand was a good-fielding, but weak-hitting catcher, whose major league career spanned three years, all with the Oakland Athletics. His main role with the A's was back-up catcher to Terry Steinbach (courtesy National Baseball Hall of Fame Library; Cooperstown, N.Y.).

two more years in the minors—one year in the Cleveland farm system and his last year as a professional in the San Diego organization.[14]

Eddie Zosky

A Jewish player who debuted in the 1990s and appeared in his final game in the major leagues in 2000 was Eddie Zosky. Zosky, a right-handed–hitting infielder, played for four teams in his widely separated five-year career in the majors, but he played in only 44 games throughout the entire period.[15]

Eddie Zosky played 12 years of professional baseball, but appeared in only 44 games in the major leagues and hit safely only 8 times for a lifetime batting average of .160. Once considered the "next best thing" for the Toronto Blue Jays organization and the "shortstop of the future," Zosky finally retired from baseball in March 2001 after wandering among the Marlins, Orioles, Giants, Brewers and Cardinals farm systems (courtesy National Baseball Hall of Fame Library; Cooperstown, N.Y.).

Eddie Zosky was born in Whittier, California, on February 10, 1968, to Yvonne Katzman Zosky and a non–Jewish father. The New York Mets drafted him out of high school in 1986, but like many of his Jewish peers, he opted for college. In his junior year at Fresno State, the six-foot, 175-pound infielder played shortstop on the varsity squad and hit .370. Both the *Sporting News* and *Baseball America* selected him for their All-American teams.[16]

The Toronto Blue Jays took Zosky in the first round of the 1989 draft, and he spent the 1989 and 1990 seasons with Toronto's AA affiliate where he played shortstop both years.[17] Zosky quickly became one of Toronto's top prospects and was considered the "next big thing" and the Blue Jays' "shortstop of the future."[18]

At the beginning of 1991, the Jays promoted Zosky to their AAA club at Syracuse where he led International League shortstops with 221 putouts, 371 assists, and 88 double plays. On September 1, Eddie debuted with Toronto where he played 18 games with the Jays and hit a disappointing .148.[19]

Although the Blue Jays felt confident that he was ready to take the shortstop position away from Manny Lee,[20] Zosky returned to Syracuse in 1992. When the minor league season ended, Toronto recalled Zosky and he batted .286 in eight games for the Jays.[21]

Zosky did not play in the majors in either 1993 or 1994. He underwent surgery in 1993 to remove a bone spur from his right elbow and rehabbed in the minors that year. Toronto invited Zosky back to spring training in 1994, but the team cut him before breaking camp, and he spent the entire season playing in Syracuse. For the first time in his professional baseball career he played second base.[22]

Eddie Zosky began to fade into the background because of his arm injury and his poor offensive production. His future with Toronto became more problematic when the Jays drafted shortstop Alex Gonzalez.[23] On November 18, 1994, the Toronto Blue Jays traded Eddie Zosky to the Florida Marlins for a player to be named later.[24]

The Marlins sent Zosky to their AAA club in Chattanooga. Late in the 1995 season, Florida brought Zosky to the majors, his third trip to the big leagues, where he played six games before returning to the minors.[25]

Zosky spent all of 1996, 1997, and 1998 in the minors. In 1996 he was in the Baltimore Orioles organization; the following year the San Francisco Giants signed Zosky; in 1998, he played for the Milwaukee Brewers' International League farm club.[26]

Zosky played twelve more games in the major leagues. In 1999 he appeared in eight games for the Milwaukee Brewers and the following year played four games for the Houston Astros.[27] The Astros granted him free agency following the 2000 season, and he retired from baseball in March 2001.[28]

Micah Franklin

Power-hitting Micah Franklin played more than seven years for five different major league organizations before he finally broke into the big leagues, but as he once said, "I wasn't in the right place at the right time."[29]

Micah Ishanti Franklin, son of a Jewish mother and an African-American father, was born April 15, 1972, in San Francisco, and always considered himself Jewish. His name honors his mixed heritage: "Micah" for his maternal great grandmother Mildred and "Ishanti" for the West African Ashanti tribe and his maternal grandfather Israel. Franklin once said that the Jewish community never made him feel out of place because "nobody at synagogue cared what color you are, as long as you're trying to be a good person."[30]

The New York Mets drafted the 6-foot, 195-pound switch-hitter on June 10, 1990, after he had graduated from Lincoln High School in San Francisco. He started out as an infielder, but switched to the outfield. After two years in the Mets organization, he signed a contract with the Cincinnati Reds March 27, 1992, and he played for the Reds in their minor league system until he was traded to the Pittsburgh Pirates in July 1994.

In November 1995, the Detroit Tigers claimed Franklin on waivers from the Pirates. Just a few months into the 1996 season, Detroit traded Franklin, along with Brian Maxcy, to the St. Louis Cardinals for Miguel Inzunza and Tom Urbani. The Cardinals sent Franklin to their Louisville farm club where he

Micah Franklin, the son of a Jewish mother and a black father, had the misfortune of having outstanding outfielders playing ahead of him. With the Cardinals in 1997, Franklin's only year in the majors, it was Ron Gant and Brian Jordan. In the Cubs' organization it was Sammy Sosa. After a brief stint playing in Japan and then for the White Sox and Diamondbacks organizations, Franklin retired from professional baseball in 2004 (courtesy of Iowa Cubs).

played from June to the end of the season. His 21 home runs for Louisville in 1996 marked his fourth consecutive 20-plus home run season.[31]

In 1997, his eighth year as a professional, Franklin finally made it to the major leagues on May 13. Unfortunately, the Cardinals were well stocked with outfielders, including Brian Jordan and Ron Gant, and Franklin was used sparingly. He appeared in only 17 games for St. Louis, and although he hit .324 with two home runs, that was the end of his major league career. The Cardinals released him September 10, 1997. He signed as a free agent with the Cubs December 18, 1997, and spent the entire 1998 season with their AAA team in Iowa. He was released after the season ended.[32]

Frustrated at his inability to gain a berth in the majors, Franklin played in Japan for two years where he was near the top of the league with 30 homers and 80 RBIs. The large meatpacking firm, Nippon Ham, sponsored his team, the Fighters. Every Friday, Nippon Ham would distribute packages of their product to every team member, and every Friday Franklin would say, "No thank you" and pass it on.[33]

When he returned to the States, he played in the minors for two years in the Brewers' and the Diamondbacks' systems. In 2003 he went abroad again, playing for the Hyundai Unicorns in South Korea before returning to the United States.[34]

On June 11, 2004, Franklin made one last attempt to find his place in professional baseball, playing 28 games for the Diamondbacks' farm club in Tucson before he retired August 25, 2004. His manager, Chip Hale, said of Franklin, "He came here to help us out because we were down bodies.... I felt like when we got him he would be a real good influence on our younger players. He has helped these guys tremendously."[35]

David Newhan

David Newhan was the last Jewish ball player to make his major league debut in the 1990s, appearing for the Padres in his first game on June 4, 1999. He was nicknamed "Son of Scribe" because his father was the *Los Angeles Times* Hall of Fame baseball writer Ross Newhan. During his major-league career, David played first, second, and third base and all three outfield positions (courtesy New Orleans Zephyrs, photograph: Joe Maitrejean).

David Newhan's major league career was built on his willingness to play almost any position needed on any given day. During more than eight seasons in the big leagues, the five-foot, ten-inch, 180-pound utility player covered first, second, and third base, and all three outfield positions.[36]

David Matthew Newhan was born September 7, 1973, in Fullerton, California. When he began playing major league baseball, he was nicknamed "Son of Scribe," because his father was Hall of Fame *Los Angeles Times* sportswriter Ross Newhan, who also happened to be David's most ardent fan.[37]

Newhan grew up in Los Angeles where he went to Hebrew school, attended synagogue, and had his bar mitzvah, but his family were not committed Jews. David became a Messianic Jew in 2000.[38]

Newhan attended Pepperdine University where he led the West Coast Conference in slugging, and the Oakland Athletics signed him in the seventeenth round of the 1995 draft.[39] Two years later, the A's traded Newhan along with pitcher Doug Wengert to the San Diego Padres for pitcher Doug Bochtler and infielder Jorge Velandia.[40] Newhan debuted in the majors on June 4, 1999, and four days later, went 3-for-4 against Oakland, becoming the first Padre in 19 years to get hits in his first two at-bats.[41] After spending July and August with the Padres AAA team, Newhan came back to the big club on September 10 and played in a total of 32 games for the Padres, but hit just .140.[42]

Newhan played most of the 2000 season with San Diego but was traded to the Phillies for the final weeks of the season. His hitting remained a problem as he posted an anemic .176.[43] During the 2001 season, Newhan appeared in only seven games for the Phillies before running into an outfield wall and having to undergo season-ending shoulder surgery on May 15.[44]

Newhan spent the 2002 and 2003 seasons in the minor leagues until Baltimore picked him up as a free agent; he made an incredible comeback with the Orioles in 2004. Appearing in 95 games, Newhan hit .311 with eight home runs and 54 runs batted in. He also scored 66 runs for the third-place Orioles.[45]

Newhan returned to the role of utility player for both 2005 and 2006 with the Orioles, appearing in a total of 135 games those two years. In 2007 with the New York Mets, Newhan hit .203 in 56 games. The following year, Newhan played for his fifth major league team, the Houston Astros, and hit .260 in 104 plate appearances. Newhan stayed with Houston for 2008, but finished the year in the Astros' minor league system. A free agent at the end of the 2008 season, in January 2009, he signed a minor league contract with Houston's AAA club and was invited to the Astros' 2009 spring training camp.[46]

Gabe Kapler

Gabe Kapler roamed the outfield for a number of major league teams, but was probably best known for his years with the Boston Red Sox.

Gabriel Stefan Kapler was born on August 31, 1975, in Hollywood, to Mike and Judy Kapler. Both of his parents were involved in the community—his father taught music and worked in the peace movement; his mother was an educator and counselor. Gabe remembers having a Christmas tree in his home when growing up, but his family became more religious when his mother began working at a Jewish preschool. The Kaplers joined a conservative synagogue where Gabe became a bar mitzvah.[47]

His parents were not big baseball fans, so he was not raised with stories of Hank Greenberg or Sandy Koufax. "It was a home where the issues of the day were discussed at top volume." However, Kapler credits his parents, particularly his father, for allowing him "to be who he was." And from the age of five, for the most part, Kapler wanted to be a professional baseball player.[48]

Gabe won a baseball scholarship to Cal State–Fullerton, but he admits he did more partying than anything else. He transferred to Moorpark Junior College where the Detroit Tigers drafted him in the fifty-seventh round of the 1995 amateur draft.[49] He was signed by Mike Lieberthal's father, Dennis, a Detroit Tigers scout, and began his professional career that year at the age of 19, playing for the Jamestown Jammers in the New York–Pennsylvania League. In 63 games for the Jammers, Kapler hit .288.[50]

Kapler received a great deal of attention before coming to the big leagues. A weightlifter with a muscular physique, the six-foot, two-inch, 190-pound outfielder was considered one of the strongest men in baseball, thanks to a rigorous training routine he had begun in high school. He had even appeared on the cover of several fitness magazines.[51]

Kapler was also noticed for the large tattoos on his legs which proclaimed the connection he felt with his Jewish heritage. On his left leg was a Star of David with the words,

"Strong Minded." On his right leg were the starting and ending dates of the Holocaust and the motto, "Never Again." Many years later, Kapler described them as telling the story of his youth and as an expression of his great pride in the Jewish community.[52]

Gabe spent nearly four years in the minor leagues. By 1998, Kapler was with the Tigers' AA affiliate at Jacksonville where he appeared in 138 games and hit .322 with 28 home runs and 146 runs batted in.[53] Named both *Baseball Weekly's* and *USA Today's* Minor League Player of the Year, he was also the MVP of both the Southern League and its All-Star team.[54]

The Tigers noted Kapler's success at Jacksonville and brought him to the big leagues briefly at the tail end of the 1998 season. He made seven appearances with the Tigers beginning on September 20, the Tigers' home finale. His average for his brief stay with the Tigers was .200, with five hits, including one triple. Kapler, not the fastest runner in the Tiger organization, also managed to steal two bases in his major league debut year.[55]

Kapler began the 1999 season with Toledo, the Tigers' AAA affiliate. But after only 14 games, the Tigers brought him to the major leagues where he remained the rest of the season. He played 130 games for the Tigers, hit 18 home runs, drove in 49 runs,

Fitness buff Gabe Kapler's picture has appeared not only on baseball cards, but also on the covers of a number of fitness magazines. While not a practicing Jew, he takes his Jewish heritage very seriously as evidenced by a Star of David tattooed on one leg and the post–Holocaust motto "Never Again" on the other (courtesy National Baseball Hall of Fame Library; Cooperstown, N.Y.).

and ended the season with a .245 batting average.[56] While in Detroit, it was inevitable that Kapler would be compared with another Jewish Tiger player, Hank Greenberg, and Kapler took the opportunity to learn about him "and the [other] people who have come before me."[57]

Despite his relatively good performance for the Tigers, on November 2, 1999, Detroit traded Kapler, minor leaguer Alan Webb, infielder Frank Catalanotto, catcher Bill Haselman, and pitchers Francisco Cordero and Justin Thompson to the Texas Rangers in exchange for catcher Greg Zaun, outfielder Juan Gonzalez, and pitcher Danny Patterson.[58]

Kapler began the 2000 season in the minors, but was soon promoted to the Rangers where he divided his time between center and right field. In 116 games, he hit .302, with 14 home runs and 66 runs batted in and he stole eight bases. Kapler's 28-game hitting streak for the Rangers that year was the longest in the majors.[59]

In his first year in Texas, Kapler's decisions about playing on the High Holidays were of interest to the press and the fans. Kapler told the *Dallas Morning Sun* that he would play on Yom Kippur that year (2000), but he might not make the same decision in later years. "I'm a totally spiritual person," said Kapler. "I have a relationship with God, but it's my own relationship and the way I choose to practice my beliefs. I'm skeptical when it comes to organized religion."[60]

The following year he again proclaimed his pride in his faith. "Nobody is more proud of their heritage than I am and nobody is more proud of being Jewish than I am."[61] As it turned out, in 2001, Kapler had a day game that ended prior to the beginning of Yom Kippur so his playing on the High Holy Day was a moot point that year. Kapler went 3-for-4 with two home runs that day in a game the Rangers lost to Seattle, 7–5.[62]

In 2001 Kapler again began the season in the minors, but after only five games, he returned to the Rangers where he played in 134 games as the regular center fielder. The Rangers struggled all year and finished in the cellar in the American League West with a record of 73–89 but for the most part, Kapler had an exceptional year. Although his batting average dropped to .267, he slammed 17 home runs, had 72 runs batted in, 29 doubles and a slugging average of .437. He also stole 23 bases. Playing exclusively in center field, Kapler had a .997 fielding percentage, with only one error in 352 total chances.[63]

For the third consecutive year, Kapler started out with the Rangers' AAA team, but soon returned to Texas. Rangers manager Jerry Narron called Kapler "the most athletic and the most versatile" of all the Texas outfielders, including Juan Gonzalez and Carl Everett. Despite the compliment, Kapler saw little playing time for the Rangers in 2002, appearing in only 72 games. Before the July 31 trading deadline, the Rangers sent Kapler and infielder-outfielder Jason Romano to the Colorado Rockies in exchange for pitcher Dennys Reyes and outfielder Todd Hollandsworth.[64] Both Kapler and the Rockies hoped that a change of scenery would help him reach his potential, and the premise seemed to be working. Kapler played 40 games for the Rockies, hitting .311 and driving in 17 runs.[65]

The next year, 2003, Kapler actually began with the Colorado Rockies but appeared in only 39 games before he was released. The Boston Red Sox purchased his contract four days later, making him the first Jewish player on the team since Brian Bark pitched for the Bosox in 1995.[66] In his Red Sox debut, Gabe went 4-for-5 with three RBIs; in his second start he hit two homers and scored and drove in four runs.[67]

In 68 games for Boston in 2003, Kapler hit .291 with four homers, 23 runs batted in, and 23 runs scored. He helped his team secure a wild-card spot in the playoffs, as Boston finished in second place in the American League East with a record of 95–67.[68] Kapler enjoyed playing in Boston, especially in 2003. "Hitting in a lineup like this," he said, "it's easy to see good pitches. Success breeds confidence. This has been an incredible experience all the way through."[69]

The Red Sox met the Oakland A's in the American League Divisional Series and lost the first two games, but came back to win the next three to capture the series. In the Divisional Series Kapler played in four games and went 0–9. The Red Sox faced their traditional rivals, the New York Yankees, in the American Championship Series and lost the pennant in a tight seven-game match-up. In the ALCS, Gabe Kapler played three games and had one hit in eight plate appearances for a .125 batting average.[70]

Kapler played the entire 2004 season with the Red Sox as a backup outfielder. He managed to appear in 136 games but started only 73, hitting .272 with six home runs and 33 RBIs. The High Holiday issue arose again in 2004, and again Kapler chose to play ball. Although he often called himself a role model for Jewish fans, he explained his choice, saying, "I am not really a practicing Jew. It would be selfish to be a practicing Jew on only one day."[71]

In 2004 the Red Sox won the wild-card slot for the second consecutive time, but this year they swept the Anaheim Angels in the American League Divisional Series, then came from behind, 0–3, against the despised New York Yankees and won the American League pennant. Boston then swept the St. Louis Cardinals for their first World Championship in 86 years.[72]

On October 28, 2004, Kapler was granted free agency in order sign with the Yomiuri Giants where he could play on an everyday basis. His agent told the press that Kapler "really wanted the guarantee to play," and Red Sox manager Terry Francona said, "Selfishly I don't want him to go. For his sake I'm thrilled."[73]

Kapler called his Japanese experience "difficult" saying that he did not play well there, and because of the language barrier, he could not explain that he was injured. He also indicated that his time in Japan made him sympathetic to the problems of Japanese players who come to the United States.[74]

Kapler returned to the United States and re-signed with the Red Sox on July 15, 2005, joining two other Jewish players, Adam Stern and Kevin Youkilis. Manager Terry Francona was elated to have Kapler back. Although Gabe was again the fourth outfielder, he became a team leader. Former Red Sox outfielder Trot Nixon, who played with Kapler in Boston, praised Kapler for his leadership in an ego-driven clubhouse. "He has a knack of caring," said Nixon. "He shed some light on things, maybe a problem that I wasn't thinking about.... Sometimes that's all a manager has to do."[75]

The Red Sox brass must have seen those qualities in Kapler, for after he played 36 games for the Sox in 2005 and 72 in 2006, they named him manager of the Greenville Drive, their farm team in the Class A South Atlantic League.[76]

Although he once said that he appreciated all his baseball experiences, by the fall of 2007, Kapler was ready to retire as a manager and un-retire as a player. On December 20, 2007, the Milwaukee Braves signed Kapler as a free agent.[77] He played 96 games for the Brewers in 2008 and for only the second time in his major league career, hit over .300. He was ecstatic about being a Brewer the moment he donned his uniform.[78]

Gabe Kapler and his wife, Lisa, who is Catholic, have two boys who both attended the Jewish preschool where Gabe's mother taught. Kapler was insistent that they know about their roots and their history.[79] In addition, Gabe and Lisa established The Gabe Kapler Foundation, a non-profit organization dedicated to stopping domestic violence. Gabe and Lisa have known each other since high school where Gabe rescued her from an abusive boyfriend. Together they set up the foundation to try to prevent such abuse and aid other victims.[80]

On January 12, 2009, Kapler signed a contract with the Tampa Bay Rays, who expected Kapler to help the younger players on the team.[81]

Ruben Amaro Jr.

Rubin Amaro Jr. was unique in two ways. First, he represented a third generation of professional baseball players although he was the first Jewish male in his family to make the majors. Second, although his playing career began and ended in the 1990s, he became active on the management side of the game and, at the age of 43, rose to the position of general manager of the Philadelphia Phillies.[82]

Amaro was born in Philadelphia on February 12, 1965, to a Jewish mother and a non–Jewish father, Ruben Amaro Sr. His grandfather, Santos Amoro, had been a legendary star in the Cuban and Mexican Leagues during the 1930s, but he had never had the opportunity to play in the United States because of the color of his skin. Ruben Amaro Sr., however, played in the majors for more than ten years, primarily in the 1960s, and coached for many years afterward.[83]

Growing up in Philadelphia, Ruben Jr. and his family, which included his older brother Dave, did not have any formal Jewish training, but they celebrated the Jewish holidays.[84] He did, however, have the opportunity to study baseball up close, serving as batboy for the Phillies from 1980 to 1983 when his father was the team's first base coach. "My father told me," said Ruben, "'Whatever you do here, watch!'"[85] It was especially good advice since he was observing baseball greats such as Manny Trillo, Steve Carlton, and Mike Schmidt. "I learned from all of them," he reflected.[86] "I think that's what turned me onto a career in baseball."[87]

Both education and baseball were obviously very important in the Amaro family. Ruben's brother Dave went to Duke and played minor league ball before an injury took him out of the game. The switch-hitting Ruben Jr. attended Stanford, earning a degree in biology and taking an outstanding role in Stanford's first NCAA Championship in 1987.[88]

After he graduated Stanford in 1987, the California Angels drafted the five-foot, ten-inch, 175-pound outfielder; he played in the Angels farm system through the 1990 season, moving steadily higher by virtue of his speed and good hitting.[89]

Amaro started the 1991 season with the AAA Edmonton Trappers, but the Angels called him to the majors in June to replace the injured Junior Felix. On June 8, 1991, Amaro debuted in the majors as a pinch-runner in a game against the Detroit Tigers. He appeared in nine more games for the Angels that year, going to the plate 23 times and hitting safely five times for a batting average of .217.[90]

The Angels traded Amaro in December 1991 to his hometown Philadelphia Phillies. Amaro knew very well the reputation of the Philadelphia fans. "When I was traded, I thought, "Wow, some of those fans are difficult.'" But he realized they were also knowledgeable and he felt he could compete. He played 126 games for the Phillies in 1992, hitting .219.[91]

In 1993 Amaro spent the bulk of the season in the minors, but managed to play 25 games that year for the Phillies and improved to a batting average of .333 with the parent club. After the 1993 season, the Phillies traded Amaro to the Cleveland Indians, where he once again spent most of the season in the minors. In 1994, a strike-shortened year, Amaro did appear in 26 games for the Indians, hitting .217.[92]

Amaro divided his time in 1995, playing mostly with the Indians' AAA franchise in Buffalo and in 28 games with the Indians. He joined the parent club just in time to participate in postseason play. One of his teammates in 1995 was bullpen catcher Jesse Levis, who was also Jewish.[93] The Indians defeated the Mariners, four games to two, to win the ALCS. Amaro, as designated hitter, appeared in three games, had one at-bat and scored a run.[94] In the World Series, which the Atlanta Braves won in six games, Amaro made two plate appearances but failed to get on base.[95]

Ruben Amaro Jr.'s baseball career is truly a Horatio Alger story. The Philadelphia native began as the team's batboy when his father was a coach on the 1980 Phillies World Champion team. Amaro Jr. later was a player with the Phillies twice and today is Philadelphia's general manager (© The Phillies 2009).

In 1996 Amaro went to still another team when the Toronto Blue Jays acquired him and assigned him to their farm club in Syracuse; a month later, the Jays released him. The Phillies picked him up again, and in 1996, he played 61 games for the Phillies and had the most successful year in his major league career. Used primarily as a pinch hitter, Amaro hit safely 37 times in 117 at-bats for an average of .316. It was the third-best average for a pinch-hitter in the National League.[96]

Amaro played two more years in the majors, both with the Phillies, who continued to use him as a pinch-hitter. In his last year as a player, 1998, Amaro appeared in 92 games, and for the only time in his eight-year major league career, he hit below .200—finishing the season with an average of .187.[97]

On September 22, 1998, Ruben Amaro made his final appearance in a major league game, but it was not his sacrifice fly that drew attention. Amaro played that game figuratively wearing two hats; the Phillies had just appointed him their assistant general manager. This dual role of player–general manager gave rise to some good-natured ribbing. His teammate, third baseman Scott Rolen, teased Amaro when he said, "It's great when front office guys get RBIs." General manager Ed Wade added, "Yeah, he's going to negotiate both sides of his arbitration case."[98]

One of Amaro's functions as assistant general manager was to interview managerial candidates when a vacancy occurred. In the fall of 2000, the Phillies were seeking a new manager, and one of the candidates was Ruben Amaro Sr. Amaro Jr. recounted the unusual experience of interviewing his father. "I tried to be as objective as possible, and I think I was." Before the interview, the assistant general manager disclosed that his father told him, "I'm awfully proud that you're one of the people interviewing me."[99] The Phillies eventually hired Larry Bowa for the managerial post. Amaro also took part in contract negotiations with players already on the Phillies' roster and with free agents.[100]

Other duties as assistant general manager included participating in public relations functions and promoting the team for the city of Philadelphia. In 2005, for example, donors to the Jewish Family and Children's Service of Greater Philadelphia enjoyed a pre-game dinner with Ruben Amaro Jr. at "JFCS Night at the Phillies."[101] He also co-founded the Richie Ashburn Foundation, which provided free baseball camps for 1,100 underprivileged children in the Delaware Valley.[102]

In November 2008, Phillies general manager Pat Gillick stepped down after fulfilling a three-year contract he had inked prior to the 2006 season. Phillies president David Montgomery selected Ruben Amaro Jr., the 43-year-old former batboy, to replace Gillick. In hiring Amaro, Montgomery said, "I feel Amaro is not only well prepared, but I believe he is extremely well qualified for this opportunity. That is evidenced by the outstanding contribution he's made to our club since he joined us 10 years ago."[103]

When then–Phillie general manager Ed Wade first asked Amaro to be his assistant in 1998, Ruben hesitated and talked it over with his family. Everyone advised him that the door might not be open very long, or maybe never again. Amaro agreed that accepting the post of assistant to Wade was "probably the second-best decision he had ever made." The first? Going to Stanford University.[104]

Jesse Levis

Jesse Levis was one of several Jewish catchers in the major leagues toward the end of the 1990s. Several of his peers had more successful careers, but none of them was more pleased about being able to make a living playing a game he loved. Like many young Jews of his generation, especially those who aspired to become professional baseball players, Sandy Koufax was an obvious hero. "I know Koufax's story and I admire him," Levis once said. "If you look at him as a player, Koufax was a Hall of Fame pitcher and deserved all the attention he got. Not many guys can throw a curve ball like he did."[105]

Levis was born in Philadelphia on April 18, 1968. His parents operated Levis's Kosher Hot Dogs Restaurant in the city and he was raised as a conservative Jew. Levis played baseball when he did not attend Hebrew School. "I got it done," Levis said. "I had a bar mitzvah and I respected the holidays. I had plenty time for school, basketball and friends."[106]

He attended Philadelphia's Northeast High School where he was both a catcher and a first baseman. The hometown Phillies drafted him when he graduated from high school in 1986, but he turned down the offer and chose a baseball scholarship to the University of North Carolina instead. He led his team to the College World Series in 1989.[107]

The stocky five-foot, nine-inch, 180-pound catcher, who batted left and threw right, accepted an offer from the Cleveland Indians in the 1989 amateur draft and he began to climb up through the Indians' farm system— the Burlington Indians, the Kinston Indians, and the Colorado Springs Sky Sox.[108] In 1991, playing for the Canton/Akron Indians, Levis led all catchers in the AA Eastern League and he came up to Cleveland early the following year, playing his first game April 24, 1992. He hit well in 28 games, but he spent most of that year in the minors.[109]

Jesse Levis's professional baseball career followed a similar pattern from 1993 through 1995. In all three of those years, he played a few games with the Indians but spent most of his time on their minor league clubs. In fact, Levis played a total of only 72 games in the majors during the four seasons from 1992 through 1995.[110]

The Indians met the Atlanta Braves in the 1995 World Series. Since Levis had been Cleveland's third-string catcher in his short stint in the majors that year, the Indians did not place him on the roster for postseason play. He did warm up the pitchers in the bullpen throughout the playoffs, however, and after the Indians lost the World Series to the Braves, four games to two, the team awarded Levis a World Series ring.[111]

On April 4, 1996, the Cleveland Indians traded Levis to the Milwaukee Brewers for minor leaguer Scott Nate and a player to be named later.[112] In 1996, his first year in Milwau-

Jesse Levis, a native of Philadelphia, was drafted out of high school by his hometown Phillies, but opted to attend the University of North Carolina instead. Eventually he signed with the Cleveland Indians as a catcher in 1992. He also caught for the Milwaukee Brewers during his nine years in the major leagues (courtesy National Baseball Hall of Fame Library; Cooperstown, N.Y.).

kee, he played in 104 games and displayed a remarkable eye at the plate, striking out only 15 times in 233 plate appearances or fewer than five percent of his at-bats.

Wherever Levis played, he tried to become part of that Jewish community by attending minyans and speaking to Jewish youth groups.[113] He also made it a point to always fast on Yom Kippur, although in 1996, he did play with the Brewers in a rescheduled game that happened to occur on the Holy Day. "I played that day," stated Levis. "I'm not like Koufax. I don't have that kind of leverage. I hope God forgives me." Levis also mentioned that in that game, he went 0-for-3, striking out once and leaving three runners in scoring position.[114]

In 1997 the left-handed swinging Levis platooned with right-handed–hitting first-string catcher Mike Matheny. In his best year in the majors, Levis brought his average up to .285, and made only two errors in 99 games. Baseball reorganization in 1998 moved the Brewers from the American League to the National League, Levis' first time playing in the senior circuit. He began the season as a back-up catcher again, but a torn rotator cuff put Levis on the disabled list and forced him to miss most of the second half of the season.[115] The Milwaukee Brewers released Levis on September 29, 1998.[116]

Levis played only a few more major league games after 1998. On July 30, 1999, the Cleveland Indians signed Jesse Levis to a one-year contract. He played 10 games for the Tribe, hitting safely four times in 26 at-bats for an average of .154. The following year, Cleveland again signed Levis but he spent the entire 2000 season playing for their AAA affiliate.[117]

By 2001, the 34-year-old Levis had added a few pounds to his already sturdy frame, and with his thinning hair, looked older than his actual age. But he still had an upbeat attitude, was extremely likable, and could still hit. After an attempt to catch on with the Atlanta Braves, he signed with the Milwaukee Brewers. At the end of the 2001 season, the Brewers called him to the majors where he played his final 12 games in the major leagues.[118]

Levis attempted to remain in the major leagues from 2001 through 2004, signing contracts with the Cincinnati Reds, the Philadelphia Phillies and the New York Mets, but never rose above AAA with any of these organizations.[119]

Jesse Levis managed the Mets farm club in Kingsport, Tennessee, in the Appalachian League in 2005.[120] In 2006 Levis began scouting for the Boston Red Sox.[121]

Levis often admitted that he had struggled throughout his career and then added, "But I loved every second of playing this game."[122]

Mike Lieberthal

Mike Lieberthal was one of the most successful Jewish players of this period. He caught 14 seasons in the majors and had the rare distinction of playing all but one of his years for the same organization, both in the minors and the majors.

Another Californian and child of an intermarriage, he was born Michael Scott Lieberthal, on January 18, 1972. His Jewish father, Dennis Lieberthal, was a baseball scout for the Detroit Tigers and encouraged his son to catch in various youth baseball leagues. Mike always credited his father as the greatest influence on his life. "He knows my swing better than I do. He's always giving me tips and pointers," he said.[123] Many years later, Lieberthal explained why he chose to become a catcher, "[Jewish kids] ... are smart. Even though a catcher takes some physical abuse, he doesn't have to be an outstanding hitter or runner. We get beat up a little bit, but it's the quickest way to the major leagues."[124]

Small for his age the first three years in high school, Lieberthal was not allowed to catch until he reached his senior year. He then became the star of the baseball team and was chosen MVP for all of Ventura County and the Cal *Hi Sport's Magazine*'s California Player of the Year.

On June 4, 1990, the Philadelphia Phillies selected Lieberthal in the first round of the amateur draft.[125] Philadelphia Phillies fans, always known as difficult to please, were unhappy with the draft pick, because the Phils had passed over Alex Fernandez, a pitcher, who they felt was a better choice.[126]

Although at six feet and 170 pounds, Lieberthal was still considered light for a catcher, Mike's defensive skills and quick footwork made him known as a key to the Phillies' future. He spent more than four years in the minors in Phillies' farm clubs in Martinsville, Spartanburg, Clearwater, Reading and Scranton.[127] His manager at Reading, Don McCormack, was well aware of how light Lieberthal was, and he made sure that he embarked on a weight program. "He is developing rapidly into a major league player," noted McCormack, "and as times goes along, he'll get bigger and stronger. I wouldn't worry about his size."[128]

On June 30, 1994, Lieberthal made his major league debut with the Phillies. He remained the Phillies' third-string catcher behind Darren Daulton and Benito Santiago until 1997 when he became the team's number one catcher.[129]

Lieberthal caught 134 games in 1997 and hit .246 with 20 home runs and 77 runs batted in. Defensively, he was third behind Brad Ausmus in steals allowed per nine innings.[130] Both Lieberthal and the Phillies were off to a good start in 1998, but on July 23, Mike suffered a pelvic injury, which ended his season. Deprived of their top catcher, the Phillies dropped out of contention.[131]

Coming back from that injury in 1999, Lieberthal had a stellar year. In addition to making the All-Star team, Mike won a Gold Glove for his play behind the plate and batted .300 with 31 home runs and 96 runs batted in. He had a career-best slugging percentage at .551 and was eighth in the league with eight sacrifice flies.[132]

Despite two periods on the disabled list in 2000 with shoulder chips, Lieberthal managed to appear in 108 games, hit .278, and was again selected for the All-Star team. With 121 fewer at-bats than the previous year, Lieberthal still hit 15 home runs, drove in 71 runs, and clouted 30 doubles (third in the league). The Phillies sorely missed his skill at handling pitchers. During his two stints on the disabled list, the Phillies' record was 13–27.[133]

In 2001 the Phillies learned again how valuable Lieberthal was to the team. On May 12, Lieberthal was picked off first base and tore the anterior cruciate ligament (ACL) in his right knee—he also tore the medial collateral ligament (MCL) and a good deal of cartilage.[134] At the time of the injury, the Phillies were in first place. Ed Wade, general manager, said, "Replacing an All-Star catcher won't be easy. Getting Lieby ready for next year will be our ultimate goal."[135]

With Lieberthal catching only 34 games for the Phillies in 2001, it became almost impossible for them to win the National League's Eastern Division. Yet, they finished the season in second place with a record of 86–76, two games behind the first-place Atlanta Braves.[136]

The Phils were happy to have a healthy Lieberthal back in 2002 as their first-string catcher once again. He hit .346 against left-handers and finished the year with an overall average of .279. In the middle of the year the Phillies gave him a three-year extension of his contract. "There's something to be said for playing your whole career with one team," said Lieberthal. "If you're happy, why change?" GM Ed Wade said that he was happy to keep Lieberthal. "He's very important to us."[137]

Catcher Mike Lieberthal played thirteen of his fourteen years in the major leagues with the Philadelphia Phillies. In 2007, his final year as a player, he caught 38 games as a backup catcher for the Los Angeles Dodgers. Lieberthal ranks fifth after Hank Greenberg, Shawn Green, Sid Gordon, and Al Rosen on the list of all time Jewish home run leaders (courtesy National Baseball Hall of Fame Library; Cooperstown, N.Y.).

Mike had an excellent year in 2003. In 131 games, his average was .313, twelfth-highest in the National League. He hit 13 home runs, drove in 81 runs, and scored 68. The following year, Lieberthal appeared once again in 131 games and hit .271, with 17 home runs, 67 RBIs, and 58 runs scored.[138]

Although 32 years old in 2004, Lieberthal became the longest-tenured athlete in Philadelphia, a town not known for sustained loyalty. True to his southern California heritage, he was laid back and easy going in his personal life, but hard-working on the field. One sports writer felt he could be the best catcher the Phillies had ever had, outpacing previous star catchers by excelling both offensively and defensively.[139] Another hailed him as an expert at guarding home plate by being "right and firm as a knight in armor" and at the same time, "nimble and flexible, both physically and mentally." He was praised for his ability to develop great working relationships with his pitchers and with his managers and coaches.[140]

Lieberthal was also known for his charitable works. He sponsored "Lieby's VIPs," which purchased game tickets for children with cancer and their families. He began to host Halloween parties for children every off-season and a celebrity billiards tournament to raise money for Philadelphia future mentors programs.[141] He also served as Chairman of the Corporate Alliance for Drug Education's 2000 fundraising drive.[142]

Lieberthal appeared in 118 games in 2005, was sixth in the league in intentional walks, and struck out only 35 times. Most importantly, he got his 1,000th hit that year, and by the end of the 2006 season, Lieberthal was the team's all-time catching leader in home runs, runs batted in, and total games caught.[143] Unfortunately, he was also injured and on the disabled list seven times during the last four years in Philadelphia, much to the displeasure of the fickle Phillie fans.[144]

On October 31, 2006, Mike Lieberthal became a free agent when the extension of his contract expired. On December 6, 2006, he signed a contract for the 2007 season with his hometown club, the Los Angeles Dodgers, at a salary of $1.15 million with an option for 2008.[145] In his final year in the major leagues, Lieberthal was primarily used as a backup catcher to Russell Martin, playing in only 38 games for the Dodgers, hitting .324 with no home runs and driving in only one run.[146] The Dodgers refused to pick up his option for the following year, and he was granted free agency.[147]

In January 2008, before a charity celebrity soccer match hosted by his Los Angeles teammate, Nomar Garciappara and his wife, soccer star Mia Hamm, Lieberthal announced that he had decided to retire. "The money was great," said Lieberthal, "but I have made (enough) money in baseball. I just didn't want to go through what I have to go through with my body to play 20–25 games a year. It's not worth it."[148]

Lieberthal was not quite through, however. On June 1, 2008, Lieberthal signed a one-day minor league contract with the Philadelphia Phillies, the team with which he had played 13 of his 14 years in the majors. The contract enabled Mike to retire officially as a Phillie. He threw out the ceremonial first ball at the game that day and, responding to the warm applause of the crowd, declared, "It's definitely an honor to come here and finish with the Phillies."[149]

In addition to the records Lieberthal set with the Phillies, he also etched several spots on the list of achievements by Jewish major leaguers. At the time of his retirement, Mike ranked fifth on the list of Jewish major league home run hitters behind Hank Greenberg, Shawn Green, Sid Gordon, and Al Rosen and seventh in both hits and RBIs by a Jewish major leaguer.[150]

Brad Ausmus

Brad Ausmus was an All-Star catcher of Jewish descent who experienced a long and successful career in the big leagues, more than half of it with the Houston Astros. He has worked with many pitchers who consider him the best catcher they ever had.

Born April 14, 1969, in New Haven, Connecticut, Bradley Davis Ausmus, the son of a Jewish mother and a non–Jewish father, was a Red Sox fan from an early age. Yet, when he began classes at Dartmouth in 1987, he had already signed as a professional baseball player with the Yankees' organization, which drafted him in the forty-eighth round of the 1987 amateur draft.[151] He completed his degree in government in 1991, taking classes during the off-season.[152]

The five-foot, eleven-inch, 195-pound right-handed hitter started his professional career in 1988, playing first in the Gulf Coast Instructional League and then progressing a level or two each year. In 1992 Ausmus played most of the season with the AAA Columbus Clippers in the International League, hitting .242.[153]

On November 17, 1992, the Colorado Rockies drafted Ausmus as the fifty-fourth pick in the 1992 expansion draft but he never played for the Rockies.[154] In 1993 Ausmus spent about half the season with the Rockies' AAA club at Colorado Springs, until on July 26, the Rockies sent him and pitchers Doug Bochtler and Andy Ashby to San Diego in

When Brad Ausmus, a graduate of Dartmouth College, played in the 1993 World Series for the Padres, he became the first Ivy League catcher in the Series since 1916. Even after many years in the majors since his 1993 rookie season, Ausmus is considered one of baseball's best defensive catchers (courtesy National Baseball Hall of Fame Library; Cooperstown, N.Y.).

exchange for pitchers Bruce Hurst and Greg Harris.[155] The games played for the Rockies' farm club would be the last he would play in the minor leagues.

Two days after the trade, July 28, 1993, Ausmus debuted in the major leagues against the Chicago Cubs. He appeared in 49 games for the Padres that year, and hit .256 in 160 plate appearances. Not known as a home run hitter, Ausmus still managed to clout five round trippers in his brief season with the Padres.[156]

Ausmus was the starting catcher for the Padres during all of 1994, 1995, and the first half of 1996. He got off to a slow start in 1994 but after the All-Star Game, he hit .308 in 22 games before the strike shortened the season. In 1995 Ausmus, normally a light-hitting batter, brought his average up to .293 and stole a career-high 16 bases, the most by any catcher since Craig Biggio stole 19 in 1991.[157] Brad also threw out 39 percent of opposing base runners, second-best in the National League.[158]

In 1996 Ausmus played in 50 games for the Padres; his batting average dipped to .181. The slumping Padres traded him to the Detroit Tigers along with shortstop Andujar Cedeno for catcher John Flaherty and shortstop Chris Gomez.[159] Ausmus played 75 games with the Tigers that year and his improved average of .248 with the Tigers brought his season mark to .221.[160]

At the end of the 1996 season, the Tigers traded Ausmus to his third major league team, the Houston Astros, as part of a ten-player swap. The Astros received, in addition to Ausmus, right-handed pitcher Jose Lima, southpaws C. J. Nitkowski and Trever Miller, and infielder Daryle Ward. The Tigers got center fielder Brian Hunter, shortstop Orlando Miller, pitchers Doug Brocail and Todd Jones, and a player to be named later. It was the largest major league deal since December 28, 1994, when the Astros and Tigers exchanged twelve players.[161]

As the first-string catcher for the Astros in 1997, Ausmus started 113 games and appeared in a total of 130. He led the National League in base runners caught stealing (44.7 percent), and he improved his batting average to .266.[162] Ausmus also participated in his first post-season play that year as he helped lead his team to the NL Central crown. The Atlanta Braves defeated the Astros in the first round of the playoffs in three consecutive games, but Ausmus went two-for-five with a double and two runs batted in.[163]

Ausmus also became a footnote to history in 1997 when, on August 12, he was the first catcher to wear a "Catcher-Cam," a small TV camera mounted on his mask to show the game over Fox Sports from a catcher's perspective.[164]

Ausmus continued his solid play for the Astros in 1998, when he appeared in 128 games and finished the season with an average of .269. For the second consecutive year, the Astros made the playoffs, but lost in the first round this year in four games to the San Diego Padres. Ausmus appeared in all four, hitting safely twice in nine plate appearances for .222.[165]

On January 13, 1999, a little more than two years after the Astros had acquired Ausmus from the Tigers, they dealt him back to the Bengals along with left-handed hurler C. J. Nitowski in return for three right-handed pitchers, Paul Bako, Dean Crow, Brian Powell, and two minor leaguers, Carlos Villalobos and Mark Persails.[166]

Unlike his previous time with Detroit, Ausmus had his best offensive season his first year back in the American League. Playing in 127 games, he hit .275 with a career-high nine home runs. He was also outstanding defensively with an almost perfect .998 fielding percentage. Because of his fine work, Joe Torre, manager of the American League All-Star team, selected him as the Tigers' lone representative to the All-Star game. He caught the final four innings of the game, and although he went 0–1 at the plate, he threw out Atlanta's speedy Brian Jordan, who was attempting to steal.[167]

The next year, 2000, Ausmus set a club record when he appeared in 150 games for the Tigers, starting 140 of them as catcher. His defense was spectacular again as he threw out 43.2 percent of base runners attempting to steal, second that year to Cardinals catcher Mike Matheny. Ausmus hit a respectable .266 with 51 runs batted in. He also stole 11 bases, the fourth consecutive year he ended the season with double figures in stolen bases, a rarity for a catcher.[168]

On December 11, 2000, almost exactly two years after Houston traded Ausmus to the Tigers, and four years after he first went to Houston, the Astros were successful in getting him back for a second stint. Along with Ausmus, the Tigers sent two right-handed pitchers, Doug Brocail and Nelson Cruz, to Houston for outfielder Roger Cedeno, catcher Mitch Meluskey and right-handed pitcher Chris Holt.[169] Houston was not only getting back a recognized all-star, but also one of the most fan-friendly players in baseball. Brad was known to get on the field early and stay after the game to sign autographs for anyone waiting for them.[170]

Back in Houston, Ausmus picked up consecutive Gold Glove awards in 2001 and 2002. His .232 batting average in 2001 was disappointing, but he displayed his stellar defensive ability. He had the second-best caught-stealing percentage (40 percent) in the majors in 2001. His coaches also gave Ausmus a great deal of credit for developing Houston's young pitchers, especially Wade Miller and Roy Oswalt. Reliever Octavio Dotel heaped praise on his veteran catcher. "Brad is a great catcher. If he feels 100 percent I should throw a pitch, then I will go with him. He knows more than me."[171]

With Ausmus back, the Astros made it to the playoffs once again as winners of the National League Central. And again they were knocked out in the first round, losing three straight games to the Atlanta Braves.[172] Ausmus received much credit for his help in bringing the Astros into the playoffs. His outstanding defense was a factor in their success—a .997 fielding percentage and only three errors out of a career-high 1,013 chances in 2001.[173]

In 2004, the Astros finally advanced to the League Championship Series. Ausmus appeared in all five games of the division playoffs, going three-for-nine for a .333 average. He also played in all seven of the NLCS games, but his hitting cooled off and the Cardinals defeated the Astros.[174] In 2004, Brad Ausmus was inducted into the National Jewish Sports Hall of Fame and Museum.[175]

In 2005 the Astros made it all the way to the World Series. It was the first year that Ausmus recorded more walks than strikeouts in his career, and his 66 hits in the season's second half led all major league catchers. On September 18, he passed Alan Ashby for the most games caught in Astros' club history with 902.[176] The only thing marring the Astros' 2005 season was their World Series loss in four games to the Chicago White Sox.[177]

Ausmus became the Astros' backup catcher in 2008, playing in only 81 games, and although his hitting slipped to .218, his defensive work remained sharp.[178] He also became a free agent after the end of the 2008 season. One of his Astro teammates, pitcher Mike Hampton, said that whatever Ausmus decided to do, the fans "will miss him more than they realize.... He's the best catcher I have ever had."[179]

Brad Ausmus signed a one-year, one million dollar contract with the Los Angeles Dodgers on January 21, 2009.[180]

ON THE MOUND

Wayne Rosenthal

The six-foot, one-half-inch, 220-pound right-handed relief pitcher, Wayne Scott Rosenthal, was one of the first Jewish players to enter the major leagues in the 1990s.[181] A native of Brooklyn, Rosenthal was born February 19, 1965. The Texas Rangers acquired him in the 1986 draft, and as a reliever in the minors, he earned a number of honors. He had the lowest ERA in the Gulf Coast League in 1986 and was named the Rangers' Minor League Player of the Year in 1987.[182]

He debuted in the majors on June 6, 1991, in relief of injured pitcher Goose Gossage, pitching one scoreless inning. Rosenthal ended that season with a record of 1–4, one save, and an ERA of 5.25 in 36 games.[183]

Wayne Rosenthal was one of the pleasant surprises at the Rangers' spring training camp in 1992, and they selected him to fill one of the bullpen spots for the season.[184] He pitched in only six games for the Rangers and finished the 1992 season with no decisions and a very high 7.71 earned run average.[185] His statistics for his brief appearances in the major leagues included appearances in 42 games and a career earned run average of 5.40.[186] The most impressive statistic Rosenthal amassed in his short career was that in the 75 innings he pitched, he walked only 39 men (one intentionally) and struck out 62 batters.[187]

Although he had been officially out of the majors for three years, Wayne Rosenthal was a replacement player or "scab" during the 1995 players' strike.[188]

In 2003 he began a different baseball role as the pitching coach of the Marlins. His "relaxed style" and an "advisory rather than an authoritative" manner worked well with the team's young, talented, and rather volatile pitching staff. Rosenthal was credited for guiding them into a group that helped their team become the 2003 World Series Champions.[189] "My role," said Rosenthal, "was to keep my charges loose and confident and I never saw anything to get concerned about."[190]

At the end of the 2004 season, the Marlins refused to renew the contracts of their bench coach Doug Davis and their pitching coach Wayne Rosenthal.[191] The official reason was that Rosenthal had not been a successful major league pitcher who commanded respect from the pitching staff.[192] Observers knew, however, that Rosenthal had clashed frequently with several of the Marlin's starters, including Josh Beckett, Brad Penny, A. J. Burnett, and Dontrelle Willis. They complained about him and eventually hardly spoke to him.[193]

Right-handed reliever Wayne Rosenthal was one of the first Jewish players to debut in the 1990s, appearing in 42 games for the Texas Rangers in 1991 and 1992. Rosenthal was the Florida Marlins' pitching coach for the 2002 and 2003 seasons before his release. In 2006 he returned to the Marlins, accepting a position as Florida's minor-league pitching coordinator (photograph, Florida Marlins, Denis Bancroft).

After the Marlins fired Rosenthal, Marlins owner Jeffrey Loria offered him a minor league coaching assignment at his major league salary.[194] In 2006 Rosenthal became minor league pitching coordinator for the Florida Marlins where he continued to enjoy working with young pitchers.[195]

Andrew Lorraine

In contrast to many players who were not practicing Jews, Andrew Lorraine was a very observant one. "I'm proud of my family," he often said, "and being Jewish is what I share with my sister and my parents. Personally, it's deeper than anything else."[196]

Andrew Jason Lorraine was born in Los Angeles on August 11, 1972. His paternal grandparents had escaped from Poland and settled in England prior to the German invasion. Unfortunately, the family members who remained in Poland perished during the Holocaust. Andrew's grandfather changed the family name to Lorraine from the original, Levine, because he had served in Alsace-Lorraine while with the British Army during World War II and liked the name.[197]

Andrew's grandmother had two sons—one became a rabbi near London and the other, Andrew's father, moved to suburban southern California. When Andrew was 14, the entire family met in Israel and visited Yad Vashem, the memorial to the Holocaust dead. "It was overwhelming," said Lorraine. "You could look up records that showed what happened to each Jewish community. It was sad to see the town where my grandmother lived. There were no survivors. They were all taken to Treblinka."[198]

The California Angels drafted Lorraine in 1993 while he was still attending Stanford University and playing ball on the college team. He pitched that summer for California's A level team in the Northwest League and ended with a record of 4–1 and an ERA of 1.29.[199]

The year 1994 was a milestone for Lorraine. He received his BA in American studies, achieved a 12–4 record with the Angels' AAA team in Vancouver, and was named the number one pitcher in the PCL by *Baseball America*. Also that summer the Angels called him up the majors. The six-foot, three-inch, 200-pound southpaw pitched in his first major league game July 17, 1994. In his four major league appearances that year, he lost two games without winning any, and his ERA was a very high 10.61.[200]

Lorraine started the 1995 season with Vancouver, but on July 27, 1995, California traded him to the Chicago White Sox along with McKay Christensen, John Snyder, and Bill Simas for Jim Abbott and Jim Fortugno.[201] The White Sox assigned Lorraine to their AAA farm club in Nashville.[202]

In January 1996, the White Sox traded Lorraine to the Oakland Athletics along with outfielder Charlie Poe for outfielder Danny Tartabull.[203] Andrew spent all of the 1996 and most of the 1997 seasons with Oakland's Pacific Coast League team. In August 1997, the A's brought him to the majors, and on August 13, Lorraine won his first major league start, allowing only one run in five innings. He finished the 1997 season with a record of 3–1, appearing in twelve games.[204] Despite his good work, the A's released Lorraine in October 1997, but the Seattle Mariners signed him the next day and assigned him to their AAA affiliate where he was used both as a starter and as a reliever. The Mariners recalled Lorraine in September, and he appeared in four games for Seattle that year with no record and an ERA of 2.46.[205]

At the end of the 1998 season, the Chicago Cubs signed Lorraine and, like all the other teams, started him with their AAA affiliate. Lorraine remained with the Iowa Cubs until

Chicago called Lorraine to the parent club. Lorraine enjoyed his stay in Chicago with its large Jewish population. "It's a part of me," said Lorraine. "People want to identify with a

Jewish player. There's a big Jewish community in Chicago. It's great." In his Cub debut, Lorraine pitched a complete game, a three-hit shutout over the Houston Astros at Wrigley Field.[206] It was the first shutout by a Jewish Cubs left-hander since Ken Holtzman's second no-hitter against the Reds on June 2, 1971.[207]

Lorraine remained with the Cubs only until May 22, 2000, when he signed with Cleveland. He appeared in eight games for the Tribe with no decisions but a 3.68 ERA.[208] Lorraine did not pitch in the major leagues in 2001, spending the entire year with the Calgary Cannons, the Florida Marlins' AAA club in the Pacific Coast League. The Marlins released Lorraine in September 2001, and two months later, the Milwaukee Brewers signed him.[209]

Lorraine finished his major league career in 2002 with the Brewers, pitching in five games, winning none and losing one. (He got the loss in his only start.) His ERA in his final year in the majors was an embarrassing 11.25. That year, the Brewers' record of 55–106 was the second worst in baseball and the worst in the National League.[210] Lorraine pitched a total of seven seasons in the major leagues with seven different major league teams. He pitched in a total of 59 games in the majors with a record of 6–11 and an ERA of 6.53.[211]

Andrew Lorraine never once felt that the constant changing of teams was due to anti–Semitism. "I just figured that I wasn't mature and settled enough in my own game to stick with one team in baseball's fickle universe," said Lorraine. Lorraine always took pride in his work ethic, noting that he never took a full day off from work

Andrew Lorraine played for seven different clubs during his seven seasons in the majors. An observant Jew, he continues to remember the many members of his paternal grandmother's family exterminated by the Nazis, calling his visit to Israel's Yad Vashem Holocaust memorial, "overwhelming" (courtesy National Baseball Hall of Fame Library; Cooperstown, N.Y.).

and always came to the ballpark. He was also quick to add that he attended services during each of the Jewish holidays. "In my own way," said Lorraine, "I'm observing the holidays."

Brian Bark

Brian Bark was another Jewish player who was drafted by a major league team after an exceptional high school baseball career, but chose college instead. Like Brian Kowitz, he, too, was a native of Baltimore and played all his major league games in 1995.[212]

Bark, the son of former minor leaguer Gerald Bark, was born August 16, 1968, and turned down an offer from the Orioles in order to attend North Carolina State. At college, the five-foot, nine-inch, 170-pound left-handed pitcher set record after record for both his pitching and his hitting.[213]

Again paralleling Kowitz, the Atlanta Braves drafted Bark in 1990, and he began playing for minor league teams in the Braves' organization.[214] By 1992, the southpaw was on the Braves' AAA team in Richmond, but even with good statistics, he remained there for more than three years. The reason was simple—in the early 1990s, Atlanta already had a premier pitching staff and was not looking for new talent.[215]

On June 1, 1995, the Braves released Bark and the Boston Red Sox signed him as a free agent, and assigned him to their AAA club.[216] A month later, on July 6, 1995, the Red Sox called Bark up to Boston; he made his major league that same day. He pitched in two more games that year for a total of 2.1 innings, allowed no runs, no hits, and only one base on balls.[217] That was the extent of Bark's major league career. The Red Sox decided to send Bark back to the minors for the 1996 season, but he refused to go, again becoming a free agent. He never returned to the majors as a player, but did some scouting for the New York Mets.[218]

Brian Bark, the son of a former minor leaguer, had little opportunity to make the majors with Atlanta, the first team that signed him, since the Braves starters were among the best in baseball. Although he did debut with the Boston Red Sox in 1995, after appearing in only three games, he never again pitched in professional baseball (courtesy of Boston Red Sox).

Mike Milchin

Mike Milchin was a first baseman–pitcher for the United States baseball team in the 1988 Olympics. Although he hit only .154 for Team USA as a backup for first sacker Tino Martinez, as a pitcher Milchin went 4–1 with two saves and a 1.93 ERA, helping the U.S. baseball team win the 1988 Olympic gold medal.[219] Despite his outstanding pitching at the Olympics, Milchin's major league career was both brief and unexceptional.

Michael Wayne Milchin, a native of Tennessee, was born on February 28, 1968. His father was Jewish, his mother was not. The six-foot, three-inch, 190-pound Milchin attended Clemson University where he and Brian Kowitz were teammates on Clemson's baseball squad.[220]

The St. Louis Cardinals acquired the left-handed pitcher on June 5, 1989, in the second

Mike Milchin excelled in baseball at Clemson University, pitching and playing both first base and the outfield. In 1988 he was a member of the United States' gold-medal winning Olympic baseball team in Seoul, South Korea. As a major league pitcher, however, the southpaw had a very brief career, appearing in only 39 games for the Minnesota Twins and the Baltimore Orioles in 1996 (courtesy Minnesota Twins/Rick Orndorf).

round of the 1989 free agent draft.[221] Milchin spent five years in the Cardinals minor league system. Although *Baseball America* consistently rated him one of the top ten prospects in the Cardinals organization, he was constantly plagued by a variety of injuries, especially during the 1991 and 1992 seasons. His final season in the Cardinals system was 1993.[222]

On October 15, 1993, the Los Angeles Dodgers selected Milchin off waivers and he was invited to the Dodgers' spring training camp in 1994, but tendinitis and elbow surgery kept him out of action the entire year. He returned relatively healthy in 1995 and spent the season at Albuquerque, turning in a 4–2 record with an ERA of 4.32. The highlight of the season was a seven-inning no-hitter Milchin threw on June 13 against the Vancouver Canadians.[223]

In late 1995, the Minnesota Twins signed Milchin as a free agent and assigned him to their AAA team. Milchin finally made it to the majors with the Twins on May 14, 1996. He got the final two outs in his inaugural game that evening. Milchin pitched in 26 games in 1996 for the Twins, winning two and losing one. He allowed 31 hits in 21.2 innings for an ERA of 8.31.[224]

After pitching three months for the Twins, the Baltimore Orioles claimed Milchin on waivers. He finished the 1996 season with the Orioles, going 1–0 with a 5.73 ERA in 13 games to conclude his major league career. He did strike out 29 batters in a career total of 32.2 innings, almost a batter an inning. The Baltimore Orioles released him November 19, 1996.[225]

After his playing days, Milchin worked for a firm in Houston that represented athletes.[226]

Keith Glauber

Only two Jewish major leaguers debuted in the 1990s and played their final games in 2000. One of these was pitcher Keith Glauber. Glauber did not start out as a pitcher. While in high school and early in his college days, Glauber played the outfield. He did not turn to pitching until he enrolled at New Jersey's Montclair State. "I discovered that I liked pitching better than playing the outfield," said Glauber."[227] The St. Louis Cardinals drafted Glauber from college in the forty-second round of the 1994 draft.[228]

He remained in the Cardinals farm system for three years while improving his ERA each year and was then acquired by the Cincinnati Reds on December 12, 1997.[229] Glauber underwent surgery for a rotator cuff tear but was expected to be ready for spring training in 1998.[230] "In retrospect," noted Glauber, "I was not rested enough before I played ball again."[231]

The Reds called Glauber to the big leagues the final two weeks of the 1998 season, and he debuted on September 9, 1998, the same day that Mark McGwire set a new home run record. "It was unbelievable," Glauber recalled of the first time he took the mound. "I felt like I belonged there. All the hard

Right-handed relief pitcher Keith Glauber spent eight years in professional baseball, but rotator cuff surgery limited his tenure in the major leagues to seven games in two seasons with the Cincinnati Reds (courtesy of Cincinnati Reds).

work I put into it was rewarded."[232] He appeared in three games in 1998, all in relief. His earned run average was 2.35.[233]

The Reds signed Glauber for 1999, but he spent the entire season in the minors.[234] In October 1999, the Reds granted Glauber free agency, but re-signed him as a free agent one month later.[235] He began the 2000 season in the Cincinnati minor league organization, but appeared in four games with the parent club at the tail end of the season, pitching 7.1 innings.[236]

Glauber had more arm surgery in 2001. He remained with the Reds in 2002, and attempted to rehab, but with a growing family, Glauber decided to retire.[237] His brief major league career consisted of only seven games in which he allowed 11 hits and 5 earned runs for an ERA of 3.00.[238]

After his playing days ended, Glauber became director of a youth day camp run by his father, Howard Glauber. He also did some scouting for the Reds, but he did not give up the idea of returning to major league baseball in some capacity. "If the right situation came around," he said, "I would go back into baseball.... I wouldn't pass up a front office job in baseball or something in player personnel."[239]

Al Levine

Al Levine was another Jewish pitcher whose career began in the middle of the 1990s. Born in the northern Chicago suburb of Parkridge, Illinois, on May 22, 1968, Alan Brian Levine grew up a Cubs fan, but his first seven years as a professional player were with the Chicago White Sox organization. That was not a problem for Levine, however, who once told a sportswriter that, "Whatever team is paying your bills, you're a fan of," an excellent philosophy for a player who would pitch for seven different teams during his ten major league seasons.[240]

Like Jesse Levis, Levine attended Hebrew School and became a bar mitzvah at a reform congregation, but thanks to his mother, who "schlepped" him from Hebrew school to practice, he also was able to play baseball.[241]

The Chicago White Sox drafted the six-foot, three-inch, 180-pound right-handed pitcher in the 1991 free agent draft out of Southern Illinois University at Carbondale. He was sent to the Sox's A level farm team, the Utica Blue Sox.[242]

The following two years, Levine pitched in the Florida State League where he won 20 games and lost 15.[243] In both 1994 and 1995, Levine split his seasons between the White Sox's AA club in Birmingham and AAA team in Nashville. In 1994 one of his teammates at Birmingham brought a lot of media attention to the team. When Levine was asked, "In a word, what was it like to be on the Double A Birmingham team in 1994 when [NBA star] Michael Jordan played," Levine answered succinctly, "Circus."[244]

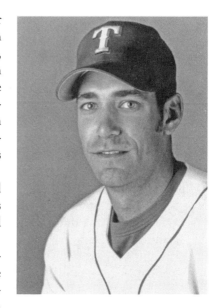

Al Levine pitched for seven major league teams in his ten-year career. He was used as a middle reliever and started only seven of the 416 games in which he appeared. Two years before the Chicago White Sox brought him to the majors, he spent a year with the Birmingham Barons, with basketball star Michael Jordan as one of his teammates (courtesy National Baseball Hall of Fame Library; Cooperstown, N.Y.).

It was around this time that Levine nearly gave up baseball. "I almost quit," he said, "because I got tired of it, but my wife helped me through it. I just changed my attitude, basically, and that really helped." That change came at just the right time.[245]

In 1996 and 1997, Levine split his time between Nashville and Chicago. He debuted with the White Sox June 22, 1996, and pitched in 16 games, all in relief. His ERA was a rather high 5.40, and the Sox returned him to Nashville. The following season was virtually a repeat of 1996. He began the 1997 season with Nashville where he appeared in 26 games before being promoted to the parent club. He appeared in 25 games for the Chisox, had a 2–2 record with a hefty 6.92 ERA and was again shipped back to Nashville.[246]

On December 19, 1997, the White Sox traded Al Levine and Larry Thomas to the Texas Rangers for infielder Benji Gil. Levine began the 1998 season with the Rangers' AAA farm club as a middle reliever. He was promoted to Arlington in June where he appeared in 30 games. His record was 0–1, but his earned run average dropped to 4.50.[247]

After the 1998 season, the Rangers placed Levine on waivers and the Anaheim Angels claimed him. He remained with the Angels for four years and became one of their most reliable relievers. Even though he pitched a few games in the minors in 2000 and 2002, he managed to appear in at least 50 games during each of the four seasons he spent at Anaheim. He was also a starter when needed and finished games when closer Troy Percival was unavailable. Angels manager Mike Scioscia praised Levine's consistency and importance to the team. In 2001 Levine appeared in 64 games and posted an ERA of 2.38, the best of his career. He also won eight games that year and struck out 40 hitters compared with only 28 bases on balls.[248]

In 2002 the Angels were the AL wild card in the playoffs, finishing the season with a record of 99–63, four games behind the Oakland A's in the AL West. They surprisingly defeated the New York Yankees in the American League Division Series, and they went on to defeat the Minnesota Twins, four games to one, in the ALCS, winning the right to represent the American League in the World Series. It was the first time the Angels had made it to the World Series in the franchise's 41-year history. In the Series, the Angels defeated the San Francisco Giants, four games to three, and became the 2002 World Champions.[249]

Al Levine won a World Series ring in 2002, but he had been left off the post-season roster and had mixed feelings about the situation. "It was a good time and a bad time," said Levine. "I was happy because I had worked with those guys for four years, and we were in the bottom for a couple of those years. We did really well, and I was left off. But, you know, I was happy. I wasn't happy with certain aspects of it."[250] While he was disappointed about not being placed on the roster for the playoffs, Levine did state, "Everyone on the team gets along so well and works incredibly hard. We persevered and look what happened."[251]

Levine became a free agent on December 21, 2002. He was signed by the Cardinals in January, but released in March. On April 2, 2003, Levine signed as a free agent with the Tampa Bay Devil Rays.[252] The 35-year-old Levine pitched 36 games for the last-place Devil Rays and had an impressive 2.90 earned run average when the Kansas City Royals, who were leading in a tight race for the American League Central title, purchased his contract. Levine was pleased to be going to a playoff contender. "It's exciting. That's what you play for. I'm happy to go, but I'm leaving a good group of guys. I'm very surprised."[253]

Tony Pena was the Kansas City manager in 2003 and was well acquainted with Al Levine, having caught him when the two were teammates with the Chicago White Sox in 1997. The Royals wanted Levine's slider in their bullpen, and Levine wanted another opportunity to participate in postseason play.[254] Al Levine pitched well for the Royals; in his 18 appearances, he allowed only six earned runs for an ERA of 2.53 and saved one game. Unfortunately, the Royals finished third in the division despite Levine's help.[255]

Although he did not have to make the choice, Levine was asked whether he would play in games on either Rosh Hashanah or Yom Kippur. Levine said that he had always made it a practice to fast on Yom Kippur and that he would play on the high holidays only in the event they were postseason. "This is a job," said Levine. "I'm a reliever and there's a chance to pitch every day. If I have to, I will. It's something I'll have to live with, nobody else. If they want to look at me a little differently because I didn't take off, so be it."[256]

On October 28, 2003, Levine once more became a free agent, and again was signed quickly, this time by the Detroit Tigers.[257] With a record of 43–119, the Tigers badly needed to improve their miserable 2003 finish as the league's worst team.[258] Levine, now pitching for his sixth major league club, posted a 3–4 record for the Tigers in 65 games, his career high. The Tigers did do better in 2004, moving up to fourth place in the AL Central.[259]

In 2005 Levine pitched in the majors for the final time and for the first time in the National League. On February 2, Levine signed with his seventh team, the San Francisco Giants. Despite pitching nine scoreless innings in spring training, the Giants assigned Levine to their AAA club before they called him up.[260] He appeared in nine games for the Giants before they released him on June 11, 2005.[261]

Despite his well-traveled career and overall losing record of 24–33, Levine was actually an effective pitcher as his career ERA of 3.96 attests. Al Levine, himself, once said, "Anyone can be a baseball player. If you put your mind to it, you can be anything."[262]

Scott Radinsky

Scott David Radinsky was not only an accomplished left-handed reliever, but also had an interesting career off the diamond. He was born March 3, 1968, to a Jewish mother and a non–Jewish father who died when Radinsky was a teenager. The Glendale, California, native did not practice Judaism or any other religion.[263]

When he was growing up, Radinsky was not really interested in professional baseball, but based on his high school prowess, the Chicago White Sox signed him when he graduated in 1986. From 1986 to 1990, the six-foot, three-inch, 204-pound southpaw pitched in the Gulf Coast League, the Carolina League, and the Midwest League where he compiled a record of 12–15. His best year, however, was in 1989, when he won seven games and had an outstanding earned run average of 1.75.[264]

His 1989 record in the Class A Midwest League impressed the White Sox, and the parent club invited him to spring training in 1990. He pitched so well there that he was placed on the White Sox roster, the first pitcher to go from Class A directly to the majors since Dwight Gooden accomplished the feat six years earlier.[265]

Radinsky debuted in the majors on opening day, April 9, 1990. The following day he won his first major league game. In 62 games his rookie year, all in relief, Radinsky had a record of 6–1, four saves and a 4.82 earned run average.[266]

For the following three seasons, Radinsky pitched very well for the White Sox in relief. In 1991 he had a low ERA at 2.02, holding the opposition scoreless in 53 of the 67 innings he hurled; in 1992, he had his career high 15 saves; and in 1993, he appeared in 73 games for the White Sox, stranded 30 of the last 34 runners, had a record of 8–2 and saved 4 games.[267] Radinsky did not fare so well in the ALCS in 1993. Facing the Toronto Blue Jays, he pitched 1.2 innings, allowed 2 earned runs and 3 hits for an ERA of 10.80. Toronto defeated the White Sox in the Series, four games to two.[268]

Radinsky was diagnosed with Hodgkin's disease, a cancer of the lymphatic system, and spent the entire 1994 season on the disabled list, undergoing chemotherapy and radiation treatment. He was well enough to spend some of the summer coaching his former high school's team in Simi Valley, California, where he was credited with mentoring future major leaguer Jeff Weaver, who was a senior that year. Weaver never forgot the time Radinsky spent with him. "He helped me with keeping my head on straight, because I was getting really rattled when I did bad. He was there to put his arm around me and tell me the team's plan," recalled Weaver.[269]

Although not at full strength in 1995, Radinsky managed to return to professional baseball. He began the season with the Class A team and finished the season with the White Sox, where he appeared in 46 games and compiled a 2–1 record.[270]

Scott Radinsky signed with the Dodgers as a free agent in 1996 and gave them three productive years. After a brief start in the Advanced A League, Radinsky appeared in 58 games for the Dodgers in 1996; he won five games and lost only one with a 2.41 ERA. In 1997 he also had a record of 5–1 with a slightly higher earned run average of 2.89 in 75 games. His last year with the Dodgers, 1998, was another successful one for Radinsky. Although he only had a .500 record, Radinsky lowered his ERA to an excellent 2.63 in 62 games.[271]

In his ten-year major league career, Scott Radinsky appeared in 557 games, more than any other Jewish major league pitcher. That number is even more remarkable considering that he was diagnosed with Hodgkin's disease in 1994. He was on the disabled list that entire year and able to pitch only part of the 1995 season. In addition to his feats on the mound, Radinsky or "Rad," was the lead singer for "Pulley," a punk rock group he formed in 1996 (courtesy National Baseball Hall of Fame Library; Cooperstown, N.Y.).

After three years pitching for the Dodgers, Radinsky filed for free agency during the winter of 1998. In December, he signed with the St. Louis Cardinals, and the following year had a winning record of 2–1 in 43 appearances.[272] In 2000 Radinsky pitched in only one game for the Cardinals before he underwent Tommy John surgery and was out for the remainder of the year.[273] At the conclusion of the 2000 season, the Cardinals chose not to exercise Radinsky's option.[274]

Radinsky signed with the Cleveland Indians organization in 2001, spending most of the season in the minor leagues. The Indians called Radinsky up to the majors at the end of the year and he made two appearances with the Tribe, his final major league games.[275]

During his 11 years in the majors, Radinsky posted a record of 42–25 with 52 saves. His ERA for 481.2 innings pitched was 3.44.[276]

Radinsky returned to organized baseball in 2004 as a guest instructor for the Cleveland Indians, and in 2005 he was the pitching coach for their Class A team. By 2008, Radinsky had worked his way up to the AAA Buffalo Bisons as pitching coach.[277]

Before, during and after his major league career, Scott Radinsky, or "Rad," was a punk rock singer during the off-seasons. With his brother, he formed his own band that became known as Ten Foot Pole. In 1996, he founded another group, Pulley, when the old group wanted to tour fulltime. In 2008, he was still doing gigs with Pulley.[278]

Scott Schoeneweis

Scott Schoeneweis was the last Jewish pitcher to debut in the 1990s. He carved out an excellent career although, like Radinsky, he had to overcome serious health problems to achieve his success.

Scott David Schoeneweis was born in Long Branch, New Jersey, on October 2, 1973, to Barbara and Mike Schoeneweis. His father is Christian, and although Barbara is Jewish, Scott did not consider himself a practicing Jew.[279]

In 1992 when Schoeneweis graduated high school, the Montreal Expos drafted him. For advice on accepting the offer, he consulted, among others, his cousin Jerry Kapstein, a former player agent, later president of the Padres, and senior adviser for the Boston Red Sox. Kapstein advised him to attend Duke University instead, and from that time on, the two cousins, although 30 years apart in age, became very close. "It's just grown from there," said Schoeneweis. "We're of similar nature and we have a lot to talk about."[280]

While attending Duke, the left-handed pitcher was chosen an All-American his freshman year. But during the next two years, the 6-foot, 185-pound pitcher faced a life-threatening situation. Diagnosed with testicular cancer, Schoeneweis overcame the disease by taking six months of chemotherapy in three months, which he said, "certainly puts things in perspective." He also had to undergo Tommy John elbow surgery.[281]

By hard work, Schoeneweis recovered his health and his pitching prowess and graduated with a history degree from Duke in 1996. On June 4 of that year, the California Angels drafted Schoeneweis in the third round of the amateur draft and assigned him to their advanced A team.[282] By 1999, he had been promoted to the Angels' AAA team in Edmonton.[283]

Schoeneweis debuted with the Angels on April 7, 1999, the same year that pitcher Al Levine joined the team. Scott was used as a middle reliever; he pitched 39.1 innings, fanned 22, and had an ERA of 5.49.[284] During the last half of the 1999 season, Schoeneweis suffered a second bout of elbow problems and his year ended with still more surgery, this time for a torn medial lateral ligament in his left elbow.[285]

Resilient as always, Schoeneweis came back to the majors for a second time in 2000 and became a starter for the Angels. In the 27 games he began that year, he posted a 7–10 record with an ERA of 5.45—the best on a struggling Angels pitching staff. He also fanned 78 batters in 170 innings with one complete game and one shutout.[286]

As the ace on the staff, Schoeneweis started the opening game for the Angels in 2001, and although he pitched effectively, the Angels began the season with a 3–2 loss to the Rangers. Schoeneweis ended the 2001 season with a record of 10–11. He registered career highs in wins, innings pitched, games started, and strikeouts for an Angels team that finished the season 12 games under .500.[287]

By 2002 Scott was not only starting games but, like Al Levine, was one of the team's most reliable relievers. His won-loss record was 9–8; he pitched in 54 games and had 65 strikeouts in 118 innings.[288] Levine did not go to the playoffs, but Schoeneweis was included on the Angels' post-season roster in 2002 as the only lefty in the bullpen. Schoeneweis pitched the first two innings of Game One of the ALCS Series and retired the only two men he faced.[289]

Although by mid-season 2003 he was the only southpaw in their bullpen, the Angels traded Schoeneweis on July 30 to the Chicago White Sox along with Doug Nickle, receiving Gary Glover, Scott Dunn, and Tim Bittner.[290]

White Sox general manager Ken Williams was delighted to have Schoeneweis. "Right now, our primary need for him is in the bullpen. He's not stretched out enough to go into the rotation. He has three quality pitches. We can visualize him in our rotation next year."[291] After he joined the White Sox, Schoeneweis won two and lost one with a 4.50 ERA and 27 strikeouts in 20 games. In his final 2003 appearances for the Chisox, though, his ERA was an impressive 1.17.[292]

Scott Schoeneweis, a graduate of Duke University, overcame testicular cancer and Tommy John surgery, while in college. He not only graduated with his class, but he was drafted by the Anaheim Angels in 1996. Now with his sixth club in 11 years in the majors, Schoeneweis has found his niche as a solid middle-inning relief pitcher (courtesy National Baseball Hall of Fame Library; Cooperstown, N.Y.).

With the White Sox in 2004, Schoeneweis was used exclusively as a starter in all 19 of the games in which he appeared. He posted a record of 6–9, but his season was cut short in August when he injured his left elbow again.[293]

Schoeneweis signed with the Toronto Blue Jays as a free agent in 2005.[294] He had an excellent 3.32 ERA that year and his record of 80 appearances was second in the American League, only one fewer than Mike Timlin's 81. Scott struck out 43 while walking only 25 batters.[295]

Schoeneweis appeared in 55 games for the Blue Jays in 2006 as a middle reliever, but he could not recapture the success he had had the previous year and was considered expendable when younger prospects began pitching well. In August he was acquired by Cincinnati, a team looking for a middle reliever to help them qualify for postseason play.[296] In the 16 games Schoeneweis pitched for Cincinnati, he went 2–0 with an amazing 0.63 ERA, but the Reds did not make it to the playoffs.[297]

A free agent again after the 2006 season, Schoeneweis signed with the New York Mets. He appeared in 143 games with the Mets in 2007 and 2008. In 2008 his ERA was 3.34, but he had a disappointing record of 2–6, and at the major league winter meetings in December of that year, the Mets traded Schoeneweis to the Arizona Diamondbacks for right-hander Connor Robertson.[298]

Throughout his many years in the majors, Schoeneweis kept a fairly low profile. He remained close to his cousin, Jerry Kapstein, who expressed his feelings about how Scott handled the many setbacks he had had to face. "I have a lot of respect and admiration for everything he's been through, the way he's handled adversity and success," said Kapstein. "The people who play with him all like him a great deal. The measure of a person is not how many innings he's thrown, it's how he treats other people."[299]

17. A New Icon Arrives

The great slugger Hank Greenberg was the idol of Jewish baseball fans from the 1930s to the 1950s. Sandy Koufax took over the role of iconic Jewish star in the 1960s. Although the Jewish community was no longer dependent on Jewish sports heroes to solidify its place in America, but after Koufax retired, Jews still longed for another Jewish superstar. They wanted a player who would be an undeniable baseball performance leader and, at the same time, proudly represent Jewish values. Shawn Green, one of the Jewish players to enter major league baseball in the 1990s, was the person who fulfilled that role.

Shawn David Green was born on November 10, 1972, in Des Plaines, Illinois, the second child and only son of Ira Green and Judy Schneider Green. Ironically the family name was originally Greenberg, but Shawn's grandfather, Leo, changed the name to Green in the 1930s.[1]

The family moved quite a bit, and for this reason Shawn received little formal Jewish education during his childhood. When Shawn was a year old, the family moved to New Jersey; they moved again when Shawn was five to San Jose, California, and then to Irvine seven years later. Ira Green, a frustrated athlete who had played NCAA basketball at DePaul University during the 1950s, transferred his love of sports to his son. Ira would play catch with Shawn and take him to baseball games at Candlestick Park. He bought Shawn a batting cage and a pitching machine and watched his son hit as many as 200 balls daily.[2]

In 1986, Shawn's father took his 13-year-old son to Angels Stadium for Game Five of the American League Championship Series where he watched the Angels eliminate Boston. "I was one of the first kids there in the seventh inning. By the ninth there were thousands," he said. That experience encouraged Shawn to try to become a major leaguer.[3] Green adopted 1980 Cy Young Award winner Steve Stone as his boyhood idol, identifying with him because they were both Jewish. Green had long felt that being Jewish "is something different and I understand that, throughout my career, it'll be something that differentiates me from other players—always separates me."[4]

Green entered Tustin High School in 1988 and was immediately recognized for both his academic and baseball talents. He tied the California Interscholastic Federation hit record with 147 during his senior year and was a first-team selection to the 1991 USA Today All–USA high school team. His 4.0 GPA helped him earn a scholarship to Stanford University.

While still in high school, a Blue Jay scout, Moose Johnson, watched Green play ball. His scouting report was simple and to the point: "A good looking, tall, left-handed hitter. Long neck. Has the resemblance in size, stature, and swing to Ted Williams."[5]

Toronto drafted Green when he graduated high school in 1991, and Green negotiated a contract that allowed him to play professional ball while he attended Stanford during the off-season, a schedule he maintained until the demands of baseball made it impossible. His contract with the Blue Jays prevented him from playing on Stanford's baseball team as his scholarship demanded, but college expenses were not a problem; he had received a $700,000 signing bonus from the Blue Jays, one of the highest signing bonuses up to that time. Green donated a portion of his bonus to a Toronto charity that provided food for poor children.[6]

Green was slender, with dark hair, dark eyes, and chiseled features. The six-foot, four-inch, 190-pound left-handed-hitting outfielder played, for the most part, in the Blue Jays farm system from 1992 through 1994, hitting consistently and well. His minor league tour of duty included stops at Dunedin (Florida State League), Knoxville (South Atlantic League), and Syracuse (International League) where his average improved each year. He played his first three games for Toronto late in the 1993 season, and although the 20-year-old Green never appeared in the Series in which the Blue Jays were victorious that year, he was given a World Series ring.[7] "It was great to get one because a lot people play their whole careers

Many consider Shawn Green, who debuted with the Toronto Blue Jays in 1993, the greatest Jewish superstar since Hank Greenberg and Sandy Koufax. In addition to playing for Toronto, Green was also outstanding with the Los Angeles Dodgers, the Arizona Diamondbacks, and the New York Mets. With a home run total only three fewer than Hank Greenberg, Green is second on the list of all-time Jewish homerun hitters (courtesy National Baseball Hall of Fame Library; Cooperstown, N.Y.).

and never get one," said Green, adding, "I really didn't earn it that year. I was up for two weeks in September. But it's still exciting to be associated with a team like this."[8] Although he played most of the 1994 season in Syracuse, Green also played in 14 games for Toronto that year. That would be the last year Green would play in the minors for the remainder of his professional career.[9]

Green's batting average his first three years in Toronto was a respectable .285, and in 1995 he became the first rookie to lead the Blue Jays in slugging percentage (.509).[10] Management was not convinced that Green could hit left-handed pitchers, and he tended to ride the bench against southpaws. Although frustrated when not playing, he used that time to quiz his pitchers, catchers, and other teammates about various situations, strategies, and techniques.[11]

One person not dismayed by Green's part-time role as an outfielder was Arthur Richman, a senior adviser in the New York Yankees media relations department and an observant Jew. He approached George Steinbrenner, boss of the Yankees, and informed him that one acquisition would greatly help boost Yankee attendance. When Steinbrenner asked the name of the player Richman had in mind, Richman answered, "This Jewish kid in Toronto—Shawnie Green."

"Give George credit," said Richman.

"He looked at Shawnie, saw he was a talent and did everything he could to bring the kid to New York. But Toronto wouldn't give him to us. Too bad."[12] Every time Richman saw Green play, he would shake his head and wonder what might have been had the Yankees been able to acquire him, and how many Jewish fans Green could have lured into Yankee Stadium. "He's probably the best Jewish hitter since Hank Greenberg," said Richman. "New York would love him."[13]

In 1998 the Blue Jays finally put Green in the lineup against both right- and left-handed pitching and both his morale and his performance improved. He played 158 games that year and hit .278 with 35 home runs and 100 runs batted in. His 35 stolen bases made him the first Blue Jay and the first Jewish major leaguer to become a 30/30 man—30 home runs and 30 stolen bases. He had always been a spray hitter, but now he was learning how to extend his arms through each swing, which allowed him to hit the ball much further.[14]

Times were changing and the mainstream media was much less interested in a player's ethnicity that it once was. Nevertheless, the Jewish press in both Canada and the United States began to welcome Green with such articles as "Shawn Green Following in Greenberg's Steps." Many in Toronto's large Jewish community eagerly welcomed Green. He received many letters from Jewish fans and he began to make numerous personal appearances before Jewish organizations. "I see it building," Green said of his Jewish fan base, "and I think it is fine. It's great to have people pull for me. A lot of Jewish fans can relate to a Jewish ballplayer. It's almost like family.... I'm proud of who I am."[15] "The Jewish community in Toronto has been great," said Green. "They have a real large and supportive community, big sports fans, so it's nice to be a member of that community."[16]

Shawn admitted that he had not been reared in a religious household and that he learned more about his religion while he was playing in Toronto than in the preceding 23 years combined. He also attended High Holy Day services for the first time in his life while in Toronto and even decided he wanted a bar mitzvah. "Since I've been in the big leagues, I've learned a lot more about my religion, my heritage," confessed Green. "I would like to have a bar mitzvah. I've got a full plate right now, but I'm going to see if I can somehow accomplish that."[17]

Shawn Green's most outstanding year in the major leagues during the 1990s was in 1999. He played in 153 games, drove in 123 runs, stole 20 bases, blasted 42 home runs, and for the only time in his major league career, his batting average topped the .300 mark at .309.[18] He was also selected to the 1999 All-Star Game. The team that year tied a record—the most number of Jewish All-Star participants—Green in the outfield and Brad Ausmus of Detroit and Mike Lieberthal of the Philadelphia Phillies behind the plate. Green had a theory why the number of Jewish players had increased during the 1990s. "I think Jewish parents are so focused on education and studying that there wasn't emphasis on sports. I think now maybe kids are getting a little more involved and playing a little more and getting out there as much as anybody."[19]

Green's manager at Toronto, Jim Fregosi, was elated that his star right fielder was selected for the 1999 All-Star Game. Mentioning such names as Larry Walker, Dave Parker, and Roberto Clemente, Fregosi said, "I'm not saying at this time that Shawn's going to be a Hall of Famer. But he has the ability, if he can do it over a long period of time, to put up the numbers that would make him that kind of player."[20]

When Green was still in high school, scout Moose Johnson had compared him to superstar Ted Williams. At the 1999 All-Star Game, the real highlight for Green was finally meeting this baseball icon. Williams even gave Green some hitting advice: try to hit the ball up the middle. Shawn said he would never forget the moment.[21] Green might have needed some advice on hitting, but certainly not on his fielding. He won a gold glove in 1999.[22]

Green was eligible for free agency in 2000, and the Blue Jays wanted to sign him to a multi-year contract, offering him $48 million for five years. However, Green asked the Blue Jays to trade him, but he placed conditions on the trade. He wanted to go to an American city with a large Jewish population, preferably on the West Coast where he had grown up.[23]

In November 1999, the Los Angeles Dodgers acquired Green from Toronto and signed him to the second-highest player contract in baseball, a six-year deal that averaged $14 million a year. "It's nice to be one of the more recognized Jewish players in the game," said Green."[24] Green also was elated about the new location. "This is a dream come true for me to play at home and play for this organization," he said.[25] The trade for Green also included Toronto's sending second baseman Jorge Nunez to the Dodgers for outfielder Raul Mondesi and left-handed pitcher Pedro Borbon.[26]

His high salary and regular playing assignment with the Dodgers, the same team where Sandy Koufax had reigned as the Jewish superstar, put pressure on Green as a Dodger and a Jew. Jewish Dodgers fans were ecstatic and Green gladly accepted his role as an example of how a Jew could rediscover his Jewish beliefs. "As a Jewish ballplayer," he said, "I'm in a fairly unique situation. I have a chance to do a lot of good. Here in Los Angeles, I can do things that will permeate the rest of the country."[27]

When he went to the Dodgers' training camp in Vero Beach, Florida, in 2000, he met Sandy Koufax for the first time. According to Green, Koufax offered him a number of helpful suggestions. "He told me to make sure I take care of baseball first. 'You'll hate to say no,' he said, 'but at the same time you have to try to do the right thing.' So I'm trying to do the things that'll have the best effect to help the most amount of people."[28]

Koufax also passed along some advice about being a Jewish ballplayer whose religion and playing stats were both in the public eye. Koufax advised Green that he had to feel comfortable with his decisions and not worry about what anyone else had to say.[29]

In 2000 his first season as a National Leaguer batting against many pitchers he had never faced before, Green hit .269, 40 points lower than the previous year. He also dropped from 42 home runs to only 24, and his RBI total went down from 123 to 99. However, he became only the seventh Dodger to hit 20 or more home runs and steal more than 20 bases in the same season. He also led the National League with 44 doubles and 90 walks. Despite his decline in run production, for the second consecutive year, Green became a member of the All-Star team.[30]

Green was still not a particularly observant Jew and had yet to affiliate with any congregation, but he began to take an active part in both the Jewish and secular communities in Los Angeles. He donated $250,000 of his salary each year to the Dodgers' Dream Foundation, an organization that built baseball fields in impoverished neighborhoods and neglected parks. He also was a supporter of the Johnny Fund, a pediatric leukemia organization.[31]

Green also became active in KOREH L.A., the child literacy program of the Jewish Federation of Greater Los Angeles. As its honorary co-chair, he filmed several public service announcements, among other things. "That's a great fit with what I like," said Green. "I like working and supporting kids. And it's a Jewish organization that helps all people, not just Jewish kids."[32]

Once Green became more comfortable with National League pitching, his numbers began to improve. Even though he did not hit .300 in 2001, he had a breakout year in all other offensive categories that year, the finest season of his major league career. He led the

Dodgers in every major batting category except average, and his batting average of .297 was just barely under the .300 mark. In 161 games, Green had 184 hits, 49 home runs, and an outstanding .598 slugging percentage. In addition, he had a .982 fielding percentage with only 6 errors. In 2001 the Dodgers won 86 and lost 76 games for the second year in a row; sportswriters felt that their record for 2001 would have been much worse had it not been for Shawn Green.[33]

Green carried into the 2001 season the longest consecutive-game playing streak in the majors—408 games. On September 5, he announced that he would end the streak on September 26 in observance of Yom Kippur. The decision to not play on the Jewish High Holy Day emphasized the value Green placed on his roles as a representative of the Jewish community and an example for Jewish youth. His decision was supported by the club and applauded by American Jews.[34]

During the 2001 off-season, Green married the former Lindsay Bear, who was not Jewish, and the couple had their first child the following year, a daughter named Presley. "Fatherhood is the best thing I've experienced in my life so far," Green said. Green planned to give his daughter an understanding of both her religious heritages. "We're going to expose her to everything. She's lucky because she gets to celebrate all the holidays."[35]

Green admitted that with the birth of his daughter, he gained a greater appreciation for his young fans that changed the way he interacted with kids around the stadium. "I understand when parents are a little pushy to get their kids to the front of the line for autographs ... because I have a daughter of my own."[36]

In 2002, with 42 home runs, Green achieved two consecutive seasons of 40-plus homers. He was also named to the All-Star Game for a third consecutive season. In May, his tenth home run of the year was his fifth homer in two games, tying a major league record. It was the twenty-fifth time a player accomplished this feat. The following night Green was perfect at the plate, going six-for-six and hitting home runs in the second, fourth, fifth and ninth innings. Together with a single and a double, he collected 19 total bases, a record for one game. He also tied the major league record for runs scored (6) and extra-base hits (5).[37] Despite Green's contributions and the Dodgers' excellent 92-70 record, the team finished the 2002 season in third place in the NL West, six games behind the Diamondbacks.[38]

Green did not have a good year offensively in 2003, nor did most of his teammates. He managed to play in 160 games even with a right shoulder that he injured in spring training, waiting until the season ended to get the needed surgery. His home run total dropped dramatically to 19, the fewest he had hit since 1997, and he drove in only 85 runs. Even so, he led the team in hits, RBIs, runs scored, doubles and walks.[39] Los Angeles finished the 2003 season with a record of 85–77, good enough for second place in the National League West although 15.5 games behind the Giants.[40] Following the 2003 season Green announced that he would be willing to move to first base "if that's the best thing for the organization."[41]

Recovered from his injury, in 2004 Green played 111 games at first base and 52 games in right field, and he was the designated hitter in three games.[42] He continued to struggle at the plate, increasing his home run total from 19 to 28, but dropping his average 14 points, from .280 to 266.[43]

By the time Green played in the major leagues, baseball was much more understanding and accommodating than in the days of Hank Greenberg. But the High Holiday observance was still an issue for Jewish players. Green, like Greenberg, Koufax, and other Jewish players who identified strongly with their religious values, always chose to observe Yom Kippur in some form, even when there was a conflict with an important game.[44]

Although Green's refusal to play on Yom Kippur ended his consecutive game record in 2001, the game itself had no particular importance. The situation was different in 2004 when the Dodgers were contesting for a playoff spot in the National League West. Near the end of the season that year, the Dodgers had a razor-thin lead for the division championship over the San Francisco Giants. Green decided to play the game on the Friday night of Kol Nidre, but sit out the Saturday game on the day of Yom Kippur.[45] As he told the Associated Press, "Playing one of the two is the most consistent with my beliefs as a Jewish person. I'm not Orthodox. I am Jewish and I respect the custom. I feel this is the most consistent way to celebrate the holiday. I feel real good about my decision."[46] He indicated that he had struggled with this issue for several days and spoken with his wife, parents, and grandmother prior to making the decision. Green also said that his teammates and others in the Dodgers organization were as supportive as they had been three years earlier.[47]

His decision stirred up much controversy in the Jewish community. In general, more traditional Jews were extremely disappointed in Green. Rabbi Reuven Bulka, of Ottawa's congregation Machzikei Hadas, stated, "You can't be half pregnant. It's like saying I'll be honest today, but I'll steal tomorrow." He added that Green's decision would "compromise the general public's understanding of what Yom Kippur is all about." However, more liberal Jewish voices supported Green's action. Rabbi Matthew Kaufman of the Lodzer Congregation said, "Green's compromise is a commendable decision and a wonderful example of how an individual has made a statement that Judaism is both relevant and compatible with modern life."[48]

On January 11, 2005, Los Angeles traded Shawn Green to the Arizona Diamondbacks for Dioner Navarro, Beltran Perez, and minor leaguers Danny Muegge and William Juarez.[49] Green said that while he had preferred to end his career with the Dodgers, the team's repeated attempts to trade him made him willing to listen to the Diamondbacks' offer.

On April 3, 2005, Shawn Green was inducted into the National Jewish Sports Hall of Fame and Museum. At his induction he stated that he couldn't be happier with being a member of the Diamondbacks in 2005. "The team that I was really hoping would work out is Arizona. It's my favorite park to play in and it's my favorite city to come to. It was a perfect fit for me and my family."[50]

That year, Green played both right and center fields for Arizona in 158 games. He hit only 22 home runs and drove in only 73 runs, his lowest number since 1997, but his batting average was .286, his highest since 2001.[51]

The next season, 2006, Green played 115 games in right field for the Diamondbacks hitting .283, smacking 11 home runs, and driving in 51 runs. On August 22, he was traded to the New York Mets who were contending for their division title.[52] Even though Green had a no-trade clause in his contract that prevented his being shipped to every team but three—San Francisco, San Diego, and Los Angeles, Green was willing to waive it and move his wife and two daughters nearly 3,000 miles for the opportunity to win a championship. "It's not like I'm going to come there and be the answer," Green said. "They obviously have a great mix. I'm just going to go there to be a piece of the puzzle and help out when I can in September and October."[53]

There was another factor which persuaded him to agree to the trade. As baseball's most prominent Jewish player, he had always been intrigued by the idea of playing in New York, the largest Jewish population center in the country, if not the world. "It will be an interesting and fun experience for me. I'm looking forward to being a part of the Jewish community there," he said.[54] "Had I played my whole career and never played in New York, I always would have wondered what it was like," said Green. "My wife and family are all for the move. We feel we're up for an adventure. At this stage in my career, it's a perfect fit." Green became the first prominent Jewish Met since Art Shamsky in the late 1960s and early 1970s and the first Jewish player in New York since Ron Blomberg's days with the Yankees ended in 1977.[55]

New York Jewish fans were delighted to have a Jewish hero on their hometown ball club. What made his arrival doubly exciting was that in Shawn Green's first scheduled game as a Met he would be facing the St. Louis Cardinals, whose starting pitcher was to be Jason Marquis, a Jewish native of Staten Island.[56]

Shawn Green hit 14 home runs, had 61 RBIs, and 159 hits for a combined batting average of .274, nine points shy of his lifetime batting average of .283.[57] Although he played in just 34 games in 2006, Green had two notable achievements. In September, he notched hit number two thousand. Also, for only the second time in his 15 seasons in the major leagues, Green appeared in post-season play but the St. Louis Cardinals defeated the Mets in the National League Championship Series, four games to three. In the playoffs Green tied for the team lead with three doubles and hit .313, second-best on a team that hit collectively only .250.[58]

During his short tenure with New York, Green participated in charitable activities as he had done in Los Angeles. In 2007, for every run he batted in, he pledged to donate $180 or 10 times *Chai* ("Life" in Hebrew with the numerological value of 18) to the United Jewish Appeal-Federation of New York.[59]

On September 11, 2007, Green told the *New York Times*, "Every year, I come in expecting to get back to where I was, and it's been very frustrating that I haven't been able to do it. It's not like I live and die by this. When you reach a certain level, a bar gets set, and there are expectations and all that."[60]

It came as no surprise, therefore, that the 35-year-old Shawn Green announced his retirement from major league baseball on February 28, 2008. "There were teams interested in me, but none close to home [California]," said Green. "I wanted to stay here with my family and not travel around the country anymore. I enjoyed playing a lot. I enjoyed New York, but for me, it was time to be home."[61] He finished his career with a lifetime batting average of .281, 1,070 runs batted in, 162 stolen bases and 328 home runs, only three fewer than Hank Greenberg.[62]

The list of Jewish baseball greats is short and sometimes confined to Koufax and Greenberg, depending on the generation of the person compiling the list. When Green is asked if he is able to identify with that lineup, he modestly responds, "It's an honor to be mentioned with those guys. Those are Hall of Famers who had incredible careers. It's important for me to be a good role model for the Jewish community."[63]

18. The First Jewish Commissioner

During the second half of the twentieth century and beyond, there were a considerable number of Jewish baseball owners, including Jerrold C. Hoffberger, president of the National Brewing Company, who purchased the St. Louis Browns from Bill Veeck and moved the team to Baltimore; Charles Bronfman, co-chairman of the Seagram Company, co-owner of the Montreal Expos from 1968 to 1990, and an ardent supporter of Jewish causes; and Walter Haas, former president and chairman of the board of Levi, Straus & Company, who purchased the Oakland Athletics from Charles O Finley.

This select group of Jewish baseball owners also included Jeffrey Loria, noted art dealer and former co-owner of the Expos along with Bronfman and more recently, principal owner of the Florida Marlins; Jerry Reinsdorf, not only the owner of the Chicago White Sox, but also of the city's NBA franchise; Fred Wilpon, who became the sole owner of the New York Mets upon the death of former owner Joan Payton; and real estate developer Ted Lerner, who assumed control of the Washington Nationals when they began playing baseball in the nation's capital in 2005.

One Jew during this period would not only own a major league baseball team, but he would become the first Jew to occupy the office of commissioner of baseball.

Allan (Bud) Huber Selig was born July 30, 1934, in Milwaukee, the son of immigrant parents, Ben and Marie Selig. Through personal contacts, Bud's father developed an auto-leasing business that eventually became the largest car dealership in Wisconsin.

His mother, who was primarily responsible for Bud's interest in baseball, was a college graduate and became a schoolteacher. When Bud was only three, his mother took him and his older brother Jerry to Borchert Field, where the Chicago Cubs' AAA farm club played. By the time Bud was in the fourth grade, he was already a true baseball fanatic. When he acquired the Brewers in 1970, Bud recalled that during the first 18 years he owned the team, his mother never missed a game. "She'd sit in the box next to mine, bring her friends, keep score," he said. "If you didn't know how the Brewers did, her face would tell you the whole story."[1]

At her funeral in 1995, Selig reminisced about his mother and her love for the national pastime. "She attended her last Brewers game about four years ago. Before then, she never missed a game. I don't think there's any question that she got me into baseball at a tender age."[2] Any ambitions Selig might have had about playing baseball professionally were dashed in an American Legion game when a pitch hit him on either the shoulder or the head. He never participated in organized sports again.[3]

242

Selig attended public schools and graduated from Washington High School in 1952 and from the University of Wisconsin three years later with a degree in American history and political science. He served two years in the Army and when he returned to civilian life, he went to work for his father, primarily in management, overseeing sales, leasing, and the family's growing real estate holdings. He had little contact with customers and often had to dispel the stories that he actually sold automobiles. "I never sold a used car," he would often tell his friends.[4]

When he was 22 years old, Selig married Donna Chaimson, a storekeeper's daughter from Northern Wisconsin. The marriage lasted 19 years and the couple divorced in 1976. According to his wife, Selig was "unduly absenting himself from the home of the parties and isolating himself ... in pursuit of his baseball interests to the detriment of his marriage."[5] During her divorce proceedings, his wife told the court, "From the day Bud became involved in baseball, he divorced me and married baseball."[6] The couple had two daughters, Sari Markenson and Wendy Selig-Prieb.[7] Less than two years after his divorce, Selig married Sue Lappins, who had been a real estate broker and who very much shared her husband's love of baseball.[8]

The young Bud Selig rooted for the minor league Brewers and the major league Chicago Cubs until the Braves moved from Boston to Milwaukee in 1953.[9] By the early 1960s, Selig was one of the major stockholders in the Milwaukee Braves. He purchased 2,000 shares at $11.38 each. When the Braves left Milwaukee in 1966 for greener pastures in Atlanta, Selig sold 1,700 of his shares for a profit. He never failed to mention how he had had to "endure the miserable play of the Braves during the early 1960s."[10] (When the National League approved the move of the Milwaukee Braves to Atlanta, it marked the first time that a team was allowed to abandon a major league city that had only one club.)[11]

Even before the Braves headed for Atlanta, Selig had put together a civic organization that was determined to keep major league baseball in Milwaukee. The group was called Teams Inc. and it had two goals: do whatever it could to keep the Braves in Milwaukee and, if that failed, attract another major league team to the city.[12]

A tactic Selig employed to demonstrate the viability of Milwaukee as a market for major league baseball was to persuade the Chicago White Sox to play 21 of its home games in both 1968 and 1969 at Milwaukee's County Stadium.[13] Despite the large crowds at those games, Milwaukee was denied an expansion team in 1969. San Diego and Montreal in the National League and Kansas City and Seattle in the American League were awarded expansion teams, but not Milwaukee.[14] Selig and his group even attempted to purchase the Chicago White Sox in 1969, but the deal fell through when one of the owners' brothers, a 50-percent shareholder, decided at the last minute that he did not wish to sell. Selig was heartbroken. "When that deal went up in smoke," he commented, "my heart sank. I knew we were coming to the end, that I couldn't hold this group together much longer."[15]

Selig defended his attempts to acquire a major league franchise for Milwaukee. Answering charges that he was a "predator raider," making unjustified negotiations for a franchise, Selig lashed out at his accusers. "Accusations that we have no institutions for a franchise are unjustified. Some people think Milwaukee is a small, hemmed-in community, but in fact it is the largest primary market area in the country without baseball and larger than three or four existing baseball markets."[16]

It was only after one of the expansion teams, the Seattle Pilots, flopped, that Selig and his associates, including Robert Uihlein of Schlitz Breweries, Ralph Evinrude of the outboard motor company, and meatpacker Oscar Mayer, among others, were successful in gaining control of a major league franchise. The American League accepted the group's offer of $10.8 million for a franchise during the 1969 World Series, but legal delays kept the deal up in the air until the following spring.[17] Years later when Bud Selig reflected on his first season as owner of the Milwaukee Brewers, he said, "Of all the marvelous things that have happened to me, including becoming commissioner of baseball, that will always be my proudest accomplishment because the odds were stacked up tremendously against Milwaukee."[18] A remarkable thing had occurred in baseball. The first city in modern baseball history to obtain a transferred team had acquired another, and Milwaukee was ecstatic.[19]

When the Pilots moved from Seattle to Milwaukee, they were immediately renamed the Brewers. They played their first game one week later on April 7, 1970, remaining a club in the American League West. Two years later they would replace the Washington Senators in the East Division of the American League.[20]

In a forewarning of things to come, the Brewers lost their opening game to Andy Messersmith and the California Angels, 12–0.[21] The entire offense for the Brewers' first season in Milwaukee was supplied by third baseman Tommy Harper, who became the second 30–30 player in history when he slugged 31 homers and stole 38 bases. Milwaukee struggled to a fourth-place tie—the highest it would go until 1978.[22] Selig did his best to eliminate nonproductive team members and bring in new players.[23]

The tall, slim, friendly but reserved Bud Selig smoked small cigars until he quit in 1983 because he finally realized that smoking was "stupid." He watched his Brewers from the press box and used his team publications to promote his car dealership.[24]

In 1977 Selig began to take drastic action to turn the ball club around. First, he fired the general manager, Jim Baumer, and replaced him with Harry Dalton, recently general manager of the California Angels. Next, he replaced the manager, Alex Grammas, who had led the Brewers to last- and sixth-place finishes the past two years, with George Bamberger, former pitching coach of the Baltimore Orioles. In addition, Selig acquired two good free agents—Sal Bando in 1977 and Larry Hisle in 1978.[25]

The new group of front office staffers, many of them formerly with the Baltimore Orioles, ushered in the most successful seasons in the history of the Milwaukee Brewers. They helped develop an internal scouting network that ultimately numbered thirty.[26] In 1978 the team went to 93–69, fourth best in major league baseball. That same year, Bud Selig was voted Major League Executive of the Year.[27]

Bamberger was replaced by Buck Rodgers during the 1980 season. Under his leadership, the Brewers won the second half title in the split season of 1981 with the best record in baseball—95–67. Unfortunately, they lost the ALCS to the New York Yankees, three games to two.[28] The following year, general manager Dalton fired Buck Rodgers and replaced him, on an interim basis, with Harvey Kuenn.[29] Under Kuenn's leadership, the Brewers became the American League East champions by one game over the Baltimore Orioles.[30] The Brewers went on to defeat the California Angels in the ALCS, three games to two, for the only pennant Bud Selig would win as owner of the Brewers. In the 1982 World Series, the Brewers faced the St. Louis Cardinals in what was dubbed the "Sudsway Series."[31] The Cardinals defeated the Brewers in seven games. The following year, Milwaukee would draw more than two million fans for the only time in the team's history.[32] During Selig's tenure as owner of the Brewers, his team won three consecutive *Baseball America* Awards—from 1985 through 1987, and seven "Organization of the Year" awards.[33]

From the moment he brought the Brewers to Milwaukee, it was Selig's dream to build a first-class stadium. It took twenty-five years and Selig's threat to move the franchise to another state before the Wisconsin State Legislature in 1995 endorsed a tax plan for the construction of a new facility.[34]

As owner of the Milwaukee Brewers and a resident of the city, Bud Selig became quite active in community life. He helped establish the Child Abuse Prevention Network and Business Against Drunk Driving. He and his wife Sue were patrons of the Milwaukee Art Museum and jointly received the 1990 Humanitarian of the Year Award from the St. Francis Children's Center. He fervently supported numerous Jewish causes as well. In July 2001, he established a scholarship at the Rothberg International School in Jerusalem.[35]

Selig was also well liked and respected by his fellow owners after he managed to bring the Seattle Pilots to Milwaukee. Gradually, Selig began to assume a leadership role among baseball's magnates, including chairing multiple committees. This came about because most owners avoided the administrative aspects of baseball, but Selig relished being involved in all the aspects of the game.

One of Selig's earliest committee assignments was to chair a four-member committee to study and advise on inter-league play. When the owners met in the summer of 1973, Bud's committee recommended the adoption of inter-league play, but the National League owners on the executive council voted down the proposal. In the summer of 1982, Selig took part in another committee that ultimately recommended revenue sharing from big-city to small-city teams. In June 1983, when the owners appointed Lee MacPhail to replace Ray Grebey as president of the Players Relations Committee, one of the six owners on the PRC board was Bud Selig. Selig was becoming quite visible as a major league baseball owner.[36]

Bud Selig, former owner of the Milwaukee Brewers, became acting baseball commissioner in 1992 and permanent commissioner in 1998. Many changes in baseball have occurred since he took office, including interleague play, the realignment of each league into three divisions, the awarding of home field advantage to the league winning the All Star Game, and instant replay in the event of a disputed home run call. Despite these changes, Bud Selig has been plagued with problems such as the use of steroids and other performance enhancing drugs by players (courtesy National Baseball Hall of Fame Library; Cooperstown, N.Y.).

It became known that when Bowie Kuhn's term as baseball commissioner expired in 1984 he would not be rehired. An announcement was made on September 6, 1983, that Bud Selig would head a search committee to "look for baseball's next commissioner." Several owners asked Selig to look no further than the chair of the committee. Selig's reply was brief and would be stated many times in the future, "I don't want to be commissioner. Under no circumstances."[37]

The task of finding a new commissioner was a tiresome one as Selig interviewed 10 to 12 candidates during a period of 15 months.[38] It was no secret that Selig's first choice for the post was A. Bartlett Giamatti, an English professor at Yale, who was currently president of the prestigious university. Selig's committee, however, recommended Peter Ueberroth, president of the Los Angeles Olympic Organizing Committee. The owners accepted the committee's recommendation, and Ueberroth became baseball's sixth "czar" on October 1, 1984.[39]

Selig was elated that the search for Kuhn's successor was finally over. While he admitted that there were certain aspects of the job he liked, he also admitted that he would never undertake anything like it again. "The task," said Selig, "became totally time consuming, an overriding passion. I forgot about my car business, I paid little attention to my ball club. I'm glad it's over."[40]

As baseball's commissioner, Ueberroth helped broker a five-year agreement between major league players and owners, which ended a one-day players' strike. He was also instrumental in opening the door to managerial and administrative positions for minorities and attempted to address the growing drug problems plaguing major league baseball. Under Ueberroth's regime, baseball increased its attendance, doubled its national television revenues and multiplied its income from merchandising 16 times.[41]

On the negative side, Ueberroth's detractors argued that during his four years as baseball commissioner, baseball's owners were found guilty of collusion, joining together to hold down players' salaries from 1985 through 1987 even though the clubs' profits increased significantly during that period.[42]

In 1988 Ueberroth announced that he would not seek a second term as commissioner. Selig, despite his earlier statements that he would never again accept the chairmanship of a committee to select a baseball commissioner, once again chaired the search committee to find a successor to Ueberroth.[43]

Selig announced that the transition from Ueberroth to his successor would be very orderly, unlike the two transitions preceding Ueberroth's appointment. Selig announced, "Baseball has often been criticized for being reactive. This time we're out in front. The institution is the important thing, and the commissioner has said he will not leave until the transition process is complete." Selig indicated that he wanted Ueberroth to remain on the job through two critical negotiation periods—the Basic Agreement with the Major League Players Association, which was due to expire in 1989, and baseball's national television contract.[44]

On October 1, 1984, A. Bart Giamatti became baseball's seventh commissioner by unanimous vote of the owners. He reorganized the administration of the office by creating a deputy commissioner position to which he appointed Fay Vincent. The most prominent issue Giamatti faced in his short career was the agreement with Cincinnati Reds manager Pete Rose that resulted in Rose's lifetime suspension on August 23, 1989. Five months after he took office, Giamatti unexpectedly died of a heart attack. Many believed that his death was a result of the stress of the Rose scandal.[45]

After Ueberroth declined the offer of a second term as commissioner, Selig was chosen once again to chair the search committee which chose deputy commissioner Fay Vincent to succeed Giamatti. Vincent assumed the post on September 13, 1989. His relationship with the owners was fragile from the start. There were a number of issues between the commissioner and the owners, but the most serious was the claim by Vincent and Richard Ravitch, chief of the PRC, that the owners were in collusion against the Major League Baseball Players Association. Many of the owners were also concerned that Vincent was too friendly toward the player representatives, or as some owners put it, Vincent was interpreting his powers too broadly to protect "the good of the game.[46] In 1992, the owners gave Vincent a no-confidence vote of eighteen-to-nine, and he resigned as commissioner on September 7, 1992.[47]

The vote to dump Vincent was held in Rosemont, Illinois, a Chicago suburb. Jerry Reinsdorf, owner of the White Sox, arranged the meeting. The leaders of the "dump Vincent" movement were Bud Selig, Jerry Reinsdorf, Stanton Cook of the Cubs, William Bartholomay of the Atlanta Braves, and Carl Pohlad of the Minnesota Twins. The Chicago media dubbed the anti–Vincent clique "The Great Lakes Gang." Bartholomay, though representing Atlanta, lived in Chicago and had been with the Braves since their days in Milwaukee.[48]

Once the owners forced Vincent to resign, he was replaced by an executive council composed of the presidents of the two major leagues plus eight owners.[49] Selig was elevated from member to chair of the MLB's executive council, which made him, in effect, the *de facto* commissioner.[50] For the first time an owner was acting commissioner. It would be quite reasonable to assume that the best interests of baseball would now be equated with the best interests of the owners. Don Fehr and the Players Association were not encouraged by this turn of events.[51] As chair, Selig began to carry out the duties of the commissioner. By the time he became the actual baseball commissioner, Selig had served or was serving on a minimum of ten to fifteen major committees. This prompted Peter O'Malley to ask, "How can he be in charge of so many things?" The truth was simply that Selig was probably the most powerful man in baseball even before he became acting commissioner.[52]

Selig did not have the title of commissioner or even commissioner *pro tem*. He was, in effect, an interim commissioner, filling the vacancy in the commissioner's office while the owners searched for Vincent's replacement. As chair, Selig was a non-voting, ex-officio member of the executive council. In addition, Selig became board chairman of the Players Relations Committee and the owners' representative to the economic study committee with the players.[53]

Shortly after he was given his new position, Bud Selig stated that a permanent commissioner must be appointed. "We expect to have our man within two to four moths. We need a strong commissioner to lead like Bart [Giamatti]." He added that in the interim, he would not make any unilateral decisions. "I operate by consensus. If there is a problem of any sort, I get in touch with the executive council immediately. And we go from there. We'd probably take a vote and consensus rules."[54]

Selig made two things clear at the outset. He resisted all suggestions that he should assume the position on some terms other than as a caretaker, and he stated that he was not interested in being a candidate for the commissioner's job on a full-time basis.[55] When Bud told his wife Sue of his new position, she asked what it meant. He answered, "It's two to four months, not more. Don't worry about it. It won't affect anything."[56] After several owners began to push Selig to become a candidate for permanent commissioner's, he restated his position—that while he was extremely flattered, he was not interested.[57]

In September 1993, the owners decided to give Selig a $1-million-a-year salary as acting commissioner, and allowed him to handle the business of the major leagues out of a new office in Milwaukee. He was also allowed to continue in his executive capacity with the Milwaukee Brewers. His compensation from MLB was referred to as an "honorarium," rather than a salary which Selig, whose official position was chair of the executive council, could not be paid. Terming the sum "honorarium" also meant that social security taxes did not have to be withheld. In Selig's final year as acting commissioner, he was supposedly being paid $2.5 million.[58]

Selig was always described as a decent, honorable man, and he set the tone quite early that he expected baseball to uphold similar values. He acted decisively in 1993 to suspend Cincinnati Reds owner Marge Schott for one year for bigoted remarks and actions.[59] In 2000 he gave a three-month suspension to Atlanta's John Rocker for offensive racial and ethnic statements attributed to him in a *Sports Illustrated* article.[60] On two separate occasions, Selig also refused to recommend reinstatement of Pete Rose.[61]

He also ordered owners to consider minorities when hiring general managers and to provide his office with a list of potential candidates. He added that he would discipline any team that "did not aggressively pursue equal opportunities."[62]

When Selig became *de facto* commissioner in 1992, baseball had some serious problems. As a result of prolonged labor disputes, baseball had slipped to number three in popularity of American sports. It was in poor financial condition and suffering a steady loss in revenues. Selig bluntly stated, "More than a third of the clubs would sell if they could find a buyer."[63] He admitted that television ratings were dropping, and the sport was faced with internal controversy between large-market and small-market teams.[64]

The issue that first placed Selig in the national spotlight was the deadlock between the Players Association and the owners over a new Basic Agreement needed in 1994. Selig took an active role in these labor-management negotiations, acting less like the head of all of baseball and more like the spokesman for the owners.[65]

After prolonged sessions during the first six months of 1994, the owners agreed to split all revenues with the players, including licensing money, with a guarantee of $1 billion for player's salaries. In return for these concessions, they asked for a salary cap and an elimination of salary arbitration. The owners were also willing to lower the free agency requirement from six to four years of major league service under certain provisions.[66]

The major obstacle in these negotiations was the insistence on the part of the owners on tying revenue sharing to a salary cap. The MLBPA would not accept this stipulation and talks were at a stalemate.[67] At the time labor negotiations broke down, attendance appeared likely to match the record set in 1993, but on August 12, 1994, the players went on strike.[68]

A month later, on September 14, 1994, with no progress toward a settlement, Selig shocked the baseball world and outraged the fans by calling off the remainder of the season, including the playoffs and the World Series. It was the first time since John McGraw refused to play Boston in 1904 that a World Series had been cancelled.[69] Selig's move allowed owners to use "scabs" both in 1995 to take part in spring training camps and to start the season, further antagonizing the press, the players, and especially the fans.[70]

Late in March 1995, the matter went to court when the National Labor Relations Board filed action, accusing the owners of not bargaining in good faith. The strike officially ended on April 2, 1995, after federal judge Sonia Sotomayor issued an injunction against the owners, which restored the terms of the old agreement.[71] Bud Selig's comments: "The players are back, the game is back and we are very happy about that. We hope to resolve our dispute so that we and our fans never have to go through the heartache we've endured for the past eight months."[72]

Nobody really could claim victory in the eight-month strike. In fact, both sides lost, but the game itself lost the most. The fans were angry and disillusioned; they lost trust in the capability of either side to preserve the game. Attendance was down 17 percent or 20 million in 1995 from the peak of 70 million two years earlier. The fans' enthusiasm and zeal for the game would not return for many years.[73] The strike also shaped Selig's reputation. For years, many fans would know Selig as the man who canceled baseball.[74]

Although the event that really brought fans back to the ballpark was the home run competition between Sammy Sosa and Mark McGwire in 1998, Bud Selig was responsible for many innovations that helped increase fan interest and support.[75]

In 1993 each league realigned into three divisions in order to create a third playoff round with a wild-card; it was to have begun in 1994.[76] After the strike was settled in 1995, league executive Selig implemented this additional round of playoffs.[77] Inter-league play, first suggested by Steve Greenberg, began in 1997. As many remembered, Selig had been on a committee that recommended inter-league play, but it was voted down at that time.[78] Baseball also experienced further expansion. The Colorado Rockies and the Florida Marlins had been added in 1993 and the Arizona Diamondbacks and the Tampa Bay Devil Rays in 1998. At the conclusion of the 1997 season, the Milwaukee Brewers became the first team ever to switch leagues, moving from the American to the National League.[79] Jackie Robinson's uniform number 42 was universally retired and finally, for the first time, the major league season was opened abroad. In 2000, the Chicago Cubs began their season in Japan against the New York Mets.[80]

Selig's efforts to restore and improve the game's status were largely successful. Roland Hemond, long-time baseball executive, credits Selig for making the game more popular through all of his initiatives.[81]

In addition, after the eight-month strike, Selig was praised for presiding over an era of labor peace.[82] The basic agreement of 2002 was the first since 1972 that was reached without a work stoppage of any kind.[83] In 2006 a five-year agreement was concluded, the longest labor contract in the history of the game.[84]

By 1998, it was rumored that the word "acting" would soon be dropped and that Selig would become the permanent baseball commissioner. There were some skeptics, however, who were not sure that Selig was the man for the job. The managing executive of the Cincinnati Reds, John Allen, was one. "Canceling the playoffs and World Series in 1994 was a huge mistake," claimed Allen. "Bud Selig has done a good job, but I don't think we should keep him. We need somebody independent, somebody with charisma, somebody who can make judgments and rulings in the best interests of baseball. I don't know who that is, but we need to find somebody quickly."[85]

Another voting member of baseball's ownership group, speaking anonymously, indicated that he had grave concerns about the status of baseball and that he felt that the commissioner ought to be someone from outside the game—someone with a clean slate.[86]

Peter Schmuck, columnist for *The Sporting News*, argued that Selig would be named permanent commissioner for two reasons. First, as interim commissioner, he had the support of the most powerful ownership faction and second, although his past actions had offended many baseball fans, the success of his later moves, such as more expansion and inter-league competition, had silenced even his most vocal critics.[87]

In addition to his duties as acting commissioner, Bud Selig was still an owner and, in 1998, was optimistically thinking about the future of his Milwaukee Brewers. The baseball field of his dreams was due to open in two years, and the club was already spending more money on salaries and selling more season tickets in anticipation of the April 2000 grand opening. Miller Park would increase revenue even more with its luxury boxes and rising broadcast rights fees. "We're headed for a new ballpark and we're changing leagues," said Selig, "and we believe that our revenue streams will improve. That's what it's all about—which franchises can generate large enough revenue streams to be able to compete."[88]

On July 8, 1998, after a six-year search for a permanent commissioner, and on Bud Selig's 2,130th day as acting commissioner, major league baseball owners named Selig the ninth commissioner of baseball. He received the unanimous vote of the other owners for a five-year term at an annual salary of at least $3 million.[89]

Not only was Selig the first Jewish baseball commissioner, but he was also the first baseball owner to hold that post, even though the owners had always paid the commissioner's salary.[90] Selig placed the ownership of the Brewers in a trust and transferred the operation of the team to his daughter Wendy in order to remove any technical conflicts of interest. It was widely presumed that Selig would still take some part in team operations.[91]

Even though Jerry Reinsdorf was a close ally of Bud Selig, many owners assumed he would oppose the idea of an owner being commissioner. He voted for Selig, however, and later said: "I don't think there's anyone in America who could do the job that he can do. The only alternative was bringing in an outsider. That just didn't make any sense at all."[92]

After the election, Selig announced he would move out of his office at County Stadium and open a new office in downtown Milwaukee, dividing his time between there and the commissioner's office on Park Avenue in New York. He was very sensitive to possible conflicts which might arise from his position as an owner, and he told a press conference that if he really believed he could not hold both jobs, he would not have accept the position of permanent commissioner. Selig's election surprised no one, neither on management's nor on the players' side.[93]

Once he was officially the commissioner, Selig believed that he had to bring more control to his office in order to accomplish all of his goals. He instituted centralized scheduling, disciplining, and umpiring in 1999 shortly after the umpires' strike that led to the loss of 22 umpires. For all practical purposes, the jobs of both league presidents were eliminated. Both of these positions predated that of baseball commissioner.[94]

In the next few years, the owners authorized even more powers. At their annual meeting they allowed the commissioner to block trades and redistribute wealth to restore competitive balance to the game.[95] Using these powers, Selig made several moves that increased team incomes. He consolidated all internet rights for major league baseball, declaring that all internet revenue should be shared equally among teams.[96] He also brought in new revenues for the teams by establishing a TV channel reaching 50 million households, which began operation in January 2009.[97]

On rare occasions, major league baseball games have been called off by an event not involving a labor dispute or a weather-related condition. In 1918, during World War I, both major leagues voted to shorten their seasons, ending on September 2. During World War II, two games scheduled to be played on June 6, 1944—D-Day—were canceled out of respect for President Franklin Delano Roosevelt's request that the nation focus its attention on the war effort in Europe. On the evening of September 11, 2001, Commissioner Selig called off 15 games because of the terrorist attack in the United States. He stated that he called off the games in "the interest of security and out of a sense of deep mourning for the national tragedy that has occurred today."[98]

In 2002 Bud Selig took steps toward addressing the ongoing issue of revenue sharing among teams from different sized markets. In fact, it was one of the major topics included in the 2002 basic agreement and although negotiators approved the plan, it was only the beginning. It did funnel some additional profits to smaller market teams.[99]

That same year, Selig's daughter resigned as president of the Milwaukee Brewers and was replaced by Ulice Payne, managing partner of the Milwaukee law firm Foley & Lardner. He became the first African-American to be head executive of a major league baseball team.[100]

Selig was also successful in convincing the home cities of numerous baseball teams that a new stadium was essential to prevent the team from moving or being eliminated. Although the tactic did not work everywhere, particularly in the case of the Florida Marlins in 2001, it did achieve its goal in 20 cities as of 2008, with two new stadiums scheduled to open in 2009. Approximately two-thirds of the funding came from the public.[101]

Not every effort at increasing revenue was successful. Although advertising signs and banners proliferate the modern baseball stadium, Selig's proposals to place advertising on the players' uniforms and on the field of play itself were short-lived. One instance was the "Spider-man" initiative of 2004. Selig ordered the logo for the movie *Spider-man 2* placed on the tops of all bases in every major league park to promote the film's release. Fan reaction caused Selig to cancel the project.[102]

Overall, Selig was able to accomplish baseball's financial turnaround—revenue of $1.6 billion in 1992, to more than $6 billion in 2007.[103]

In 2004 with the new Milwaukee stadium completed and $18 million yearly in revenue-sharing, Selig finally felt the time was "right," and he put the ownership of the Milwaukee Brewers up for sale. He sold the team to Los Angeles investor Mark L. Attanasio late that year for $220 million.[104]

On the non-financial side, in one instance, Selig was able to take a very embarrassing situation and turn it into an effort to make baseball more meaningful and more interesting. The 2002 All Star Game, being played in Milwaukee's new stadium, was tied in the 11th inning when both squads ran out of pitchers. The participants turned to Selig for direction. Appearing unsure of what action he should take, the commissioner simply stopped the game and called the players off the field, which many felt emphasized that the traditional All-Star game served only for "bragging rights."[105]

Although caught off-guard at the game, Selig later analyzed the situation and acknowledged that the argument against his actions had some merit. In response to these arguments, Selig decided to make victory in the All-Star game more significant. He declared that beginning in 2003, the league winning the All-Star game would have the home field advantage in that year's World Series. This edict satisfied many, but outraged traditionalists and provoked much criticism.[106]

Selig has often been the object of controversy, but in the end his core values usually led him to do the right thing. The manner in which he dealt with steroids and other performance enhancement drugs is a case in point. Selig's critics claim that although the problem of bulked-up players was obvious for many years, baseball did nothing until Jose Canseco's book and subsequent Congressional hearings in 2005 forced Selig to take action.[107]

Supporters, however, praised the actions he took. His 2005 proposal to impose a 50-game ban for the first positive drug test and lifetime expulsion from the game for the third infraction seemed the needed solution, although in hindsight, he failed to implement the sanctions strongly enough. He also got high marks for tackling the problem of amphetamines.[108]

His most effective action in the drug controversy was bringing in former Senator George Mitchell in March 2006 as an independent investigator. When the Mitchell Report was released in December 2007, Selig accepted its recommendations, stating that he would immediately enact all that did not require approval by the players union and also that he would call a summit to discuss finding an easier test for human growth hormone.[109] A few weeks later, a Congressional committee commended baseball for its actions.[110]

Bud Selig was also one of the architects of the World Baseball Classic. The first WBC was played in 2006 and won by Japan. Many baseball media pundits gave the WBC little chance to succeed, but it was considered an unqualified success on every level. Selig admitted that at the outset even he was skeptical of its success, but he later said, "Anything you do for the first time is not going to be perfect. But by any stretch of the imagination, this tournament exceeded my expectations in a myriad of ways. Absolutely."[111]

The baseball owners renewed Selig's contract through 2012. His salary was estimated at more than $15 million, but Selig remains quiet, self-assuming and down-to-earth. He enjoys hot dogs for lunch, taking out his five granddaughters, shopping at Target, and communicating endlessly by phone with players, the press, and owners.[112]

Bud Selig has won a number of awards and honors. The National Conference for Community and Justice awarded him the "Human Relations Award," the Boy Scouts of America awarded him its "Good Scout Award," and he has received the "Distinguished Service Award" from the U.S. Sports Academy. Two prominent Jewish groups have also recognized him—he has been the recipient of the "World of Difference" Award from the Anti-Defamation League, and the "International B'nai B'rith Sportsman of the Year Award." One of his greatest honors was when major league baseball ownership bestowed on Selig the "August A. Busch, Jr. Award" which is given annually for "long and meritorious service to baseball." It is equivalent for off-field personnel to the players' Most Valuable Player award.[113]

Bud Selig has become one of the most visible person to hold the office of baseball commissioner, and he has also been the most controversial. Many still view him as the voice of the owners rather than the "non-baseball man" described in the original definition of the commissioner. Yet his accomplishments are many and even his detractors usually admit that while problems in baseball still remain, under Selig major league baseball has become a stronger game in many respects.

19. The Twenty-First Century

From 2000 to 2008, 13 players of Jewish descent debuted in the major leagues, joining those still active from the 1990s to create a small, but viable pool of Jewish players. Just as before, many of the new athletes came from intermarried families. As adults, some did not identify themselves with Judaism; others expressed their Jewish values in both traditional and non-traditional ways. In many cases, especially for players who lacked typically "Jewish" names, only the most knowledgeable fans even realized they were Jewish. Nine of the 13 players had either brief careers, or by the end of the 2008 season, were not yet considered "stars."

Justin Wayne

The first new Jewish player in the big leagues after 2000 was Justin Wayne in 2002. Wayne was an exceptional college athlete who never quite caught on in the majors.

Wayne was born in Honolulu, April 16, 1979, and was a member of an athletic family. Both his father and his brother played college baseball, and Justin ran cross country and played soccer in high school as well as baseball. He was an outstanding pitcher at Stanford University, tying for first in Stanford history in strikeouts (363). He was also in the school's top ten for wins (31), won–loss percentage (.861), innings pitched (342.1), and strikeouts per nine innings (9.54).[1]

The six-foot, three-inch, 200-pound right-hander left Stanford following his junior year when the Montreal Expos drafted him in as the fifth pick of the 2000 amateur draft.[2] He signed with the Expos on July 20, 2000. (The Boston Red Sox had drafted him in the 1997 amateur draft, but he did not sign.)[3]

Wayne played in the Expos system from 2000 until July 2002, making stops at Jupiter in the Florida State League and Harrisburg, the Expos' AA affiliate in the Eastern League. He had a record of 16–13 while playing in the Montreal organization.[4]

Wayne never reached the big leagues as an Expo. After playing 17 games for Harrisburg in 2002, Wayne was traded on July 11 to the Florida Marlins. In addition to Wayne, the Expos sent the Marlins pitchers Graeme Lloyd and Carl Pavano, infielder Mike Mordecai, and a player to be named later. In return, the Expos received outfielder Cliff Floyd, infielder Wilton Guerrero and pitcher Claudio Vargas.[5]

Florida manager Jeff Torborg was delighted with Wayne whom he considered a good athlete. In his second start, Wayne, backed by home runs from Andy Fox and Derek Lee, defeated the Philadelphia Phillies, 2–1, for his first major league victory.[6]

Wayne made five starts for the Marlins in 2002 and finished the season with a record of 2–3 and an ERA of 5.32. In his 23.2 innings of work, he struck out 16 and walked 13 as the Marlins finished in fourth place in the National League East with a record of 79–83.[7]

In 2003 instead of starting with the Marlins as planned, Wayne was placed on the fifteen-day disabled list with a leg problem. He returned to the Marlins on April 11, but appeared in only two games for Florida in 2003, winning none, losing two, and compiling an ERA of 11.81.[8] Following an inauspicious start on May 3 in which he allowed two hits and three runs without retiring a single batter, the Marlins optioned him to their AAA club in Albuquerque, where he finished the season with a record 4–12.[9] Unfortunately for Wayne, he was not on the Marlins roster when they won the World Series in 2003.[10]

Although Justin Wayne's statistics were mediocre, the Marlins still felt he had his ability to win in the major leagues. They claimed that his ERA of 4.24 at Albuquerque was respectable for pitching in the high New Mexico altitude. He struck out 82 hitters while walking only 40. At the Marlins' complex in Jupiter, Florida, in November 2003, Marlins' pitching coach Wayne Rosenthal watched Justin throw in a bullpen session and stated, "We'll work with his two-seam fastball, [but] I'd like to see him get his sinker working again, giving hitters something else to handle."[11]

Hawaiian born Justin Wayne was an outstanding pitcher for three years at Stanford before the Montreal Expos drafted him. He then signed with the Florida Marlins, and during his major league career from 2002 to 2004, he compiled a record of five wins and eight losses (photograph, Florida Marlins, Denis Bancroft).

After a solid 2004 spring training, the Marlins decided that Wayne's best opportunity was in the bullpen. "Whatever they want me to do," said Wayne. "If it's in Miami, I'll do it. If I'm with the team, I'll do anything it takes to get into the game."[12] Wayne began the 2004 season with the parent club, appearing in 19 games, all but one in relief. His record for the Marlins was 3–3 with an ERA of 5.79.[13] On July 30, the Marlins sent Wayne back to Albuquerque where he completed the 2004 season with a record of 1–5.[14]

The Florida Marlins released Wayne on April 1, 2005. His last appearances in professional baseball were that year, pitching for the Newark Bears and the Las Vegas 51s.[15]

John Grabow

John Grabow grew up a fan of both the Giants and the Dodgers in San Gabriel, California, about fifteen minutes from Dodger Stadium. Through 2008, the left-handed pitcher played his entire professional career for the Pittsburgh Pirates organization.[16]

Grabow was born in Arcadia, California, on November 4, 1978. His father was not Jewish, but his maternal grandmother came from a Jewish community in Beirut, Lebanon. Much of the family moved to Israel while others settled in Brooklyn or California. His aunt's family was Orthodox and his mother and grandmother kept kosher. While John attended a Jewish Sunday School as a child, he admitted that baseball drew him "away from religion" and that his parents did not attempt to force their religious beliefs on him. Even if he wanted to be more observant, he stated, his constant travel made it difficult for him to observe the Jewish dietary laws.[17]

Although he grew up about fifteen minutes from Dodger Stadium, left-handed relief pitcher John Grabow signed with the Pittsburgh Pirates in 1997. He was brought up to the major leagues in 2003 and became the Pirates' most reliable relief pitcher, used both in long relief and as a closer (courtesy Pittsburgh Pirates).

Grabow, an effective pitcher for his San Gabriel High School team, was drafted by the Pittsburgh Pirates in the third round of the 1997 amateur draft.[18] The hard throwing six-foot, two-inch, 185-pound leftie was primarily a fastball pitcher, often clocked between 90 and 92 mph at his best. He could also throw a change-up and had an effective slider.[19]

Grabow spent 1997 through most of 2003, or from age 18 through 24, pitching for various minor league teams, all in the Pirates organization. As he worked his way up from the rookie league to AAA, he was used almost exclusively as a starting pitcher. While he was with the AA club in Altoona, his progress was stopped for a time near the end of the 2000 season by arm surgery. During the next two seasons, Grabow had a difficult time throwing strikes.[20]

In 2003 Grabow was in his fourth year starting for Altoona when his minor league manager decided to move him to the bullpen. It was the right move. Everything seemed to fall into place. Grabow was 3–0 with an earned run average of 2.25 and one save in 15 relief appearances. His performance earned him a promotion to AAA Nashville that year where he pitched exclusively in relief. "I definitely like pitching out of the pen," said Grabow. "When you're a starter and you lose a game, you can beat yourself up for a couple of days. In the bullpen you can always redeem yourself the next game. The role suits me better."[21]

Grabow was a September callup to the major leagues. He debuted with the Pirates September 14, 2003, after hurling 722 innings in the minor leagues.[22] Unfortunately, he made a rather unimpressive appearance in his first game, allowing six hits and three runs, two of them earned, in 1.1 innings. "It was just one of those days," Grabow said of his outing. "They hit everything I threw. Maybe I was a little pumped up that day and left some pitches up. We were getting blown out. I just took it as a good experience and tried to make some adjustments from there."[23]

His adjustments worked, for in his final four appearances, Grabow allowed no runs and no hits and struck out eight in 3.2 innings. He finished the 2003 season with the Pirates with no record but a respectable 3.60 ERA. In five innings, he struck out nine hitters without walking a single one.[24]

Grabow was asked to try out for the 2004 U.S. Olympic baseball team. In six games during the Olympic Qualifying Trials, he posted an ERA of 1.42 and was selected to the squad. Unfortunately, Team USA lost in the qualifying tournament.[25]

From 2004 to 2008, Grabow pitched exclusively for the Pirates except for a brief rehab stop with AAA Indianapolis at the beginning of 2007. He had suffered a left elbow injury during spring training and started the season on the disabled list.[26]

Grabow established himself as the team's most reliable and frequently used left-handed middle reliever. In 2005, he led major league baseball with the lowest percentage of inherited runners scored.[27] From 2004 to 2008, Grabow was a real "workhorse" for the Pirates. He pitched 311 innings, striking out 276 opposing hitters, and walking only 139—a ratio of nearly two-to-one.[28] He was counted on to carry the load in the Pirates bullpen for the 2009 season, but was traded to the Cubs on July 30 of that year.[29]

Grabow was always proud of his Jewish heritage and credited his mother with teaching him his values, such as being responsible and patient.[30] Since he did not receive a lot of media attention, his identity as a Jewish player "slipped under the radar" during his years in the minors. In 2004, however, the Pittsburgh community discovered he was Jewish and he soon became their "favorite son." For his part, Grabow was very pleased with the designation, knowing it would make his grandmother extremely happy.[31]

Adam Stern

Adam Stern was the second Jewish Canadian to play in the major leagues, and the first since Goody Rosen was a member of the Brooklyn Dodgers in the 1930s and 1940s. Stern was also one of four Jewish players to debut in the major leagues in 2005.[32]

Adam James Stern was born in London, Ontario, Canada, on February 12, 1980. His parents, Joe and Jane Stern, and older brother Jason would often travel to Montreal to spend Passover with Adam's aunt and uncle.[33]

As a boy, Stern played a number of sports, but he began concentrating on baseball. "Family and friends commented on how good I was becoming in baseball, which led to phasing out the other sports." He stayed with track and field, partially to help keep in shape for baseball.[34]

The five-foot, eleven-inch, 180-pound left-handed-hitting outfielder was known primarily as a line drive hitter, spraying the ball to all parts of the field and occasionally hitting with power. Stern attended the University of Nebraska on a baseball scholarship after turning down a draft offer from the Toronto Blue Jays in 1998.[35] Seven years later, in an interview Stern explained that accepting the Jays' offer, "was not the best thing for him to do at the time." He believed that going to a top-tier school, getting an education, and going pro later, seemed like a better long-term option.[36]

During his junior year at Nebraska, Stern was named to the 2001 Academic All-Big-12 team. The Atlanta Braves drafted him in June of that year in the third round and this time, he signed a contract.[37]

From 2001 until 2004, Stern played at four different levels of minor league ball in the Braves organization for four different teams, including Jamestown, Myrtle Beach, Bradenton, and Greenville, the Braves' AA club in the Southern League.[38] His parents were his biggest supporters; they would often drive down to spring training to root for him wherever he played.[39]

In 2004 Stern was selected the center fielder on Canada's Olympic baseball team at the summer games in Athens where Canada finished fourth in the competition. He considered being chosen to participate in the Olympics an experience that comes once in a lifetime.[40]

After the Summer Games, Stern returned to Greenville where he finished the year with a .321 batting average, a .480 slugging percentage, and 27 stolen bases. Even though he had missed a month of the season, Stern was named center fielder of the year, a member of the Southern League's All-Star team, and Atlanta's AA Player of the Year.[41]

On December 13, 2004, the Boston Red Sox drafted Stern from the Atlanta Braves in the 2004 Rule 5 draft, which meant he was required to remain on the Red Sox roster an entire season or be returned to the Braves.[42] The Red Sox were impressed with Stern's speed, his ability to play all three outfield positions, and his developing offensive ability. Ben Cherington, Red Sox director of player development, said that Stern "can be a good defensive player, and he showed considerable growth in his plate discipline and power production."[43]

During spring training in 2005, Stern fractured his thumb and was placed on injured reserved; he rehabbed with the Pawtucket Red Sox, Boston's AAA team in the International League. After 20 games for Pawtucket, he was finally called up to the Red Sox and made his major league debut on July 7, 2005.[44]

Adam Stern was the second Jewish Canadian to play in the majors and the first since Goody Rosen played for the Brooklyn Dodgers in the 1930s and 1940s. When he made his debut with the Boston Red Sox on July 7, 2005, he joined Jewish teammates Kevin Youkilis and Gabe Kapler. In addition to his time in the major leagues, Stern played for Team Canada at the first World Baseball Classic in March 2006 (courtesy Brita Meng Outzen, Boston Red Sox).

Stern's manager, Terry Francona, later confirmed that his rookie outfielder "handled himself well" when he joined the team. As a Rule 5 player whom veterans sometimes resent, Francona described Stern as "quiet when he first came up, paid respect to the veterans, and slowly but surely began to show his personality." He also played well, but he sprained the same thumb in August, and in September he had to have shoulder surgery.[45] Because of his injuries, Stern appeared in only 36 games for the Red Sox in 2005; he came to the plate only 15 times and finished the season with a .133 batting average.[46]

Once he fully recovered from his injuries, Stern was a standout for the Canadian baseball team in the first World Baseball Classic in March 2006. According to the press, Stern played "the greatest baseball ever by a Canadian." In an 8–6 upset over the U.S. Team, Stern hit a single, a triple, and an inside-the-park homer, and made two incredible catches—a sinking liner from the bat of Jeff Francoeur and a leaping stab against the center field wall that denied an extra base hit to Chase Utley.[47]

Because he had lost so much major league playing time in 2005, Stern fell 17 games short of the time Rule 5 picks were required to remain on the 25-man major league roster.

To make up this time, the Red Sox kept him on the roster to start the 2006 season. He joined two other Jewish players, Gabe Kapler and Kevin Youkilis.[48]

Although he was able to play all three outfield positions, Stern began the 2006 season in center field, filling in for the injured Coco Crisp. Crisp had high praise for the young outfielder. "Stern has a great arm, above-average speed, good wheels on him, a good glove, a good hitter. Everything he needs to be a successful big leaguer."[49]

Stern was with Boston only 18 days, just long enough to fulfill his Rule 5 obligations, and the Red Sox sent him back to Pawtucket.[50] He worked hard with the AAA team in 2006, earning the approval of PawSox manager Don Johnson. "He's been doing a nice job. He's getting himself back playing again. Once he gets some consistency, you're going to see his numbers start to go up."[51]

Unfortunately, the injury-prone Stern damaged his right hamstring on August 16 and once again landed on the disabled list. On August 29, Pawtucket announced that he was out for the entire season.[52]

On August 4, 2006, the Red Sox acquired catcher Javy Lopez from Baltimore for cash and a player to be named later. The Red Sox completed the trade on October 3, 2006, by naming Stern as that player.[53] In his two years at Boston, the oft-injured Stern had played 46 games for the Red Sox, made 25 plate appearances, hit one home run, drove in six runs, and had a .143 batting average.[54]

Stern was invited to the Orioles spring training camp in 2007, but was limited to only 14 games because of a strained oblique muscle and a bout of food poisoning.[55] Stern started the 2007 season with the Orioles AAA team, the Norfolk Tides; on April 17, the Orioles called him up to Baltimore. In his last appearance in the majors, he played in two games for the Orioles without any at-bats, and then was sent back to Norfolk for the remainder of the year. Stern appeared in 78 games for the Tides and hit .270.[56]

In 2008 Stern played 38 games for the Tides, hitting .221 before being released on June 10.[57] He participated in the summer Olympics for Team Canada, playing center field in all seven of its games and getting four hits, including two triples.[58] According to Norfolk Tides general manager Dave Rosenfield, Stern did not play professional baseball after his release from the Oriole organization.[59]

Craig Breslow

Craig Breslow was an Ivy League graduate and southpaw pitcher who deferred medical school in order to try his chances at professional baseball.

Craig Andrew Breslow was born August 8, 1980, in New Haven, Connecticut. Both his parents were educators—his mother Ann taught math, and his father Abe taught health and physical education in addition to coaching tennis. The Breslows attended B'nai Israel, a Reform temple in Bridgeport. Craig got his start in baseball early, playing t-ball at the age of three.[60]

After graduating from Trumbull High School in Trumbull, Connecticut, in 1998, where he was outstanding in both soccer and baseball, the six-foot, one-inch, 180-pound Breslow was accepted at Yale University. He majored in biochemistry and molecular biophysics and played on the Bulldogs baseball team all four years, serving as captain part of the time. He graduated in 2002.[61]

On June 4, the Milwaukee Brewers drafted Breslow in the twenty-sixth round of the

2002 amateur draft. He spent the remainder of the 2002 season playing for the Brewers' rookie-level club and in 2003, moved up to their Class A team, performing well both years and striking out a total of 136 batters while walking only 51.[62]

Breslow began the 2004 season for the High Desert Mavericks, an advanced A team in the California League known for being a hitter's dream and a pitcher's nightmare. Not unexpectedly, he struggled there, winning only one game while losing three with a high ERA of 7.19. On July 6, 2004, much to Breslow's astonishment, the Brewers released the 23-year-old pitcher. "I was somewhat surprised by the fact that they would give up on a 23-year-old lefthander," said Breslow. "I was brought up by the adage that if you were a lefty and you can pitch, you'd keep your job. But, looking back, it was the best thing that could have happened to me. I started to enjoy the game again."[63]

After his release, Breslow considered applying for medical school, but he opted to give baseball another try, and he signed with the independent New Jersey Jackals. He enjoyed his stay there and felt more relaxed playing with teammates who really found fun in the game. "The fear of getting released was gone," said Breslow. "It was like playing summer league baseball."[64]

In the winter of 2004, Breslow tried out with the San Diego Padres, and on March 3, 2005, they signed him as a free agent.[65] He threw well in the spring and the Padres assigned him to their AA team, the Mobile Bay Bears in the Southern League. In 40 games with Mobile, Breslow's record was 2–1 with an excellent 2.75 ERA. His strikeout-to-walk ratio continued at a remarkable pace—47 strikeouts and 17 walks.[66]

He was unexpectedly called to the majors while still with Mobile in 2005 because the Padres, playing in Philadelphia, needed a lefty with strikeout ability, and their AAA team was too far away to send a pitcher who could arrive in time.[67] Padre's general manager Kevin Towers turned to the Mobile squad, asking for a lefty who could throw strikes. Breslow—a pitcher Towers had never seen—was nominated. The Padres GM personally gave Breslow the good news.[68]

Breslow was awestruck when he described his first impression of the big leagues. "Beyond my wildest dreams would be a fair assessment," stated Breslow, as he entered a major league clubhouse as an active member of the team for the first time.[69] Breslow debuted on July 23, 2005, becoming the first Yale pitcher to reach the major leagues since Ron Darling. When he left the game, the home plate umpire, Gary Davis, tossed him the ball he had thrown in his first major league appearance as a memento.[70]

Breslow had to return to the minors the next day to make room for

Craig Breslow, an Ivy League graduate and southpaw pitcher, deferred medical school in order to try his chances at professional baseball. When the Connecticut native debuted with the San Diego Padres on July 23, 2005, he became the first Yale pitcher to reach the major leagues since Ron Darling broke in with the Mets in 1963 (courtesy Minnesota Twins/ Rick Orndorf).

the Padres' newly acquired third baseman Joe Randa. GM Towers, impressed with Breslow, rewarded him by allowing him to stay in a big-league hotel (the Ritz-Carlton) for a night and giving him two days of big-league meal money.[71]

Just six days later, the Padres recalled Breslow from Mobile. He faced six batters in a game with the Cincinnati Reds and was thrilled when he forced Ken Griffey Jr., to pop up.[72] He pitched a total of fourteen games for the Padres in 2005 with an ERA of 2.20 and struck out a total of 14 batters in 16 innings.[73] Even though he ended the season pitching in the minors, Breslow was upbeat about his experience. "I've traveled through 30 states I never would have seen without baseball and I believe I'll get to see a lot more in the years to come."[74]

Breslow was to have more years ahead in organized baseball but not in the Padres organization. On December 21, 2005, the Padres granted Breslow free agency even though he had held left-handed hitters to a .063 batting average.[75] They invited him back on a minor league deal, but Breslow chose to sign with the Boston Red Sox. He had met Red Sox general manager and fellow Yale alumnus Theo Epstein when his college coach, former major league pitcher John Stuper took the team for a workout at Fenway Park. "I don't know if he remembers," said Breslow.[76]

Breslow was considered one of the top prospects in the Red Sox organization. He was assigned to Pawtucket, the Red Sox's AAA farm club, and turned in not only a 2.69 earned run average, but also averaged 10.3 strikeouts per 9 innings.[77]

Breslow appeared with the Red Sox twice in 2006. On July 16, the Red Sox brought Breslow to Boston for a few days as a replacement for pitcher Jason Johnson.[78] They re-called him on September 1, making Breslow the fourth Jewish player on the 2006 Red Sox team along with Adam Stern, Gabe Kapler, and Kevin Youkilis. Breslow appeared in 13 games for the Red Sox in 2006. In his 12 innings of work, he had a record of 0–2, a 3.75 ERA, and twice as many strikeouts as walks.[79]

Although he sat on the bench most of his time during his few weeks with the Red Sox in 2006, Breslow, as always, was grateful for the opportunity, and took this opportunity to learn from the veteran pitchers on the Red Sox staff, just as he had in San Diego. When I was at San Diego," said Breslow, "I learned a lot from [Trevor] Hoffman—a great character. Here it's the same thing with the established guys—Schilling, Timlin, and Foulke."[80]

Despite his good work in his brief tenure with the Red Sox, Breslow did not pitch a single inning in the major leagues in 2007. The Red Sox promoted him to the major leagues on September 1, 2007, but he did not make an appearance, and on the following day he was sent back to Pawtucket to make room for Bosox pitcher Jon Lester.[81]

In a complete turn-around from the previous year, Breslow spent the entire 2008 season in the major leagues. Out of options that year, Breslow was selected off waivers on March 23, 2008, by the Cleveland Indians.[82] When the Indians broke their spring training camp, Breslow won the final spot on the opening day roster.[83]

Breslow appeared in seven games for the Indians in 2008 with no record and a 3.24 ERA. On May 23, the Indians designated him for assignment, and one week later, the Minnesota Twins claimed him.[84]

The Twins' fans learned much about Breslow from an interview on Minnesota Public Radio. For example, when Breslow pitched for the Beloit, Wisconsin, team in 2003, the parents of one of his teammates were both professors at Yale in Breslow's fields, biochemistry and biophysics. "We had much in common," said Breslow.

Breslow also spoke about his sister having been diagnosed with thyroid cancer at the age of 14 and how this brought about his interest in childhood cancer research. Finally, he indicated that when his career as a major leaguer ended, he would give serious thought to going to medical school unless he had family obligations.[85]

In an effort to not only help victims of childhood cancer but also to become involved with a charity where he could maintain a connection to the medical field, Breslow established the Strike 3 Foundation in his home state of Connecticut. "I founded the Strike 3 Foundation in 2008 with a compelling inspiration to reciprocate my good fortune. Privileged by a healthy and prosperous upbringing, yet forever touched by the childhood cancer of my sister, I now seek to raise awareness and support for this devastating disease."[86]

Breslow finished the 2008 season with the Twins. His record was 0–4, but with an exceptional ERA of 1.63; he struck out 32 batters and walked only 14. Craig Breslow remained with the Twins until May 20, 2009, when the Oakland A's claimed him.[87]

Adam Greenberg

Adam Daniel Greenberg had the shortest major league career of the Jewish players entering the game from 2000 through 2008. The Guilford, Connecticut, native, born on February 21, 1981, received his Jewish education at Temple Beth Tikvah in Madison. He was a star athlete at Guilford High School, playing baseball, basketball and soccer, but baseball was always his favorite sport. "He wanted to play professional baseball ever since I could remember," his father Mark said.[88]

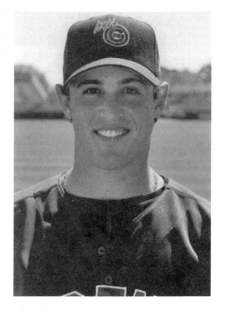

A communications major at the University of North Carolina, he was named Atlantic Coast Conference Rookie of the Year, and both *Collegiate Baseball* and *Baseball America* picked Greenberg for their Freshman All-American team.[89] During his three outstanding years for the University of North Carolina, Greenberg batted well above .300 each year.[90]

Surprisingly, in an era that was supposedly free of anti–Semitism, Greenberg experienced ignorant remarks about his religion in the South.[91] In an article on mlb.com, Greenberg explained that life for a Jew was a little different in North Carolina where he attended college. There were not many Jews there, and about ninety percent of the team had never met a Jewish person. "People would want to talk to me about it," said Greenberg. "Yes, comments would be made, but uneducated people are going to make uneducated comments. But it was never a detriment."[92]

Following his junior year at UNC, the Chicago Cubs signed the five-foot, nine-inch, 180-pound outfielder in the ninth round of the 2002 amateur draft.[93] From the summer of 2002 until July 2005, Greenberg played in the Cubs minor league system, working his way up to

On July 9, 2005, Chicago Cub outfielder Adam Greenberg tied an unenviable major league baseball record—he became the second major leaguer to get hit in the head by the very first and only pitch he ever saw in his big league career. The gritty, 5-foot, 9-inch, left-handed batter did not have an at-bat in the major leagues after the incident, although at the end of the 2008 season, he was still hoping for a comeback (courtesy Iowa Cubs).

the AAA Iowa Cubs.[94] He was not a power hitter, getting only a total of 15 home runs during these years, but he was able to get on base and score runs.[95]

On July 7, 2005, the Cubs called Greenberg up to the big leagues, and two days later, he debuted as a pinch-hitter in the ninth inning against the Florida Marlins. His parents and three of his siblings were in the stands, having flown to Chicago to watch Adam make his major league debut. On the first pitch thrown, Marlin pitcher Valerio de Los Santos unintentionally hit Greenberg in the head with a 91-mile per hour fastball. Greenberg was helped off the field by the team trainer and led to the training room where doctors from both the Cubs and Marlins checked him out. The following morning he was taken to a hospital for a CAT scan, which showed that he had suffered a mild concussion.[96]

"I went down fast. I was really scared. It was the first time I was ever scared on the baseball field," he said. He was placed on the disabled list and, after a few weeks of rehab, returned to the Double A team in Tennessee thinking he would go back up to the Cubs to finish the season. He soon realized he still had after-effects from the beaning. "Just bending over to tie my shoe left me with headaches for hours," he said. For weeks, Greenberg slept upright, the only way he could tolerate the unbearable headaches. During the winter he played ball in Venezuela, batting .264.[97]

The Cubs released Greenberg in June 2006. One week later he signed a contract with the Los Angeles Dodgers but was released again at the end of the season. He next signed with the Kansas City Royals and played the 2007 season with their AA farm club in Wichita, posting good stats in many offensive categories.[98] Greenberg began the 2008 season with the Independent Bridgeport Bluefish near his hometown of Guilford before signing with the Los Angeles Angels who assigned him to the AA Arkansas Travelers. He has not played a single game in the major leagues since his beaning in 2005.[99]

At the beginning of 2009, Greenberg was still determined to return to the majors. "I am going to accomplish what I set out to do. They'll have to tear my uniform off me before I quit."[100] Adam Greenberg hoped to avoid being the second player whose major league career was ended by being hit in the head in his one and only big-league at-bat. The first player to hold that dubious distinction was Fred Van Dusen, a member of the Philadelphia Phillies, who was beaned on September 11, 1955.[101]

Scott Feldman

Scott Feldman, a right-handed reliever, was the fourth player to enter major league baseball in 2005, and like Justin Wayne, he was born in Hawaii. The towering six-foot, five-inch, 210-pound Feldman who was born on February 7, 1983, played high school baseball in California. Overweight and known more for his hitting than his pitching, Feldman lost 40 pounds between high school and his first year at San Mateo Junior College where he compiled a 25–2 record over two years with an ERA of 1.30.[102]

On June 3, 2003, the Texas Rangers drafted Feldman in the thirtieth round of the amateur draft and he spent all of 2003 and 2004 and portions of 2005 in the Rangers minor league system. Feldman's most productive year was 2005 when he appeared in 46 games for Frisco, the Rangers' AA affiliate in the Texas League. All 46 games were in relief and he had 14 saves.[103]

Feldman made his major league debut on August 31, 2005, and appeared in a total of eight games for the Rangers that year, all in relief. His ERA was a brilliant 0.96, and although he did not save any games, he finished three of the eight games in which he pitched.[104]

Feldman was primarily a fastball/slider pitcher who was relaxed and friendly off the field, but possessed a "killer instinct" in the bullpen. He often stated, "To make it to the majors, you have to be able to flip that switch."[105] He began the 2006 season with the Rangers, but he was shipped to the minors after making 36 appearances and pitching 41.1 innings.[106]

Scott Feldman gained limited national attention for the first time as a major league pitcher in 2006, but it was not for an admirable feat. Feldman was one of a number of players thrown out of a Rangers-Angels game in Arlington on August 16. Earlier in the month, two Ranger pitchers, Adam Eaton and Vincente Padilla, had been ejected for throwing at Angels' batters. In the August 16 game between the two division rivals, before Feldman took the mound, two other Angel pitchers, Kevin Gregg and Brendan Donnelly, had been thrown out of the game for hitting batters. Angels manager, Mike Scioscia, and bench coach, Ron Roenicke, were also sent to the showers. In the ninth inning, with only one out remaining in the game and the Rangers ahead, 9–3, Feldman hit Angels batter Adam Kennedy. Kennedy immediately charged the mound. Feldman took a swing and Kennedy swung back as players on both teams joined the melee. Both Feldman and Kennedy, along with Rangers manager Buck Showalter were ejected, even though Feldman claimed, "The pitch just got away from me." In addition to his ejection, Feldman was suspended for six days.[107]

In 2007 and 2008, Feldman remained with the Ranger organization, where he split each season between the minor and major leagues. In 2008 he again began the season with Frisco, but after starting and winning only two games, Feldman was promoted to the majors and became one of the Rangers starting pitchers. He finished the 2008 season with a 6–8 record, starting 25 of the 28 games in which he appeared. His ERA dropped slightly from 5.77 in 2007 to 5.29.[108]

Feldman's 2008 ERA would have been even lower were it not for one game. On August 12, the Boston Red Sox defeated the Rangers, 19–17. Feldman was not the losing pitcher in that game, but he was charged with 12 of the 19 Red Sox runs. It had been more than 90 years since Gene Packard had allowed 12 runs in one game without taking the loss.[109]

In 2008, as a starter for the first time in his major league career, Feldman pitched admirably on a very weak Ranger pitching staff. The Rangers looked to him to improve in 2009 and he more than lived up to expectations. With a record of 17 wins and 8 losses, Feldman became the ace of the Rangers starting rotation.[110]

Jason Hirsh

Jason Hirsh was distinctive for several reasons. At six feet, eight inches, and 250 pounds, he was one of the largest Jewish players ever to make it to the majors, and during his second season, he displayed incredible endurance while pitching with a severe injury.

Another of the many California natives, Jason Michael Hirsh was born February 20, 1982, in Santa Monica, to Jewish parents, Michael and Karen Hirsh. His maternal step-grandfather, born in Europe, had changed his name numerous times to avoid being sent to concentration camps.

Hirsch's parents never "hammered" him or his younger brother Matthew with religion when they were young. "My brother and I are not particularly religious," wrote Hirsh, "but I do attempt to observe as many Jewish holidays as I can. I carry on the Jewish traditions with my wife Pam, who is Lutheran."

Hirsh's interest in baseball began at a young age. His father loved the game and passed that love onto his son. Hirsh remembers when one of his teachers asked the class to write down what he/she wanted to be in life, Hirsh wrote Professional Baseball Player.

Growing up in Southern California, he became an avid Los Angeles Dodgers fan. Although Hirsh never saw Sandy Koufax pitch, he read of his exploits and the motivation he gave to aspiring baseball players. Hirsh's earliest baseball mentor was Mike Boyd, brother of former major league pitcher "Oil Can" Boyd. "He along with my father," wrote Hirsh, "were tremendous influences on my career choice and the reason I have had any success at this level."[111]

Jason Hirsh, a former hurler for the Colorado Rockies, who broke into the big leagues with the Astros, is unusual in a number of ways. At six feet, eight inches tall and weighing 250 pounds, he is one of the largest Jewish players ever to make it to the majors. During his second season in the majors, he displayed remarkable endurance, pitching with a broken leg. Finally, although he is Jewish, he received his formal education at a Catholic high school and a Lutheran college (courtesy of Houston Astros).

Hirsh attended St. Francis High School in La Canada, California, and graduated in 2000. His primary reason for attending the Catholic School was baseball; friends of his family had played there, but his experience at St. Francis was disappointing. During high school, Hirsh did meet a scout from the San Diego Padres who was impressed with his pitching, but his high school coaches never gave Hirsh the team's paper work nor did they ever return the scout's call.

Being Jewish at a Catholic high school never was an issue, primarily because Hirsh kept his religion hidden from most students and the faculty. One benefit was his course on the Old Testament where he learned a great deal about the history of the Jewish people. A detriment was that he was forced to attend Mass once a month, and he felt awkward because he "didn't have a clue what he was doing there."[112]

After he left high school, Hirsh enrolled at California Lutheran University because it, too, was supposed to have a good baseball program and was near his home. He studied graphic arts and web page design before being drafted in 2003 by the Houston Astros in the second round of the amateur draft.[113] He was Houston's first pick because they had lost their first-round choice by signing veteran infielder Jeff Kent. The Astros liked Hirsh's collegiate statistics— 9–1 record, 3.68 ERA, 126 strikeouts, 22 walks, and 97 hits allowed in 100 innings.[114]

After the season ended, he did the work needed to complete his bachelor of arts degree in multi-media. "Once I sent in my project, my advisor gave me the go ahead for graduation and I flew home during spring training to walk down the aisle and grab my diploma. It was very important to me and my family."[115]

When Hirsh began his minor league career in 2003, a close friend who had some extensive experience with major league baseball advised him to not bring up being Jewish because hatred and intolerance of other faiths still existed. "I took him at his word," stated Hirsh. "I never divulged my 'true identity' unless someone asked. I get asked a lot now because I wear a mezuzah around my neck and a lot of people are very intrigued as to what it is and its significance. I usually give them the short answer, 'It's the Jewish version of the cross that Christians might wear' and they are usually satisfied with that."[116] Hirsh added that during his three years in the minors, he never had a negative experience with his religious beliefs.[117]

During every season in the minors, from 2003 to 2006 when the Astros brought him to the major leagues, Jason Hirsh was a dominant pitcher in the Astros organization. Before the 2006 season, he was named the Astros' top prospect and also touted by *Baseball America* as possessing the best breaking pitch in the Pacific Coast League. In addition to a breaking slider, Hirsh also threw a 92 to 93 mile-per-hour fastball and a changeup.[118] In 2006 he was 13–2 with a 2.10 ERA for the AAA Round Rock Express and was allowing hitters a mere .193 average when the Astros called him to the majors in August.[119]

Hirsh made his major league debut for the Astros on August 12, 2006; to make room for him on the roster, outfielder Preston Wilson was sent out on assignment. With the Astros, Hirsh and catcher Brad Ausmus became the first all Jewish battery in major league baseball since Sandy Koufax and Norman Sherry had teamed up in the 1960s. In his first three games, Hirsh allowed 17 earned runs in just 12 innings, but in his last six starts, he was 2–2, and had an earned run average of 3.58. Houston won four of the six games in which he pitched.[120]

On December 12, 2006, the Houston Astros traded Willie Taveras, Taylor Buchholz and Jason Hirsh to the Colorado Rockies for pitchers Jason Jennings and Miguel Ascencio.[121] Hirsh, who thought he had a future with Houston, soon focused on earning a spot in the Rockies' starting rotation. "It was disheartening when I found out about the trade," said Hirsh. "I thought I was a key part of that organization for years to come. I knew everybody over there. I was raised (in pro ball) by the Astros. They drafted me. They gave me the opportunity for success. And then I was gone." Realizing that there was a business side to the game, Hirsh tried to get himself excited about the move. "I have a lot of pride, and what this has done is make me work real hard so when the Rockies fans see me they will realize they got a good deal," he said. "I realize I got a good deal. Colorado has young talent. We have a chance to develop together and be good for a long time together."[122]

Denver sportswriters compared Hirsh's laidback lifestyle and use of yoga to increase his flexibility with his intimidating presence on the mound and his intense competitiveness. They found him to be very articulate and a computer whiz. In addition, Hirsh was a writer who kept a journal for mlb.com beginning in 2005 that documented his minor league baseball experiences.[123]

With the Rockies, just as in high school and college, Hirsh's religion set him apart from the majority of his teammates. Many of them stated that they were "devout" Christians, who participated in weekly chapel and Bible meetings. Nevertheless, Hirsh said he always felt very comfortable in the Rockies clubhouse. "There are guys who are religious, sure, but they don't impress it upon anybody. It's not like they hung a cross in my locker or anything. They've accepted me for who I am and what I believe in."[124]

For the first time in their division history, the Rockies won the NL pennant in 2007, but the Boston Red Sox swept them in the World Series. Hirsh started 19 games for the Rockies that year with a 5–7 record and an ERA of 4.81.[125] His season was cut short by an unusual incident. In the first inning of the game on August 7 against the Milwaukee Brewers, Hirsh was hit in the right calf by a line drive off the bat of J. J. Hardy. After he threw Hardy out at first, Hirsh completed an additional five innings, allowing Milwaukee two earned runs and three hits in the Rockies' 11–4 win. X-rays taken after the game revealed that the ball had fractured his fibula and that he had pitched almost the entire game on a broken leg.[126]

During the 2008 season Hirsh was hurt again, suffering a strain to a rotator cuff muscle that kept him rehabbing with Colorado's AAA team most of the year. He was recalled in September and made a total of four appearances, including one start, finishing the season with no decisions and an 8.31 ERA in 8.2 innings.[127]

Hirsh's only goal in baseball was to return to the pitcher he had been in 2005 and 2006. On July 29, 2009, the Rockies traded Hirsch to the New York Yankees, who assigned him to their AAA club, the Scranton/Wilkes-Barre Yankees.[128]

Sam Fuld

Sam Fuld was an athletic standout at his prestigious prep school and academically acclaimed university, but even though he literally threw himself into professional baseball, his major league career did not start out successfully.

Fuld was born in Durham, New Hampshire, on November 20, 1981, to an intermarried family; his Jewish father was a college professor and his Christian mother, a doctor. Samuel Babson Fuld grew up in a home where he experienced both religious cultures. For example, they had a Christmas tree, but also lit candles in a Chanukah menorah.[129]

Fuld was diagnosed with juvenile diabetes when he was just ten. He learned to treat his condition himself and applied the same discipline to playing baseball, crediting his father as his most influential coach. As an adult, Sam continued monitoring his blood sugar and giving himself insulin shots.[130]

The five-foot, ten-inch, 185-pound left-handed outfielder graduated from Exeter Academy where his lowest batting average during his four years was .489. He won numerous baseball awards and in 2000 was named by *Baseball America* one of the top twenty high school prospects in the nation. Fuld chose to attend Stanford University because he wanted "a school with good academics and good baseball." He continued his hot hitting at Stanford, was a starter for the baseball team all four years, and also demon-

The Chicago Cubs first drafted Sam Fuld in 2003, but through the 2008 season, the Stanford University graduate had only six at-bats in the major leagues. Fuld, who was diagnosed with juvenile diabetes at the age of ten, learned to cope with his condition while pursuing a career in professional baseball (courtesy Iowa Cubs).

strated his defensive skills, posting no errors in conference games in both his sophomore and junior years.[131]

The Chicago Cubs drafted Fuld in 2003, but he chose to finish his studies at Stanford, graduating in 2004 with a degree in economics. During his four years at Stanford, he set the school record for runs (266) and was second in hits with 353.[132]

When the Cubs drafted Fuld again in 2004, he was ready and began his professional career in the Cubs A farm system at Peoria. By 2007, Fuld had been promoted to the Cubs AAA farm club in Iowa; the Cubs called him up to the major leagues in September 2007.[133]

Fuld made his major league debut September 5, 2007, as a defensive substitute for Alfonso Soriano. In Chicago, he bonded with fellow Type 1 diabetes sufferer Ron Santo, former Cubs star and broadcast analyst, who had had to keep his condition secret throughout his playing career. Fuld did not get an at-bat until his ninth game with the Cubs. He came to the plate as a pinch-hitter for pitcher Kevin Hart, but was hitless then and in all of his other plate appearances that year.[134]

Late in the 2007 season, Fuld became an instant hero to Cub fans with an almost unbelievable game-saving catch as the Cubs were attempting to solidify their division lead. Against the Pittsburgh Pirates on September 22, in front of a crowd that packed Wrigley Field, Fuld crashed into the vines in right center, robbing Nyger Morgan of a hit; he then threw a sizzling one-hopper to first to double Nate McLouth. Despite his heroics, he did not make the post-season roster.[135]

Sam Fuld spent the entire 2008 year in the minor leagues, playing 85 games for the Chicago Cubs AA Southern League affiliate and 20 games for the Iowa Cubs, their AAA affiliate. Recalled by the parent club midseason in 2009, Fuld made 97 plate appearances; he hit his first major league home run, and picked up his first big league RBI.[136]

Brian Horwitz

Brian Jeffrey Horwitz, nicknamed "Rabbi" by his teammates, was the only Jewish player to make his major league debut in 2008. He was the first Jewish Giants player since pitcher Jose Bautista in 1995 and 1996, and the eighth since the team moved to San Francisco. He was also the second player in major league history to be tabbed with a "Rabbi" nickname. The other, also a Giant, was Mose Solomon, who played in the 1920s and was termed "the Rabbi of Swat."[137]

Horwitz, a right-handed hitting outfielder, was born in San Mateo, California, on November 11, 1982, and attended Crespi High School and the University of California.[138] While Horwitz was raised a reform Jew, he credited one set of grandparents, who were Conservative, for "instilling a lot of Jewish traits in our family." He attended religious school and had his bar mitzvah at Temple Judea in Tarzana. He also played in the Jewish Community Center Maccabi Games when he was 15 and 16, leading his Los Angeles area team to national titles in 1996 and 1997.[139]

Horwitz was drafted by Oakland after he finished his junior year at Cal, but he wanted a larger bonus than the A's were willing to give. He returned to school for his senior year where his batting average dropped from .347 to .288, and no team approached him during the 2004 draft.[140]

The San Francisco Giants finally gave Horwitz an opportunity to play in 2004, sending him to their low A farm club, the Salem-Keizer Volcanoes in the Northwest League. The six-foot, one-inch, 180-pound Horwitz rose through the minor league ranks for four seasons in San Francisco's minor league system ending his stint in the minors with a .319 average, 18 home runs, and 253 runs batted in.[141]

Brian Horwitz was the only Jewish major leaguer to make his debut in 2008, appearing in his first major league game on May 30 for San Francisco. Nicknamed "Rabbi" by his teammates, Horwitz was the first Jewish player in the Giants' organization to reach the majors since Jose Bautista pitched in 1995 and 1996 (courtesy Fresno Grizzlies).

Horwitz debuted with the San Francisco Giants on May 30, 2008. Prior to his debut, he had played in 425 minor league games, and *Baseball America* described him as the "player with the best strike-zone defense in the Giants' organization."[142]

Horwitz banged out two homers in his first 13 at-bats, and he soon became known for his desire not only to become a success in the majors, but also to remain there. He did not get much playing time in his rookie year, appearing in only 21 games with 36 at-bats and compiling a .222 batting average. Horwitz was optioned back to the Giants' AAA team in Fresno late in September 2008.[143]

Horwitz was not deterred by his demotion to the minors, and he hoped to return to the Giants in 2009. One of those who also rooted for Horwitz's success was Al Rosen, former great third baseman for the Cleveland Indians. When Rosen played in the major leagues, there was a great deal of ill feeling about Jews playing in the big leagues. "There are prejudices that run deep," said the former star. "But today, with the advent of international players, a great deal of that is gone. There's no more bench jockeying. There used to be some very nasty things coming out of the dugout. It's different now, and it should be."[144]

Horwitz often echoed Rosen's analysis of increasing tolerance in major league baseball. "Stars are aligning. Things are happening. Opportunities are coming."[145]

20. Certified Stars

As the 2009 major league baseball season opened, team rosters included slightly more than a minyan of Jewish players. Some had been playing for a number of years and were in the twilight of their careers. Many players who started in 2000 or after had come and gone or were utility players, but four of the 2000-and-after group had established themselves as outstanding.

Jason Marquis

Right-handed pitcher Jason Marquis was not a star in the traditional sense, but during his long career he contributed significantly to his various teams, in several instances helping his clubs qualify for post-season competition. A native of Manhasset, New York, Marquis was born on August 2, 1978; his name is of English descent, and is pronounced Mar-kee.[1]

Marquis was raised in a conservative Jewish home; he attended Hebrew School and had a bar mitzvah. He also focused on baseball, but he readily admitted that he had no Jewish sports heroes. At the age of 13, Jason was the number-one pitcher and hitter for the Staten Island team in the Little League World Series.[2] After he pitched his high school to a second consecutive Public School Athletic League title, the World Series champion Atlanta Braves signed him as a special selection between the first and second rounds of the June 1996 free agent draft.[3]

Marquis, used chiefly as a right-handed starter, spent 1996 through the middle of the 2000 seasons in the Braves' minor league organization. His stops included Danville, Myrtle Beach, Greenville, and ultimately Richmond, the Braves' AAA team in the International League.[4]

By 2000, Marquis had developed a sinking fastball clocked in the mid–90s to complement an effective curve and change-up. He soon became one of the most promising pitchers in the Braves' system.[5] In early June, John Rocker was demoted for threatening a reporter, creating an opening in Atlanta's roster. The Braves brought Marquis up from Richmond on June 5, 2000, to supplement an already good pitching staff. He made his pitching debut one day later, throwing one inning in relief. Between stints in the minors in 2000, Marquis managed to appear in fifteen major league games and had a 1–0 record that year.[6]

Marquis spent the following year with Atlanta as both a spot starter and a reliever. In his first start on May 12, 2001, Marquis faced Shawn Green twice, retiring the Dodger slugger both times. When he was asked about his experiences facing a Jewish batter, Marquis replied that it was not really a big thing. "Now, it seems more and more [Jews] are playing and hopefully I can be a role model for those kids growing up," he said, adding, "It's nice for little kids of Jewish ancestry to know that there are guys who did make it and not have them be discouraged."[7]

On June 24, 2001, Marquis made his first start in his hometown of New York. He was so excited about his many family and friends in the stands that his pitching coach, Leo Mazzone, had to come to the mound to settle him down after he had thrown only two pitches. The Braves defeated the Mets, 8–4, for Marquis's first major league win. Marquis finished the 2001 season with a record of 5–6 and an excellent 3.48 ERA.[8]

The Atlanta Braves won the National League East Division in 2001 by two games over the second-place Philadelphia Phillies. The Braves then went on to defeat the Astros in three consecutive games in the NLDS. Although Marquis was on the roster for the playoffs, he was not included because of the strength of his arm, but because of his speed on the base paths. He appeared as a pinch runner in Game Two of the NLCS against the Arizona Diamondbacks in Atlanta's 8–1 victory. He did manage to pitch one inning in Game Three and another in Game Four; he did not allow any runs and struck out two hitters. The Braves lost to Arizona in five games.[9]

After starting the 2002 season at Richmond, Marquis returned to the Braves starting rotation behind Greg Maddux, Tom Glavine, Kevin Milwood, and Damian Moss. Even though Marquis was the fifth starter in the rotation, he appeared in 22 games and finished the season with a record of 8–9.[10]

The Braves had the best record in the National League—101–59—in 2002, but in the division series, the wild card San Francisco Giants defeated the Braves three games to two. Marquis did not appear in the series in any capacity.[11]

In 2003 the Braves overhauled their starting rotation. They acquired Mike Hampton, Russ Ortiz, and Shane Reynolds and promoted Horacio Ramirez from their AA affiliate, the Greenville Braves. After starting 22 games in 2002, Marquis experienced shoulder problems and fell out of favor with his pitching coach. He made only two starts in 2003, before the Braves shipped him to Richmond where he spent most of the year in AAA.[12]

When he learned of his demotion, Marquis was upset but resolute. "I'm going to work hard, do my best and hopefully be the first guy called back up," he said. "Maybe I'll be able to look back a year from now and laugh about this." He insisted his confidence wasn't shaken by the move. "My goal is to be a solid big league starter. Whether it's two days from now or two years from now, I know it's going to happen."[13]

On December 13, 2003, the Braves traded Marquis and pitchers Ray King and Adam Wainwright to the St. Louis Cardinals for outfielder J. D. Drew and catcher Eli Marero.[14] The Cardinals were elated that they were able to acquire Marquis. They were positive that the six-foot, one-inch, 185-pound Marquis would not be frustrated with the Redbirds, who had already slated him as the fifth starter behind Matt Morris, Woody Williams, Chris Carpenter, and Jeff Suppan. Cardinal manager Tony La Russa said, "He's got an exciting arm and he's got exciting athletic ability. He also helps himself offensively. You can't run on him. A lot of poise."[15]

Pitching coach Dave Duncan also liked Marquis' attitude. "You have to understand that Jason has thoughts about himself and what his strengths are, and I think that the conflict [with his previous pitching coach] was because they didn't see his strengths the same as he sees his strengths."[16]

Marquis pitched for the Cardinals from 2004 through 2006. Although he had a winning record of 39–37 during those three years his ERA kept increasing—from 3.71 to 4.13 to 6.02.[17] He credited his pitching coach for helping him accomplish what he had been attempting to do in Atlanta—stop trying to overpower the batter and become a "finesse guy," relying more on his sinker.[18]

The Cardinals made the playoffs in 2004 and defeated both the Giants and the Astros to win the National League pennant. The Boston Red Sox swept the Cardinals four straight games in the World Series. Marquis appeared in Game One not as a pitcher, but as a pinch runner. He made his World Series pitching debut throwing a perfect seventh inning in relief in Game Two. His first World Series start came in Game Four and although he lost the game, 3–0, he pitched very well. He was voted the most effective of all the Cardinals starters in the 2004 World Series.[19]

Marquis' ability with the bat was evident in 2005; he won the Silver Slugger Award as the best hitting pitcher in the National League.[20] In 2006 his final season with the Cardinals, Marquis had his worst year since entering the major leagues and one of the worst in Cardinals history. He led the major leagues in runs allowed (136) and the National League with 16 losses. However, in games that were close in the late innings that year, Marquis held the opposing hitters to a .188 batting average.[21]

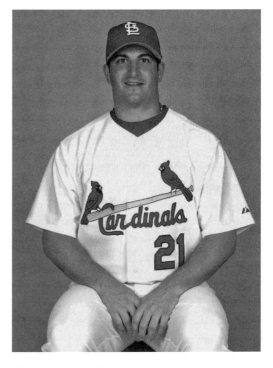

When right-handed pitcher Jason Marquis was traded to Colorado early in 2009, the Rockies became the fourth National League team for the native of Manhassat, New York. Marquis was the first Jewish player to debut in 2000 when he made a relief appearance for Atlanta against the Toronto Blue Jays on June 6, one day after he had been recalled from Greenville. He also pitched for the St. Louis Cardinals and the Chicago Cubs (courtesy St. Louis Cardinals).

The Cardinals made the playoffs in 2006, and they placed Marquis on the roster for the first round match-up against the San Diego Padres. He did not appear in that series, and he was not on the roster when the Cardinals won the NLCS against the New York Mets and went on to defeat the Detroit Tigers in the World Series.[22]

On December 19, 2006, the Chicago Cubs signed Marquis as a free agent to a three-year contract worth $21 million.[23] From the beginning of the 2007 season, Marquis was in Chicago's rotation and finished the season with a record of 12–9. His ERA of 4.60 was better than in 2006, but still rather high.[24]

In his first year with the Cubs, Marquis avoided the conflict of pitching on Yom Kippur. He was scheduled to pitch a day game that would likely end before the holy day began. When he had faced the same problem during his first years in the majors with the Braves, he elected to play on the night of Kol Nidre, but went to Temple the following morning. His manager in Atlanta, Bobby Cox, had no problem allowing Marquis to do what he felt was right. Marquis, explaining his decision to pitch, stated, "Baseball and religion fall into place, and I try not to make one more important than the other."[25]

Marquis remained with the Cubs for the 2008 season. Late in the year at Shea Stadium, he became the first Jewish pitcher to hit a grand slam since Saul Rogovin in 1950. He also raised his record to 11–9 for the season.[26]

On January 5, 2009, the Cubs traded Jason Marquis to the Colorado Rockies for reliever Luis Vizcaino.[27] By the end of the 2009 season, Marquis had appeared in 290 games, winning 94 and losing 83, while compiling an ERA of 4.48.[28]

Kevin Youkilis

Kevin Youkilis, nicknamed the Greek God of Walks by Oakland general manager Billy Beane in Michael Lewis' 2003 book, *Moneyball*, is not Greek, nor is he very Greek-godlike in appearance.[29] Youkilis is of Romanian lineage and one of the best Jewish players to debut in the major leagues between 2000 and 2008.

Kevin Edmund Youkilis was born March 15, 1979, in Cincinnati, the son of Mike and Caroline Youkilis. He was raised in a Conservative Jewish household and celebrated his bar mitzvah, but today most of the Youkilis family, including Kevin, attend synagogue only on the high holidays and do not keep kosher homes. "We keep the faith," he says. "We believe in what we believe."[30]

According to family lore, Kevin's great-great-great-grandfather, whose last name was Weiner, escaped to Greece in the nineteenth century to avoid Cossack persecution. After two years, he became homesick and returned to Romania, but in order to avoid the army, he changed his name to Youkilis. During the late 1920's, Kevin's great-uncle Paul immigrated to America. To raise enough money to move his siblings from Europe to the United States, Paul became a "rum-runner" during Prohibition, working with Al Capone, to "run" alcohol out of Canada into the United States. According to family legend, the Bronfman family in Canada wanted to make Paul a partner, but he refused. Kevin's dad, Mike, said, "My uncle told the Bronfmans that I take on no partners." Eventually, the entire Youkilis clan immigrated to the States and settled in Canada.[31]

Mike Youkilis was a wholesale diamond dealer and a third baseman in Cincinnati's Jewish Community Center softball league. It was he who taught Kevin to hit, to be a Reds fan and to respect the game of baseball. Kevin Youkilis had no Jewish baseball heroes growing up. "There weren't that many," he explained.[32]

Youkilis attended the University of Cincinnati where he played on the college baseball team, setting a number of school records. He was a two-time All-American selected by the Boston Red Sox in the eighth round of the 2001 draft.[33]

Many scouts overlooked the right-handed third baseman who could also play several other positions because he seemed shorter than his official height of six-feet, one-inch. He also appeared "chubby" at 220 pounds, could not run very fast, and possessed only average throwing ability. In addition, he had a strange batting crouch. Being ignored and told he could not compete only fueled Youkilis' determination.[34]

In addition to determination and discipline, which he credited to his Jewish beliefs,[35] Youkilis possessed other valuable assets that became apparent in the minors. He had the ability to see pitches well because of his 20/11 eyesight. This visual acuity explained his most obvious skill, excellent strike zone judgment, which resulted in few strikeouts and many free passes.[36]

Youkilis began playing professional baseball with the Lowell Spinners in the low A league, and by the end of 2003, he had worked his way up to the Red Sox AAA affiliate, the Pawtucket Red Sox.[37] Although "everyone" knew he was Jewish, he said that he experienced no anti–Semitism in the minors. "I believe," he asserts, "that just like in any workplace, one's faith, among other things, should not strongly influence his association with his co-workers."[38]

In mid–May 2004, the Red Sox called Youkilis up from Pawtucket to replace their regular third baseman, Bill Mueller, who was sidelined for a few days with inflammation in his right knee. Youkilis, with his parents present, made his major league debut in Toronto on May 15, 2004. He left a runner on third base with no outs his first time at bat, but Youkilis, in his second plate appearance hit a Pat Hentgen fastball for a 402-foot home run. When he returned to the dugout after circling the bases, his teammates gave the rookie their traditional silent treatment. Nonplussed, Youkilis went around the dugout giving "air high-fives" until his teammates broke down and mobbed him with congratulations.[39]

Youkilis appeared in 72 games for the Red Sox in 2004, finishing the season with a .260 batting average and a .367 OBP.[40] The Red Sox clinched the American League wild card spot and in the AL Divisional Series defeated the Anaheim Angels in three games. In that series, Youkilis appeared in one game and went 0–2. The Red Sox were down, three games to none, against the Yankees in the ALCS when they won four straight, and then did the same to the St. Louis Cardinals in the World Series.[41]

One of the World Series games in 2004 took place during Yom Kippur. Although Youkilis was in the dugout in uniform on the Day of Atonement, he did not play that day. "Everyone has to make their own personal decisions. Unfortunately, as a professional ballplayer, my decision comes under public scrutiny. I try not to judge whether a person's level of observance is right or wrong. You're your own person, and you have to make the decisions that are right for you."[42]

A disappointed Youkilis started the 2005 season in the minor leagues, but said that the demotion was motivating. "The biggest thing for me," said Youkilis, "was getting here and then getting sent back to the minor leagues. I realize how tough it is to be here in the major leagues and that has allowed me to be humble. I had to push myself harder and harder to prove to these guys that I belonged here."[43] After 2005, Youkilis did not play in the minors again.[44]

In 2006 Kevin Youkilis played the entire season for the Red Sox. He was switched to first base because the Red Sox had acquired third baseman Mike Lowell in a trade with the Florida Marlins. Although first base was a relatively new position for Youkilis, he made only two errors in 147 games at that position. He hit .279 for the season; his 42 doubles placed him in the top ten in doubles in the American League. He hit an impressive .372 with runners on base and two outs, earning him the reputation as one of the league's great young clutch hitters.[45]

Youkilis began to take on a distinctive look in 2007, equally recognizable both on and off the field. His shaved head and his facial hair, combined with his intense, down-to-earth approach to the game, made him a favorite of the home town fans who would chant "Yooouuk! Yooouuk!" at games and often in public.[46] His teammates marveled at the intensity with which he played. Red Sox second baseman Dustin Pedroia described his passion. "The fire he plays with is not going to change, and he's not going to apologize for it."[47]

That year Youkilis's performance got even better. He hit .424 during a 23-game hitting streak throughout the month of May, including nine straight games with two hits each. In the 2007 ALCS, in which the Red Sox defeated the Cleveland Indians in seven games, Youkilis hit three home runs and had an average of .421. He also helped the Red Sox defeat the Rockies in the World Series in another four-game sweep.[48] Defensively, Youkilis won the American League Gold Glove at first base and established an American League record for the most consecutive errorless games (179) at first. He was the first American League player in history to have an errorless season at first base.[49] Youkilis joined first baseman George Scott, three-time Gold Glove winner, as only the second Red Sox first baseman to win that defensive award.[50]

In 2008 Youkilis, one of the lowest paid players on the Red Sox roster in 2007, signed

a one-year contract for $3 million.[51] He picked up his streak of consecutive errorless games where he had left off in the 2007 regular season, extending it past Steve Garvey's major league record. Youkilis' streak of 238 errorless games, begun July 4, 2006, was finally broken on June 7, 2008, against the Seattle Mariners after 2,002 fielding attempts.[52]

Youkilis was elected to the 2008 All-Star team, one of three Jewish players in the game, along with Ian Kinsler and Ryan Braun. According to Kinsler, Youkilis always acknowledged him on the bases by saying something like "Happy Passover."[53] His performance at the plate continued to improve. Youkilis hit .312 for the Bosox in 2008, drove in 115 runs and clouted 29 home runs. He was third in balloting for the MVP behind his teammate Dustin Pedroia. The fans also honored him, awarding Youkilis the American League's Henry Aaron Award as the player with the greatest offensive contribution.[54]

Kevin Youkilis is one of the outstanding players in the American League. Since he broke in with the Red Sox in 2004, he has played on two championship teams (2004, 2007), set a record for most consecutive games of errorless play by a first baseman (238 games), and was the starting first baseman for the American League in the 2008 All Star Game. He was nicknamed "the Greek god of walks" for his amazing strike zone judgment, which earns him many free passes. Youkilis batting (courtesy Mike Ivins, Boston Red Sox). Youkilis Fielding (courtesy Brian Babeneau, Boston Red Sox).

A strong believer in his Jewish values, Youkilis created a charitable foundation in 2007 called Hits for Kids that focused on health, advocacy, and medical healing for children in Massachusetts and beyond. He even re-shaved his head during the 2007 Series to demonstrate solidarity with a child cancer patient and shaved off his goatee after the World Series for a $5,000 donation to the foundation from Gillette.[55] "In my religion, the Jewish religion," said Youkilis, "that's one of the biggest things ... giving a mitzvah. I was always taught as a kid giving to charity. You're supposed to give a good amount of charity each and every year. That probably started in my youth ... I just wish more people, not just athletes, would give people just a little bit of their time. It doesn't take much ... it can make a huge difference."[56]

On November 9, 2008, Kevin Youkilis married his fiancée, Enza Sambataro, in Mexico. She is a native of Newton, Massachusetts, and serves as CEO of Youk's charity, Hits for Kids.[57] The following month, Youkilis signed on as a member of Team USA for the March 2009 World Baseball Classic.[58] In January 2009, Youkilis signed a four-year $41 million contract with the Red Sox with an option for the year 2013.[59]

Ian Kinsler

An outstanding second basemen and leadoff hitter, Ian Kinsler, like Kevin Youkilis, played for only one team organization throughout his first six years as a professional and seemed likely to remain with that team for many more years.

Kinsler was born in Tucson, Arizona, on June 6, 1982. His father, Howard, was Jewish; his mother, Kelly, was not. Kinsler, however, always identified himself as Jewish.[60]

Ian's father, a Yankee fan from New York, taught him to root for the Mets growing up merely to create some controversy. "Everyone knows how New Yorkers are," Kinsler said of his father. "They need adversity at all times. When he moved to Arizona he didn't have any, so he decided to make some by making me a Mets fan. Try to figure that out."[61]

Kinsler's high school won two state titles in baseball while he was on the team. "We were a very dominant high school team and we all knew what we were capable of doing," said Kinsler. Some of his teammates included future major leaguers Scott Hairston, Brian Anderson, Chris and Shelly Duncan, and Ryan Schroyer.[62]

The Diamondbacks drafted Kinsler twice—first on June 5, 2000, in the nineteenth round of the amateur draft and again a year later in the twenty-sixth round of the 2001 amateur draft. Kinsler refused to sign either time because he felt unprepared for minor league ball and preferred college experience to help him become a more rounded player.[63]

The six-foot, 200-pound, right-handed-hitting Kinsler, originally a shortstop, first attended junior college and then Arizona State, known for its baseball team. Unfortunately, Kinsler sat on the bench in Arizona and then in his junior year, transferred to the University of Missouri, which he called "a perfect fit."[64] He was the best hitter for the Missouri Tigers in the 2002 Fall World Series, batting a resounding .619.[65]

The Texas Rangers drafted Kinsler in the seventeenth round of the 2003 amateur draft.[66] The Rangers selected Kinsler primarily for his glove, but he was also a very good hitter and base runner, described in a scouting report as possibly "one of the better prospects in the major leagues."[67]

Kinsler remained in the Rangers minor league system from late 2003 until 2006, moving from shortstop to second base in 2005 while with AAA Oklahoma in the Pacific Coast League. He also hit .274 there, drove in 94 runs, and powered 23 home runs.[68]

Texas called Kinsler to the major leagues early in 2006 to replace their regular second baseman, Alfonso Soriano, who had signed with the Chicago Cubs. Kinsler made his major league debut on April 3, 2006, even though he had been placed on the disabled list with a dislocated thumb.[69]

Despite his sore thumb, Kinsler played 120 games for the Rangers in 2006 and was named the team's Rookie of the Year. He was the first Texas rookie to get more than 100 hits (121), more than 10 home runs (14), and more than 10 stolen bases (11). He joined teammate Scott Feldman who had debuted with the Rangers a year earlier.[70]

Even with his outstanding abilities, Kinsler approached the game quietly and respectfully, concentrating when on the field. This demeanor won over the veterans on the squad, who accepted their young teammate and helped him learn from their experience.[71]

The 2006-2007 off-season was a busy time for Kinsler. He married Tess Brady in November 2006, and the two became involved in numerous charities in the North Texas area. They both served as Honorary Chairs for the Marine Corps' Toys for Tots program.[72] Kinsler also began a weight and agility program between seasons and worked on his fielding and speed all spring.

Nevertheless, in 2007, Kinsler was once again on the disabled list, this time for five weeks because of a stress fracture in his foot.[73] Despite his injury, he still became a 20–20 player, hitting 20 home runs and stealing 23 bases. His teammates praised him, including 2006 All-Star MVP Michael Young, his role model. "I love when people compare me to Michael Young," said Kinsler. "I know my career will not be the same as his, but as far as preparation and mental toughness, I want to emulate him and learn from him. He's like my big brother. Can't hope for any better type of mentor than that."[74]

Kinsler began sharing the leadoff duties with Frank Catalanotto during the second half

Ian Kinsler proved to be a positive surprise to the Texas Rangers when they picked him in the 17th round of the 2003 amateur draft. Chosen primarily for his glove, Kinsler did so well offensively his first three years in the majors, that at the end of the 2008 season, the Rangers extended his contract through 2012, with a team option for 2013 (courtesy Oklahoma City RedHawks, photograph: Kyle Nosal).

of the 2007 season. "I want to hit leadoff," said Kinsler. "I want to be the table setter. I'm normally an aggressive hitter, but you've got to be a little more patient when you hit lead-off." By 2008, Kinsler was the undisputed number one in the batting order.[75]

In 2008 Kinsler was selected for the American League All-Star team. His season totals included 102 runs scored, 165 hits, 41 doubles, 18 home runs, 71 runs batted in, and a .319 batting average.[76] On May 26, 2008, Ian Kinsler, according to Jewish Major Leaguers, Inc., hit the 2,500th home run by a Jewish player in the history of major league baseball.[77]

At the beginning of the 2008 season, the Texas Rangers had signed Kinsler to a five-year deal worth $22 million with an extra $10 million for the option year, 2013. With the option, the commitment was the largest the Rangers had made to a player that they drafted and developed.[78]

After the deal was finalized, Thad Levine, the Rangers assistant general manager, said, "Ian represents the past, present and future of this organization. It was important to us that he is the first of that next wave of young players to commit. We think he will have a huge impact on those young players."[79]

Ryan Braun

Ryan Braun was credited with being one of the prime reasons the Milwaukee Brewers began a dramatic improvement in 2007, the year he debuted.

Ryan Joseph Braun was born November 11, 1983, in Mission Hills, California, to Diane and Joe Braun, a non–Jewish mother and an Israeli father who had come to the United States when he was seven years old and did not practice his religion.[80] Ryan was raised in "no faith" and never observed any Jewish holidays, yet he considered himself "half–Jewish" and took much pride in his heritage. "There aren't too many Jewish athletes who have achieved success at the highest level, so it's something I'm very proud of," he often said.[81]

Ryan Braun had an interesting connection with the only two Jewish major leaguers enshrined at Cooperstown. Sandy Koufax's name was "Braun" before he took his stepfa-ther's name. "There's no (family) connection that I know of," said Ryan, "but it's kind of cool."[82] Also, as a child, Braun spent vacations with his maternal grandfather whose house was previously owned by Hank Greenberg, the idol of Jewish boys of earlier generations. Braun spoke often of having spent time in that house. "It's very cool, and ironic."[83]

Braun's parents encouraged Ryan and his younger brother Steve to take an interest in baseball. Their mother set up a hitting cage in the yard while their father pitched batting practice to the two boys. He pitched left-handed to Ryan to get him used to hitting south-paws. Ryan's parents firmly believe that it helped contribute to Braun's .450 average against left-handers as a rookie.[84]

In his senior year at Granada Hills High School, *Baseball America* named the six-foot, two-inch, 190-pound Braun the sixth-best shortstop in the country.[85] Yet, he received no draft offers out of high school. His mother recalled that one scout asked Ryan why his organ-ization ought to draft him. Ryan answered, "Because I'll make you look like a genius." There were still no takers.[86]

Braun did get a scholarship offer to attend Stanford, however, but he turned it down. Instead he attended the University of Miami, majoring in business and playing on Miami's baseball team. A designated hitter who occasionally played shortstop, Braun became the third Hurricane to win *Baseball America*'s Freshman of the Year Award. During his junior year, Braun divided his time between playing shortstop and third base, and in 2005 he was named College All-American.[87]

The Kansas City Royals drafted Braun in the sixth round of the 2003 amateur draft, but he did not sign. He did sign two years later with the Milwaukee Brewers who picked him in the first round of the 2005 amateur draft.[88]

Braun's outstanding hitting and speed on the base paths moved him up quickly through the Milwaukee minor league farm system, from Helena in the rookie Pioneer League to the Nashville Sounds in the AAA Pacific Coast League, where *Baseball America* dubbed him the Brewer organization's "best power hitter," and having the "best infield arm."[89] Braun was also considered one of the best Jewish minor league prospects in 2006 even though the Brewers had switched him from shortstop to third and he was having difficulty adjusting to this new position.[90]

During 2007 spring training, Braun competed for the third base job, but he began the season with the AAA Sounds to get more fielding experience. After he played 34 games for Nashville, during which he hit .342, with 10 home runs, the Brewers recalled him for his bat because the Brewers' third-base platoon, veteran infielders Craig Counsell and Tony Graffanino was not hitting.[91] Braun made his major league debut on May 25, 2007, in San Diego.[92]

Management, the press, and the fans were impressed with Braun's maturity and quiet self-assurance. Braun realized that he would have to make some adjustments, but "I know I'll get to where I want to be," he stated confidently.[93] As the regular third baseman, Braun still needed to work on his defense. His fielding percentage was only .895, the first time a regular major leaguer's fielding was under .900 since Butch Hobson's in 1978.[94]

While Braun may have been less than an asset in the field, he was spectacular with the bat. In his rookie season, despite missing the first seven weeks, Braun began to emerge as a top contender for Rookie of the Year honors. Near the end of July, his .387 on-base percentage led the team and his slugging percentage of .648 topped that of Prince Fielder, the National League's home run leader. Braun was third on the team with 14 home runs, 39 runs batted in, and a .337 batting average despite playing in only half as many games as the Brewers' leaders in those same categories.[95]

For his outstanding statistics, Ryan Braun won National League Player of the Month and Rookie of the Month awards for July, becoming the first player to win both awards in the same month since the rookie honor was first established in 2002. Braun had also taken home NL Rookie of the Month honors in June.[96] "He's just a special player," said Geoff Jenkins, Brewers left fielder. "He's got a world of ability and is obviously coming into his own." Braun's

Soon after becoming a major leaguer in 2007, third baseman-turned-outfielder Ryan Braun established himself as one of the game's top stars. He was the first Jewish player to be voted Rookie of the Year, and the first member of the Milwaukee Brewers to be voted an All-Star by the fans (Mike Strasinger/Nashville Sounds).

reaction to the accolades was, "It certainly is a great honor, something I'm proud of, but right now, I think the focus is on the team and trying to win games."[97]

One person not surprised by Braun's statistics was Jack Zduriencik, Brewers' scouting director, who said that Braun was doing exactly what the scouts thought he could do. "The big knock was that people questioned him defensively, whether he could play third in the long term," said Zduriencik." We all thought that he would, that he had too much athletic ability not to handle it. They also thought that he had a hitch in his swing. I don't hear anyone complaining now."[98]

In 2007 the Milwaukee Brewers and the Chicago Cubs headed toward the home stretch, vying for first place in the National League Central Division. This caused many people to question whether Ryan Braun would play on Yom Kippur or take a day off in the tradition of Hank Greenberg, Sandy Koufax, and Shawn Green. The fans did not have to wait long for their answer, as Braun announced that he would play during the Jewish Holy Day against the Atlanta Braves. "I don't really celebrate the (Jewish) holidays, so it won't be much of an issue with me, "said Braun. "Growing up half–Jewish, half–Catholic, I've never celebrated one holiday over the other."[99]

The Milwaukee Brewers finished in second place in the NL Central, two games behind the Cubs. Braun ended the season with a batting average of .324, 97 runs batted in, 34 home runs, and 15 steals in 21 attempts. He set the all-time major league rookie record with a slugging percentage of .634. His 34 home run total was fifth-highest for a Jewish major leaguer in one season."[100]

For his outstanding work in 2007, Ryan Braun received the Rookie of the Year Award in the National League from the Baseball Writers of America, edging out Colorado Rockies shortstop Troy Tulowitzki, 128–126, in the closest voting since the current system was adopted in 1980.[101] Braun was the first Jew to win that honor. Although not raised Jewish, when he accepted the award, he spoke of the pride he took in his Jewish heritage.[102]

In 2008 the Brewers acquired Michael Cameron to play centerfield and moved Braun to left, a less stressful position than third base. Braun accepted the challenge with his usual confidence, using his natural athletic ability to adjust to his new assignment.[103]

Braun was the first Brewers player elected by the fans as an All-Star starter. An outfielder in the 2008 All-Star game, he was the only Jewish player on the National League squad, although Ian Kinsler and Kevin Youkilis were on the American League team. Braun finished third in the annual home run derby held prior to the All-Star Game.[104]

Braun played in 151 games for the Brewers in 2008, and although his batting average dropped from .324 to .285, his homerun output increased from 34 to 37 and his RBIs also increased from 97 the previous year to 106.[105]

In May 2008, Braun signed the largest contract in Brewers' history—an eight-year deal running through 2015 for $45 million, including a $2.3 million bonus for 2008. After the deal was announced, Braun said, "For me, the opportunity to secure my future financially is something that really means a lot to me. I feel I was ready to make this commitment to the city of Milwaukee, to the fans and to the Brewers' organization. For them obviously to step up and give me this type of offer is unprecedented and it means a lot to me."[106]

With the Brewers' pitching staff decimated in 2009, the team counted on Braun's big bat for any chance to contend in the National League Central Division.

Epilogue

The Jewish community and professional baseball grew up together in America and continue to enjoy a close, mutually beneficial relationship. In fact, the story of Jews and baseball is a microcosm of the history of Jews in the United States.

From 1871, the generally accepted date for the beginning of major league baseball, through the first decade of the twentieth century, virtually all of the Jews in baseball were of German or Western European descent, reflecting the first major wave of Jewish immigration that began in 1848. These educated newcomers were relatively few in number and as they spread throughout the small towns and cities east of the Mississippi, they did not encounter organized anti–Semitism. They had come to America confident that if they became acculturated to American society, the non–Jews living here would accept them; they saw baseball as an excellent way to become part of the American mainstream.

Great changes came to the Jewish community and to the dynamics between Jews and the rest of the country when huge numbers of Eastern European or Russian Jews arrived in America between 1881 and 1914. These strangely dressed, more observant Jews lived in tightly-knit communities primarily on the East Coast and triggered more widespread and deep-seated feelings of anti–Semitism as they competed for jobs with American working-men.

The newly arrived Russian Jews were often fearful of becoming too much a part of American culture. They viewed baseball as a worthless distraction and tried to prevent their children from playing. But these children were huge baseball fans and loved the game because it was fun and allowed them show that they were "real Americans." Those who defied parental objections and became professional baseball players during the 1910s and 1920s, found more general anti–Semitism. Some even felt they had to change their names when they entered professional baseball.

By the 1930s, the Jewish community had changed again. American Jews were becoming more acculturated and many were moving to suburbs where children could play baseball on sandlots rather than on the streets. Still fascinated by the game, more Jews were playing professional baseball and more good Jewish players were beginning to reach the major leagues, including the first, and many say, the greatest, Jewish superstar, Hank Greenberg. His fierce pride in his heritage and his incredible physical skills demonstrated to the world that someone could be both a superior player and a committed Jew. Many of the Jewish players who came after him credited Greenberg with making it easier for them to achieve success in baseball.

Just as Greenberg was pivotal for Jews in baseball, World War II was pivotal for all Jews in America. Many Jewish Americans, including the majority of Jewish major leaguers, had proven their loyalty through their military service, usually fighting side by side with GIs of diverse ethnic and geographic backgrounds. The common war effort, and especially the establishment of the State of Israel in 1948, erased the divisions between the German Jew and the Russian Jew, creating the American Jew.

For these American Jews, the changes brought about by the War were, for the most part, positive. Jews were able to become upwardly mobile, attend colleges of their choice, and take advantage of a myriad of economic opportunities available to them. For some, professional baseball was one of these opportunities.

Not only did professional baseball accept the Jew into its ranks, but parents of aspiring Jewish players were more than willing to help their children reach their goals. Jews could still remain "the people of the book," (they graduated from prestigious colleges such as Stanford, Duke, Dartmouth, and Yale) but they could also professionally don the tools of ignorance or deliver an unhittable curve ball.

As proof of how thoroughly Jews were becoming assimilated into the American mainstream, many of the Jewish major leaguers after World War II were the children of mixed marriages—a Jewish father and a non–Jewish mother or vice versa. In turn, some Jewish players married out of their faith, but many still respected their Jewish traditions. The religiosity of the Jews who played in the majors ran the gamut from fairly observant to "Jew in name only."

Anti-Semitism certainly did not disappear after the War, but it was no longer publicly acceptable or "politically correct." Few Jewish players since World War II encountered any organized or "official" anti–Semitism although many, especially during the 1950s and 1960s, suffered various instances of verbal abuse.

Jews were so much accepted in baseball after 1948 that not one Jewish major leaguer found it necessary to change his name in order to play. In contrast, seven non–Jewish ballplayers converted to Judaism for various reasons.

Furthermore, the ethnicity and religion of players entering professional baseball was rarely, if at all, to be found anywhere in the media, much less in the sports pages or the broadcast booth. Today, even well-informed fans are often unaware of whether a player is Jewish.

During the second half of the twentieth century, Jews also played crucial roles in bringing about enormous changes in the relationship between players and owners. Marvin Miller taught the players that they had certain basic rights and how to organize themselves into what many have called the most powerful union in the country. On the management side, not only were more Jewish owners accepted and respected, but one of them, Bud Selig, was unanimously elected by his peers as baseball commissioner, nominally the most influential position in the game.

Experts calculate that the total number of Jewish major leaguers totaled approximately 160; roughly half played major league ball before 1948 and half entered the big leagues afterwards. These 160 represent less than one percent of the more than 16,000 major league players since 1871, although over the years, Jews made up between two and three percent of the U.S. population.

But the story of Jews and baseball is much more than the story of Jewish players. In addition to playing, owning teams, and leading the players union, Jews were executives, sports writers, radio and TV broadcasters, statisticians, umpires, coaches, and managers. Above all, Jews were devoted and knowledgeable baseball fans. From baseball, Jews gained acceptance into American culture, a means of making a living, and for most, the sheer joy of playing and following a game that challenged their physical skills and their mental acuity. In return, Jews gave to baseball not only their great love for the game, but also a number of good and a few great players, the World Series, innovative statistics, equal rights for players, and even the music for baseball's national anthem.

From all indications, this love affair between Jews and baseball—a passion that many historians feel is unique in how deeply Jews have identified with the game—will continue. Despite the lure of other sports, Jewish baseball fans will not only immerse themselves in every pitch, every statistic, and every play of the season and post-season, they will also follow the trade talks and the player signings, and eagerly look forward to the next time they can hear the first strains of "Take Me Out to the Ball Game" and the siren call of "Play Ball!"

Notes

Prologue

1. Oscar Theodore Barck, Jr., and Nelson Manfred Blake, *Since 1900: A History of the United States in Our Times* (New York: Macmillan, 1974), 553, 620.
2. *Ibid.*
3. Edward S. Shapiro, *A Time for Healing: American Jewry Since World War II* (Baltimore: Johns Hopkins University Press, 1992), 39.
4. *Ibid.*, 38–39.
5. Hasia R. Diner, *The Jews of the United States, 1654–2000* (Berkeley: University of California Press, 2004), 283–285.
6. Howard M. Sachar, *A History of the Jews in America* (New York: Macmillan, 1992) 755.
7. John Thorn, Phil Birnbaum, and Bill Deane, eds., *Total Baseball: The Ultimate Baseball Encyclopedia* (Wilmington, DE: Sports Media Publishing), 185, 187, 195.
8. Thorn, *et al.*, *Total Baseball*, 179.
9. Boxerman and Boxerman, *Ebbets to Veeck to Busch: Eight Owners Who Shaped Baseball* (Jefferson, NC: McFarland, 2003), 106.
10. Thorn, *et al.*, *Total Baseball*, 195.
11. *Ibid.*, 193.
12. Ron Kaplan, "Literary Hitters," 1, found at www.njewishnews.com; John Bowman and Joel Zoss, *Diamonds in the Rough: The Untold History of Baseball* (New York: Macmillan, 1989), 279; Walter L. Harrison, "Six-Pointed Diamond: Baseball and American Jews," *Journal of Popular Culture* 15 (September 1981): 117; Allen Guttmann, *From Ritual to Record: The Nature of Modern Sports* (New York: Columbia University Press, 1978) 105.
13. Kaplan, "Literary Hitters," 1.
14. Harrison, "Six-Pointed Diamond," 117.
15. Steven A. Riess, ed., *Sports and the American Jew* (Syracuse: Syracuse University Press, 1998), 250–251; Guttmann, *From Ritual to Record*, 104–105; Eric Solomon, "Jews, Baseball, and the American Novel," *Arete* 1 (Spring 1984): 53–54.
16. Kaplan, "Literary Hitters," 4.
17. Solomon, "Jews, Baseball, and the American Novel," 47–50; Riess, *Sports and the American Jew*, 251–252.
18. Undated article by Joshua Meckler in *Jewish News of Greater Phoenix*; Solomon, "Jews, Baseball, and the American Novel," 52.

Chapter 1

1. *Chicago Tribune*, May 11, 1948.
2. Marvin Rotblatt, telephone interview with authors, July 11, 2008.

3. Peter S. Horvitz and Joachim Horvitz, *The Big Book of Jewish Baseball* (New York: SPI Books, 2001), 155.
4. www.jewsinsports.org.
5. Rotblatt telephone interview.
6. Horvitz and Horvitz, *The Big Book of Jewish Baseball*, 155.
7. Gary Gillette and Pete Palmer, eds., *The ESPN Baseball Encyclopedia* (New York: Sterling, 2008), 1497.
8. *Chicago Tribune*, June 2, 1951.
9. *Ibid.*, April 1, 1949; Horvitz and Horvitz, *The Big Book of Jewish Baseball*, 155.
10. Gillette and Palmer, *The ESPN Baseball Encyclopedia*, 1497.
11. Rotblatt telephone interview.
12. *Ibid.*
13. Richard Lindberg, *Who's on Third? The Chicago White Sox Story* (South Bend, IN: Icarus Press, 1983), 73.
14. *Chicago Tribune*, July 31, 1951.
15. Gillette and Palmer, *The ESPN Encyclopedia of Baseball*, 1497.
16. *Chicago Tribune*, August 31, 1951.
17. Horvitz and Horvitz, *The Big Book of Jewish Baseball*, 155.
18. www.jewsinsports.org; Horvitz and Horvitz, *The Big Book of Jewish Baseball*, 155.
19. *Wall Street Journal*, June 3, 1980; www.carlwiki.org/Rotblatt.
20. Rotblatt telephone interview.
21. Joe Ginsberg, telephone interview with authors, July 16, 2008.
22. www.Sun-Herald.com, July 4, 2006.
23. Horvitz and Horvitz, *The Big Book of Jewish Baseball*, 69–70.
24. *Chicago Tribune*, September 14, 1948.
25. Bob Cairns, *Pen Men: Baseball's Greatest Bullpen Stories Told by the Men Who Brought the Game Relief* (New York: St. Martin's Press, 1992), 98.
26. *Chicago Tribune*, September 7, 1950; *New York Times*, September 2, 1950.
27. Gillette and Palmer, *The ESPN Baseball Encyclopedia*, 525.
28. www.major-league-baseball.suite101.com.
29. *New Jersey Jewish Standard*, April 12, 2007.
30. *Washington Post*, May 16, 1951.
31. Gillette and Palmer, *The ESPN Baseball Encyclopedia*, 525.
32. Ginsberg telephone interview.
33. Horvitz and Horvitz, *The Big Book of Jewish Baseball*, 70.
34. Encyclopedia of Baseball Catchers—Joe Ginsberg found at www.members.tripod.com.

35. *Washington Post*, December 8, 1952.
36. Ginsberg telephone interview.
37. *Washington Post*, June 16, 1953.
38. *Chicago Tribune*, June 1, 1954, *New York Times*, June 1, 1954.
39. www.jewsinsports.org.
40. Ginsberg telephone interview.
41. *Chicago Tribune*, August 18, 1956; *Washington Post*, August 18, 1956.
42. Cairns, *Pen Men*, 98.
43. Rotblatt telephone interview.
44. Cairns, *Pen Men*, 100–101.
45. *Washington Post*, June 12, 1960.
46. *Ibid.*, May 18, 1961.
47. Horvitz and Horvitz, *The Big Book of Jewish Baseball*, 70.
48. *New York Times*, October 14, 1961.
49. *Chicago Tribune*, January 31, 1962.
50. Horvitz and Horvitz, *The Big Book of Jewish Baseball*, 70.
51. Ginsberg telephone interview.
52. *Chicago Tribune*, April 17, 1962.
53. Thorn *et al.*, *Total Baseball*, 1237.
54. Horvitz and Horvitz, *The Big Book of Jewish Baseball*, 70.
55. Ginsberg telephone interview.
56. Horvitz and Horvitz, *The Big Book of Jewish Baseball*, 143.
57. Inductee details concerning Rogovin's induction into the National Jewish Sport Hall of Fame, www.jewishsports.org.
58. Ralph Berger, "Saul Rogovin," The Baseball Biography Project, www.bioproj.sabr.org, 1.
59. "My Heroes—Where Are They Now?" *Old Tyme Baseball News*, Fall 1989, 16.
60. Berger, "Saul Rogovin," 1.
61. *Ibid.*, 1702.
62. Horvitz and Horvitz, *The Big Book of Jewish Baseball*, 144.
63. Gillette and Palmer, *The ESPN Baseball Encyclopedia*, 1494.
64. Berger, "Saul Rogovin," 1.
65. *Washington Post*, August 4, 1950.
66. "My Heroes," 16.
67. *Chicago Tribune*, May 16, 1961; *New York Times*, May 16, 1951.
68. Horvitz and Horvitz, *The Big Book of Jewish Baseball*, 144; Gillette and Palmer, *The ESPN Baseball Encyclopedia*, 1494.
69. *New York Times*, October 27, 1951.
70. "My Heroes," 16; *New York Times*, July 29, 1953; *Chicago Tribune*, August 18, 1953; Horvitz and Horvitz, *The Big Book of Jewish Baseball*, 145.
71. Berger, "Saul Rogovin," 2; Rotblatt telephone interview.
72. Harold U. Ribalow and Meir Z. Ribalow, *Jewish Baseball Stars* (New York: Hippocrene Books, 1984), 119–120; *Chicago Tribune*, December 11, 1953; *New York Times*, December 11, 1953.
73. Berger, "Rogovin," 2.
74. *Sporting News*, February 9, 1955.
75. *New York Times*, April 10, 1955.
76. Berger, "Saul Rogovin," 2.
77. Gillette and Palmer, *The ESPN Baseball Encyclopedia*, 1494.
78. *Chicago Tribune*, July 17, 1955.
79. Berger, "Saul Rogovin," 2.
80. Horvitz and Horvitz, *The Big Book of Jewish Baseball*, 145.
81. Gillette and Palmer, *The ESPN Baseball Encyclopedia*, 1494.

82. *New York Times*, July 2, 1957.
83. Berger, "Saul Rogovin," 2.
84. *New York Times*, April 25, 1979.
85. Berger, "Saul Rogovin," 2.
86. *New York Daily News*, September 15, 1994.
87. "Jewish Sports Hall of Fame," www.jewishsports.org.
88. Donald Dewey and Nicholas Acocella, *The Biographical History of Baseball* (New York: Carroll & Graf, 1995), 3.
89. Peter Golenbock, *Bums: An Oral History of the Brooklyn Dodgers* (New York: G. P. Putnam's Sons, 1984), 263.
90. Charles Dexter, "Cal Finally Scores!" *Baseball Digest*, March 1954, 36.
91. Elli Wohlgelernter, "Interview: Calvin R. Abrams and May Abrams," *American Jewish History* 83 (March 1955): 112.
92. www.Jews in Sports.org; Horvitz and Horvitz, *The Big Book of Jewish Baseball*, 15.
93. *Ibid.*
94. Golenbock, *Bums*, 265.
95. Lawrence Baldassaro and Richard A. Johnson, eds. *The American Game: Baseball and Ethnicity* (Carbondale, Ill.: Southern Illinois Press, 2002), 127; Golenbock, *Bums*, 263.
96. Peter Levine, *Ellis Island to Ebbets Field: Sport and the American Jewish Experience* (New York: Oxford University Press, 1992), 124.
97. *Ibid.*, 125.
98. Carl E. Prince, *Brooklyn's Dodgers: The Bums, the Borough, and the Best of Baseball, 1947–1957* (New York: Oxford University Press, 1996), 125.
99. Horvitz and Horvitz, *The Big Book of Jewish Baseball*, 15.
100. Golenbock, *Bums*, 265; Wohlgelertner, "Interview: Calvin R. Abrams and May Abrams," 109.
101. Horvitz and Horvitz, *The Big Book of Jewish Baseball*, 15; www.jeogle.com.
102. Golenbock, *Bums*, 265.
103. Cal Abrams Baseball Stats by Baseball Almanac—www.baseball-almanac.com.
104. Harold Friend, "The Year Was 1950," found at www.major-league-baseball.suite101.com.
105. Prince, *Brooklyn's Dodgers*, 52.
106. Friend, "The Year Was 1950."
107. Larry Powell, "Cal Abrams Recalls Play That Ruined Flag Hopes of Dodgers in 1950," *Baseball Digest*, September 1992, 73–74.
108. *Ibid.*
109. Powell, "Cal Abrams Recalls Play That Ruined Flag Hopes of Dodgers in 1950," 74.
110. Golenbock, *Bums*, 256.
111. *New York World Telegram*, October 2, 1950.
112. *New York Times*, October 2, 1950.
113. *New York World Telegram*, October 2, 1950.
114. *Ibid.*
115. Golenbock, *Bums*, 254.
116. *Ibid.*, 258.
117. *Ibid.*, 259.
118. www.baseball-almanac.com; www.jewsinsports.org.
119. Wohlgelernter, "Interview Calvin R. Abram and May Abrams," 110.
120. Golenbock, *Bums*, 266.
121. *Ibid.*, 267.
122. Wohlgelernter, "Interview: Calvin R. Abrams and May Abrams," 114.
123. *New York Times*, undated issue found in Cal Abrams files, Baseball Hall of Fame, Cooperstown, New York.
124. Wohlgelernter, "Interview: Calvin R. Abrams and May Abrams," 119–122.
125. *Chicago Tribune*, June 9, 1952.
126. Roger Kahn, *The Era, 1947–1957: When the Yankees,*

the Giants, and the Dodgers Ruled the World (New York: Ticknor & Fields, 1993), 303.

127. *Washington Post*, August 27, 1952.

128. Gillette and Palmer, *The ESPN Baseball Encyclopedia*, 272.

129. Horvitz and Horvitz, *The Big Book of Jewish Baseball*, 16.

130. Dexter, "Cal Finally Scores," 37; Wohlgelernter, "Calvin R. Abrams and May Abrams," 110.

131. *New York Times*, October 15, 1952; *Washington Post*, October 15, 1952.

132. www.jewsinsports.org; Horvitz and Horvitz, *The Big Book of Jewish Baseball*, 16; www.jeogle.com.

133. *Chicago Tribune*, May 26, 1954; *Los Angeles Times*, May 26, 1954; *New York Times*, May 26, 1954.

134. Gillette and Palmer, *The ESPN Baseball Encyclopedia*, 272; www.jewogle.com.

135. *Chicago Tribune*, October 19, 1955.

136. *New York Times*, May 11, 1956; *Chicago Tribune*, May 11, 1956.

137. www.jewogle.com; www.jewsinsports.org.

138. www.thedeadballera.com; *New York Post*, February 27, 1997.

139. *Newark Star-Ledger*, February 27, 1997.

140. www.major-league-baseball.suite101.com; www.mlb.com; *Jewish Exponent* (Philadelphia, Pa.), April 26, 2007.

141. *Jewish Ledger* (W. Hartford, CT), January 26, 2006; *New Jersey Standard*, April 12, 2007.

142. Max Silberman, "Lou Limmer, One of Baseball's Nice Guys," found on www.philadelphiaathletics.org; www.jewsinsports.org.

143. *Sporting News*, May 31, 1950.

144. *Chicago Tribune*, September 2, 1950; *New York Times*, September 2, 1950.

145. Glenn Liebman, "Sometimes Even 'Experts' Misjudge Baseball Talent," *Baseball Magazine*, August, 1988, 55–56.

146. *Sporting News*, January 24, 1951.

147. *Washington Post*, January 26, 1951; "Lou Limmer," www.thebaseballcube.com.

148. www.major-league-baseball.suite101.com.

149. *Chicago Tribune*, March 24, 1952; *Los Angeles Times*, March 24, 1952; *Washington Post*, March 24, 1952.

150. *Sporting News*, April 2, 1952.

151. *Chicago Tribune*, April 9, 1954.

152. Thorn *et al.*, *Total Baseball*, 1391.

153. Gillette and Palmer, *The ESPN Baseball Encyclopedia*, 679.

154. Horvitz and Horvitz, *The Big Book of Jewish Baseball*, 107.

155. *New York Times*, April 1, 1955.

156. www.baseball-reference.com.

157. www.baseball-reference.com; *New Jersey Standard*, October 12, 2007; *News Transcript*, November 6, 2002.

158. *News Transcript*, November 6, 2002.

159. Horvitz and Horvitz, *The Big Book of Jewish Baseball*, 57; www.jewsin sports.org.

160. Horvitz and Horvitz, *The Big Book of Jewish Baseball*, 58.

161. *Washington Post*, March 26, 1950.

162. *New York Times*, September 13, 1951.

163. Gillette and Palmer, *The ESPN Baseball Encyclopedia*, 484; www.baseballdigestdaily.com; www.baseball-reference.com.

164. www.people.virginia.edu; *Chicago Tribune*, July 15, 1952.

165. Horvitz and Horvitz, *The Big Book of Jewish Baseball*, 58; jewsinsports.org.

166. *Los Angeles Times*, March 26, 1953, May 3, 1953; www.jewsinsports.org; www.baseball-reference.com.

167. Horvitz and Horvitz, *The Big Book of Jewish Baseball*, 76–77.

168. *Los Angeles Times*, November 22, 1951.

169. *Ibid.*, February 12, 1952.

170. Horvitz and Horvitz, *The Big Book of Jewish Baseball*, 77; www.baseball-almanac.com; www.jewsinsports.org.

171. *Los Angeles Times*, April 6, 1953; *Chicago Tribune*, April 6, 1953; *Washington Post*, April 6, 1953.

172. *New York Times*, April 6, 1953.

173. *Los Angeles Times*, April 7, 1953.

174. Horvitz and Horvitz, *The Big Book of Jewish Baseball*, 48; www.jewsinsports.org.

175. www.sportsillustrated.cnn.com; www.baseball-reference.com.

176. Horvitz and Horvitz, *The Big Book of Jewish Baseball*, 48.

177. *Ibid.*

178. www.jewsinsports.org.

179. *Ibid.*

180. Horvitz and Horvitz, *The Big Book of Jewish Baseball*, 176l; www.jewsinsports.org.

181. Unnamed article dated June 21, 1955, Al Silvera files, Baseball Hall of Fame, Cooperstown, New York.

182. *Los Angeles Times,* June 10, 1955, June 17, 1975.

183. Unnamed article dated June 21, 1955, Al Silvera files, Hall of Fame.

184. www.baseball-reference.com; www.baseball-almanac.com; jewsinsports.org.

185. Horvitz and Horvitz, *The Big Book of Jewish Baseball*, 176.

186. Unnamed article dated March 31, 1956, Al Silvera files, Hall of Fame.

187. Gillette and Palmer, *The ESPN Baseball Encyclopedia*, 914.

188. *New York Times*, May 16, 1956.

189. Unnamed article dated May 17, 1956, Al Silvera files, Hall of Fame.

190. www.jewsinsports.org.

191. *Ibid.*

192. www.sonofsamhorn.net.

193. *Ibid.*

194. www.baseball-reference.com.

195. Horvitz and Horvitz, *The Big Book of Jewish Baseball*, 142.

196. *Sporting News*, May 6, 1953.

197. Horvitz and Horvitz, *The Big Book of Jewish Baseball*, 142.

198. *Ibid.*

199. www.baseball-reference.com.

200. Horvitz and Horvitz, *The Big Book of Jewish Baseball*, 160.

201. *Sporting News*, July 7, 1954.

202. www.baseball-reference.com.

Chapter 2

1. www.usgennet.org.

2. Boxerman and Boxerman, *Jews and Baseball, Volume I: Entering the American Mainstream, 1871–1948* (Jefferson, NC: McFarland, 2007), 40, 44–45, 134.

3. Gillette and Palmer, *The ESPN Baseball Encyclopedia*, 1557.

4. Horvitz and Horvitz, *The Big Book of Jewish Baseball*, 163.

5. *Ibid.*; www.jewsinsports.org.

6. *Sporting News*, March 29, 1950.

7. www.thebaseballpage.com; Horvitz and Horvitz, *The Big Book of Jewish Baseball*, 163.

8. *Chicago Tribune*, May 14, 1951; *Los Angeles Times*, May 14, 1951.

9. www.thebaseballpage.com; www.baseball-almanac.com.

10. www.jewsinsports.org.

11. Undated note written by Duke Markell, Duke Markell files, Baseball Hall of Fame, Cooperstown, New York.

12. Horvitz and Horvitz, *The Big Book of Jewish Baseball*, 112; Markell minor league statistic sheet, Duke Markell files, Hall of Fame.

13. Markell Stats, Duke Markell files, Hall of Fame.

14. Horvitz and Horvitz, *The Big Book of Baseball*, 113.

15. *New York Times*, September 28, 1951; *Washington Post*, September 28, 1951.

16. Gillette and Palmer, *The ESPN Baseball Encyclopedia*, 1370.

17. *New York Herald Tribune*, December 28, 1953.

18. *New York Times*, March 31, 1952.

19. www.jewsinsports.org.

20. *Chicago Tribune*, August 7, 1953; *New York Times*, August 7, 1953.

21. Horvitz and Horvitz, *The Big Book of Jewish Baseball*, 113.

22. *New York Times*, April 30, 1955; *Washington Post*, April 30, 1955.

23. *Sporting News*, July 2, 1984.

24. Horvitz and Horvitz, *The Big Book of Jewish Baseball*, 128.

25. *Sporting News*, October 18, 1980.

26. David Pietrusza, Matthew Silverman, and Michael Gershman eds., *Baseball: The Biographical Encyclopedia* (Kingston, NY.: Sports Illustrated, 2002), 871.

27. *Ibid.*; Horvitz and Horvitz, *The Big Book of Jewish Baseball*, 129.

28. *Ibid.*

29. Tom Cuneff, "Max Patkin, the Goofball Laureate of Baseball, Scores in *Bull Durham* and—Holy Cow—It's a Grand Ham," *People Weekly*, July 11, 1988, 61–62.

30. Horvitz and Horvitz, *The Big Book of Jewish Baseball*, 129.

31. Max Patkin and Stan Hochman, *The Clown Prince of Baseball* (Waco, TX: WRS Publishing, 1994), 133.

32. Horvitz and Horvitz, *The Big Book of Jewish Baseball*, 129; www.baseball-reference-com; *Los Angeles Times*, August 8, 1973.

33. *Sporting News*, January 20, 1997.

34. *Los Angeles Times*, August 8, 1973.

35. *New York Times*, November 1, 1999; *Sporting News*, January 20, 1997.

36. *Washington Post*, September 1, 1946.

37. Horvitz and Horvitz, *The Big Book of Jewish Baseball*, 130.

38. Bill Veeck, "Baseball and Me: I Believe in Fireworks," *Sport*, April 1950, 30–31.

39. *Sporting News*, May 21, 1947; Fred Lieb, *Comedians and Pranksters of Baseball* (St Louis: Charles C. Spink & Son, 1958), 38.

40. *Sporting News*, March 2, 1949.

41. *Ibid.*, January 21, 1948.

42. www.baseball-reference.com.

43. *Sporting News*, February 15, 1950.

44. Lieb, *Comedians and Pranksters of Baseball*, 38.

45. *Ibid.*

46. Ed Mickelson, telephone interview with authors, July 11, 2008.

47. *Sporting News*, June 29, 1954.

48. *Ibid.*, June 17, 1967.

49. *Ibid.*, July 1, 1967.

50. *Ibid.*, May 22, 1971.

51. *Ibid.*, April 21, 1973.

52. *Ibid.*, October 18, 1980.

53. *Ibid.*, November 23, 1987; Horvitz and Horvitz, *The Big Book of Jewish Baseball*, 130.

54. Horvitz and Horvitz, *The Big Book of Jewish Baseball*, 130.

55. www.espn.com.

56. www.deadballera.com

57. *Sporting News*, July 13, 1960.

58. *Ibid.*, October 19, 1955.

59. *New York Times*, May 15, 1974.

60. *Sporting News*, October 19, 1955.

61. *New York Times*, May 15, 1974.

62. Boxerman and Boxerman, *Ebbets to Veeck to Busch*, 133–134; Ronald J. Oakley, *Baseball's Last Golden Age, 1948–1960: The National Pastime in a Time of Glory* (Jefferson, NC: McFarland, 1994), 92.

63. *New York Times*, May 15, 1974.

64. *Sporting News*, October 19, 1955.

65. *Ibid.*, October 20, 1962.

66. *Ibid.*, October 19, 1955.

67. *Ibid.*, January 21, 1972; May 15, 1974.

68. An excerpt from "Veeck as in Wreck," found at www.press.uchicago.edu.

69. *Ibid.*, July 18, 1988.

70. *Sporting News*, February 24, 1954, August 19, 1954.

71. *Ibid.*, October 19, 1955.

72. *New York Times*, May 1, 1960.

73. *Sporting News*, October 20, 1962.

74. *Chicago Tribune*, January 21, 1972; www.baseball-almanac.com; *New York Times*, January 30, 1972.

75. Bill Madden and Moss Klein, *Damned Yankees: A No-Holds Barred Account of Life with "Boss" Steinbrenner* (New York: Warner Books, 1990), 227; *Sporting News*, September 14, 1974; *Chicago Tribune*, September 1, 1974; *Washington Post*, September 1, 1974.

76. *Sporting News*, December 26, 1981.

77. *Ibid.*, July 11, 1988.

78. *Ibid.*, April 17, 1989.

Chapter 3

1. Baldassaro and Johnson, *The American Game*, 130.

2. Al Rosen, telephone interview with authors, January 14, 2005.

3. Ralph Berger, "Al Rosen," The Baseball Biography Project," www.bioproj.sabr.com, 1.

4. www.jewsinsports.org.

5. Levine, *Ellis Island to Ebbets Field*, 128.

6. Horvitz and Horvitz, *The Big Book of Jewish Baseball*, 145.

7. Berger, "Al Rosen," 2.

8. *Ibid.*, 146.

9. Harry T. Paxton, "That Clouting Kid from Cleveland," *Saturday Evening Post*, August 11, 1951, 26.

10. David Spaner, "From Greenberg to Green, Jewish Ballplayers," in Thorn *et al.*, *Total Baseball*, 175; Rosen telephone interview.

11. Horvitz and Horvitz, *The Big Book of Jewish Baseball*, 175.

12. Rosen telephone interview.

13. Ribalow and Ribalow, *Jewish Baseball Stars*, 130–131; Berger, "Al Rosen," 2; Cynthia J. Wilber, *For the Love of the Game* (New York: William Morrow, 1992), 99.

14. *Ibid.*, 100.

15. Arthur Daley, "Rosen Rises to 'Most' Past," *Baseball Digest*, September 1959, 30.

16. *Sporting News*, September 10, 1947; www.baseball-almanac.com.

17. *Sporting News*, October 22, 1947.

18. Jack Torry, *Endless Summers: The Fall and Rise of the Cleveland Indians* (South Bend, IN: Diamond Communications, 1995), 3–4.

19. Wilber, *For the Love of the Game*, 100; Gillette and Palmer, *The ESPN Baseball Encyclopedia*, 875.

20. *Sporting News*, October 1, 1947.

21. *Chicago Tribune*, April 15, 1948; *Sporting News*, April 28, 1948.

22. *Sporting News*, August 18, 1948.

23. *Ibid.*, September 1, 1948.

24. Horvitz and Horvitz, *The Big Book of Jewish Baseball*, 146; Thorn *et al.*, *Total Baseball*, 378; *Chicago Tribune*, September 4, 1948; Berger, "Al Rosen," 2.

25. Wilber, *For the Love of the Game*, 100–101.

26. Horvitz and Horvitz, *The Big Book of Jewish Baseball*, 146.

27. *Sporting News*, March 16, 1949.

28. Gillette and Palmer, *The ESPN Baseball Encyclopedia*, 638.

29. William Marshall, *Baseball's Pivotal Era: 1945–1951* (Lexington: University Press of Kentucky, 1999), 264.

30. *Sporting News*, March 1, 1950.

31. Rosen telephone interview.

32. *Ibid.*

33. Torry, *Endless Summers*, 4–5.

34. Spaner, "From Greenberg to Green," 175; Levine, *Ellis Island to Ebbets Field*, 128.

35. Roger Kahn, *The Passionate People: What It Means to be a Jew in America* (New York: William Morrow, 1968), 108–109.

36. Rosen telephone interview.

37. Levine, *Ellis Island to Ebbets Field*, 140.

38. Torry, *Endless Summers*, 5.

39. Don Cuddy, "Big Chief Rosen," *Sport*, April 1954, 82.

40. www.mlb.com.

41. Wilber, *For the Love of the Game*, 101–102.

42. "Rebuilt Indians," *Newsweek*, August 14, 1950, 74–75.

43. Pietrusza *et al.*, *Baseball: The Biographical Encyclopedia*, 971.

44. Horvitz and Horvitz, *The Big Book of Jewish Baseball*, 146; Dewey and Acocella, *The Biographical History of Baseball*, 400; Berger, "Al Rosen," 2; Gillette and Palmer, *The ESPN Baseball Encyclopedia*, 875.

45. Roger Kahn, *October Men: Reggie Jackson, George Steinbrenner, Billy Martin and the Yankees Miraculous Finish in 1978* (New York: Harcourt, 2003), 174.

46. *Sporting News*, July 12, 1950.

47. *Ibid.*

48. *Ibid.*, March 21, 1951.

49. Horvitz and Horvitz, *The Big Book of Jewish Baseball*, 146.

50. Ribalow and Ribalow, *Jewish Baseball Stars*, 132.

51. Pietrusza *et al.*, *Baseball: The Biographical Encyclopedia*, 971.

52. Ribalow and Ribalow, *Jewish Baseball Stars*, 134–135.

53. *Ibid.*,126; Levine, *Ellis Island to Ebbets Field*, 128.

54. *Washington Post*, February 5, 1952.

55. Ribablow and Ribalow, *Jewish Baseball Stars*, 125.

56. Gillette and Palmer, *The ESPN Baseball Encyclopedia*, 875; Berger, "Al Rosen," 3.

57. *Sporting News*, July 9, 1952.

58. Don Cuddy, "Big Chief Rosen," 85.

59. Charles C. Alexander, *Our Game: An American Baseball History* (New York: Henry Holt, 1991), 225.

60. Pietrusza *et al.*, *Baseball: The Biographical Encyclopedia*, 971; Gillette and Palmer, *The ESPN Baseball Encyclopedia*, 875.

61. www.jewsinsport.org; *Sporting News*, October 7, 1953.

62. Pietrusza *et al.*, *Baseball: The Biographical Encyclopedia*, 971; Berger, "Al Rosen," 3.

63. *Washington Post*, May 2, 1954.

64. Horvitz and Horvitz, *The Big Book of Jewish Baseball*, 146.

65. Berger, "Al Rosen," 3; Ribalow and Ribalow, *Jewish Baseball Stars*, 128; *Los Angeles Times*, November 28, 1953.

66. Ribalow and Ribalow, *Jewish Baseball Stars*, 124; *Sporting News*, September 23, 1953; Robert Slater, *Great Jews in Sports* (Middle Village, NY: Jonathan David, 2000), 221.

67. *Sporting News*, September 2, 1953.

68. Hal Lebovitz, "How Rosen Rocks Em." *Colliers*, May 28, 1954, 72–73.

69. Gordon Cobbledick, "They'll Follow Rosen Now," *Baseball Digest*, March 1954, 29.

70. *Sporting News*, May 5, 1954.

71. *Ibid.*, May 12, 1954.

72. "Top of the League, *Time*, July 5, 1954, 38; *Sporting News*, July 7, 1954.

73. Gillette and Palmer, *The ESPN Baseball Encyclopedia*, 875.

74. Al Rosen, "The Game I'll Never Forget," *Baseball Digest*, July 1984, 47–48.

75. Ribalow and Ribalow, *Jewish Baseball Stars*, 133.

76. www.jewsinsports.

77. Torry, *Endless Summers*, 2.

78. Pietrusza *et al.*, *Baseball: The Biographical Encyclopedia*, 971.

79. www.jewsinsports.org.

80. Torry, *Endless Summers*, 2.

81. *Washington Post*, March 29, 1955.

82. Berger, "Al Rosen," 3; Gillette and Palmer, *The ESPN Baseball Encyclopedia*, 875.

83. *Sporting News*, September 28, 1955.

84. Dewey and Acocella, *The Biographical History of Baseball*, 401.

85. *Sporting News*, January 25, 1956.

86. Torry, *Endless Summers*, 29–30.

87. *Chicago Defender*, March 12, 1956.

88. *Sporting News*, April 11, 1956.

89. Ribalow and Ribalow, *Jewish Baseball Stars*, 133–134.

90. *Sporting News*, May 30, 1956.

91. *Los Angeles Times*, September 18, 1956; *Washington Post*, September 18, 1956.

92. *Sporting News*, September 16, 1956.

93. Gillette and Palmer, *The ESPN Baseball Encyclopedia*, 875.

94. *Sporting News*, December 19, 1956.

95. Torry, *Endless Summers*, 30–31.

96. *Los Angeles Times*, February 13, 1957.

97. Torry, *Endless Summers*, 31.

98. Gillette and Palmer, *The ESPN Baseball Encyclopedia*, 875; Berger, "Al Rosen," 3.

99. *Chicago Defender*, September 18, 1963.

100. Kahn, *October Men*, 175.

101. *New York Times*, March 28, 1978; *Sporting News*, April 15, 1978.

102. Kahn, *October Men*, 213.

103. Jack Sands and Peter Gammons, *Coming Apart at the Seams: How Baseball Owners, Players, and Television Executives Have Led Our National Pastime to the Brink of Disaster* (New York: Macmillan, 1993), 7.

104. Pietrusza *et al.*, *Baseball: The Biographical Encyclopedia*, 971.

105. *Sporting News*, August 4, 1979; Kahn, *October Men*, 255.

106. Madden and Klein, *Damned Yankees*, 37; *Washington Post*, July 20, 1979; *New York Times*, July 20, 1979.

107. Berger, "Al Rosen," 4.

108. Pietrusza *et al.*, *Baseball: The Biographical Encyclopedia*, 971.

109. *New York Times*, October 7, 1980.

110. *Sporting News*, November 8, 1980; Pietrusza *et al.*, *Baseball: The Biographical Encyclopedia*, 971; Berger, "Al Rosen," 4.

111. Bowie Kuhn, *Hardball: The Education of a Baseball Commissioner* (New York: Times Books, 1987), 237.

112. Berger, "Al Rosen," 4.

113. *Sporting News*, November 22, 1980.

114. *New York Times*, January 13, 1981.

115. *Sporting News*, February 21, 1981.

116. *Ibid.*, October 24, 1981.

117. Pietrusza *et al.*, *Baseball: The Biographical Encyclopedia*, 971; Berger, "Al Rosen," 5.

118. *Chicago Tribune*, September 14, 1985; *Los Angeles Times*, September 14, 1985.

119. *Los Angeles Times*, September 19, 1985.

120. *Sporting News*, October 7, 1985.

121. *Ibid.*, October 5, 1987.

122. *Washington Post*, November 19, 1987; *Sporting News*, December 14, 1987; Berger, "Al Rosen," 5.

123. www.mlb.com; www.classzone.com.

124. *New York Times*, November 21,1992.

125. www.jewishsports.org; www.jewsinsports.org; Slater, *Great Jews in Sports*, 222

126. Major League Baseball News at www.mlb.com.

127. Wilber, *For the Love of the Game*, 107.

128. *New York Times*, February 3, 1980; *Los Angeles Times*, July 27, 1980; www.jewsinsports.org.

129. Kahn, *The Passionate People*, 111.

Chapter 4

1. *Jewish News Weekly*, January 6, 2006, found at www.jewishf.com.

2. Ed Mayer, interview with authors, August 13, 2007.

3. *Jewish News Weekly*, January 6, 2006.

4. Joe Sargent, "Ed Mayer," www.bioproj.sabr.org, 1.

5. *Ibid.*

6. *Jewish News Weekly*, January 6, 2006.

7. Sargent, "Ed Mayer," 2; Mayer interview.

8. Horvitz and Horvitz, *The Big Book of Jewish Baseball*, 113; www.baseball-almanac.com.

9. Horvitz and Horvitz, *The Big Book of Jewish Baseball*, 114.

10. Sargent, "Ed Mayer," 2.

11. Horvitz and Horvitz, *The Big Book of Jewish Baseball*, 114.

12. *New York Times*, September 11, 1957.

13. Horvitz and Horvitz, *The Big Book of Jewish Baseball*, 114; Gillette and Palmer, *The ESPN Encyclopedia of Baseball*, 1378.

14. *New York Times*, January 11, 1958.

15. *Chicago Tribune*, March 31, 1958.

16. Sargent, "Ed Mayer," 3.

17. *Ibid.*

18. Mayer interview.

19. Sargent, "Ed Mayer," 4; *Jewish News Weekly*, January 6, 2006.

20. Gillette and Palmer, *The ESPN Baseball Encyclopedia*, 1378.

21. *Jewish News Weekly*, January 6, 2006.

22. Mayer interview.

23. *Ibid.*

24. www.jewsinsports.org; www.thebaseballpage.com; Gillette and Palmer, *The ESPN Baseball Encyclopedia*, 961.

25. Horvitz and Horvitz, *The Big Book of Jewish Baseball*, 184.

26. *Ibid.*

27. *New York Times*, January 19, 1958.

28. *Ibid.*, February 26, 1958.

29. *Ibid.*

30. *Chicago Tribune*, June 22, 1958.

31. *Sporting News*, September 17, 1958.

32. *Ibid.*, April 19, 1961.

33. www.thebaseballpage.com.

34. *New York Times*, October 11, 1961.

35. *Ibid.*, May 10, 1962.

36. *Ibid.*, July 31, 1962; *Washington Post*, July 31, 1962, *Los Angles Times*, August 18, 1962.

37. www.jewsinsports.org.

38. *Ibid.*

39. *Chicago Tribune*, April 19, 1960; *Los Angeles Times*, December 24, 1960.

40. Barry Latman, telephone interview with authors, August 31, 2008.

41. Horvitz and Horvitz, *The Big Book of Jewish Baseball*, 101.

42. Latman interview.

43. *Ibid.*

44. Barry Latman, "Ty Cobb's Letters to Barry Latman," *Sport*, February 1962, 18.

45. *Ibid.*, 69.

46. *Ibid.*, 21; *Los Angeles Times*, March 28, 1962.

47. Horvitz and Horvitz, *The Big Book of Jewish Baseball*, 101.

48. *Ibid.*; Dave Condon, *The Go-Go Chicago White Sox* (New York: Coward-McCann, 1960), 127.

49. *Los Angeles Times*, January 30, 1956.

50. *Chicago Defender*, September 5, 1957; *Los Angeles Times*, September 5, 1957; www.baseball-almanac.com.

51. *Sporting News*, March 7, 1964.

52. www.baseball-almanac.com.

53. *New York Times*, March 31, 1958.

54. *Chicago Defender*, April 21, 1958.

55. Latman interview.

56. *Chicago Tribune*, July 28, 1958; *Washington Post*, July 28, 1958.

57. www.jewsinsports.org.

58. Gillette and Palmer, *The ESPN Baseball Encyclopedia*, 1340.

59. Horvitz and Horvitz, *The Big Book of Jewish Baseball*, 102.

60. *Chicago Tribune*, April 19, 1960; *Sporting News*, April 27, 1960.

61. Gillette and Palmer, *The ESPN Baseball Encyclopedia*, 1340; www.baseball-almanac.com.

62. *Sporting News*, September 14, 1960.

63. *Ibid.*, October 12, 1960.

64. *Washington Post*, July 21, 1961.

65. *Ibid.*

66. Horvitz and Horvitz, *The Big Book of Jewish Baseball*, 102.

67. *Sporting News*, September 1, 1962.

68. *Ibid.*, April 6, 1963.

69. *Chicago Tribune*, December 3, 1963.

70. *Los Angeles Times*, December 3, 1963.

71. *Ibid.*, December 24, 1963.

72. *Sporting News*, January 11, 1964.

73. *Chicago Tribune*, July 1, 1965; *Los Angeles Times*, July 1, 1965; Horvitz and Horvitz, *The Big Book of Jewish Baseball*, 1340; Gillette and Palmer, *The ESPN Baseball Encyclopedia*, 1341.

74. *Chicago Tribune*, December 16, 1965.

75. *Ibid.*, August 16, 1967.

76. www.jewsinsports.org

77. Latman interview.

78. www.findarticles.com

79. John B. Old, "He Almost Quit Baseball Four Years Ago," *Baseball Digest*, Dec 1959-Jan 1960, 12.

80. Cairns, *Pen Men*, 200

81. Milton Gross, "The Dodgers' Precocious Pitcher," *Saturday Evening Post*, March 12, 1960, 100.

82. *Ibid.*

83. *Ibid.*

84. Herbert Simons, "The Sherry Flip," *Baseball Digest*, Dec 1959-Jan 1960, 10.

85. Old, "He Almost Quit Four Years Ago," 11.

86. Horvitz and Horvitz, *The Big Book of Jewish Baseball*, 172.

87. *Los Angeles Times*, May 14, 1958; www.baseball-refer ence.com.

88. Pietrusza *et al.*, *Baseball: The Biographical Encyclopedia*, 1031; Cairns, *Pen Men*, 201.

89. Cairns, *Pen Men*, 207; Pietrusza *et al.*, *Baseball: The Biographical Encyclopedia*, 1031; Roy Terrell, "No Relief for Sherry," *Sports Illustrated*, March 28, 1960, 63.

90. Gross, "The Dodgers' Precocious Pitcher," 99.

91. *New York Times*, April 3,1959.

92. *Los Angeles Times*, July 4, 1959; Cairns, *Pen Men*, 201.

93. www.findarticles.com.

94. Cairns, *Pen Men*, 201–202.

95. David Quentin Voigt, *American Baseball: From Postwar Expansion to the Electronic Age* (University Park, PA: Pennsylvania State University Press, 1983), 40.

96. Cairns, *Pen Men*, 109, 203.

97. Ribalow and Ribalow, *Jewish Baseball Stars*, 173, 175–176.

98. Cairns, *Pen Men*, 203–204; Horvitz and Horvitz, *The Big Book of Jewish Baseball*, 172; Ribalow and Ribalow, *Jewish Baseball Stars*, 176–178; "Fun for the Fireman," *Time*, October 19, 1959, 87; Thorn *et al.*, *Total Baseball*, 389.

99. *Los Angeles Times*, October 9, 1959.

100. *Washington Post*, October 9, 1959.

101. *Los Angeles Times*, February 11, 1960.

102. David Anderson, "The Dangers of Being a World Series Hero," *Saturday Evening Post*, November 1965, 94; *Sporting News*, November 18, 1959.

103. Anderson, "The Dangers of Being a World Series Hero," 94.

104. Horvitz and Horvitz, *The Big Book of Jewish Baseball*, 172; Cairns, *Pen Men*, 204–205.

105. *Chicago Tribune*, June 6, 1960.

106. www.baseball-almanac.com; Dan Schlossberg, "How Rookie Pitcher Rallied '59 Dodgers," *Baseball Digest*, November 1993, 42.

107. Horvitz and Horvitz, *The Big Book of Jewish Baseball*, 173; Ralph Berger, "Larry Sherry," www.bioproj.sabr.org., 2.

108. *New York Times*, April 10, 1964; *Washington Post*, April 10, 1964.

109. Pete Waldmeier, "What Vintage the Sherry?" *Baseball Digest*, July 1966, 56; *Washington Post*, August 4, 1964.

110. www.baseball-almanac.com.

111. *Sporting News*, July 15, 1967.

112. *Chicago Tribune*, March 27, 1968, July 13, 1948; *Los Angeles Times*, July 3, 1968.

113. Gillette and Palmer, *The ESPN Baseball Encyclopedia*,1524.

114. *Sporting News*, March 26, 1969.

115. *Ibid.*, May 16, 1970, May 29, 1971, July 31, 1971, June 10, 1972; *Washington Post*, July 6, 1971; *Chicago Tribune*, October 8, 1971.

116. *Washington Post*, December 2, 1976; *Los Angeles Times*, October 30, 1978, January 15, 1981; *Sporting News*, November 25, 1978, October 29, 1984.

117. Spaner, "From Greenberg to Green: Jewish Ballplayers," 175.

118. Berger, "Larry Sherry," 3.

119. www.findarticles.com.

120. *Los Angeles Times*, September 8, 1976; Wilbur, *For the Love of the Game*, 170.

121. Wilbur, *For the Love of the Game*, 170.

122. *Los Angeles Times*, June 16, 1960.

123. *Ibid.*, March 7, 1958.

124. Jane Leavy, *Sandy Koufax: A Lefty's Legacy* (New York: HarperCollins, 2002), 103.

125. *Los Angeles Times*, June 6, 1960.

126. Wilbur, *For the Love of the Game*, 170.

127. Horvitz and Horvitz, *The Big Book of Jewish Baseball*, 174; *Los Angeles Times*, June 16, 1960.

128. Wilbur, *For the Love of the Game*, 172.

129. *New York Times*, April 1, 1958.

130. Horvitz and Horvitz, *The Big Book of Jewish Baseball*, 174.

131. *Chicago Tribune*, October 15, 1958.

132. *Los Angeles Times*, February 16, 1959.

133. *Ibid.*, April 10, 1962.

134. *Ibid.*, May 8, 1960.

135. Wilbur, *For the Love of the Game*, 172.

136. *Los Angeles Times*, June 16, 1960; July 31, 1960.

137. *Ibid.*, May 8, 1960; Wilbur, *For the Love of the Game*, 173.

138. *Sporting News*, August 31, 1960; *Los Angeles Times*, August 24, 1960; *New York Times*, August 24, 1960.

139. *Sporting News*, February 14, 1962.

140. *Washington Post*, July 13, 1961.

141. Edward Gruver, *Koufax* (Dallas: Taylor, 2000), 125–126.

142. Spaner, "From Greenberg to Green: Jewish Ballplayers," 175.

143. *Sporting News*, February 14, 1962.

144. *Ibid.*

145. Horvitz and Horvitz, *The Big Book of Jewish Baseball*, 174.

146. *New York Times*, October 14, 1962; *Washington Post*, October 14, 1962.

147. Horvitz and Horvitz, *The Big Book of Jewish Baseball*, 174; www.jewsinsports.org.

148. *Los Angeles Times*, October 17, 1963, September 8, 1976.

149. Wilber, *For the Love of the Game*, 173.

150. *Sporting News*, March 2, 1974.

151. *Ibid.*, November 8, 1975.

152. *Los Angeles Times*, July 24, 1976.

153. *Sporting News*, August 7, 1976.

154. *Ibid.*, August 14, 1976.

155. Spaner, "From Greenberg to Green: Jewish Ballplayers," 175.

156. Gillette and Palmer, *The ESPN Baseball Encyclopedia*, 1704.

157. *Los Angeles Times*, September 25, 1976.

158. *Ibid.*, October 5, 1976.

159. *Sporting News*, May 28, 1977.

160. *Los Angeles Times*, July 11, 1977.

161. *New York Times*, July 12, 1977.

162. *Sporting News*, July 30, 1977.

163. *Los Angeles Times*, October 13, 1977.

164. *Ibid.*, March 22, 1978.

165. *Ibid.*, November 26, 1981; *Sporting News*, February 6, 1982.

166. *Sporting News*, October 29, 1984.

167. *New York Times*, December 6, 2006.

168. Dick Williams and Bill Plaschke, *No More Mr. Nice Guy: A Life of Hardball* (New York: Harcourt Brace Jovanovich, 1990), 275.

169. *Los Angeles Times*. October 6, 1985; Wilbur, *For the Love of the Game*, 174.

170. *Sporting News*, October 28, 1991.

Chapter 5

1. Barck and Blake, *Since 1900*, 631–632.
2. Arthur Hertzberg, *Jews in America: Four Centuries of an Uneasy Encounter* (New York: Simon & Schuster, 1989), 347–348.
3. *Ibid.*, 348.
4. Sachar, *A History of Jews in America*, 802–804.
5. Alexander, *Our Game*, 244–245.
6. Thorn *et al.*, *Total Baseball*, 199.
7. Alexander, *Our Game*, 249–256.
8. Gillette and Palmer, *The ESPN Baseball Encyclopedia*, 1330.
9. Gruver, *Koufax*, 64.
10. Al Silverman, *Heroes of the World Series* (New York: G. P. Putnam's Sons, 1964), 231; Gruver, *Koufax*, 65.
11. Golenbock, *Bums*, 383–385; Gruver, *Koufax*, 55.
12. Gruver, *Koufax*, 66; "Sandy Koufax—Baseball's Enigmatic Participant, found at wwwpasacard.com, 2.
13. Gruver, *Koufax*, 66–67.
14. *Ibid.*,68.
15. *Ibid.*,69.
16. Silverman, *Heroes of the World Series*, 231.
17. "Sandy Koufax at All Experts," www.en.allexperts.com.
18. Pietrusza *et al.*, *Baseball: The Biographical Encyclopedia*, 621.
19. Silverman, *Heroes of the World Series*, 231,
20. Gruver, *Koufax*, 71.
21. "Sandy Koufax at All Experts," 2; Leavy, *Sandy Koufax*, 54.
22. Alexander Peters, "Heroes of the Major Leagues," (New York: Random House, 1947), 44–45; Pietrusza *et al.*, *Baseball: Biographical Encyclopedia*, 621.
23. Melvin Durslag, "Sandy Koufax the Strikeout King," *Saturday Evening Post*, July 14, 1962, 70.
24. "Sandy Koufax at All Experts," 2.
25. Leavy, *Sandy Koufax*, 65.
26. Horvitz and Horvitz, *The Big Book of Jewish Baseball*, 97.
27. Peters, *Heroes of the Major Leagues*. 46.
28. Jack Olsen, "The Very Best Act in Town," *Sports Illustrated*, July 29, 1963, 22.
29. Pietrusza *et al.*, *Baseball: The Biographical Encyclopedia*, 621.
30. *Ibid.*; www.baseballlibrary.com.
31. Palmer and Gillette, *The ESPN Baseball Encyclopedia*, 1330.
32. Peters, *Heroes of the Major Leagues*, 46.
33. Ed Linn, "Koufax Remembered," *Sport*, February 1972, 42; Baldassaro and Johnson, *The American Game*, 131.
34. www.jewz.com.
35. Leavy, *Sandy Koufax*, 72.
36. *Ibid.*, 73.
37. Brent Kelley, *Baseball's Biggest Blunder: The Bonus Rule of 1953-1957* (Lanham, MD: Scarecrow Press, 1997), 111; www.pubquizhelp.com.
38. Palmer and Gillette, *The ESPN Baseball Encyclopedia*, 1330.
39. Pietrusza *et al.*, *Baseball: The Biographical Encyclopedia*, 621.
40. Palmer and Gillette, *The ESPN Baseball Encyclopedia*, 108.
41. Kelley, *Baseball's Biggest Blunder*, 111–112.
42. *Washington Post*, September 1, 1959.
43. Silverman, *Heroes of the World Series*, 232; Peters, *Heroes of the Major Leagues*, 48–49; "Sandy Koufax for All Experts, 3–4.
44. Gruver, *Koufax*, 124.
45. Olsen, "The Very Best Act in Town," 22.

46. *Ibid.*
47. "Sandy Koufax at AllExperts, 4; Slater, *Great Jews in Sports*, 165.
48. Olsen, "The Very Best Act in Town," 22.
49. Pietrusza *et al.*, *Baseball: The Biographical Encyclopedia*, 621.
50. Palmer and Gillette, *The ESPN Baseball Encyclopedia*, 1330.
51. Mordecai Richler, "Koufax the Incomparable," *Commentary*, November 1966, 89.
52. Gruver, *Koufax*, 125.
53. Leavy, *Sandy Koufax*, 106.
54. Silverman, *Heroes of the World Series*, 232.
55. Gruver, *Koufax*, 125.
56. "Wild Man Tamed," *Newsweek*, July 10, 1961, 46.
57. Donald Honig, *Baseball America: The Heroes of the Game and the Times of Their Glory* (New York: Macmillan, 1985), 303.
58. Olsen, "The Very Best Act in Town," 22; Peters, *Heroes of the Major Leagues*, 50; "Sandy Koufax, Baseball's Enigmatic Participant," 3; Glenn Hibdon, "Sandy Koufax Recalls Advice That Helped His Career," *Baseball Digest*, May 1985, 67.
59. Leavy, *Sandy Koufax*, 103–106.
60. Silverman, *Heroes of the World Series*, 232; Palmer and Gillette, *The ESPN Baseball Encyclopedia*, 1330; *Chicago Tribune*, September 28, 1961; Thorn *et al.*, *Total Baseball*, 201; Peters, *Heroes of the Major Leagues*, 50–51; Horvitz and Horvitz, *The Big Book of Jewish Baseball*, 98.
61. Pietrusza *et al.*, *Baseball: The Biographical Encyclopedia*, 622.
62. *Los Angeles Times*, July 1, 1962; *Washington Post*, July 2, 1962.
63. Silverman, *Heroes of the World Series*, 234.
64. *Washington Post*, July 2, 1962.
65. "Sandy Koufax at AllExperts," 4.
66. Peters, *Heroes of the Major Leagues*, 52; Slater, *Great Jews in Sports*, 165.
67. www.niams.nih.gov.
68. Silverman, *Heroes of the World Series*, 234.
69. "Sandy Koufax at AllExperts, 4.
70. Palmer and Gillette, *The ESPN Baseball Encyclopedia*, 1330; *Chicago Tribune*, December 29, 1962; www.baseball-almanac.com.
71. *Sporting News*, February 14, 1963.
72. *Los Angeles Times*, May 12, 1963; "Sandy Koufax at AllExperts," 4–5.
73. Pietrusza *et al.*, *Baseball: The Biographical Encyclopedia*, 622.
74. Bill Libby, "The Sophistication of Sandy Koufax," *Sport*, September 1963, 69.
75. *Los Angeles Times*, August 30, 1963.
76. *Chicago Defender*, September 12, 1963.
77. *New York Times*, September 18,1963; Pietrusza *et al.*, *Baseball: The Biographical Encyclopedia*, 622; *Los Angeles Times*, September 19, 1963.
78. Gillette and Palmer, *The ESPN Baseball Encyclopedia*, 1330; *Los Angeles Times*, October 18,1963, October 21, 1963; *Chicago Tribune*, October 25,1963; *Washington Post*, October 25, 1963; Slater, *Great Jews in Sports*, 165; www.info-pedia. net; Silverman, *Heroes of the World Series*, 236; Peters, *Heroes of the Major Leagues*, 51–52; Pietrusza *et al.*, *Baseball: The Biographical Encyclopedia*, 622.
79. Thorn *et al.*, *Total Baseball*, 205.
80. "Sandy Koufax at AllExperts," 5.
81. Pietrusza *et al.*, *Baseball: The Biographical Encyclopedia*, 622; www.info-pedia.net.
82. Silverman, *Heroes of the World Series*, 230–231.
83. *Los Angeles Times*, November 20, 1963; *Chicago Defender*, December 26,1963, January 21, 1964; *Washington Post*,

December 27, 1963, January 7, 1964; *New York Times*, January 4, 1964, February 16, 1964.

84. Gruver, *Koufax*, 125.

85. Olsen, "The Very Best Act in Town," 21.

86. *Ibid.*

87. Leavy, *Sandy Koufax*, 177; Milton Gross, "Sandy Koufax; The Pressure's on a World Series Hero," *Sport*, November 1964, 33.

88. *New York Times*, February 29, 1964.

89. *Los Angeles Times*, June 5, 1964; Thorn *et al.*, *Total Baseball*, 207.

90. *New York Times*, June 5, 1964.

91. *Washington Post*, August 9, 1964.

92. "Sandy Koufax at AllExperts," 5.

93. *Chicago Defender*, December 15, 1964; "Sandy Koufax-Baseball's Enigmatic Participant, 3; Peters, *Heroes of the Major Leagues*, 52.

94. Joe Jares, "Koufax Makes a Pitch for Posterity," *Sports Illustrated*, August 2, 1965, 10–12; "Sandy Koufax at AllExperts," 5.

95. "Sandy Koufax at AllExperts," 5.

96. "Sport's 19th Annual Award Sandy Koufax Man of the Year," *Sports Illustrated*, February 1966, 20; Pietrusza *et al.*, *Baseball: The Biographical Encyclopedia*, 622; *Chicago Tribune*, September 10, 1965; *Los Angeles Times*, September 10, 1965.

97. Pietrusza *et al.*, *Baseball: The Biographical Encyclopedia*, 623; Gillette and Palmer, *The ESPN Baseball Encyclopedia*, 92; Thorn *et al.*, *Total Baseball*, 209; Horvitz and Horvitz, *The Big Book of Jewish Baseball*, 97.

98. *New York Times*, October 2, 1965.

99. Leavy, *Sandy Koufax*, 182.

100. Durslag, "Sandy Koufax The Strikeout King," 71; Richler, "Koufax the Incomparable," 88.

101. Spaner, "From Greenberg to Green," 176.

102. Levine, *Ellis Island to Ebbets Field*, 246.

103. Spaner, "From Greenberg to Green," 176.

104. "Sandy Koufax—Baseball's Enigmatic Participant," 3; Gruver, *Koufax*, 52.

105. Slater, *Great Jews in Sports*, 166; Horvitz and Horvitz, *The Big Book of Jewish Baseball*, 98.

106. Levine, *Ellis Island to Ebbets Field*, 245–246.

107. Leavy, *Sandy Koufax*, 194.

108. *San Francisco Chronicle*, October 30, 2002.

109. Leavy, *Sandy Koufax*, 172,

110. *Ibid.*, 176.

111. Baldassaro and Johnson, *The American Game*, 131.

112. *Chicago Defender*, October 20, 1965; *Chicago Tribune*, November 4, 1965, January 24, 1966; *Washington Post*, December 5, 1965; *New York Times*, January 12, 1966; www.historicbaseball.com; *Sporting News*, November 12, 1996.

113. Neil J. Sullivan, *The Diamond Revolution: The Prospect for Baseball After the Collapse of Its Ruling Class* (New York: St. Martin's Press, 1992), 185.

114. "Sic Transit Tradition," *Time*, April 8, 1966, 75; "Sandy Koufax at AllExperts," 7.

115. Stan Hochman, "Koufax: This Is How It Was," *Baseball Digest*, February 1966, 11–12.

116. Sullivan, *The Diamond Revolution*, 186.

117. Slater, *Great Jews in Sports*, 166.

118. "Sic Transit Tradition" 75; *Los Angeles Times*, March 18, 1966.

119. Linn, "Koufax Remembered," 84.

120. *Los Angeles Times*, February 28, 1966; *Washington Post*, February 26, 1966.

121. *New York Times*, March 27, 1966.

122. Mike Coffey, *27 Men Out* (New York: Atria Books, 2004), 112,

123. *Chicago Tribune*, March 31, 1966; "Sic Transit Tradition," 75; Pietrusza *et al*; *Baseball: The Biographical Encyclopedia*, 623; www.info-pedia.net, 2; "Sandy Koufax at AllExperts, 7.

124. Ribalow and Ribalow, *Jewish Baseball Stars*, 231.

125. Andrew Zimbalist, *May the Best Team Win: Baseball Economics and Public Policy* (Washington, D.C.: Brookings Institution, 2003), 76.

126. Benjamin G. Rader, *Baseball: A History of America's Game* (Urbana: University of Illinois Press, 1992), 204.

127. Slater, *Great Jews in Sports*, 166.

128. Phil Collier, "Memories of Koufax's Well-Kept Secret," *Baseball Digest*, November 1972, 88.

129. Milton Gross, "Goodbye, Sandy," *Sport*, March 1967, 84.

130. Palmer and Gillette, *The ESPN Baseball Encyclopedia*, 1330; Slater, *Great Jews in Sports*, 166; "Sandy Koufax—Baseball's Enigmatic Participant," 3; Pietrusza *et al.*, *Baseball: The Biographical Encyclopedia*, 623.

131. www.info-pedia.com; *Los Angeles Times*, October 3, 1966; *Chicago Defender*, November 2, 1966

132. www.pubquizhelp.com.

133. Peters, *Heroes of the Major Leagues*, 56; Pietrusza *et al.*, *Baseball: The Biographical Encyclopedia*, 623; Gross, "Goodbye, Sandy," 35.

134. Gruver, *Koufax*, 211–212.

135. "Goodbye, Sandy," 57; Gruver, *Koufax*, 211; *Chicago Tribune*, November 19,1996; *Los Angeles Times*, November 19, 1966; *New York Times*, November 19, 1966; Slater, *Great Jews in Sports*, 166.

136. Gross, "Goodbye, Sandy," 85.

137. Horvitz and Horvitz, *The Big Book of Jewish Baseball*, 99; www.info-pedia.com; "Sandy Koufax at AllExperts, 7.

138. Thorn *et al.*, *Total Baseball*, 211.

139. "Koufax Retires," *Baseball Digest*, February 1967, 67.

140. Phil Collier, "Sandy Koufax," *Sport*, May 1969, 49.

141. *Los Angeles Times*, December 30, 1966.

142. Linn, "Koufax Remembered," 85.

143. *Sporting News*, March 22, 1969.

144. "Sandy Koufax at AllExperts," 8.

145. Gruver, *Koufax*, 217.

146. *Ibid.*

147. *Ibid.*, 217–218.

148. *Los Angeles Times*, December 25, 1968; *Washington Post*, January 2, 1969; "Sandy Koufax at AllExperts," 8.

149. *Chicago Tribune*, January 30, 1970; *New York Times*, January 30, 1970.

150. Horvitz and Horvitz, *The Big Book of Jewish Baseball*, 96; Pietrusza *et al.*, *Baseball: The Biographical Encyclopedia*, 620.

151. *Chicago Defender*, January 20, 1972; *Sporting News*, February 5, 1972.

152. www.espn.go.com.

153. *Los Angeles Times*, January 21, 1972.

154. "Sandy Koufax at AllExperts," 8.

155. Libby, "The Sophistication of Sandy Koufax," *Sport*, September 1963, 69.

156. *Sporting News*, February 10, 1979, February 17, 1979; *Los Angeles Times*, March 25, 1979; Slater, *Great Jews in Sports*, 167; "Sandy Koufax at AllExperts," 8.

157. Gruver, *Koufax*, 13; "Sandy Koufax at AllExperts," 8.

158. "Jewish Sports Hall of Fame," www.jewishsports.org.

159. www.cbs2.com.

160. Gruver, *Koufax*, 12.

161. Levine, *Ellis Island to Ebbets Field*, 243.

162. Gruver, *Koufax*, 245.

Chapter 6

1. Pietrusza *et al.*, *Baseball: The Biographical Encyclopedia*, 972.

2. Leonard Koppett, *The Thinking Fan's Guide to Baseball* (Kingston, NY: Total Sports, 2001), 206–207.

3. Tom Meany, "The Figger Filbert," *Baseball Magazine*, September 1949, 332.

4. Alan Schwarz, *The Numbers Game: Baseball's Lifelong Fascination with Statistics* (New York: St. Martin's Press, 2004), 56.

5. Pietrusza *et al.*, *Baseball: The Biographical Encyclopedia*, 972.

6. *Ibid.*

7. *Los Angeles Times*, September 13, 1963.

8. Schwarz, *The Numbers Game*. 56.

9. *Los Angeles Times*, September 13, 1963; *New York Times*, March 22, 1992; Meany, "The Figger Filbert," 332,

10. Schwarz, *The Numbers Game*, 56; Jonathan Eig, *Opening Day: The Story of Jackie Robinson* (New York: Simon & Schuster, 2007), 169.

11. *Washington Post*, February 26, 1960.

12. Meany, "The Figger Filbert," 331; Eig, *Opening Day*, 169; Schwarz, *The Numbers Game*, 57; *Los Angeles Times*, September 13, 1963.

13. Oakley, *Baseball's Last Golden Age*, 188.

14. Meany, "The Figger Filbert," 332.

15. Schwarz, *The Numbers Game*, 57.

16. *Ibid.*, 54–55; *Los Angeles Times*, June 28, 1960.

17. *Los Angeles Times*, April 14, 1958; Schwarz, *The Numbers Game*, 56.

18. Schwarz, *The Numbers Game*, 169.

19. Branch Rickey, "Goodbye to Some Old Baseball Ideas," www.baseballthinkfactory.org.

20. Schwarz, *The Numbers Game*, 218.

21. Ed Linn, *Hitter: The Life and Turmoil of Ted Williams* (New York: Harcourt Brace, 1993), 174.

22. *Los Angeles Times*, September 13, 1963; Meany, "The Figger Filbert," 332.

23. Rickey, "Goodbye to Some Old Baseball Ideas."

24. *Ibid.*, Pietrusza *et al.*, *Baseball: The Biographical Encyclopedia*, 972; Schwarz, *The Numbers Game*, 58–59; Meany, "The Figger Filbert, 331; *New York Times*, October 31, 1951, June 21, 1952.

25. "Dodgers All-Time General Managers" found at www.losangeles.dodgers.mlb.com; Schwarz, *The Numbers Game*, 57.

26. *New York Times*, March 22, 1992.

27. Schwarz, *The Numbers Game*, 57–58.

28. *Ibid.*, 59.

29. Pietrusza *et al.*, *Baseball: The Biographical Encyclopedia*, 972.

30. *Los Angeles Times*, August 11, 1963.

31. "Allan Roth—BR Bullpen," www.baseball-reference.com.

32. *Washington Post*, August 4, 1957.

33. Leavy, *Sandy Koufax*, 106.

34. *New York Times*, February 19, 1961.

35. *Los Angeles Times*, February 7, 1962.

36. *Ibid.*, September 3, 1964.

37. Schwarz, *The Numbers Game*, 142; Pietrusza *et al.*, *Baseball: The Biographical Encyclopedia*, 972; "Allan Roth—BR Bullpen; www.netshrine.com.

38. *New York Times*, March 5, 1992; Pietrusza *et al.*, *Baseball: The Biographical Encyclopedia*, 272.

39. Pietrusza *et al.*, *Baseball: The Biographical Encyclopedia*, 272; www.retrosheet.org.

40. www.baseball-almanac.com; *New York Times*, March 5, 1992; *Chicago Defender*, June 22, 1965.

Chapter 7

1. *Sporting News*, June 19, 1968.

2. It was not until late in the century that the advent of computers and the internet made a form of written play-by-play possible.

3. "Jewish Sports Hall of Fame," www.jewishsports.com.

4. Pietrusza *et al.*, *Baseball: The Biographical Encyclopedia*, 1084; John A. Garraty and Mark C. Carnes, eds., *American National Biography* (New York: Oxford, 1999), 677; Jerry Gorman and Kirk Calhoun. *The Name of the Game: The Business of Sports* (New York: John Wiley, 1994), 90.

5. Garraty and Carnes, *American National Biography*, 677.

6. *Sporting News*, December 4, 1971; *New York Times*, May 21, 1939; Leonard Koppett, "A Little Game That Turned TV Loose on Sports," *Sports Illustrated*, May 10, 1965, M3.

7. Huston Horn, "Baseball's Babbling Brook," *Sports Illustrated*, July 9, 1962, 58.

8. G. Edward White, *Creating the National Pastime: Baseball Transforms Itself, 1903-1953* (Princeton, NJ: Princeton University Press, 1996), 237.

9. Horn, "Baseball's Babbling Brook," 58.

10. Stephen Borelli, *How About That! The Life of Mel Allen* (Champaign, IL: Sports Publishing, 2005), 14.

11. Levine, *From Ellis Island to Ebbets Field*, 93.

12. Borelli, *How About That!*, 14.

13. *Ibid.*

14. Horn, "Baseball's Babbling Brook," 58.

15. Slater, *Great Jews in Sports*, 16.

16. Mel Allen and Ed Fitzgerald, *You Can't Beat the Hours: A Long, Loving Look at Big-League Baseball Including Some Yankees I Have Known* (New York: Harper & Row, 1964), 4.

17. Horn, "Baseball's Babbling Brook," 60; Allen and Fitzgerald, *You Can't Beat the Hours*, 1.

18. Curt Smith, *The Voice: Mel Allen's Untold Story* (Guilford, CT: Lyons Press, 2007), 14.

19. Borelli, *How About That!*, 18.

20. Allen and Fitzgerald, *You Can't Beat the Hours*, 4.

21. Smith, *The Voice*, 15.

22. Ted Patterson, *The Golden Voices of Baseball* (Champaign, IL: Sports Publishing, 2002), 60.

23. Slater, *Great Jews in Sports*, 16.

24. Pietrusza *et al.*, *Baseball: The Biographical Encyclopedia*, 16; Warren Corbett, "Mel Allen," www.bioproj.sabr.org, 1.

25. Allen and Fitzgerald, *You Can't Beat the Hours*, 6.

26. Horn, "Baseball's Babbling Brook," 62.

27. Curt Smith, *Voices of Summer: Ranking Baseball's 101 All-Time Best Announcers* (New York: Carroll & Graf, 2005), 96; Corbett, "Mel Allen," 2.

28. Horn, "Baseball's Babbling Brook," 62; Slater, *Great Jews in Sports*, 16; Curt Smith, *Voices of the Game: The First Full-Scale Overview of Baseball Broadcasting, 1921 to the Present* (South Bend, IN: Diamond Communications), 1987.

29. Smith, *The Voice*, 22.

30. Patterson, *The Golden Voices of Baseball*, 61.

31. Corbett, "Mel Allen," 2

32. Smith, *The Voice*, 26.

33. David J. Halberstam, *Sports on New York Radio: A Play-by-Play History* (Indianapolis: Masters Press, 1999), 248.

34. Corbett, "Mel Allen," 4.

35. Horn, "Baseball's Babbling Brook," 63.

36. Halberstam, *Sports on New York Radio*, 248.

37. Aaron Goldstein, "The Extraordinary Life of Mel Allen," www.intellectualconservative.com., 5.

38. Slater, *Great Jews in Sports*, 17; Corbett, "Mel Allen," 3; "Radio Hall of Fame—Mel Allen, Sportscaster www.radiohof.org.

39. Smith, *Voices of the Game*, 59.

40. Corbett, "Mel Allen," 3.

41. White, *Creating the National Pastime*, 238.

42. Halberstam, *Sports on New York Radio*, 250.

43. *Ibid.*, 251; Corbett, "Mel Allen," 3.

44. Halberstam, *Sports on New York Radio*, 252–253; Smith, *Voices of the Game*, 64; Borelli, *How About That!*, 77.

45. Oakley, *Baseball's Last Golden Age*, 118.
46. "Radio Hall of Fame," www.radiohof.org.
47. Corbett, "Mel Allen," 3–4; White, *Creating the National Pastime*, 238–239; Halberstam, *Sports on New York Radio*, 250.
48. Smith, "The Voice," 167.
49. Smith, *Voices of the Game*, 256–257.
50. Curt Smith, *The Storytellers: From Mel Allen to Bob Costas: Sixty Years of Baseball Tales from the Broadcast Booth* (New York: Macmillan, 1995), 201
51. "Mel Allen," www.jewishvirtuallibrary.org.
52. Corbett, "Mel Allen," 2.
53. Goldstein, "The Extraordinary Life of Mel Allen," 5.
54. Smith, *The Storytellers*, 201–202; "Mel Allen," www.jewishvirtuallibrary.org; Patterson, *The Golden Voices of Baseball*, 62.
55. "Mel Allen," www.jewishvirtuallibrary.org; Richard Ben Cramer, *Joe DiMaggio: The Hero's Life* (New York: Simon & Schuster, 2000), 263.
56. Tommy Henrich and Bill Gilbert, *Five O'Clock Lightning: Ruth, Gehrig, DiMaggio, Mantle and the Glory Years of the NY Yankees* (New York: Carol Publishing Group), 195; Roger Kahn, *The Era, 1947–1957: When the Yankees, the Giants and the Dodgers Ruled the World* (New York: Ticknor & Fields, 1993), 177.
57. Slater, *Great Jews in Sports*, 17.
58. Smith, *The Voice*, 49.
59. Corbett, "Mel Allen," 3–4.
60. Horn, "Baseball's Babbling Brook," 57; Corbett. "Mel Allen," 4.
61. Goldstein, "The Extraordinary Life of Mel Allen," 7; Smith, *Voices of the Game*, 47.
62. Borelli, *How About That!*, 152.
63. Corbett, "Mel Allen," 3.
64. Smith, *Voices of the Game*, 66.
65. Borelli, *How About That!*, 91.
66. Halberstam, *Sports on New York Radio*, 253.
67. *Ibid.*, 254–255.
68. Corbett, "Mel Allen," 3; Halberstam, *Sports on New York Radio*, 256; Henrich and Gilbert, *Five O'Clock Lightning*, 288.
69. David Quentin Voigt, *American Baseball, Volume III: From Postwar Expansion to the Electronic Age* (University Park, PA: The Pennsylvania State University Press, 1983), 105.
70. Kahn, *The Era*, 285.
71. Halberstam, *Sports on the New York Radio*, 258.
72. Smith, *The Storytellers*, 61.
73. Halberstam, *Sports on New York Radio*, 260.
74. Smith, *Voices of Summer*, 99.
75. Corbett, "Mel Allen," 3.
76. Halberstam, *Sports on New York Radio*, 258, 260.
77. Bill Davidson, "Mel Allen: Baseball's Most Controversial Voice," *Look*, September 22, 1960, 98.
78. Goldstein, "The Extraordinary Life of Mel Allen," 7.
79. *Washington Post*, September 26, 1963; Goldstein, "The Extraordinary Life of Mel Allen," 8; Corbett, "Mel Allen," 4; Borelli, *How About That!* 192.
80. Pietrusza et al., *Baseball: The Biographical Encyclopedia*, 16.
81. Borelli, *How About That!*, 197–198.
82. *Ibid.*, 201; Slater, *Great Jews in Sports*, 17; *New York Times*, October 7, 1964.
83. Corbett, "Mel Allen," 4; *New York Times*, December 18, 1964.
84. Smith, *The Voice*, 175.
85. Smith, *Voices of Summer*, 101.
86. White, *Creating the National Pastime*, 241.
87. *Ibid.*; Pietrusza et al., *Baseball: The Biographical Encyclopedia*, 16.
88. Smith, *Voices of the Game*, 263.

89. Borelli, *How About That!* 206.
90. *New York Times*, March 10, 1965; *Washington Post*, March 10, 1965; Slater, *Great Jews in Sports*, 17
91. Corbett, "Mel Allen," 5
92. *Chicago Tribune*, October 29, 1965.
93. *Washington Post*, October 29, 1965.
94. *Ibid.*, September 1, 1966.
95. *Ibid.*, October 1, 1966.
96. Corbett, "Mel Allen," 5; *Chicago Tribune*, August 17, 1976.
97. *New York Times*, February 27, 1968; *Washington Post*, February 27, 1968; Corbett, "Mel Allen," 5.
98. Corbett, "Mel Allen," 6–7; Halbestram, *Sports on New York Radio*, 263.
99. Pietrusza et al., *Baseball: The Biographical Encyclopedia*, 7.
100. Borelli, *How About That!*, 221.
101. White, *Creating the National Pastime*, 242.
102. Smith, *The Voice*, 198–201.
103. David Levine, "Say Good Night, Mel," *Sport*, October 1983, 100.
104. Borelli, *How About That!* 222–223.
105. Smith, *Voices of Summer*, 101.
106. Smith, *The Voice*, 239–240.
107. Pietrusza et al., *Baseball: The Biographical Encyclopedia*, 7.
108. Quoted in Halberstam, *Sports on New York Radio*, 263.
109. *Sporting News*, August 5, 1978; Corbett, "Mel Allen," 6; Smith, *The Voice*, 202; Smith, *Voices of Summer*, 50; Borelli, *How About That!*, 233.
110. Slater, *Great Jews in Sports*, 18; Smith, *The Voice*, 219.
111. Henrich and Gilbert, *Five O'Clock Lightning*, 70; Davidson, "Mel Allen: Baseball's Most Controversial Voice," 101.
112. Smith, *Voices of Summer*, 103.
113. Smith, *The Voice*, 85; Borelli, *How About That!* 151.
114. Borelli, *How About That!*, 151.
115. *Ibid.*, 152.
116. *Ibid.*, 235.
117. Corbett, "Mel Allen," 6.
118. Smith, *The Voice*, 237.
119. *New York Times*, June 20, 1996; Joshua Hammerman, "A Tribute to Mel Allen," June 19, 1996, found on www.tbe.org.
120. Goldstein, "The Extraordinary Life of Mel Allen," 10.
121. Borelli, *How About That!*, 240.
122. "Two New Stadiums on Deck: Baseball Brings Jobs to the Big Apple, *The Carpenter*, Summer 2006, 16.
123. Corbett, "Mel Allen," 7.
124. Borelli, *How About That!*, 241.

Chapter 8

1. Shapiro, *A Time for Healing*, 42.
2. Diner, *The Jews of the United States*, 306; Shapiro, *A Time for Healing*, 43.
3. Spaner, "From Greenberg to Green: Jewish Ballplayers," 178.
4. Thorn et al., *Total Baseball*, 213.
5. *New Jersey Jewish News*, November 18, 2004.
6. *Chicago Tribune*, July 26, 1963.
7. Gillette and Palmer, *The ESPN Baseball Encyclopedia*, 1328.
8. *New York Times*, June 25, 1961; www.jewsinsports.org.
9. Horvitz and Horvitz, *The Big Book of Jewish Baseball*, 42.

10. Conrad Cardinal at www.jewsinsports.org
11. Rob Trucks, *Cup of Coffee: The Very Short Careers of Eighteen Major League Pitchers* (New York: Smallmouth Press, 2002), 106.
12. Horvitz and Horvitz, *The Big Book of Jewish Baseball*, 191.
13. Larry Yellen at www.jewsinsports.org.
14. *Ibid.*; *Jewish News of Greater Phoenix*, September 3, 2004; *The Jewish Ledger*, September 3, 1004.
15. Trucks, *Cup of Coffee*, 114; Horvitz and Horvitz, *The Big Book of Jewish Baseball*, 191.
16. Palmer and Gillette, *The ESPN Baseball Encyclopedia*, 1621.
17. *Ibid.*
18. Trucks, *Cup of Coffee*, 110.
19. Steve Hertz, telephone interview with authors, October 2, 2008.
20. Horvitz and Horvitz, *The Big Book of Jewish Baseball*, 86; Steve Hertz at www.jewsinsports.org; Gillette and Palmer, *The ESPN Baseball Encyclopedia*, 581; www.baseballalmanac.com; www.baseball-reference.com.
21. Hertz telephone interview.
22. Horvitz and Horvitz, *The Big Book of Jewish Baseball*, 85.
23. *Ibid.*, 85–86.
24. Hertz telephone interview.
25. www.israelbaseballleague.com.
26. *Sporting News*, May 28, 1966.
27. Horvitz and Horvitz, *The Big Book of Jewish Baseball*, 169; Art Shamsky at www.jewsinsports.org; *Chicago Tribune*, February 15, 1979; *Sporting News*, October 26, 1963.
28. Thorn *et al.*, *Total Baseball*, 905; George Vass, "What They Want for '67: It Could Be an Inside Job!," December 1966, 5.
29. *Sporting News*, August 27, 1966.
30. *Washington Post*, August 17, 1966; *Chicago Defender*, August 18, 1966; *New York Times*, August 21, 1966.
31. *Chicago Defender*, December 13, 1966.
32. *Los Angeles Times*, February 23, 1967.
33. *New York Times*, November 9, 1967; Gillette and Palmer, *The ESPN Baseball Encyclopedia*, 905; Horvitz and Horvitz, *The Big Book of Jewish Baseball*, 169.
34. *Chicago Defender*, November 9, 1967.
35. *Ibid.*
36. *Sporting News*, March 2, 1968.
37. *Chicago Tribune*, April 28, 1969; *Washington Post*, April 28, 1968.
38. Gillette and Palmer, *The ESPN Baseball Encyclopedia*, 905.
39. Art Shamsky at www.jewsinsports.org; www.jewishsports.org.
40. *Chicago Tribune*, September 12, 1969; www.baseballsavvy.com.
41. www.baseballsavvy.com.
42. *New York Times*, October 19, 1971, April 4,1972; *Chicago Tribune*, October 19, 1971; *Sporting News*, October 30, 1971, January 29, 1972, April 15, 1972.
43. *Chicago Tribune*, April 11, 1972; *Sporting News*, April 22, 1972.
44. *Chicago Tribune*, June 29, 1972; *Washington Post*, June 29, 1972; *Sporting News*, July 15, 1972; *Sporting News*, August 5, 1972.
45. *Chicago Tribune*, July 1, 1972.
46. *New York Times*, August 4, 1977.
47. *Chicago Tribune*, February 15, 1979; *Sporting News*, April 28, 1979.
48. "Jewish Sports Hall of Fame," www.jewish sports.org.
49. *Sporting News*, August 16, 1969.
50. *Ibid.*, September 23, 1972.
51. Horvitz and Horvitz, *The Big Book of Jewish Baseball*, 121–122.
52. Norman Miller at www.jewsinsports.org.
53. www.jewsinsports.org.
54. *Sporting News*, April 27, 1968.
55. *Ibid.*, October 5, 1968, October 19, 1968.
56. Horvitz and Horvitz, *The Big Book of Jewish Baseball*, 122.
57. Maxwell Kates, "Of Horsehides and Hexagrams," *National Pastime* 24 (2004): 123.
58. Maury Wills, "The National League's 9 Most Underrated Players," *Sport*, July 1970, 13.
59. *Sporting News*, May 12, 1973.
60. Horvitz and Horvitz, *The Big Book of Jewish Baseball*, 122.
61. *Sporting News*, March 21, 1970.
62. *Ibid.*, May 9, 1970.
63. *Ibid.*, November 7, 1970.
64. Norman Miller, telephone interview with authors, October 10, 2008.
65. *Sporting News*, May 12, 1973; *Chicago Tribune*, April 22, 1973.
66. Horvitz and Horvitz, *The Big Book of Jewish Baseball*, 122.
67. Gillette and Palmer, *The ESPN Baseball Encyclopedia*, 751; Horvitz and Horvitz, *The Big Book of Jewish Baseball*, 122.
68. Miller telephone interview.
69. *Los Angeles Times*, January 30, 1975.
70. Miller telephone interview.
71. Gillette and Palmer, *The ESPN Baseball Encyclopedia*, 751.
72. Miller telephone interview.
73. *Los Angeles Times*, June 2, 1964; Greg Goossen at www.jewsinsports.org.
74. Horvitz and Horvitz, *The Big Book of Jewish Baseball*, 73; *Chicago Tribune*, April 11, 1965.
75. Gillette and Palmer, *The ESPN Baseball Encyclopedia*, 533.
76. *New York Times*, December 2, 1965.
77. *Ibid.*, August 6, 1965.
78. Gillette and Palmer, *The ESPN Baseball Encyclopedia*, 533.
79. Greg Goossen at www.jewsinsports.org.
80. *Chicago Tribune*, August 14, 1970; Gillette and Palmer, *The ESPN Baseball Encyclopedia*, 533.
81. *New York Times*, November 4, 1970.
82. Greg Goossen at www.jewsinsports.org., Spaner, "From Greenberg to Green," 171.
83. Richie Scheinblum at www.jewsinsports.org.
84. Marc Katz, "'I Didn't Think Baseball Players Were Real People,' An Interview with Richie Scheinblum," in *Batting Four Thousand: Baseball in the Western Reserve* (Cleveland: Society for American Baseball Research, 2008), 69.
85. Maury Allen, "Richie Scheinblum Finally a Star," *Baseball Digest*, November 1972, 67.
86. Katz, "I Didn't Think Baseball Players Were Real People," 69.
87. Richie Scheinblum, E-mail interview with authors, January 28, 2009.
88. Katz, "I Didn't Think Baseball Players were Real People," 69.
89. *Ibid.*, Horvitz and Horvitz, *The Big Book of Jewish Baseball*, 165.
90. Richie Scheinblum at www.jewsinsports.org.
91. Katz, "'I Didn't Think,'" 71.
92. *Sporting News*, September 11, 1965; Palmer and Gillette, *The ESPN Encyclopedia of Baseball*, 893.
93. Horvitz and Horvitz, *The Big Book of Jewish Baseball*, 166; *Los Angeles Times*, June 27, 1973; *Sporting News*, July 7, 1973.
94. Horvitz and Horvitz, *The Big Book of Jewish Baseball*, 166.
95. *Sporting News*, January 13, 1968, March 2, 1968; *Chicago Defender*, February 7, 1968.

96. *Sporting News*, October 5, 1968; Gillette and Palmer, *The ESPN Baseball Encyclopedia*. 893.

97. *Washington Post*, July 4, 1971; *Sporting News*, November 13, 1971.

98. *Sporting News*, March 29, 1969.

99. Horvitz and Horvitz, *The Big Book of Jewish Baseball*, 166.

100. *Sporting News*, December 27, 1969.

101. *Washington Post*, October 24, 1970; Horvitz and Horvitz, *The Big Book of Jewish Baseball*, 166.

102. Horvitz and Horvitz, *The Big Book of Jewish Baseball*, 166.

103. *Sporting News*, September 25, 1971; Horvitz and Horvitz, *The Big Book of Jewish Baseball*, 166–167.

104. *Washington Post*, July 4, 1971.

105. *Sporting News*, November 6, 1971.

106. *Ibid.*, December 16, 1972.

107. Richie Scheinblum at www.jewsinsports.org.

108. *Los Angeles Times*, August 7, 1972.

109. *Sporting News*, December 16, 1972; *Chicago Tribune*, December 2, 1972.

110. *Los Angeles Times*, March 1, 1973.

111. *Ibid.*, June 16, 1973.

112. *Ibid.*, June 17, 1973.

113. *Ibid.*

114. *Sporting News*, March 23, 1974.

115. Gillette and Palmer, *The ESPN Baseball Encyclopedia*, 893.

116. *Sporting News*, May 18, 1974; *Los Angeles Times*, May 1, 1974.

117. *Sporting News*, August 24, 1974, September 21, 1974; *Washington Post*, September 22, 1974

118. Gillette and Palmer, *The ESPN Baseball Encyclopedia*, 893.

119. *New York Times*, December 4, 1974; Katz, "'I Didn't Think,'" 71, 74.

120. *Providence Journal*, November 22, 2006.

121. *Los Angeles Times*, August 17, 1978.

122. Katz, "'I Didn't Think,'" 74.

123. *Ibid.*, 76.

124. Horvitz and Horvitz, The *Big Book of Jewish Baseball*, 55; Levine, *Ellis Island to Ebbets Field*, 239.

125. Levine, *Ellis Island to Ebbets Field*, 239.

126. *Chicago Tribune*, March 23, 1967.

127. Levine, *Ellis Island to Ebbets Field*, 239–240.

128. *Washington Post*, November 6, 1964; *Chicago Tribune*, March 23, 1967.

129. Horvitz and Horvitz, *The Big Book of Jewish Baseball*, 55.

130. *Sporting News*, September 24, 1966.

131. Spaner, "From Greenberg to Green," 176.

132. *Chicago Tribune*, September 10, 1966; Gillette and Palmer, *The ESPN Baseball Encyclopedia*, 475.

133. Spaner, "From Greenberg to Green," 176.

134. *Sporting News*, December 3, 1966.

135. *New York Times*, March 23, 1967.

136. Berry Stainback, "Socrates in a Jockstrap," *Sport*, June 1965, 8; *New York Times*, March 3, 1957.

137. *Los Angeles Times*, May 11, 1967.

138. "Mike's Little Rebellion," *Newsweek*, June 12, 1967, 58; *Chicago Tribune*, May 11, 1967.

139. *Los Angeles Times*, May 23, 1967, May 25, 1967.

140. James Edward Miller, *The Baseball Business: Pursuing Pennants and Profits in Baltimore* (Chapel Hill: The University of North Carolina Press, 1990), 128.

141. *Chicago Tribune*, May 30, 1967; *New York Times*, May 30, 1967.

142. *Sporting News*, June 10, 1967.

143. *Washington Post*, June 7, 1967; *New York Times*, June 7, 1967.

144. "Mike Epstein SuperJew" at www.jewsinsport.org.

145. *Los Angeles Times*, June 30, 1967.

146. Levine, *Ellis Island to Ebbets Field*, 242.

147. "Jewish Players Celebrated at Hall," found at www.mlb.com.

148. Levine, *Ellis Island to Ebbets Field*, 242.

149. *Ibid.*

150. *Sporting News*, January 20, 1968.

151. *Chicago Tribune*, May 23, 1968; *Washington Post*, May 23, 1968; *Sporting News*, June 8, 1968.

152. *Chicago Tribune*, June 4, 1968.

153. *Sporting News*, August 25, 1968.

154. Gillette and Palmer, *The ESPN Baseball Encyclopedia*. 475.

155. *Ibid.*, 1699.

156. Spaner, "From Greenberg to Green," 176.

157. *Sporting News*, March 22, 1969.

158. Gillette and Palmer, *The ESPN Baseball Encyclopedia*, 474; "Mike Epstein 'SuperJew,'" at www.jewsinsports.org; Arnold Hano, "Mike Epstein: Somewhere Between Journeyman & Superstar," *Sport*, November 1972, 86.

159. *Washington Post*, September 21, 1969.

160. *Sporting News*, June 13, 1970.

161. Gillette and Palmer, *The ESPN Baseball Encyclopedia*, 465.

162. *Chicago Tribune*, May 8, 1971; *Washington Post*, May 8, 1971; *New York Times*, May 9, 1971.

163. *Sporting News*, May 22, 1971; *The New York Times*, May 9, 1971.

164. *Sporting News*, July 17, 1971.

165. "About Mike Epstein Hitting," at www.baseball-hitting.com.

166. "Mike Epstein SuperJew," at www.jewsinsports.org.

167. *The Sporting News*, October 9, 1971.

168. Hano, "Mike Epstein," 69.

169. Thorn *et al.*, *Total Baseball*, 241

170. *Sporting News*, December 23, 1972; Hano, "Mike Epstein," 87; Williams and Plaschke, *No More Mr. Nice Guy*, 148–149.

171. Gillette and Palmer, *The ESPN Baseball Encyclopedia*, 474.

172. Thorn *et al.*, *Total Baseball*, 409–410.

173. *Washington Post*, September 7, 1972; Kates, "Of Horsehides and Hexagrams," 122–123.

174. *Washington Post*, January 30, 1973; *Sporting News*, January 13, 1973.

175. *Sporting News*, December 23, 1972.

176. *Chicago Tribune*, May 21, 1973; *Washington Post*, May 21, 1973.

177. *Washington Post*, June 29, 1973; *Sporting News*, July 14, 1973

178. *Los Angeles Times*, May 5, 1974; *Washington Post*, May 5, 1974.

179. *Sporting News*, May 18, 1974.

180. "Mike Epstein Baseball Stats," at www.baseball-almanac.com.

181. *Washington Post*, May 23, 1968; Spaner, "From Greenberg to Green," 176.

182. Horvitz and Horvitz, *The Big Book of Jewish Baseball*, 56.

183. "Jewish Sports Hall of Fame," www.jewishsports.org.

Chapter 9

1. Berger, "Ken Holtzman," at www.bioproj.sabr.org., 1; Ken Holtzman," www.jewsinsports.org.

2. Horvitz and Horvitz, *The Big Book of Jewish Baseball*, 88; Andrew Hazucha, "Leo Drencher's Last Stand: Anti-

Semitism, Racism, and the Cubs Player Rebellion of 1971," *Nine* 15, Fall 2006: 3.

3. www.baseball-reference.com; www.ballparkdigest.com; "Ken Holtzman," www.thebaseballcube.com.

4. *Chicago Tribune*, September 2, 1965.

5. Gillette and Palmer, *The ESPN Baseball Encyclopedia*, 1285.

6. *Washington Post*, April 26, 1966; *Sporting News*, April 16, 1966.

7. *Sporting News*, May 7, 1966.

8. *Ibid.*, September 10, 1966.

9. *Ibid.*, October 8, 1966.

10. www.reference.com/Encyclopedia/Ken Holtzman; www.jewsinsports.org.

11. *Chicago Tribune*, September 26, 1966.

12. Spaner, "From Greenberg to Green," 177.

13. Carrie Muskat, *Banks to Sandberg to Grace: Five Decades and Frustration with the Chicago Cubs* (Chicago: Contemporary Books, 2001), 120–121.

14. *Chicago Tribune*, June 3, 1967.

15. *Los Angeles Times*, May 8, 1967; *Sporting News*, August 26, 1967; Horvitz and Horvitz, *The Big Book of Jewish Baseball*, 87.

16. www.reference.com.

17. *Ibid.*

18. George Vass, "Can Holtzman Beat the Rap?" *Baseball Digest*, July 1970, 35.

19. Glenn Dickey, *The Great No-Hitters* (Radnor, PA: Chilton Books, 1976).

20. Pietrusza *et al.*, *Baseball: The Biographical Encyclopedia*, 509.

21. Muskat, *Banks to Sandberg to Grace*, 118–119.

22. Gillette and Palmer, *The ESPN Baseball Encyclopedia*, 1285.

23. *Chicago Tribune*, June 4, 1971; *Chicago Defender*, June 5, 1971.

24. Hazucha, "Leo Durocher's Last Stand," 4.

25. *Ibid.*

26. Quote found in Ribalow and Ribalow, *Jewish Baseball Stars*, 243–244; Hazucha, "Leo Durocher's Last Stand," 4.

27. Letter, Richard Bladt to authors, October 17, 2008.

28. Hazucha, "Leo Durocher's Last Stand," 4–5.

29. Vass, "Can Holtzman Beat the Rap?" 38–39.

30. *Chicago Tribune*, November 30, 1971; *Los Angeles Times*, November 30, 1971.

31. Williams and Plaschke, *No More Mr. Nice Guy*, 122–123.

32. Ribalow and Ribalow, *Jewish Baseball Stars*, 248.

33. www.reference-com.

34. Thorn *et al.*, *Total Baseball*, 409–410.

35. *Sporting News*, February 17, 1973.

36. Thorn *et al.*, *Total Baseball*, 412–413; www.baseball-reference.com.

37. www.jewsinsports.org.

38. Horvitz and Horvitz, *The Big Book of Jewish Baseball*, 87; Berger, "Ken Holtzman, 2.

39. Gillette and Palmer, *ESPN Baseball Encyclopedia*, 1285.

40. Pietrusza *et al.*, *Baseball: The Biographical Encyclopedia*, 510; Thorn *et al.*, *Total Baseball*, 415.

41. www.reference.com.

42. Berger, "Ken Holtzman," 2.

43. Bob Hayes, "From Thrower to Pitcher: The Education of Ken Holtzman," *Baseball Digest*, December 1974, 73.

44. Gillette and Palmer, *The ESPN Baseball Encyclopedia*, 1285.

45. Thorn *et al.*, *Total Baseball*, 418.

46. Berger, "Ken Holtzman," 2–3; *Los Angeles Times*, September 4, 1975.

47. *Sporting News*, February 21, 1976.

48. Pietrusza *et al.*, *Baseball: The Biographical Encyclopedia*, 510; www.jewsinsports.org; Berger, "Ken Holtzman, 2.

49. *Chicago Tribune*, April 3, 1976.

50. *Ibid.*

51. Gillette and Palmer, *The ESPN Baseball Encyclopedia*, 1285.

52. *Los Angeles Times*, June 16, 1976; *Sporting News*, July 3, 1976.

53. Pietrusza *et al.*, *Baseball: The Biographical Encyclopedia*, 510; Horvitz and Horvitz, *The Big Book of Jewish Baseball*, 87–88.

54. *Sporting News*, November 13, 1976; Berger, "Ken Holtzman," 2.

55. *Chicago Tribune*, October 7, 1977.

56. Slater, *Jews in Sports*, 139–140; www.reference.com.

57. Spaner, "From Greenberg to Green," 177.

58. www.reference.com.

59. *Los Angeles Times*, June 11, 1978; *Washington Post*, June 11, 1978; *Sporting News*, June 24, 1978.

60. Gillette and Palmer, *The ESPN Baseball Encyclopedia*, 1285.

61. *Washington Post*, September 21, 1979; baseball-reference.com; Slater, *Great Jews in Sports*, 140.

62. Ken Holtzman, interview with authors, July 30, 2002.

63. www.jewsinsports.org; www.jewishsports.net.

64. Steve Hertz, telephone interview with authors, October 2, 2008; *St. Louis Jewish Light*, March 28, 2007; *Chicago Tribune*, April 20, 2007.

65. www.mlb.com.

66. *Sporting News*, October 20, 1979.

Chapter 10

1 Marvin Miller, interview with authors, August 12, 2007.

2. Horvitz and Horvitz, *The Big Book of Jewish Baseball*, 219.

3. James B. Dworkin, *Owners Versus Players: Baseball and Collective Bargaining* (Boston: Auburn House, 1981), 29.

4. *Ibid.*

5. Horvitz and Horvitz, *The Big Book of Jewish Baseball*, 219; Marvin Miller, *A Whole Different Ballgame: The Sport and Business of Baseball* (New York: Birch Lane Press, 1991), 17.

6. Marvin Miller Interview found at www.baseballreliquary.org, 2; Marvin Miller at www.jewsinsports.org., 1.

7. John Helyar, *Lords of the Realm: The Real History of Baseball* (New York: Villard, 1994), 18; Voigt, *American Baseball*, 209; Dworkin, *Owners and Players*, 29–30; Miller, *A Whole Different Ball Game*, 19.

8. Pietrusza *et al.*, *Baseball: The Biographical Encyclopedia*, 783; Miller, *A Whole Different Ball Game*, 21.

9. *Los Angeles Times*, August 10, 1964; Dworkin, *Owners Versus Players*, 30; Dewey and Acocella, *The Biographical History of Baseball*, 319.

10. Robert H. Boyle, "This Miller Admits He's a Grind," *Sports Illustrated*, March 11, 1974, 25.

11. Robert F. Burk, *Much More Than Just a Game: Players, Owners & American Baseball Since 1921* (Chapel Hill: The University of North Carolina Press, 2001), 147–148; *Chicago Sun-Times*, August 11, 1987.

12. Bryan Di Salvatore, *A Clever Base-Ballist: The Life and Times of John Montgomery Ward* (New York: Pantheon Books, 1999), 176–178; "Major League Baseball Players Association: MLBPA History," found at www.mlbplayers.mlb.com; Paul D. Staudohar, ed., *Diamond Mines: Baseball and Labor* (Syracuse: Syracuse University Press, 2000), xx.

13. Joe Glickman, "Union Man: Marvin Miller Disses

Vincent, Giamatti, and the Rest of Baseball's Old-Boy Network," *Village Voice*, July 2, 1991, 158; Curt Flood, *The Way It Is* (New York: Trident Press, 1970) 157; David Q. Voigt, "They Shaped the Game: Nine Innovators of Major League Baseball," *Baseball History* 1 (Spring 1986): 19; Voigt, *American Baseball*, 207; Zimbalist, *May the Best Team Win*, 76; Andrew Zimbalist, *Baseball and Billions: A Probing Look Inside the Big Business of Our National Pastime* (New York: Basic Books, 1992) 17.

14. Lee Lowenfish and Tony Lupien, *The Imperfect Diamond: The Story of Baseball's Reserve System and the Men Who Fought to Change It* (New York: Stein and Day, 1980), 196.

15. John E. Dreifort (ed.), *Baseball History From Outside the Lines: A Reader* (Lincoln: University of Nebraska Press, 2001), 251; Burk, *Much More Than a Game*, 146; Flood, *The Way It Is*, 157; Charles P. Korr, *The End of Baseball as We Knew It: The Players Union, 1960-1981* (Urbana, IL: University of Illinois Press, 2002), 36; Lowenfish and Lupien, *The Imperfect Diamond*, 196; Sullivan, *The Diamond Revolution*, 188.

16. Burk, *Much More Than a Game*, 146; Dworkin, *Owners Versus Players*, 30–31.

17. "Marvin Miller Interview," www.baseballrelikquary.org, 2.

18. Dewey and Acocella, *The Biographical History of Baseball*, 319; *Sporting News*, March 23, 1974; Korr, *The End of Baseball as We Knew It*, 28; Miller, *A Whole Different Ball Game*, 7.

19. "Marvin Miller Interview," 2–3; Burk, *Much More Than a Game*, 148.

20. Dworkin, *Owners Versus Players*, 31.

21. Voigt, *American Baseball*, 207.

22. Lowenfish and Lupien, *The Imperfect Diamond*, 197.

23. Burk, *Much More Than a Game*, 148; Lowenfish and Lupien, *The Imperfect Diamond*, 197

24. Glickman, "Union Man," 158.

25. Korr, *The End of Baseball as We Knew It*, 37.

26. *Sporting News*, March 23, 1974.

27. Burk, *More Than Just a Game*, 149; Voigt, "They Shaped the Game," 20.

28. Miller, *The Business of Baseball*, 143.

29. *Los Angeles Times*, March 11, 1966.

30. Burk, *Much More Than a Game*, 149–150; Korr, *The End of Baseball as We Knew It*, 40.

31. Flood, *The Way It Is*, 160.

32. *Sporting News*, March 23, 1974.

33. Flood, *The Way It Is*, 160.

34. *Chicago Tribune*, April 16, 1966; Voigt, "They Shaped the Game," 20.

35. Burk, *Much More Than a Game*, 150.

36. Pietrusza et al., *Baseball: The Biographical Encyclopedia*, 783.

37. Miller interview; "Marvin Miller Interview," 3; Korr, *The End of Baseball as We Knew It*, 39; "Marvin Miller," www.jewsinsports.org.

38. Helyar, *Lords of the Realm*, 29.

39. *Ibid.*, 27; Miller, *A Whole Different Ball Game*, 46–47; Dewey and Acocella, *The Biographical History of Baseball*, 319; Boyle, "This Miller Admits He's a Grind," 25–26.

40. Glickman, "Union Man," 158; Miller, *A Whole Different Ball Game*, 143–147; Lowenfish and Lupien, *The Imperfect Diamond*, 200–201; Helyar, *Lords of the Realm*, 28; Flood, *The Way It Is*, 163–165; Boyle, "This Miller Admits He's a Grind," 25–26.

41. *Ibid.*

42. Voigt, *American Baseball*, 210.

43. Helyar, *Lords of the Realm*, 28.

44. Korr, *The End of Baseball as We Knew It*, 60–61, 189–190; Miller, *The Baseball Business*, 143.

45. Flood. *The Way It Is*, 166; mlbplayers.mlb.com.

46. *Ibid.*; Voigt, "They Shaped the Game," 20.

47. Dewey and Acocella, *The Biographical History of Baseball*, 319; Alexander, *Our Game*, 273; Voigt, "They Shaped The Game," 20; Dworkin, *Owners Versus Players*, 32; Miller, *A Whole Different Ball Game*, 97–98; Helyar, *Lords of the Realm*, 36; Kenneth M. Jennings, *Balls and Strikes: The Money Game in Professional Baseball* (New York: Praeger, 1990) 23.

48. *Washington Post*, August 2, 1967.

49. Dworkin, *Owners Versus Players*, 32; *Sporting News*, September 21, 1968.

50. *Sporting News*, December 21, 1968.

51. *Ibid.*, February 15, 1969.

52. *Los Angeles Times*, January 31, 1969.

53. *Sporting News*, May 24, 1969.

54. *Chicago Tribune*, February 11, 1969.

55. *Chicago Defender*, February 19,1969.

56. Dewey and Acocella, *The Biographical History of Baseball*, 319; Alexander, *Our Game*, 273; Voigt, "They Shaped the Game," 20.

57. *New York Times*, February 26, 1969.

58. Alexander, *Our Game*, 273; Korr, *The End of Baseball as We Knew It*, 71; Voigt, "They Shaped the Game," 20; "History of the MLBPA" found at mlbplayers.com.

59. Helyar, *Lords of the Realm*, 109.

60. Alexander, *Our Game*, 273; Dewey and Acocella, *The Biographical History of Baseball*, 319; Miller interview.

61. Miller, *The Baseball Business*, 182.

62. Sands and Gammons, *Coming Apart at the Seams*, 187; *Washington Post*, June 10, 1970; Alexander, *Our Game*, 281; Miller, *The Business of Baseball*, 182; Lowenfish and Lupien, *The Imperfect Diamond*, 208–209; Burk, *Much More Than a Game*, 177–180; James Quirk and Rodney D Fort, *Pay Dirt* (Princeton, NJ: Princeton University Press) 193; David Whitford, "Curt Flood," *Sport*, December 1986, 105.

63. Sullivan, *The Diamond Revolution*, 37, 40–41.

64. *Sporting News*, March 25, 1972; *New York Times*, April 1, 1972.

65. *Los Angeles Times*, April 2, 1972.

66. *Chicago Tribune*, April 3, 1972.

67. Alexander, *Our Game*, 280; Pietrusza et al., *Baseball: The Biographical Encyclopedia*, 783; Dewey and Acocella, *The Biographical History of Baseball*, 319; David Q. Voigt, *America Through Baseball* (Chicago: Nelson Hall, 1976) 137.

68. Kuhn, *Hardball*,106; Sands and Gammons, *Coming Apart at the Seams*, 186; Voigt, *American Baseball*, 212.

69. Korr, *The End of Baseball as We Knew It*, 113–114; Pietrusza et al., *Baseball: The Biographical Encyclopedia*, 783.

70. *Los Angeles Times*, April 6, 1972.

71. *Sporting News*, April 15, 1972; April 22, 1972.

72. Kuhn, *Hardball*, 107.

73. *Los Angeles Times*, February 12,1973

74. *Sporting News*, April 29, 1972.

75. *Los Angeles Times*, February 13, 1973.

76. *Los Angeles Times*, February 26, 1973; Dewey and Acocella, *The Biographical History of Baseball*, 319; Pietrusza et al., *Baseball: The Biographical Encyclopedia*, 873; Voigt, "They Shaped the Game," 20; "Marvin Miller at www.jewsinsports.org; "Marvin Miller Interview," at www.baseballreliquary, 3; Quirk and Fort, *Pay Dirt*, 195; Miller, *The Baseball Business*, 183.

77. *Sporting News*, March 3, 1973.

78. Voigt, *American Baseball*, 212; *Sporting News*, March 16, 1974.

79. Voigt, *Baseball History*, 213.

80. Pietrusza et al., *Baseball: The Biographical Encyclopedia*, 784.

81. Helyar, *Lords of the Realm*, 110.

82. Dreifort, *Baseball History from Outside the Lines*, 252; Dewey and Acocella, *The Biographical History of Baseball*, 319; Marvin Miller at www.jewsinsports.org; Miller, *The Baseball Business*. 216–217.

83. Pietrusza et al., Baseball: The Biographical Encyclopedia, 784.

84. Voigt, American Baseball, 213–214.

85. Miller, The Baseball Business, 216–217; Dreifort, Baseball History from Outside the Lines, 252; "Marvin Miller," at www.jewsinsports.org; Dewey and Acocella, The Biographical History of Baseball, 319

86. "The Union Rep Who Changed Baseball," Newsweek, April 3, 1989, 48; Dewey and Acocella, The Biographical Directory of American Baseball, 320.

87. Sands and Gammon, Coming Apart at the Seams, 218.

88. Ibid., 50–51; "Collective Bargaining," found at www.sabr.org; "MLBPA History," at www.mlbplayers.mlb.com.

89. New York Times, February 24,1976; Voigt, American Baseball, 214.

90. Jerome Holtzman, The Commissioners (New York: Total Sports, 1998), 163; New York Times, July 13, 1976.

91. Voigt, American Baseball, 215; Alexander, Our Game, 297.

92. Voigt, American Baseball, 215.

93. Korr, The End of Baseball as We Knew It, 185.

94. Alexander, Our Game, 313.

95. Ibid.

96. Los Angeles Times, March 5, 1980, March 20, 1980; Dewey and Acocella, The Biographical History of Baseball, 320; Korr, The End of Baseball as We Knew It, 194.

97. Korr, The End of Baseball as We Knew It, 190.

98. Helyar, Lords of the Realm, 224; Burk, Much More Than a Game, 224.

99. Sporting News, May 24, 1980.

100. Pietrusza et al., Baseball: The Biographical Encyclopedia, 784; Washington Post, May 22, 1980.

101. Alexander, Our Game, 314.

102. Los Angeles Times, February 26, 1981.

103. Washington Post, May 17, 1981; Chicago Tribune, May 27, 1981, June 5, 1981; Los Angeles Times, May 27, 1981, June 13, 1981, June 14, 1981; New York Times, June 7, 1981.

104. Alexander, Our Game, 314.

105. Helyar, Lords of the Realm, 225–226; Korr, The End of Baseball as We Knew It, 193–194.

106. Los Angeles Times, July 16, 1981.

107. Ibid., July 30, 1981.

108. Chicago Tribune, August 1, 1981.

109. Dewey and Acocella, The Biographical History of Baseball, 320; Helyar, Lords of the Realm, 286; Quirk and Fort, Pay Dirt, 196; John P. Rossi, The National Game: Baseball and American Culture (Chicago: Ivan R. Dee, 2000), 194; Miller, Baseball Business, 253; Alexander, Our Game, 315.

110. Chicago Tribune, August 1, 1981.

111. New York Times, August 16, 1981.

112. "Marvin Miller Interview," 3–4.

113. Burk, Much More Than a Game, 234.

114. Alexander, Our Game, 314; Pietrusza et al., Baseball: The Biographical Encyclopedia, 784.

115. Burk, Much More Than a Game, 229.

116. Korr, The End of Baseball as We Knew It, 43.

117. "Marvin Miller Interview," 4.

118. Pietrusza et al., Baseball: The Biographical Encyclopedia, 784.

119. Korr, Baseball as We Knew It, 42.

120. Pietrusza et al., Baseball: The Biographical Encyclopedia, 784.

121. Horvitz and Horvitz, The Big Book of Jewish Baseball, 219.

122. Joe Morgan and Richard Lally, Long Balls and No Strikes (New York: Crown, 1999), 189.

123. Voigt, "They Shaped the Game," 21.

124. Sporting News, December 13, 1982, December 20, 1982; Los Angeles Times, December 3, 1982; New York Times, December 9, 1982.

125. Chicago Tribune, March 22, 1983.

126. Ibid., November 23, 1983.

127. Los Angeles Times, November 24, 1983.

128. New York Times, December 9, 1983; Dewey and Acocella, The Biographical Directory of Baseball, 320.

129. "Marvin Miller Interview," 4; Miller interview; Helyar, Lords of the Realm, 550.

130. Marvin Miller Interview," 1.

131. Ibid., 2.

132. "Jewish Sports Hall of Fame 1999," found at www.jewishsports.com; "The Pillar of Achievement," at www.jewishsports.net.

133. Korr, The End of Baseball as We Knew It, 40, 45, 65.

134. Wall Street Journal, February 5, 2003.

135. New York Sun, June 16, 2008.

136. "Marvin Miller," at www.baseballlibrary.com.

137. Dewey and Acocella, The Biographical History of Baseball, 319.

138. Sporting News, March 23, 1974.

139. Voigt, "They Shaped the Game," 20; www.jewsinsports.org.

140. Sullivan, The Diamond Revolution, 188–189.

141. Miller, A Whole Different Game, inside front jacket.

142. Roland Hemond, telephone interview with authors, December 5, 2008.

Chapter 11

1. The Jewish Advocate, October 11, 2006; Chicago Tribune, April 7, 1973; Los Angeles Times, April 7, 1973.

2. Washington Post, July 1, 1973.

3. Ron Blomberg and Dan Schlossberg, Designated Hebrew: The Ron Blomberg Story (Champaign, IL: Sports Publishing, 2006), 15–16.

4. Sporting News, July 8,1967.

5. Ibid.

6. Ron Blomberg, interview with authors, October 8, 2006; Blomberg and Schlossberg, Designated Hebrew, 14.

7. The Jewish Advocate, October 11, 2006; "The Ron Blomberg Interview," 1, found at www.nyfans.com.

8. Slater, Great Jews in Sports, 43.

9. Washington Post, June 22, 1967; New York Times, August 13, 1971; Blomberg and Schlossberg, Designated Hebrew, 22; Horvitz and Horvitz, The Big Book of Jewish Baseball, 35.

10. Dick Schaap, "What's a Nice Georgia Cracker Doing in the Bronx?" Sport, October 1973, 50.

11. Los Angeles Times, August 12, 1971.

12. Washington Post, February 27, 1972.

13. Slater, Great Jews in Sports, 43; Sporting News, May 11, 1968; Spaner, "From Greenberg to Green," 176.

14. "Jewish Players Celebrated at Hall," found at www.mlb.com; "Blomberg Interview," www.nyfans.com.

15. Blomberg and Schlossberg, Designated Hebrew, 57–59.

16. Slater, Great Jews in Sports, 43; Horvitz and Horvitz, The Big Book of Jewish Baseball, 35; "Ron Blomberg Baseball Stats," www.baseball-almanac.com; Gillette and Palmer, The ESPN Baseball Encyclopedia, 329.

17. Slater, Great Jews in Sports, 43; Horvitz and Horvitz, The Big Book of Jewish Baseball, 36; Sporting News, September 5, 1970.

18. Los Angeles Times, June 25, 1971

19. "Blomberg Stats," www.baseball-almanac.com.

20. Sporting News, October 16, 1971.

21. Washington Post, February 27, 1972.

22. New York Times, March 17, 1972.

23. Blomberg Stats, www.baseball-almanac.com; Gillette and Palmer, The ESPN Baseball Encyclopedia, 329.

24. *Ibid.*, May 22, 1978.

25. Spaner, "From Greenberg to Green," 176–177.

26. Levine, *From Ellis Island to Ebbets Field*, 236.

27. "Joltin Jew," found at www.newyorkmetro.com; Blomberg and Schlossberg, *Designated Hebrew*, 23.

28. Slater, *Great Jews in Sports*, 44; *Los Angeles Times*, August 13, 1971; Spaner, "From Greenberg to Green," 177.

29. Levine, *From Ellis Island to Ebbets Field*, 241.

30. Blomberg interview.

31. *Jewish Advocate*, October 11, 2006.

32. Horvitz and Horvitz, *The Big Book of Jewish Baseball*, 35.

33. "Blomberg First Permanent Pinch Hitter," www.sports.espn.go.com.

34. *Ibid.*

35. *Ibid.*

36. *Ibid.*

37. "Blomberg First Permanent Pinch Hitter," www.sports.espn.go.com; "Where Are They Now—Ron Blomberg" www.baseballsavvy.com.

38. Blomberg and Schlossberg, *Designated Hebrew*, 3–7; *Chicago Tribune*, April 7, 1973; *Los Angeles Times*, April 7, 1973; *Washington Post*, April 7, 1973; *The Jewish Advocate*, October 11, 2006; John C. Skipper, *Inside Pitch: A Closer Look at Classic Baseball Moments* (Jefferson, NC: McFarland, 1996), 73.

39. Blomberg and Schlossberg, *Designated Hebrew*, 7; *Sporting News*, April 28, 1973.

40. Blomberg and Schlossberg, *Designated Hebrew*,11; *The Jewish Advocate*, October 11, 2006; Horvitz and Horvitz, *The Big Book of Jewish Baseball*, 36.

41. Pietrusza et al., *Baseball: The Biographical Encyclopedia*, 96.

42. "The New Yankees," *Newsweek*, July 16, 1973, 46; *Washington Post*, July 1, 1973; *New York Times*, August 8, 1971; Skipper, *Inside Pitch*, 74; Schaap, "What's a Nice Georgia Cracker Doing in the Bronx?" 52, 54; Blomberg and Schossberg, *Designated Hebrew*, 8; *Sporting News*, June 30, 1973.

43. "Blomberg Stats," www.baseball-almanac.com; Gillette and Palmer, *The ESPN Baseball Encyclopedia*, 329.

44. Schaap, "What's a Nice Georgia Cracker Doing in the Bronx?" 54.

45. *New York Times*, March 4, 1975.

46. *Chicago Tribune*, April 8, 1978; Pietrusza et a.l, *Baseball: The Biographical Encyclopedia*, 96; Slater, *Great Jews in Sports*, 43–44; *Sporting News*, September 6, 1975; *Washington Post*, April 6, 1977.

47. *New York Times*, April 13, 1978.

48. Kahn, *October Men*, 250–251.

49. *New York Times*, November 15, 1977.

50. Blomberg and Schlossberg, *Designated Hebrew*, 138–140.

51. *New York Times*, April 13, 1978.

52. Slater, *Great Jews in Sports*, 44; "Ron Blomberg Stats," www.baseball-almanac.com; Pietrusza et al., *Baseball: The Biographical Encyclopedia*, 96; *Chicago Tribune*, May 25, 2978, March 28, 1979, March 31, 1979; *Sporting News*, July 29, 1978; Bruce Nash and Allan Zullo, *The Baseball Hall of Shame* (New York: Wallaby Books, 1985), 162.

53. *Chicago Tribune*, March 31, 1979.

54. Skipper, *Inside Pitch*, 75; Marty Appel, *Yesterday's Heroes: Revisiting the Old-Time Baseball Stars* (New York: William Morrow, 1988), 49.

55. Horvitz and Horvitz, *The Big Book of Jewish Baseball*, 36; "Ron Blomberg Stats," www.baseball-almanac.com; Thorn et al., *Total Baseball*, 1041.

56. Blomberg and Schlossberg, *Designated Hitter*, 144; Slater, *Great Jews in Sports*, 44.

57. www.baseballsavvy.com.

58. "Jewish Sports Hall of Fame," www.jewishsports.org

59. "Ron Blomberg," at www.kjmpromotions.com.

60. Hertz interview.

61. *The Jewish Advocate*, October 11, 2006.

Chapter 12

1. www.usinfo.state.gov; Diner, *The Jews of the United States, 1654-2000*, 320, 324; Shapiro, *A Time for Healing*, 122, Baldasarro and Johnson (eds.), *The American Game*, 131,132; Spaner, "From Greenberg to Green," 178.

2. *Florida Jewish News*, November 11, 2008.

3. *Sporting News*, May 30, 1970.

4. "Dave Roberts," www.jewsinsports.org.

5. Horvitz and Horvitz, *The Big Book of Jewish Baseball*, 143.

6. *Sporting News*, October 26, 1968.

7. Jack Murphy, "Dave Roberts on the Road to Stardom," *Baseball Digest*, November 1971, 39.

8. *Chicago Tribune*, July 4, 1969

9. Murphy, "Dave Roberts on the Road to Stardom," 39; "Dave Roberts," www.jewsinsports.org; Gillette and Palmer, *The ESPN Baseball Encyclopedia*, 1489; Thorn et al., *Total Baseball*, 2191.

10. Gillette and Palmer, *The ESPN Baseball Encyclopedia*, 1489.

11. *Sporting News*, January 16, 1971.

12. Murphy, "Dave Roberts on the Road to Stardom," 40.

13. *Los Angeles Times*, December 4, 1971; "Dave Roberts," www.jewsinsports.org.

14. *Sporting News*, November 6, 1971.

15. *Ibid.*, December 18,1971; *The Los Angeles Times*, December 4, 1971.

16. *Sporting News*, January 22, 1972.

17. "Dave Roberts," www.jewsinsports.org.

18. *Chicago Tribune*, December 7, 1975; *Los Angeles Times*, December 7, 1975; Gillette and Palmer, *The ESPN Baseball Encyclopedia*, 1489.

19. *Chicago Tribune*, December 7, 1975; *Los Angeles Tribune*, December 7, 1975.

20. *Sporting News*, March 13, 1976.

21. *Washington Post*, July 31, 1977.

22. *Sporting News*, August 20, 1977.

23. "Dave Roberts," www.jewsinsports.org.

24. *Sporting News*, February 17, 1979.

25. *Los Angeles Times*, June 28, 1979.

26. Horvitz and Horvitz, *The Big Book of Jewish Baseball*, 143; Gillette and Palmer, *The ESPN Baseball Encyclopedia*, 1489.

27. *New York Times*, January 18, 1984.

28. "Dave Roberts," www.jewsinsports.org.

29. www.sports.yahoo.com.

30. "Statement from Tal Smith regarding death of Dave Roberts," found at www.chicago.cubs.mlb.com.

31. Ross Baumgarten, telephone interview with authors, September 6, 2006.

32. *Chicago Tribune*, June 10, 1979.

33. *Ibid.*

34. Baumgarten interview.

35. *Ibid.*; *Chicago Tribune*, June 10, 1979.

36. *Chicago Tribune*, June 10, 1979.

37. Baumgarten interview.

38. *Chicago Sun-Times*, June 19, 1903; *Chicago Tribune*, August 17, 1978.

39. Hemond interview.

40. Horvitz and Horvitz, *The Big Book of Jewish Baseball*, 24.

41. *Sporting News*, July 29, 1978.

42. *Chicago Tribune*, August 17, 1978.
43. *Ibid.*
44. Gillette and Palmer, *The ESPN Baseball Encyclopedia*, 1077.
45. *Chicago Sun-Times*, June 29, 2003.
46. *Chicago Tribune*, June 10, 1979.
47. Baumgarten interview.
48. *Sporting News*, January 13, 1979.
49. *Chicago Tribune*, September 13, 1979.
50. *Sporting News*, September 15, 1979.
51. *Chicago Tribune*, June 10, 1979.
52. *Ibid.*
53. *Chicago Tribune*, June 10, 1979; Vass, "7 Candidates for Stardom in 1980 and Beyond, *Baseball Digest*, June 1980, 24–25; "Ross Baumgarten, www.jewsinsports.org.
54. *Chicago Sun-Times*, June 29, 2003; Horvitz and Horvitz, *The Big Book of Jewish Baseball*, 25; Gillette and Palmer, *The ESPN Baseball Encyclopedia*, 1077; "Ross Baumgarten," www.jewsinsports.org.
55. *Chicago Tribune*, July 31, 1980; *New York Times*, August 24, 1980.
56. *Chicago Tribune*, February 22, 1981.
57. *Sporting News*, March 7, 1981.
58. Gillette and Palmer, *The ESPN Baseball Encyclopedia*, 1077; Thorn *et al.*, *Total Baseball*, 1789; *Sporting News*, February 6, 1982.
59. Baumgarten interview.
60. *Chicago Tribune*, March 22, 1982.
61. Gillette and Palmer, *The ESPN Baseball Encyclopedia*, 1076.
62. *Ibid.*, March 29, 1983
63. Baumgarten interview.
64. Horvitz and Horvitz, *The Big Book of Jewish Baseball*, 139.
65. *Ibid.*, 140.
66. "Steve Ratzer Baseball Stats" at www.baseball-almanac.com; "Steve Ratzer," www.jewsinsports.org.
67. *New York Times*, February 25, 1983.
68. Horvitz and Horvitz, *The Big Book of Jewish Baseball*, 140.
69. "Steve Rosenberg Statistics," found at www.thebaseballcube.com.
70. *Ibid.*, 150–151; "Steve Rosenberg," www.jewsinsports.org "Steve Rosenberg Statistics," at www.baseball-reference.com.
71. "Steve Rosenberg Statistics," www.thebaseball.com.
72. Gillette and Palmer, *The ESPN Baseball Encyclopedia*, 1496.
73. Slater, *Great Jews in Sports*, 294.
74. "Jose Bautista," www.jewsinsports.org.
75. *USA Today Baseball Weekly*, September 14, 1994.
76. *Ibid.*; Horvitz and Horvitz, *The Big Book of Jewish Baseball*, 26; Kates, "Of Horsehides and Hexagrams, 123; Slater, *Great Jews in Sports*, 294.
77. *USA Today Baseball Weekly*, September 14, 1994.
78. *Washington Post*, December 9, 1987.
79. "Jose Bautista," at www.jewsinsports.org; Horvitz and Horvitz, *The Big Book of Jewish Baseball*, 26; "Bautista Baseball Stats," at www.baseball-almanac.com; "Jose Bautista-Pitching," at www.sportsillustrated.com.
80. *Washington Post*, June 19, 1989; Gillette and Palmer, *The ESPN Baseball Encyclopedia*, 1077.
81. Horvitz and Horvitz, *The Big Book of Jewish Baseball*, 26; *Washington Post*, April 23, 28, 1990.
82. Slater, *Great Jews in Sports*, 294.
83. "Jose Bautista," www.jewsinsports.org.
84. Kates, "Of Horsehides and Hexagrams," 123.
85. *USA Today Baseball Weekly*, September 14, 1994.
86. Horvitz and Horvitz, *The Big Book of Jewish Baseball*, 26

87. "ESPN Classic-Green, Koufax and Greenberg," at www.espn.go.com.
88. Gillette and Palmer, *The ESPN Baseball Encyclopedia*, 1078; Thorn *et al.*, *Total Baseball*, 1790.
89. Horvitz and Horvitz, *The Big Book of Jewish Baseball*, 26.
90. Gillette and Palmer, *The ESPN Baseball Encyclopedia*, 1078; "Jose Bautista Baseball Stats," www.baseball-almanac.com; "Jose Bautista-Pitching," at www.sportsillustrated.cnn.com.
91. Horvitz and Horvitz, *The Big Book of Jewish Baseball*, 26.
92. *Sporting News*, May 27, 1972; Horvitz and Horvitz, *The Big Book of Jewish Baseball*, 170.
93. *New York Times*, November 28, 1972.
94. *Ibid.*, March 31, 1973.
95. *Sporting News*, December 16, 1972.
96. *Chicago Tribune*, May 13, 1973.
97. Horvitz and Horvitz, *The Big Book of Jewish Baseball*, 170.
98. *Sporting News*, July 28, 1973.
99. "Sharon Baseball Stats," www.baseball-almanac.com; "Dick Sharon Stats," www.thebaseballcube.com.
100. *Sporting News*, December 29, 1973.
101. *Ibid.*, September 14,1974.
102. *Chicago Tribune*, November 19, 1974; *Los Angeles Times*, November 19, 1974.
103. *Sporting News*, March 22, 1975.
104. Sharon Baseball Stats," www.baseball-almanac.com; "Dick Sharon Statistics," www.thebaseballcube.com.
105. Horvitz and Horvitz, *The Big Book of Jewish Baseball*, 171; *Chicago Tribune*, October 21, 1975; New York Times, October 21, 1975
106. *Los Angeles Times*, January 14, 1976; Chicago Tribune, March 4, 1976.
107. Gillette and Palmer, *The ESPN Baseball Encyclopedia*, 906.
108. Spaner, "From Greenberg to Green," 178; *Chicago Tribune*, July 25, 1985; "Mark Gilbert," www.jewsinsports.org; Horvitz and Horvitz, *The Big Book of Jewish Baseball*, 68.
109. "Mark Gilbert," www.jewsinsports.org; Horvitz and Horvitz, *The Big Book of Jewish Baseball*, 68.
110. Spaner, "From Greenberg to Green," 178; Horvitz and Horvitz, *The Big Book of Jewish Baseball*, 68.
111. "Mark Gilbert," www.jewsinsports.org; *Chicago Tribune*, December 27, 1984.
112. Horvitz and Horvitz, *The Big Book of Jewish Baseball*, 68.
113. *New York Times*, March 27, 1985.
114. *Ibid.*, 68; *Chicago Tribune*, December 27, 1984.
115. *Ibid.*, July 25,1985.
116. Horvitz and Horvitz, *The Big Book of Jewish Baseball*, 68–69; "Mark Gilbert Statistics," at www.baseball-reference.com; "Mark Gilbert," at www.baseball-almanac.com.
117. *Washington Post*, August 1, 1985.
118. "Mark Gilbert," jewsinsports.org.
119. Gillette and Palmer, *The ESPN Baseball Encyclopedia*, 1505.
120. Horvitz and Horvitz, *The Big Book of Jewish Baseball*, 159.
121. *Washington Post*, July 20, 1988; "Roger Samuels Stats," at www.baseball-almanac.com.
122. Gillette and Palmer, *The ESPN Baseball Encyclopedia*, 1505.
123. *Sporting News*, May 22, 1989.
124. Thorn *et al.*, *Total Baseball*, 2207.
125. *Sporting News*, July 31, 1989.
126. Horvitz and Horvitz, *The Big Book of Jewish Baseball*, 1505.

Chapter 13

1. Spaner, "From Greenberg to Green," 178.
2. *Washington Post*, July 5, 1980; *Chicago Tribune*, July 10, 1978; Horvitz and Horvitz, *The Big Book of Jewish Baseball*, 180; Slater, *Great Jews in Sports*, 273.
3. *Chicago Tribune*, July 10, 1978.
4. *Washington Post*, July 5, 1980.
5. Slater, *Great Jews in Sports*, 273; Horvitz and Horvitz, *The Big Book of Jewish Baseball*, 180.
6. "Kent State Shootings," at www.ohiohistorycentral. org.
7. Ribalow and Ribalow, *Jewish Baseball Stars*, 268.
8. *Ibid.*
9. *Sporting News*, April 10, 1971.
10. *Ibid.*, May 1, 1971.
11. *Washington Post*, April 24, 1971.
12. Gillette and Palmer, *The ESPN Baseball Encyclopedia*, 1549.
13. Levine, *From Ellis Island to Ebbets Field*, 243.
14. *New York Times*, March 1, 1973; *Sporting News*, December 16, 1972.
15. Ribalow and Ribalow, *Jewish Baseball Stars*, 269.
16. *Sporting News*, September 9, 1972.
17. *Ibid.*, March 10, 1973.
18. Horvitz and Horvitz, *The Big Book of Jewish Baseball*, 181; Slater, *Great Jews in Sports*, 273; Gillette and Palmer, *The ESPN Baseball Encyclopedia*, 1549.
19. *Chicago Tribune*, December 12, 1973; *Sporting News*, December 23, 1973.
20. *Sporting News*, January 5, 1974.
21. *Chicago Tribune*, March 4, 1974; *Sporting News*, May 17, 1975; Horvitz and Horvitz, *The Big Book of Jewish Baseball*, 181; Slater, *Great Jews in Sports*, 273; Gillette and Palmer, *The ESPN Baseball Encyclopedia*, 1549; Thorn *et al.*, *Total Baseball*, 2250; Ribalow and Ribalow, *Jewish Baseball Stars*, 270.
22. *Sporting News*, March 20, 1976.
23. Horvitz and Horvitz, *The Big Book of Jewish Baseball*, 181.
24. Gillette and Palmer, *The ESPN Baseball Encyclopedia*, 1549; *Sporting News*, September 25, 1976; *Chicago Tribune*, November 13, 1980.
25. Ribalow and Ribalow, *Jewish Baseball Stars*, 270–271; "kinesiologist," at www.thefreedictionary.com; Horvitz and Horvitz, *The Big Book of Jewish Baseball*, 181; *Los Angeles Times*, July 8, 1980; *Chicago Tribune*, August 11, 1980; Muskat, *Banks to Sandberg to Grace*, 133–134.
26. Muskat, *Banks to Sandberg to Grace*, 134; Gillette and Palmer, *The ESPN Baseball Encyclopedia*, 1549; Horvitz and Horvitz, *The Big Book of Jewish Baseball*, 181; Slater, *Great Jews in Sports*, 274; *Chicago Tribune*, November 25, 1976; *Sporting News*, December 18, 1976.
27. *Los Angeles Times*, July 8, 1980.
28. *Chicago Tribune*, July 10, 1978.
29. *Ibid.*, November 29, 1978; *Los Angeles Times*, November 30, 1978; *Washington Post*, November 30, 1978; Ribalow and Ribalow, *Jewish Baseball Stars*, 272.
30. *Sporting News*, December 16, 1978, December 23, 1978.
31. Ribalow and Ribalow, *Jewish Baseball Stars*, 272.
32. Pietrusza *et al.*, *Baseball: The Biographical Encyclopedia*, 1090; Slater, *Great Jews in Sports*, 274.
33. *Sporting News*, October 29, 1977.
34. Ribalow and Ribalow, *Jewish Baseball Stars*, 273.
35. *Ibid.*, 275–276; Horvitz and Horvitz, *The Big Book of Jewish Baseball*, 182; Thorn *et al.*, *Total Baseball*, 431.
36. *Sporting News*, April 19, 1980.
37. *Ibid.*, June 14, 1980.
38. *Ibid.*, August 23, 1980.
39. *Ibid.*, September 6, 1980.
40. David McQuay, "Superstitions Are Still Part of Baseball Scene." *Baseball Digest*, January 1982, 60.
41. Ribalow and Ribalow, *Jewish Baseball Stars*, 284–285; Gillette and Palmer, *The ESPN Baseball Encyclopedia*, 1549; Thorn *et al.*, *Total Baseball*, 2250; Horvitz and Horvitz, *The Big Book of Jewish Baseball*, 182.
42. Pietrusza *et al.*, *Baseball: The Biographical Encyclopedia*, 1090.
43. *Los Angeles Times*, November 12, 1980; *Chicago Tribune*, November 13, 1980; *New York Times*, November 13, 1980; Ribalow and Ribalow, *Jewish Super Stars*, 285; *Sporting News*, November 15, 1980.
44. Horvitz and Horvitz, *The Big Book of Jewish Baseball*, 182.
45. Ribalow and Ribalow, *Jewish Baseball Stars*, 281.
46. Steve Stone, "The Game I'll Never Forget," *Baseball Digest*, March 1963, 91.
47. John Kuenster, "Steve Stone Thinks He Can Improve on His Cy Young Award Year," *Baseball Digest*, June 1981, 15; Slater, *Great Jews in Sports*, 274–275.
48. *Washington Post*, May 20, 1981; *Sporting News*, June 6, 1981; Slater, *Great Jews in Sports*, 274.
49. *Chicago Tribune*, March 12, 1982.
50. *Washington Post*, March 13, 1982.
51. *Chicago Tribune*, March 26, 1982.
52. *Ibid.*, June 2, 1982; *Washington Post*, June 2, 1982.
53. Gillette and Palmer, *The ESPN Baseball Encyclopedia*, 1549; Horvitz and Horvitz, *The Big Book of Jewish Baseball*, 172.
54. Steve Stone, *Where's Harry? Steve Stone Remembers His Years with Harry Caray* (Dallas: Taylor, 1999), 8.
55. *Sporting News*, June 14, July 5, 1982.
56. *Washington Post*, November 10, 1982; *Sporting News*, November 29, 1982; Stone, "Where's Harry?" 8–9; Slater, *Great Jews in Sports*, 275; Pietrusza *et al.*, *Baseball: The Biographical Encyclopedia*, 1090.
57. *Chicago Tribune*, June 7, 1983.
58. Press Release, 8/19/2002 found at www.chicago. cubs.mlb.com; "Steve Stone's Resignation Letter," found at www.cubschronicle.com; "Cubs Broadcaster Stone gets last word in battle with team," at www.cbs.sportsline.cubs; "Longtime broadcaster Steve Stone Steps Down," 10/28/ 2004 at www.usatoday.com.
59. "Steve Stone Joins WSCR in Chicago," 2/4/05 at www.radio.about.com.
60. Horvitz and Horvitz, *The Big Book of Jewish Baseball*, 181; Slater, *Great Jews in Sports*, 275; Pietrusza *et al.*, *Baseball: The Biographical Encyclopedia*, 1090; *Chicago Tribune*, July 10, 1978.
61. Spaner, "From Greenberg to Green," 177–178.
62. Ribalow and Ribalow, *Jewish Baseball Stars*, 289.
63. Slater, *Great Jews in Sports*, 275.

Chapter 14

1. Horvitz and Horvitz, *The Big Book of Jewish Baseball*, 88; Joe Horlen Interview with Mark Liptak, found at www. whitesoxinteractive.com (hereafter referred to as Liptak Interview w/Horlen.
2. *Ibid.*
3. Litvak Interview w/Horlen; Gillette and Palmer, *The ESPN Baseball Encyclopedia*, 1287.
4. "Joe Horlen," on jewsinsports.org.
5. Horvitz and Horvitz, *The Big Book of Jewish Baseball*, 89; "The Ballplayers—Joe Horlen," www.baseballlibrary.com.
6. Gillette and Palmer, *The ESPN Baseball Encyclopedia*, 1287; *Sporting News*, February 13, 1965.

7. "Joe Horlen," www.jewsinsports.org.

8. *New York Times*, July 9, 1967; September 11, 1967.

9. *Ibid.*, December 20, 1967; *Sporting News*, December 30, 1967.

10. *Ibid.*, November 11, 1967.

11. Horvitz and Horvitz, *The Big Book of Jewish Baseball*, 89.

12. *Sporting News*, June 24, 1967; Horvitz and Horvitz, *The Big Book of Jewish Baseball*, 89; "The Ballplayers," www.baseballlibrary.com.

13. Horvitz and Horvitz, *The Big Book of Jewish Baseball*, 89; "The Ballplayers," www.baseballlibrary.com.

14. www.whiteinteractive.com.

15. *Sporting News*, August 15, 1970, June 12, 1971; "Joe Horlen," jewsinsports.org; "Joe Horlen," www.thebaseballnexus.com; Gillette and Palmer, *The ESPN Baseball Encyclopedia*, 1287; Thorn *et al.*, *Total Baseball*, 1994.

16. *Sporting News*, April 15, 1972; *New York Times*, March 28, 1972.

17. Gillette and Palmer, *The ESPN Baseball Encyclopedia*, 1287.

18. Thorn *et al.*, *Total Baseball*, 409–410.

19. "Joe Horlen," www.jewsinsports.org.

20. *Sporting News*, October 21, 1972.

21. *Ibid.*, September 29, 1973; November 17, 1973; July 6, 1974.

22. *Ibid.*, February 9, 1987; September 4, 1989.

23. Horvitz and Horvitz, *The Big Book of Jewish Baseball*, 89–90.

24. *Ibid.*, 90.

25. Larry DeFillipo, "Point Men," *National Pastime* 25 (2005), 120; Horvitz and Horvitz, *The Big Book of Jewish Baseball*, 16; "Lloyd Allen," www.jewsinsports.org.

26. Horvitz and Horvitz, *The Big Book of Jewish Baseball*, 16.

27. *Sporting News*, June 8, 1968.

28. DeFillipo, "Point Men," 120; Horvitz and Horvitz, *The Big Book of Jewish Baseball*, 17.

29. Gillette and Palmer, *The ESPN Baseball Encyclopedia*, 1057.

30. *Washington Post*, October 1, 1970.

31. "Lloyd Allen Stats," www.baseball-almanac.com; *Los Angeles Times*, July 17, 1971.

32. DeFillipo, "Point Men," 120; "Lloyd Allen," www.jewsinsports.org; Horvitz and Horvitz, *The Big Book of Jewish Baseball*, 17; *Los Angeles Times*, April 23, 1971.

33. DeFillipo, "Point Men," 120; *Sporting News*, September 18, 1971.

34. "Lloyd Allen Stats," at www.baseball-almanac.com; *Los Angeles Times*, July 1, 1972; Thorn *et al.*, *Total Baseball*, 1770.

35. *Los Angeles Times*, May 14, 1973.

36. *Ibid.*, May 21, 1973; *Sporting News*, June 2, 1973.

37. "Lloyd Allen Stats," at www.baseball-almanac.com; Thorn et al., *Total Baseball*, 1770.

38. *Chicago Tribune*, July 2, 1974.

39. Horvitz and Horvitz, *The Big Book of Jewish Baseball*, 17.

40. *Sporting News*, February 7, 1976, January 22, 1977.

41. Horvitz and Horvitz, *The Big Book of Jewish Baseball*, 17; DeFillipo, "Point Men," 120.

42. Spaner, "From Greenberg to Green," 178; *Sporting News*, June 27, 1970.

43. Smith, "Old Order Changeth: From Dimag to Mick to Maddox," *Black Sports*, February 1975, 23.

44. *Ibid.*; Horvitz and Horvitz, *The Big Book of Jewish Baseball*, 108.

45. Spaner, "From Greenberg to Green," 178.

46. "Elliott Maddox," at www.jewsinsports.org; Horvitz and Horvitz, *The Big Book of Jewish Baseball*, 108.

47. *Washington Post*, November 12, 1970.

48. Smith, "Old Order Changeth," 46.

49. *Washington Post*, October 10, 1970.

50. "Elliott Maddox," www.jewsinsports.org.

51. *Washington Post*, February 25, 1971.

52. Smith, "Old Order Changeth," 46.

53. "Elliott Maddox Baseball Stats," at www.baseball-almanac.com; Thorn et al., *Total Baseball*, 1409.

54. Smith, "Old Order Changeth," 46.

55. *New York Times*, March 24, 1974.

56. *Ibid.*, June 4, 1974.

57. Smith, "The Old Order Changeth," 46.

58. *Ibid.*, Gillette and Palmer, *The ESPN Baseball Encyclopedia*, 697.

59. "Elliott Maddox," www.jewsinsports.org.

60. Thorn *et al.*, *Total Baseball*, 1409.

61. Gillette and Palmer, *The ESPN Baseball Encyclopedia*, 697; "Elliott Maddox Baseball Stats," www.baseball-almanac.com.

62. Thorn *et al.*, *Total Baseball*, 422.

63. *Los Angeles Times*, January 21, 1977; *New York Times*, January 21, 1977; *Sporting News*, February 5, 1977.

64. *Washington Post*, October 29, 1977; *New York Times*, December 1, 2, 1977; *Sporting News*, December 17, 1977.

65. *Ibid.*, May 13, 1978.

66. *New York Times*, February 6, 1981, March 21, 1981.

67. Gillette and Palmer, *The ESPN Baseball Encyclopedia*, 697; "Elliott Maddox," www.jewsinsports.org.

68. *Jerusalem Post*, September 28, 2006.

69. "Jewish Sports Hall of Fame," at www.jewishsports.org.

70. *Utica-Observer Dispatch*, August 20, 2004.

71. *Jerusalem Post*, September 28, 2006.

72. Horvitz and Horvitz, *The Big Book of Jewish Baseball*, 91.

73. *Sporting News*, October 28, 1972.

74. "Skip Jutze Statistics," at www.thebaseballcube.com.

75. *Ibid.*

76. *Sporting News*, July 22, 1972.

77. *Ibid.*, September 16, 1972.

78. "Skip Jutze Statistics," at www.baseball-reference.com; Gillette and Palmer, *The ESPN Baseball Encyclopedia*, 631.

79. *Sporting News*, October 28, 1972.

80. *Chicago Tribune*, November 30, 1971; *Sporting News*, December 16, 1972; "Skip Jutze Statistics," www.thebaseballcube.com.

81. *Sporting News*, January 20, 1973.

82. *Ibid.*, July 14, 1973.

83. "Baseball Stats," at www.baseball-almanac.com.

84. *New York Times*, April 4, 1974; *Sporting News*, April 20, 1974.

85. Horvitz and Horvitz, *The Big Book of Jewish Baseball*, 92; *Sporting News*, September 7, 1974.

86. Gillette and Palmer, *The ESPN Baseball Encyclopedia*, 631; "Skip Jutze Statistics," www.thebaseballcube.com; *Sporting News*, December 6, 1975.

87. "Skip Jutze Statistics," www.thebaseballcube.com; *Sporting News*, January 29, 1977; *Chicago Tribune*, January 13, 1977.

88. *Sporting News*, February 5, 1977.

89. Horvitz and Horvitz, *The Big Book of Jewish Baseball*, 92; "Jutze Baseball Stats," www.baseball-almanac.com; *Sporting News*, June 11, 1997.

90. Thorn *et al.*, *Total Baseball*, 1343.

91. Horvitz and Horvitz, *The Big Book of Jewish Baseball*, 189.

92. "Steve Yeager," at www.jewsinsports.org.

93. Pietrusza *et al.*, *Baseball: The Biographical Encyclopedia*, 1266.

94. Gillette and Palmer, *The ESPN Baseball Encyclopedia*, 1941; Thorn *et al.*, *Total Baseball*, 1754.

95. *Los Angeles Times*, March 30, 1972.

96. *Sporting News*, July 1, 1972.

97. Horvitz and Horvitz, *The Big Book of Jewish Baseball*, 189; Gillette and Palmer, *The ESPN Baseball Encyclopedia*, 1041.

98. "Steve Yeager," www.jewsinsports.org.

99. *Los Angeles Times*, March 23, 1973.

100. *Ibid.*

101. *Ibid.*, August 31, 1973.

102. *Sporting News*, March 23, 1974.

103. *Ibid.*

104. *Ibid.*

105. *Ibid.*

106. *Ibid.*, August 31, 1974.

107. Gillette and Palmer, *The ESPN Baseball Encyclopedia*, 1941,

108. Thorn *et al.*, *Total Baseball*, 416.

109. "Steve Yeager Fielding Stats," at sportsillustrated. com.

110. Horvitz and Horvitz, *The Big Book of Jewish Baseball*, 189.

111. *Los Angeles Times*, September 8, 1976; July 24, 1977; *Sporting News*, September 26, 1976.

112. "Steve Yeager," www.jewsinsports.org; Pietrusza *et al.*, *Baseball: The Biographical Encyclopedia*, 1266; "Steve Yeager," at www.baseball-reference.com; www.addict.sports. com.

113. *Sporting News*, February 12, 1977.

114. "Baseball Catcher Steve Yeager," www.members.tripod.com; Gillette and Palmer, *The ESPN Baseball Encyclopedia*, 1041.

115. Thorn *et al.*, *Total Baseball*, 625.

116. Doug Krikorian, "The Indispensable Dodger: Catcher Steve Yeager," *Baseball Digest*, July 1978, 37–39.

117. Thorn *et al.*, *Total Baseball*, 428.

118. "Steve Yeager," at www.jewsinsports.org; Thorn *et al.*, *Total Baseball*, 441.

119. Horvitz and Horvitz, *The Big Book of Jewish Baseball*, 190; "The Dodgers' Most Valuable Trio," *Sport*, January 1982, 13; *Sporting News*, November 14, 1981.

120. "The Dodgers Most Valuable Trio," 13.

121. *Los Angeles Times*, October 18, 1983.

122. *Ibid.*, September 7, 1984.

123. *Sporting News*, February 13, 1984.

124. Horvitz and Horvitz, *The Big Book of Jewish Baseball*, 189.

125. Thorn *et al.*, *Total Baseball*, 445, 451.

126. *Los Angeles Times, December 12, 1985; Sporting News*, December 23, 1985.

127. *Washington Post*, June 20, 1986; November 12, 1986.

128. "Steve Yeager," www.members.tripod.com.

129. "Steve Yeager," www.jewsinsports.org.

130. Pietrusza *et al.*, *Baseball: The Biographical Encyclopedia*, 1266.

131. www.pe.com.

132. *Sporting News*, April 12, 1993; Pietrusza *et al.*, *Baseball: The Biographical Encyclopedia*, 1266; Horvitz and Horvitz, *The Big Book of Jewish Baseball*, 190; *New York Times*, July 25, 1983

133. *Los Angeles Times*, October 30, 1975, July 25, 1983; Horvitz and Horvitz, *The Big Book of Jewish Baseball*, 190.

134. Horvitz and Horvitz, *The Big Book of Jewish Baseball*, 127.

135. *Ibid.*

136. "Jeff Newman," at www.jewsinsports.org.

137. Horvitz and Horvitz, *The Big Book of Jewish Baseball*, 127.

138. "Jeff Newman," at www.thebaseballcube.com.

139. "Jeff Newman Baseball Stats," at www.baseball-almanac.com.

140. "Jeff Newman Statistics," at www.baseball-reference.com; "Jeff Newman Statistics," at www.fangraphs.com.

141. "Jeff Newman Statistics," www.baseball-reference. com; Horvitz and Horvitz, *The Big Book of Jewish Baseball*, 127.

142. Horvitz and Horvitz, *The Big Book of Jewish Baseball*, 128; *Sporting News*, July 28, 1979.

143. *Sporting News*, January 10, 1981.

144. Thorn *et al.*, *Total Baseball*, 438, 440.

145. *Washington Post*, December 21, 1982; "The Ballplayers—Jeff Newman," at www.baseballlibrary.com; "Jeff Newman—The Baseball Cube," at www.baseballcube.com.

146. Gillette and Palmer, *The ESPN Baseball Encyclopedia*, 783.

147. *Ibid.*, November 1, 1985; *Sporting News*, November 18, 1985; "Jeff Newman," www.jewsinsports.org.

148. *New York Times*, June 27, 1986; *Washington Post*, June 27, 1986; Horvitz and Horvitz, *The Big Book of Jewish Baseball*, 128

149. Horvitz and Horvitz, *The Big Book of Jewish Baseball*, 128; *New York Times*, March 2, 2002; www.sports.go.com.

150. *Sporting News*, June 10, 1978.

151. Bob Tufts, E-mail interview with authors, July 18, 2008.

152. *Los Angeles Times*, August 5, 1981.

153. Tufts inteview.

154. Gillette and Palmer, *The ESPN Baseball Encyclopedia*, 1574; "Bob Tufts, at www.jewsinsports.org.

155. *Chicago Tribune*, March 31, 1982; *Washington Post*, March 31, 1982.

156. *Sporting News*, September 17, 1982.

157. Gillette and Palmer, *The ESPN Baseball Encyclopedia*, 1574.

158. *Sporting News*, September 27, 1982.

159. *New Jersey Jewish News*, April 9, 2007; Tufts interview.

160. *New Jersey Jewish News*, April 19, 2007.

161. "Dowbrigade News," at www.blogs.law.harvard.edu; Tufts interview.

162. *New York Times*, June 24, 1983.

163. *Chicago Tribune*, May 14, 1983; *Washington Post*, May 14, 1983; *Sporting News*, June 13,1983.

164. *Chicago Tribune*, June 8, 1983; "Bob Tufts," www. jewsinsports.org.

165. *New Jersey Jewish News*, April 19. 2007.

166. *Ibid.*

167. *Ibid.*, July 20, 2006, April 19, 2007.

168. *Ibid.*, April 19, 2007.

Chapter 15

1. "Lefty Phillips," at www.jewsinsports.org.

2. *The Sporting News*, April 25, 1970.

3. Roy Blount Jr., "Lefty Makes the Angels Sing," *Sports Illustrated*, June 8, 1970, 29; "Lefty Phillips," www. jewsinsports.org; *The Sporting News*, April 25, 1970.

4. *Ibid.*

5. *Washington Post*, May 28, 1969; *Los Angeles Times*, May 26, 1969; *New York Times*, June 1, 1969; *Sporting News*, April 25, 1970.

6. *Ibid.*; "Lefty Phillips," www.jewsinsports.org; Horvitz and Horvitz, *The Big Book of Jewish Baseball*, 132; "Lefty Phillips," www.jewsinsports.org.

7. *Sporting News*, April 25, 1970.

8. *Los Angeles Times*, March 30, 1965.

9. *Sporting News*, April 27, 1968.

10. *Ibid.*, May 4, 1968.

11. *Ibid.*, May 18, 1968.

12. *Los Angeles Times*, September 30, 1968, February 20, 1969; *Sporting News*, October 19, 1968.

13. "Los Angeles Angels of Anaheim," at www.sportsen cyclopedia.com.

14. *Chicago Tribune*, May 18, 1969.

15. *Chicago Defender*, May 29, 1969; *Chicago Tribune*, May 28, 1969; *Sporting News*, June 7, 1969; *Washington Post*, May 28, 1969.

16. *Los Angeles Times*, May 28, 1969.

17. *Ibid.*, May 30, 1969.

18. *Sporting News*, July 19, 1969.

19. Gillette and Palmer, *The ESPN Baseball Encyclopedia*, 85.

20. *Sporting News*, October 18, 1969; *Los Angeles Times*, October 1, 1969; *New York Times*, October 1, 1969; *Washington Post*, October 1, 1969.

21. Blount Jr., "Lefty Makes the Angels Sing," 23.

22. "Lefty Phillips," www.jewsinsports. org.

23. *Washington Post*, October 1, 1969.

24. *Chicago Defender*, August 8, 1970; "Angels of Anaheim," www.sportsencyclopedia.com.

25. Gillette and Palmer, *The ESPN Baseball Encyclopedia*, 83.

26. *Sporting News*, September 5, 1970; *Los Angeles Times*, September 12, 1970; *Washington Post*, September 12, 1970.

27. *Sporting News*, September 19, 1970.

28. *Ibid.*, February 6, 1971.

29. *Los Angeles Times*, March 7, 1971.

30. *The World Almanac and Book of Facts*, 890.

31. *Chicago Defender*, August 8, 1970; *Los Angeles Times*, June 4, 1971.

32. *Los Angeles Times*, March 22, 1971, May 17, 1971.

33. *Ibid.*, June 5, 1971.

34. *Ibid.*, June 17, 1971.

35. *Ibid.*, June 18, 1971.

36. *Washington Post*, June 27, 1971; *Los Angeles Times*, June 27, 1971.

37. *New York Times*, August 11, 1971.

38. *Los Angeles Times*, August 18, 1971.

39. *Chicago Defender*, September 29, 1971.

40. *Washington Post*, September 29, 1971.

41. John Kuenster, "Warm Up Tosses," *Baseball Digest*, October 1971, 4.

42. Gillette and Palmer, *The ESPN Baseball Encyclopedia*, 81; "Lefty Phillips," www.jewsinsports.org.

43. *Los Angeles Times*, October 6, 1971.

44. *Chicago Tribune and New York Times*, October 8, 1971.

45. *Los Angeles Times*, May 12, 1972.

46. "Angels of Anaheim," www.sportsecyclopedia.com.

47. Horvitz and Horvitz, *The Big Book of Jewish Baseball*, 133; "Lefty Phillips," www.Jewsinsports.org; *Chicago Tribune*, June 13, 1973; *Los Angeles Times*, June 13, 1972; *Washington Post*, June 13, 1972; *New York Times*, June 13, 1962.

48. *Sporting News*, July 1, 1972.

49. Horvitz and Horvitz, *The Big Book of Jewish Baseball*, 156.

50. "Rothschild Always Rooted for the Cubs," found at www.mlb.com.

51. "Chicago Cubs Team," at Chicago.cubs.mlb.com.

52. *Ibid.*; Horvitz and Horvitz, *The Big Book of Jewish Baseball*, 156.

53. Gillette and Palmer, *The ESPN Baseball Encyclopedia*, 1497; "Larry Rothschild Baseball Stats," at www.baseball-almanac.com.

54. Thorn *et al.*, *Total Baseball*, 2199.

55. *New York Times*, February 23, 1990.

56. *Ibid.*, November 17, 1989.

57. Thorn *et al.*, *Total Baseball*, 468.

58. *Sporting News*, October 28, 1991, November 11, 1991; *New York Times*, November 1, 1992, May 25, 1993; Horvitz and Horvitz, *The Big Book of Jewish Baseball*, 156–157; "Larry

Rothschild," www.jewsinsports.org. "Chicago Cub Team," at www.cubs.mlb.com.

59. *Sporting News*, October 17, 1994.

60. Thorn *et al.*, *Total Baseball*, 498; "Larry Rothschild," www.jewsinsports.org.

61. Horvitz and Horvitz, *The Big Book of Jewish Baseball*, 157.

62. *Sporting News*, November 17, 1997; *New York Times*, November 8, 1997; "Chicago Cubs' Team," www.cubs.mlb.com; *The Kentucky Post* at www.cincypost.com; *USA Today Baseball Weekly*, March 29, 2005.

63. Gillette and Palmer, *The ESPN Baseball Encyclopedia*, 1703; "Chicago Cubs Team," www.chicago.cubs.mlb.com; *Sporting News*, February 1, 1999.

64. *Ibid.*, January 31, 2000.

65. "Rays Fire Manager Rothschild," at www.sportsillustrated.cnn.com.

66. "Chicago Cubs Team," www.chicago.cubs.mlb.com; "Larry Rothschild," www.jewsinsports.org.

67. *Sporting News*, November 5, 2001; "Manager and Coaches," at www.chicago.cubs.mlb.com.

Chapter 16

1. Spaner, "From Greenberg to Green," 178.

2. "Brian Kowitz," www.baseball-reference.com.

3. "Brian Kowitz," www.jewsinsports.org; "Brian Kowitz Stats," www.baseball-almanac.com.

4. Gillette and Palmer, *The ESPN Baseball Encyclopedia*, 654.

5. *New York Times*, June 19, 1995.

6. "Brian Kowitz," www.jewsinsports.org.

7. Horvitz and Horvitz, *The Big Book of Jewish Baseball*, 99.

8. "Aberdeen Arsenal," at www.baseball-reference.com.

9. Horvitz and Horvitz, *The Big Book of Jewish Baseball*, 84; "Eric Helfand at www.jewsinsports.org.

10. *Ibid.*

11. "Eric Helfand Statistics," www.baseballalmanac.com.

12. *New York Times*, November 18, 22, 1992.

13. Gillette and Palmer, *The ESPN Baseball Encyclopedia*, 574; Thorn *et al.*, *Total Baseball*, 1286.

14. "Eric Helfand," www.jewsinsports.org; "Eric Helfand," www.thebaseballcube.com.

15. Horvitz and Horvitz, *The Big Book of Jewish Baseball*, 193.

16. "Eddie Zosky," www.jewsinsports.org.

17. "Eddie Zosky," www.thebaseballcube.com; www.retrosheet.org.

18. "Eddie Zosky," www.member.tripod.com.

19. Horvitz and Horvitz, *The Big Book of Jewish Baseball*, 192.

20. *New York Times*, March 1, 1992.

21. "Eddie Zosky," www.thebaseballcube.com.

22. Horvitz and Horvitz, *The Big Book of Jewish Baseball*, 193; "Eddie Zosky," www.thebaseballcube.com.

23. "Eddie Zosky," www.members.tripod.com; "Eddie Zosky," www.jewsinsports.org.

24. "Eddie Zosky," www.retrosheet.org.

25. "Eddie Zosky," www.thebaseballcube.com.

26. *Ibid.*

27. Gillette and Palmer, *The ESPN Baseball Encyclopedia*, 1048; www.sportsillustrated.com; "Eddie Zosky Statistics," www.baseball-reference.com; *New York Times*, March 26, 1998, April 1, 1998, October 13, 1998, September 12, 2000.

28. "Eddie Zosky," www.jewsinsports.org.

29. *USA Today Baseball Weekly*, March 24, 1999.

30. Horvitz and Horvitz, *The Big Book of Jewish Baseball*, 63; "Micah Franklin," at www.jewsinsports.org.

31. Horvitz and Horvitz, *The Big Book of Jewish Baseball*, 63; "Micah Franklin—Armchair," at www.armchairgm.wikia.com; "Micah Franklin Statistics," www.baseball-reference.com.

32. *Sporting News*, April 21, 1997; *USA Today Baseball Weekly*, March 24, 1999; "Micah Franklin," www.armchairgm.wikia.com; "Micah Franklin Statistics," www.baseball-reference.com; Horvitz and Horvitz, *The Big Book of Jewish Baseball*, 64.

33. Micah Franklin," www.jewsinsports.org.

34. *Ibid.*; "Micah Franklin," www.baseball-reference.com.

35. *Tucson Citizen*, August 25, 2004.

36. "David Newhan," www.jewsinsports.org; *USA Today*, July 26, 2004; *Washington Post*, March 22, 2005.

37. *USA Today*, July 26, 2004; "David Newhan," www.jewsinsports.org.

38. "David Newhan," www.jewsinsports.org; www.jewishtimes.com.

39. Horvitz and Horvitz, *The Big Book of Jewish Baseball*, 278.

40. *New York Times*, November 27, 1997.

41. "David Newhan," www.jewsinsports.org.

42. "David Newhan Baseball Stats," www.baseball-almanac.com; Gillette and Palmer, *The ESPN Baseball Encyclopedia*, 783.

43. "David Newhan Baseball Stats," www.baseball-almanac.com.

44. "David Newhan," www.jewsinsports.org.

45. "David Newhan Baseball Stats," www.baseball-reference.com; "David Newhan," www.jewsinsports.org; *Washington Post*, March 22, 2005; *Boston Globe*, July 22, 2004; *USA Today*, July 26, 2004.

46. *USA Today Sports Weekly*, February 4–10, 2009.

47. Joe Eskenazi, "The Tattoos of Gabe Kapler," at www.jewsweek.com; *Boston Globe*, July 22, 2007.

48. *Boston Globe*, July 22, 2007; Jonathan Mayo, "Gabe Kapler: Your Everyday Bodybuilding Jewish Outfielder," found at www.jewishsports.com; Gabe Kapler, telephone interview with authors, December 19, 2008.

49. "Gabe Kapler Statistics," www.baseball-reference.com.

50. Horvitz and Horvitz, *The Big Book of Jewish Baseball*, 275; Jeff Goodman, "Kaplan Hoping to Rejuvenate Career, "Interviews and Profiles," at www.interfaithfamily.com; Eskenzai, "The Tattoos of Gabe Kapler."

51. Horvitz and Horvitz, *The Big Book of Jewish Baseball*, 275; "Gabe Kapler," www.jewsinsports.org; Eskenazi, "The Tattoos of Gabe Kapler."

52. Kapler telephone interview; Eskenazi, "The Tattoos of Gabe Kapler"; "Gabriel Kapler," www.jewishvirtuallibrary.org.

53. "Gabe Kapler," www.thebaseballcube.com.

54. Horvitz and Horvitz, *The Big Book of Jewish Baseball*, 276; *Jewish World Review*, June 16, 1999.

55. "Gabe Kapler," www.thebaseballcube.com; "Gabe Kapler Player Page," www.sportsillustrated.cnn.com; "Gabe Kapler Statistics," www.baseball-reference.com.

56. Gillette and Palmer, *The ESPN Baseball Encyclopedia*, 632; Thorn *et al.*, *Total Baseball*, 1344.

57. Jonathan Mayo, "Your Everyday Bodybuilding Jewish Outfielder."

58. "Gabe Kapler Statistics," www.baseball-reference.com; "Gabe Kapler," www.jewsinsports.org.

59. "Gabe Kapler," www.jewsinsports.org; "Gabe Kapler—The Babe" www.freewebs.com.

60. Jeff Merron, "Green, Koufax and Greenberg—same dilemma, different decisions," September 26, 2001, at www.espn.go.com.

61. *Ibid.*

62. "Gabe Kapler," www.jewsinsports.org; "Gabe Kapler—The Babe," at www.freewebs.com.

63. "Gabe Kapler," www.jewsinsports.org; Gillette and Palmer, *The ESPN Baseball Encyclopedia*, 21, 632.

64. "Gabe Kapler Statistics," www.baseball-reference.com.

65. "Gabe Kapler," www.thebaseballcube.com.

66. *New York Times*, June 29, 2003.

67. "Gabe Kapler—The Babe," www.freewebs.com.

68. Gillette and Palmer, *The ESPN Baseball Encyclopedia*, 17, 632.

69. "Gabe Kapler," wwwjewsinsports.org.

70. Thorn *et al.*, *Total Baseball*, 537–540.

71. "Gabe Kapler," www.jewishvirtuallibrary.org.

72. *Ibid.*

73. Kapler Changes Red Sox," at www.sports.espn.go.com.

74. Kapler telephone interview.

75. *Boston Globe*, July 22, 2007.

76. *Ibid.*

77. "Gabe Kapler Statistics," www.baseball-reference.com.

78. "Kapler Interview with www.onmilwaukee.com, May 5, 2008.

79. Jeff Goodman, "Kapler Hoping to Rejuvenate Career."

80. "The Gabe Kapler Foundation," at www.kaplerfoundation.org; *Boston Globe*, July 22, 2007.

81. www.mlb.com.

82. "Ruben Amaro" at www.jewsinsports.org; Horvitz and Horvitz, *The Big Book of Jewish Baseball*, 18–19; "Ruben Amaro Jr. at www.baseballreference.com; "Ruben Amaro Jr." at www.news.prnewswire.com.

83. *New York Times*, April 15, 1992; Horvitz, *The Big Book of Jewish Baseball*, 18; "Ruben Amaro," www.jewsinsports.org.

84. *New York Times*, April 15, 1992.

85. www.prenewswire.com; *New York Times*, April 15, 1992.

86. *New York Times*, April 15, 1992.

87. *Baseball USA Today*, June 14, 1995.

88. Horvitz and Horvitz, *The Big Book of Jewish Baseball*, 18; "Ruben Amaro Jr.," www.jewsinsports.org; *New York Times*, April 15, 1992.

89. Horvitz and Horvitz, *The Big Book of Jewish Baseball*, 18.

90. "Ruben Amaro Stats," www.baseball-almanac.com; Gillette and Palmer, *The ESPN Baseball Encyclopedia*, 283; Thorn *et al.*, *Total Baseball*, 995.

91. "Amaro Baseball Stats," www.baseball-almanac.com.

92. Gillette and Palmer, *The ESPN Baseball Encyclopedia*, 283.

93. "Ruben Amaro," www.jewsinsports.org.

94. Thorn *et al.*, *Total Baseball*, 483.

95. *Ibid.*, 484.

96. "Ruben Amaro Baseball Stats," www.baseball-almanac.com; Horvitz and Horvitz, *The Big Book of Jewish Baseball*, 19.

97. Gillette and Palmer, *The ESPN Baseball Encyclopedia*, 283.

98. *Sporting News*, October 5, 1998.

99. *New York Times*, October 15, 2000.

100. *Philadelphia Inquirer*, November 3, 2008.

101. "Jewish Family and Children's Service of Greater Philadelphia," at www.jfcsphil. org.

102. "Ruben Amaro, Jr." at www.news.prnewswire.com.

103. "Amaro Takes Over Reins for Phillies," at www.philadelphia.phillies.mlb.com.

104. *Ibid.*

105. Gruver, *Koufax*, 55.

106. *Jews News Weekly of Northern California*, August 16, 1996.

107. Horvitz and Horvitz, *The Big Book of Jewish Baseball*, 105; Steve Feldman, "He's One of a Rare Breed: Jewish Big-League Catcher," *Jewish Exponent*, January 8, 1983, 6.

108. "Jesse Levis," www.thebaseballcube.com.

109. *New York Times*, August 22, September 27, 1992; "Jesse Levis," www.thebaseballcube.com; "Jesse Levis Baseball Stats," www.baseball-almanac.com.

110. *New York Times*, May 12, 1994.

111. *Cincinnati Enquirer*, March 17, 2002.

112. "Jesse Levis Stats," www.baseball-reference.com.

113. *Jewish News Weekly of Northern California*, August 16, 1996.

114. *Ibid.*, September 27, 1996.

115. Gillette and Palmer, *The ESPN Baseball Encyclopedia*, 677; Horvitz and Horvitz, *The Big Book of Jewish Baseball*, 106.

116. "Jesse Levis Statistics," www.baseball-reference.com; *New York Times*, October 7, 1998.

117. *New York Times*, July 312, 1999; "Jesse Levis Baseball Stats," www.baseball-almanac.com; "Jesse Levis," www.thebaseballcube.com; "Jesse Levis Statistics," www.baseball-reference.com; *Atlanta Jewish Times*, March 30, 2001.

118. "Jesse Levis Statistics," www.baseball-almanac.com; "Levis Statistics," www.baseball-almanac.com; "Jesse Levis," www.thebaseballcube.com.

119. "Jesse Levis," www.thebaseballcube.com; *Cincinnati Enquirer*, March 17, 2002; *Cincinnati Post*, March 11, 2002

120. www.tarheelblue.cstv.com.

121. www.commonwealthtimes.com.

122. www.mlb.com, February 2, 2004.

123. Joe O'Laughlin, "Mike Lieberthal: Phillies' Leader Behind the Mask: Philadelphia Catcher Works Diligently with His Coaches and Pitching Staff to Perfect Their Strategic Approach to Defeating an Opponent," June, 2004 found at www.findarticles.com.

124. *New York Times*, July 18, 1999.

125. "Lieberthal Statistics," www.baseball-reference.com.

126. Alan Schwarz, "Lieberthal Satisfies His Naysayers," *Baseball America*, December 10, 1991, 14.

127. "Mike Lieberthal," www.thebaseballcube.com.

128. *Baseball USA Today*, September 30, 1992.

129. Horvitz and Horvitz, *The Big Book of Jewish Baseball*, 276.

130. *Ibid.*; Gillette and Palmer, *The ESPN Baseball Encyclopedia*, 678; "Mike Lieberthal Statistics, www.baseballreference.com.

131. "Mike Lieberthal," www.jewsinsports.org.

132. Thorn et al., *Total Baseball*, 1390; "Mike Lieberthal," www.jewsinsports.org; "Mike Lieberthal," at www.losangelesdodgersonline.com.

133. "Mike Lieberthal," www.jewsinsports.org.

134. O'Laughlin, "Mike Lieberthal," *Baseball Digest*, June 2004.

135. "Mike Lieberthal, www.jewsinsports.org.

136. Gillette and Palmer, *The ESPN Baseball Encyclopedia*, 20.

137. "Mike Lieberthal," www.jewsinsports.org; *South Jersey News*, March 31, 2004.

138. Gillette and Palmer, *The ESPN Baseball Encyclopedia*, 678; "Mike Lieberthal," www.thebaseballcube.com; "Mike Lieberthal," www.jewsinsports.org.

139. *South Jersey News*, March 31, 2004.

140. O'Laughlin, "Mike Lieberthal," June 2004.

141. *South Jersey News*, March 31, 2004.

142. "Mike Lieberthal," www.losangelesdodgersonline.com.

143. *Ibid.*

144. "Mike Lieberthal Retires," www.cbs3.com.

145. "Mike Lieberthal," www.losangelesdodgersonline.com; "Mike Lieberthal Statistics," www.baseball-reference.com.

146. Gillette and Palmer, *The ESPN Baseball Encyclopedia*, 679; "Mike Lieberthal," www.thebaseballcube.com.

147. "Mike Lieberthal Statistics," www.baseball-reference.com.

148. "Mike Lieberthal Hangs Up Spikes," www.scout.com; "MLB Catcher Mike Lieberthal Retires," at www.sports.outsidethebeltway.com.

149. "Lieberthal Retires as a Phillie," www.abclocal.go.com.

150. "Mike Lieberthal," www.losangelesdodgersonline.com.

151. "Brad Ausmus Statistics," www.baseball-reference.com.

152. Bill Palmer, "Ausmus Catching On," *Baseball America*, September 10, 1991, 15; Horvitz and Horvitz, *The Big Book of Jewish Baseball*, 22; "Brad Ausmus," www.jewsinsports.org.

153. "Brad Ausmus." www.thebaseballcube.com.

154. "Ausmus Statistics," www.baseball-reference.com.

155. *Ibid.*; "boys of tireball," www.tireball.com; *New York Times*, July 27, 1993.

156. Gillette and Palmer, *The ESPN Baseball Encyclopedia*, 292.

157. "Nation Master—Encyclopedia," at www.nationmaster.com.

158. "Brad Ausmus," www.jewsinsports.org; "boys of tireball." www.boysoftireball.com; "Brad Ausmus," www.thebaseballcube.com.

159. *New York Times*, June 19, 1996; "Brad Ausmus Statistics," www.baseball-reference.com.

160. "Brad Ausmus," www.fantasybaseball.usatoday.com.

161. *New York Times*, December 11, 1996; "Brad Ausmus Statistics," www.baseballreference.com; "Nation Master—Encyclopedia, www.nationmaster.com; "Jewish Sports Hall of Fame," at www.jewishsports.org.

162. "Brad Ausmus Statistics," www.baseball-reference.com.

163. "boys of fireball," www.boysoffireball.tireball.com; "Brad Ausmus," www.jewsinsports.org; Thorn et al., 493.

164. Horvitz and Horvitz, *The Big Book of Jewish Baseball*, 23.

165. Thorn *et al.*, *Total Baseball*, 499.

166. *New York Times*, January 15, 1998; "Brad Ausmus Statistics," www.baseball-reference.com; "NationMaster—Encyclopedia," www.nationmaster.com.

167. "Boys of Tireball," www.boysoftireball.tireball.com; "Jewish Sports Hall of Fame," www.jewishsports.org; "Brad Ausmus," www.jewsinsports.org.

168. "Jewish Sports Hall of Fame," www.jewishsports.org; Gillette and Palmer, *The ESPN Baseball Encyclopedia*, 292; Thorn *et al.*, *Total Baseball*, 1004; "boys of tireball," www.boysoftireball.tireball.com; "Brad Ausmus," www.jewsinsports.org.

169. *New York Times*, December 12, 2000; "Brad Ausmus Statistics," www.baseball-reference.com; "NationMaster—Encyclopedia, www.nationmaster.com.

170. "boys of tireball," www.boyofsoftireball.tireball.com.

171. "Brad Ausmus," www.jewsinsports.org.

172. Thorn *et al.*, *Total Baseball*, 521.

173. Gillette and Palmer, *The ESPN Baseball Encyclopedia*, 292.

174. *Ibid.*, 1752; "Brad Ausmus," www.jewsinsports.org.

175. "Jewish Sports Hall of Fame," www.jewishsports.org.

176. "boys of tireball," www.boysoftireball.tireball.com.

177. Gillette and Palmer, *The ESPN Baseball Encyclopedia*, 1752.

178. *Ibid.*, 292.

179. *Houston Chronicle*, September 28, 2008.

180. www.mlb.com.

181. Horvitz and Horvitz, *The Big Book of Jewish Baseball*, 154.

182. *Ibid.*

183. "Wayne Rosenthal Baseball Stats," at www.baseball-almanac.com; Gillette and Palmer, *The ESPN Baseball Encyclopedia*, 1496; Thorn *et al.*, *Total Baseball*, 2198.

184. *Sporting News*, March 30, 1992.

185. Thorn *et al.*, *Total Baseball*, 2198.

186. "Wayne Rosenthal," www.jewsinsports.org; Wayne Rosenthal Baseball Stats," www.baseball-almanac.com.

187. Gillette and Palmer, *The ESPN Baseball Encyclopedia*, 1496.

188. *San Diego Union Tribune*, June 8, 2003.

189. *Ibid.*

190. *USA Today*, April 27, 2004.

191. "Garciaparra Eligible to Become Free Agent," at sports.espn.go.com.

192. *Sporting News*, October 11, 2004.

193. "Rosenthal vs. Burnett," at www.cantstopthebleeding.com.

194. *Sporting News*, October 11, 2004.

195. "Greensboro Grasshoppers," at www.gsohoppers.com.

196. Spaner, "From Greenberg to Green," 178.

197. *Jewish World Review*, September 22, 1999; Horvitz and Horvitz, *The Big Book of Jewish Baseball*, 107; Spaner, "From Greenberg to Green," 178.

198. *Ibid.*

199. "Andrew Lorraine," www.thebaseballcube.com.

200. Gillette and Palmer, *The ESPN Baseball Encyclopedia*, 1357; "Andrew Lorraine," www.sports.espn.go.com.

201. "Andrew Lorraine," at www.armchairgm.wikia.com.

202. "Andrew Lorraine," www.thebaseballcube.com; Thorn *et al.*, *Total Baseball*, 2062; "Andrew Lorraine," www.jewsinsports.org.

203. *New York Times*, January 23, 1996.

204. Horvitz and Horvitz, *The Big Book of Jewish Baseball*, 108; *New York Times*, March 19, 1996; "Andrew Lorraine," www.thebaseballcube.com.

205. *New York Times*, September 9, 1998; Gillette and Palmer, *The ESPN Baseball Encyclopedia*, 1357; *Jewish World Review*, September 22, 1999.

206. *Las Vegas Sun*, April 25, 2003.

207. *Jewish World Review*, September 22, 1999.

208. Gillette and Palmer, *The ESPN Encyclopedia*, 1357; "Andrew Lorraine," www.jewsinsports.org.

209. "Andrew Lorraine," www.thebaseballcube.com.

210. "Andrew Lorraine," www.jewsinsports.org.

211. "Andrew Lorraine Baseball Statistics, www.baseball-almanac.com; "Andrew Lorraine," www.thebaseballcube.com.

212. Horvitz and Horvitz, *The Big Book of Jewish Baseball*, 24; "Brian Bark," www.jewsinsports.org.

213. Horvitz and Horvitz, *The Big Book of Jewish Baseball*, 24.

214. "Brian Bark Statistics," www.thebaseballcube.com.

215. "Brian Bark," www.jewsinsports.org.

216. "Brian Bark Statistics," www.thebaseballcube.com.

217. Gillette and Palmer, *The ESPN Baseball Encyclopedia*, 1073; Thorn *et al.*, *Total Baseball*, 1786.

218. "Brian Bark," www.jewsinsports.org.

219. "Mike Milchin," www.baseball-reference.com.

220. Horvitz and Horvitz, *The Big Book of Jewish Baseball*, 99, 120.

221. "Mike Milchin Statistics," www.baseball-reference.com.

222. Horvitz and Horvitz, *The Big Book of Jewish Baseball*, 121; "Mike Milchin," www.baseball-reference.com.

223. Brian Milchin," www.baseball-reference.com.

224. Gillette and Palmer, *The ESPN Baseball Encyclopedia*, 1397.

225. Thorn *et al.*, *Total Baseball*, 2102; "Mike Milchin Statistics," www.baseball-reference.com; "Mike Milchin," www.jewsinsports.org; Horvitz and Horvitz, *The Big Book of Jewish Baseball*, 121.

226. "SFX Sports Group," at www.linkedin.com.

227. Keith Glauber, telephone interview with authors, December 28, 2008.

228. Horvitz and Horvitz, *The Big Book of Jewish Baseball*, 275.

229. "Keith Glauber Statistics," www.baseball-reference.com.

230. *Cincinnati Enquirer*, December 16, 1997.

231. Glauber telephone interview.

232. *Farmingdale* (N.J.) *News Transcript*, July 2, 2003.

233. Gillette and Palmer, *The ESPN Baseball Encyclopedia*, 1235.

234. "Keith Glauber," www.thebaseballcube.com.

235. "Keith Glauber Statistics," www.baseball-reference.com.

236. "Keith Glauber," www.thebaseballcube.com; Thorn et al., *Total Baseball*, 1943.

237. Glauber telephone interview.

238. www.sports.yahoo.com; "Keith Glauber Baseball Stats" www.baseball-almanac.com.

239. Authors Interview with Keith Glauber, December 28, 2008; *Farmington* (N.J.) *News Transcript*, July 2, 2003.

240. Horvitz and Horvitz, *The Big Book of Jewish Baseball*, 104; *St. Petersburg Times*, July 6, 2003.

241. *Jewish Journal*, October 19, 2006; *Kansas City Jewish Chronicle*, August 8, 2003.

242. "Al Levine," www.thebaseballcube.com.

243. *Ibid.*

244. *St. Petersburg Times*, July 6, 2003.

245. *Kansas City Jewish Chronicle*, August 8, 2003.

246. "Al Levine," www.thebaseballcube.com; Horvitz and Horvitz, *The Big Book of Jewish Baseball*, 105; "Levine Statistics," www.baseball-reference.com.

247. "Al Levine," www.thebaseballcube.com; Levine Statistics," www.baseball-reference.com; "Al Levine," www.jewsinsports.org.

248. "Levine Stats," www.baseball-almanac.com; "Al Levine," wwwthebaseballcube.com; "Al Levine," www.jewsinsports.org.

249. "Al Levine," www.jewsinsports.org; Thorn *et al.*, *Total Baseball*, 529, 532.

250. *Kansas City Jewish Chronicle*, August 8, 2003.

251. *Jewish Journal*, October 19, 2006.

252. "Levine Statistics," www.baseball-reference.com.

253. *Sporting News*, July 31, 2003.

254. *Kansas City Jewish Chronicle*, August 8, 2003.

255. Gillette and Palmer, *The ESPN Baseball Encyclopedia*, 1349, 17.

256. *Kansas City Jewish Chronicle*, August 8, 2003.

257. "Levine Statistics," www.thebaseballcube.com; "Al Levine Baseball Stats," www.baseball-almanac.com.

258. Gillette and Palmer, *The ESPN Baseball Encyclopedia*, 17.

259. "Al Levine," www.thebaseballcube.com; Gillette and Palmer, *The ESPN Baseball Encyclopedia*, 15.

260. *San Francisco Chronicle*, April 27, 2005.

261. "Levine Baseball Stats," www.baseball-almanac.com.

262. Gillette and Palmer, *The ESPN Baseball Encyclopedia*, 1349; *Jewish Journal*, October 19, 2006.

263. Horvitz and Horvitz, *The Big Book of Jewish Baseball*, 138.

264. "Scott Radinsky, at www.thebaseballcube.com.

265. Horvitz and Horvitz, *The Big Book of Jewish Baseball*, 138.

266. Gillette and Palmer, *The ESPN Baseball Encyclopedia*, 1472; "Scott Radinsky Baseball Stats," at www.baseball-reference.com.

267. Thorn *et al.*, *Total Baseball*, 2175; Horvitz and Horvitz, *The Big Book of Jewish Baseball*, 138.

268. Thorn *et al.*, *Total Baseball*, 476.

269. *The New York Times*, March 9, 2003.

270. "Scott Radinsky," www.thebasdballcube.com.

271. "Scott Radinsky Baseball Stats," www.baseball-almanac.com.

272. "Scott Radinsky Statistics," www.baseball-almanac.com.

273. "Buffalo Bisons Roster," at www.buffalo.bisons.mlb.com.

274. *New York Times*, October 31, 2000.

275. "Scott Radinsky," www.thebaseballclube.com.

276. Gillette and Palmer, *The ESPN Baseball Encyclopedia*, 1472; "Scott Radinsky Baseball Statistics," www.baseball-almanac.com.

277. "Eastern League Baseball," at www.easternleague.com; "Buffalo Bisons: Roster," at www.buffalo.bisons.mlb.com.

278. Horvitz and Horvitz, *The Big Book of Jewish Baseball*, 138–139; "Scott Radinsky's Double Life," at www.bisoninsider.com.

279. Horvitz and Horvitz, *The Big Book of Jewish Baseball*, 279; *Jewish Journal*, October 25, 2002.

280. *Pawtucket Times*, September 29, 2005.

281. Horvitz and Horvitz, *The Big Book of Jewish Baseball*, 279; "Scott Schoeneweis," www.jewsinsports.org; *Baseball USA Today*, April 21, 1993.

282. "Scott Schoeneweis," www.thebaseballcube.com; "Scott Schoeneweiss Statistics," www.baseball-reference.com.

283. "Scott Schoeneweis," www.thebaseballcube.com.

284. "Scott Schoeneweis," www.jewsinsports.org.

285. Horvitz and Horvitz, *The Big Book of Jewish Baseball*, 279.

286. "Scott Schoeneweis," www.thebaseballcube.com.

287. "Scott Schoeneweis," www.jewsinsports.org.

288. Gillette and Palmer, *The ESPN Baseball Encyclopedia*, 1513.

289. Thorn *et al.*, *Total Baseball*, 532.

290. "Schoeneweis Statistics," www.baseball-reference.com.

291. "Scott Schoeneweis," www.jewsinsports.org.

292. "Scott Schoeneweis Player Page," www.skids.com.

293. Gillette and Palmer, *The ESPN Baseball Encyclopedia*, 1513.

294. *Pawtucket Times*, September 29, 2005.

295. "Schoeneweis Baseball Stats," www.baseball-reference.com.

296. "Schoeneweis Statistics," www.baseball-reference.com; "Jays Ship Schoeneweis to Reds," www.cbc.ca.

297. Gillette and Palmer, *The ESPN Baseball Encyclopedia*, 1513.

298. *New Jersey Star-Ledger*, December 12, 2008.

299. *Pawtucket Times*, September 29, 2005.

Chapter 17

1. Spaner, "From Greenberg to Green," 179; Leavy, *Sandy Koufax*, 174.

2. Slater, *Great Jews in Sports*, 111; Tom Green, "*Atlanta Jewish Times*, August 4, 2000.

3. Slater, *Great Jews in Sports*, 111.

4. "Shawn Green," at www.jewishvirtuallibrary.org; "Jewish Sports Hall of Fame," at www.jewish sports.org.

5. *Atlanta Jewish Times*, August 4, 2000; Slater, *Great Jews in Sports*, 111.

6. Horvitz and Horvitz, *The Big Book of Jewish Baseball*, 77; Slater, *Great Jews in Sports*, 111; *New York Times*, July 18, 1999.

7. Slater, *Great Jews in Sports*, 111.

8. *St. Clair County Journal*, October 16, 1977 found at www.angelfire.com.

9. "Shawn Green," www.thebaseballcube.com; Horvitz and Horvitz, *The Book of Jewish Baseball*, 77.

10. Horvitz and Horvitz, *The Big Book of Jewish Baseball*, 78.

11. Slater, *Great Jews in Baseball*, 112; *New York Times*, August 2, 1999; *St. Clair College Journal*, October 16, 1997.

12. *New York Times*, August 2, 1999; Slater, *Great Jews in Sports*, 111–112.

13. "The Kosher Kid," found at www.shawgreen.net; *Atlanta Jewish Times*, August 4, 2000.

14. Slater, *Great Jews in Sports*, 112; Gillette and Palmer, *The ESPN Baseball Encyclopedia*, 540; "Shaw Green," www.the baseballcube.com; "Shawn Green Player Page," at www.sportsillustrated.cnn.com; "Shawn Green Baseball Stats," www.baseball-almanac.com.

15. Spaner, "From Greenberg to Green," 179.

16. "Shawn Green," at www.jewishsports.com.

17. *Atlanta Jewish Times*, August 4, 200; *New York Times*, August 2, 1999; www.jvibe.com.

18. "Shawn Green," www.thebaseballcube.com; Gillette and Palmer, *The ESPN Baseball Encyclopedia*, 540; Thorn et al., *Total Baseball*, 1252.

19. *New York Times*, July 18, 1999.

20. *Ibid.*, August 2, 1999.

21. Slater, *Great Jews in Sports*, 112.

22. *New York Times*, August 24, 2006.

23. Slater, *Great Jews in Sports*, 113; *New York Times*, August 2, 1999, August 9, 1999.

24. Slater, *Great Jews in Sports*, 113.

25. *New York Times*, November 9, 1999.

26. *Ibid.*; "Shawn Green," www.jewishvirtuallibrary.org; "Jewhoo!-Biographies," at www.jewhoo.com.

27. *Atlanta Jewish Times*, August 4, 2000.

28. *Ibid.*

29. "Hadassah Magazine," dated April 20003 found at www.hadassah.org.

30. www.jewishsports.org; "Shawn Green," www.jewishvirtuallibrary.org.

31. *Jewish Journal* dated July 7, 2004, at www.jewishjournal.com.

32. www.jewishvirtuallibrary.com; *Atlanta Jewish Journal*, August 4, 2000; "Shawn Green Steps up to the Plate," at www.babaganewz.com.

33. "Shawn Green," at www.jewishvirtuallibrary.org; "Shawn Green," at www.losangelesdodgersonline.com.

34. *New York Times*, December 5, 2001, December 9, 2001.

35. www.jewishjournal.com; www.hadassah.org.

36. www.jewishjournal.com.

37. *New York Times*, May 25, 2002.

38. Gillette and Palmer, *The ESPN Baseball Encyclopedia*, 18.

39. "Shawn Green," www.thebaseballcube.com; "Shawn Green Baseball Stats, www.baseball-reference.com; www.jewishvirtuallibrary.org.

40. Gillette and Palmer, *The ESPN Baseball Encyclopedia*, 16.

41. www.jewishvirtuallibrary.org; www.losangelesdodgersonline.com.

42. Gillette and Palmer, *The ESPN Baseball Encyclopedia*, 540

43. "Shawn Green Baseball Stats," www.baseball-reference.com.

44. *New York Times*, September 9, 2001.

45. "Green Will Play Friday, Sit Saturday," at msnbc.com.
46. *Canadian Jewish News*, December 7, 2006.
47. "Green Will Play Friday, Sit Saturday," msnbc.com.
48. *Jewish News Daily of Northern California* (undated) found at www.jewishf.com
49. "LA Getting Navarro in Deal," www.sports.espn.go.com.
50. "Jewish Sports Hall of Fame," www.jewishsports.org.
51. Gillette and Palmer, *The ESPN Baseball Encyclopedia*, 540; www.thebaseballcube.com; www.baseball-reference.com.
52. "Shawn Green Stats," www.baseball-reference.com.
53. *New York Times*, August 24, 2006.
54. *Ibid.*; August 26, 2006; www.ynetnews.com.
55. "Mets Acquire Shawn Green from Arizona," at www.usatoday.com; www.sports.yahoo.com; www.jewishpress.com.
56. "Jewish Fans Say Mazel Tov to Green," at www.WCBSTV.com.
57. Gillette and Palmer, *The ESPN Baseball Encyclopedia*, 540.
58. "Shawn Green Announces Retirement," at www.tireball.com.
59. *Ibid.*
60. "Mets Shawn Green Retires," at www.upi.com.
61. www.tireball.com.
62. *Ibid.*; Gillette and Palmer, *The ESPN Baseball Encyclopedia*, 540.
63. www.Hadassah.org.

Chapter 18

1. Andrew Zimbalist, *In the Best Interests of Baseball? The Revolutionary Reign of Bud Selig* (Hoboken, NJ: John Wiley & Sons, 2006), 111–112; Holtzman, *The Commissioners*, 272–273.
2. *Milwaukee Sentinel*, January 9, 1995.
3. Holtzman, *The Commissioners*, 273.
4. Zimbalist, *In the Best Interests of Baseball?*, 115.
5. *Sporting News*, July 31, 1976.
6. Nicholas Thompson, "A Baseball Hero, Really," found at www.slate.com.
7. Holtzman, *The Commissioners*, 274.
8. *Ibid.*
9. Chuck Carlson, *True Blue: A Quarter Century with the Milwaukee Braves* (Dallas: Taylor, 1993), 86.
10. Pietrusza et al., *Baseball: The Biographical Encyclopedia*, 1019.
11. Zimbalist, *In the Best Interests of Baseball?*, 117.
12. *Ibid.*; Dewey and Acocella, *The Ball Clubs* (New York: Harper Collins, 1996), 313; Pietrusza et al., *Baseball: The Biographical Encyclopedia*, 1019; John Garrity, "Sing Along with Bambi's Brewers," *Sport*, September 1969, 58; *Sporting News*, April 29, 1967.
13. *The Sporting News*, June 15, 1968.
14. Dewey and Acocella, *The Ball Clubs*, 313; www.baseball-reference.com.
15. Zimbalist, *In the Best Interests of Baseball?*, 121–122; Dewey and Acocella, *The Ball Clubs*, 313; Dewey and Acocella, *The Biographical History of Baseball*, 421; *Sporting News*, October 14, 1967.
16. *Sporting News*, January 31, 1970.
17. Dewey and Acocella, *The Ball Clubs*, 313; Dewey and Acocella, *The Biographical History of Baseball*, 421; Pietruisza et al., *Baseball: The Biographical Encyclopedia*, 1019.
18. Zimbalist, *In the Best Interests of Baseball?*, 123.
19. *Sporting News*, April 19, 1970; *Washington Post*, April 1, 1970.
20. *Washington Post*, October 10, 1971.
21. Pietrusza et al., *Baseball: The Biographical Encyclopedia*, 1019; John Garrity, "Sing Along with Bambi's Brewers," 58.
22. Dewey and Acocella, *The Ball Clubs*, 313.
23. *Ibid.*, 313–315.
24. Zimbalist, *Baseball and Billions*, 33; Sands and Gammons, *Coming Apart at the Seams*, xiii; Garrity, "Sing Along with Bambi's Brewers," 58; *Chicago Tribune*, July 7, 1983; Burk, *Much More Than a Game*, 268.
25. Garrity, "Sing Along with Bambi's Brewers," 60.
26. *Sporting News*, December 3, 1977, February 4, 1978; Dewey and Acocella, *The Biographical History of Baseball*, 421; Dewey and Acocella, *The Ball Clubs*, 315.
27. Horvitz and Horvitz, *The Big Book of Jewish Baseball*, 214.
28. Thorn et al., *Total Baseball*, 437; Dewey and Acocella, *The Ball Clubs*, 316.
29. *Chicago Tribune*, June 3, 1982.
30. Gillette and Palmer, *The ESPN Baseball Encyclopedia*, 59.
31. *Chicago Tribune*, July 7, 1983.
32. Dewey and Acocella, *The Ball Clubs*, 316; Dewey and Acocella, *The Biographical History of Baseball*, 421; Thorn et al., *Total Baseball*, 443–444; Pietrusza et al., *Baseball: The Biographical Encyclopedia*, 1020.
33. "National Press Club—Bud Selig," at www.npr.org.
34. Dewey and Acocello, *The Ball Clubs*, 317.
35. "Bud Selig," at www.sportsecyclopedia.com.
36. Zimbalist, *In the Best Interests of Baseball?*, 126–139; John Feinstein, *Play Ball: The Life and Troubled Times of Major League Baseball* (New York: Villard, 1993), 176.
37. *New York Times*, September 6, 1983; Zimbalist, *In the Best Interests of Baseball?*, 132.
38. *Sporting News*, December 19, 1983.
39. "Major League Baseball Commissioners," www.baseball-almanac.com.
40. *Sporting News*, March 26, 1984.
41. "Peter Vincent Ueberroth," at www.answers.com.
42. Zimbalist, *In the Interests of Baseball?*, 132.
43. *Ibid.*
44. *Sporting News*, June 27, 1988.
45. "A. Bartlett Giamatti," www.baseball-reference.com; "Bart Giamatti Biography," www.baseball-almanac.com.
46. Burk, *Much More Than a Game*, 267; Dewey and Acocella, *The Biographical History of Baseball*, 421; Rossi, *The National Game*, 204.
47. Zimbalist, *In the Best Interests of Baseball?*, 132; "Major League Baseball Commissioners," www.baseball-almanac.com.
48. *Sporting News*, September 19, 1994; Dewey and Acocella, *The Ball Clubs*, 317.
49. Rossi, *The National Game*, 204.
50. Sands and Gammon, *Coming Apart at the Seams*, 207.
51. Zimbalist, *May the Best Team Win*, 87–88.
52. Zimbalist, *In the Best Interests of Baseball?*, 132–133.
53. *New York Times*, September 10, 11, 1992.
54. *Ibid.*, September 17, 1992, August 28, 2002; Zimbalist, *In the Best Interests of Baseball?* 135; Holtzman, *The Commissioners*, 272..
55. Dewey and Acocello, *The Biographical History of Baseball*, 42; Pietrusza et al., *Baseball: The Biographical Encyclopedia*, 1020; "Bud Selig," www.infopedia.net; *New York Times*, December 19, 1992, October 29, 1993, January 20, 1994; June 20, 1996.
56. Zimbalist, *In the Best Interests of Baseball?*, 135.
57. *Sporting News*, September 27, 1993, December 20, 1993.
58. Zimbalist, *In the Best Interests of Baseball?*, 142–143.
59. "Bud Selig," www.info-pedia.com.

60. "Bud Selig Biography," www.baseball-almanac.com.
61. *New York Times*, September 12, 1997, February 17, 2000.
62. *Ibid.*, April 25, 1999.
63. Sands and Gammons, *Coming Apart at the Seams*, 188.
64. Zimbalist, *In the Best Interests of Baseball?*, 135; "Bud Selig Biography," www.baseball-almanac.com.
65. *Sporting News*, September 19, 1994; Dewey and Acocella, *The Biographical History of Baseball*, 422.
66. Holtzman, *The Commissioners*, 274.
67. Pietrusza et al., *Baseball: The Biographical Encyclopedia*, 1020; Tom Verducci, "What's All the Shouting About?" *Sports Illustrated*, January 31, 1994, 86.
68. *Cincinnati Enquirer*, August 12, 2004.
69. Horvitz and Horvitz, *The Big Book of Jewish Baseball*, 214; *New York Times*, September 15, 1994; "Bud Selig," www.infopedia.net; Holtzman, *The Commissioners*, 275.
70. Rossi, *The National Game*, 206; Pietrusza et al., *Baseball: The Biographical Encyclopedia*. 1020; Staudohar, *Diamond Mines*, 66; Thompson, "Bud Selig," www.slate.com.
71. Pietrusza et al., *Baseball: The Biographical Encyclopedia*, 1020; 1994–1996 at www.bizofbaseball.com.
72. *New York Times*, April 3, 1995.
73. Rossi, *The National Game*, 207; Rader, *Baseball*, 240.
74. Morgan and Lally, *Long Balls, No Strikes*, 12.
75. Rossi, *The National Game*, 207.
76. Thorn et al., *Total Baseball*, 283.
77. Pietrusza et al., *Baseball: The Biographical Encyclopedia*, 1020.
78. Horvitz and Horvitz, *The Big Book of Jewish Baseball*, 214; Thorn et al., *Total Baseball*, 291.
79. Pietrusza et al., *Baseball: The Biographical Encyclopedia*, 1020; *Sporting News*, November 17, 1997; *New York Times*, November 6, 1997.
80. "The Sports Network" at www.sportsnetwork.com.
81. Hemond telephone interview; *New York Daily News*, May 14, 2004.
82. *Sporting News*, March 13, 2008.
83. Paul D. Staudohar, "Baseball Negotiations: A New Agreement," *Monthly Labor Review* 125 (December 2002): 21; Zimbalist, *May the Best Team Win*, 105.
84. "MLB Executives," at www.mlb.com.
85. *Sporting News*, February 7, 1997.
86. *Ibid.*, August 4, 1997.
87. *Ibid.*, January 26, 1988.
88. *Ibid.*, February 2, 1998.
89. Zimbalist, *In the Best Interests of Baseball?*, 157.
90. Pietrusza et al., *Baseball: The Biographical Encyclopedia*, 1019; Horvitz and Horvitz, *The Big Book of Jewish Baseball*, 214; "National Press Club—Bud Selig," www.npr.org.
91. "Bud Selig," www.info-pedia.net; *USA Today*, July 9, 1998; Staudohar, *Diamond Mines*, xxvii, 61.
92. *New York Times*, July 10, 1998.
93. *Ibid.*
94. Pietrusza et al., *Baseball: The Biographical Encyclopedia*, 1020.
95. *New York Times*, January 20, 2000.
96. Pietrusza et al., *Baseball: The Biographical Encyclopedia*, 1020.
97. *Orlando Sentinel*, June 5, 2008.
98. *New York Times*, September 12, 2001.
99. Staudohar, "Baseball Negotiations: A New Agreement," 21; Pietrusza et al., *Baseball: The Biographical Encyclopedia*, 1020; Zimbalist, *May the Best Team Win*, 105.
100. *New York Times*, September 26, 2002.
101. Zimbalist, *May the Best Team Win*, 31; Zimbalist, *In the Best Interests of Baseball?*, 173; "MLB Executives," www.mlb.com.
102. "Bud Selig," at www.nndp.com.
103. "Commission Agrees to 3-year Extension," www.espn.go.com.
104. Zimbalist, *In the Best Interests of Baseball?*, 178, 199; "Bud Selig," www.info-pedia.net; *Sports Business Daily*, September 28, 2004.
105. Thompson," Bud Selig," www.slate.com.
106. *New York Times*, July 15, 2003; "Bud Selig," www.nndp.com.
107. "Bud Selig," www.nndb.com.
108. Thompson, "Bud Selig," www.slate.com; *Sporting News*, March 13, 2008.
109. *New York Times*, December 14, 2007.
110. www.espn.go.com.
111. "Sports Business News," www.sportsbiznews.blogspot.com; "Looking Back at the World Baseball Classic," www.usatoday.com.
112. *Sporting News*, March 13, 2008.
113. "Bud Selig Biography," www.baseball-almanac.com.

Chapter 19

1. "Justin Wayne," www.virtuallibrary.org; "Justin Wayne," www.jewsinsports.org.
2. *New York Times*, June 12, 2000.
3. "Justin Wayne Statistics," www.baseball-reference.com.
4. "Justin Wayne," www.thebaseballcube.com.
5. *New York Times*, July 11, 2002; "Justin Wayne Statistics," www.baseball-reference.com.
6. "Justin Wayne," www.jewishvirtuallibrary.org; *New York Times*, September 12, 2002.
7. "Justin Wayne," www.thebaseballcube.com; "Justin Wayne Statistics," www.fangraphs.com; "Justin Wayne Baseball Stats," www.baseball-almanac.com; Gillette and Palmer, *The ESPN Baseball Encyclopedia*, 1593.
8. Gillette and Palmer, *The ESPN Baseball Encyclopedia*, 1593.
9. "Justin Wayne," www.jewsinsports.org.
10. *Ibid.*
11. "Florida Marlins News," www.mlb.com.
12. "Wayne Ready and willing," www.mlb.com.
13. Gillette and Palmer, *The ESPN Baseball Encyclopedia*, 1593; "Justin Wayne Statistics," www.fangraphs.com.
14. "Justin Wayne," www.thebaseballcube.com.
15. *Ibid.*
16. *Pittsburgh Tribune-Review*, August 5, 2004; "Baseball America," www.baseballamerica.com. "Pittsburgh Pirates News," www.mlb.mlb.com.
17. "John Grabow," www.baseball-reference.com; Jonathan Mayo, "Pittsburgh's Newest Star Athlete," at www.jewishsports.com.
18. "John Grabow Statistics," www.baseball-reference.com.
19. "Baseball America," www.baseballamerica.com.
20. *Pittsburgh Post-Gazette*, March 23, May 11, 2004; "John Grabow, www.thebaseballcube.com.
21. *Ibid.*
22. Mayo, "Pittsburgh's Newest Jewish Star Athlete."
23. *Pittsburgh-Post Gazette*, May 11, 2004.
24. "John Grabow," www.thebaseballcube.com; "John Grabow, www.baseball-reference.com; Gillette and Palmer, *The ESPN Baseball Encyclopedia*, 1240; "John Grabow Player Page, www.sportsillustrated.cnn; "John Grabow Stats," www.sports.espn.com. "John Grabow Baseball Stats," www.baseball-almanac.com.
25. *Pittsburgh Post-Gazette*, March 23, 2004; "Baseball America," www.baseballamerica.com; "Nashville Sounds," www.nashvillesounds.com.
26. "John Grabow," www.baseball-reference.com.
27. *Pittsburgh Tribune-Review*, March 10, 2006.

28. "John Grabow," www.thebaseballcube.com; Gillette and Palmer, *The ESPN Baseball Encyclopedia*, 1240.

29. "John Grabow Stats," www.sports.espn.go.com; roto world.com.

30. "Pittsburgh Pirates News," www.mlb.mlb.com.

31. "John Grabow," www.jewishsports.com. "The Baseball Reader," www.baseballpiggies.blogspot.com.

32. "Adam Stern," www.jewishvirtuallibrary.org.

33. *Jewish Tribune*, September 16, 2004.

34. *Ibid.*

35. "Adam Stern," www.jewishvirtuallibrary.org; "Adam Stern," www.jewsinsports.org.

36. "Adam Stern on RedSoxNation.com." found at www.baseball-almanac.com.

37. "Adam Stern Statistics," www.baseball-reference.com.

38. "Adam Stern," www.thebaseballcube.com.

39. *Jewish Tribune*, September 16, 2004.

40. "Baseball Canada," www.baseball.ca./eng.doc; "Adam Stern," www.jewsinsports.org.

41. "Adam Stern," www.thebaseballcube.com; *Jewish Tribune*, September 16, 2004; *Rhode Island News*, May 18, 2006.

42. "Adam Stern," www.jewsinsports.org.

43. "Boston Red Sox News," www.boston.redsox.mlb.com.

44. "Adam Stern," www.jewsinsports.org; "Adam Stern," www.thebaseballcube.com; "Adam Stern," www.soxprospects.com.

45. *Boston Globe*, April 12, 2006.

46. Gillette and Palmer, *The ESPN Baseball Encyclopedia*, 943; "Adam Stern," www.soxprospects.com; "Adam Stern," www.thebaseballcube.com; "Adam Stern," www.fantasybaseball.usatoday.com.

47. *Boston Globe*, March 9, 2006.

48. *Ibid.*

49. *Ibid.*, April 12, 2006.

50. "Adam Stern," www.thebaseballcube.com.

51. *Providence Journal*, May 18, 2006.

52. "Adam Stern" www.sportsline.com.

53. "Adam Stern Statistics," www.baseball-reference.com; www.cbc.ca.

54. "Adam Stern," www.sportsline.com.

55. "Bowie Baysox," www.bowiebaysox.com.

56. "Adam Stern," www.thebaseballcube.com.

57. "Adam Stern," www.soxprospects.com; "Adam Stern," www.thebaseballcube.com.

58. *Stratford Gazette*, October 24, 2008.

59. Dave Rosenfeld, E-mail interview with authors, January 16, 2009.

60. *Jewish Ledger*, April 12, 2006.

61. "Craig Breslow," www.jewsinsports.org; "Craig Breslow," www.baseball-reference.com; *Jewish Ledger*, April 12, 2006; *New Haven Register*, May 21, 2006.

62. "Craig Breslow," www.2sportsnet.ca; "Craig Breslow." www.thebaseballcube.com.

63. *New Haven Register*, May 21, 2006.

64. "Craig Breslow," www.2.sportsnet.ca; *New Haven Register*, May 21, 2006.

65. "Craig Breslow" www.baseball-reference.com.

66. *Ibid.*

67. "Major League Baseball News," www.mlb.mlb.com; *North County Times* (San Diego), July 24, 2005.

68. "Major League Baseball News, www.mlb.mlb.com.

69. *Trumbull Times*, August 17, 2005.

70. *Ibid.*

71. *North County Times*, July 24, 2005; www.yalealumni magazine.com.

72. *Trumbull Times*, August 17, 2005.

73. "Craig Breslow Stats," www.baseball-almanac.com; "Craig Breslow," www.thebaseballcube.com.

74. *Trumbull Times*, August 17, 2005.

75. "Breslow Statistics," www.baseball-reference.com; *Boston Globe*, January 27, 2006.

76. *Boston Globe*, February 26, 2006.

77. "Craig Breslow," www.thebaseballcube.com.

78. *Providence Journal*, July 13, 2006.

79. Gillette and Palmer, *The ESPN Baseball Encyclopedia*, 1105.

80. Undated article *Standard Times* (New Bedford, MA).

81. "Craig Breslow," www.thebaseballcube.com; "Craig Breslow," www.rotoworld.com. (9/1/2006); "Major League Baseball Transactions," www.mlb.mlb.com.

82. "Breslow Statistics," www.baseball-reference.com; *Canton Repository*, March 23, 2008.

83. *Boston Globe*, March 14, 2008.

84. "Craig Breslow Statistics," www.baseball-reference.com.

85. "MPR" www.minnesota.publicradio.org.

86. "Baseball Prospectus," www.baseballprospectus.com.

87. "Craig Breslow," www.hardballtimes.com; www.sports.espn.go.com.

88. *Jewish Ledger*, April 17, 2006.

89. *Ibid.*

90. "Adam Greenberg," www.thebaseballcube.com.

91. "Adam Greenberg," www.baseball-reference.com.

92. "Adam Greenberg," www.jewsinsports.org.

93. "Adam Greenberg Statistics," www.baseball-reference.com.

94. *Jewish Ledger*, April 17, 2006.

95. "Adam Greenberg," www.thebaseballcube.com.

96. "Chicaco Cubs Call up Greenberg," www.jta.org; *International Herald Tribune*, August 23, 2005.

97. "Adam Greenberg," www.royalboard.com; *Jewish Ledger*, April 17, 2006.

98. www.mintherawfield.squarespace.com/baseball-transactions.

99. Adam Greenberg," www.thebaseballcube.com; "Andrew Greenberg Stats," www.baseball-reference.com.

100. *Shore Line Times*, January 22, 2009.

101. *Jewish Press*, June 6, 2007.

102. "Scott Feldman," www.jewsinsports.org; *San Mateo Daily Journal*, April 6, 2006; "Scott Feldman BR Bullpen," www.baseball-reference-com.

103. "Scott Feldman," www.thebaseballcube.com; "Scott Feldman—BR Bullpen," www.baseball-reference.com.

104. "Scott Feldman Baseball Stats," www.baseball-almanac.com; "Texas Rangers Player Information," www.mlb.com; "Scott Feldman MLB Baseball," www.cbs.sportsline.com.

105. *San Mateo Daily Journal*, April 6, 2006.

106. "Scott Feldman-BR Bullpen," www.baseball-reference.com.

107. "Nation master-Encyclopedia," www.nationmaster.com; *USA Today*, August 16, 2006; *Ft. Worth Star-Telegram*, August 16, 2006.

108. "Scott Feldman," www.thebaseballcube.com; "Scott Feldman Statistics," www.baseball-reference.com.

109. "Scott Feldman—BR Bullpen," www.baseball-reference.com.

110. *Dallas Morning Star*, September 16, 2008; www.baseballamerica.com.

111. Jason Hirsh, E-mail interview with authors, January 27, 2009.

112. *Ibid.*; *New York Times*, October 23, 2007.

113. "Jason Hirsch Statistics," www.baseball-reference.com; "Official Sight Colorado Rockies," www.mlb.com.

114. "Jason Hirsh—BR Bullpen," www.baseball-reference.com.

115. Hirsh E-mail interview.

116. *Ibid.*

117. *Ibid.*

118. "Jason Hirsh—BR Bullpen" www.baseball-reference. com; "CLU Sports," www.clubsports.com.

119. "Jason Hirsh—BR Bullpen," www.baseball-refer ence.com; "Texas League," www.texas.league.com; "Profile: Jason Hirsh," www.projectprospect.com.

120. "Astros Recall Hirsh," www.wsotv.com; "Jason Hirsh—Colorado Rockies," www.sports.yahoo.com; "Official Site of Colorado Rockies," www.mlb.com; *Rocky Mountain News,* February 13, 2007; *Denver Post,* February 15, 2007.

121. "Official Site of the Rockies," www.mlb.com; "Jen nings Dealt to Houston," www.purplerow.com.

122. *Rocky Mountain News,* February 13, 2007.

123. *Denver Post,* February 15, 2007; "Profile—Jason Hirsh," www.projectprospect.com; "Official Site of Colorado Rock ies," www.mlb.com.

124. *New York Times,* October 23, 2007.

125. "Jason Hirsh—Colorado Rockies," www.sports.yahoo. com; "Jason Hirsh—THT Stats," www.hardballtimes.com; "Jason Hirsh Statistics," www.baseball-reference.com.

126. "ESPN-X-rays show Hirsh pitched with broken leg," www.sports.go.com; "Posts tagged Jason Hirsh at FanHouse," www.sports.aol.com.

127. "Hirsh Not 100% percent, but back in bigs," www. colorado.rockies, mlb.com; "Jason Hirsh," www.fantasybase ball.usatoday.com.

128. Hirsh E-mail interview; *New Jersey Star-Ledger,* July 29, 2009.

129. "Sam Fuld—BR Bullpen," www.baseball-reference. com; "Q&A with Sam Fuld," www.chicago.cubs.mlb.com.

130. "Cubs Hub—A Scouting Report on Sam Fuld," www. cubshub.com; "Chat Wrap—Sam Fuld," www.espn.go.com.

131. "Cubs Hub—A Scouting Report on Sam Fuld," www.cubshub.com; "Sam Fuld—BR Bullpen" www.base ball-reference.com; "Chat Wrap—A Scouting Report on Sam Fuld," www.espn.go.com.

132. "Sam Fuld—BR Bullpen," www.baseball-reference.com.

133. "Sam Fuld," www.thebaseballcube.com.

134. "Sam Fuld Stats," www.chicago.cubs.mlb.com.

135. *Chicago Daily Herald,* March 4, 2008; "Sam Fuld Re joins Southern League," www.mln.therawfeed.squarespaces. com.

136. www.thebaseballcube.com.; www.chicago.cubs.mlb. com.

137. Boxerman and Boxerman, *Jews and Baseball,* 85; *Jew ish Forward,* June 5, 2008.

138. "Brian Horwitz, www.thebaseballcube.com; *San Francisco Chronicle,* June 20, 2008.

139. *New Jersey Jewish News,* June 26, 2008.

140. *San Francisco Chronicle,* June 22, 2006, June 20, 2008.

141. "Brian Horwitz," www.thebaseballcube.com.

142. *San Francisco Chronicle,* June 20, 2008.

143. www.thebaseballcube.com; "Brian Horwitz," www. cbssports.com.

144. *San Francisco Chronicle,* June 20, 2008.

145. *Ibid.*

Chapter 20

1. *Canadian Jewish News,* August 23, 2001; Horvath and Horvath, *The Big Book of Jewish Baseball,* 277.

2. *New York Times,* August 15, 1990, August 22, 1991; *Canadian Jewish News,* August 23, 2001.

3. *New York Times,* June 11, 1996.

4. "Jason Marquis," www.mahalo.com; "Jason Mar quis," www.thebaseballcube.com.

5. Horvitz and Horvitz, *The Big Book of Jewish Baseball,* 277; "Jason Marquis," www.jewsinsports.org; Brian Walton, "Interview: Jason Marquis," at www.sportsblurb.com.

6. *New York Times,* June 6, 2000, September 2, 2000;

"Jason Marquis Statistics," www.fangraphs.com; "Jason Mar quis Statistics," www.baseball-reference.com; Gillette and Palmer, *The ESPN Baseball Encyclopedia,* 1371.

7. *Canadian Jewish News,* August 3, 2001.

8. "Jason Marquis," www.jewishvirtuallibrary.com; "Ja son Marquis, www.thebaseballcube.com; Thorn *et al., Total Baseball,* 1871–1872.

9. *Ibid.,* 524; "Jason Marquis," www.jewishvirtuallibrary. com.

10. "Jason Marquis," www.thebaseballube.com; "Jason Marquis Statistics," www.baseball-reference.com; Gillette and Palmer, *The ESPN Baseball Encyclopedia,* 1371.

11. Thorn *et al., Total Baseball,* 527.

12. Walton, "Interview: Jason Marquis"; www.espn.go. com; "Jason Marquis," www.jewsinsports.org.

13. www.espn.go.com.

14. "Jason Marquis Statistics," www.baseball-reference. com; "Jason Marquis," www.jewsinsports.org; "Jason Mar quis," www.sports-library.com.

15. "Marquis Gets Fresh Start in St. Louis," www.mlb.com.

16. *Ibid.*

17. Gillette and Palmer, *The ESPN Baseball Encyclopedia,* 1371; "Jason Marquis," www.thebaseballcube.com.

18. "Jason Marquis," www.jewsinsports.org.

19. *Ibid.,* "Jason Marquis," www.sports-library.com; Gillette and Palmer, *The ESPN Baseball Encyclopedia,* 1752.

20. "Jason Marquis," www.sports-library.com.

21. www.baseball-reference.com.

22. "Jason Marquis," www.sports-library.com.

23. "Jason Marquis," www.baseball-reference.com; "Ja son Marquis," www.sports-library.com.

24. "Jason Marquis Statistics," www.fangraphs.com; Gillette and Palmer, *The ESPN Baseball Encyclopedia,* 1371; "Jason Marquis," www.mahalo.com.

25. www.chicago.cubs.mlb.com.

26. *Jewish Ledger,* October 2, 2008; *Canadian Jewish News,* October 2, 2008

27. www.mlb.com.

28. www.sports.espn.go.com.

29. *Hardball Times,* May 2, 2005.

30. *Pawtucket Times,* May 15, 2004; "Jewseek—Pray Ball," www.jewsweek.com.

31. "The Bonus," www.vault.sportsillustrated.cnn.com.

32. "Jewsweek," www.jewsweek.com; *New York Times,* May 23, 2007; "The Bonus," www.vault.sportsillustrated. com; *Hardball Times,* May 2, 2005.

33. "Kevin Youkilis Baseball Stats," www.baseball-alma nac.com; "Kevin Youkilis," www.thebaseballcube.com; "Kevin Youkilis," www.sonofsamhorn.net.

34. "The Bonus," www.vault.sportsillustrated.cnn.com; *New York Times,* May 23, 2007; "Kevin Youkilis," www.the baseballcube.com.

35. "Jewsweek," www.jewsweek.com.

36. "ESPN.com:MLB," www.espn.go.com; *Pawtucket Times,* May 15, 2004; "The Bonus," www.vault. Sportsillustrated.com.

37. "Kevin Youkilis," www.thebaseballcube.com; "Kevin Youkilis," www.soxprospects.com.

38. "Jewsweek," www.jewsweek.com.

39. *Pawtucket Times,* May 15, 2004.

40. Gillette and Palmer, *The ESPN Baseball Encyclopedia,* 1042.

41. "Kevin Youkilis," www.jewsinsports.org; Gillette and Palmer, *The ESPN Baseball Encyclopedia,* 1749–1750.

42. "One on One with Kevin Youkilis," undated inter view with "Jvibe," at www.jewishsports.com; "Kevin Youk ilis—BR Bullpen," www.baseball-reference.com; "Kevin Youkilis," www.absoluteastronomy.com.

43. *New York Times,* May 23, 2007.

44. "Kevin Youkilis," www.thebaseballcube.com; "Kevin Youkilis-BR Bullpen," www.baseball-reference.com.

45. "Kevin Youkilis," www.mahalo.com; "Kevin Youkilis," www.thebaseballcube.com; "Kevin Youkilis Statistics, www.baseball-reference.com.

46. "The Bonus," www.vault.sportsillustrated.com.

47. "Intensity is Youkilis' trademark," www.boston.red sox.com; "Youkilis' defense is as good as it gets," www.boston.redsox.mlb.com.

48. Gillette and Palmer, *The ESPN Baseball Encyclopedia*, 1753.

49. "Intensity is Youkilis' Trademark," www.bostonred sox.com; "Kevin Youkilis," www/sonofsamhorn.net.l; "Kevin Youkilis," www.absoluteastronomy.com.

50. "Youk wins Gold Glove," www.boston.com.

51. "Kevin Youkilis," www.absoluteastronomy.com.

52. *Ibid.*, "Kevin Youkilis," www.mlb.com; "Boston Red Sox," www.fenwayfanatics.com.

53. "Kevin Youkilis," www.absoluteastronomy.com.

54. "Report: Youkilis to play in world baseball," www.upi.com; "Kevin Youkilis wins 2008 Hank Aaron Award," www.overthemonster.com.

55. "Kevin Youkilis," www.absoluteastronomy.com.

56. *Ibid.*, "Intensity is Youkilis' trademark," www.boston.redsox.mlb.com; "Hits for Kids," www.youkskids.org.

57. "Youk ties the knot," www.boston.com.

58. "Youikilis to play in world baseball," www.upi.com.

59. "Kevin Youkilis," www.mlb.com.

60. "Celebrity Jews," www.jewishsf.com.

61. "Ian Kinsler Interview," www.texasrangerstrade.blog spot.com; "Q & A with Ian Kinsler," www.mlb.com.

62. "Ian Kinsler Interview," www.texasrangerstrade.blog spot.com.

63. "Ian Kinsler Statistics," www.baseball-reference.com; "Ian Kinsler Interview," www.texasrangerstrades.blogspot.com.

64. "Ian Kinsler," www.mlbplayers.mlb.com.

65. "Ian Kinsler," www.thebaseballcube.com. "Player Information," www.texasrangers.mlb.com; "Ian Kinsler Interview," www.texasrangerstrades.logspot.com; "Player Bio: Ian Kinsler," www.mutigers.cstv.com.

66. "Ian Kinsler Statisics," www.baseball-reference.com; "Ian Kinsler, www.mahalo.com.

67. *Ibid.*, "Prospect in the Spotlight: Ian Kinsler," www.athomeplate.com.

68. "Ian Kinsler," www.thebaseballcube.com; "Ian Kinsler," www.mlbplayers.mlb.com.

69. "Ian Kinsler Interview," www.texasrangerstrades. blogspot.

70. "Ian Kinsler," www.thebaseballcube.com; "Ian Kinsler Statistics," www.baseball-reference.com; "Official Site of the Texas Rangers," www.texas.rangers.mlb.com. "Ian Kinsler," www.arlington.org.

71. *Dallas Morning News*, April 2, 2007.

72. "Ian Kinsler," www.arlington.org; *Dallas Morning News*, April 2, 2007.

73. "Ian Kinsler," www.arlington.org.

74. *Dallas Morning News*, September 27, 2007.

75. "Ian Kinsler," www.arlington.org.

76. "Ian Kinsler," www.thebaseballcube.com.

77. *Jewish Forward*, August 28, 2008.

78. *Dallas Morning News*, February 20, 2008.

79. "Ian Kinsler," www.arlington.org.

80. "Ryan Braun—BR Bullpen," www.baseball-reference.com.

81. *Ibid.*; *Racine Journal Times*, July 23, 2007; *Forward*, July 30, 2007; "Suspense Builds Around Brewers' Braun," www.jta.org; "IsraGood: Ryan Braun," www.isragood.com.

82. "Ryan Braun: BR Bullpen," www.baseball-reference.com.

83. *New York Times*, July 30, 2007; *Forward*, July 30, 2007.

84. *Los Angeles Times*, August 17, 2008.

85. "Ryan Braun," www.jewishvirtuallibrary.org.

86. *Los Angeles Times*, August 17, 2008.

87. "Baseball America," www.baseballamerica.com; "Ryan Braun," www.jewishvirtuallibrary.org; "Player Bio: Ryan Braun," www.hurricanesports.cstv.com; *Racine Journal Times*, July 23, 2007.

88. "Braun Statistics," www.baseball-reference.com.

89. "Ryan Braun," www.thebaseballcube.com; "First Inning-Ryan Braun," www.firstinning.com; "Nashville Sounds," www.nashvillesounds.com.

90. *Racine Journal Times*, July 23, 2007; "Ryan Braun—BR Bullpen," www.baseball-reference.com.

91. "Brewers Promote Top Prospect Braun," www.mlb.mlb.com.

92. "Ryan Braun—BR Bullpen," www.baseball-reference.com; *Racine Journal Times*, July 23, 2007; *Milwaukee Journal Sentinel*, M ay 24, 2007.

93. *Racine Journal Times*, July 23, 2007.

94. "Ryan Braun—BR Bullpen," www.baseball-reference.com.

95. *Wisconsin Sports Daily*, July 23, 2007.

96. "Ryan Braun," www.baseball.about.com; "Ryan Braun Fan," www.ryanbraunfan.com.

97. "Braun Top NL Player," www.mlb.mlb.com. (August 2, 2007).

98. *USA Today*, August 29, 2007.

99. *Wisconsin Journal Sentinel*, September 17, 2007.

100. "Ryan Braun," www.thebaseballcube.com; "Ryan Braun Statistics," www.baseball-reference.com; "First Inning—Ryan Braun," www.firstinning.com; "Ryan Braun Player Page," www.sportsillustrated.cnn.com.

101. "IsraGood: Ryan Braun," www.isragood.com; "Pedroia, Braun Named Rookies of the Year," www.vaildaily.com; "Braun Named Rookie of the Year," www.mlb.mlb.com; *Denver Post*, November 13, 2007.

102. *Jerusalem Post*, November 14, 2007.

103. "Ryan Braun," www.jewishvirtuallibrary.org; *Wisconsin State Journal*, March 4, 2008.

104. "Ryan Braun," www.jewishvirktuallibrary.org; *Los Angeles Times*, August 17, 2008.

105. "Ryan Braun," www.thebaseballcube.com; "Ryan Braun Statistics," www.baseball-reference.com; "First Inning-Ryan Braun," www.firstinning.com; "Ryan Braun Player Page," www.sportsillustrated.cnn.com.

106. "Left Fielder Braun Signs 8 year, 45 million dollar deal," www.kdka.com; "Braun's contract latest in trend of deals for young MLB stars," www.sportsbusinessdaily.com; "ESPN: Braun Signed through 2015," www.mobileapp.espn.go.com.

Bibliography

Books

Alexander, Charles C. *Our Game: An American Baseball History*. New York: Henry Holt, 1991.

Allen, Mel, and Ed Fitzgerald. *You Can't Beat the Hours*. New York: Harper & Row, 1964.

Andreano, Ralph. *No Joy in Mudville*. Cambridge, MA: Schenkman, 1965.

Angell, Roger. *Five Seasons A Baseball Companion*. New York: Simon & Schuster, 1977.

Appel, Marty. *Yesterday's Heroes*. New York: Dial Press, 1988.

Baldassaro, Lawrence, and Richard A. Johnson, eds. *The American Game: Baseball and Ethnicity*. Carbondale: Southern Illinois University Press, 2002.

Barck, Oscar Theodore, Jr., and Norman Manfred Blake. *Since 1900: A History of the United States in Our Time*. New York: Macmillan, 1974.

Bjarkman, Peter. *Encyclopedia of Major League Baseball Team Histories: American League*. Westport, CT: Meckler, 1991.

_____. *Encyclopedia of Major League Baseball Team Histories: National League*. Westport, CT: Meckler, 1991.

Blomberg, Ron, and Dan Schlossberg. *Designated Hebrew: The Ron Blomberg Story*. Champaign, IL: Sports Publishing, 2006.

Borelli, Stephen. *How About That! The Life of Mel Allen*. Champaign, IL: Sports Publishing, 2005.

Bowman, John, and Joel Zoss. *Diamonds in the Rough: Untold History of Baseball*. New York: Macmillan, 1989.

Boxerman, Burton A., and Benita W. Boxerman. *Ebbets to Veeck to Busch: Eight Owners Who Shaped Baseball*. Jefferson, NC: McFarland, 2003.

_____ and _____. *Jews and Baseball. Volume I: Entering the American Mainstream, 1871–1948*. Jefferson, NC: McFarland, 2007.

Broeg, Bob, and William J. Miller, Jr. *Baseball from a Different Angle*. South Bend, IN: Diamond Communications, 1988.

Burk, Robert F. *Much More Than a Game: Players, Owners & American Baseball Since 1921*. Chapel Hill: University of North Carolina Press, 2001.

Cairns, Bob. *Pen Men: Baseball's Greatest Bullpen Stories Told by the Men Who Brought the Game Relief*. New York: St. Martin's Press, 1992.

Carlson, Chuck. *True Brew: A Quarter Century with the Milwaukee Brewers*. Dallas: Taylor, 1993.

Clark, Tom. *Champagne and Baloney: The Rise and Fall of Finley's A's*. New York: Harper & Row, 1975.

Coffey, Mike. *27 Men Out: Baseball's Perfect Games*. New York: Atria Books, 2004.

Cohen, Stanley. *Dodgers: The First 100 Years*. New York: Carol Publishing Group, 1990.

Condon, Dave. *The Go-Go Chicago White Sox*. New York: Coward-McCann, 1960.

Cramer, Richard Ben. *Joe DiMaggio: The Hero's Life*. New York: Simon & Schuster, 2000.

Crasnick, Jerry. *License to Deal: A Season on the Run with a Maverick Baseball Agent*. Emmaus, PA: Rodale, 2005.

Dewey, Donald, and Nicholas Acocella. *The Ball Clubs*. New York: HarperCollins, 1996.

_____ and _____. *The Biographical History of Baseball*. New York: Carroll & Graf, 1995.

Dickey, Glenn. *The Great No-Hitters*. Radnor, PA: Chilton Books, 1976.

_____. *The History of American League Baseball Since 1901*. New York: Smith and Day, 1980.

_____. *The History of National League Baseball Since 1876*. Lanham, MD: Rowman & Littlefield, 1979.

Diner, Hasia R. *The Jews of the United States, 1654–2000*. Berkeley: University of California Press, 2004.

DiSalvatore, Bryan. *The Life and Times of John Montgomery Ward*. New York: Pantheon Books, 1999.

Dreifort, John E., ed. *Baseball History from Outside the Lines: A Reader*. Lincoln: University of Nebraska Press, 2001.

Dworkin, James B. *Owners Versus Players*. Boston: Auburn House, 1981.

Eig, Jonathan. *Opening Day: The Story of Jackie Robinson's First Season*. New York: Simon & Schuster, 2007.

Feinstein, John. *Play Ball: The Life and Troubled Times of Major League Baseball*. New York: Villard, 1993.

Flood, Curt. *The Way It Is*. New York: Trident Press, 1970.

Frick, Ford. *Games, Asterisks and People*. New York: Crown, 1973.

Garraty, John, and Mark C. Carnes, eds. *The American National Biography*. New York: Oxford University Press, 1999.

Goldstein, Richard. *Superstars and Screwballs: 100 Years of Brooklyn Baseball*. New York: Dutton, 1991.

Golenbock, Peter. *Bums: An Oral History of the Brooklyn Dodgers*. New York: Putnam's, 1984.

_____. *Dynasty: The New York Yankees, 1949–1964*. Englewood Cliffs, NJ: Prentice-Hall, 1975.

Gordon, Milton M. *Assimilation in American Life*. New York: Oxford University Press, 1964.

Gorman, Jerry, and Kirk Calhoun. *The Name of the Game: The Business of Sports*. New York: John Wiley, 1994.

Gould, Stephen J. *Triumph and Tragedy in Mudville: A Lifelong Passion for Baseball*. New York: W. W. Norton, 2003.

Gruver, Edward. *Koufax*. Dallas: Taylor, 2000.

Guttmann, Allen. *From Ritual to Record: The Nature of Modern Sports*. New York: Columbia University Press, 1978.

_____. *The Jewish Writer in America: Assimilation and the Crisis of Identity*. New York: Oxford University Press, 1971.

Halberstam, David J. *Sports on New York Radio: A Play-By-Play History*. Indianapolis: Masters Press, 1999.

Helyer, John. *Lords of the Realm: The Real History of Baseball*. New York: Villard, 1994.

Hendricks, Randal A. *Inside the Strike Zone*. Austin: Eakin Press, 1994.

Henrich, Tommy, with Bill Gilbert. *Five O'Clock Lightning: Ruth, Gehrig, DiMaggio, Mantle and the Glory Years of the NY Yankees*. New York: Carol Publishing Group, 1992.

Hertzberg, Arthur. *Jews in America: Four Centuries of an Uneasy Encounter*. New York: Simon & Schuster, 1989.

Hollander, Zander. *Great American Athletes of the 20th Century*. New York: Random House, 1966.

Holtzman, Jerome. *The Commissioners: Baseball's Mid-Life Crisis*. New York: Total Sports, 1998.

_____. *No Cheering in the Press Box*. New York: Holt, Rinehart, & Winston, 1974.

Honig, Donald. *Baseball America: The Heroes of the Game and the Times of Their Glory*. New York: Macmillan, 1985.

_____. *Baseball Between the Lines: Baseball in the 40's and 50's as Told by the Men Who Played It*. New York: Coward-McCann and Geoghegan, 1976.

Horvitz, Peter S., and Joachim Horvitz. *The Big Book of Jewish Baseball*. New York: SPI Books, 2001.

Hynd, Neil J. *The Giants of the Polo Grounds*. New York: Doubleday, 1988.

Jennings, Kenneth M. *Balls and Strikes*. New York: Praeger, 1990.

_____. *Swings and Misses: Moribund Labor Relations in Professional Baseball*. Westport, CT: Praeger, 1997.

Kahn, Roger. *The Era, 1947 to 1957: When the Yankees, the Giants, and the Dodgers Ruled the World*. New York: Ticknor & Fields, 1993.

_____. *October Men: Reggie Jackson, George Steinbrenner, Billy Martin, and the Yankees' Miraculous Finish in 1978*. New York: Harcourt, 2003.

_____. *The Passionate People: What It Means to be a Jew in America*. New York: William Morrow, 1968.

Kelley, Brent. *Baseball's Biggest Blunder: The Bonus Rule of 1953–1957*. Lanham, MD: Scarecrow, 1997.

Koppett, Leonard. *The Thinking Fan's Guide to Baseball*. Kingston, NY: Total Sports, 2001.

Korr, Charles P. *The End of Baseball as We Knew It: The Players Union, 1960–81*. Champaign: University of Illinois Press, 2002.

Kowet, Don. *The Rich Who Own Sports*. New York: Random House, 1977.

Kuhn, Bowie. *Hardball: The Education of a Baseball Commissioner*. New York: Times Books, 1997.

Langford, Jim. *The Game Is Never Over: An Appreciative History of the Chicago Cubs, 1948–1980*. South Bend, IN: Icarus Press, 1980.

Lansche, Jerry. *Forgotten Championships: Post-Season Baseball, 1882–1981*. Jefferson, NC: McFarland, 1989.

Leavy, Jane. *Sandy Koufax: A Lefty's Legacy*. New York: HarperCollins, 2002.

Levine, Peter. *Ellis Island to Ebbets Field: Sport and the American Jewish Experience*. New York: Oxford University Press, 1992.

Lieb, Fred. *Comedians and Pranksters of Baseball*. St. Louis: Charles C. Spink & Son, 1958.

Lindberg, Richard. *Stealing First in a Two-Team Town: The White Sox from Comisky to Reinsdorf*. Champaign, IL: Sagamore, 1994.

_____. *Who's on 3rd? The Chicago White Sox Story*. South Bend, IN: Icarus Press, 1983.

Linn, Ed. *Hitter: The Life and Turmoil of Ted Williams*. New York: Harcourt Brace, 1993.

Lowenfish, Lee. *Branch Rickey: Baseball's Ferocious Gentleman*. Lincoln: University of Nebraska Press, 2007.

_____ and Tony Lupien. *The Imperfect Diamond: The Story of Baseball's Reserve System and the Men Who Fought to Change It*. New York: Stein and Day, 1980.

Madden, Bill, and Moss Klein. *Damned Yankees*. New York: Warner Books, 1990.

Marburger, Daniel, ed. *Stee-Rike Four: What's Wrong with the Business of Baseball*. Westport, CT: Praeger, 1997.

Marshall, William. *Baseball's Pivotal Era: 1949–1951*. Lexington: University Press of Kentucky, 1999.

Menke, Frank. *Sports Tales and Anecdotes*. New York: A.S. Barnes, 1953.

Miller, James Edward. *The Baseball Business: Pursuing Pennants and Profits in Baltimore*. Chapel Hill: University of North Carolina Press, 1990.

Miller, Marvin. *A Whole Different Ball Game: The Sport and Business of Baseball*. New York: Birch Lane Press, 1991.

Morgan, Joe, and Richard Lally. *Long Balls, No Strikes: What Baseball Must Do to Keep the Good Times Rolling*. New York: Crown, 1999.

Muskat, Carrie. *Banks to Sandberg to Grace: Five Decades of Love and Frustration with the Chicago Cubs*. Chicago: Contemporary Books, 2001.

Nash, Bruce, and Allan Zullo. *The Baseball Hall of Shame*. New York: Pocket Books, 1985.

Oakley, Ronald J. *Baseball's Last Golden Age, 1946–1960: The National Pastime in a Time of Glory and Change*. Jefferson, NC: McFarland, 1994.

Olson, James C. *Stuart Symington: A Life*. Columbia: University of Missouri Press, 2003.

Palmer, Pete, and Gary Gillette, eds. *The 2007 ESPN Encyclopedia*. New York: Sterling, 2006.

Patkin, Max, and Stan Hochman. *The Clown Prince of Baseball*. Waco, TX: WRS Publishing, 1994.

Patterson, Ted. *The Golden Voices of Baseball*. Champaign, IL: Sports Publishing, 2002.

Peters, Alexander. *Heroes of the Major Leagues*. New York: Random House, 1967.

Pietrusza, David, Matthew Silberman, and Michael Gershman, eds. *Baseball. The Biographical Encyclopedia*. Kingston, NY: Sports Illustrated, 2002.

Porter, David, ed. *The Biographical Directory of American Sports*. New York: Greenwood Press, 1987.

Postal, Bernard, Jesse Silver, and Roy Silver. *The Encyclopedia of Jews in Sports*. New York: Bloch, 1965.

Preston, Joseph G. *Major League Baseball in the 1970's: A Modern Game Emerges*. Jefferson, NC: McFarland, 2004.

Prince, Carl E. *Brooklyn's Dodgers: The Bums, The Borough, and the Best of Baseball, 1947–1957*. New York: Oxford University Press, 1996.

Quirk, James, and Rodney Fort. *Paydirt: The Business of Professional Team Sports*. Princeton, NJ: Princeton University Press, 1993.

Rader, Benjamin G. *Baseball: A History of America's Game*. Urbana: University of Illinois Press, 1992.

Ribalow, Harold U., and Meir Z. Ribalow. *Jewish Baseball Stars*. New York: Hippocrene Books, 1984.

Rielly, Edward J. *Baseball: An Encyclopedia of Popular Culture*. Santa Barbara: ABC-CLIO, 2000.

Riess, Steven A. *Sports and the American Jew*. Syracuse: Syracuse University Press, 1998.

Rossi, John P. *The National Game: Baseball and American Culture*. Chicago: Ivan R. Dee, 2000.

Sachar, Howard M. *A History of the Jews in America*. New York: Alfred A. Knopf, 1992.

Sands, Jack, and Peter Gammons. *Coming Apart at the Seams: How Baseball Owners, Players, and Television Executives Have Led Our National Pastime to the Brink of Disaster*. New York: Macmillan, 1993.

Schwarz, Alan. *The Numbers Game*. New York: St. Martin's Press, 2004.

Scully, Gerald W. *The Business of Major League Baseball*. Chicago: University of Chicago Press, 1989.

Shapiro, Edward S. *A Time for Healing: American Jewry Since World War II*. Baltimore: Johns Hopkins University Press, 1992.

Silverman, Al. *Heroes of the World Series*. New York: Putnam's, 1964.

Skipper, John C. *Inside Pitch: A Closer Look at Classic Baseball Moments*. Jefferson, NC: McFarland, 1996.

Slater, Robert. *Great Jews in Sports*. Middle Village, NY: Jonathan David, 1992.

Smith, Curt. *The Storytellers, from Mel Allen to Bob Costas: Sixty Years of Baseball Tales from the Broadcast Booth*. New York: Macmillan, 1995.

_____. *The Voice: Mel Allen's Untold Story*. Guilford, CT: Lyons Press, 2007.

_____. *Voices of Summer*. New York: Carroll & Graf, 2005.

_____. *Voices of the Game: The Acclaimed Chronicle of Baseball Radio and Television Broadcasting—from 1921 to the Present*. New York: Simon & Schuster, 1992.

Smith, Leverett, Jr. *The American Dream and the National Game*. Bowling Green, OH: Bowling Green University Popular Press, 1975.

Staudohar, Paul D., ed. *Diamond Mines: Baseball & Labor*. Syracuse, NY: Syracuse University Press, 2000.

Stern, Bill. *The Taste of Ashes*. New York: Henry Holt, 1959.

Stone, Steve. *Where's Harry? Steve Stone Remembers His Years with Harry Carey*. Dallas: Taylor, 1999.

Sullivan, Neil J. *The Diamond Revolution: The Prospects for Baseball After the Collapse of Its Ruling Class*. New York: St. Martin's Press, 1992.

_____. *The Dodgers Move West*. New York: Oxford University Press, 1987.

Thomas, Evan. *The Man to See: Edward Bennett Williams Ultimate Insider; Legendary Trial Lawyer*. New York: Simon & Schuster, 1991.

Thorn, John, Phil Birnbaum, and Bill Deane, eds. *Total Baseball: The Ultimate Baseball Encyclopedia*. Wilmington, DE: Sports Media Publishing, 2004.

Torry, Jack. *Endless Summers: The Fall and Rise of the Cleveland Indians*. South Bend, IN: Diamond Communications, 1995.

Trucks, Rob. *Cup of Coffee: The Very Short Careers of Eighteen Major League Pitchers*. New York: Smallmouth Press, 2002.

Vanderberg, Bob. *Sox: From Lane and Fain to Zisk and Fisk*. Chicago: Chicago Review Press, 1982.

Voigt, David. *America Through Baseball*. Chicago: Nelson-Hall, 1976.

_____. *American Baseball. Volume 3: From Postwar Expansion to the Electronics Age*. University Park: Pennsylvania State University Press, 1974.

Wallop, Douglas. *Baseball: An Informal History*. New York: W. W. Norton, 1969.

White, G. Edward. *Creating the National Pastime: Baseball Transforms Itself, 1903–1953*. Princeton, NJ: Princeton University Press, 1996.

Wilber, Cynthia J. *For the Love of the Game*. New York: William Morrow, 1992.

Williams, Dick, and Bill Plaschke. *No More Mr. Nice Guy: A Life of Hardball*. San Diego: Harcourt Brace Jovanovich, 1990.

Zimbalist, Andrew. *Baseball and Billions: A Probing Look Inside the Big Business of Our National Pastime*. New York: HarperCollins, 1992.

_____. *In the Best Interests of Baseball? The Revolutionary Reign of Bud Selig*. Hoboken, NJ: John Wiley, 2007.

_____. *May the Best Team Win: Baseball Economics and Public Policy*. Washington, DC: The Brookings Institution, 2003.

Magazine Articles

Allen, Maury. "Richie Scheinblum Finally a Star." *Baseball Digest*, November 1972, 67–68.

Anderson, David. "The Dangers of Being a World Series Hero." *Sport*, November 1965, 29–32, 94.

Blount, Roy, Jr. "Lefty Makes the Angels Sing." *Sports Illustrated*, June 8, 1970, 28–29.

Boyle, Robert H. "This Miller Admits He's a Grind." *Sports Illustrated*, March 11, 1974, 22–26.

Cobbledick, Gordon. "They'll Follow Rosen Now." *Baseball Digest*, March 1954, 29.

Collier, Phil. "Memories of Koufax's Well-Kept Secret." *Baseball Digest*, November 1972, 87–89.

_____. "Sandy Koufax: What I Miss Most About Baseball." *Sport*, May 1967, 48–50.

Cuddy, Don. "Big Chief Rosen." *Sport*, April 1954, 82–87.

Cunneff, Tom. "Max Patkin, The Goofball Laureate of Baseball Scores in Bull Durham and Holy Cow—It's a Grand Ham." *People Weekly*, July 11, 1988, 61–62.

Daley, Arthur. "Rosen Rises to 'Most' Past." *Baseball Digest*, September 1950, 30.

Davidson, Bill. "Mel Allen: Baseball's Most Controversial Voice." *Look*, September 22, 1960, 97, 100–102.

DeFillipo, Larry. "Point Men." *National Pastime* 25 (2005): 116–122.

Dexter, Charles. "Cal Finally Scores." *Baseball Digest*, March 1954, 35–39.

"The Dodgers' Most Valuable Trio." *Sport*, January 1982, 13.

Durslag, Melvin. "Sandy Koufax The Strikeout King." *Saturday Evening Post*, July 14, 1962, 69–72.

Feldman, Steve. "He's One of a Rare Breed: Jewish Big-League Catcher." *Jewish Exponent*, January 8, 1993, 6, 57.

"Fun for the Fireman." *Time*, October 19, 1959, 87.

Garrity, John. "Sing Along with Bambi's Brewers." *Sport*, September 1979, 58–64.

Glickman, Joe. "Union Man: Marvin Miller Disses Vincent, Giamatti, and the Rest of Baseball's Old Boy Network." *Village Voice*, July 2, 1991, 158.

Gross, Milton. "The Dodgers' Precocious Pitcher." *Saturday Evening Post*, March 12, 1960, 31, 98–100.

_____. "Goodbye, Sandy." *Sport*, March 1967, 35–36, 83–84.

_____. "Sandy Koufax: The Pressures on a World Series Hero." *Sport*, November 1964, 33, 71.

Hano, Arnold. "Mike Epstein: Somewhere Between Journeyman and Superstar." *Sport*, November 1972, 66–69, 86–88.

Harrison, Walter L. "Six-Pointed Diamond: Baseball and the American Jews." *Journal of Popular Culture* 15 (September 1981): 112–118.

Hays, Bob. "From Thrower to Pitcher: The Education of Ken Holtzman." *Baseball Digest*, December 1974, 72–73.

Hazucha, Andrew. "Leo Durocher's Last Stand: Anti-Semitism, Racism, and the Cubs' Player Rebellion of 1971." *Nine* 15 (Fall 2006): 1–5.

Hibdon, Glenn. "Sandy Koufax Recalls Advice That Helped His Career." *Baseball Digest*, May 1985, 66–68.

Hochman, Stan. "Koufax: This Is How It Was." *Baseball Digest*, February 1966, 11–12.

Horn, Huston. "Baseball's Babbling Brook." *Sports Illustrated*, July 9, 1962, 54–63.

Jares, Joe. "Sandy Makes a Pitch for Posterity." *Sports Illustrated*, August 2, 1965, 10–12.

Kates, Maxwell. "Of Horsehides and Hexagrams." *National Pastime* 24 (2004): 118–126.

Katz, Fred. "Larry Sherry—Career Reliever." *Baseball Digest*, May 1962, 45.

_____. "Little Old Yankee." *Sport*, February 1968, 12.

Katz, Marc. "'I Didn't Think Baseball Players Were Real People': An Interview with Richie Scheinblum" in *Batting Four Thousand: Baseball in the Western Reserve* (Cleveland, OH: Society for American Baseball Research, 2008, 68–76.

Koppett, Leonard. "A Little Game That Turned TV Loose on a Sport." *Sports Illustrated*, May 10, 1965, M3–M4.

"Koufax Retires." *Baseball Digest*, February 1967, 67.

Krikorian, Doug. "The Indispensable Dodger: Catcher Steve Yaeger." *Baseball Digest*, July 1978, 37–39.

Kuenster, John. "Steve Stone Thinks He Can Improve on His Cy Young Award Year." *Baseball Digest*, June 1981, 15.

_____. "Warm Up Tosses" *Baseball Digest*, October 1971, 4–6.

Latman, Barry. "Ty Cobb's Letters to Barry Latman." *Sport*, February 1962, 8, 19–21, 68–69.

Lebovitz, Hal. "How Rosen Rocks 'Em." *Colliers*, May 25, 1954, 72–73.

Levine, David. "Say Goodnight, Mel." *Sport*, October 1983, 100.

Libby, Bill. "The Sophistication of Sandy Koufax." *Sport*, September 1963, 61–69.

Liebman, Glenn. "Sometimes Even 'Experts' Misjudge Baseball Talent." *Baseball Digest*, August 1988, 55–56.

Linn, Ed. "Koufax Remembered." *Sport*, February 1972, 41–42.

McQuay, David. "Superstitions Are Still Part of Baseball's Scene." *Baseball Digest*, January 1982, 60–61.

Meany, Tom. "The Figger Filbert." *Baseball Magazine*, September 1949, 331–332.

"Mike's Little Rebellion." *Newsweek*, June 12, 1967, 58.

Murphy, Jack. "Dave Roberts on the Road to Stardom." *Baseball Digest*, November 1971, 39–40.

"My Heroes—Where Are They Now?" *Old Tyme Baseball News*, Fall 1989, 16.

"The New York Yankees." *Newsweek*, July 16, 1973, 46.

Old, John B. "He Almost Quit 4 Years Ago." *Baseball Digest*, December 1959-January 1960, 11–12.

Olsen, Jack. "The Very Best Act in Town." *Sports Illustrated*, July 29, 1963, 20–22, 53.

Palmer, Bill. "Ausmus Catching On." *Baseball America*, September 10, 1991, 15.

Paxton, Harry T. "That Clouting Kid from Cleveland." *Saturday Evening Post*, August 11, 1951, 87–88.

Perry, Jim. "Koufax Player of the Decade." *Baseball Digest*, May 1970, 37–39.

Powell, Larry. "Cal Abrams Recalls Play That Ruined Flag Hopes of Dodgers in 1950." *Baseball Digest*, September 1992, 73–75.

"Rebuilt Indians." *Newsweek*, August 14, 1950, 74–75.

Richler, Mordecai. "Koufax the Incomparable." *Commentary*, November 1966, 87–89.

Rosen, Al. "The Game I'll Never Forget." *Baseball Digest*, July 1984, 47–48.

Schaap, Dick. "What's a Nice Georgia Cracker Doing in the Bronx?" *Sport*, October 1973, 48–54.

Schlossberg, Dan. "How Rookie Pitcher Rallied '59 Dodgers." *Baseball Digest*, November 1993, 42.

Schwarz, Alan. "Lieberthal Satisfies His Nay Sayers." *Baseball America*, December 10, 1991, 14.

"Sic Transit Tradition." *Time*, April 8, 1966, 75.

Simons, Herbert. "The Sherry Flip." *Baseball Digest*, December 1959-January 1960, 9–10.

Smith, Sam. "Old Order Changeth: From DiMag and Mick to Maddox." *Black Sports*, February 1975, 23, 46.

Solomon, Eric. "Jews, Baseball, and the American Novel." *Arete* 1 (Spring 1984): 47–57.

"Sports' 19th Annual—Sandy Koufax Man of the Year." *Sport*, February 1966, 20.

Stainback, Berry. "Socrates in a Jock Strap." *Sport*, June 1965, 8.

Staudohar, Paul D. "Baseball Negotiations—A New Agreement." *Monthly Labor Review* 125 (December 2002): 1–21.

Stone, Steve. "The Game I'll Never Forget." *Baseball Digest*, March 1983, 91.

Terrell, Roy. "Hawkeye and His Boy Scouts." *Sports Illustrated*, April 17, 1961, 14–15.

____. "No Relief for Sherry." *Sports Illustrated*, March 28, 1960, 62–64.

"The Union Who Changed Baseball." *Newsweek*, April 10, 1989, 48.

"Top of the League." *Time*, July 5, 1954, 38.

"Two New Stadiums on Deck—Baseball Brings Jobs to the Big Apple." *The Carpenter*, Summer 2006, 16–17.

Vass, George. "Can Holtzman Beat the Rap?" *Baseball Digest*, July 1970, 35–41.

____. "7 Candidates for Stardom in 1980 and Beyond." *Baseball Digest*, June 1980, 20–25.

____. "What They Want for 1967—It Could Be an Inside Job." *Baseball Digest*, December 1966, 5.

Veeck, Bill. "Baseball and Me." *Sport*, April 1950, 30–31.

Verducci, Tom. "What's All the Shouting About?" *Sports Illustrated*, January 31, 1994, 84.

Voigt, David Q. "They Shared the Game: Nine Innovators of Major League Baseball." *Baseball History* 1 (Spring 1986): 5–22.

Waldmeier, Pete. "What Vintage the Sherry?" *Baseball Digest*, July 1966, 56.

Whitford, David. "Curt Flood." *Sport*, December 1986, 103–105.

Wild Man Tamed." *Newsweek*, July 10, 1961, 46.

Wills, Maury. "The National League's 9 Most Underrated Players." *Sport*, July 1970, 12–13, 59.

Wohlgelertner, Elli. "Interview: Calvin R. Abrams and May Abrams." *American Jewish History* 83 (March 1995): 109–122.

Newspapers

Atlanta Jewish Times
Canadian Jewish Times
Canadian Jewish News
Canton (OH) Registry
Chicago Daily Herald
Chicago Defender
Chicago Sun-Times
Chicago Tribune
Cincinnati Enquirer
Cincinnati Post
Dallas Morning News
Dallas Morning Star
Denver Post
Farmingdale (NJ) News Transcript
Florida Jewish News
Fort Worth Star-Telegram
Hardball Times
Houston Chronicle
International Herald Tribune
Jerusalem Post
Jewish Advocate
Jewish Exponent (Philadelphia, PA)
Jewish Forward
The Jewish Journal
Jewish Ledger (W. Hartford, CT)
Jewish News of Greater Phoenix
Jewish News Weekly
Jewish Tribune (Canada)
Jewish World Review
Jews News Weekly of Northern California
Kansas City Jewish Chronicle
Kentucky Post
Las Vegas Sun
Los Angeles Times
Milwaukee Journal-Sentinel
Milwaukee Sentinel
New Haven Register
New Jersey Jewish News
New Jersey Jewish Standard
New Jersey Star-Ledger
New York Herald Tribune
New York Sun
New York Times
News Transport (NJ)
North County Times (San Diego, CA)
Orlando Sentinel
Pawtucket (RI) Times
Pittsburgh Post Gazette
Pittsburgh Tribune Review
Providence Journal
Racine (WI) Journal Times
Rhode Island News
Rocky Mountain News
San Diego Union Tribune
San Francisco Chronicle
San Mateo Daily Journal
Shore Line Times (Guilford, CT)
South Jersey News
Sporting News
Sports Business Daily
St. Clair College Journal
St. Louis Jewish Light
St. Petersburg Times
Standard Times (New Bedford, MA)
Stratford Gazette
Trumbull (CT) Times
Tucson Citizen
USA Today
USA Today Baseball Weekly
Utica Observer-Dispatch
Wall Street Journal
Washington Post
Wisconsin Sports Daily
Wisconsin State Journal

Internet

2sportsnet.com
abclocal.go.com
absoluteastronomy.com

angelfire.com
answers.com
arlington.org
athomeplate.com
babaganewz.com
ballparkdigest.com
baseball.about.com
baseball.ca/eng.doc
baseballaddict.com
baseball-almanac.com
baseballamerica.com
baseballdigestdaily.com
baseball-hitting.com
baseballlibrary.com
baseball-reference.com
baseballreliquary.org
baseballsavvy.com
baseballthinkfactory.org
bioproj.sabr.org
bisoninsider.com
bizofbaseball.com
bostonredsoc.mlb.com
buffalobisons.mlb.com
can'tstopthebleeding.com
cbc.ca
cbs2.com
cbs3.com
cbssports.com
cbssportsline.com
chicago.cubs.mlb.com
classzone.com
clusports.com
coloradorockies.com
commonwealthtimes.com
cubschronicle.com
cubshub.com
easternleague.com
enalexperts.com
espn.com
fangraphs.com
fantasybaseball.usatoday.com
findarticles.com
firstinning.com
freewebs.com
gsohoppers.com
hadassah.org
hardballtimes.com
historicbaseball.net
hurricanesports.cstv.com
info-pedia.net
intellectualservative.com
interfaithfamily.com
israelbaseballleague.com
israelgood.com
jewhoo.com
jewishf.com
jewishsf.com
jewishsports.net
jewishvirtuallibrary.org
jewogle.com
jewsinsports.com
jewsweek.com
jewz.com
jfcsphil.org

jstandard.com
jta.org
jvibe.com
kaplerfoundation.org
kdka.com
kjmpromotions.com
linkedin.com
losangeles.dodgers.mlb.com
losangelesdodgersonline.com
mahalo.com
members.tripod.com
minnesotapublicrelations.org
mlb.com
mlbplayers.mlb.com
mlbtraderumors.com
mlndstherawfeed.squarespace.com
mobileapp.espn.go.com
msnbc.com
multigers.cstv.com
nashvillesounds.com
nationmaster.com
neilkeller.com
netshrine.com
newyorkmetro.com
niams.nih.gov
nndp.com
npr.org
nyfans.com
ohiohistoricalcentral.org
onmilwaukee.com
overthemonster.com
pasacard.com
pe.com
people.virginia.edu
philadelphiaathletics.org
philadelphiaphillies.mlb.com
pressuchicago.edu
prnewswire.com
projectprospect.com
publicquizhelp.com
purplecow.com
radio.about.com
radiohof.com
reference.com
retrosheet.org
rotoworld.com
royalboard.com
ryanbraunfanclub.com
sabr.org
scout.com
shawngreen.net
skids.com
slate.com
sonofsamhorn.net
soxprospects.com
sports.aol.com
sportsbiznews.blogspot.com
sports.espn.go.com
sports.outsidethebeltway.com
sports.yahoo.com
sportsblurb.com
sportsecyclopedia.com
sportsillustrated.cnn.com
sportslibrary.com

sportsline.com
sportsnetwork.com
sportspool.com
tarheelblue.cstv.com
tbe.org
texasrangers.mlb.com
texaxleague.com
thebaseballcube.com
thebaseballnexuc.com
thebaseballpage.com
thedeadballera.com
thefreedictionary.com
tireball.com
ultimatemets.com
Upi.com
usatoday.com
usgannett.org
usinfo.state.gov
ussportspool.com
vaildaily.com
vault.sportsillustrated.com
wcbstv.com
whitesoxinteractive.com
wsoctv.com
yalealumnimagazine.com
ynet.com
yourkids.org

Personal Communications

Baumgarten, Ross. Telephone Interview. September 6, 2006.

Blomberg, Ron. Telephone Interview. October 8, 2006.

Ginsberg, Joe. Telephone Interview. July 11, 2008.

Glauber, Keith. Telephone Interview. December 29, 2008.

Hemond, Roland. Telephone Interview. December 5, 2008.

Hertz, Steve. Telephone Interview. October 2, 2008.

Hirsh, Jason. E-Mail Interview. January 27, 2009.

Holtzman, Ken. Interview. July 30, 2002.

Kapler, Gabe. Telephone Interview. December 19, 2008.

Latman, Barry. Telephone Interview. August 31, 2008.

Mayer, Ed. Telephone Interview. August 13, 2007.

Mickelson, Ed. Telephone Interview. July 11, 2008.

Miller, Marvin. Interview. August 12, 2007.

Miller, Norman. Telephone Interview. October 10, 2008.

Reinsdorf, Jerry. Telephone Interview. August 31, 2006.

Rosenfield, Dave. E-Mail Interview. January 16, 2009.

Rotblatt, Marvin. Telephone Interview. July 11, 2008.

Scheinblum, Richie. E-Mail Interview. January 28, 2009.

Tufts, Bob. E-Mail Interview. July 18, 2008.

Index

Numbers in **bold italics** indicate pages with photographs.